Management Science

Management Science

As per the Latest Syllabus
JNTU (Hyderabad, Kakinada, Anantapur)
(Common to B Tech., ECE, CSE, EEE and IT Branches)

P Ramamurthy

BE, M Tech., Gr.IIIE, PGDBA,CEM, FIIIE

Former
Professor, Mechanical Engineering
JNTU College of Engineering, Anantapur
Principal, PVKK College of Engineering, Anantapur
Principal, Intell Engineering College, Anantapur

Y Kesava Reddy

MA, MBA, PhD

Associate Professor, Management
Intell Engineering College, Anantapur

NEW AGE
JNTU

An Imprint of

NEW AGE INTERNATIONAL (P) LIMITED, PUBLISHERS
New Delhi • Bangalore • Chennai • Cochin • Guwahati
Hyderabad • Kolkata • Lucknow • Mumbai
Visit us at **www.newagepublishers.com**

Published by New Age International (P) Ltd., Publishers
First Edition: 2014

BRANCHES

- **Bangalore** 37/10, 8th Cross (Near Hanuman Temple), Azad Nagar, Chamarajpet, Bangalore-560 018
  Tel.: (080) 26756823, Telefax: 26756820, **E-mail: bangalore@newagepublishers.com**
- **Chennai** 26, Damodaran Street, T. Nagar, Chennai-600 017
  Tel.: (044) 24353401, Telefax: 24351463, **E-mail: chennai@newagepublishers.com**
- **Cochin** CC-39/1016, Carrier Station Road, Ernakulam South, Cochin-682 016
  Tel.: (0484) 2377004, Telefax: 4051303, **E-mail: cochin@newagepublishers.com**
- **Guwahati** Hemsen Complex, Mohd. Shah Road, Paltan Bazar, Near Starline Hotel, Guwahati-781 008
  Tel.: (0361) 2513881, Telefax: 2543669, **E-mail: guwahati@newagepublishers.com**
- **Hyderabad** 105, 1st Floor, Madhiray Kaveri Tower, 3-2-19, Azam Jahi Road, Nimboliadda, Hyderabad-500 027
  Tel.: (040) 24652456, Telefax: 24652457, **E-mail: hyderabad@newagepublishers.com**
- **Kolkata** RDB Chambers (Formerly Lotus Cinema) 106A, 1st Floor, S.N. Banerjee Road, Kolkata-700 014
  Tel.: (033) 22273773, Telefax: 22275247, **E-mail: kolkata@newagepublishers.com**
- **Lucknow** 16-A, Jopling Road, Lucknow-226 001
  Tel.: (0522) 2209578, 4045297, Telefax: 2204098, **E-mail: lucknow@newagepublishers.com**
- **Mumbai** 142C, Victor House, Ground Floor, N.M. Joshi Marg, Lower Parel, Mumbai-400 013
  Tel.: (022) 24927869, Telefax: 24915415, **E-mail: mumbai@newagepublishers.com**
- **New Delhi** 22, Golden House, Daryaganj, New Delhi-110 002
  Tel.: (011) 23262368, 23262370, Telefax: 43551305, **E-mail: sales@newagepublishers.com**

ISBN: 978-81-224-3537-5

₹ 250.00

C-13-03-6828

Printed in India at Nisha Enterprises, Delhi.

Typeset at In House, New Delhi.

PUBLISHING FOR ONE WORLD
NEW AGE INTERNATIONAL (P) LIMITED, PUBLISHERS
7/30 A, Daryaganj, New Delhi - 110002
Visit us at **www.newagepublishers.com**

The book is dedicated to

My Students Who Are on Jobs
All Over The World

Preface

For any professional executive, may be an Engineer, a Lawyer or a Doctor, the knowledge of basic principles of management is highly essential. It is because everyone has to plan their work, plan for the resources to meet the needs of their work, and control all the resources to achieve success in their profession. But for an engineer, who always deals with various resources in his work, the knowledge of Management Science and Industrial Engineering is very much essential. Today the demands of the society need engineer managers rather than purely an engineer or a manager. The technology is advancing very fast and the human relations are also changing on other side, at the same time the scarcity of resources is posing a problem. At this juncture, it is necessary to prepare all professionals with management knowledge and make them to fulfill the needs of the society.

This book **MANAGEMENT SCIENCE** has got the objective to help engineering students to become full-fledged engineering professionals with the knowledge of management principles and functions.

The subject is written on the basis of the revised syllabus of J.N.T. University, Hyderabad. It will cater to the needs of EEE, ECE, CSE and IT branches of engineering. In many chapters, the students may feel that the matter provided may be too detailed. But this is inevitable. The author of a book always bears in mind that the students have to face various competitive examinations after completing their graduation. Then, the students will feel that they need a book, which will help them to face the competitive examination. I sincerely hope that this book will help students of all disciplines to face the competitive examinations with confidence.

Units 2 and 1 explain the basic principles of management and structures and needs of an organization. Unit 3 discusses the production engineering aspects of the subject, such as layout, work-study, quality control with suitable examples and solutions to help the students to prepare for their B.Tech. examination and also for competitive examination.

Unit 4 deals with materials management, the important topic catching the attention of industrial managers and also the functions of purchase management, stores management and marketing management are discussed.

In Unit 5, the human resource part of the management is discussed. This resource is very important, as this the only resource which has life and reacts with the feelings of business executives and is directly responsible for increasing productivity and has larger percentage of effort in industrial growth. Topics like job evaluation, merit rating and wage payment system, incentive schemes are discussed.

Unit 6 gives the description and application of PERT and CPM techniques of scheduling, which is a powerful tool of an engineer in planning his work and controlling resources.

Unit 7 deals with strategic management giving objectives, policies and SWOT analysis to help the students to face the problems in their real life successfully.

In the last unit, some latest concepts of management (Contemporary management practice) have been discussed to alert the students in which direction the growth is advancing and what problems they have to face when they go out of the college. It also enables them to analyze what they should be and how they should be in facing the challenges of their carrier.

I sincerely feel that the book will remain as a handy reference to the students and teachers as well.

Any comments on the contents of the book are welcome. I thank Mr. V.V.Venkata-Ramana, M.Tech., Associate Professor in Mechanical Engineering, Intell Engineering College, Anantapur and Mr. Jagadish, M.Tech. for all the help done in bringing out this book.

It is my duty to express my thanks to the publishers for taking all pains in bringing out this book in time to the market.

—Author

Syllabus

MANAGEMENT SCIENCE
(Common to all Branches of B.Tech. of J.N.T. University, Hyderabad, Anantapur and Kakinada)
(COMMON TO EEE, ECE, CSE AND IT STUDENTS)
(07A6HS01)

UNIT 1: Introduction to Management

Concepts of Management and Organization – Nature, Importance and Functions of Management, Evolution of Management Thought - Taylor's Scientific Management Theory, Fayol's Principles of Management, Mayo's Hawthorne Experiments, Maslow's Theory of Human Needs, Douglas McGregor's Theory X and Theory Y. Herzberg's Two-Factor Theory of Motivation, Systems Approach to Management, Leadership Styles, Social Responsibilities of Management.

UNIT 2: Designing Organizational Structure

Basic Concepts Related to Organization – Departmentation and Decentralization, Types of Mechanistic and Organic Structure of Organization (Line organization, Line and Staff Organization, Functional Organization, Committee Organization, Matrix Organization, Virtual Organization, Cellular Organization, Team Structure, Boundary Less Organization, Inverted Pyramid Structure, Lean and Flat Organization Structure) and their Merits, Demerits and Suitability.

UNIT 3: Operations Management

Plant Location – Definition, Factors Affecting the Plant Location – Comparison of Rural and Urban Sites – Methods for Selection of Plant – Matrix Approach-Plant Layout Definition Objectives – Various Data Analyzing Forms – Travel Charts - Principles and Types of Plant Layout – Methods of Production (Job, Batch and Mass Production), Work study – Basic Procedure Involved in Method Study and Work Measurement – Statistical Quality Control: X Chart, R Chart, C Chart, P Chart (Simple problems). Acceptance Sampling, Deming's Contribution to Quality.

UNIT 4:

(a) Materials Management

Objectives — Need for Inventory Control, EOQ, ABC Analysis, Purchase Procedure, Stores Management and Stores Records.

(b) Marketing

Functions of Marketing, Marketing Mix, and Marketing Strategies Based on Product Life Cycle, Channels of Distribution.

UNIT 5: Human Resource Management (HRM)

Concepts of HRM, HRD and Personnel Management and Industrial Relations (PMIR), HRM Vs PMIR. Basic Functions of HR Manager: Manpower Planning, Recruitment, Selection, Training and Development, Placement, Wage and Salary Administration, Promotion, Transfer, Separation, Performance Appraisal, Grievance Handling and Welfare Administration, Job Evaluation and Merit Rating.

UNIT 6: Project Management (PERT/CPM)

Network Analysis, Programme Evaluation and Review Technique (PERT), Critical Path Method (CPM), Identifying Critical Path, Probability of Completing the Project within given Time, Project Cost Analysis, Project Crashing. (Simple Problems).

UNIT 7: Strategic Management

Mission, Goals, Objectives, Policy, Strategy, Programmes, Elements of Corporate Planning Process, Environmental Scanning, Value Chain Analysis, SWOT Analysis, Steps in Strategy Formulation and Implementation, Generic Strategy Alternatives.

UNIT 8: Contemporary Management Practices

Basic Concepts of MIS, End User Computing, Materials Requirement Planning (MRP), Just-in-Time (JIT) System, Total Quality Management (TQM), Six Sigma and Capability Maturity Model (CMM) Levels, Supply Chain Management, Enterprise Resource Planning (ERP), Performance Management, Business Process Outsourcing (BPO), Business Process Re-engineering and Bench Marking, Balanced Score Card.

Contents

Unit 1 Concept of Management

1.1. INTRODUCTION

The knowledge of Management Science is very much essential for an engineer as he is the man who deals with utilization of useful resources of the country to produce useful products for the use of human kind. In the process of conversion he must be very careful in using the available resources, which belongs to the public at large. He must use them optimally to produce goods and services. The knowledge of management science helps him to use his analytical ability to sharpen enough to see that he does his work in such a way; for the best advantage of the country and his fellowmen. Everyone of us are involved in the management processes every day while planning our activities from morning till evening, without the knowledge of management science. The knowledge of management will sharpen our thinking in the direction of optimal utilization of available resources.

1.2. NATURE OF MANAGEMENT

To run any business a central directing and controlling agency is a must. This agency is very much similar to our mind, which directs and controls our body, which is an assembly of flesh and bones. Without mind this body has no meaning. Similarly any business house is a collection of men, machines, labour and equipment, which does not serve any purpose, without the proper guiding and controlling agency. For efficient functioning of business, it is necessary that all the above said factors are put to work in co-coordinated and meaningful way. Management does this work. All the resourses available inside and outside of the organization are put to right use in a planned manner by the management. Management is a word used by different people with different meanings. The noun 'management' is used as a collective noun to refer all those who manage with in a particular organization including the decision makers (like managers), including those who help or advise them in decision making process (staff personnel). The word management is also used to refer to a particular activity such as scientific management or to distinguish a special class of peoples 'management' and labor. Peter Drucker says that 'management is a multi-purpose organ that manages a business, managers, workers and work.' He adds that 'neither results nor resources exist inside the business. Both exist outside.' It is the function of a management to use resources for the realization of results in such a way that the business firm is not only able to pay its way but also able to earn some surplus to meet the needs of growth and expansion. It is the management that provides planning, organization and direction, which are necessary for business operations. Whatever may be the size of the firm it is the function of the management or people responsible for management to chalk out the course of action that the business has to follow to fulfill the objectives for which the business has started. *Management is a vital function concerned with all aspects of the working of enterprise.*

In any enterprise, people will associate together to run it, with specific objectives, may be maximization of profit, or render service to the community. These people plan the work of the organization, direct the people in the organization, pool up resources and direct the men under them to use these resources in a meaningful way to achieve the desired objectives. The process employed by this group is the process of management. **Management is the function of guiding, directing, coordinating human effort and activities for the accomplishment of given task.** Or, we can say that the task of planning, co-coordinating, motivating and controlling the efforts of others (people working in the organization) towards the specific objectives. Or it is the act of getting things done by the people to achieve the goals. Luther Gullick says that the functions of management as **POSDCORB**. That is:

P = Planning,
O = Organization,
S = Staffing,
D = Directing,
CO = Coordinating,
R = Reporting, and
B = Budgetting.

1.3. ADMINISTRATION, MANAGEMENT, AND ORGANIZATION

Although the words 'administration' and 'management' are often used synonymously, some authors have sought to make a distinction between the two. Sheldon describes **administration** as *the function in industry concerned with the determination of the corporate policy, the coordination of finance, production and distribution, the settlement of the compass of the organization and the ultimate control of the executive.* Sheldon says the **management** as the *function in industry concerned with the execution of policy, within the limits set by the administration and employment of the organization to fulfill the objective for which it has been established.* With this we can understand that the administration relates to the duties of top management, who are more concerned with determining the corporate policy and ensuring coordination among the functional departments. As against to this, management is more involved in ensuring adequate execution of policy decisions prescribed at the top management level. But in real practice, there is a certain overlap between the two and it is very difficult to demark the two, as many managers are involved in both the activities i.e. thinking and doing aspects. It can be explained that as one of them say thinking aspect, i.e. administration work descends, and the execution work i.e., managerial work increases. This is shown in Fig.1.1.

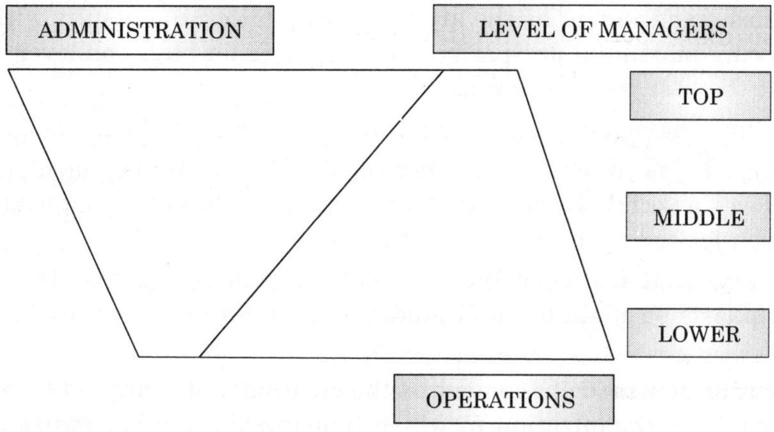

Fig. 1.1. Administration and Management

The word **organizing** or **organization planning** is generally taken to refer:

(a) The logical combining or grouping of activities,

(b) The delineating of authority and responsibility, and

(c) The establishment of working relationships among the human beings within the organization.

Organizing sometimes also refers to combining appropriately materials, machines, equipment and efforts of manpower with a view to accomplish the desired goals and objectives of the company. The word organization is also used to refer to the structure or network showing the relationship between the individual managers in the organization. In this context, the management function is divided into two aspects, namely **(i) Administrative management, and (ii) Operative management.**

Administrative management is concerned with the laying down of policies and the preparing of plans as well as with evaluating the performance against predetermined goals or targets or standards. Operative management, on the other hand is concerned with the actual execution of the plans, through the use of resources. To summarize:

Administration is the function in industry concerned with the determination of the corporate policy, the coordination of resources, production and distribution, the settlement of the compass of the organization and the ultimate control of the executive.

Management is the function in industry concerned with the execution of policy, within the limits set up by the administration and the employment of the organization for the particular objects set before it.

Organization is the process of combining the work, which individuals or groups have to perform with the faculties necessary for its execution that the duties, so formed, provide the best channels for the efficient, systematic, positive and coordinated application of the available effort.

1.4. DEFINITION OF MANAGEMENT

John F. Mee defines management as the art of securing maximum results with a minimum of effort so as to secure maximum prosperity and happiness for both employer and employee and give the public the best possible service.

R.C. Davis defines management as tough function of executive leadership anywhere.

Mary Cushing Niles defines management as Good Management, or Scientific Management, achieves a social objective with the best use of human, material energy, time and with satisfaction for the participants and the public.

E.F.L. Brech says that management is concerned with seeing that the job gets done —its tasks put emphasis on planning and guiding the operations that are going on in the enterprise.

Prof. A. Dasgupta defines management as the creation and control of technological and human environment of an organization in which human skill and capacities of individuals and groups find full scope for their effective use in order to accomplish the objective for which an enterprise has been set up. It is involved in the relationships of the individual, group, organization and the environment.

Many authors defined management in their own way of learning. Many definitions concentrate on getting things done by the people through coordinating, using the resources of the organization to fulfill the goal for which the organization is set up.

Management is also looked upon as a process concerned with planning, executing and controlling the activities of an enterprise.

1.4.1. Different Meanings of Management

The word management can be referred **as a field of learning, a body of organized knowledge, which is taught in universities and business schools.**

Another way of thinking is collective sense of the managerial group of an organization; say for example, 'the *management* of the college has declared the vacation period'.

Management may also be taken as an occupation or a career.

1.5. IS MANAGEMENT AN ART OR SCIENCE?

Art refers to know-how or systematic skills for the effective accomplishment of desired results. Every art is practical in that the proof of the practitioner's competence lies in the tangible results that he can show. Art is used in creating things; hence it is creative in nature. Any manager's work is to get the things done by the people for getting the desired targets. In this process, many a time he has to use his skills to deal with human beings so that they cooperate with manager and fulfill the mission without any difficulty. Instead of ordering by using his official power, he can as well guide them in a friendly way, so that they may feel a sense of working. A manager must use his skills to motivate the people under him by creating a friendly atmosphere in the organization, so that everybody feel that he is working for his organization and he realizes the benefits when the goal of the organization is reached. Hence, we can say management as an art of getting things done by the people for the accomplishment of desired goals.

Science refers to organized theoretical knowledge empirically derived, critically tested and generalized into theories, laws and principles. Many a time manager, who is making a decision, has to deal with the data on his hand and use mathematical techniques. While making decisions, he has to use logical thinking and scientific methods to obtain optimal results. Hence, we can say that *management is both art and science.* The science of management provides certain general principles, which can guide managers in their professional effort. The art of the management consists in tackling every situation in an effective manner. Hence, we can summarize the nature of management as:

1. It is an art.
2. It is a science or a discipline.
3. It is a process of achieving results.
4. It is a social process involving integration of people for common objectives.
5. It is organized to lead to the achievement of predetermined objectives.
6. It is a profession, which involves specialized training and is governed by an ethical code arising out of its social obligations.

1.6. DEVELOPMENT OF MANAGEMENT THOUGHT

Before, we study the evolution of management thought, it is better we understand some of the works of pioneers in management. The most important persons are:

(a) Fredric Winslow Taylor (F.W. Taylor):1856–1916: U.S.A.
(b) Henry Robinson: 1844–1924: U.S.A.
(c) Harrington Emerson: 1853–1931: U.S.A.
(d) Fredric Arthur Halsey: 1856–1935: U.S.A.
(e) Henry Laurence Gantt (H.L. Gantt): 1861–1919: U.S.A.
(f) Mary Parker Follet: 1868–1933: U.S.A.
(g) Frank Bunker Gilbreth: 1868–1924: U.S.A.
(h) George Elton Mayo: 1880–1949: Australia.

Let us now briefly discuss the contributions of the above-mentioned persons to the field of industrial management.

(a) Fredric Winslow Taylor: F.W. Taylor coined the word scientific management and his work *Principles of Scientific Management was published* in the year 1911. From that time onwards greater attention has been given to scientific management as a separate discipline worth studying. F.W. Taylor has been accepted as father of scientific management in spite of severe criticism about his works. Taylor received training as a machinist in 1873 and took position in 1878 in Midvale Steel Works at Philadelphia and become chief engineer of the plant in the year 1884, at the age of 31 years. He began to concentrate attention on such basic industrial problems as *which is the best way to do a work? What should constitute a day's work?* He deliberately set out to give answers to many of these questions. He extended his studies further and endeavored to establish basic principles of management, which would apply to all fields of industrial activity. He explained his objectives as:

The development of a science for each element of a man's work, thereby replacing the old thumb rule method.

(i) The selection of the best worker for each particular task and then training, teaching and developing the workman; in place of the former practice of allowing the worker to select his own task and train himself as best as he could.

(ii) The development of a spirit of hearty cooperation between management and the men to carry the activities in accordance with the principles of the developed science.

(iii) The division of the work into almost equal shares between management and the workers, each department taking over the work for which it is best fitted; instead of the former condition in which almost all of the work and the greater part of the responsibility were thrown on the men.

It were these principles, extended and applied, which formed the basis of what has been called ***'Scientific Management'.***

In the year 1989, Taylor went to Bethlehem Steel Works, where he undertook his famous studies of shoveling. He designed an optimal shovel and by which the productivity increased. He also started planning department in order to determine in advance the amount of work to be done in the yard during the ensuing day. The credit must go to him for naming his technique ***'time study'*** for necessity of time studies became the principal feature of his scientific management.

(b) Henry Robinson Towen: Towne's most significant contribution to management was the leading part he played in persuading his fellow engineers to extend the traditional scope of their professional interest to include management subjects. He also elaborated an important management technique when he presented the results of the ***gain sharing*** system operating in his own works. Under this system gains were awarded to the departments on the basis of relative efficiency. This was a modified form of profit sharing on a group basis and an attempt for improving the traditional piece rate system.

(c) Harrington Emerson: He is well known as ***efficiency engineer***; he popularized scientific management and expounded the concepts of standard time, standard costs, preventable wastes etc. He was the first man to call attention to the lessons to be learnt from military experienced by business management.

(d) Frederic Arthur Halsey: He originated first successful **incentive scheme** of wage payment in the American industry and improved upon the ordinary piece rate system. His incentive schemes have advantages over piece rate system, day rate system and Twine's gain sharing system. Halsey's **premium plan of paying labour** aimed at eliminating rate cutting. It guaranteed daily or hourly rate for fixed quantity of work as agreed with the worker based on customary performance in the past. The premium payment was provided for any additional work of about one-half to one-third of the sum normally payable for such work. As the employer gets benefit from increased output, he should not indulge in rate cutting.

(e) Henry Laurence Gantt: He is very much bothered about human beings in industry. He considered human resource as the most important one in all problems of management. He is also described as ***'The forerunner of modern industrial***

democracy'. He was famous for one particular chart, which bears his name although he evolved many charts. This chart is known as **Gantt chart**, which is used for scheduling the work. He also devised incentive schemes to motivate human beings to work.

(f) **Mary Parker Follett:** Her contribution to industrial management is the application of ***'psychological insight* and findings of *social science'***. She was herself a political and social philosopher. She offered a new conception of the nature of management and of human relationships within industrial groups. She showed that conflict can be constructive and could be harnessed to the service of the groups.

(g) **Frank Bunker Gilbreth:** The industrial world owes an incalculable debt to Frank and Lillian Gilbreth, for the development of what they named ***'motion study'***, an intensification of the broad pioneering method studies of Robert Owen and many others. Frank B. Gilbreth was a New England contractor and industrial consultant and another pioneer in the field of scientific management. He was always greatly assisted by his wife, Dr. Lillian Gilbreth, a trained psychologist, who until her death played an active part in the continuation of her husband's work. Gilbreth started as a bricklayer and become a successful contractor. His wife worked for many years to win her doctorate in psychology; yet she was able at the same time to assist her husband materially in his work to develop the technique motion study, which concentrates on finding the best way of doing the work.

(h) **George Elton Mayo:** Elton Mayo is famous for his contribution to management on the human and the social factors in industrial relationships and the great difficulty in developing true scientific techniques applicable to the study of social behaviour. He is very famous for his investigation at Hawthorne. His experiments at Hawthorne emphasized that the emotional, non-logical attitudes and sentiments are more important even in economic relationships than the logical, economic ones.

1.7. THE EVOLUTION OF MANAGEMENT DISCIPLINE

Until Industrial revolution after World War II, adequate thought was not given to the practice of management as separate discipline. Development of management theory on a systematic basis began in twentieth century because of industrial revolution and advent of factory system. Economists, psychologists, sociologists, engineers etc. Made contributions to the theory of management to promote management as separate discipline. Development of management thought in a time perspective can be divided into four stages, as:

1. The Scientific Management Stage,
2. The Organizational Stage,
3. The Management Process Stage, and
4. The General Management Theory Stage.

1.7.1. The Scientific Management Stage

During early 20th century, man was very much interested in using human effort effectively. His intention was to reduce the waste and unnecessary operations from human work and to increase the productivity. In this direction, the work was divided as *operative work* and *planning work.* Top level management was responsible for planning the work effectively and the lower level managers or operative management was responsible for executing the plan. Thus the line organization, line and staff organization structures developed during this period. Wage payment plans were aimed at providing incentives for the worker for maximum motivation. Thus a major break-through was affected during this decade of World War I with the greatest contributions being that of Taylor and Fayol. In short it was conceived as mental attitudes towards intelligent use of human effort to increase the productivity by reducing the wastages and at the same time taking care of labour welfare.

1.7.2. The Organizational Stage

In the next decade, that is during 1930s more attention was given to organization as a structure for carrying out managerial assignments. Administration was concerned with formulation of polices and the establishment of the organization through which the plan was executed and the organization structure become a management mechanism for carrying out the work assignment. Management's main concern was to control and ensure proper work performance with the organization structure. Later on certain people divided the work of management as *administrative management* and *operative management* where administrative management was responsible for formulation of policies, plans and the operative management was responsible for execution of plans.

1.7.3. The Management Process Stage

In the next decade, i.e. during 1940, more emphasis is placed on two management functions ***planning*** and ***control*** to crystallize the objectives, so that all activities are directed to achieve the desired objectives. Thus achievement of objectives of an enterprise as a whole became the basis of conceptual framework of the management and more stress was placed on the process of *managing.* In this stage more emphasis is placed on setting of objectives, goals and also on the functions of management such as organizing, staffing, motivating etc. to fulfil the organizational objectives.

1.7.4. The General Management Theory Stage

In this stage, the management concepts so far evolved is synthesized into a conceptual framework for a general management theory. The process of managing was influenced by *technology.* Developments in communication and information technology, advent of computers in database management, use of operations research techniques in decision-making have dramatically changed the process of management. Especially after World War II, one can recognize the changes in management approach and then onwards, due to changes in technology, introduction of computers in decision-making process, a new wave swept the general management theory, due to which *new schools of management thought* began to evolve.

1.8. SCHOOL OF MANAGEMENT THOUGHT

Several schools of management thought have evolved over a period of time depending on the learning and philosophy of the exponents. A study of literature in the field of management is necessary to the modern manager, so as to develop his own way of solving the managerial problems and managing the resources of an enterprise effectively. The mental philosophy of the manager will be automatically conditioned by his own thinking and frame of reference. His leaning will automatically be in favour of certain philosophy or school of thought. Various schools of management thought available are:

1. The Empirical or Management by Custom School
2. The Human Behaviour or Human Relations School
3. The Social System School
4. The Decision Theory or Decisional Management School
5. The Mathematical or Quantitative Measurement School
6. The System's Approach or Systems Management School
7. The Management Process School
8. Contingency School.

1.8.1. The Empirical or Management by Custom School

Those who believe in this thought, is of the opinion that the management is a study of the experiences of managers. If managerial experiences can be studied closely, management knowledge would emerge and grow out of it. Other managers in making their own decisions and solving managerial problems faced by them can use this knowledge. But this school of thought depends heavily on the historical methods of study. The *basic assumption of this approach to the study of management is* that the study of actual business situation contributes to the development of management skill. Even today we can see that in management courses much importance is given to the case studies to train students to understand and solve the managerial problems. By studying the management situations, which are unique the manager gets on idea about what could be the good managerial decisions and what makes the decisions poor. By studying the cases he can also develop the analytical and problem solving abilities, which are very essential for the successful practice of management in actual life. This school of thought is based on the proverb ***'learn from experience'.***

Empirical school of thought goes mainly by precedents in so far as it studies the managerial situations handled by the mangers and their own experience. However, the exponents of this school do not fully realize that a manager has to work under dynamic conditions and that history does not exactly repeat by itself. The situations of the past may not be exactly same as that of the present because of the development of technology, information system and changes in the social system. Hence manager may face a problem if he tries to transfer the ideas gained by study of experiences of previous managers straight away.

While making decisions, manager must use his knowledge from previous case studies as guidelines, study the present problem, try to combine his experience, knowledge from cases and commonsense to solve the problem. In the words of Harold Koontz ***"Management unlike law is not a science based on precedents and situations in the future exactly comparable to the past are exceedingly unlikely to occur. There is a positive danger in relying too much of the past experience and on undistilled history of managerial problems solving for the simple reason that the technique of approach found right in the past may not fit the situation of the future".*** The principle tool of study for the empirical school of thought is the case method. The case is considered to be the most convenient way of acquiring skill of decision-making. However, this method is not necessarily the best method in imparting training for decision-making. In decision-making, there are several complex variables, which change under dynamic conditions. It is because of this, case study method has its own limitations. The main contributors of this school of thought are: *Harvard Business School, Ernest Dale and the Management Associations in various countries, especially American Management Association.* The main features of this school of thought are:

(a) Management is the study of experience.

(b) The management experience can be passed over to the practitioners and students.

(c) The success and the failure of management in the process of decision-making could provide guidance to the manager in the similar situation.

(d) Theoretical research has to be based on practical experience.

1.8.2. The Human Behaviour or Human Relation School

Management could be rightly thought of as the process of getting things done through or with people. If that is so, any organization could be compared to a structure made up of human beings. The relationship among these people is the cementing force that binds them together in pursuit of common organizational goals. According to this school of thought *management is the study of behavior of people at work.* This school had its origin in a series of experiments conducted by *Professor Elton Mayo* and his associates in Harvard School of Business at the Western Electric Company's Hawthorns works near Chicago. These studies brought out for the first time the importance of relationship between social factors and productivity. Until then the productivity of the employee was considered to be a function only on physical conditions of work and money wages paid to them. For the first time it was realized that productivity depended heavily upon the satisfaction of the employee in work situations.

Following the Hawthorne Experiments, a great deal of work has been carried on by *behavioral Scientists* belonging to variety of disciplines including psychology, sociology, anthropology and philosophy in studying the behavior of people at work in organizations. Those who subscribe to the Human Relations or the Human Behavior School of thought are of the view that the effectiveness of any organization depends upon the quality of relationships among the people working in the organization. Supporters of this school are of the opinion that the management should concern itself with the analysis of organizational behavior or the interaction among the people at work. Apart from the study of formal organization and techniques used by such organizations, this school studies the psychological change, motivation and relationships among the various groups of people constituting organization and the climate of the organizations. In short this school of thought concentrates on people and their behavior, within formal and informal organization. To summarize, the main features of this school are:

(a) Since management is getting things done through or with people, a manager must have a basic understanding of human behavior in all its aspects, particularly in the context of work groups and organizations.

(b) Management must study inter-personal relations among people.

(c) Motivation of people and higher productivity can be achieved only through good human relations.

(d) Motivation, leadership, communicating, trading, participative management and group dynamics are critical to the study of management.

(e) The study of management draws upon the concepts and principles of various behavioral sciences like psychology and social psychology.

The main thinkers subscribing to this school of thought are Elton Mayo, Roethlisbergar, Mc Gregor and Keith Davis. This school has also benefited from the contributions of psychologists like Maslow, Argyris, Herzberg and Mc Clelland.

1.8.3. The Social System School

This school of thought is closely related to the Human Behavior or Human Relations School of thought. In this school of thought, an organization is considered as a *Social System* consisting of various groups of people. The founder of this thought is *Chester Bernard*, who considered an organization as a cooperative system involving collaboration and cooperation among various groups of people. In real world, we can see that cooperation among the people exists, the society will not have any problem, so also, in an organization, which is considered to a social system consisting various groups of people working together to fulfil organizational goals must work with common understanding and cooperation. The major contribution of this school of thought is in the development of concepts and theories related to the formal organization, that is, the organization as formerly planned by the entrepreneurs or the top management. Another area in which valuable contribution has been made by the pioneers belonging to this school is that of the informal organization.

An important aspect of the Social System School of thought in management is its focus on the cultural factors in the working of an organization. It is recognized by the exponents of this school that people working together in groups have their own norms and values, which have a bearing on the contribution that they are likely to make towards the goals of the organization. More over the organization has its own cultural environment made of norms and values, which in turn has affect on the functioning of the organization. If the elements of society are highly disciplined one, then the employees will also are of high culture and discipline. The main features of this school are:

(a) An organization is a social system. It is a system of cultural relationship and management concerned with the effectiveness of an organization must study it as such.

(b) Formal organizations represent cultural relationships of the social groups working within the organization.

(c) Cooperation among the working members and to groups is essential which is the core of the effective management.

(d) Management has to direct its efforts towards establishing harmony between the goals of organization and the needs, aims and aspirations of the people comprising the various groups in the organization.

(e) Relationship exists between internal and external environments may change from time to time depending upon social changes.

The main pioneers and contributors to this field are Max Weber, Moreno, Simon and Rensis Likert.

1.8.4. Decision Theory School or Decisional Management School

The main work of Management is to make decisions. Whatever a manager does is the outcome of a decision made by him from the data on hand and the alternatives available to him. The decision theory school of management thought concentrates its attention on decision-making and treats the various aspects of decision-making as constituting the scope of the study of management. This school of thought has its origins in the theory of consumer's choice, which has been the favorite preoccupation of the economists since early 19th century. Economists have been trying to determine the process through which a consumer makes a rational choice from among a number of alternative commodities or products available to him. It also takes into account some of the relatively rational or logical aspects of consumer's choice. While the Decision Theory School of Thought accepts the basic assumptions that decisions are taken through rational choice from among different alternatives given different constrains, it does not confine itself to the process of decision-making. In fact analysis of this school includes the behavior of the person or organizational groups making the decision. Going further into the question of decision-making, the exponents of this school also concern themselves with the various factors involved in decision-making including the implementation of the decisions, the psychological and sociological foundation of decisions and even the cultural background of the decision-makers. This school of thought is very close to the Social System School of thought. The main features of this school of thought are:

(a) Decision-making is very important in the study of management.

(b) The field of management theory is in essence the field of decision-making.

(c) The members of any organization are essentially decision-makers and problem-solvers irrespective of their cadre. Hence, management is the study of the process of decision-making, the personalities and behavior of the decision-makers.

(d) Management Information System, the process and techniques of decision-making form the subject matter of the study of management according the decision theory school of thought.

The main contributors and thinkers of this school of thought are Chester Bernard, James March, Herbert Simon, Forrester and Richard Cyert.

1.8.5. The Mathematical School of Thought or Quantative Measurement School of Thought

Mathematics has been universally recognized as an important tool of analysis and a language for precise expression of concepts and relationships among concepts. Mathematics has now made entry in the field of management and is used by modern managers in decision-making process. Now all branches of study have been considered as optimal blend of mathematics and the principle subject. The scientific, technological developments as well as the introduction of computers have brought management and mathematics closer to each other. Mathematics is being used in management to study various problems and analyze them to find an optimal and rational solution to these problems. In this sense, mathematics is closely related to the Mathematical School of Thought or Decision Theory School of Management.

The exponents of the mathematical school of thought believe that effective solutions to the problems of management can be achieved through application of simulation and by the use of analytic and synthetic mathematical techniques. The contributors this school of thought have been using mathematical and quantitative techniques in developing models of the various kinds of decision and problems involved in managing organization with a view to understanding them also finding optimal solutions to them. For example a manager can use inventory models to solve the problems of inventory, Maintenance models to solve the problems of maintenance and Resource allocation models to have optimal utilization of existing resources. Now-a-day, the mathematical branch *Operations Research* has become indispensable tool of a modern manager in making decisions. In fact it is Fredric Winslow Taylor (F.W.Taylor), father of scientific management has advocated the use of science in management. The thinkers of this school have been labeled as *Management Scientists.* The main features of mathematical school of thought are:

(a) Management is concerned with problem solving and it must make use of mathematical tools and techniques for the purpose.

(b) The different factors involved in management can be quantified, expressed in the form of models and with the help of mathematics they can be solved.

(c) Management problems can be expressed in mathematical symbols.

(d) Operations Research, mathematical tools simulation and model building are the basic methodologies developed by this school of thought.

But one thing we have to remember is that mathematical models cannot be substitutes for sound judgement, they are only the means to make decisions. The results of the decision depend on the experience and insight of the decision-maker. The main contributors of this school of thought are, F.W. Taylor, Gilbreth, Henry Gantt, Joel Dean, Newmann, Ackoff and Hicks. Mathematics has certainly helped management in systematizing thinking and has lent a certain measure of exactness to the management discipline.

1.8.6. The System Approach or Systems Management School

No doubt that major contribution in the development of management thought since 1960s have come basically from the quantitative and behavioral science schools of thought. However, a new direction in management thought has evolved which is named as ***Systems Approach.*** Though the systems approach is very much common in natural and physical sciences, this application is new to the field of management. The system is composed of related and interdependent elements, which form a unitary whole. It may be considered an assembling or a combination of things or parts forming a complex whole. Every system is made up of a number of sub-systems arranged in a hierarchy. From this point of view that an organization may be considered as a system made of number of sub-systems as marketing department, personal department, finance department and production department. Once again each sub-system may be considered as an independent system for detailed analysis. According to the Systems Approach School of thought, attention must be given to the overall effectiveness of the system rather than the effectiveness of a sub-system in isolation. The major concerns here are inter-relationship and inter dependence of various sub-systems, from the point of view of the total effectiveness of main system. According to the traditional schools of management thought developed before the Systems Approach, each department or function of management has to be studied separately. However, with the introduction of the Systems Approach, this approach or method of study has to be changed. In an organization, for instance, a project management approach may be introduced by forming teams drawn from different specialization coordinated by a project manager. This team represents a combination of sub-systems brought together in pursuit of goals of the organization (main system). Systems could be simple or complex. Simple systems can be studied in terms of input, the process and the output. In addition, feedback from the output could be linked with the input so that improvements could be brought about in input or process. To study large and complex systems, computers are used to build up models and to simulate. The major features of this school are:

(a) A system consists of interdependent and inter-related parts known as sub- systems.

(b) The systems approach emphasizes the study of the various parts in their inter-relationships rather than in isolation from each other.

(c) The systems approach to management brings out the complexity of a real life management problem much more sharply than any of the other approaches.

(d) The systems approach can be utilized by any of the other approaches including the process approach, the mathematical approach etc.

(e) The systems approach has been utilized in studying the function of complex organizations.

The major contributors to the Systems Approach School of thought are Kenneth, Boulding, Johnson, Cast, Rosen Zweig and C.W. Churchman. We can also remember here Martin, particularly in the area of management audit system. The Systems Approach has an edge over the other approaches in so far as the closeness to reality is concerned.

1.8.7. Management Process School or the Operational Approach School

This approach is also known as *Traditional Approach, the Universalistic Approach* or the *Classicist Approach.* Henry Fayol, a French management practitioner is the founder of this school of thought. According to this school of thought, management can be best studied in terms of the process consisting of five broad categories of functions, namely, *Planning, Organizing, Staffing, Directing* and *Controlling.* Based on this, this school of thought has evolved some universal principles of management. The subscribers of this school are of the view that management principles are universally applicable. These principles can be applied to any type of organization, may be business, trade, manufacturing organizations or government organizations. Main features of this school of thought are:

(a) The study of management should focus on the role and functions of managers.

(b) The functions of managers are the same irrespective of the type of organization.

(c) The conceptual framework of management can be built through an analysis of the processes of management and identification of principles.

(d) The five functions, namely, planning, organizing, staffing, directing and controlling are the core of management.

This school of thought has been criticized on the following:

(a) This school is loosing ground as hardly any significant contribution has been made after Henry Fayol's contribution.

(b) The so-called universal principles of management do not always stand the test of empirical scrutiny.

(c) Organizations functions under dynamic conditions and therefore searching for universal principles may not always be a fruitful exercise.

With all these criticisms, the management process school does prove a concept on framework, which could be efficiently utilized in understanding the basics of management.

The chief contributors of this school of thought are Henry Fayol, J.D.Mooney, A.C. Reiley, Lyndall Urwick, Haroled Koontz, Newman and McFarland.

1.8.8. The Contingency Approach School of Management

From all the above discussions we can see that the whole field of management is divided into two streams.

1. *Behavioral Approach,* and
2. *Quantitative Approach.*

Quantitative approach is applied in some situations while the behavioral approach works in some other situations. Those who work in the fields of psychology, sociology, anthropology and philosophy are the followers of behavioral approach and provide useful insight to the field of management from their works. Those who come from disciplines like mathematics; physical sciences have been trying to apply quantitative techniques of analyses to an understanding of management problems. The main problem however is that while quantitative people could not overcome behavioral problems, the behavioral people could not cope up with operational problems adaptable to quantitative solutions. In recent years it is seen neither of the two have answers to all the situations. When manager faces with a problem, he must use the basic principles of the two approaches and blend them with his experience and apply systems approach to get a reliable answer. In view of this, the thinkers and writers in the field of management is now veering round the view that the study of management calls for a contingency approach, which falls *somewhere between simplistic and specific principles and complex and vague notions.* According to this approach, management is situational. Study of management according to this approach, lies in identifying the important variables in the situation. This approach has been used in important sub-systems of management like organization, design, leadership, behavior and operations. In present scence of management this approach is more suitable one. Major contributors to this school are: Woodward, Fiedler, Lorsch and Lawrence.

1.9. FAYOL'S PRINCIPLES OF MANAGEMENT

The search for fundamental truths has resulted in the identification and the defining of certain principles of management. Some people avoid theories and emphasize merely practice. Their view is that management is purely an art and not a science. Through lack of appreciation of the alliance between theory and practice (both reinforcing the other) some businessmen and mangers proudly state that they never read a book on management. Their view is that they do not want to follow textbook approach to solve management problems, and they laugh at management principles. Some managers even say that they are very successful in spite of breaking every principles of management. But they are forgetting that they are using the principles of management without their knowledge of application and they say that their success is due to their own way of managing. Koontz and O'Donnell describe a theory as *'systematic grouping of interrelated principles'*. They divide principles into two types, namely, (1) Descriptive, and (2) Prescriptive. The *descriptive principle* simply describes the relationship between variables while the *prescriptive* or *normative principle* indicates what a person should do, it prescribes the action. By increasing the effectiveness of management, management principles contribute to the attainment of social objectives through a more efficient way of material and human resources available to an organization. The importance of management principles lies in increasing the efficiency of a manager in operating his organization.

Fayol's Principles of Management

Henry Fayol emphasized, "The soundness and good working order of the corporate body depend on a certain number of conditions, termed as ***principles, laws and rules***". He is of the opinion that there is nothing rigid or absolute in management affairs and it all being a question of proportion. He said that the principles are flexible and can be adaptable to any need. Only difficult task is to know *how to use them*, which needs intelligence, experience decision and proportion. The given below are the *fourteen principles of management* given by Henry Fayol.

1. Division of work,
2. Authority and Responsibility,
3. Discipline,
4. Unity of command,
5. Unity of direction,
6. Subordination of individual interest to the general interest,
7. Remuneration,
8. Centralization,
9. Scalar chain (Line of Authority),
10. Order,
11. Equity,
12. Stability or tenure of personnel,
13. Initiative, and
14. Esprit de corps.

1.9.1. Division of Work

Fayol describes that higher productivity can be achieved by division of work with the same effort. He says that the division of work and specialization as the best means of increasing the productivity and he also says that division of work has its limits, which should not be exceeded. The principle here is the whole work which can be divided into small units then each unit is allocated to one worker and train him in that work, so that he become proficient in that work and does it without much strain thus increasing productivity. But there is a danger of monotony and boredom, which may have effect on the worker.

1.9.2. Authority and Responsibility

According to Fayol, ***Authority is the right to give orders and the power to exact obedience***. Manager has two types of authority one being derived from his position in the office, i.e. *official authority,* and other derived from his experience, qualification, intelligence, moral worth and ability to lead etc, which is known as *personal authority.* He describes *responsibility* as a corollary of authority, as its natural consequence and essential counterpart. It is interesting to note that his stress on responsibility being feared as much as authority is sought then after requires the good leader to infuse in persons around him –'***courage to accept responsibility.***' In fact authority and responsibility are the two faces of the same coin. If one comes automatically other exists. Authority can be delegated to the subordinate but responsibility cannot be. Ultimately, manager who handles the project is responsible for all results of the project, even though he has delegated the authority to his subordinate.

1.9.3. Discipline

Fayol believes that *discipline* is absolutely essential for the smooth running of business. Here, *'discipline is respect for agreements, which are, directed at achieving obedience, application, energy, and the outward marks of respect.'* The best means of establishing and maintaining discipline are (a) To appoint good superiors at all levels, (b) have clear and fair agreement between management and employees and (c) The punishment or penalty or sanctions must be judiciously applied.

1.9.4. Unity of Command

Unity of command means an employee must receive orders from one superior only for any action whatsoever. An individual or a department feels uneasiness if he or it receives orders from two different superiors and the person or the department will be under confusion in deciding to whom he has to obey. He also says that the dual command is a perpetual source to many conflicts. Consider in a house if a child receives command from both father and mother at the same time, the child will be in dilemma as to obey whom. In case, the child receives command from either father or mother or from mother through father, it will feel happy. By unity of command duplication of work may be avoided.

1.9.5. Unity of Direction

This is best explained as *'one head and one plan for a group of activities having the same objective'* This is essential for 'unity of action, coordination of strength and focusing of effort'. Unity of direction refers to *'one head, one plan'* whilst unity of command emphasizes' *one employee to have orders from one superior only'*. In real life situation also we can see that if a person receives orders or command from one person only, it will be easy for him to do work without confusion. Also we see that employees of group must have one objective to fulfill. If individuals of a group have different objectives, then nothing can be achieved. Here objectives refer to organizational objective and not personal objectives.

1.9.6. Subordination of Individual Interest to the General Interest

For the well being of an organization, its employee or group of employees must consider the institutional objective/interest is superior that their personal goals and interests. But in general, due to human characteristics like-ignorance, ambition, selfishness, laziness and weakness, man ignores institutional interest and tries to satisfy the personal interests.

1.9.7. Remuneration of Personnel

The remuneration is the price paid to the worker/employee by the firm for the services rendered by him. The remuneration should be on par with the existing market rate and must be quite enough for the employee to lead his life happily and satisfy his mere needs. At the same time the remuneration paid should not be too excess. It should be fair enough that both employee and the employer are satisfied.

1.9.8. Centralization

Here he refers to the centralization of authority. The importance of role of subordinate and executive depends on the degree of centralization exists in the organization. More the centralization, of authority more will be the importance of executive and more the decentralization, the subordinate's role is important. Any way certain amount of centralization and decentralization exists in all the organizations. This is necessary for smooth running of the organization. But the manager must be careful to see that there will be an optimum degree of combination of both in the organization to get fruitful results.

1.9.9. Scalar Chain

Scalar chain concerned with the flow of authority from the top management to the low level managers. It also indicates line of communication. It clearly shows who is accountable to whom. General scalar chain indicates line of communication and flow line of authority. Thus the line of authority is routed via every link in the chain by all communications, which commence from or reach the ultimate authority. This path is disastrously lengthy in large concerns, notably in government organizations. One should not depart needlessly from the line of authority but it is even a greater error to stick to it when detrimental to the business.

1.9.10. Order

Order refers to indicate where one should be. Here the rule is *'a place for everything and everything must be in its place'* for materials and for men 'a *place fore everyone and everyone must be in his place'*. It is the principle of organization for arrangement of material things and human beings. It is a must for both *material order* and *social order*. When this principle is followed, one car find the required material/person when needed without much difficulty and without wasting time.

1.9.11. Equity

Equity refers to the act of creating a sense of loyalty and devotion among the employees of all levels. This makes them to feel that they are also important in the organization and the organization belongs to them and it is their duty to see that they have to work with commitment, so that the unit will grow healthily, which in turn help their personal growth.

Equity results from kindness and justice. When these two exists, the loyalty and devotion automatically will be the characteristics of the employees.

1.9.12. Stability of Tenure of Personnel

This refers to the stay of an employee/manager in an organization. Whenever an employee joins the organization, he takes sometime to learn the job and get proficiency in that job, after which his higher productivity will benefit the organization. If the employee remains in the organization for a small length of time and when he has no guarantee of his stay in the organization, he will not show interest in the job and his work is a mere waste. It is a loss to the organization. It is the responsibility of the manager to see that labor turnover is kept at a minimum, so that trained workers will not leave the organization. Employee must have confidence that his job is secured and he will be with the organization until he retires. This point (Stability of Tenure) is as important as remuneration. These are the two factors required to keep good relation between management and workers.

1.9.13. Initiative

Every manager must think that he should develop his subordinates and try to create *initiative* in them, so that they work with commitment and cultivate the power of thinking to execute the given work. For this the manager may have to sacrifice some of his personal vanity. When the employees are encouraged to develop the power of thinking to execute the work, they take initiative and do the work.

1.9.14. Esprit de Corps

As *'union is strength'*, harmony and union among the personnel constitute the great strength of a concern. The dangers to be avoided are a misguided interpretation of the motto *'divide and rule'* and misunderstandings caused through poor communication. At the time of crisis, everyone must stand united and work to achieve the desired goal. Unity is to work and not to fight. Instead of unity for fighting, unity to bargain is healthier.

The principles enunciated are not aimed at being exhaustive but are the ones to which Fayol had recourse most often. He stresses the universality of such principles and their application not only to business but also for the success of all associations of individuals.

1.10. FUNCTIONS OF MANAGEMENT (OR THE MANAGEMENT PROCESS)

The basic aim of managing is to achieve certain objectives and goals. The manager must be sure of the objective or objectives he desires to attain or of the end results to be ensured. A precise and complete statement in this regard would make the objective clear and understood by all concerned, who have to direct their activities towards its attainment. Performing certain fundamental management functions, which can be listed as, attains the desired results, goals or objectives: *Planning, Organizing, Staffing, Motivating and Controlling.*

Among those who tried to analyze the functions of management, Henry Fayol's name is easily the most outstanding. According to Fayol, Managerial activities consists mainly *Forecasting and Planning, Organizing, Commanding, Coordinating and Controlling.* Fayol's approach to the functions of management has been most widely accepted and practically all authorities on management have based their description of such functions on it.

Gullick gave a formula word to indicate the principal functions of management. According to him, management functions may be indicated by the word **'PODSCORB'**.

P for Planning,
O for Organizing,
D for Directing,
S for Staffing,
CO for Coordinating,
R for Reporting and
B for Budgetting.

Out of all these Reporting covers Controlling activity. Budgetting represents Planning.

Taking everything into account, the principal functions of management in most of the business and non-business enterprises are:

1. **Planning**, this is aimed at achieving the desired results. This includes *Forecasting, Formulation of Objectives, Policies, Programs, Schedules, Procedures and Budgets.*
2. **Organizing,** This seeks to integrate the available factors into an optimum relationship, so that the plan can be put into effect. This includes *identification and grouping of work activities, Definition and delegation of responsibility and authority and Establishment of Authority-Responsibility relationship.*
3. **Staffing**, which attempts to select and develop right type of personnel suitable to the job on hand. This includes, *Selection, Communication, Participation, Appraisal, Counseling, Training, Compensation and Dismissal, etc.*
4. **Directing,** which aims at giving instructions to the concerned and directing them to do the work. This includes, *Decision-making, Guiding, Supervising, Communication and Motivating.* Motivating is to inspire and induce the people in the organization to direct their activities towards implementing the plan.
5. **Controlling**, this constantly evaluates to ensure that activities are being executed in terms of achievement of plans. This includes, *Laying down performance standards, Measurement, Interpretation, and Corrective action.*

The above-mentioned functions are briefly described below:

1.10.1. Planning

We have to *plan* in advance, if we want to accomplish satisfactorily anything of importance. Consider for example, you want to write an examination commencing on certain date. Then depending on the time available at your disposal, and the subjects that you have to write, you prepare a schedule of your activities indicating the allocation of time for each subject, so that you can attend the examination with confidence. This type of planning the activities well in advance to accomplish the desired results is very much common in our day-to-day life. This is sometimes referred as **Primacy of Planning**. All the facts relevant to a situation have to be collected so that the action taken is in accordance with what the facts dictate. The facts when analyzed will often generate more than one alternative course of action. The manager must select the alternative, which has the highest probability of yielding the maximum benefit or gains for his organization. Often the word *optimum* is used instead of *maximum,* as the word maximum may not constitute the most desirable objective. The selection from alternative courses of action is sometimes referred to as the **Principle of Alternative Planning** and involves decision-making, which is very closely connected with planning.

Planning involves the forecasting of *future* problems, events, selecting courses of actions to handle these foreseen or anticipated problems and events. Some describe planning, as decision-making because planning requires decision making based on:

(a) What should be done?

(b) How it should be done?

(c) Who will be responsible for doing it?

(d) Where action is to be taken?

(e) Why it is to be done?

This involves taking decisions in advance of action. Planning emphasizes the fact that if one knows where he is going, he is more likely to get there. Good managers endeavor to draft a plan, which will make things happen in the desired way. This can be put in a better way as: "Good managers make things happen and things do not just happen to themselves." To put shortly, planning is concerned with the fixing of objectives, determining the strategies and policies and the prescription of procedures as guidelines to future action.

1.10.2. Organizing

The function of organizing is the creation of a *structure* of duties and functions for the attainment of the objectives of the concern. The organization structure consists of a series of relationships at all levels of authority. Urwick defined organization as "determining what activities are necessary to any purpose and arranging them in groups which may be assigned to individuals.

It is an important function of management to organize the enterprise by grouping the activities necessary to carry out the plans into administrative units, and defining the relationships among the executives and workers in such units. Organization deals with the human and material factors in business. Mostly, when the resources are given it is the headache of the organizer to organize them properly. Many managers take a easy way trying to mould his organization according to the fancy and peculiarities of the men under him. But this is not proper. An outline of the organization must be thought out before hand, and the organizer should try to fit men to his ideas, rather than ideas to men. He may have to make deviations here and there, but such deviations should be temporary to be given up as soon as an opportunity comes. Fayol says in this connection "See that human and material organizations are suitable and ensure material and human order."

1.10.3. Staffing

Staffing is concerned with ensuring that right type of personnel is available to man and execute the varied activities required to attain the planned objectives of the organization. Therefore, staffing deals with forecasting manpower requirements search for right personnel through advertising, selection procedure and training and placement activities. It also includes manpower appraisal and development.

1.10.4. Directing

In practice, management is essentially the art and process of getting things done. The managers have, therefore, the responsibility not only of planning and organizing the operations but also of guiding and supervising the subordinates. This is the managerial function of *direction.*

The function of direction includes (a) Issuing of orders and instructions, (b) Guiding and teaching the subordinates in the proper methods of work; and (c) Supervising the subordinates to ensure that their performance confirms to the plans.

Henry Fayol, as the function of command identified directing. In modern times, the following aspects of the important managerial function are usually identified:

(a) Leadership,

(b) Communication,

(c) Motivation, and

(d) Supervision.

(a) Leadership: The function of direction involves the exercise of the function of leadership. Leadership, according to Chester I. Bernard, "is the quality of the behavior of individuals whereby they guide people or their activities in organized effort." A leader has the function of interpreting the objectives of group efforts and guiding or leading the group as a team towards the realization of these objectives. Managers at all levels act as leaders because they have subordinates, whose efforts are to be canalized in a definite direction. As leaders, they have not only to show the way but also to lead the group towards it. In doing this, the manager leading the whole or a part of the organization has to set an example to his followers. He has to establish both by conduct and expression the community of interests, which prompts people in a group; to work together for certain given objectives.

(b) Communication: The process of leadership as part of the function of direction requires effective communication between the leader and the subordinate as well as among the subordinates. Simply stated, the process of communication is the passing of information and understanding. In fact communication is what one does when he wants to create understanding in the mind of another. Here communication involves *systematic and contentious process of* ***telling, listening, understanding.*** It is the responsibility of management to establish and maintain channels whereby it can convey its own thinking and policies to the subordinates and can receive their reactions and an account of their problems.

(c) Motivation: Motivation means the creation among the personnel in the organization to work and cooperate for the accomplishment of common objectives. A manager, in managing, must motivate people to highest productivity. All administrative actions lose its point unless the members of the enterprise are willing to contribute their effort for the fulfillment to their assigned tasks. The role of motivation is to develop and intensify a desire in every member of the organization to work effectively with commitment in his position. The task of creating effective motivation calls for a proper appreciation of human behavior. Management has to reply on the insights provided by sociologists, psychologists and social anthropologists for such appreciation. A manager's personal philosophy and values are perhaps felt the most in the field of motivating or getting things done through people. A good manager should analyze whether his leadership is that of ***paternalism*** so common in India and Japan. Happy people do not necessarily work hard. Again, if one is good to his subordinates, it does not inevitably follows that they will work hard out of gratitude. A manager may be ***autocratic***, believing that his subordinates are lazy, indifferent, unambitious, do not want additional responsibility and do not like to work. As against this, the truly ***democratic*** type of leader is convinced that his subordinates are ambitious, desire more responsibility and want to work hard. He believes that it is his obligation to supply as a leader to the quality, which integrates the needs, goals of his subordinates with the ultimate objectives and goals of his organization. Thus the type of leadership, which will emanate from a manager, will depend upon the basic values of and management philosophy. A good manager would also know which type of leadership style is appropriate in a given situation with the type of subordinates or followers involved.

(d) Supervision. Literally supervision means overseeing. In directing their subordinates, the managers have generally to exercise supervision over them in the sense that they have to personally watch, direct and control their performance. While doing this, they have to plan the work of their subordinates, give them directions and instructions, guide them, what is most important, exercise leadership in gearing the subordinates together into a team. He has to listen to their grievances, complaints, maintain discipline and work standards. Thus the function of supervision has two broad aspects and they are: (*a*) Technical guidance and direction, and (*b*) Human relations and leadership. This function assumes greater importance at the lower levels of management as compared to the top or higher levels of management.

1.10.5. Controlling

In terms of managerial function, controlling is said to be consists of steps taken to ensure that the performance of the organization confirms to the set plans. A manager is responsible for controlling the work for which he is accountable. The managerial function of control is inseparably connected with the functions of planning. Unless the management is able to fix in clear terms the objectives of the organization which can chart out a clear and realistic course of action for their attainment, effective control is almost impossible. Most notable feature of the process of control is that it is forward-looking or futuristic. A manager cannot, for obvious reasons, control or do anything about past. He can study the past, note the pitfalls and avoid them in future with a view to preventing their reoccurrence. Many a time, adequate control can lead to innovation and improvements or modifications in previously determined objectives. Here again manager's personal philosophy and personal values play a vital role. If manager institute very strict control, then the subordinates may loose their initiative an enthusiasm. As against to this another manager may accept a more modern management philosophy of laying down standards of performance expected and provide that only the significant exceptions to such standards be brought to his attention. He will thus accept the ***Principle of Management by Exception.***

1.10.6. Co-ordination

Co-ordination is concerned with synchronizing and unifying the actions of a group of people or departments. Mooney and Ralley define co-ordination as "The orderly arrangement of group efforts to provide unity of action to provide in pursuit of a common purpose." Some authorities emphasize co-ordination as a separate function of management. This approach has not been adopted here because it is felt that co-ordination is emphasized in each of the functions of management process. Co-ordination must be sought from the very first step, namely planning, so that the plans of all departments are integrated into a master plan ensuring adequate co-ordination. Co-ordination should be considered as essence of manager ship.

Mary Parker Follet gave the following principles of co-ordination:

1. **Early Beginning:** Co-ordination must be sought in the early stages of activity. It may often be impossible or at least very difficult if this is attended to after work has preceded un-coordinated.
2. **Direct Contact:** Co-ordination should be attained by direct contact among the parties concerned. This would ensure promptness and avoid red-tapism.
3. **Reciprocity:** Co-ordination should be regarded as a reciprocal relating to all factors in the situation. Factors here mean: production, sales, finance, men and management.

Continuity: Co-ordination must be maintained as a continuous process.

1.11. TECHNIQUES OF CO-ORDINATION

Louis A. Allen suggests "a manager, in managing, must co-ordinate the work for which he is accountable by *balancing, timing and integrating*". Hence balancing, timing and integrating are the techniques of co-ordination.

- **Balancing** means that appropriate thing is provided to support or counterbalance the other.
- **Timing** involves the adjustment of the time schedules of different activities in such a way that they support and reinforce each other.
- **Integrating** implies the unification of the variety of diverse interests for the accomplishment of the organizational goals.

For effective co-ordination the following measures are taken in an organization:

(a) **Simplified Organization:** In the modern large-scale organizations, there is a tendency towards over-simplification. The organization gets divided into a series of department and each department works for its goals by side tracking the organizational goal. In such situations lots of problem arises in managing the organization. Sometimes it may need to re-organize the departments to get greater harmony among the departments. The need for clear-cut organization and procedures can hardly be over-emphasized. Organizational procedures should cover all activities and each person must be given clear understanding for which he is responsible and how his work is related to that of other individuals.

(b) **Harmonized Programs and Policies:** Planning should provide good opportunities for good co-ordination. All the departmental plans should be checked for consistency. The manager must ensure all plans of the departments that they add up to unified program and balance among the conflicting plans must be secured by proper course of action. Co-coordinated activities must not only be consistent with each other, but also to be performed at the proper time.

(c) **Well-designed Methods of Communication:** Good communication is the basic for proper co-ordination. Proper communication of information department to department is essential to prepare a workable plan and modification of future plans. Communication should be effective in both directions that are from top to bottom for giving orders, directions and from bottom to top to communicate the progress of work.

(d) **Voluntary Co-operation:** By establishing the dominant objectives among the people, voluntary co-operation may be obtained; this is possible in ideal conditions of the organization. Generally accepted customs and terms create easiness among the people working. Sometimes encouraging informal contacts among people help to supplement formal communication, providing liaison men to maintain close contact with various departments and using committees for informal exchange of ideas and views.

(e) **Co-ordination Through Supervision:** The supervising staff has a great thing to do in co-ordination of the activities of all people working under their purview through effective communication.

1.12. DECISION-MAKING

The task of management involvers making of countless decisions, so much so that some believe that management is decision-making. Peter.F. Drucker rightly said that "What ever manager does, he does through making decisions". Malvin T. Copeland writes, "Administration is essentially is a decision-making process and authority is responsible for making decisions and for ascertaining that the decisions made are carried out". Decision-making is very important in all the functions of management. It is described that the decision-making is choosing the best among the available alternatives and this can be done by using scientific methods or unconsciously in an automatic and responsive way. A decision may relate to the end or means or both. The characteristics of decision making are:

(a) It is the end process preceeded by deliberation and reasoning.

(b) It is the choice of optimal course among alternatives.

(c) It may be negative and may just be a decision not to decide.

(d) It relates the means to the end.

Types of Decisions

According to P.F. Drucker, there are four basic criteria, which determine the nature of a decision, and the level of authority that should make it. They are:

(a) The degree of futurity in it,

(b) Its impact on other functions,

(c) Number of qualitative factors that enter into it, and

(d) Whether it is periodically recurrent or rare, if not unique.

If the decision does not commit to the organization for a longer time or is immediately reversible, it is made at lower levels. The moment basic principles of conduct, ethical values, social and political beliefs have to be taken into account to make decisions, the higher level of management does it.

Steps of Decision Making

Stanley Vance has identified the following steps in decision-making:

(i) *Perception*: A state of awareness, out of which a consciousness of being arises,

(ii) *Conception*: **That power of the mind, which develops ideas out of perceptions. Concepts may term as schemes or designs for actions.**

(iii) *Investigation*: The search for, and the acquisition of information pertinent in specific concepts so that the relative advantages and limitations of alternative courses of action can be compared.

(iv) *Deliberations*: A mental weighing of relative merits and consequences attached to the alternative schemes of action.

(v) *Selection*: Discrimination among the available alternatives so that the most desirable course of action is selected as the decision.

(vi) *Promulgation*: A declaration or public anouncement of the decision so that all persons concerned are adequately notified.

1.13. MANAGERIAL OBJECTIVES

We have seen that first step in the managerial functions is planning. Planning starts with crystallizing the objectives and goals towards which the activities of the organization are to be directed. Objectives result in direction of action towards accomplishment of certain results described as goals/aims/mission or purposes. Though these words are used interchangeably, there slight difference in the shade of meaning. ***Mission*** refers to overall reason for which the organization exists, *purpose* refers to the commitment to a desired future and *objective* is a specific category of purpose. More specific than an objective or purpose is a ***goal.*** But for practical purposes all these words are synonymous. As objectives being a part of planning are concerned with the future or attainment at some future period of time. They may be classified as:

(a) Depending on the time period:

(i) Short term objectives or objectives of immediate achievement, and

(ii) Long term objectives or objectives attainable in distant future.

(b) Depending on the purpose:

(i) General or Overall Objectives, and

(ii) Specific objectives in each area such as Production, Marketing etc.

"The intended goal, which describes definite scope and suggests directions to efforts of a manager", defines Managerial Objectives"(Terry).

Benefits or Advantages of Objectives: The following are the *benefits* or *advantages* of objectives:

(a) Objectives always provide guidelines for planning; in fact they are the foundation of planning. All types of planning, such as budgeting, scheduling, procedures and policies etc can be effectively framed if we have clearly defined objectives.

(b) Objectives result in a better appreciation of what the organization is attempting to achieve, and *give meaning and direction to the people* working in the organization.

(c) As the duly established objectives are communicated to the people in the organization, all the groups work in the same direction, i.e. towards the attainment of objectives and hence a good *co-coordinated behavior exists among the working groups.*

(d) Objectives serve as *standards for control* of the organization and human effort.

(e) Objectives serve as *motivation device* by giving proper directions to the workers, who are thus motivated to direct their efforts in achieving the desired goals.

(f) They give direction and *force management to think ahead,* as the process of establishing objectives (both long-term and short-term) forces the incharge managers of accomplishing to look ahead, plans for eventualities and take a course of action which will help the organization or department concerned towards the right path for future success.

1.13.1. Management by Objectives (MBO)

The word **Management by Objectives or MBO** has become very popular today because of the advantages derived from that. Management by Objectives is also known as *Results Oriented Management* or *Management By Results.* MBO aims at *increasing the effectiveness of managers by placing the responsibility on each manager for achieving results for his part of the organization's activities.* Thus manager either with participation or consultation or through the "top-down approach" sets objectives. Where the subordinate concerned is actively associated in formulating his own objectives or goals in the light of the broader departmental or overall company objectives, he is more likely to achieve such goals or objectives as he has participated in the decision making process. The *essentials* of MBO are:

(a) **The individual and departmental objectives must dovetail into overall organizational objectives.** The departmental and individual objectives are framed after organization's overall objectives are framed and care must be taken to see that they are integrated into overall objective and all the people in the organization are motivated towards the *organizational objective.*

(b) Objectives must be **clearly defined and communicated to all concerned well in advance.** Objectives are to be specific in nature. Suppose the objective is to increase the market returns in the coming year. It should be clearly stated in what period it is to be achieved? By what means it is to be achieved? And by what percentage it should be increased?

(c) Objectives and goals must **reasonably attainable**. Before fixing the objectives, the manager must have clear idea about the *Strengths of the organization, Opportunities available, External and Internal threats and Weakness of the Organization.* If the objectives or standards are fixed too high, the result would be frustration and from the very beginning a decision by the individual concerned not just to try but to achieve the impossible.

(d) Objectives fixed for an individual **must consider factors controllable** by the individual, which might affect the achievement of individual goals.

(e) As both external and internal environment changes periodically, to suit the existing conditions the objectives **must be periodically reviewed.**

1.14. GENERAL OR OVERALL OBJECTIVES

General or overall objectives are set by top management level such as Chairman of the board or Board of Directors, and the Chief Executive. Top Management is also concerned with the establishment of *long-range* objectives, which is high-level responsibility. The general objectives may be stated as:

(a) Nature of the business,
(b) Economic contribution,
(c) The survival objective,
(d) The growth objective,
(e) The profit objective,
(f) Increasing productivity objective, and
(g) Social obligations objective.

(a) Nature of Business: The manager of an organization must have clear idea about his business. He should not think that he is doing business to earn profit only. But he is serving the consumers. He should have broad idea about the nature of his business. Many business fail in early stages because of wrong understanding of the objectives of the business and nature of business by the top-level managers. If they understand the nature of the business correctly, the business will grow. The success of *Lijjat Papad* and *Nirma washing powder* are the examples of such success. To find what the nature of business is, one must start with the prospect or the potential customer. What does he really buy? Where is he to be found? How can he be reached? And what is our business? We get the best answer to our questions, when we see the business from outside and think about it from market point of view.

(b) Economic Contribution: In the long-range perspective, a business unit must contribute to the economic needs of the society and that of nation. This can be done in the form of providing goods or services or a combination of both to the society. By doing so, some need of the customer and society has to be satisfied. The need of the human being thus constitutes the basic foundation of the business. If business cannot provide satisfaction to the consumer/market it cannot survive for a long time.

(c) The Survival Objective: Every organization wishes to survive and continue profitably. This is possible only if it makes an economic contribution and offers satisfaction of a need of the community. The chances of survival (and growth) will be higher, if organization is giving satisfaction to the community. The economic and political environment change such that organization must continue its profitable existence despite such changes. To survive, the organization must earn sufficient profits and pay proper dividends or otherwise it will be difficult in the future to get more outside capital. Survival of a business will depend upon its ability to cover the costs of staying in business, such as costs of replacement, obsolescence and uncertainty in the market risks. The survival of a business mostly depends upon the financial strength of the company, the general business conditions as well as managerial skill.

(d) The Growth Objective: If an industry/company/business wants to contribute to the economy of the country and it has to serve the community in true sense, it must grow as it goes. In fact the growth objective is more important than the profit objective. A business may be willing to sacrifice immediate profits for the sake of growth. Here two things are important, one is to see that existing business remain and the management has to maintain with the existing situation and the other is constant efforts has to be made to see that the business will grow steadily. Especially, where competitive market situation exists, growth objective is utmost important as it increases the strength of the business and provides employment opportunities to the people and job prospectus to the employees. Growth objective helps or promotes survival objective too. As the company grows, it can manufacture in large scale and when it manufactures in large scale, cost of production is less and it can meet the market competition successfully. Growth objective make the management to convert future possible economic and political environments as well as social factors operating into product and market opportunities. The growth should be steady, and grown up size should be optimal.

(e) The Profit Objective: The word *profit* has assumed an unpleasant flavor in the modern context and particularly in the socialistic pattern of society envisaged for the Indian economy. This is because of lack of appreciation of the role of profit. A distinction has to be made between *"profiteering"* and making of *"reasonable profits"*. In a seller's market there is undoubtedly a temptation to profiteer, which must be curbed, in the national interest and in the long- term interests of the organization itself. But the survival objective dictates that a certain minimum profit must be made. The interest in profits both in short and long term will show measure of performance.

(f) Increasing Productivity Objective: Allied with the profit objective is the productivity objective. The productivity objective concentrates on:

(*i*) To secure optimum utilization of available resources for higher operational efficiency,

(*ii*) To plan and organize better working methods on the shop floor and in the office, and

(*iii*) To analyze various other aspects like substitution of imported machinery and components by indigenous ones, in plant standardization, cost control, inventory control and product development.

When the profit margins are shrinking, it becomes more essential for organization in such industries to become cost-conscious and productivity-oriented.

(g) Social Obligation Objective: As the organization has to satisfy economic needs of the country, satisfy the needs of the prospective market, and operates by consuming the national resources, which otherwise used for some useful purpose, it has a social commitment/obligation to fulfil. The obligation extends to supply adequate products at reasonable prices to customers, a reasonable return on investment to shareholders and so on. However, frowning on profits in this context is erroneous. Unless a business unit makes sufficient profits how can it pay adequate dividends to its shareholders or provide continuous research and development with a views to improve its products for its consumers or customers? Unless sufficient income is generated, how can the organization continuously increase the wages and salaries of its employees? This is only when reasonable profits are made, that an organization in this sense can fulfil its social obligations. Thus reasonable profits constitute on measure of a business unit's efficiency. For example, it would be better if public sector undertaking provide products and services at reasonable prices and ended up in a small surplus rather than proudly claimed, as some do, of making *a loss in the public interest.* A loss is generally a sign of inefficiency and has to be borne by someone, generally the taxpayer in the ultimate analysis, in the case of the public sector. An undertaking running on loss will have more difficulty in convincing an outsider of its contributions to the society.

1.15. SPECIFIC OBJECTIVES

In addition to the general or overall objectives discussed above, an organization must have more specific objectives evolved in each area of its operation such as marketing, production, personnel and so on. To evolve specific objectives the questions given below are of great help:

1. What is the nature of goods or services to be produced by the company?
2. What is the extent of diversification into different groups of products to be manufactured desired by the organization?
3. What is the extent of geographical market to be covered, such as local, national, or international?
4. Who are Company's customers–whether consuming public industry or government or a combination of both or general public?
5. What type of skill (labor) company needs to provide efficient service and quality product to the customer?

This type of questions will have to be answered to arrive at more specific objectives. For example, from the *overall marketing objectives* regarding (*a*) the nature of business, (*b*) the extent of diversification or (*c*) minimum return desired on investment, specific objectives will have to be evolved in the area of product, pricing, distribution and production. In the light of market segment to be aimed at:

(a) The type of product to be manufactured will have to be decided;
(b) Pricing objective will have to be established;
(c) The extent and type of distribution required will have to be determined which would depend on the nature of control desired, and
(d) More specific objective in connection with advertising will have to be established with regard to creating consumer and dealer awareness creating a favorable image and encouraging immediate sales.

These specific objectives then must be dovetailed or to be integrated into the company's overall objectives.

1.15.1. Multiplicity of Objectives

We have a large variety of business objectives but Drucker has classified these depending on performance and results such as:
(a) Market standing,
(b) Innovation,
(c) Productivity,
(d) Physical and financial resources,
(e) Profitability,
(f) Manager's performance and development,
(g) Worker's performance and attitude, and
(h) Public responsibility.

1.16. SOCIAL RESPONSIBILITIES OF MANAGEMENT

Today's manager has greater responsibility as far as the society is concerned in addition to his organizational responsibilities i.e. to run the organization profitably. Professor Dasgupta rightly points out that, whether in the public or the private sector, every enterprise *"must be so conducted that it can serve its own objective as well as social purpose"* *According to him social responsibility was not fixed and had always to be related to the pressures at a particular point of time.* Any organization uses the material, land and other resources belonging to society. In case that organization would have not started, these resources have been used for some other purposes useful to society. As the organization promoters of an organization using the social resources, they have a commitment to serve some or the other social purpose. Dasgupta points out that current pressure as far as social responsibilities concerned are:
(a) To remove or to reduce the quantum of centralized authority;
(b) To make all positions accessible to persons who have the qualities;
(c) To remove authoritarian attitude by top management in relation to employees;
(d) To provide opportunities to all employees for growth and advancement through participation in management problems;
(e) To use modern technology and science in business for development of innovational personnel;
(f) To create additional jobs each year for absorbing young trained persons; and
(g) To help Government in increasing the rate of economic growth.

1.16.1. Social Responsibilities of a Manager and Beneficiaries

Actions of a manager of an organization have effects on society. In India, in the context of socialistic pattern of society, these obligations increase in importance. These responsibilities can be divided into four groups depending on the benefits enjoyed by the public/groups of people or the beneficiaries. They are responsibility towards:

1. The owners or promoters or shareholders of a company,
2. The employees,
3. The customers and consumers, and
4. The community at large.

1. **Responsibility to the Owners:** It is the responsibility of top management to ensure that the resources available are used for the benefit of the owners or shareholders in a company. The managers are using the properties of the owners and are in a position of trust to them. They thus owe honesty and dedication to the interest of the owners. The manager must use his experience and judicious knowledge while submitting the reports to the Board of Directors regarding the various aspects, such as marketing, financial commitment, product design etc. He must also do justice in translating the opinion of Board to the subordinate with effective communication. The shareholders will look to the chief executive of the company and the board of directors to see that the company will produce reasonable profits and pay them reasonable dividends out of such profits as well as protect their investment. The dividend is the return legitimately expected by shareholders on their investment. Therefore, wise and safe use of such resources dictates the making of profits whilst keeping in view long-range stability and security of the enterprise. Again, if the management runs the company effectively, the shareholder is likely to gain in the form of capital appreciation or increase in the market price of his share. Hence, it is the management's responsibility to the owners to ensure that the organization is strengthened and grows adequately in the interests of the owners.

2. **Responsibility to the Employees:** If any organization is running on well, no doubt the credit goes to the management, at the same time the credit should be equally shared by the employees, it is because their contribution in the form of commitment and dedication towards the work makes the enterprise to earn profit and grow. Cooperation and harmonious relations between workers and management alone ensure maximum productivity and successful operation of the organization. If there is no cooperation, then the labor problem arises and organization has to face lots of problems. They must be viewed in the larger context of social responsibilities employees as well as responsibility for increased productivity of the enterprise. It is management's responsibility to provide adequate monetary and psychological rewards as well as appropriate job security. In Indian context, where job opportunities are scarce and unemployment has raised its ugly head with the influence of unstable political scene, responsibility for job security is of greater importance. Apart from providing job security, selection of employees must be made fairly and without discrimination on ground of caste, community and sex., which is at large in India, because of ugly politics. Emphasis must consistently be on suitable educational

qualifications and merit in terms of possible effectiveness on the job for which the person is selected. Existing employees must be encouraged to develop themselves with further education where necessary so that they may be ready for taking up higher responsibility by future promotions. In fact today's responsibilities extend even in providing such educational opportunities and job training to the employees at the company's expenses. In addition to this a fair and reasonable wage or salary must be paid in terms of the effort required by the employee. Improved payments should results from improved productivity or performance. Besides all the above, a safe and good working environment must be provided to the worker, so that worker must be motivated by himself to work in such environment. All the amenities governed by the factory law should be provided. Insurance and medical aid should be provided to the workers. Once the worker starts his work he should not think of other problems (may be personal or domestic), and feel himself that he is one among the group in which he is working and wholeheartedly contribute his might to the success of the organization. The environment and work conditions provided by management must initiate and motivate the employee towards the work.

3. **Responsibility to the Consumers:** In today's scenario, almost all enterprises are working in the sellers market; hence, the modern outlook of any enterprise based on the marketing concept ***should be consumer oriented.*** Its objective is to *identify the needs* of the consumer and convert them into products or services of the company aiming at satisfaction of consumer. It is the social responsibility of the management to assure that the consumers are provided with adequate quality products at reasonable price. It is the responsibility of the management to look after ***five rights***, such that consumer must get ***right product*** at ***right time*** at ***right place*** at ***right price***, of ***right quality*** and ***quantity***. Organization must give equal importance for after sales services so that they can create confidence in the minds of a consumer regarding the product of the company. They must see that required spares are available in the market at reasonable price and without any difficulty. The confidence that the management create in the minds of the consumer should make the consumer a permanent customer of the company's products. In case the organization neglects the consumer and harass him, then the Government may get certain legislative measures in to action.
4. **Responsibility to Community:** All organizations, irrespective of their business, owe a responsibility to community at large. It is because the organization is using the community's resources and the community around the organization supplies the required labors, it has to feel responsible that it has to help the community in certain aspect. In this context some of the organizations adopt the villages around the organization and provide some infrastructure facilities such as good roads, water facilities, schools, hospitals transport facilities etc. to these villages, so that the community feels happy and always have a soft corner towards the organization. For example, M/S A.C.C. Ltd. has a social philosophy to provide village welfare schemes, which benefits the villagers a lot. The management philosophy at M/S India Tobacco Companies is: (*a*) Consumers are their ultimate customers, (*b*) Concern for their intermediate customers i.e. traders, (*c*) concern for their suppliers, (*d*) concern for

their employees, who are their most valued asset, (*e*) concern for their competitors, whom they wish to have healthy and happy competition (*f*) Concern of the investors and finally, (*g*) Concern for India's future.

Most important than all these is that organization must take all measures to prevent air pollution and sound pollution. In addition to this you might have seen in cities some companies adopt some roads and maintain them in a decent way for the sake of the public. Fertilizer manufacturing firms and pesticide manufacturing firms adopt some villages and help the peasants in increasing the yield.

1.17. MOTIVATION

What makes people to work? Why some people perform better than others? Perhaps one of the biggest questions confronting organization today is the *manpower question*. Performance results from the interaction of three resources. They are *Physical resources, Financial Resources and Manpower resources*. The first two are inanimate; they are translated into *productivity* only when the human element is introduced. However, the human element is a resource, a variable over which the management has limited control. When dealing with inanimate resources, the management can accurately predict the input-output relationship and can even vary the factor to choose in order to achieve a desired rate of production. In dealing with manpower, however, an intangible factor of will, violation or freedom of choice is introduced and workers can increase or decrease their productivity as they choose. This human quality gives raise to the need for positive motivation. Hence, the question is: *How the management has to motivate the employees to achieve the goals of an organization and at the same time satisfy the needs of employees? How to tap the latent human capabilities in organization endeavors?* The manager's problem here is: the manager is responsible for the results of the work entrusted to him. But he alone cannot finish the work to achieve the desired result. He and his fellowmen i.e. subordinate, in real sense, the combined efforts of manager and the subordinates are necessary and vital in achieving the desired results. With the *authority* given to him, the manager by using the *delegation powers* has to delegate the work to the subordinates and *motivate* them to get the things done in an optimal way. Here *human quality* gives rise to the need for *positive motivation*. In fact, the level of the performance of an employee is a function of his abilities and motivation. A manager must stimulate people to action to accomplish the desired goals; he must fuse the varied individual human capacities and powers of many people employed into a smoothly working team with high productivity. How do we get the people to work at a higher than normal percent of their physical and mental capacities and also maintain satisfaction? For this, first we determine what an employee *can do?* Secondly determine what he *will do?* We can observe two things here: (a) Where there is *strong positive motivation* the employee's output increases and he will have higher satisfaction and (b) Where there is pessimism, his performance level is low. This gives us a *key* in managing the people. That is one of the key element in personnel management is *motivation*. It is the core of management, which shows that every human being earnestly seeks a secure, friendly and supportive relationship, which gives him a sense of worth in face-to-face groups, which are most important to him. A supervisor should strive to treat individuals with dignity and recognition of their personal worth.

Unfortunately, motivation is not a simple concept. It involves a complex combination of individual needs, drives, tensions, discomforts and expectations. The motivation of any organism, even the simplest one, is at present only partly understood. Moreover, needs vary significantly with the individual and lead to differential behavior patterns. The most important one is the individual's needs vary over time. It is peculiar to note here that man's needs are to be evaluated periodically because it varies continuously. If one need is satisfied, it becomes less significant to the employee and he looks at higher level need. Thus understanding individual motivation requires continual updating in order to reflect the most current mix of goals. As employees become better educated and economically blessed, the traditional *carrot and stick policies* only scratch the surface. The constraints imposed by internal and external environment restrict the powers of the manager to motivate the workers. It is really a Herculean task for the manager to find out a way to motivate the employees towards the achievement of goal. This is where the motivational theory helps as a guideline for the manager. Motivational theory provides a great deal of insight into the reasons that different individuals exhibit different behavioral patterns in an organization. It is useful in explaining why the same individual exhibit different reactions to the same stimulus at different times. We can define ***motivation*** as 'a willingness to expand energy to achieve a goal or reward.' It is a force that activates dormant energies and sets in motion the action of the people. It is the function that kindles a burning passion for action among the human beings of an organization.'

1.17.1. Importance of Motivation

Motivation of employees has become very important in recent times so as to stimulate people to achieve the desired goals in a highly competitive market situation.

(a) People are very important factor in production. The other two resources, finance and physical can be effectively controlled, whereas men because of their behavioral nature, they are to be motivated towards the achievement of goal.

(b) Motivation as a concept is pervasive and a highly complex activity that affects and is affected by a host of factors in the organizational milieu.

(c) To meet the increasing demand of the market and limited physical resources available, the management has to motivate its employees to increase the productivity. Unless human resource co-operates with the management in increasing the productivity, management cannot improve productivity with the physical resources or improved technology available with it. Hence motivation of human resource is very important for organizational existence and growth.

1.17.2. Theories of Motivation

During the last century, numerous thinkers, experts and researchers have studied different aspects and theories of organizational behavior and individual interactions, which have a bearing on motivation. These studies can be classified under two groups as *traditional theories and modern theories.*

The Traditional Theories are based on mostly the *human relation approach in management*, with little attention to psychological process that occur. These theories works on basic assumptions:

(a) Personnel primarily are economically motivated and secondly desire security and good working conditions.

(b) Providing the above rewards to the personnel will have a positive effect or the work morale.

(c) There is a positive correlation between morale and productivity.

As these theories neglect behavioral approach and psychological aspects of employees and complex features of motivation could not work well. Around fifties of previous century behavioral approach to motivation started to search new facts and techniques for motivation. These theories were termed as ***modern theories of work motivation.*** These have been classified depending on the assumptions made.

(a) **Prescription Theories:** These theories guide management to find a way to motivate employees. These models include theories such as *Taylor's Scientific Management, Hawthorne's Human Relation Model and McGregor's Y theory*. The basis for these models is Trial and Error experience or popular beliefs.

(b) **Content Theories:** These models think logically what makes behaviors to occur and stop. The basis for these theories is needs, motives, or desires that drive employees to get satisfaction in the job. Some of the theories, which deal with above, mentioned items are Maslow's Need Hierarchy, Fredrick Herzberg's Two Factor Theory and David McClelland's Need for Achievement Theory.

(c) **Process Theory:** This type of model is known as *Behaviorist's model.* This theory deals with the matter how behavior originates and is performed.

(d) **Cognitive Theory:** Cognition means thinking and feelings of individuals. This model deals with the individual thinking, feelings and expectations. Vroom's Expectancy Theory comes under this category.

1.17.3. Traditional Theories of Motivation

Important theories come under this category are McGregor's theory-X, Fear and Punishment theory; Reward Theory, Carrot and Stick Theory.

1.17.3.1. McGregor's Theory–X

Professor Douglas McGregor has presented two opposite sets of assumptions about employees and management views the nature of man at work. Theory X and Theory Y have represented these factors. Theory X based on a set of traditional beliefs, whereas theory Y based on researches in behavioral science. Theory X was presented by Prof. McGregor in 1957 and later elaborated in his work 'The *human side of an enterprise in 1960'*

Theory X assumes that:

(a) Typical individuals basically dislike work, as by nature they are indolent, and will avoid work whenever they can.

(b) Because most people dislike work, they have to be pushed, closely supervised, threatened, coerced, persuaded and even punished to get them to achieve the objective of the organizations.

(c) Most people basically are lazy, have little ambition, prefer to avoid responsibility and desire security as a major goal; and prefer to be directed or led.

(d) Typical worker is self-centered and has little concern for organizational goals.

(e) A worker by nature resistant to change.

(f) He is gullible, not very bright, the ready dupe of the charlatan and the demagogue.

Managers who accept this theory think as follows:

(a) In the interests of economic achievements, the management has to pool up productive resources such as money, material, equipment and men.

(b) With respect to people, this is a process of directing their efforts motivate them to control their actions and modifying their behavior to fit the needs of the organization.

(c) Without the active involvement of management and intervention by management, people would be passive and even resistant to organizational needs.

Managers who believe in Theory X, put emphasis on *discipline, incentive programme, welfare measures, close supervision, pension and other benefit programme. They take a somewhat pessimistic view of humanity.*

1.17.3.2. McGregor's Theory–Y

This Theory states that:

(a) Management is responsible for organizing the elements of productive enterprise in the interest of economic ends.

(b) People are not by nature passive or resistant to organizational needs. The average person within a favorable human relations climate, learn not only to accept but seek responsibility. Avoidance of responsibility, lack of ambition, and emphasis on security are generally consequences of experience, not inherent human characteristics.

(c) Work is as natural as play or rest and people develop an attitude toward work related to their experience with it.

(d) The Motivation, the potential for development, the capacity for assuming responsibility, the readiness to direct behavior towards organizational goals are all present in people. Management does not put them there. It is the responsibility of the management to make it possible for people to recognize and develop these human characteristics for themselves.

(e) A large percentage of population has a high degree of imagination, ingenuity, and creativity in the solution of organizational problems

(f) Under the condition of modern industrial life, the intellectual potentialities of the average human being are only partially utilized.

(g) The essential task of management is to arrange organizational conditions and methods of operation so that people can achieve their own goals efficiently by directing their own efforts towards organizational objectives. This process primarily of creating opportunities, releasing potential, removing obstacles encouraging growth, providing guidance.

(h) Close control and threats of punishment, are not the only ways to get people to do things.

(i) Commitment to objectives is determined by the rewards associated with their achievement.

(j) Motivation occurs at the social esteem and self-actualization levels, as well as at the physiological and security levels.

The essence of Theory Y is that " Workers will do fare more than expectation if treated like human beings and permitted to experience personal satisfaction on the job. The theory places the programmes squarely in the lap of management. If employees are lazy, indifferent, unwilling to take responsibility, intransigent, uncreative, non-cooperative, the causes lie in management's methods of organization and control. The managers, who believe in Theory Y, put emphasis on consultation, participation, motivation, communication, and opportunities in formulating managerial and personal policies. McGregor suggested a number of innovative ideas, which are consistent with Theory Y and are practiced in America. They are:

(a) *Greater decentralization and delegation of authority:* Too much of control on subordinates must be avoided and a sense of responsibility must be created in them so that they enjoy greater freedom in their work.

(b) *Job Enlargement:* To increase the responsibility among the rank and file workers, so as to satisfy their social and ego needs.

(c) *Participation and consultative management:* Employees are given opportunities to take part in decision-making and their suggestions are listened and if they are really good one they are adopted. This makes employees happy and they feel that they are not merely workers but they are a part of the system in which they are working.

(d) *Target setting for performance:* A self-evaluation of performance periodically is introduced in consultation with employees, so that each one will have sense of leadership and motivation by them to work.

Further clarification to the above theories offered by McGregor in his work are:

(a) Theory X and Theory Y are not the only two possible theories of management. These are only two examples among many managerial tools.

(b) These are not managerial strategies. They are the beliefs about the nature of man that influence the managers to choose appropriate strategies.

Usefulness of McGregor's Theory

(a) McGregor's Theory was extensively discussed and influenced by management thought significantly.

(b) Several studies have been made to test the relevance of theory X and Theory Y.

(c) They are consistent with the modern notions and dignity and decency of work significantly.

(d) Several studies have been made to test the relevance of theory X and Theory Y.

(e) They guide managers to be sensitive to the feelings and needs of their subordinates.

(f) They encourage freedom and flexibility to the workers so that they can develop and contribute toward the betterment of the organization.

Comparison of Theory X and Theory Y

S. No.	Theory X	Theory Y
	People by nature:	People by nature:
1.	Lack of integrity	Have integrity
2.	Fundamentally lazy	Work hard if committed.
3.	Avoid responsibility	Assume responsibility within their commitments.
4.	Are not bothered about achievements	Desires to achieve.
5.	Are incapable of directing their own behavior.	Are capable of directing their own behavior.
6.	Are indifferent to organizational needs.	Want their organization to survive and grow and succeed.
7.	Prefer to be directed by others	Are not passive and submissive.
8.	Avoid making decisions.	Will make decisions within their commitments.
9.	Are not very bright.	Are not stupid.

Criticisms of theory X and theory Y

(a) Human beings display different behavior and hence it is very difficult to find employees as described in Theory X and Theory Y.

(b) As there are many employees who are lazy and resistant to change and indifferent and there are several employees who are intelligent, dynamic and healthy, application of these theories to individuals uniformly is impossible.

(c) Similarly, we can see managers of two extremes, one being too liberal an democratic and other being autocrat and arrogant.

(d) The two theories are two extremes designed for two peculiar classes of people. But it is very difficult to find these class of people categorically. Hence, it is very difficult to apply these in practice.

(e) The situational aspect, nature of work, nature of subordinate etc. are completely ignored.

(f) When there are senior managers who handle the other managers this theory is not suitable.

(g) Nothing has been mentioned about managerial motivation. Concentration is made only on control and motivation of subordinates.

1.18. THEORY Z

Theory Z represents the adoption of Japanese management practice by the American Organizations. The *Hybrid type of System* incorporates the strengths of Japanese management such as *Group decision making, Social cohesion, Job security, Holistic concern for employees, etc.* and American management strengths such as *Quick decision making, Individual freedom, Risk taking by individuals etc.*

Professor Quachi has introduced theory Z and provided a new paradigm to the normal science of management. Theory Z concentrates on the organizational behavior aspect of management. The most important point in Theory Z is that it does not give any weightage to the traditional adversarial relationship between management and employees. It advocates tackling of productivity problems through coordinating individual efforts in a productive manner. Theory Z believes in truly democratic and dynamic philosophy of management. In this type of management philosophy, decisions are made by the consensus and where employer and employee relationship is based on the family like loyalty, strong and mutual. Theory X emphasizes external control of human behavior. Theory Y emphasizes self-control and self-direction. Whereas Theory Z exclusively rely upon corporate team work and compromise as two essential factors for its successful application. The philosophy of theory Z is committed and involved workers are the key factors in increasing the productivity. Now we have seen the three theories, the manager's duty is to select appropriate theory in his organization to manage the things. Which theory he has to select. He finds the workers of different behavior. No one theory can be selected exclusively to motivate people. An optimal and timely blend suitable to situation on hand will be helpful for him. He must behave like a parent–who sometimes provide love and affection to their children and sometimes carrot and stick policy, sometimes treatment advocated by Theory X and Theory Y (who does not have the knowledge of theory X and Theory Y or in fact any management policies.

The features of Theory Z or United States–Japanese system of management are as under:

1. *Strong bond between the Company and the Employees*: Theory Z advocates lifetime employment in the company as followed in Japan. Retrenchment, Lay-offs etc. should be avoided as far as possible. Along with the financial incentives, the management should also use non-financial incentives to motivate the workers. To strengthen the relationship between company and workers, the management should follow the paternalistic style. The needs of workers must be satisfied.
2. *Employee's participation*: To increase the commitment of workers in productivity affairs, they must be given a free approach in decision-making process and in case their suggestions are really worthy, they must be considered. This will give a moral boost to workers. Theory Z supports less centralized and more consensus seeking decision making approach.
3. *Mutual Trust*: There should be trust between employees, supervisors, workers, unions and management. According to the Quchi. Trust, Integrity and openness are closely related. All these are necessary for an effective organization. To develop trust, there should be complete openness and can dour in relationships. The changes of conflicts should be reduced to the minimum. Attempts should be made to achieve win-win relationships in the organization. This will increase the commitment of employees towards organization.
4. *Integrated Structure*: Theory Z recommends no formal structure. The organization structure should be based on the team-work. For example, the structure represents

a basketball team where there are no formal reporting relationships and the players play together. Integrated organizations do not have any chart or visible structure. The employees must develop group spirit.

5. *Human Resources Development*: The management must work to develop new skills among the employees. In Theory Z, human resources potential is recognized and the greater emphasis is laid on the job enlargement and career planning as well as socialization. Technical training, research and development are also emphasized.
6. *Informal Control*: Theory Z advises the managers to reduce their reliance of formal control system. As far as possible, organizational controls should be informal and flexile. In other words, the managers should emphasize mutual trust and cooperation rather than their authority over the subordinates. There should be free flow of information throughout the organization so that corrective actions could be taken quickly whenever needed.

The Japanese firms operating in United States of America have practiced theory Z successfully. With the collaboration of Indian Organizations and Japanese firms, there has been a lot of talk about the application of Theory Z to Indian conditions. In Maruti Udyog, which has collaboration with Suzuki Motors of Japan, an attempt has been made to implement Theory Z. The company provides Japanese work environment. To avoid class feeling among employees, same canteen, same dress code is being observed at Maruti Udyog Limited. In one word, Theory Z concentrates on the *organizational behavior side of management.*

1.19. FEAR AND PUNISHMENT THEORY

This theory supports close supervision and strict control of behavior and the use of coercion and threat. The thinking behind this theory is that people work for the sake of money and that will work only to ensure that the job is not lost. Management assumed that workers were imbued with self-interest and self-preservation. This type of theory approach authoritarian and military in tone and individual had no option but either to respect the command or to leave the job. This is *do or die* approach. This theory is useful; when for a worker the job alone is his and his family's livelihood.

1.20. REWARD (SOFT OR WEAK) THEORY

This theory has some positive factors when compared to above. This theory offers some reward and good working conditions to motivate people to work better and harder; their demands are satisfied and harmony achieved. This theory assumes that people are motivated to work to the extent to which they are rewarded. The originator of this theory is F.W.Taylor, father of scientific management. He said *'give a man more money and he will produce more.'* This theory forgets that satisfaction with more money is not sufficient motivation. Men are not machines. They are blend of psychological, physiological, social and economic needs. Money alone will not give satisfaction to the worker.

1.21. CARROT AND STICK THEORY

This theory assumes that the people can be motivated to work if rewards are offered or withheld. The rewards are attached to the effective performance of the work at the same time punishment is attached if performance falls below the level of expectation or the target set. This theory works well until an individual is struggling for subsistence. Once an individual has reached an adequate subsistence level and is motivated primarily by higher needs.

1.22. MODERN THEORIES OF WORK MOTIVATION

These theories are based on McGregor's Theory Y and believe that man can be motivated if he is given more responsibility and his task is made more eciting and challenging. Most important among them are:

(a) Maslow's Need Priority Theory

Maslolw's need priority theory is one of the most popular theories of motivations in the management and organizational behavior literature. The model presents the student of work motivation with an interesting paradox. Maslow's model provides both a theory of human motives by classifying human needs in a hierarchy and a theory of human motivation that links these needs to general behavior. Essential elements of the model are:

(i) Adult motives are complex. No single motive determines behavior, rather, a number of motives operate at the same time.

(ii) Needs form hierarchy. Lower level needs must at least partly be satisfied before higher level needs emerge. In other words, a higher order need cannot become an active motivating force until the preceding lower need is essentially satisfied.

(iii) A satisfied need is not a motivator. A need that is unsatisfied activates seeking behavior. If a lower level need is satisfied, a higher level need emerges.

(iv) Higher level needs can be satisfied in many more ways than can the lower level needs.

(v) People seek growth. They want to move up the hierarchy of needs. No person is content at the physiological level. Usually people seek the satisfaction of higher order needs.

Maslow proposed that basic needs are structured in a hierarchy of prepotency and probability of appearance as shown in the fig. 1.2.

(b) Maslow's Hierarchy of Needs

1. **Physiological Needs:** Physiological needs are the biological needs required to preserve human life; these needs include needs for food, clothing and shelter. These needs must be satisfied to certain extent before higher level need arises. These needs tremendously influence the behavior of workers and they are the most powerful of motivating stimuli, as they are the basic needs of survivability. These needs take precedence over other needs when thwarted. As food is most important for man for survival, and when there is no food Physiological needs dominate when all needs are unsatisfied. Common features of Physiological needs are:

(i) They are relatively independ on each other.

(ii) In many cases they can be identified with a particular organ in the body.

(iii) In any affluent culture these needs are unusual rather than typical motivators.

(iv) Physiological needs are essentially finite. An individual demands only a particular amount of these needs. Once these are satisfied, there will be no more demand and hence not motivational.

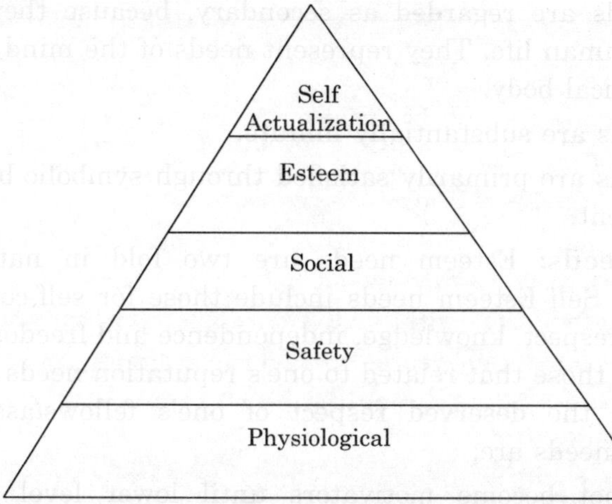

Fig.1.2. Maslow's Hierarchy of Needs.

(v) They must be met repeatedly within relatively short time periods to remain fulfilled.

(vi) Satisfaction of Physiological needs is not usually associated with money itself but what it can buy. The value of money reduces as one goes up in the hierarchy.

(vii) Most of the Physiological needs require some conscious provision for their future satisfaction.

2. Safety Needs: Once the Physiological needs are relatively satisfied the safety needs dominate the human behavior. Safety needs includes (a) Protection from physiological dangers such as accident and causality etc. (b) Economic security such as fringe benefits, health care and insurance programme, (c) Desire for an orderly, predictable environment and (d) The desire to know the limits of acceptable behavior. These needs are concerned with protection from hazards of life. Organizations influence these security needs either positively, through pension schemes, insurance plans or negatively by arousing fears of being fired or laid off. Safety aspect covers emotional and physical safety. That is why these needs concerned with protecting from hazards of life; from danger, deprivation and threat. Safety needs are primarily satisfied through economic behavior. Organizations can influence these security needs either positively by providing pension schemes or/and insurance schemes or by negatively through fears of being fired or laid off. They are motivational until they are satisfied and they have finite limits.

3. **Higher Order Needs (The love needs):** Once the lower order needs are satisfied, the social or love needs become important motivators of behavior. As man is an element in society, he wants belong, associate, gain acceptance from associates, give and take friendship; and affection. Social needs tend to be stronger for some people than for others and stronger in certain situations. Social needs have certain features in common such as:
   (*i*) They provide a meaning for work life.
   (*ii*) Social needs are regarded as secondary, because they are not essential to preserve human life. They represent needs of the mind and spirit rather than of the physical body.
   (*iii*) Social needs are substantially infinite.
   (*iv*) Social needs are primarily satisfied through symbolic behavior of psychic and social content.
4. **The Esteem Needs:** Esteem needs are two fold in nature: self esteem and esteem of others. Self-Esteem needs include those for self-confidence, achievement, competence, self-respect, knowledge, independence and freedom. The second group of esteem needs are those that related to one's reputation needs for status, recognition, appreciation and the deserved respect of one's fellows/associates. The common features of these needs are:
   (*i*) They do not become motivators until lower level needs are reasonably satisfied.
   (*ii*) These needs are insatiable; unlike lower order needs, these needs are rarely satisfied.
   (*iii*) Satisfaction of esteem needs produces feelings of self-confidence, worth, strength, capability, adequacy, of being useful and necessary in the world. If these are not satisfied, it results in inferiority feeling, weakness and helplessness.
   (*iv*) Satisfaction of esteem needs is not always obtained through mature or adaptive behavior. It is generated by irresponsible actions.
   (*v*) The modern organizations offer few opportunities for the satisfaction of these needs to people at lower level in the hierarchy.
5. **The Self-Actualization Needs:** These are the needs for realizing one's own potentialities for continued self-development, for being creative in the broadest sense of that term. Self fulfilling people are rare individuals who come close to living up to their full potential for being realistic, accomplishing things, enjoying life, and generally exemplifying classic human virtues. Self-actualization is the desire to become what one is capable of becoming. These needs are growth oriented. The common features of these needs are:
   (*a*) The specific form of these needs vary greatly from person to person.
   (*b*) The self-realization is not necessarily a creative urge.
   (*c*) The way self-actualization is expressed can change over the life cycle.

(*d*) These needs are continuously motivators. They do not have end in satisfactions.

(*e*) These needs are psychological in nature and are substantially infinite.

(*f*) The condition of modern life give only limited opportunity for these needs to obtain expression.

1.23. HERZBERG'S TWO–FACTOR THEORY

Managers are not in a position to understand why their fancy personal policies and fringe benefits offered by them were not increasing employee motivation on the job. For this Fredric Herzberg has provided an interesting extension to Maslow's need hierarchy theory and developed a specific content theory of work motivation. This theory is known as ***Dual Factor Theory*** and the ***motivation-hygiene theory of motivation.*** This theory's approach is very simple and built around the question: ***"Think of a time when you felt exceptionally good or exceptionally bad about your job, either your present job or other job you have had."*** This approach has been repeated many times with a variety of jobholders in various countries. The result indicated that when people talked about feeling good or satisfied they mentioned features intrinsic to the job and when people talked about feeling dissatisfied with the job they talked about factors extrinsic to the job. Herzberg called these **Motivation and Maintenance factors respectively.**

1.23.1. Hygiene Factors

Hygiene Factors, when absent, increase dissatisfaction with the job. When present, help in preventing dissatisfaction but do not increase satisfaction or motivation. Hygiene factors represent the need to avoid pain in the environment. They are not intrinsic part of a job, but they are related to the condition under which a job is performed. They are associated with negative feelings. They are environment related factors-**hygiene**. They must be viewed as preventive measures that remove sources of dissatisfaction from the environment. These factors are: Environmental, external to job, prevent dissatisfaction, and zero level motivation if maintained, never satisfied completely and *money* is most important hygiene factor.

1.23.2. Motivators

Motivators are associated with positive feelings of employees about the job. They make people satisfied with their job. If mangers wish to increase motivation and performance above the average level, they must enrich the work and increase a person's freedom on the job. Motivators are necessary to keep job satisfaction and job performance high. On the other hand, if they are not present they do not prove highly satisfying. Motivators are content factors affect satisfaction and spur individuals to superior performance. Herzberg advised job enlargement and job enrichment. He wanted jobs to be made more interesting, meaningful and challenging. His theory is very appealing to practicing managers.

In addition to the above, many more theories are available in management literature, which deals with motivation theory. They are: (a) Achievement Theory of David C.Mc Celland, (b) Expectancy/valence Theory of victor Vroom, (c) Porter and Lawler's Model, (d) Adam's Equity Theory, (e) Gillerman on Motivation, (f) Path-Goal Hypothesis and (g) Employee-Centered Approach of Likert.

1.24. NEOCLASSICAL THEORY OF ORGANIZATION

The classical organizational theory provides a restricted organizational structure and always concentrates on exploiting the workmen and forgets about their welfare. It concentrates on discipline and control rater than on morale. Neoclassical theory modified the classical theory by considering the behavioral aspect (i.e. psychology, sociology and anthropology) of the workmen. This theory advocates that the organization is a *social system* and emphasized that human factor is most important in it.

Development of neoclassical theory was crystallized in the famous ***Hawthorne experiments*** conducted by *Elton Mayo and his Harvard associates from 1924 to 1932, at the Hawthorne Plant of Western Electric Company, located near Cicero, Illinois.*

This experiment was performed in order to obtain answers to the following questions:

1. Do employees actually get tired out?
2. Are rest pauses desirable?
3. Is a shorter working day desirable?
4. What is the attitude of the employee towards their work and toward the Company?
5. What is the effect of changing the type of working equipment?
6. Why does the production fall off in the afternoon?

In this experiment, six girls (five assemblers and one material handler) were selected from a group of one hundred assembling telephone relays. Previous to the selection, it had not been customary to keep individual production records and the entire group of one hundred was paid on the basis of the output of the group. For a period of two weeks a record was kept of the individual production of the six selected girls to provide a base record. This record was kept without their knowledge.

The six girls were then told of the purposes of the experiment and, after agreeing to participate, were moved into a test room physically separated from the large group. They worked in the test room for five weeks, without any other changes in the condition of work, with no change on the basis of computing pay, in order to establish a base recoded for the new condition.

For the next eight weeks they were paid on a new basis, a group rate based on the production of the five assemblers in the test room, rather than on the basis of the whole group of one hundred as previously. Production increased by about 4 per cent. For the next four weeks, the group was given ten-minutes rest pauses twice a day, and again daily and weekly output rose.

For the next four weeks, the group was given six five-minutes rest pauses, further reducing the working time. The girls expressed some dislike of this constant interruption of the flow of work and the output curve showed a small decrease. For the next eleven weeks, the group was given a fifteen-minutes rest pause in the morning with refreshment-supplied by the company, and ten-minutes break in the afternoon. Despite of loss of production time, output returned to the highest-level previously obtained in the experiment.

For the next seven weeks, the group stopped a half-hour earlier each day. This was accompanied by a spectacular rise in both daily and weekly output. (At this point in the experiment unforeseen circumstances necessitated replacing two of the operators.). For the next four weeks, the working day was shortened by an additional half-hour. The hourly output rose so that the daily and weekly output diminished only slightly.

For the next twelve weeks, the group returned to working the full day but retained the fifteen-minutes mid-morning refreshment break and the ten-minutes afternoon break. Daily and weekly output reached new high.

For the next twelve weeks, the half-day of work on Saturday was eliminated. Daily output increased. Weekly output fell somewhat, but remained above all but two of the previous highs. For the next twelve weeks, the workers returned to all but one of the original condition of work; no rest pauses, no refreshments, no shortened hours, but they were paid as a group of six. The daily and weekly outputs rose to record highs and continued to rise throughout the entire twelve weeks.

For the next thirty-one weeks, the group returned to rest pauses with the company supplying the morning-break beverage and the girls supplying their own food. The output rose again, establishing a new high. It became obvious that more was happening than was attributable directly and mechanically to the experimental changes. Mr. Pennock, in charge of the investigation, explained, "The results are mainly due to changes in the mental attitude". Elton Mayo further explained the increase in productivity as follows: The supervisor took a personal interest in each girl and her achievement; he showed pride in the record of the group. He helped the group to feel that its duty was to set its own conditions of work (oriented with organization's objectives); he helped the workers find the "*freedom*" of which they so frequently spoke in the course of the experiment. The remarks of Dr. Mayo have great importance in understanding that the supervisor (representing the organization) and the workers understood each other and *communicated successfully.* Successful communication between individuals depends upon something more than a common language, a common set of words. People and groups with different experiences and social places, although having in common many of the same words, may vary widely in mental attitudes. These differences in modes of thought and ways of viewing things may make communication in some instances almost impossible. The trained expert with his precise and logical vocabulary has difficulty in communicating with the layman. The attitude of higher ups also differs. As it is commonly expressed, people with different ways of thinking do not **"get"** each other.

In brief, the Hawthorne experiment resulted an increase in productivity because of mutual understanding and acceptance of the changes as compatible with the objectives of both parties.

The summary of findings of the study is given below:

The following statements are taken from a report of the Hawthorne Experiment.

There has been a continual upward trend in output, which has been independent of the change in rest pauses. The upward trend has continued too long to be ascribed to an initial stimulus from the novelty of starting a special study.

The instruction of muscular fatigue has not been the primary factor in increasing output. Cumulative fatigue in not present.

There has been an important increase in contentment among the girls working under test room condition.

There has been a decrease in absences of about 80 percent among the girls since entering the test room group. Test-room operates have had approximately one-third as many sick absences as the regular department during last six months.

Observations of operators in the relay assembly test room indicate that their health is being maintained or improved and that they are working within their capacity.

Important factors in the production of a better mental attitude and greater enjoyment of work have been greater freedom, less strict supervision and the opportunity to vary from a fixed pace without reprimand from a gang boss.

The operators have no clear idea as of why they are able to produce more in the test room; but as shown in the replies to questionnaires. There is the feeling that better output is in some way related to the distinctly pleasanter, freer, and happier working conditions.

The Hawthorne studies have an important impact on industry. The result emphasized human relations and worker's needs. Questions continued to be raised about ways of motivating employees.

1.25. LEADERSHIP

Among the duties/objectives of managers, the most important thing is to run the organization in a profitable path and make it to grow to larger size. For this he has to motivate the personnel of all levels to work effectively and see that the resources are used optimally. For this he needs some qualities in him, which are known as **'Leadership qualities'** to lead the organization.

Management and Leadership often regarded as the same activity. Although it is true that the most effective manager will almost certainly be an effective leader and that leading is an essential function of managers, there is more meaning than just leading. In a very fundamental sense, leadership also is follower ship, and we must discover why people follow. Basically, people tend to follow those in whom they see a means of satisfying their own desire and needs. The task of manager is to encourage to contribute effectively towards the accomplishment of enterprises goals and to satisfy their own desire and needs in the process. Hence, the managerial function of leading is defined as the process of influencing people so that they will strive willingly and enthusiastically towards the achievement of organizational goals.

In fact all organized efforts are undertaken to achieve enterprise objectives; in general, the objectives is to produce and make available some kind of goods or services. This effort is by no means restricted to business activity; it may be understood that it also applies to universities, hospitals, charitable associations, government organizations and is also applicable to families, because a good manager of a family (mother) see that family achieves it goals effectively. In this context the meaning and definition of leadership, qualities and types of leadership are discussed below.

1.25.1. Meaning and Definition of Leadership

Effective leadership is one of the great importance in an enterprise to enable the enterprise in achieving its goals. Leadership is most important mans of direction. It is the process by which an executive directs his subordinate and influences the work and behavior of others for the common benefit of the organization as well as its members. To **lead** means to **guide**, to **direct** and to **integrate** the efforts of the people of an organization towards a common goal. An effective leader directs the activities of his followers and integrates their activities for the accomplishment of some pre-determined objectives. He motivates them to work more and better i.e., effectively contribute their efforts. This success of an enterprise largely depends upon the quality of its **leadership**.

(a) **Definition: Chester I Koontz and O'Donnell** defines that "Leadership may be defined as the influence, the art or the process of influencing people so that they will strive willingly towards the achievement of group goals".

(b) **Characteristics:**

(i) Followers

(ii) Personal Qualities,

(iii) A Common Goal,

(iv) Achieve relations,

(v) Practical Approach and

(vi) It is a Process.

(c) **Nature:** Leadership is the quality, which enables a person to direct other persons of the organization and by that other persons become his followers. A leader directs and guides the activities of his followers and influences them to contribute their wholehearted efforts to achieve the common objectives of the enterprise. Therefore, it becomes essential that there must be followers of a leader. He must have a complete and clear knowledge of his organization. He must have the clear knowledge of objectives of his organization also. Only then he may direct, guide and regulate the activities of his followers. However, it is important to note that an effective leader is not necessarily a good manger also.

There are two opinions about the origin of the qualities of leadership. Some are the scholars who are of the opinion that leadership is an inborn quality. Leaders take birth, they cannot be made, and on the contrary, some authors of the opinion that leadership is not an inborn quality. Giving training to them may make leaders. Every person has the quality of leadership. ***The only need is to develop and explores that quality.***

Keith Davis states "It is a human factor which binds a group together and motivated it towards the particular goals."

1.25.2. Qualities of Leadership

Success of leadership in an enterprise depends upon the qualities of its leader. If the leader is capable enough to lead and direct his followers, he can motivate them to achieve targets. If on the other hand, the leader of the enterprise does not possesses the required qualities of leadership, he will not be able in directing and regulating the activities of his followers and the objectives of his enterprise will not be achieved. Many eminent scholars have described different qualities of leadership as given below.

(a) **Mr. Ordway Tead** has described the following 10 qualities in leadership:

1. Physical Strength
2. Knowledge of object and ability of direction
3. Enterprise
4. Honesty
5. Intelligence
6. Technical Knowledge
7. Friendship and affection
8. Efficiency
9. Decision making Power and
10. Faith and Trust.

(b) **Chester I, Bernard** has described the 5 qualities of Leadership shown below:

1. Vitality and endurance,
2. Decision Making Power,
3. Initiative,
4. Responsibility, and
5. Intellectual Capacity.

(c) **Henry Fayol** has described **5** qualities of Leadership as given below:

1. Health and physical Stamina,
2. Capability and Balance,
3. Moral Qualities,
4. Knowledge and efficiency, and
5. Mental ability.

We can see from the above most comment qualities referred are:

(a) **Physical Strength:** (vitality and endurance, health and physical stamina) It is true that a manager must be physically and mentally fit to take up the leadership responsibility. In fact the followers will respect and obey an healthy leader than a week and unhealthy person. When they have a healthy leader, they believe that he will give them proper guidance and direction. The followers like a healthy, smiling, person than a grim faced unhealthy man–however intellectual he may be.

(b) **Knowledge of Work:** The leader must be well aware of knowledge of his work and his subordinate's work. When he has full knowledge of what is going on in the organization, then only he can give effective guidance to the subordinates and command them to work.

(c) **Technical Knowledge:** The manager/leader must aware of technicality of the work going on in the organization/or at least he must have support of a technical team, so that he can give effective guidance to subordinates in technical matters.

(d) **Initiative:** The leader must take initiative in guiding and directing the subordinates and if time comes he must stand in the front to get the work done to fulfill the objective of the organization.

(e) **Honesty:** A leader should be honest in his duties and towards his subordinates. Then only the subordinates will respect him. If he is dishonest, he cannot command the subordinate and subordinates will overlook his directions with a smile. This you can understand from the profiles of our national leaders, who are most dishonestly honest.

(f) **Decision-making Power:** The manager/leader must have full knowledge of the activities of his organization and enough technical and managerial ability to take timely decision. This quality in a manager helps him to command respect and obedience from subordinates.

(g) **Responsibility:** The leader must accept the responsibility, which authorizes him to use his authority to get the things done. If does not accept responsibility, it is very difficult for him to apply his authority.

1.25.3. Types of Leadership or Leadership Styles

The manner in which the leader/manager apply his powers to get the things done by the subordinates is known as leadership style. This depends on the personal traits of the manager, personal background i.e., the environment in which he brought up, family background, social culture in which he lives etc. Some of the types of leadership are given below:

1. **Democratic Leader:** He is a leader, who believes in the co-operation and co-ordination among groups. He permits his subordinates to participate in the decision-making. He believes in decentralization of authority, two-way communication and joint participation in decision-making process. He creates system and harmony in individuals. This type of leadership is based on the principles of mutual co-operation and co-ordination. It relies on respect for all the followers. He takes his decision according to the option of majority. He makes his best efforts to improve job satisfaction and morale of his followers. He believes in both types of incentives – monetary incentives and non-monetary incentives. The basic aim of democratic leadership is to improve the productivity and ensure the achievement of predetermined objectives of the enterprise. This type of leadership style is also known as **Participation Leadership**.
2. **Laissez Faire Leadership:** It is the type of leadership under which the leader does not direct the activities of his followers. He leaves it the subordinates to decide and control them. Under this type of leadership, every member is free to take the decision for his activities and to do his activities in the manner, he likes. He is responsible only to collect necessary data for his group and to make the factors of production available. This type of leadership is based on the assumption that all the subordinates are competent, willing to work and self-motivated. It is believed that they will perform better if they are free to decide and to do on their own. This is ***not popular form of leadership these days.***
3. **Autocratic Leadership:** It is completely opposite to democratic leadership style. It is based on the principle of centralization of power. Under this type of leadership, the autocratic leader himself performs all the important functions like to take decisions, to plan, to make the allotment of work etc. Thus, autocratic leader wants to concentrate all the powers with him. He believes that all the subordinates are lazy and are not capable of decide how to proceed with work.

4. **Institutional Leadership:** It means a leader who is in a position to influence his followers simply by the position, he holds. Under this type, all the members of the group work according to the directions of their leader. All the members of the group have deep faith and loyalty in their leader. They follow what their leader orders. There may be some persons who follow the orders of their leader because of their disabilities.
5. **Personal Leader:** He is a leader, who becomes in an enterprise on the basis of personal relations. Such leader influences his followers in his personal capacity only. He gives his orders and directions to his subordinates only in his personal capacity. **This type of leader influences the followers only because of his personality, personal abilities and character.**
6. **Impersonal Leader:** He develops through the employees of an enterprise under a direct leader. Under this type, all the directions, policies, plans etc. are in writing. This type of leadership is found in the organizations in which there is a large number of followers, it is not possible for the leader to have personal contact with all of them. **This type of leadership style is very much popular these days.**
7. **Persuasive Leadership:** The leader of this type has complete domination over his subordinates/followers mainly because of his polite behavior and qualities. The followers of such leader love him; respect him and express their complete faith in him. Followers of such leader treat the orders and directions of such leader as the rules and laws. This type of leadership is most effective.
8. **Creative Leadership:** This type of leader is one, who believes in free and frank discussions with his followers. He gives due recognition to the opinions and feelings of his followers. Such leader appraises the good performance of his followers. Under this type, **free exchange of ideas and opinions is found occasionally.**
9. **Bureaucratic Leadership:** The leader of this type is one, who depends upon the rules and regulations developed by him. He decides the rules for the duties, rights and responsibilities of all his followers. He issues these rules to his followers and wants them to do only in accordance with these rules. **He does not provide any opportunity to his subordinates to apply their mind to do the work and for any clarification they have to approach him.**

QUESTIONS

1. Explain the nature and meaning of management briefly.
2. Distinguish between administration, management and organization with examples.
3. Give definition of management and explain whether management is an art or science.
4. Write short notes on Fredric Winslow Taylor and explain his contribution to the management.
5. Write a note on H.L. Gantt and briefly narrate his contribution to management.
6. Write a short notes on F.B. Gilberth and what are his contributions to management discipline.

7. Who is Elton Mayo? What he contributed to management?
8. Explain the stages of evolution of management discipline.
9. List out the schools of management thought. Explain any two of them in detail.
10. Explain the mathematical or quantative measurement school.
11. Explain human behavior school of though.
12. List out Fayol's principles of management. Explain any three of them briefly with examples.
13. Write short notes on any three of the following:
    - (i) (a) Division of work (b) Scalar chain
      (c) Discipline (d) Authority and Responsibility.
    - (ii) (a) Unity of Direction (b) Esprit de Corps
      (c) Order (d) Centralization.
14. List out the functions of management and explain any two of them in detail with examples.
15. What is PODSCORB? Explain briefly.
16. Write notes on:
    (a) Leadership (b) Communication
    (c) Motivation (d) Controlling.
17. List out the techniques of coordination and explain any three of them briefly.
18. What is a decision? Explain the process of decision-making.
19. What is objective? What are managerial objectives? Explain briefly.
20. What do you understand by management by objectives? Explain briefly with examples.
21. Explain what is survival objective.
22. Write notes on:
    (a) The growth objective
    (b) The profit objective
    (c) Social obligation objective.
23. Explain what are social responsibilities of Management–Give examples.
24. What is motivation? Why is it important to a manager? Briefly explain the theories of motivation.
25. Explain what is McGregor's theory X and theory Y. And explain their applicability.
26. Is criticize the theory X and theory Y and explain what is theory Z.
27. Write notes on:
    (a) Fear and Punishment theory (b) Reward theory
    (c) Carrot and Stick theory.
28. List out modern theories of work motivation. Explain briefly Maslow's need priority theory.

29. Briefly explain Maslow's hierarchy of needs.
30. Briefly explain what is herzreberg's two-factor theory of motivation.

MULTIPLE CHOICE QUESTIONS

1. Is management
   (a) A science (b) An art
   (c) Both science and art (d) None.
2. .... is the function of the industry concerned with the determination of the corporate policy, plans and programs.
   (a) Administration (b) Management
   (c) Organization (d) All.
3. .... involves a structure of relationships among people working for the desired results.
   (a) Administration (b) Management
   (c) Organization (d) All.
4. .... is the function in industry concerned in the execution of the policies, plans and programs.
   (a) Administration (b) Management
   (c) Organization (d) All.
5. Father of scientific management is
   (a) Luther Gullick (b) Maslow
   (c) Elton Mayo (d) F.W. Taylor.
6. Human needs hierarchy and behavior science is provided by
   (a) Luther Gullik (b) Maslow
   (c) Elton Mayo (d) F.W. Taylor.
7. Use of human effort effectively described in
   (a) the scientific management stage
   (b) the organization stage
   (c) the management process stage
   (d) the general management stage.
8. According to McGregory theory Y people by nature
   (a) accept responsibility (b) avoid responsibility
   (c) accept and skip (d) neutral
9. The unity of command means an employee must receive orders from
   (a) one superior (b) two superiors
   (c) any superiors (d) by none.

10. .... is the process of stimulation the employees to perform more effectively.
(a) Direction (b) Guiding
(c) Training (d) Motivating.

11. General or overall objectives are set by:
(a) Lower level management (b) Middle management
(c) Top level management (d) All level management.

12. According to McGregor's theory X people by nature
(a) Accept responsibility (b) Avoid responsibility
(c) Both (a) and (b) (d) None.

13. .... introduced two factor theory.
(a) Maslow (b) O. Henry
(c) Hertz Berg (d) Elton Mayo.

14. The theory of hierarchy of needs introduced by
(a) Maslow (b) Henry Fayol
(c) F.W. Taylor (d) Gilberth.

15. How many stages in hierarchy of Needs?
(a) 2 (b) 3
(c) 4 (d) 5.

16. .... assumes that people can be motivated to work if reward is offered.
(a) Theory X (b) Theory Y
(c) Theory Z (d) Carrot and stick.

17. In M.B.O. the letter 'O' denotes
(a) Order (b) Organization
(c) Organizing (d) Objectives.

18. Management is .... of getting things done by others.
(a) Science (b) An art
(c) Work (d) Process.

19. Management is as important in the business as .... in the human body.
(a) Heart (b) Blood
(c) Nervous system (d) Brain.

20. .... is known as father of principles of management.
(a) F.W.Taylor (b) Henry Fayol
(c) Gilberth (d) H.L.Gantt.

21. .... has coined the term POSDCORB.
(a) Hery Fayol (b) Luther Gullick
(c) Elton Mayo (d) Lillian Gilberth.

22. In the term POSDCORB the letter 'O' refers to

(a) Order (b) Organization

(c) Observation (d) Organizing.

23. In POSDCORB the letter 'S' refers to

(a) Scaling (b) Simplify

(c) Search (d) Staffing.

24. In the term POSDCORB the letter "D" refers to

(a) Designing (b) Drafting

(c) Directing (d) Demand.

ANSWERS

1. (c)	**2.** (a)	**3.** (c)	**4.** (b)	**5.** (d)	**6.** (b)	**7.** (a)	**8.** (a)
9. (a)	**10.** (d)	**11.** (c)	**12.** (b)	**13.** (c)	**14.** (a)	**15.** (d)	**16.** (c)
17. (d)	**18.** (b)	**19.** (a)	**20.** (b)	**21.** (b)	**22.** (d)	**23.** (d)	**24.** (c).

❍❍❍

Unit 2 Designing Organizational Structure

2.1. ORGANIZATION

The word ***ORGANIZATION*** is given a variety of interpretations. We can stress here on two terms namely, (a) Organization is understood as a dynamic process and a managerial activity, which is necessary for bringing people together and trying them together in the pursuit of common objectives. This may well be the process of **organizing.** (b) Secondly, it can be used in the sense, which refers to the **structure of relationship** among positions jobs, which is built-up for the attainment of common objectives or goals. In this sense, organization can be considered as a vehicle through which goals are supposed to be achieved. Organization structure is considered in different views. Some consider it as a network of relationships, a blueprint of how the management will like the various functions and activities to be assigned and connected together. Some others look upon it as a social system, consisting of the human relationships existing among people performing different types of activities. For some people, organizations are a system with inputs (such as men, materials, money and machines), and processes through which product or service is produced. Hence, the common features, we can identify are (characteristics of organization):

(a) Division of Labor: When total work involved in achievement of goals and objectives are divided into activities and functions and allocated to an individual or a group of people, as whole work may be too heavy for an individual or a group of people, the organization structure comes into existence. Say for example, marketing, financial, personnel and production, etc.

(b) Co-ordination: Once the functions are decided and allocated to group of people or an individual next is to see that all the activities of the groups or individuals must be directed towards the organizational goals. That is activities are unified and harmonized.

(c) Accomplishment of Goals or Objectives: The organization structure has no meaning, if it doesn't serve in its mission of achieving the objectives, it is because the structure is framed in such a way that the works are allocated to different goals in such a way that they are unified and harmonized towards the achievement of a common goal or objective.

(d) **Authority-Responsibility Structure:** An organization structure consists of various positions arranged in a hierarchy with a clear definition of the authority and responsibility associated with each of these. An organization cannot serve certain specific purposes or goals unless some positions are placed above others and given authority to bind them by their decisions. In fact, an organization structure is quite often defined as a structure of authority–responsibility relationships.

All the above discussion confirms that organization structure is a structure of positions arranged in a hierarchy for the pursuit of common objectives through specialization and division of work.

2.2. THE PROCESS OF ORGANIZATIONS

Organizing is the managerial function as already discussed and this function of organizing is known as *process of organization.* To organize is to harmonize, co-ordinate or arrange in a logical and orderly manner. Making the rational division of work into groups of activities and trying together the positions representing grouping of activities for accomplishment of desired objectives is the function of management and this function is known as ***organizing***. Various steps involved in this process are:

(a) **Determination of Objectives:** Any business is established or started by entrepreneurs to achieve some objectives. These objectives must be clearly stated so as to understand the very purpose and existence of the business. Depending on the objectives the work to be done is decided and it is divided into groups and they are organized in an orderly way. It is to say that organizations are built around objectives; hence deciding the objectives is the first step in building up an organization.

(b) **Enumeration of Activities:** The work of an industrial concern is divided into essential activities. For example, it is divided as **production, financing, purchasing, marketing, personnel**, like wise.

(c) **Classification of Activities:** The next step is to classify activities according to similarities and common purposes and function by taking the available human and material resources into account. For each class of activities there will be a *department* and for each sub-class there will be *section of the department* and so on. For example, marketing may be one department, in which packing, dispatching, sales, consumer service etc. may be sections.

(d) **Fitting Individuals into Functions:** Once the departmentalization and formation of sections is over, each section should be allocated to a subordinate and each department should be allocated to one executive. Hence, next duty is to fix a *suitable and well-qualified and capable* person to fit into these activities. The rule is *right peg in a right hole.* Each person in the group is given a specific work and made responsible correctly and effectively. This step consists of appointment of workers and defining their responsibility of each one of them.

(e) **Assignment of Authority for Action:** Now suitable persons are fitted in their respective jobs and made responsible to accomplish the job. He can only proceed to do the work, when he is given adequate *authority* to proceed to do the work. The delegation authority to take steps to complete the assigned part of the job is next step in organization. Once, the authority is given the concerned manager will have power to command his subordinates and get the work done by them.

All the above supports the definition of organization i.e. organization embraces the duties of designating the departments and the personnel that are to carry on the work, defining their functions and specifying the relations that are to be exist between departments and individuals.

2.3. ANALYSIS OF ORGANIZATION

Since the process of organizing is related to specific needs and purposes it is important that an organization structure is created with a careful and comprehensive analysis of the needs of the proposed organization. Peter Duckers recommends three types of analysis. They are:

(a) Activities analysis,

(b) Decisions analysis, and

(c) Relations analysis.

(a) Activities Analysis: This refers to very purpose of analyzing the purpose of existence of organization. That is objective of the organization. Once this is known, the manager will be able to find the activities required to accomplish desired goals and group them in an order, handover each department to suitable and capable person and delegate the authority, so that everybody work to get the desired objective.

(b) Decisions Analysis: Once a person made responsible to do a job and given adequate authority, he decides what kind of decisions will need to be made to carry out the work of the organization. He must also see that where or at what level these decisions will have to be made and how each manager must be involved in them. In other words this analysis will help the managers to fix up decision levels of organization.

(c) Relations Analysis: It will include the examination of the various types of relationships that develop within the organization. These relationships are *Vertical, Lateral* and *Diagonal*. Where a superior subordinate relationship envisaged it is vertical relationship. In case of an expert or specialist advising a manager at the same level, the relationship is lateral. Where a specialist exercises authority over a person in subordinate position in another department in the same organization, it is known as diagonal relationship.

2.4. FORMAL AND INFORMAL ORGANIZATION

While discussing organization and organization structures, one should not forget that in an organization both formal and informal organization and organizational relationships exists. The formal organization refers to the structure of jobs and positions with clearly defined functions and relationships as prescribed by the top management. This type of organization is built by the management to realize the objectives of an enterprise and is bound by rules, regulations, systems and procedures. In the formal organization every employee has a position and he will carry out the work for which he is responsible. Chester Bernard says that the organization is formal when the activities of two or more persons are consciously co-coordinated towards a common objective.

2.5. INFORMAL ORGANIZATION

Informal organization refers to the relationships between people in an organization based not on procedures and regulations but on personal attitudes, whims, prejudice, likes and dislikes etc. For example, when the members of an organization goes to deputy general manager for advise, because he is kind and easily available to them, when the organizational rule stipulates that they have go to general manager, is a clear indication of informal organization. Many a time, the management makes use of this informal organization to get the things done in a more easy way. If proper use is made of informal organization it will be more effective than the formal organization.

2.6. IMPORTANCE OF ORGANIZATION

One cannot over-emphasize the importance of sound organization structure. An organization is not merely lifeless structure, it comprises people and is the agency through which the management performs the important functions of direction, co-ordination and control. In fact it is the foundation of the management on which the success of managerial functions depends. Sound organization is important because,

(a) It facilitates administration,

(b) It makes growth and diversification possible,

(c) It provides for optimum use of available resources and technological improvements, and

(d) It stimulates independent, creative thinking and initiative through well defined areas of work.

2.7. PRINCIPLES OF ORGANIZATION

We say that an organization is efficient and successful, if it achieves the desired objectives, otherwise it is understood that there is something wrong in the organization. An organization can successfully conduct its mission, if it follows certain principles, known as *Principles of Organization*. These principles are:

1. **Unity of Objective:** All the parts of the organization and organization as a whole must have only one objective to achieve and everybody should work to achieve that objective, which is determined by the top level management of the enterprise. It is analogous with the proverb saying that, two bullocks of a cart must lead the cart in the same direction to reach the destination. An enterprise is like a cart. When all the departments in the enterprise works together towards the same objective, the enterprise can achieve the desired goals, otherwise, nobody knows where they are going and what they have to achieve.
2. **Efficiency:** Whenever an organization achieves the desired goals, with minimum cost, it will satisfy the test of efficiency. So, as far as the enterprise is concerned, it

must achieve the desired goals with minimum cost. As far the individual employee is concerned, it must give him maximum job satisfaction. Regarding investors, it must be in a position to reasonable profits and provide them the dividends. From the social point of view, it must contribute maximum towards the welfare of the society. When all these are fulfilled, the organization wins the test of efficiency and is termed as efficient organization.

3. **Span of Control or Span of Management:** The problem of span of control or span of management or span of supervision rose its ugly head ages ago. The main problem involved is posed by a question, 'How many subordinates can a manager manage efficiently? 'Lyndall Urwick found " the ideal number of subordinates for a supervising authority is four. He also said that the lowest level of the organization, where what is delegated is responsibility for the performance of a specific job and not supervision of others, the number may be eight to twelve. French management consultant, V.A. Graicunaas, after analyzing supervisor-subordinate relationship, developed a mathematical formula. He identifies three types of relationships between subordinate and supervisor. They are: (a) Direct single relationships, (b) Direct group relationships, and (c) Cross relationships. He felt that single direct relationships were easy to understand and recognized but one should not forget the relationships with different grips of subordinates and the cross relationships between all the subordinates. According to Urwick, if A has two subordinates B and C, then the relation ships are: A can deal with them individually or as a pair. The behavior of B in presence of C and C in presence of B will differ from their behavior when each is with A alone. Further, what B thinks of C and C thinks of B constitute two cross relationship which A must keep in mind when delegating the work on which B and C must work together in absence of A. That means here the superior has to deal with six relationships when one supervisor has two subordinates. As the number of subordinates increases, cross relationships goes on increasing. When there are four subordinates, the relationships increase to 44. To understand this, Graicunas gave a mathematical formula:

$$N = \text{Total number of relationships} = n\{(2^n/2) + n - 1\}$$

or $$N = n\{2^{n-1} + (n - 1)\}.$$

Where n = number of subordinates.

In general, no supervisors can directly control the work of more than five subordinates.

4. **Division of Work:** Activities of an enterprise must be broken down effectively and each is handed over to one department to carry out the work effectively. The work of all the departments should be coordinated towards the objective of the enterprise. Proper grouping of activities and forming department is another principle of a sound organization.
5. **Functional Definition:** Once the departments are formed, the duties and authority relationships of every incharge of the department, workers in the department should be clearly defined, so that here is no scope for confusion and overlapping of authority. This is a must for trouble free operation of the enterprise.

6. **Scalar Principle (Chain of Command):** The line of authority or the chain of command must be clearly defined for building sound organization. This is necessary because everybody must know to whom he has to give orders and who are reporting to him. The subordinates should know that to whom he has to consult in policy matters to make decisions, which are beyond his capacity.
7. **Exception Principle**: Every organization must be designed and arranged in such a way, only exceptionally complex problems are referred to the higher levels of management and routine matters are dealt with executives at lower levels. This principle is known as exception principle.
8. **Unity of Command:** In a good organization, each subordinate should have one superior whose command he has to obey. If too many superiors command a single subordinate, he will be in confusion to know, whom he has to obey and to whom he is responsible. In case if some other superior wants to get the work done by a particular subordinate, he should pass his command in a proper channel, so that the subordinate receives orders from his superior. This will avoid conflict of command and help in fixing responsibility.
9. **Unity of direction:** There must be only one plan for a group of activities directed towards the same end. If each person in the department begins to work under different plan or program of action, nothing but confusion will follow. Unity of direction is embodied in the organizational plan is, therefore, is a must for sound organization.
10. **Responsibility:** In a good organization it is a practice that the superiors is responsible for the duties of his subordinates and the subordinates must be held responsible to their duties for the performance of the tasks assigned to them.
11. **Authority and Responsibility:** Authority and responsibility are the two faces of same coin. They co-exit in any organization. Once a man is made responsible for some work, sufficient authority should be given to him to get the things done by the subordinates. If this is not so, then a subordinate cannot discharge his duties properly for want of necessary authority or power to proceed with the assigned task.
12. **Balance**: A sound organization must have a balanced structure with regards to the following:
    (a) *Centralization and Decentralization*: This refers to delegation of decision-making power. Some matters may be left to be disposed by the subordinates at lower level while some others, such as financial matters and policy matters must be centralized and a balance between centralization and decentralization should thus be achieved.
    (b) Authority allocation to departments and staff at various levels and
    (c) Limited span of management and length of line of communication.
13. **Flexibility:** The organization must avoid complicated procedures, which encourages red-tapism and excessive complication of control, so that it can adopt itself easily and economically to suit the changing needs in business and technology.

14. **Continuity**: The organization must be so arranged as to provide for the continuity of the enterprise, by providing proper executive development and training programs.
15. **Facilitation of Leadership:** The organization structure should be so designed that there is enough opportunity for the management to give effective lead to the enterprise. This will help the organization in getting certain persons trained to take up the leadership in case of necessity.

2.8. DEPARTMENTATION

Koontz and O' Donnell define a **department** as designating – "a distinct area, division, or branch of an enterprise over which a manager has authority for the performance of specified activities". Most enterprises are involved in producing a product or a service for the benefit of others. The latter aspect requires marketing or distribution so that the persons for whom the product or service is intended will accept it if it satisfies his needs. These activities require money or sufficient capital or finance. Thus for every organization or enterprise there are three fundamental activities or functions to be performed, namely:

1. Production,
2. Marketing and
3. Finance.

Thus functional departmentation consists of grouping of common activities in the form of an organizational unit. In short, units are formed around common functions. The term functional departmentation is used at the higher organizational levels. In addition to the functional departmentation on the basis of production, marketing and finance, it is possible to attempt departmentation in different ways such as by product, by territory, by customer, by process and by task force. Top management is at liberty to use any means of departmentation while forming an organization structure. Usually for the top and bottom organization levels, functional departmentation is followed and for the intervening organization levels other means of departmentation is used. The selection of the media of departmentation will be determined on the basis of the extent to which it is likely to achieve the objective. Basically, departmentation can be in the following ways:

1. By Function,
2. By Product,
3. By Territory, region, or geographical area,
4. By Customer,
5. By Process,
6. By Task force and
7. By Appropriate combination of these types.

1. **By Product or Service:** Department may set up for each product or service manufactured and/or supplied. This makes it possible for the management to take advantage of specialized product knowledge and place responsibility for results achieved.

The *advantages* of this type of structures are:

(a) When this is extended right down to the lower level operating managers, better customer service may be given. For example in marketing department, the salesmen, who are in direct contact with the customers, can give better service to them.

(b) It simplifies determination of the profitability of each product line.

(c) When a new product is introduced a new division can be added without interrupting the existing operation by merely extending the line and having another-marketing manager and staff for that new product line or group of products.

(d) Top management secures more detailed and intimate information regarding the markets in relation to specific products.

(e) It is extremely suitable where product lines are complex and diverse and require specialized knowledge for selling and marketing as well as salesmen with specialized knowledge.

The following are the *disadvantages* of the structure:

(a) It may cause customer annoyance and confusion as a number of salesmen from the same company may plead him for different products.

(b) It involves extra costs of maintaining separate sales force for each product group.

(c) There is a duplication of costs such as traveling expenses etc.

2. **By Function:** For each of the functions, such as Personnel, Finance, Production and Marketing etc. so as to enable each manager has to attend the specialized functions of his department. This is the most popular way of departmentalization

The *advantages* of this type of structure are:

(a) Benefits of occupational specialization;

(b) Easier inter-departmental coordination; and

(c) Logical and simple easy-to-understand structure.

The *disadvantages* of the functional departmentation include:

(a) Excessive centralization;

(b) Unsuitable where geographical centralization is required;

(c) Unsuitable where emphasis on product lines is called for; and

(d) Lower potency for developing managers for promotion.

3. **By Location:** Territorial divisions may be created where activities are widely dispensed. It takes advantage of the intimate knowledge of local conditions possessed by the executive.

The following are the *advantages* of this type of departmentation:

(a) The regional managers and his staff become experts with regard to their particular region in connection with the customers as well as competition prevailing in that specific region.

(b) It is very useful where proximity to local conditions will result in low cost of operation and opportunities to enjoy the benefits of attractive local conditions.

(c) It gives an edge where the customer requires different selling in terms of geographical market segmentation.

(d) It provides good training ground for the salesmen to become sales supervisors and rise up to the ladder.

(e) It helps the executive to demonstrate his ability in a certain territory and press his claim for promotion to another important area.

The following are the *disadvantages* of the territorial type of structure:

(a) It involves higher costs of coordination and control from headquarters.

(b) It results in more managerial levels, which increases overhead costs.

4. By Time: When individuals working together in their normal working hours cannot cope with the volume and rush of work evening or night shifts may be run. Thus activities are divided into divisions on the basis of time.

5. By Customers: Departments or divisions may sometimes be earmarked on the basis of customers served. For example, we can quote, wholesale purchasers, retail purchasers etc.

The *advantages* are:

(a) It is very much suitable where the major emphasis is placed on better service to specialized types of customers using the company's products or services.

(b) It is useful where a product or service of wide appeal is offered through many marketing channels and outlets.

The *disadvantages* are:

(a) There may not be enough work in case of certain types of customers, which may result in certain salesmen remaining idle.

(b) There is the problem of coordinating department formed on the customer type basis with those organized on another basis.

(c) It may foster an unequal development of customer groups in times of expansion and disappearance of certain customer groups in times of recession.

(d) It may generate the tendency to remain rigid, with the result that it may be difficult to adjust to problems in case there is a fluctuation in the enterprise's activities.

6. By Process: This type of divisions we can see in manufacturing concerns. For example: Welding Department, Fabricating Department, Assembly Department etc.

The *advantages* are:

(a) Operators/managers/employees get specialized in their area of operation.

(b) Employees will become experts in the operations/works entrusted to them.

(c) This type of specialization reduces operation or cycle time.

The *disadvantages* are:

(a) For specialization the work is to be divided into parts suitable for an employee to get specialized in that work.

(b) Routing of work will be a tedious job.

7. **Departmentation by Task Force:** Under this system the responsibility for the completion of work rests upon an entire task-team and normally one individual acts as the leader of the task force. Every member of the task force identifies the objectives and fully comprehends them. This type of departmentation is also termed as *project organization* and is a refinement of advanced planning and controlling techniques such as PERT and CPM. This system helps to build an organization unit aimed at completing a series of evens utilizing the best available talents. After the completion of the project, the organization is dissolved and a different project is given to them.

The *advantages* are:

(a) The possibility of developing managers who can use different types of resources.

(b) The specialized complete team set up for performing the task results in greater concentration and more productive results.

The *disadvantages* are:

(a) The fostering of a feeling of frustration caused by being a separate unit and not a part of the whole organization.

(b) The sense of insecurity engendered by the feeling of not being part of the whole team with chances of promotions to the highest positions being less.

2.8.1. Factors in Departmentation

The following factors are basic to divide an organization into departments:

(a) Specialization: Department should yield the advantages of specialization. Specialization may be *functional* such as in marketing, we have advertising, sales promotion etc. or *by products* such as cosmetics, condiments etc.

(b) Control: Departmentation should serve to make control as effective as possible. One activity intended to serve, as a check on another should be under specific executive. Territorial departments (zonal or districts) may be established in such a way that the performance of one can be checked by comparison with the other. A clean break made between two departments will help in fixing responsibility clear and squarely.

(c) Co-ordination: Quite different activities may be grouped together under one executive because they need to be co-coordinated. In case of *orphan activities* like filing, or other service function, the *most–use* criterion may be applied. That is such activities may be clubbed together with the function that relies on it the most.

(d) Attention: An activity that is considered to be basic to the success of an enterprise may be given greater attention than others and may, for this purpose, be placed in separate division.

(e) Local Conditions: While forming departments, attention must be given to local conditions, at the places concerned, for example, the personalities of individuals who will man the organization, or the pattern of informal relationships among people, or the need to combine activities into full-time jobs.

(f) Economy: The expenses involved in creating a separate division for an activity or activities should also be considered though this should not become the all-important factor.

2.9. TYPES OF ORGANIZATION STRUCTURES IN PRACTICE

While developing a sound organization structure, it is important to understand not only the nature of the authority delegated but also the authority relationships which exist between managers and among themselves, and between managers and their subordinates. It involves an appreciation of (a) the line-staff relationships, which have caused considerable misunderstanding and confusion in practice; (b) The use of committees and the organizational relationships so created; and (c) the technical tools such as charting, which would help a better appreciation of the existing organizational relationships. The problem of organization is to select and combine the efforts of men of proper characteristics so as to obtain the desired result. The character and type of organization will depend largely on the size and nature of the enterprise.

Different types of organizational structures in practice are:

1. Line organization or Military organization,
2. Staff organization or Functional organization, and
3. Line and Staff organization. These three are the basic organization structures. As the knowledge of scientific approach developed many more are added to the list. They are:
   (a) Committee Organization,
   (b) Matrix Organization,
   (c) Virtual Organization,
   (d) Team Structure,
   (e) Boundary less organization,
   (f) Inverted Pyramid structure, and
   (g) Lean and Flat Organization structures.

2.9.1. Line or Military Organization

This organization is given name "Military organization" as it refers to the flow of authority in Army. In army the authority flows from the men at the top; to the lowest man vertically. This shows that the directions are issued by the man at the top i.e. the man incharge of the organization and is directly conveyed to the man incharge of execution of the work. Here the line of authority is straight and vertical. Sometimes it is also known as *pure organization.* Here line managers are responsible for result obtained. They have full authority to control the organizational work. For example consider the district administration. In the district administration, the district collector is the head of the district. He has authority to control the affairs of the district. All the district level officers, such as, Mandal Officers, Revenue officers, Medical officers, Educational officers are all departmental heads working under the district collector. The orders flow from directly from the collector the departmental officers and it then flows within the department from the departmental head to the subordinates who execute the work. The progress of the work is communicated from the bottom most workmen to higher ups and then to departmental heads and the same is communicated to the district collector. So the type of organization we have for district administration is of Military type. The departmental heads such as Mandal officers, Medical officers, and Commissioner are independent of each other and would enjoy equal status. For example, consider an industrial organization where one foreman, who is incharge of a particular group, neither he receives instruction from other foreman and does not issues orders to any other foreman.

Each foreman is the boss of his group of workers. Workers cannot approach any other boss for their problems. In case they want to approach any other boss, they have to do it through their head of the group only. Similarly in case any other departmental head wants to give instructions to the subordinate of other department, he has to strictly follow the line of authority and go up the line and communicate the same to the top man and then the information has to flow from top man to the concerned person through proper channel. The necessary characteristics of this type of organization are: (a) Commands should be given to subordinates through the immediate superior to that subordinate. There should be no skipping of links in the chain of command. (b) There should be only one chain that means the command should be received from only one immediate superior. (c) The number of subordinates under one superior should be limited i.e. the span of control should be moderate. If the above principles are followed the advantages of the organization chart can be realized effectively.

Advantages of Line Organization

(a) It is easiest to understand and follow. Every employee knows whom he has to obey and from whom he receives commands and to whom he has to report.

(b) In line organization unity of command control is confirmed, which is a must as per the principles of organization.

(c) This organization ensures perfect discipline. This is because of unified command and unified control. Every person knows from whom he get orders and to whom he is responsible. The subordinate will try to satisfy his superior in his own interest.

(d) Because of unification of authority and responsibilities, quick effective decisions are made by the decision makers.

(e) As each head of the department is solely responsible for the work of his department, he can easily get adjusted to the changing needs of the business.

Disadvantages

The following are some of the weakness of the line organization.

(a) As the person in authority directs the entire department, the efficiency of the department depends on the managerial skills and leadership qualities of that person. The performance of the department will show the qualities of the person heading the department.

(b) Line organization suffers from the lack of specialized skill of the expert. When the person in authority wants to take decision in the field of activity, which is not related to him, he will be in difficulty. If he takes decision without proper knowledge, the organization has to suffer. For example consider the Principal of an Engineering College. He may be of particular discipline, say for example Computer Science. When he wants to take a decision regarding the purchase of Electrical Equipment for the electrical engineering laboratory, He cannot take a right decision, without the help of an Electrical Engineering staff.

(c) One more drawback of line organization is lack of adequate communication. The lower rank people do not receive commands/orders directly from the departmental head and they receive it through the line of communication, which may be very lengthy. This may cause delay and also correct information may not be delivered at the lower level. Similarly, if the lower level managers or workers want to communicate any thing to the higher ups, it will be very difficult and sometimes the higher level managers may not be in a position to utilize the ideas/suggestions of lower ranks.

(d) Because of the full authority given to the higher-level managers, they may favor their own people and may do injustice to the organization.

(e) It suffers from the drawbacks of autocratic control.

This type of chart is more suitable for small business concerns where we have small number of subordinates and one or two higher-level managers. Especially suitable for ownership organizations. It is also suitable for organizations where routine type of work or job is being carried out. It is also suitable for industries where line production or continuous process is being used. It can also be helpful for industrial units where automatic machines are the main production machines. The figure below shows the structure for line or military organizations.

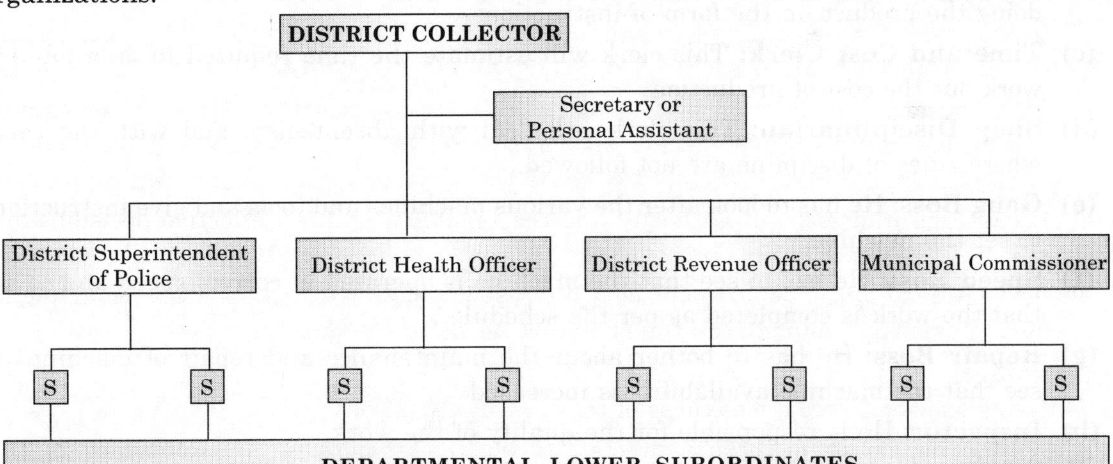

Fig. 2.1. Line Organization or Military Organization.

2.9.2. The Functional Organization or Staff Organization

As the modern business functions are very much complicated, the manager at the top alone cannot take decision on certain specialized matters. In such cases he needs advise from the people who have technical ability in the matter concerned. For example, when district collector has to deal draught situation or any epidemic health problem, he may lack of specialized knowledge in the problem concerned. Then he may take advice from an environmental specialist or from the district health officer as the case may be. So also in industrial concerns, the general manager may take advice from personal manager when he wants to take decision regarding recruiting suitable persons for the jobs, or he can take advice from production manager when a production problem arises. In fact every organization while have functional organization to certain extent. The line manager is responsible for making decisions and the staff managers may assist the line managers in making decisions. The line manager, while making a decision, may take the advice given by the staff manager into account or simply he may neglect. But ultimately line manager is responsible for the results obtained by the decision made by him. A staff function is a support function. In this type of organization, the whole work of the organization is divided on functional basis. This is to say one particular department will look after the affairs of a particular function, which is needed by entire organization. For example, Personal department will recruit all the workers required by various departments of the origination and train them. Similarly materials department will purchase and supply materials required by all other departments. F.W. Taylor, the father of scientific management, introduced functional type of organization. He has extended his functional management theory even at the lower levels also, i.e. he advised that there should be separate foreman at shop floor to look after specified activities. He recommended the following staff for various works.

(a) **Route Clerk:** He decides the actual path to be traveled by material during production of a product.

(b) **Instruction Card Clerk:** The duty of this clerk is to lay down the exact method of doing the product, in the form of instructions.

(c) **Time and Cost Clerk:** This clerk will estimate the time required to do a job and work out the cost of production.

(d) **Shop Disciplinarian:** This clerk will deal with absenteeism and with the cases where rules of discipline are not followed.

(e) **Gang Boss:** He has to look after the various machines and tools and give instructions to set the machine.

(f) **Speed Boss:** He has to see that the machine is operated at correct speed and to see that the work is completed as per the schedule.

(g) **Repair Boss:** He has to bother about the maintenance and repair of machines to see that the machine availability is increased.

(h) **Inspector:** He is responsible for the quality of the work.

He called each of the above persons as ***functional Foreman*** and kept them in charge of specified work. In this type of organization, the worker receives instructions from many bosses (foremen) instead of one. At higher levels all related works are clubbed together on functional basis and each department is allocated one function. The following Fig. 2.2. shows the structure of a functional type of organization.

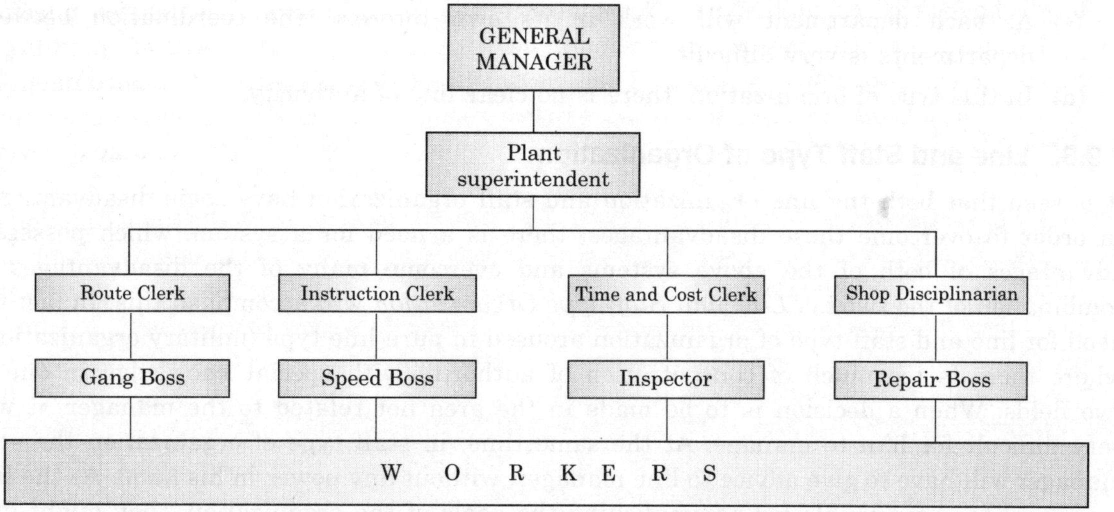

Fig. 2.2. Functional Organization (Type 1).

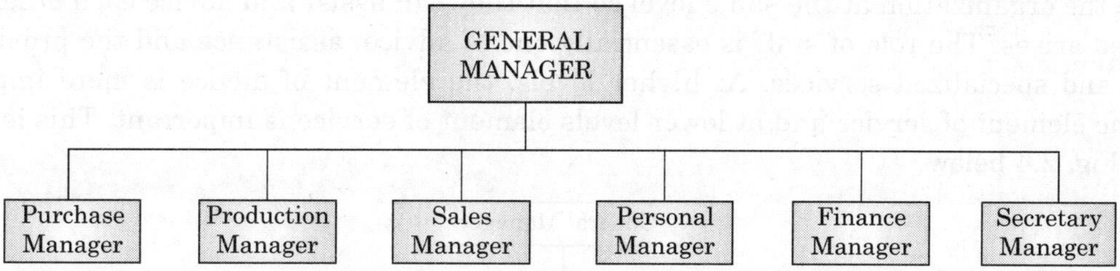

Fig. 2.3. Functional Organization (Type 2).

2.9.2.1. Advantages of functional or staff type organization

(a) Because of greater division of work, workers will get specialized in their trade so that the quality workpieces can be produced and waste can be reduced, so that the cost of production will be kept under control.

(b) It enables the organization to have clear demarcation between brainwork and manual work.

(c) This type of organization is most suitable for a unit working on mass production techniques, as planning and design (mental) is looked after by separate people and execution of job is done by separate people (manual).

2.9.2.2. Disadvantages of functional or staff type organization

(a) As the workers will get instructions or orders from too many bosses, they will be in a state of confusion because they do not know to whom they are responsible. This may spoil organizational discipline.

(b) Staff-managers will give only advice and they do not hold any responsibility.

(c) As each department will work in its own interest, the coordination between departments is very difficult.

(d) In this type of organization, there is no clear line of authority.

2.9.3. Line and Staff Type of Organization

It is seen that both the line organization and staff organization have some disadvantages. In order to overcome these disadvantages, there is a need for a system, which possesses advantages of both of the above systems and overcome many of the disadvantages. A combination of the two i.e. *Line and Staff type Organization* will accomplish this. In fact the need for line and staff type of organization aroused in pure line type (military organization), where there is too much of concentration of authority with special knowledge in one or two fields. When a decision is to be made in the area not related to the manager, it was very difficult for him to manage. At the same time, in staff type of organization the staff manager will have to give advice to line manager, without any power in his hand. As the line managers are responsible for accomplishing the goals of the organization, they might give due weightage for the advises of the staff or simply overlook them. All staff managers are kept in the organization at the same level so that they can assist and advise each other when the need arises. The role of staff is essentially one of advice, assistance and the provision of expert and specialized services. At higher levels, the element of advice is more important than the element of service and at lower levels element of service is important. This is shown in the Fig. 2.4 below.

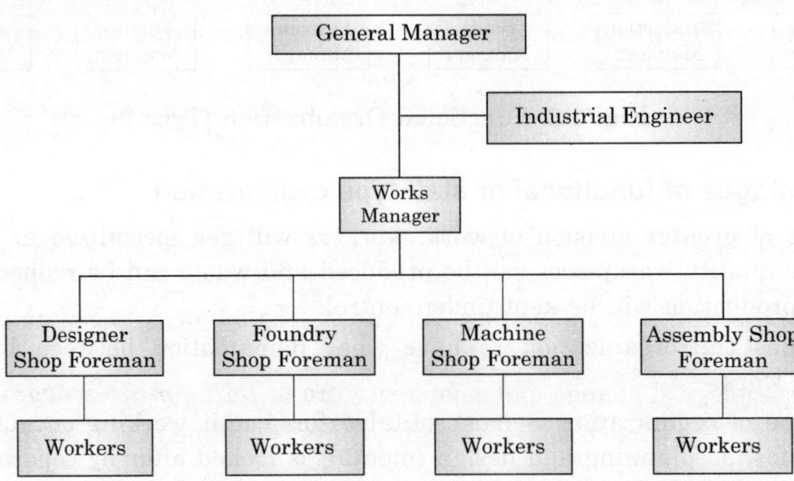

Fig. 2.4. Line and Staff Organization.

2.9.3.1. Types of staff

Depending on the advisory function done by the staff officials, they have been classified as below:

(i) **Personal Staff:** Here the staff is attached to the Line officials, to give advice to them when asked for. Personal assistant or a Secretary to an officer, advises the officer in important matters so as to enable the line manager to take effective decisions. For example, consider the district collectors. These people are transferred from one place to other place. When they go to new places, they need somebody to provide them data or information regarding the place for which they are transferred and assumed the charges. The personal assistant does this advisory function.

(ii) Specialized Staff: This type of staff officials will have professional knowledge in a particular field of knowledge and they help the line manager to take decisions. Consider for example, materials manager, who have specialized knowledge in inventory management may assist the general manager to control the material cost. Similarly, an environmental officer can advise the district collector to take decisions at the time of floods or any other environmental problems.

(iii) General Staff: This type of staff consists of a set of experts in different areas who are located at the central office and are meant to advise and assist the top management on matters calling for expertise.

Advantages: This organization has planned specialization. It accommodates required staff personals with specialized knowledge, which will help line managers in taking optimal decisions. In that way it provides the benefit of expert advice to the line management.

Disadvantages: Because of demarcation of line function and staff function confusion may arise between line and staff executives regarding their role in the organization. The staff personal may feel that they are ineffective because they do not get the authority to implement their recommendations. At the same time the line manager who takes advise from the staff person may feel that the staff personal may undermines their authority. This may lead to friction between the both at some times.

This type of structure is more suitable for any type of organization both private and government owed engaged in any type of activity.

2.9.4. Matrix Organization

Organization is an instrument, a powerful tool designed to fill certain specific organizational needs. As the organization grow the needs of the organization also changes. Then we seek new ways to organize the things to suit to new conditions. The following social and technological changes press the need for new organizational design.

(a) Rapid technological change and complexity are fostering ***matrix organizations.***

(b) The magnitude of some corporate commitments is leading to ***external, independent staff.***

(c) Increasing involvement in social issues the need for existence of a ***president's office.***

(d) Current success of organized pressure groups raises the question of how to deal with the ***interest representation.***

(e) Fascination with electronic computers calls for examination of the ***impact of computers on organization.***

In addition to the above many more social and environmental changes impinges on organization and show how a basic social institution such as managerial organization is adapted rather than scrapped.

Matrix organization was used while dealing with a problem of launching a rocket in space. Along with space program it had its own applications in variety of enterprises. ***Matrix organization based on the need for coordinated, focused action.*** A drawback of the typical organization with functional departments is that unusual, complex projects often get shunted about, progress slowly and are the cause of endless meetings of key executives representing the various departments. The more unique and complicated the project, the more likely is fumbling to occur. Matrix organization strives to:

(a) Ensures the coordinated, focused attention that such projects require, and

(b) At the same time retain the benefits of specialized expertise and capabilities that only functional departments can provide.

For example, when a project needs special materials, special and highly specialized knowledge and guidance to complete the project within the stipulated time and at a reasonable cost, the matrix organization will provide a solution. For organizations involved in manufacturing nuclear reactors, special aircrafts and defense needs, heavy-equipment manufacturing, matrix organization chart is very useful. The matrix organization proposes to make a manager responsible for a project or a clear-cut mission and then to assign from each of the functional departments the talent needed to complete the mission. When a functional specialist is working on the project he looks to the project manager for direction i.e. *he is out on loan.* When the project is finished, or when he is no longer needed, each man returns to his functional departments for assignment to other duties. The project manager must rely heavily on these assigned men for counsel and decision in their respective areas. If the team is small, its members will have frequent contact with one another and will be fully informed of the current status of the project. In these circumstances most of the coordination will be voluntary. From time to time, though, trade-off decisions may be necessary, and the project manager will make these decisions. The personal relations within a project team are delicate. Although the project manager is the nominal boss, each member of his team is on temporary assignment and will return to his functional department where his long-run career is primarily determined. To draw the best from his group, the project manager must therefore rely on both the challenge of the job and his personal leadership. Because of this heavy reliance on voluntary cooperation, project teamwork best on projects for which the quality of the finished product or service, its deadline, and its cost are clearly specified. Usually a functional department does more than supply the project team with its members. It also provides backup service. The matrix organization utilizes the blend of specialized knowledge of project manager and the experience of functional departments to complete complicated products/projects/services in an optimal way. The Fig. 2.5 below shows the arrangement of the matrix chart.

2.9.5. Committee Organization

The committee organization is not a distinctive type of organization. It is only an organizational mechanism used as a supplementary to any type of organization an undertaking has adopted.

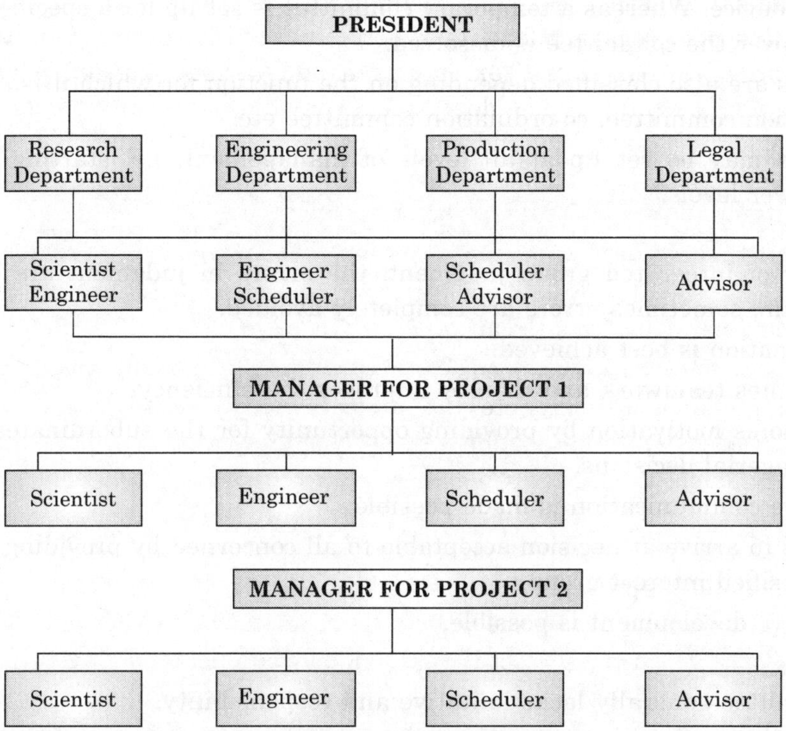

Fig. 2.5. Matrix Organization Chart.

The committee is a device widely used practically in all kinds of organization. The purposes for which committees are generally used are:

Information Gathering, Education and Training, Expert Advice, Promoting Co-ordination, facilitating communication and co-operation and sometimes the committees are formed for decision-making purpose.

Urwick defines a committee as a **group of persons to whom certain functions have been assigned on condition that they discharge those functions conjointly and in a corporate capacity.** This clarifies that a committee is organized, consisting of two or more people and some functions are assigned to it that are expected to be carried out by its members through **group action.** Whenever, for solving an issue, the need is felt for discussion and discourse among the concerned members of organization and/or the members from outside, a committee is formed and it is entrusted with a defined task. That way it is basically a **discussion group.**

Committees may be of different nature. They are classified as formal type, which is formally constituted as a part of the organization, which has to do definite duties and follow certain procedures laid by the organization. Another one is an informal committee, which is formed by an executive as the need arises to have discussion before a decision is made. Formalities are not strictly observed.

A committee may be permanent or temporary. Permanent committee is also known as standing committee generally performs on a continuing basis vital managerial functions. There is a possibility to dissolve the standing committee and replace it by a different organizational device. Whereas a temporary committee is set up for a specific purpose. Once the mission is over the committee is dissolved.

Committees are also classified depending on the function for which it is constituted. For example, selection committee, co-ordination committee etc.

Committees may be set up at all levels of management, i.e. starting form Board of Directors to lower levels.

Advantages

1. By way of integrated group judgment, the errors in judgment are brought to the minimum; sometimes errors are completely avoided.
2. Co-ordination is best achieved.
3. It promotes teamwork and thereby improves the efficiency.
4. It promotes motivation by providing opportunity for the subordinates to participate in managerial decisions.
5. Effective communication is made possible.
6. It helps to arrive at decision acceptable to all concerned by providing representation to diversified interest group.
7. Executive development is possible.

Disadvantages

1. A committee generally lacks imitative and responsibility.
2. Group discussion may turn out to be mere compromises rather than best decisions.
3. Committees will be quite frequently intensive.
4. It is an expensive means of managerial action.
5. The domination of leader is possible if other members are only *yes men.*

2.9.6. Vertical / Tall Organizations

Vertical and Tall organization refer to increase in the length of the organization's hierarchy chain of command. The hierarchical chain of command represents the company's authority – accountability relationship between superiors and subordinates. Authority and responsibility flows from the top to the bottom through all the levels of hierarchy. Accountability flow from the lowest level to the highest level as in figure 2.6, which shows the vertical/tall organization employees at each level should report to their superior, who in turn should report his boss. Thus the activities are reported to the top. Authority is more centralized in tall organization.

2.9.7. Flat / Horizontal Organizations

Horizontal/flat organization refers to an increase in breadth of an organization's structure as shown in Fig. 2.7.

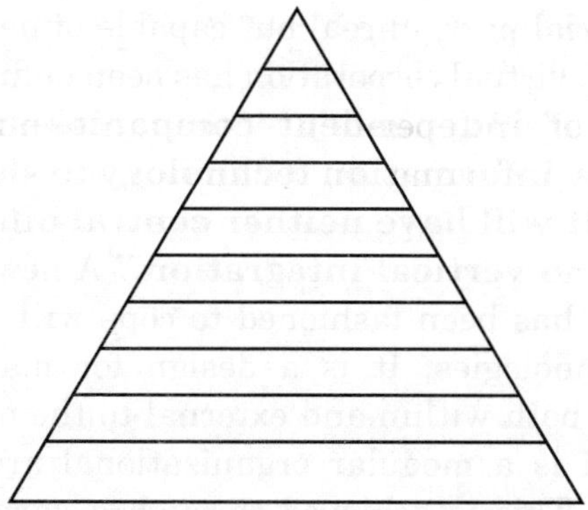

Fig. 2.6. Tall / Vertical Organizational Structure.

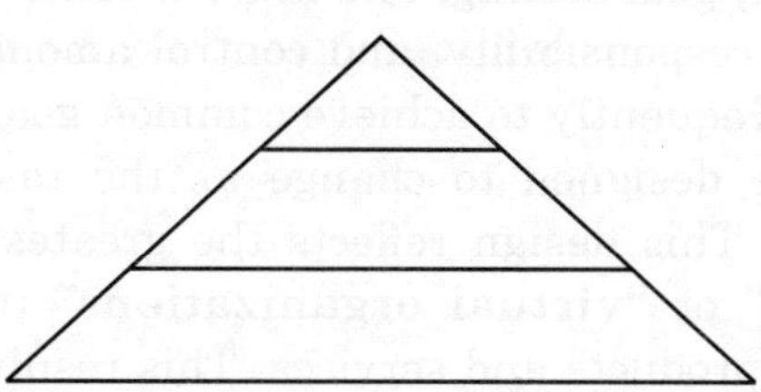

Fig. 2.7. Horizontal/Flat Organizational Structure.

The number of levels in organizational hierarchy is few. The span of control is relatively large. The increasing bio-professionalization and wide acceptance for empowerment allowed even the large bossiness firms to reduce the number of hierarchical levels of their organizations. Consequently, large sized firms also started adopting horizontal/flat organization by de-layering. In fact, this structure is well suited for small size business firms.

Authority is more decentralized in relatively flat structures. Manager with broad span of control must grant more authority to his subordinates. Decisions are more likely to be made by the employees who are at the helm of affairs and more familiar with the situations and ground realities. Organizational activities are mostly performed informally. Professional managers are treated as real professionals.

The major advantage of flat structure is quick decision-making. Thus, it enables the management to take decisions in right time. Other advantages of this organization structure include: low administrative cost, freedom and autonomy to the managers to operate, decision making by the manager who are at helm of affairs and empowerment themselves towards organizational objectives. Further, these characteristics enable the organization to be duly sensitive to the environmental demands. The employees also become innovative and creative.

Horizontal/Flat organizational structures are appropriate for the organizations with horizontal and vertical growth strategies. Thus, these structures are useful for competitive and dynamic business firms.

2.9.8. Virtual Organization

The concept of **Virtual Organization or Virtual Corporation** along with virtual team or office has entered management field very recently. The literal meaning of virtual is having the efficacy without the material part; unreal but capable of being considered as real for the purpose. Based on the concept, virtual corporation has been defined as: **"virtual corporation is a temporary network of independent companies–suppliers, customers, even erstwhile rivals — linked by information technology to share skills, costs and access to one another's markets. It will have neither central office nor organization chart. It will have no hierarchy, no vertical integration."** A new organizational design in the form of network organization has been fashioned to cope with the demand of the turbulent global environment and technologies. It is a design for managing complex relationship between group and divisions, both within and external to the organization. This design goes beyond matrix structure and is a modular organizational architecture in which business teams operate as a network. This is achieved through a variety of lateral communication channels and decision-making, goal setting, and mutual control processes. It focuses on how to mutually share authority, responsibility, and control among people and units that must cooperate and communicate frequently to achieve common goals. In a network organization, many different networks are designed to change as the tasks to be performed and the goals to be achieved change. This design reflects the greatest change in corporate future, that **"virtual corporations"** or **"virtual organizations"** (in fact, meaning of virtual is novelistic) will produce more products and services. This results in network contacts, but by sharing costs, skills and access to markets. This way every function and process would be of international standard – something no single company could think off. Figure 2.8 shows the network organization.

S. No.	Advantages	Disadvantages
1.	Has greater flexibility.	Has less control over production.
2.	Needs less capital.	Faces threat of competition from suppliers.
3.	Carries lower overhead expenses.	Increase dependence on others.
4.	Display more entrepreneurship.	Loses specialist's knowledge of problems.
5.	Facilitate use of outside technology.	Causes fluctuations in earnings.

Features of a virtual organization, which is as follows:

- *Technology*: Informal network will provide far-flunged companies and entrepreneurs to link up work together from start to finish. The partnership will be based on the electronic contracts to keep the lawyers away and speed the linkups.
- *Opportunism*: Partnership is less permanent, less formal, and more opportunistic. Companies will bond together to meet a specific market opportunity and, more often than not, fall apart once the need evaporates.
- *Excellence*: Because each partner brings its core competence to the effort, it may be possible to create a best-of-everything organization. Every function and process could be world class–something that no single company could achieve.

- *Trust*: These relationships make companies far more reliant on each other and require far more trust than even before. They will share a sense of co-destiny, meaning that the fate of each partner's dependent on other.
- *No borders*: The new corporate model redefines the traditional boundaries of the company. More cooperation among competitors, suppliers, and customers make it hard to determine where on company ends and other begins.

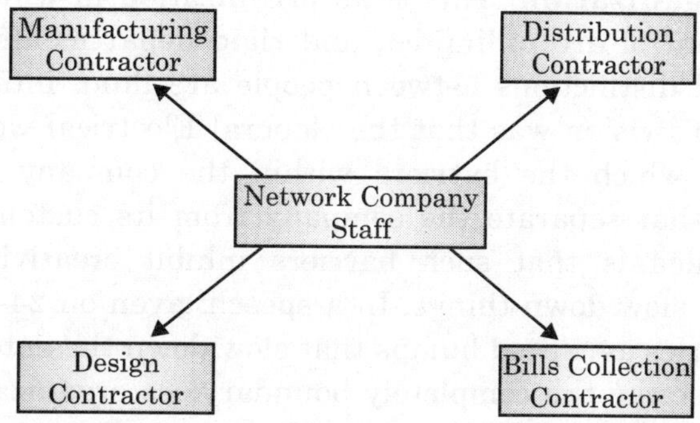

Fig. 2.8. Network (virtual) Organization.

The basic reason behind creating a virtual organization is to generate synergy through temporary alliance. Creating synergy is the process of putting two or more elements together to achieve a sum total greater than the sum total of individual elements separately. This effect is described as 2 + 2 = 5 effect.

2.9.9. The Team Structure

In the present management scenario, **teams** have become an extremely popular means around which to organize work activities. When management uses teams as its central coordination device, you have a **team structure.** The primary characteristics of the team structure are that it breaks down departmental barriers and decentralizes decision making to the level of the work team. Team structure also requires employees to be generalists as well as specialists.

In smaller companies, the team structure can define the entire organization. We have seen in some small scale industries all the people, starting from the owner cum manager and workers will work like a team while working and at the time of decision making and all of them feel oneness as far as the affair of the unit is concerned.

In larger companies the team structure complements what is typically a bureaucracy. This allows the organization to achieve the efficiency of bureaucracy's standardization, while gaining the flexibility that teams provide. To improve productivity at the operating level, some companies make use of self-managed teams.

2.9.10. The Boundaryless Organization (A New Corporate Architecture)

We may come across a situation, where someone is asked to do something but responds defiantly, saying, "It is not my job". This seems to be highly uncooperative, but such a comment may make a great deal of sense when it comes to the traditional kind of organizational structure we have seen earlier where various layers demarking authority and responsibility. These organizational charts, clearly define roles of managers and employees. Everyone knows precisely what he or she is supposed to do. The problem with such arrangements, however, is that they are inflexible. As a result, they do not lend themselves to the rapidly changing condition in which today's organizations operate.

Sensitive to this limitation, Jack Welch, C.E.O of General Electric Company proposed the **boundaryless organization.** This is an organization in which chain of command are eliminated, span of control are unlimited, and rigid departments give way to empowered teams. Replacing rigid distinctions between people are fluid, intentionally ambiguous and ill-defined roles. Welch's vision was that the General Electrical would operate like a family grocery store, one in which the barriers within the company that separate employees from each other and that separate the company from its customers and suppliers would be eliminated. The idea is that such barriers inhibit creativity, waste time, smother dreams, and generally slow down things. In a speech given on 24-4-1990, Welch referred to organizational boundaries as "speed bumps that slow down the enterprise. Although General Electric has not yet become the completely boundaryless organization Welch envisioned, it has made significant strides towards breaking down boundaries.

2.9.11. Modular Organizations

Many of today's organizations outsource non-core functions to other companies while retaining full strategic control over their core business. Such companies may be thought of as having a central hub surrounded by networks of outside specialists that can be added or subtracted as needed. As such, they are referred as **modular organizations.** For example, Toyota, one of the world's largest and most successful automakers, has taken the modular form to the extreme. Its network of 230 suppliers (two of which are owned by Toyota itself) does just about everything the company needs, from making molds for machine parts, to general contracting. The key to the success of this arrangement is Toyota's very close tie to its suppliers–providing assurance that they will meet its stringent qualities standards. Of course, companies that outsource any proprietary work (High tech breakthroughs) must be assured that their trade secrets will not be compromised.

2.9.12. Cellular Organization

Cellular Organization or Group Technology is a new concept in organization structure. In this organization, various cells re created to look after different organizational work. Each cell looks after a particular activity related to certain function. For example, Accounts cell looks after all activities of financial matters such as maintenance of accounts, payment of bills, payment of salaries, preparation of balance sheet and P & L account. Similarly, marketing cell looks after all activities related to marketing of company's products, such as advertising, sales promotion, after sales service and so on. (For all companies owned by individual owners, located at different places).

This sort of organization facilitates a person who approach appropriate cell to get his work done, also avoids overlapping or duplication of activities, this organization helps to utilize the better skills in a person to do the allocated work. The Fig. 2.9. Shows the chart.

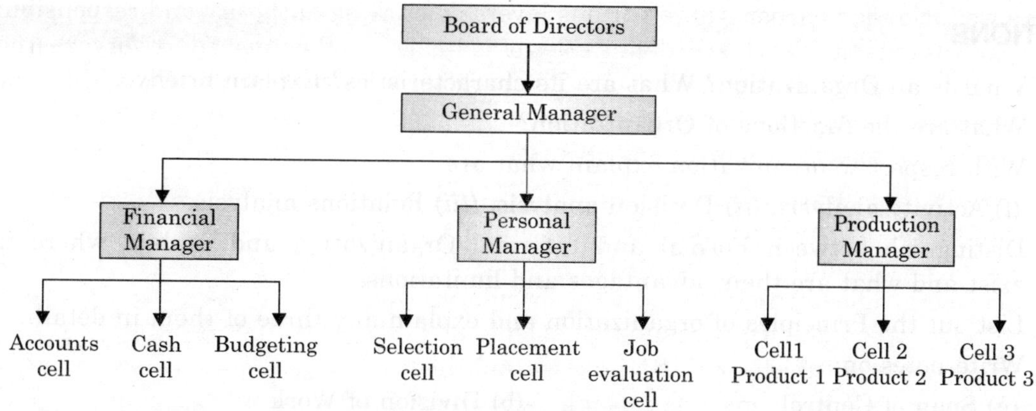

Fig. 2.9. Cellular Cell.

2.9.13. Inverted Triangle Organization

In a conventional upright triangular organization, we will have few people at the apex of the triangle, known as top management. In the middle of the triangle, we have more number of managers known as middle level management and at the operational level; we have larger number of people to do the necessary operation to satisfy the goal of the organization. This was accepted because, in olden days top management concerned with decision making from the data/information supplied by middle level managers. Because of the constraints of organization always a decision maker has to relay on the lower level managers for information needed.

But, in today's scenario advent of high-speed computers with MIS network made required data is available to all levels through networking. Where top-level managers are not depend on lower level managers for the required information. Availability of computers, necessary software today's organization needs more top level managers to make in-time and qualitative decision than operational level people. Availability of Internet and Extranet facilities will help a decision maker to get whatever information needed at the finger tips with in fraction of seconds. This sort of organization, we can see in some banks and Software Industries. Figure 2.10 shows the arrangement of the chart.

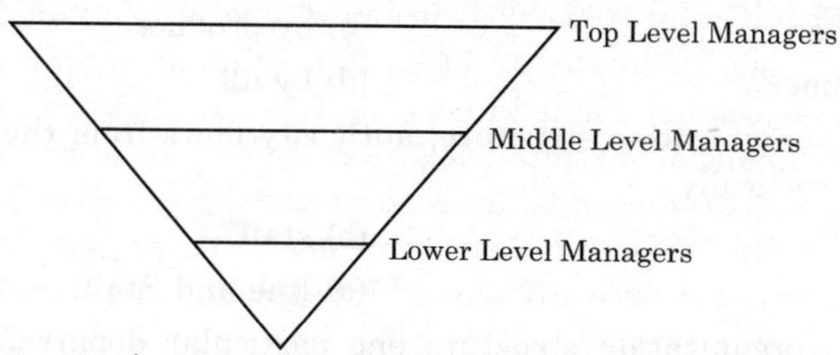

Fig. 2.10. Inverted Triangle Organization.

QUESTIONS

1. What is an Organization? What are its characteristics? Explain briefly.
2. What are the functions of Organization?
3. With respect to organization explain what are:
   (*i*) Activity analysis, (*ii*) Decision analysis, (*iii*) Relations analysis.
4. Distinguish between Formal and Informal Organization and explain where they exist and what are their advantages and limitations.
5. List out the Principles of organization and explain any three of them in detail.
6. Write notes on:
   (a) Span of Control (b) Division of Work
   (c) Unity of Command (d) Authority and Responsibility.
7. Explain what is a department and explain its importance in an organization.
8. Draw a neat sketch of Line type organization and explain its advantages and limitations and suitability.
9. Explains the Staff type organization by a neat sketch and explain its advantages and limitations and suitability.
10. By means of neat sketch explain Line and Staff type of organization and give its advantages and disadvantages and its suitability.
11. What is a committee and give the sketch of committee type organization chart and explain its advantages and limitations?
12. Explain what are Vertical and Horizontal organization explain with examples.
13. What is Virtual organization explain by means of neat sketch?
14. Explain by means of a neat sketch what is a Cellular Organization and give its applicability.
15. Write a note on Inverted triangle organization.

MULTIPLE CHOICE QUESTIONS

1. The departmentation can be described by................
   (a) by function (b) by product
   (c) by consumer (d) by all.
2. In .... organization structure, authority flows from the man at the top to the lowest man vertically.
   (a) line (b) staff
   (c) matrix (d) line and Staff.
3. In .... organization structure one particular department will look after the affair of a particular function to facilitate expertise, which is needed by entire organization.
   (a) line (b) staff
   (c) matrix (d) cellular.

4. .... organization structure most preferred while dealing with a problem launching a rocket.

(a) Line (b) Staff

(c) Matrix (d) Line and Staff.

5. .... organization refers to the structure of jobs and position with clearly defined functions and relationships as prescribed by top management.

(a) Formal (b) Informal

(c) Both a and b (d) None.

6. H.R. Manager comes under .... type of organization.

(a) line (b) staff

(c) line and staff (d) matrix.

7. Matrix organization is also called as ------------------organization.

(a) line (b) staff

(c) committee organization (d) product.

8. Dividing the organization on the basis of department is called

(a) division (b) section

(c) departmentation (d) sector.

9. Organizing the managerial functions is known as;

(a) Enumeration of activities (b) Process of organization

(c) Planning the activities (d) Stream lining.

10. In analysis of organization Peter Drucker's one of the recommendation is:

(a) Activity analysis

(b) Analysis of managerial qualities

(c) Analysis of worker behavior

(d) Analysis of financial status of organization.

11. The foundation of the management on which the success of managerial functions depends is

(a) managerial authority (b) good qualities in a manager

(c) organization (d) responsibility of all workers.

12. The factor which makes growth and diversification possible is:

(a) Good Leadership (b) Attitude of Manager

(c) Honesty of workers (d) Organization.

13. The proverb *"two bullocks of a cart must lead the cart in the same direction to reach the destination" analogs to:*

(a) Unity of objective (b) Unity of command

(c) Unity of order (d) Unity of plans.

14. As found by Lyndall Urwick ideal number of subordinates a manager can control is:

(a) 2 (b) 4

(c) 6 (d) 10.

15. Every organization must be designed in such a way that exceptionally complex problems are referred to higher level managers and routine matters are dealt by lower level managers. This is known as:

(a) Dividing Managers (b) Level of Decisions

(c) Exception Principle (d) Solution to problems.

16. In this Military type of organization we find:

(a) Unification of Authority and Responsibility

(b) Good Managers

(c) Good workers

(d) Co-ordination.

17. The person who decides the actual path to be traveled by material during production is known as:

(a) Direction Manager (b) Route Clerk

(c) Road Clerk (d) Speed boss.

18. The organization which refer to increase in the length of the organization's hierarchy chain of command is:

(a) Line Organization (b) Staff Organization

(c) Matrix Organization (d) Vertical Organization.

19. An organization structure using the group technology is referred as:

(a) Modular Organization (b) Virtual Organization

(c) Cellular Organization (d) Horizontal Organization.

20. In an organization, where chain of command is eliminated is known as:

(a) Commandless Organization (b) Informal Organization

(c) Boundaryless Organization (d) Virtual Organization.

ANSWERS

1. (d)	**2.** (a)	**3.** (b)	**4.** (a)	**5.** (a)	**6.** (b)	**7.** (c)	**8.** (c)
9. (b)	**10.** (a)	**11.** (c)	**12.** (d)	**13.** (a)	**14.** (b)	**15.** (c)	**16.** (a)
17. (b)	**18.** (d)	**19.** (c)	**20.** (c).				

❍❍❍

Unit 3 Production Systems

3.1. INTRODUCTION

Before we try to understand, what is batch production or what is Job Production, it is better for us to understand what a Product is or what is a Service or what is a Project? It is because the principles we use in production management are equally applicable for service management and project management. At the same time let us try to understand the meaning of management, so that we can clearly understand Production Management.

3.2. PRODUCT

Though many authors define the product with consumer orientation, it is better for us to deal with different angles, because it will be helpful for us to understand the subject Production Management.

(i) **For a Consumer:** The product is a combination of or optimal mix of *potential utilities.* This is because every consumer expects some use or uses from the product. Hence, he/she always identifies the product in terms of the uses. Say for example, soap can be identified by complexion, cleanliness of body, freshness, fragrance or health, etc. Because of this producers advertise that they are selling health or they are selling a cine star complexion or they are selling freshness and so on.

(ii) **For a Production Manager:** Product is the combination of various surfaces and processes (or operations). Because the production manager is solely responsible for producing product, he has to think of the various surfaces by which the product is made of, so that he can plan for processes by which a particular surface can be made and plan for required capacity of the facility by which the surface is produced. It is his duty to see that the required surface is made by cheapest method to keep the cost at low.

(iii) **For a Financial Manager:** For the Financial Manager, the product is a mix of various cost elements as he is responsible for the profitability of the product and arrangement of required finance for production.

(iv) For a Personnel Manager: As personnel manager is concerned with providing the required labour for production, he looks to the product as a combination of different skills required to produce the product.

Now we have seen what a product is. Let us try to understand what is Production?

3.2.1. Production

Production means application of processes (technology) to the raw material to add the ***use and economic values*** to arrive at desired product by the best method, without sacrificing the desired quality. We have three ways production, they are:

(a) **Production by Disintegration:** By separating the contents of crude oil or mixture, the desired products are produced. For example crude oil is disintegrated into various fuel oils. Similarly salt production is also an example for product produced by disintegration. We can use mechanical means or chemical means for disintegration.

(b) **Production by Integration:** Here the components are assembled to manufacture a product. Take for example an automobile; it is the assembly of various components. In this process, physical and chemical properties of the materials used may change. Mainly mechanical methods are used for assembly.

(c) **Production by Service:** Here the chemical and mechanical properties of material are improved without any physical change. For example Heat treatment of metals.

In actual production all the above may be used or any combination of the above three may be used to produce the desired product.

3.3. MANAGEMENT

Management can be explained as an art or science, (in fact it is a combination of art and science) of getting things done by the people, by planning, coordinating, organizing, directing and controlling the activities to meet the specified goals, within the framework of agreed policies. The above explanation put emphasis on ***getting things done*** by Planning, Organizing, Coordinating and Controlling the specific objectives and agreed policies. Today's manager needs scientific base as well as personal tactics to manager the people under him to achieve the desired goals.

The above discussion on Product, Production and Management will help us to understand what ***Production management*** is.

3.3.1. Definition of Production Management

Production Management is defined as management function which plans, organizes, co-ordinates, directs and controls the material supply and processing activities of an enterprise, so that specified products are produced by specified methods to meet an approved sales programme. These activities are being carried out in such a manner that labour, plant and capital available are used to the best advantage of the organization.

3.3.2. Objective of Production Management

The objective of production management is to produce the desired product or specified product by specified method so that the optimal utilization of available resources is met with.

Hence, the production management is responsible to produce the desired product, which has marketability at the cheapest price by proper planning the manpower, material and processes. Production management must see that it will deliver right goods of right quantity at right place and at right price. When the above objective is achieved, we can say that we have effective production management system.

3.3.3. Scope of Production Management

In fact, we apply principles of management and function of management in our day-to-day life. We all know, from morning till night, we plan our activities; we co-ordinate the available resources and control our activities to achieve certain goals. So also any organization must follow the principles of management for its survival and growth. The same is applicable to production management also. Reading and learning production management will enable one to be capable of solving the problems of the organization, may be an educational institution, or a hospital, or a grocery shop or a production shop. The problem, a manager face in various organizations is more or less similar to that of a production department but smaller in magnitude. Hence, the knowledge of production management will help any professional manager to tackle the problems of his business easily. Hence, the as far scope of Production Management is concerned; we can say that the principles and functions are applicable to any sort of human activities (personal activities to international activities) to achieve the desired results.

Before going to discuss the functions of Production Management, let distinguish between Product, Service and the Project. Because, all the functions of production management are more or less applicable to the above three.

(i) **Product:** Manufacturing system often produces standardized products in large volumes. The plant and machinery have a finite capacity. The facilities constitute fixed costs, which are allocated to the products produced. Variable costs, such as labour cost and material costs are accounted for cost calculation. While manufacturing the product use value and economic value are added to the product. Hence, the product is a store of values added during manufacture. Because input and output costs are measurable, the productivity can be measured with certain degree of accuracy. Product can be transported to the markets and stored physically until it is sold.

(ii) **Service:** Service system present more uncertainty with respect to capacity and costs. Service are produced and consumed in the presence of consumer. We cannot physically store the service. Because of this the service organizations, such as hospitals, transport organizations and many other service organizations capacity must be sufficiently or consciously managed to accommodate highly variable demand. Sometimes services like legal practice and medical practice involve professional or intellectual judgments, which cannot be easily standardized. Because of this the calculation of cost and productivity is difficult.

(iii) **Project:** Project system does not produce standardized products. The plant, machinery, men and materials are often brought to project site and the project is completed. The project is of big size and remains in the site itself after completion. As the costs can be calculated and allocated to the project with considerable accuracy, productivity can be measured. Once the project is completed, all the resources are removed from the project site. Examples are construction of a house, laying of roads etc.

3.4. BENEFITS OF GOOD PRODUCTION MANAGEMENT

Efficient production management will give benefits to the various sections of the society. They are:

(i) **Consumer:** Consumer benefits from improved industrial productivity, increased use value in the product. Products are available to him at right place, at right price, at right time, in desired quantity and of desired quality.

(ii) **Investors:** They get increased security for their investments, adequate market returns and creditability and good image in the society.

(iii) **Employee:** He gets adequate wages, job security, improved working conditions and increased personal and job satisfaction.

(iv) **Suppliers:** They will get confidence in management and their bills can be realized without any delay.

(v) **Community:** Community enjoys benefits from economic and social stability.

(vi) **The Nation:** Nation will achieve prospects and security because of increased productivity and healthy industrial atmosphere.

3.5. FUNCTIONS OF PRODUCTION MANAGEMENT

The functions of production management depend upon the size of the firm. In small firms the production manager may have to look after production planning and control along with personnel, marketing, finance and purchase functions. In medium sized firms, there may be separate managers for personnel; marketing and finance functions. But the production planning and control and purchases and stores may be under the control of production management department. In large size firms the activities of production management is confined to the management of production activities only. As such, there is no hard and fast rule or guidelines to specify the functions of production management, but in the academic interest we can mention some of the functions, which are looked after by the production management department. They are:

1. **Materials:** The selection of materials for the product: Production manager must have sound knowledge of materials and their properties, so that he can select appropriate materials for his product. Research on materials is necessary to find alternatives to satisfy the changing needs of the design are his duties.
2. **Methods:** Finding the best method for the process, to search for the methods to suit the available resources, identifying the sequence of process are some of the activities of production management.
3. **Machines and Equipment:** Selection of suitable machinery for the process desired, designing the maintenance policy and design of layout of machines are taken care of by the production management department.

4. **Estimating:** To fix up the production targets and delivery dates and to keep the production costs at minimum, production management department does a thorough estimation of production time cost. In competitive situations this will help the management to decide what should be done in arresting the costs at desired level.
5. **Loading and Scheduling:** The production management department has to draw the timetable for various production activities, specifying when to start and when to finish the process required. It also has to draw the timings of materials movement and plan the activities of manpower. The scheduling is to be done keeping in mind the loads on hand and capacities of facilities available.
6. **Routing:** This is the most important function of production management department. The routing consists of fixing the flow lines for the various raw materials, components, etc., from the stores to the packing of finished product, so that all concerned knows what exactly is happening on the shop floor.
7. **Dispatching:** The production management department has to prepare various documents such as job cards, move cards, inspection cards, and route card etc. for each and every component of the product. These are prepared in a set of five copies. These documents are to be released from production management department to give green signal for starting the production. The activities of shop floor will follow the instructions given in these documents. Activity of releasing the documents to production shops is known as dispatching.
8. **Expediting or Follow up:** Once the documents are dispatched the management wants to know whether the activities are being carried out as per the plans or not. Expediting engineers go round the production floor along with the plans, compare the actual with the plan and send feedback information regarding the progress of the work to the management. This will help the management to evaluate and or update the plans.
9. **Inspection:** Here inspection is generally concerned with the inspection or activities during production, but a separate quality control department does the quality inspection, which is not under the control of production department. This is true because, if the quality inspection is given to production management, then there is a chance to qualifying the defective products also.
10. **Evaluation:** The production department must evaluate itself and its contribution in fulfilling the corporate objectives and the department's objectives. This is necessary for setting up the standards for future.

3.6. TYPES OF PRODUCTION SYSTEMS

The organization of manufacturing system, also planning and control of production greatly depends on the type of product, type of the product line. Basic principles that guide the formation of planning policy and its execution may be the same for all the manufacturing concerns. But emphasis on a particular aspect of production management in fulfilling of specific requirement of the plant and the management approach to the problems of inventory, machine selection, machine setting, tooling, routing and scheduling, trading follow up and evaluating will differ from system, to system.

3.6.1. Selection of the System

Selection of a particular system depends on:

(a) **Type of Production** i.e. quantities of finished products and regularity of manufacture.

(b) **Size of Plant:** Small Industry, Medium Sized Industry or Large Industry.

In general there are three classifications in types of production system. They are discussed below:

3.6.1.1. Job production

In this system jobs are manufactured to meet the requirements of a specific order. The quantity involved is small and the manufacturing of the product will take place as per the specifications given by the customer. The system uses general-purpose machines with some specific attachments, if required. The system requires the services of skilled labour. The system may further classify as:

(a) ***Job produced only once***: Here the customer visit the firm and book his order. After the completion of the product, he takes delivery of the product and leaves the firm. He may not visit the firm to book the order for the same product. The firm has to plan for materials, process and manpower only after receiving the order from the customer. The firm has no scope for pre-planning the production of the product.

(b) ***Job produced at irregular intervals***: Here the customer visits the firm to place orders for the same type of the product at irregular intervals. The firm will not have any idea of customer's visit. Here also planning for materials, process and manpower will start only after taking the order from the customer. In case the firm maintains a record of the jobs produced by it, it can refer to the previous documents and use the same data when customer visits the firm successively.

(c) ***The jobs produced periodically at regular intervals***: In this system, the customer arrives at the firm to place orders for the same type of product at regular intervals. Here the firm knows very well that the customer visits at regular intervals, it can plan for the resources required by referring the documents maintained previously. Soon after the booking of order the firm can start production. It need not prepare fresh plans once again. As the frequency of visit of the customer increases, the job production slowly becomes *batch production*.

Examples of Job Production are: Tailor shops, Cycle and Vehicle repair shops, Job typing shops and Small workshops.

3.6.2. Batch Production

It is the system of manufacture where number of identical products either to meet the customer's order or to satisfy the market requirements. When the production of the batch is terminated, the plant and equipment may be used for producing similar product or different products, demanding the same process. This system can also be classified under three categories:

(a) ***A Batch produced only once***: Here customer places order with the firm, for the product of his specification. The size of the order is greater than that of job production order. The firm has to plan for the resources required only after getting the order.

(b) ***A Batch produced at irregular intervals as per customer's order or when the need arises***: As the frequency is irregular, the firm can maintain a file of its detailed plans for the product and can refer to the same as and when customer visits or the need arises.

(c) ***A Batch produced periodically at known intervals***: Here the firm either receives order from the customer at regular intervals or it may produce the product to satisfy the demand of the market. It can maintain records of production and refer to the required details and start production without any delay. It can also purchase materials well in advance and give instructions to the workers. As the frequency increases, the batch production slowly transfers to *continuous production.*

Examples of Batch Production are: Tire manufacturing units, Readymade dress units, Cosmetic manufacturing units etc.

3.6.3. Continuous Production

Continuous production system is the specialized manufacturing of identical products in large volume on which the machinery and equipment are fully engaged. The continuous production is normally associated with large quantities and with high rate of demand. Hence, the advantage of automatic production is utilized. We use automatic machines, semi-skilled and unskilled labour. For setting up of machine, skilled worker is needed. The system may be classified as:

(a) ***Mass production***: Here same type of product is produced to meet the demand of an assembly line or the market. The system needs good planning for material, process, maintenance of machines and instructions to operations. Purchase of material in bulk quantities is advisable.

(b) ***Flow production***: The difference between mass and flow production is the type of product and its relation to the plant. In mass production identical products are produced in large numbers. If the demand falls or ceases, the machinery and equipment, after slight modifications may be used for manufacturing products of similar nature. In flow production, the plant and equipment are designed for a specified product. Hence, if the demand falls for the product or ceases, the plant cannot be used for manufacturing other products. It has to be scraped.

The examples of mass production are components of industrial products, bolts and nuts etc.

Examples of Flow production are Sugar production, Cement production etc.

The Fig. 3.1 shows the relationship between the types of production. The table given below gives distinction between the types of production. Here Job and Batch production systems are considered as intermittent production systems.

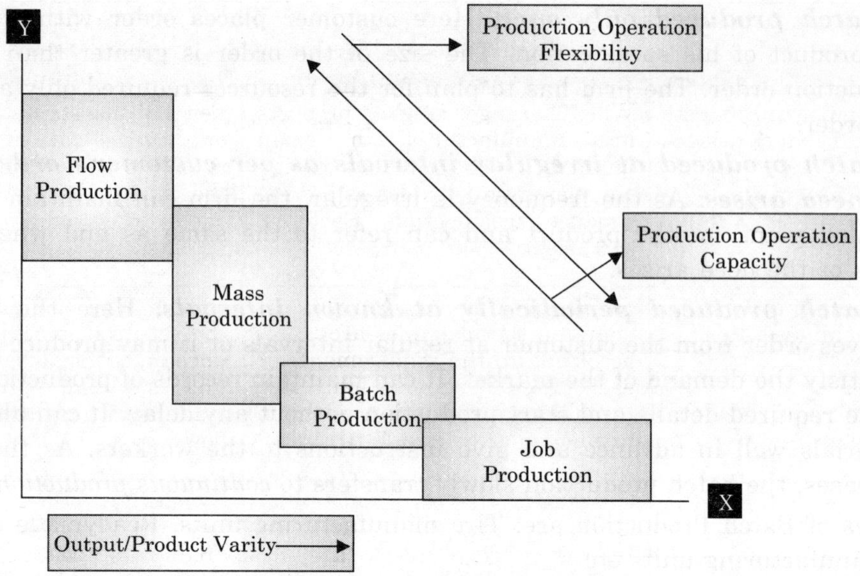

Fig. 3.1. Production Systems

Table 3.1. Characteristics of Intermittent and Continuous Production Systems

S. No.	Particulars	Intermittent Production Systems (Job and Batch Production)	Continuous Production System (Mass and Flow Production)
1.	Type of Plant Layout	Process layout is more suitable.	Product layout designed according to a separate line for each product is considered.
2.	Type of Machines	As it necessitates frequent changes in the machine set-ups, required by the specification of each order, general-purpose machines are more suitable. Also they have good flexibility. In batch production, special purpose machines automatic and semi-automatic machines are used.	As production flow is permanently in the form of product line, special or automatic machines are used. In flow production specialized machines are used.
3.	Type of Labour	The type of production pre-supposes frequent changes in product design and machine setups; which requires highly skilled labour. Repair and maintenance of machines have done by these labourers.	The manufacturing activity becomes a routine function and as the machines are designed to suit the processes required for product and automatic in nature unskilled or semi-skilled labour is required. A specialized team of maintenance staff is looking after the repair and maintenance of machines.

(contd.....)

S. No.	Particulars	Intermittent Production Systems (Job and Batch Production)	Continuous Production System (Mass and Flow Production)
4.	Number of Products and Product design.	Wide range of products are manufactured in small quantities. The product design changes from lot to lot as per the product specification. Each lot produced is similar in size.	Few or one standard products or product is manufactured in large quantities. Usually the product line is designed to one or two product of standard specification.
5.	Changes in Machine set-ups.	As specification of each product changes, the machines are to set according to the requirements or each order. Frequent changes in machine set-ups are a common phenomenon.	In this type of manufacturing, the set-up of machine remains unchanged for a longer period. The standard products are manufacturing a continuous flow.
6.	Nature and size of orders.	Generally the size of order is small and they are not repeated. The orders are for non-standardized products. The order may involve the production of single product or products in limited lot. Usually the production is done according to first in first out principle. First orders are received and then they are translated into production.	Generally, the production is carried on for stock. The production of standardized products if the nature of this type of production. Products are produced in anticipation of demand. The size of the order is large. Same type of products is produced in every cycle to satisfy the demand.
7.	Investment in Machines and Equipment.	As the machines are arranged in process layout and general-purpose machines are require for job production, the investment comparatively less. For batch production as automatic and semi-automatic machines are involved the investment will be higher than job production.	The machines are arranged according to process layout and because of this duplication of machines are fairly high. The machines are fully automatic; the cost is higher than intermittent production.
8.	Investment in inventories.	Here operation cycle takes more time and it is necessary to have standard materials for long period hence inventory cost per product is considerably large.	Bulk purchases of materials are done at periodic intervals. Due to continuous process, less in process inventory exists hence material cost per product is less.
9.	Material Handling Equipments.	Because of verities of products, different routes are followed by materials also volume of order small, mechanization of material handling is not possible.	Mechanization of material handling is possible. Generally conveyors, pipelines, automatic material handling equipment are used.

(contd.....)

S. No.	Particulars	Intermittent Production Systems (Job and Batch Production)	Continuous Production System (Mass and Flow Production)
10.	Material Handling Cost.	Material handling per product is costlier because of long distance handling (manual) and backtracking.	Due to mechanized material handling, material-handling cost per product is less.
11.	Plant Maintenance and Service.	It is desirable to have a maintenance department to avoid losses due to break down of machinery.	It is essential to have a god plant maintenance department to avoid stoppage of production due to break- down of machines.
12.	Balancing of Production Capacity.	Due to different products and different types of machines with different capacity blocks, possibility of imbalance in plant capacity occurs.	The chances of imbalance in plant capacity are very much less.
13.	Production Planning and Control.	The functions of routing, scheduling and loading becomes relatively complicated due to odd size of order, non-repetitive nature of the order, different delivery dates, etc.; production planning and control is complicated.	The functions of routing, scheduling and lodging are carried on smoothly due to standardized precuts, and rated capacity. Here production planning and control is simpler.

QUESTIONS

1. What is a product? What is management? And what is production management? Explain with examples.
2. Explain the scope of production management. Explain the benefits of good production management.
3. List out the functions of production management and explain any three of them briefly with examples.
4. Explain the job production system. Give its applicability, advantages and limitations.
5. Explain batch production system and give its applicability, advantages and disadvantages.
6. Explain continuous production system and give its applicability, advantages and limitations.
7. Distinguish between continuous production and mass production systems.

3.7. PLANT LAYOUT

3.7.1. Introduction

A plant is a place where men, materials, money, machinery and equipment etc.; are brought together for manufacturing a product. Plant location and Plant layout decisions are crucial because they commit organizations to a long time financial, employment and distribution problems. In one word, they commit organization's available resources to the future manufacturing activities. If management commit any mistake either in selecting the location for the plant or in preparing the plant layout, it has to face problems which are of serious nature and the cost of production will also be high, which makes it impossible to face competition in the market. Hence, while selecting a location for a plant, the management has to evaluate the location before the selection is made. The factors of evaluation are:

- Define the location objectives and related constraints.
- Identify the relevant decision criteria both qualitative and quantitative factors.
- Relate the objective to the criteria using appropriate mathematical models/economic models such as break-even analysis, economic cost models, linear programming and qualitative factor analysis.
- Do field research to generate relevant data and use the models to evaluate alternate location.
- Select the location that best satisfies the criteria.

The optimum location is the outcome of proper reconciliation of various considerations relevant to the question on hand.

Weber's theory is referred while selecting a plant location. This theory recommends two factors i.e.:

(i) Primary actors which influence the distribution of industrial units over different regions, and

(ii) Factors either cause concentration of industries in certain regions or their dispersal from the original regions, known as **secondary factors.**

3.7.2. Factors Influencing Plant Location

Decision regarding location requires a careful balancing of several factors. Some of them are more important and are known as primary factors, while the less important, known as secondary factors. Sometimes in real problem secondary factors may show greater influence in selecting the location for a plant.

3.7.2.1. Primary factors

1. **Availability of raw material:** In order to minimize the transport cost of raw material to the industrial plant, the nature of raw material is of great importance. A good deal of economy in transport cost may be achieved, if the industries, which are using **weight losing** materials, are located nearer to the source of raw materials. In case the industries use **ubiquities** materials, i.e. materials available everywhere, the material transport cost may not have much influence on location of site. Hence, the location to be selected has to be nearer to the source of raw materials.

(a) **Nearness to the Market for the Finished Goods:** Industries using pure raw materials (non weight loosing materials) are generally located nearer to the market for the product produced. By locating the plant nearer to the market for the goods manufactured, the transportation cost of the finished goods can be kept at minimum. In addition to this factor, the chances of finished goods getting damaged or spoiled during transport can be reduced. It also helps the unit to catch big share of the market.

(b) **Availability of Fuel and Power:** The problem of fuel and power can also be solved with reference to nature of raw materials. Industries, which use coal as the source of power for their unit, are located nearer to the coal bed. It is because coal loses weight during process. Now-a-days as the electricity is generally used as power source, this factor losing importance. But we can consider the State, which encourages the industrial units by giving power at reasonable rate and uninterrupted supply of power.

(c) **Transport Facilities:** Transportation cost forms major portion of the total cost of manufacturing the product. Depending upon the nature of raw material or the finished goods, a proper method of transport, like water, rail, air, road transport has to be selected and accordingly plant location is decided. Here the criteria is to keep the transportation cost at minimum, as **movement of material simply adds to the cost and nothing to value.**

(d) **Availability of Labour:** Another important factor influencing the location of industrial unit is availability of suitable and adequate number of labour at a reasonable labour wages. This is particularly true in units, which are labour intensive industries, where labour is main element in producing the goods. However labour alone will not attract the location, as the labour is mobile in nature.

(e) **Availability of Water:** If water is one of the raw materials used in processing the product (example: Paper, Chemical industrial units etc.), the plant has to be located nearer to source of water. Water is also required for drinking and sanitary purposes.

3.7.2.2. Secondary factors

1. **Soil and climate:** The question of soil and climate is really an influencing factor for a unit processing agricultural products like tea, coffee and rubber, etc. But in today's scenario, because of advanced technology, which helps us to get suitable atmosphere and temperature required through heating and air conditioning, this factor is not that much important. But natural atmosphere is more favorable.
2. **Industrial atmosphere:** The industrial atmosphere cannot be measured in tangible terms, but it has a very important advantage in selecting a location for a plant. Industrial atmosphere may be said to exist where people living at a place think instinctively of industry and learn the intricacies of machines without much effort. This is an added advantage for the growth of industries in a particular area.
3. **Financial and other aids:** The plant should be located in an area where financial institutions are available to get a part of capital as loan and getting working capital and for other financial aids.

4. **Availability of facilities like housing, schools, hospitals and recreation:** The site should be nearer to infrastructure facilities like, housing facility for employees at reasonable rent, hospitals for health care, schools for educating the children of the employees and recreation facilities to give relaxation for the employees in the leisure period.
5. **Momentum of an early start:** There are number of places where to begin with, only one or two factories were started. With the passage of time these places gained importance and attract industries. As the number of industries increases, certain facilities like Banking, Schools, etc. are developed in that area. Chances of availability of skilled labour also increase.
6. **Special advantages of the place:** Sometimes special facilities are offered by the state, in case the particular region is selected for starting the unit. Facilities like, providing subsides, tax holidays etc. In this way State can develop the underdeveloped areas.
7. **Personal factors:** Sometimes, promoters, irrespective of economic factors, prefer to start their unit in their place of origin to develop the area and help the fellow community.
8. **Historical factors:** Factors like personal fancies of entrepreneurs of historical incidents may in many cases lead to the development of a place as the center of an industry.
9. **Political stability:** The lack of political stability in a State makes uncertainty in the attitude of State Government to industries. In locating industrial plant it must be seen whether the State has a record of political and economic stability.

In addition the promoter has to consider the factor of locating the unit in **Rural / Sub-urban/urban** area.

3.8. OBJECTIVES OF PLANT LAYOUT

Layout decisions are concerned with arrangement of production, support customer service and other facilities used in operation so as to achieve the desired objective at cheapest cost. The flow pattern for future work activities affect the efficiency of handling materials, the utilization of capital equipment, inventories storage levels, the number and productivity of workers and even behavioral characteristics such as group communications and employee moral.

Plant layout is a companion problem to facilitate location. The word layout is used here to indicate the physical arrangements of the plant and of the various parts of the plant. The layouts will therefore encompass both location of equipment within a department or shop and arrangement of departments upon site, which include offices, warehouses, rest rooms and other facilities associated with the total system. Thus facility layout is the overall arrangement of machines, men, materials, material handling facilities, service facilities and passage required to facilitate efficient operation of the production system. It integrates all aspects of production.

3.8.1. Types of Plant Layouts

Whether one is preparing the layout for a new plant or want to change the existing layout of a unit for some reason or the other the below mentioned points will generally help the operations manager. The type of layout is determined by:

(a) **Type of Product:** This concerns whether the product, goods or service, the product design and quality standards and whether the product is produced for stock or for order.

(b) **Type of Production Process:** This relates to the technology used, the type of materials handled and/or the means of providing service.

(c) **Volume of Production:** Volume affects the present facility design and capacity utilization, plus provisions for expansion or change.

3.9. FACTORS AFFECTING THE PLANT LAYOUT

While preparing a layout, the layout engineer has to remember the factors, which influence the type of layout and the location of machinery or facilities in the layout. Some of the factors, which are important in nature, are discussed below:

(i) **Product and material specification:** The form of material, weight of material, physical and chemical characteristics of material used has great influence in locating a facility. These factors influence all parameters of the layout. Products requiring hazardous and dangerous operation call for isolation of the facility instead of integration on a line basis.

(ii) **Location and site of the plant:** The site, which has been selected, has great influence while preparing layout. A plant has to get raw material from source of material and send the manufactured product to the market. Hence, the receiving department and the shipping department must properly be located so that the receiving and shipping will not become a problem. The attitude of the community, availability of power supply and water has influence in locating the departments appropriately.

(iii) **Manufacturing Process:** This is a very important factor to be considered while preparing a layout. The manufacturing process decides the flow of material, type of machines required and the material handling facilities required. Depending on the size and weight of the machine and raw materials, the working area required and additional space required to store in process inventory has to be decided. In case this problem is not given due consideration at the layout design stage, the management has to face lot of problems at production stage.

(iv) **Material Handling:** In any manufacturing process, material handling is inevitable. Not only inevitable, but also material handling adds to cost and nothing to value. Hence, handling of materials is kept as low as possible, so that the production cost will be under control. This point applies to all aspects of manufacturing, i.e. raw material handling, handling of in-process inventory, handling of scrap, waste and finished product. Material handling and plant layout are closely related; hence, the layout engineer should integrate these two, while preparing a layout.

(v) **Storage of in-process inventory:** While preparing layout, the material waiting time should be kept at minimum, as it adds to the cost. Hence, the layout should be designed in such a way, as far as possible material does not wait in-between two processes. If possible thought should be given to integrate movement of material while it is being processed (for example, process like drying, painting cleaning etc.).

(vi) **Plant personnel and employee facilities:** Facilities like rest rooms, cloak- rooms, vehicles parking facilities, canteen, emergency medical aides and safety guards for machines should be considered while preparing layout.

(vii) **Service facilities:** Service facilities related to personnel, material, machinery and equipment, and operations should be given due considerations while preparing layout, because, they play a significant role in cost reduction and in increasing productivity.

(viii) **Design of building:** The building should be designed in such a way that ample of natural ventilation and lighting is obtained. Also care should be taken to see that in case of expansion or modification there should not be much headache.

(ix) **Flexibility:** At the time of starting, the entrepreneur might have selected best available machinery and process, but as the time passes, the method may become absolute. In such cases, the plant needs a change. Because of change in product design or change in the material used or change in the process used, the layout may need to be changed. In such cases, these changes must be accommodated with least difficulty. Hence, while preparing the layout, one should incorporate the factor of flexibility.

(x) **Work areas and equipment:** Work areas are properly designed; so that workers can move without much difficulty and material can be handled with least difficulty. Sufficient space should be provided for maintenance personnel to attend, to repair or maintenance of the machine.

(xi) **Working conditions:** If this fact is given due consideration, it will maximize human data sensing, processing and transmitting abilities. The work area should have sufficient light intensity and quality without direct or indirect glare. Provisions should be provided to reduce the noise due to process, control of temperature and humidity, so that the personnel can work comfortably.

(xii) **Disposal of waste and dangerous gases:** Proper waste disposal facility should be provided at appropriate places, so that they are disposed to a remote place, so that they will not be harmful to the workers or to the community living around the plant.

3.10. OBJECTIVES OF A GOOD PLANT LAYOUT

The primary goal of plant layout is to arrange all the factors of production in a most optimal way to that the production cost is kept at minimum and returns are increased and employee moral is boosted up. To fulfil the above goal, the plant engineer must remember certain objectives, while preparing the layout. The objectives of good plant layout are:

1. Material handling and transport is minimized and efficiently controlled, so that the handling cost is minimized.

2. Bottlenecks and points of congestions are eliminated by using the line balancing techniques, so that raw material and semi-finished goods will move fast from one workstation to the other.
3. Workstations are deigned and located suitably, so that there will be least resistance to the smooth flow of material and movement of men.
4. Sufficient space and proper location should be allocated to production centers and service centers.
5. Waiting line of semi-finished goods should be minimized.
6. Safe and proper working conditions are provided to avoid accidents and casualties.
7. Designed layout should be provided with sufficient flexibility to accommodate future minute changes in product design or change in the material specification.
8. Care should be taken to see that the space available is used optimally. Not only length and breadth of the building but also the height of the building has to be used.
9. Plant layout should make the plant maintenance simple and easy.
10. The layout should promote the effective utilization of manpower.
11. A good layout should maintain high turnover of work-in-process.

3.11. PRINCIPLES OF A GOOD PLANT LAYOUT

Plant layout engineer has to follow certain principles to design a good layout. There are certain principles to guide him; still the common sense is a must to get optima result. Important principles are discussed below:

(a) **Integration:** The first principle is to integrate production centers, other facilities and means of production in a logical and balanced manner. While preparing layout one has to think of all factors of production to achieve the objectives of a good plant layout.

(b) **Minimum movement and materials handling:** The movement of materials and men should be minimized. Because the movement will add only to the cost and consume time unproductively. There are instances where plant manager after recognizing the defect in the layout and after careful work study, changing the layout, have saved quite a good amount of money per year.

(c) **Smooth and continuous flow of materials:** Bottlenecks, congestion points and back tracking should be removed by proper line balancing techniques so that productivity is increased.

(d) **Cubic space utilizations:** Besides using the floor space of a shop, if the ceiling height is also utilized more material can be accommodated in the same shop. The vertical space may be used to stock raw material, semi-finished goods or sometimes tools. When the unit is dealing with continuous production, it is better to use the vertical space for movement of material.

(e) **Safe and Improved Environments:** Working places should be free from noise, dust, odors and other hazardous conditions so that the workers can concentrate on their work. Work place should have safety when work is being done and they are well ventilated so that the workers will work happily. This will improve the operating efficiency of workers and boosts their morale. All these lead to satisfaction among the workers and thus better employer–employee relations.

(f) **Flexibility:** In automotive and other industries, where models of product/ component will change after sometime, it is better to permit all possible flexibility in layout to accommodate the change required to meet the demand of the market. The machinery is arranged in such a way that the changes of the production process can be achieved at the least cost or disturbance.

3.12. ADVANTAGES OF GOOD PLANT LAYOUT

A good layout provides many advantages to workers and to the management.

(i) **Advantages to Workers:**

(a) Lesser number of material handling and lesser operations.

(b) Reduction of length of hauls and motions between operations minimize the throughput time and activities of workers.

(c) Improved labour productivity and hence higher wages.

(d) More safety and security because of reduced accidents and severity of accidents.

(e) Better working conditions and improved efficiency.

(ii) **Manufacturing Costs:**

(a) Reduced maintenance and replacement costs.

(b) Minimized costs due to reduced waste and spoilage of work.

(c) Improved quality of the product and reduced handling costs.

(d) Better cost control.

(iii) **Advantages to Production Control:**

(a) More space for production operations.

(b) Better storage facility for in-process inventory.

(c) Scope for better supervision.

(d) Better utilization of machinery and labour.

3.13. TYPES OF PLANT LAYOUT

Although it is convenient to classify layouts, into two or three basic types, in reality there is a continuum of different types of layouts, which can be combined in a variety of ways. Classified on the basis of volume of identical product, these layouts range from fixed position facilities assembled to produce just one product, to contentious flow facilities that produce millions of identical units.

3.13.1. Process Layout (Functional Layout)

This layout is also known as *Functional layout*, characterized by keeping similar machines or similar operations at one location or place. In other words all turning machines are placed in turning department and all drilling machines are arranged in drilling department and so on. The machines are arranged according to their functions. This type of layout is generally employed for industries engaged in job order production and non-repetitive kind of manufacturing and maintenance activities. The batch production shops and job production shops prefer Process Layout.

Advantages:

1. Flexibility in equipment or manpower allotment for specific tasks. This load distribution can be controlled and this is particularly of importance in case of breakdowns for maintenance schedules and for multi product manufacture.
2. Better utilizations of machines and available time. Consequently fewer machines are required for same volume of production by other layouts (in a limited sense).
3. Comparatively low investment on machines.
4. Better product quality because of effective supervision.
5. The diversity of task offers a more interesting and satisfying occupation for the operator.
6. Each section can be benefited from specialized supervision.
7. Workers in one section are not affected by the nature of operations carried out in another section.

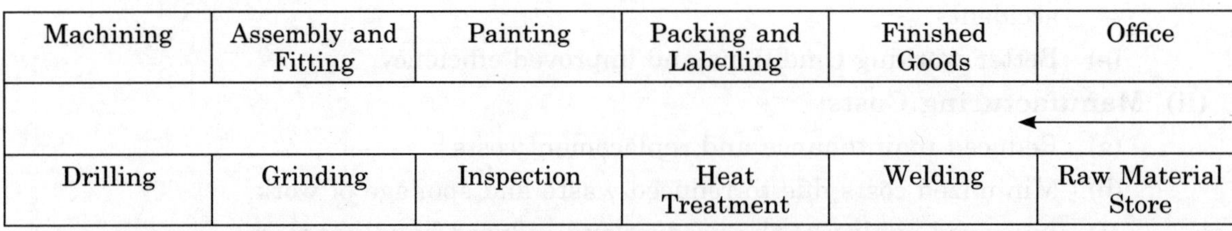

Fig. 3.2. Process Layout.

Limitations or Disadvantages:

1. Long flow lines, hence more expensive handling per product.
2. Comparatively large amounts of work-in-process materials waiting for the next operation.
3. Space and capital are tied up by work-in-process.
4. Production planning and control systems are more complicated when compared to other layouts.
5. Total production time (through put time) is longer, owing to time consumed in material handling and in waiting times.
6. Because of the diversity of the jobs in specialized departments, higher grades of skills are required.
7. For the same amount of production (volume of production), process layout needs more space.
8. Automatic material handling is extremely difficult.

Table 3.2. Showing the Characteristics of Different Types of Layouts

Types of Layouts	Types of Product	Type of Process	Volume of Production
Fixed Position (Ship Building, Railway coach building, etc.)	Customized (influenced by location)	Individual Projects (Unique or tailored specifications)	Very low. (Possibly only once)
Job Shop (e.g. Machine shop, Repair shop, Hospitals etc.)	Customized	Flexible Process	Relatively low (short runs)
Batch Processing (Batch production of components)	Many different products Compete via features and services	Materials and labour requirements less certain Labour is higher percentage of total costs	More work-in-process Inventory Planning horizon is relatively short
Line Production (Automobile assembly line)	Compete via distribution and price Fewer new products	Labour is lower percentage of total costs Material and labour Requirement is More certain	Planning horizon is relatively large More finished goods Inventory
CONTINUOUS FLOW PRODUCTION (OIL, CEMENT, SUGAR PLANTS)	MORE STANDARDIZED	STANDARDIZED PROCESS	RELATIVELY HIGH (Long runs)

Characteristics: This layout is used when:

- Volume is low
- Variety of products is many.

- The demand for the product is small or intermittent.
- General purpose and low cost machines are desirable.
- Machines or processing produces unbearable noise, vibration, fumes or heat. Such machines are located in isolated place.
- Skilled labours are required.

3.13.2. Product Layout or Line Layout

In product layout, machines and ancillary services are located along the product flow line. The layout is suitable for continuous type of production and can employ one of the basic horizontal flow lines or their combinations. The raw material enters at one side and gets processed along the line and finished product leaves the system at the other end. The various operations on the product are performed in a sequence and the machines are placed along the material flow line that is the machines are arranged in the sequence in which a given product will be processed upon (refer Fig. 3.3).

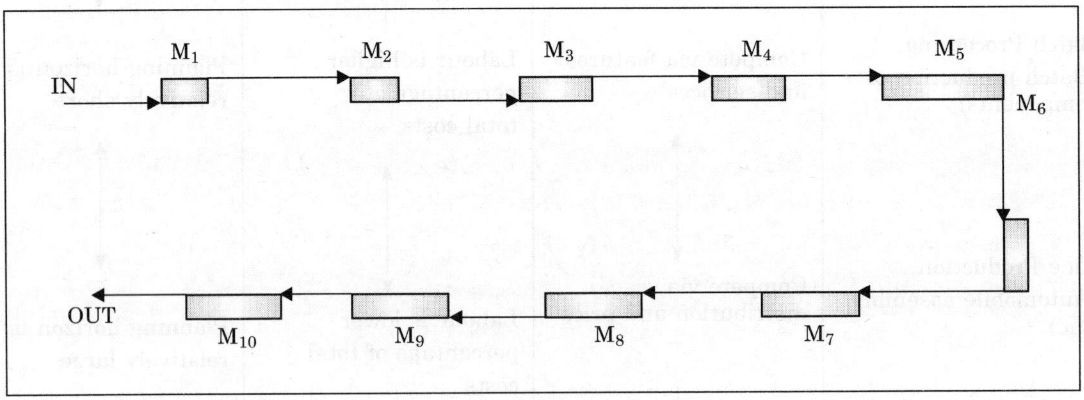

Fig. 3.3. Product Layout.

In the figure M_1 to M_{10} are machines arranged in sequence of operations desired by the product. Material enters at Machine M_1 and finished product leaves the system at machine M_{10}.

Advantages:

1. Layout corresponds to sequence of operations, resulting in smooth and logical flow lines.
2. Reduced material handling, since the machines are so located as to minimize distance between two operations.
3. Small amounts of work-in-process, as the work from one process is directly fed into the next.
4. Less space is occupied by work in transit and for temporary storage.
5. Total output time per unit is short.
6. Simple production planning and control system and simplified supervision.
7. Little skill is usually required by operators at the production line. Hence training is simple, short and inexpensive.

8. Automatic materials handling is quite common and materials handling cost per unit is less.

Disadvantages:

1. Layout is determined by the product and leaves little room for flexibility. A change in product design may need major alterations in layout.
2. The pace of production is determined by the slowest machine, hence speed of the machine is deliberately reduced or other machines remain idle for more time.
3. Break-down of one machine may lead to complete stoppage of the line that follows the broken machine.
4. Comparatively high investments are required, as identical machines (a few not fully utilized) are some times distributed along the line. Also sometimes for some critical machines, we may require a stand by to pass the production through stand by at the time of breakdown of critical machines.
5. Supervision is general but not specialized.
6. It is difficult to increase production beyond the capacity of the production line.

Characteristics:

This type of layout is used where:

1. The number of end products is limited (may be one or two).
2. The products are highly standardized and interchangeable.
3. The volume of production for the product is large.
4. The demand of the product is fairly steady.
5. The continuity of material flow can be maintained.

3.13.3. Static Product Layout or Layout by Fixed Position

When the product is very big or too heavy and very difficult to move from one process to another, this type of layout is used. Here the product is fixed in one position and machine, men, materials, components and equipments are brought to the product to do the required operations. This layout is typical of job production in construction work, such as ship building, railway coach building, locomotive building and building construction etc. (Figure 3.4)

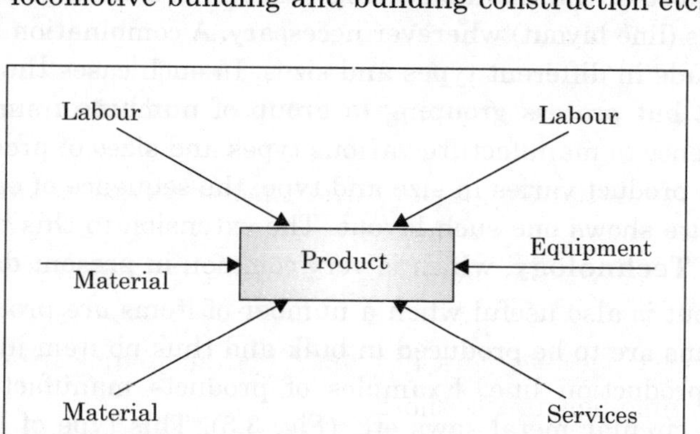

Fig. 3.4. Fixed Position Layout.

Advantages

1. Comparatively, material movement is minimum.
2. The task is usually carried out by a group of operators; hence continuity of operations and responsibility are ensured.
3. Production centers often operate independently of each other, and effective scheduling can be planned to ensure minimum total production time.
4. It is more flexible in all aspects.

Disadvantages

1. Movement of machines and equipment to the production center may be costly as well as time consuming.
2. Positioning the material or object or machine may be cumbersome and costly.
3. Machine and equipment utilization is usually low, owing to handling and positioning time, even if schedule provides for successive employment of the equipment at several production centers.
4. Highly skilled workers are required.

Characteristics

The layout is suitable when:

1. Material forming or treating operations requires only tools or simple portable machines.
2. Only one of the few pieces of a product/item are manufactured.
3. The cost of moving major piece of material is high.
4. Skill of the workmanship lies in the abilities of the workers or when it is desired to fix the responsibility of product quality on the workmen or a group of workers.

3.13.4. Combination of Process and Product Layout or Functional and Line Layouts or Matrix Layout

A combination of functional and line layout to a large extent takes the advantages of both the layouts into account. Moreover, these days pure product (line) or process (functional) layouts are rare. Most of the manufacturing sections are arranged in process layout with manufacturing lines (line layout) wherever necessary. A combination layout is feasible where an item is being made in different types and sizes. In such cases the machinery is arranged in a process layout but process grouping (a group of number of similar machines) is then arranged in a sequence to manufacture various types and sizes of products. A point to note is that, no matter the product varies in size and type; the sequence of operations remains same or similar. The figure shows one such layout. The extension to this type of layout is **Group Layout or Group Technology**, which is very common in present day production scenario.

A combination layout is also useful when a number of items are produced in same sequence but none of the items are to be produced in bulk and thus no item justifies for an individual and independent production line. Examples of products manufactured using this layout is: files, hacksaws, circular metal saws etc. (Fig. 3.5). This type of layout is also known as **Matrix layout,** as it resembles a matrix.

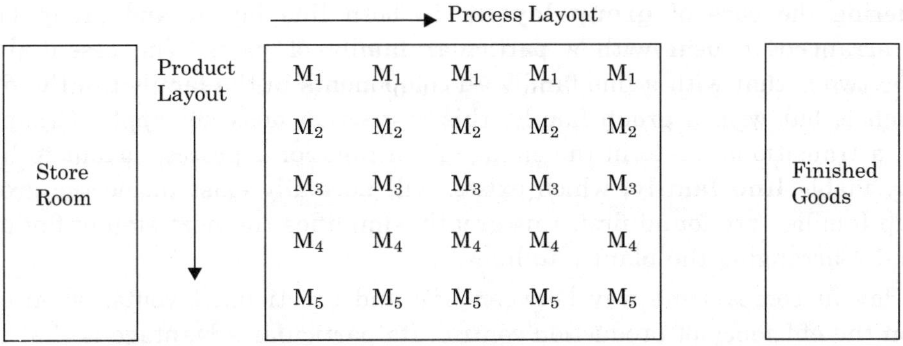

Fig. 3.5. Combinations of Process and Product Layout.

3.13.5. Group Layout

Group layout is the type of plant layout in which the plant is divided into groups, each of which contains all the facilities necessary to carry out all the operations applied to a given **family** of parts. The parts or components in the **group or family** are generally similar in form, but the essential criterion is that they can all be completed in special plant group, laid out for that purpose. It will be noted that a change from **functional layout** to **group layout** changes the emphasis from **process specialization** to **product specialization.** Each group consists of a set of machines, which can process a wide range of products of different sizes, each requiring processing on the same group of machines, may be in same sequence or different sequence. The figure 3.6 shows one such layout.

GROUP I	GROUP II	GROUP III
Lathe Turning	Grinding Grinder	Milling Milling Machine
Milling Milling Machine	Shaper Shaping Machine	Lathe Turning
Shaper Shaping Machine	Milling Milling Machine	Grinding Grinder

Fig. 3.6. Group Layouts.

3.14. THE EFFECT OF LAYOUT ON PRODUCTION CONTROL

Differences in layout have an important effect on the efficiency of production control. In line layout the controlling of production can be done more effectively and cheaply than in process layout. Line layout will give better utilization of labour, plant and capital. Even in the small to medium-sized concern, where the mathematics of the subjects will sometimes seem, to show that the line layout would give poor machine and labour utilization, the simplicity of control and the psychological effect of flow and of the **pace line**, will often make nonsense of the mathematics.

Considering the case of **group layout**, in both line layout and group layout each section is arranged to deal with a particular family of parts. The essential difference between the two is that with a line family all components in the family use the plant in the same sequence, but with a group family, this restriction does not apply. Group layout is, in a sense, a transitional state in the change from functional/process layout to line/product layout. Any viable **line family,** which exists, will normally exist inside the group family. If the group families are found first, this greatly simplifies the next step of finding the line families and rearranging the plant into lines.

Group layout comes some way between line and functional layouts, when considering its effect on the efficiency of production control. Its particular advantage is that it offers an alternative method by which the small or medium-sized firm, which makes a large variety of products, can reduce throughput time and thereby improve capital utilization and delivery promises. It also has the advantage that in comparison with process layout, it simplifies and ease production control and makes it more effective and efficient.

3.15. SYMPTOMS OF BAD LAYOUT

A plant layout usually, once well designed and established it helps in increased productivity and improves the employee morale. Not every minor change in the production programme or additions of machines or sections justify redesign of the plant layout, but these changes accumulate and gradually alter the basic pattern of flow lines in the plant, until re-planning of the layout becomes inevitable. The symptoms of layout in need of redesign are:

1. Congestion of materials, components and assemblies.
2. Excessive amounts of work-in-process.
3. Poor utilization of available space.
4. Production bottlenecks at certain machines while similar or identical machines have idle time.
5. Long waiting lines of components (because of inefficient handling).
6. Excessive handling by skilled operators.
7. Long production cycles and delay in delivery.
8. Mental or physical strain of operators.
9. Difficulties in maintaining effective supervision and control.

QUESTIONS

1. What is a Plant? What factors you consider for selecting a suitable location for the plant?
2. Think that you want to produce certain Electronic Components and give your views regarding the selection for a location for your project.
3. Explain the Primary factors to be considered by an entrepreneur while selecting a location for a manufacturing plant.
4. Explain the Secondary factors to be considered by an entrepreneur while selecting a location for a manufacturing plant.

5. What is Plant Layout? What factors affect the Plant Layout?
6. What are the objectives of a good Plant layout? Explain the Principles of a good Plant Layout.
7. List out the different types of Layouts and discuss the advantages of a good Plant Layout.
8. Explain with a neat sketch Process/Functional layout and give its suitability, Characteristics, Advantages, and Disadvantages.
9. Explain the Product/Line Layout with a neat sketch and give its suitability, Characteristics, Advantages and Limitations.
10. Explain by means of a neat sketch Static Product Layout and give its suitability, Characteristics, Advantages and Limitations.
11. Explain with a neat sketch combination of Process and Product Layout gives its advantages and limitations.
12. Write a note on Group Layout. What are the symptoms of Bad Layout?

MULTIPLE CHOICE QUESTIONS

1. The product can be defined as:
   (a) Which can be purchased
   (b) Which can be sold
   (c) Which can be seen
   (d) Optimal combination of potential utilities.
2. These are the two important duties of production management:
   (a) Planning and directing (b) Controlling and staffing
   (c) Scheduling and loading, (d) Pricing and selling.
3. When items are manufactured to meet the requirements of a specific order it is known as:
   (a) Batch production (b) Mass production
   (c) Line production (d) Continuous production.
4. A system in which identical products are manufactured in large volume by utilizing the plant fully engaged to manufacture the product.
   (a) Mass production (b) Batch production
   (c) Continuous production (d) Job production.
5. For intermittent production this type of layout is most suitable:
   (a) Process layout (b) Product layout
   (c) Combination layout (d) Matrix layout.
6. When products are manufactured by Job or Batch production we require:
   (a) Semi-skilled labour (b) Highly skilled labour
   (c) Casual labours (d) None.

7. In intermittent production the size of the order is:
   (a) Large and repetitive (b) Small and repetitive
   (c) Small and non-repetitive (d) Large and repetitive.
8. One of the factors to be considered while selecting Plant Location is:
   (a) Define the location objectives and related constraints
   (b) Urban or Rural site
   (c) Type of the product
   (d) Type of the labour.
9. One of the primary functions influencing plant location is:
   (a) The attitude of the entrepreneur
   (b) The qualification of managers
   (c) The money available with the entrepreneur
   (d) Nearness to the raw-material.
10. Materials which are available everywhere are known as
    (a) Localized material (b) Ubiquitous martial
    (c) Raw material (d) Special material.
11. One of the important secondary factors to be considered while deciding plant location is:
    (a) Availability of labour (b) Availability fuel and power
    (c) Availability of transport facilities (d) Industrial atmosphere.
12. One of the factors influencing the plant layout is:
    (a) Manufacturing process (b) Type of labour available
    (c) The manager's will (d) The capital available.
13. One of the objectives of good plant layout is:
    (a) To manufacture good products
    (b) To reduce the number of workers
    (c) To increase the efficiency of managers
    (d) Handling and Transport costs are minimized.
14. One of the principles of a good plant layout is:
    (a) Minimum movement and material handling
    (b) Easy to control labour
    (c) To use less raw material
    (d) To minimize the number of managers.
15. Process layout is also known as:
    (a) Line layout (b) Combination layout
    (c) Functional layout (d) Fixed product layout.
16. The line layout is also known as:
    (a) Process layout (b) Functional Layout
    (c) Matrix layout (d) Military Layout.

17. A layout in which similar machines are kept in one location is known as:

(a) Line layout (b) Product layout

(c) Process layout (d) Matrix layout.

18. A layout corresponds to sequence of operation is known as:

(a) Matrix layout (b) Group layout

(c) Line layout (d) Process layout.

19. A combination of process and product layout is known as:

(a) Group layout (b) Static product layout

(c) Common layout (d) Matrix layout.

20. To Manufacture Railway Coach this type of layout is suitable.

(a) Line layout (b) Matrix layout

(c) Process layout (d) Static product layout.

21. One of the symptoms of bad layout is:

(a) Product cannot be manufactured

(b) Labours are not available

(c) Non availability of raw-material

(d) Congestion of materials components and assemblies.

ANSWERS

1. (d)	**2.** (c)	**3.** (d)	**4.** (c)	**5.** (a)	**6.** (b)	**7.** (c)	**8.** (a)
9. (d)	**10.** (b)	**11.** (d)	**12.** (a)	**13.** (d)	**14.** (a)	**15.** (c)	**16.** (d)
17. (c)	**18.** (c)	**19.** (d)	**20.** (d)	**21.** (d).			

○○○

3.16 WORK STUDY

Work-Study: Basic Procedures involved in Method Study and Work Measurement:

3.16.1. Introduction

Man for some reason or the other always try to simplify his work. For example, a person wants to reach destination B from his place A. He always leaves the main road joining the two places A and B and follows a cross path which save his **energy** and **time.** In fact, every man is a good expert in the techniques of simplifying his work. But is very difficult for us to tell where and when exactly the science of simplifying the work has begun. But in the interest of knowing much about the subject, we can identify some of the pioneers, who contributed to spread the knowledge of science of simplifying the work and measuring the work in terms of time units. While there is noting essentially new in work-study the novelty is apparent in the intensity of the analytical approach. It has always been practiced as an unconscious art and attitude of individuals, gained through experience and lost in the same way. In real sense work-study is 10 percent technical and 90 percent common sense.

To understand the history of work-study, let us discuss some of the persons who have done remarkable work in the area.

(i) Fredric Winslow Taylor (F.W. Taylor)—(1856–1915): He is the first man who evolved the principle of breaking the job down into detailed elements to determine by time study a time to be allowed for the job. He is rather a remarkable man. He joined Midvale Steel Works as an apprentice and reached the position of chief engineer at the age of 31 years. He has given scientific base in analyzing the work. The objectives of his scientific management are:

(a) The development of science for each element of a man's work, thereby replacing the old practice of thumb rule method.

(b) The selection of right worker for each particular task and give training and develop him as skilled worker, rather than allowing man to select his work and learn the work by himself.

(c) To develop hearty co-operation between workers and management.

(d) Dividing the work into almost equal shares between management and the workers and each department is allocated the work, which is best suited.

Taylor undertook his famous studies of shoveling at Bethlehem Steel Works during 1898 and designed optimal size of the shovels, which increased the productivity of workers. He is the man who devised functional management also initiated the method of measuring work in terms of time units, by breaking down the work into measurable elements. He also invented high-speed steel, which has a longer life than the conventional tool material.

Henry L. Gantt: (1861–1919) H.L. Gantt is famous for his work known as Gantt Chart, widely used in work-study and scheduling of works. He has developed incentive and planning and control system.

Frank and Lillian Gilbreth: Mr. Gilbreth is the founder of Method Study (Motion Study—1869–1924). He eschewed his education at the age of 17 and learnt bricklayer's work. He studied various hand motions adopted by workers while laying the bricks and found the best pattern of movement of hands for laying the bricks. Later he became a contractor and an industrial consultant. His wife, Dr. Lillian Gilbreth, a trained psychologist helped in his work. The knowledge of psychology and scientific thinking of work given a wonderful contribution to the industrial world, which is Method Study. He developed laws of human motions and principles of motion economy.

3.16.2. Productivity and Work-Study

Productivity is the relationship between inputs used and output produced. As far the inputs are concerned, we have to take all the resources that go into production, such as material, man-hour, machine hours, money etc. Therefore, when we talk about productivity, the question arises whether it is the material productivity or machine productivity? Hence while calculating; if we take one particular resource, then we say it is the productivity of that particular resource. For example, if we consider the total man-hours used to produce the goods, we say that it is the labour productivity and so on. If we put together all the resources and calculate productivity, it is total productivity. The factors affecting productivity are:

1. Nature and quality of raw material.
2. Basic nature of process employed.
3. Amount of plant and equipment employed.
4. Efficiency of plant and equipment employed.
5. Volume, quantity, continuity and uniformity of production.
6. Utilization of manpower.

3.16.2.1. Methods of improving productivity

(i) Either by improving the basic process by research and development or by providing more and improved physical means of production. This needs lot of time to implement, hence are considered as long term strategies.

(ii) It can also be improved by simplifying and reducing the variety, which enable us to save scarce resources and improve the use value of the product also reduce the cost of the product. This may not take much time as above, but need considerable time and hence considered as medium term strategy.

(iii) Productivity can also be improved by improving the method of operation and by increasing manpower efficiency at all levels and practicing effective planning and organization. This can be achieved by following scientific management in day-to-day work; hence this is considered as short-term strategy. One of the techniques used to improve manpower utilization and improve the methods of production is the application of work-study technique.

3.16.3. Definition of Work Study, Method Study and Work Measurement

Work-study is the study of human work in all its contexts. It is defined as:

Work-study is a management service based on those techniques, particularly method study and work measurement, which are used I the examination of human work in all its contexts and which lead to the systematic investigation of all the resources and factors which affect the efficiency and economy of the situation being reviewed in order to effect improvement.

The definition says that the work-study is the combination of method study and work measurement that means on one hand we have to examine the method of doing the work and on the other hand, we have to find the time required to do the work. Studying the method is to improve the method of production, which results in more effective use of material, manpower and equipment. Work measurement on the other hand assess the human effectiveness and gives guidelines to improve the planning and control methods also serves as the basis of sound incentive schemes. These two techniques are used to achieve optimal utilization of available resources and to improve productivity.

Method study is defined as the systematic recording and critical examination of the factors and resources involved in existing and proposed ways of doing work as a means of developing and applying easier and more effective method of reducing costs.

Work measurement is defined as the application of techniques designed to establish the time for a qualified worker to carry out a specified job at a desired level of performance.

The purpose or objective of work-study is to use the resources required for production in the best possible way to improve productivity. That is available manpower, equipment and machinery (plant) and material have to be used optimally.

3.16.3.1. Introduction to method study

Method study can be applied to any type of work. But to get the best advantages, it is better we apply method study to repetitive type of work. The method study man must be in a position to understand the human factors of method study and must have desire, determination and ability to produce the best results by taking economic and technical considerations of the work. Method study is basically concerned to finding the better way of doing work. Hence its objectives are to:

- Improve layout and design of factory, plant and the work place.
- Improve working procedures.
- Optimal utilization of material, manpower and plant and equipment.
- Improve the working environment.
- Improve the design or specification of the product.

In method study, we analyze the true facts concerning the situation and examine those facts critically and develop the best method of doing the work.

3.16.3.2. Steps in method study

There is a step-by-step procedure to conduct method study. The **first step** is to **Select the Job or Work,** which needs method study. When the job is examined, if it shows the following defects, we can apply method study to this job to improve the method of doing work.

If work-study team finds that there are unnecessary movements of men, material and equipments due to bad planning or bad layout, they have to select this situation for conducting method study.

When work-study team notices that there is unnecessary over time production, they have to analyze the situation.

When they notice too much of reprocessing of material it has to be analyzed by method study.

When workers complain about inconvenience or fatigue or strain while doing work it should be analyzed by method study.

When they notice bottlenecks in flow of material, men should be analyzed by method study.

Anyone of the above or a combination of the above are noticed, it has to be understood that the situation needs the application of method study. To decide whether to conduct method study or not, the benefits gained from the application of method study are weighed in the light of cost of method study. If the benefits are really worthwhile, the job is selected for method study. The benefits may include:

- Increased productivity.
- Savings in materials.
- Improved quality of product.
- Improved safety to workers and equipment.
- Reduction in scrap.
- Improved house keeping.

The second step in method study is **to record the facts.** Recording of the facts regarding the job selected for analysis is very much essential because it happens in critical examination of the facts and to compare the conditions before and after the improvement. Also, the records will serve as guidelines to train the employees in method study. There are many ways of recording the facts. The selection of a particular method depends on the purpose for which the record is prepared and cost of recording. The recording methods are classified into three categories. They are:

1. Charts (for process and time records).
2. Diagrams and models (for path and movement records).
3. Photographic aids. (For recording the movement of two hands, legs etc.) Depending on the need and the purpose, sometimes more than one method has been used for recording. In order to make recording easy certain **symbols** (Recording symbols or Method study symbols) are used for recording the facts. The symbols and the description is given below:

Table 3.3. Showing the Symbols used in Method Study

S. No.	Symbols	Description	For which the symbol is used
1.	○	OPERATION	Showing the operation for e.g. pressing, writing etc.
2.	→	TRANSPORT, MOVEMENT	Movement, Traveling etc.
3.	▽	STORAGE	Holding, Stocking, Storing.
4.	D	DELAY	Waiting for transport, Waiting for verifying, Inspection, Quality checking.
5.	□	INSPECTION	Checking the dimension etc.

3.17. CHARTS

There are different types of charts, depending on the need and purpose. Principle types are:

(i) Out line Process Chart: This chart is used for recording operations and inspections. This chart is mainly used in the initial state, to know the overall position of the problem and to assess the problem to know whether method study is necessary or not (This chart uses only Inspection and Operation Symbols).

(ii) Flow Process Chart: This chart uses all symbols mentioned in the chart given above and record the movement of men, material and equipment.

(iii) Two Hand Process Chart: This chart records activities of both hands of the worker. Here the symbol chart is used for indicating, "hold" i.e. holding a job in hand.

(iv) Multiple Activity Chart: Multiple Activity Chart records the activities of men, machine or both on a common time scale in the form of a bar chart. This chart is generally drawn on a graph sheet.

(v) Simultaneous Motion Chart: (SIMO Chart): On SIMO Chart, the activities of worker's hands, legs and other body movements are recorded on a common time scale. For recording cine cameras are used.

3.17.1. Diagrams and Models

Sometimes, it will be necessary to study the problem by using the diagrams and models, which will give enough scope to study the movement of men and materials.

(i) Flow Diagram: Same symbols, used in charting, are used in preparing the diagrams. These diagrams are prepared on a paper to scale by indicating flow lines. This diagram will be helpful to study the quality of layout.

(ii) String Diagram: This diagram is also used for studying a layout. The difference between the string diagram and flow diagram is, in flow diagram we draw different coloured lines to indicate the movements of different subject. In string diagram we use different coloured threads to indicate the movements of different subjects.

(iii) Two and Three-dimensional Models: These are models prepared to study the problem in detail. Two-dimensional models use templates and three-dimensional models uses actual working model, for example, we can construct the model of the plant to scale, so that it will be easy for one to study the movement of men and material in all directions.

Cyclographs and Chrono-cyclographs: This diagram is used for recording high speed, short-cycle operations. Generally a cine camera is used to record the movements. In cyclograph, a bulb tied to one of the fingers of worker's hand, which receives power from a battery with the worker and the whole movement, is photographed. The movement of worker's hand will appear as a white line on the film. In this it is very difficult to know the direction of movement of the hand. In chrono-cyclograph, the bulb is arranged to off and on mode, so that on the picture an oval-shaped dot appears, which shows the direction of movement of hand.

3.18. POINTS TO BE REMEMBERED WHILE DRAWING CHARTS AND DIAGRAMS

While drawing charts or diagrams, certain information is to be provided regarding the chart or diagram so as to understand to which job the chart belongs, where the job begins and where it ends.

(a) Name of the organization is to be written at the top of the chart.

(b) Title of the chart or diagram is to be written below the name of the company.

(c) On the right hand top corner against the name of the chart, the page number should be written as a fraction number. For example, a/b, where 'b' indicates the total number of pages in the study and 'a' indicates the serial number of pages. Thus 4/10 means the study consists of 10 pages and the present page is 4th page.

(d) Below the name of the chart, type and subject of the chart has to be mentioned. For example, *'present method'* or *'proposed method'* and *'material type'* or *'man type'*. This indicates whether the chart belongs to present method or proposed method and also indicates, whether the chart is drafted for showing movements of material or man.

(e) Below the above information, write a brief description of the job. For example, *packing the pencils in a carton.*

(f) Below the description of the job, we have to give, information regarding where the job begins and where it ends. For example, *Job begins: Operator switch on the machine.*

Job Ends: Operator put the finished job aside.

The above statement tells us that the study is conducted between the above two events.

(g) Just below the 'Job ends' statement, it is better we present the layout of the workstation.

(h) Then draw the actual chart or diagram.

(i) At the end of the chart, a summary of the study along with the date of study and name of the person who conducted the study is to be presented.

The general information to be given on the chart is shown below.

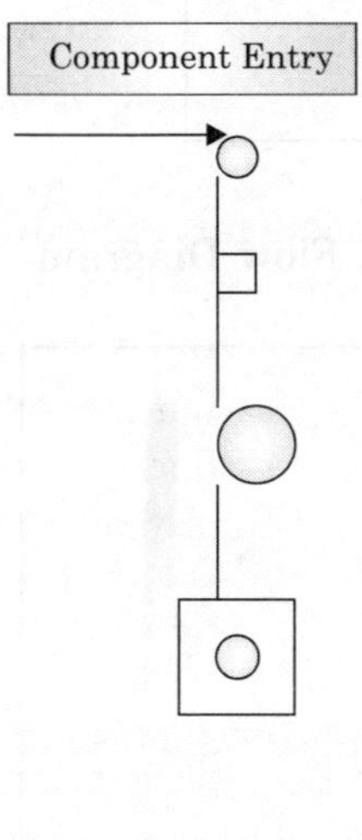

Fig. 3.7. Out Line Process Chart.

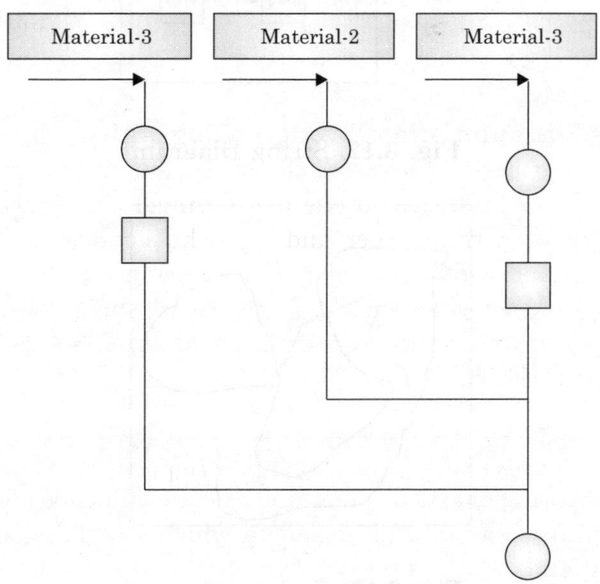

Fig. 3.8. Flow Process Chart.

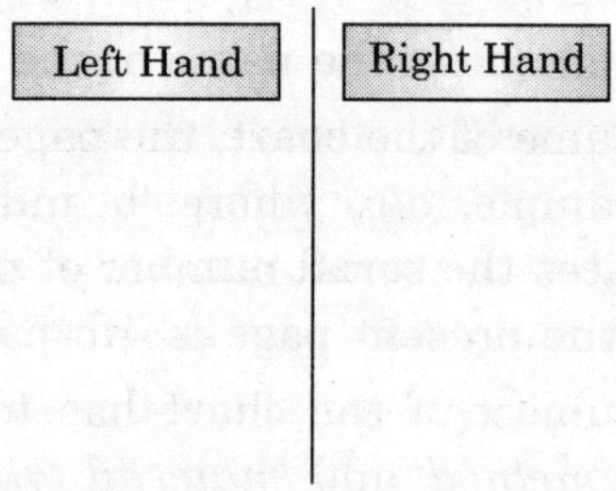

Fig. 3.9. Two Hand Process Chart.

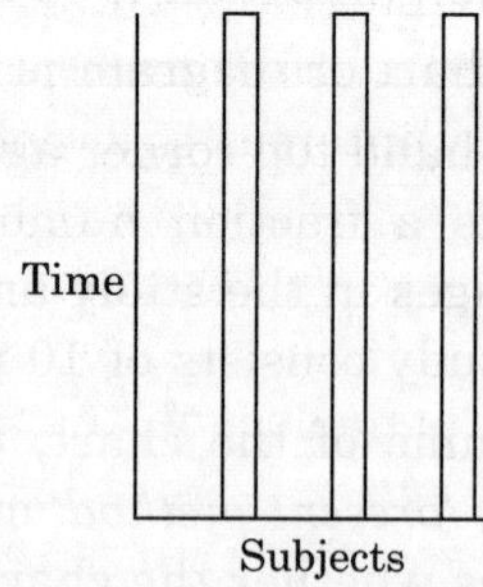

Fig. 3.10. Multiple Activity Chart.

LEFT HAND			FRAME NUMBER	RIGHT HAND		
DESCRIPTION	TIME	THERBLIG		THERBLIG	TIME	DESCRIPTION

Fig. 3.11. Simultaneous Motion Chart (SIMO Chart)

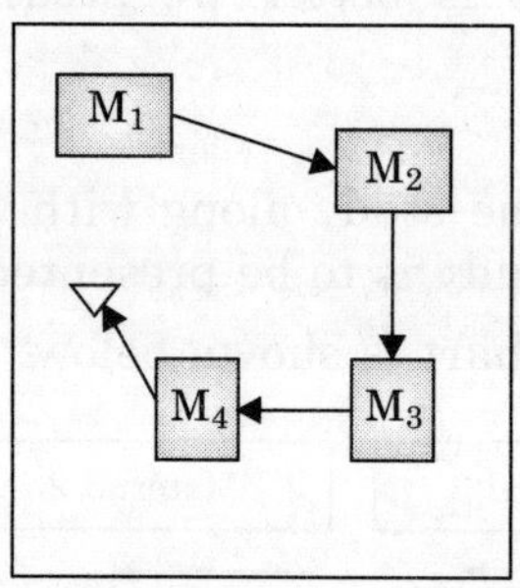

Fig. 3.12. String Diagram

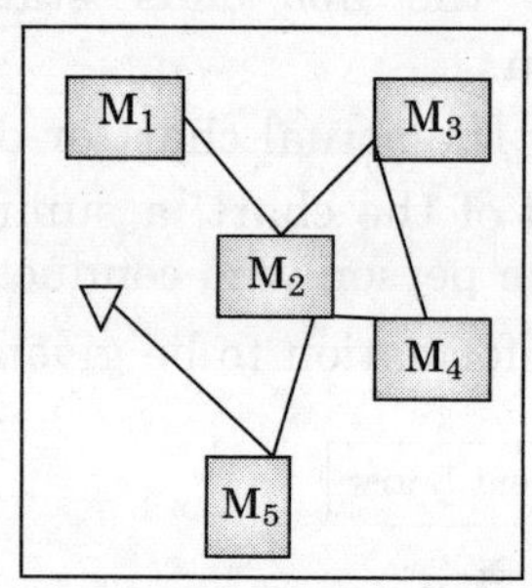

Fig. 3.13. Flow Diagram

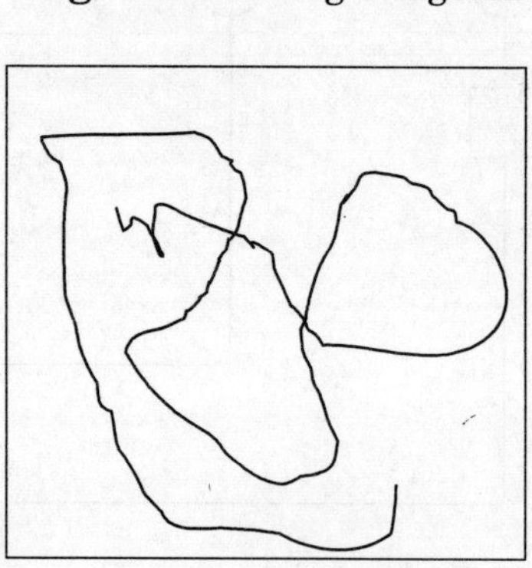

Fig. 3.14. Cyclograph

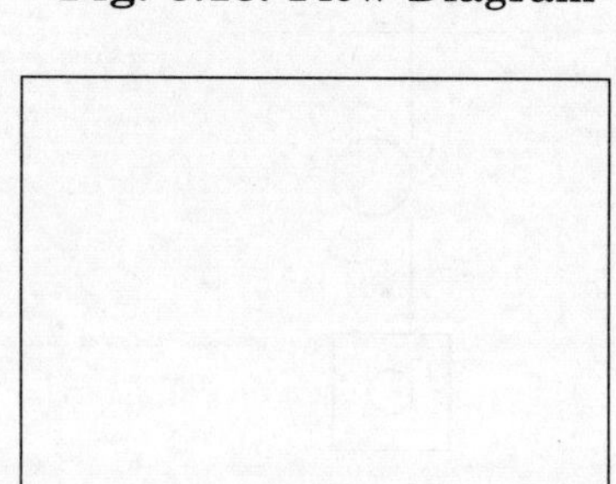

Fig. 3.15 Chrono-cyclograph

While constructing a chart, an arrow is to be shown at the top indicating the entry of the first material and a brief description of material is to be given above the arrow. The other particulars are entered, say, operation, movement, storage, inspection etc., as they occur by means of symbols and the description of the event and for movement the distance, if any has to be entered on the right hand side. When we are showing the assembly of a component the first material is entered on the left hand side with particulars as mentioned above and the next component to the right of the first component and so on. The following figures show the various means of showing assembly disassembly, repetition of operation etc. All facts, which are entered, should be numbered in the order as they exist.

1. Method of writing a chart. Fig. 3.16

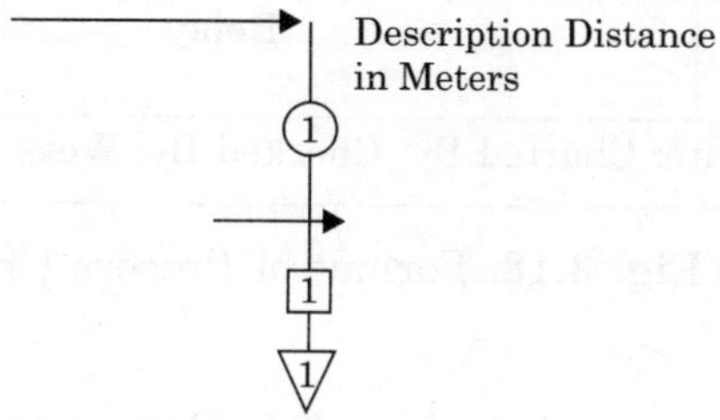

Fig. 3.16. Method of Writing a Chart

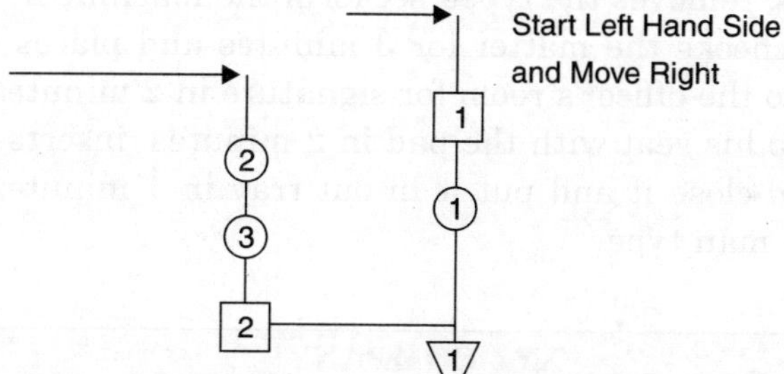

Fig. 3.17. Process Chart Showing the Assembly of Components.

XYZ COMPANY, ABC CITY
Name of the Chart: FLOE PROCESS CHART. **Page No.: a/b**
Method: Present Method / Proposed Method.
Type: Man type / Material type / Machine type.

Job:

Job begins:
Job ends:

WORK STATION
Layout

CHART OR DIAGRAM

SUMMARY

S. No.	Symbol	Description	Present Method	Proposed Method	Savings
1.	○	Operation			
2.	→	Transport			
3.	□	Inspection			
4.	▽	Storage			
5.	D	Delay			
6.	Date: Charted By: Checked By: Work-study Manager				

Fig. 3.18. Format of Process Chart

Problem 3.1:

A steno typist waiting for dictation from his officer leaves to his officer's room, which is 5 meters away in 2 minutes, takes dictation for 3 minutes, returns to his seat in 2 minutes. He prepares typing set for 2 minutes and inserts it in the machine in 2 minutes and types the letter for 10 minutes, removes the typed set form the machine in 1 minute, separates the copies in two minutes, checks the matter for 3 minutes and places the set on the pad in 1 minute. Takes the pad to the officer's room for signature in 2 minutes, wait for the signature for 3 minutes, returns to his seat with the pad in 2 minutes, inserts the original copy in the envelop in 1 minute and close it and put it in out tray in 1 minute. Write the flow process chart of the problem for man type.

Solution:

XYZ COMPANY
Flow Process Chart / Material Type / Present Method
Job: Writing a letter using a Steno Typist
Chart Begins: Contents awaiting dictation by author
Chart Ends: Contents of letter to out tray

Chat	Description	Distance in Mts	Times in Minutes
→			
○	1 Dictation		3
→	1 To typist	5	2
○	2 Type		10

(Contd....)

XYZ COMPANY
Flow Process Chart / Material Type / Present Method
Job: Writing a letter using a Steno Typist
Chart Begins: Contents awaiting dictation by author
Chart Ends: Contents of letter to out tray

	2	To typist	–	–
	1	Check		3
	3	To officer	5	2
	1	Wait for signature		3
	4	To typist	5	2
	3	In envelope		1
	4	Out tray		0.5

Fig. 3.19. The Chart for Problem 2.1

Summary:

S. No.	Symbol	Description	Present Method	Proposed Method	Savings
1.		Operation	4		
2.		Transport	4		
3.		Inspection	1		
4.		Storage	--		
5.		Delay	1		
6.	Dt.: Manager:	Checked By:		Checked By:	W/S

Summary for the above chart.

3.19. CRITICAL EXAMINATION

Critical examination stage is a very important stage in method study. During critical examination stage, all the recorded facts are critically examined by asking a set of questions to develop an improved method of doing work. A group of work-study experts sit together, and subject each event of the record to a set of **primary** and a set of **secondary** questions to find alternative ways of doing the subject under examination. While doing so, they must avoid any hasty judgment. Any hint for improvement must be committed in writing for future investigation. And new method should not even be considered until all the undesirable features of the existing method have been exposed by systematic examination. The objective of critical examination is to determine the true reasons underlying each event and to draw up a systematic list of all possible improvement for later development into a new and improved method.

3.19.1. Examination Procedure

Two sets of questions are asked. First, **the primary set of questions** to indicate the facts and reasons underlying the subject examined, and the **secondary set of questions** to indicate alternatives and consequently the means of improvement. The questions are asked under five headings, which examines the purpose of operation or event, place where it is done, person by whom it is done, the sequence in which it is carried out and the means by which the operation is carried out.

3.19.2. Primary Questions

(i) ***Purpose***: The question *what is achieved?* And *is it necessary?* And *Why?* is asked to challenge the existence of the action. The answer will guide us to remove this operation or to improve the operation or to include this as it is in the proposed method or to combine the operation with any other event.

(ii) ***Place***: The questions are, *Where is it done? And why there?* These questions help us to find alternate place for the work to have a better environment or to have a better layout.

(iii) ***Sequence***: *When is it done? And why there?* Questions are asked regarding the sequence of operation with reference to other operations would enable us to develop a better sequence of carrying out the operation or combining the operation with some other operation.

(iv) ***Person***: The question refers to the person performing the activity. *Who does it? And why that person?* These questions will help us to know why a particular person is chosen for the work.

(v) ***Means***: Finally the means of carrying out the activity is challenged by asking *How is it done? And why that way?*

3.19.3. Secondary Questions

The secondary questions seek to establish suitable alternatives to existing or previously proposed method. While doing so, we may get many numbers of alternatives. To select the particular alternative, once again a third question is asked. The questions are:

1. ***Purpose***: *What else could be done? And what should be done?*
2. ***Place***: *Where else could it have to be done? And where should it have to be done?*
3. ***Sequence***: *When else could it be done? And when it should be done?*
4. ***Person***: *Who else could do it? And who should do it?*
5. ***Means***: *How else could it be done? And how it should be done?*

The answers to these questions indicate the lines along with a new method for the overall process should be developed. A further examination of proposed alternative may give us a better way of doing work. These questions may be tabulated as under for better understanding.

Table 3.4. Showing Questions of Critical Examination

Description of the element:..

S. No.	Present Facts (Primary questions)	Secondary Questions	Alternatives
1.	**PURPOSE:** What is achieved? Is it necessary : Yes / No.	What else could be done?	What?
2.	**PLACE**: Where is it done? Why there?	Where else could it have to be done?	Where?
3.	**SEQUENCE:** When is it done? Why then?	Where else could it be done?	When?
4.	**PERSON:** Who does it? Why that person?	Who else could do it?	Who?
5.	**MEANS:** How is it done? Why that way?	How else could it be done?	How?

3.20. DEVELOP THE NEW METHOD

During critical examination, some of the operations or events might have been eliminated or combined or improved. These changes form the basis of proposed method. Before finalizing the proposed method certain factors regarding working environment and working conditions of workers are to be given due consideration to have a comfortable and economical working conditions. Present – day trend is to adopt man's working environment to his needs and capabilities. This led to the study of man at work and his needs at workstation for comfortable working, and is given the name – **Human engineering or Ergonomics.** Ergonomics is the study of relations between man and his occupation, equipment and environment and particularly, the application of anatomical, physiological and psychological knowledge to the problem arising there from. Other factors have considered to design the comfortable workstation are sight and lighting, colour contrast, ventilation and heating, noise, seating and amenities.

As far as the sight and lighting are concerned, the work place must be provided with suitable lighting, preferably natural lighting and the work should not cause strain to the eyes of the person working. The actual place of working should be within the normal visual range. When man is working with the material, within the normal visual range, the eyes will at rest when looking, otherwise eye muscles get strained. Colour is generally used to improve or increase contrast or can be used as codes to indicate different items. Colour can also be used to give a sense of pleasure and well-being to the employees of a particular department.

The ventilation and temperature directly affects health and comfort of employees. Therefore, proper care should be taken to see that good ventilation and comfortable temperature are maintained so that the workers are self-motivated to work. Good ventilation will also minimize the risk of infection among the people working together. Any production process producing heavy noise should be isolated, so that it will not cause damage to the ears of other workers. The workers working on machines, producing noise should be provided with earplugs or provisions may be made to damp the noise. Properly designed seating is also an important factor in increasing the efficiency of the worker. Amenities like safety of personal belongings, good toilet facilities, and canteen, drinking water, and transport facility must be provided.

Improvement of plant and workplace layout, material used, design specifications of end product, process used, materials handling, work environment should be given due consideration while working for an improved method. Another factor to be considered is the motion of hand at the workplace. This enables one to design a better workstation layout. It is recognized that there are certain basic movements of hand, which will ease the working procedure. These are known as **characteristics of easy movement or principles of motion economy.** Before discussing the principles of motion economy, let us see how the movement of body is classified. Gilbreth gives this classification. They are:

Table 3.5: Showing Class of Movements

S. No.	Class of Movements	Description of Movements
1.	I	Fingers only.
2.	II	Fingers and Wrist.
3.	III	Fingers, Wrist and Lower arm.
4.	IV	Fingers, Wrist, Lower arm and Upper arm.
5.	V	Fingers, Wrist, Lower arm, Upper arm and Shoulder.

There are six basic principles of motion economy. They are:

1. **Principle of minimum movement:** This principle states that, tools, materials and equipment should be positioned so that the worker can use them with minimum movement of his hand. At the same time ensure that the movement classification used is to the lowest practicable group in the circumstances. If the distance moved is to be kept to a minimum, knowledge of working areas is required. When worker seated at his workstation there is an area in front of him, which can be called his normal working area in the horizontal plane and is bound by the arcs drawn by his right and left hands with the lower arms pivoted from the elbows, which are held naturally by the side of the body. If the tools used by the worker are kept in the normal working area then least movement is required to reach the tools by the worker. Where all the tools used by the worker cannot be located in normal working area, and then they should be placed in maximum working area. The maximum working area is the area covered by the arcs drawn by the right and left hands, with the arms pivoting from the shoulders. Objects placed in the normal working area may require class I type of movement and those placed in maximum working area requires class III and IV type movements. Application of this principle of minimum movement has resulted in the use of semi-circular workplaces. When considering layouts of workplaces, it is obvious that movements will be kept at a minimum if the most frequently used equipment/ tool is nearest to hand. In vertical plane, the minimum and maximum working areas can be found by the arcs drawn with hand hinged at the elbows and at the shoulder.

2. **and 3. Principles of simultaneous and symmetrical movements:** These two principles are considered together, which suggest that the movement of the arm and hands should be balanced by being simultaneous and/or symmetrical. The anatomy of human beings is such that if movements are unbalanced, excessive fatigue is caused. Perhaps you might have experienced that it is very difficult to walk with different loads in two hands than with equal load in both hands. Also it is very easy to move hand in the hand in the form of an arc than in the form of a right angle. Example for symmetrical movement is one feels it is difficult to write a square with right hand and a circle with left hand. It is easy to move both hands simultaneously in the form of the movement of one hand is the mirror image of the other.
3. **Natural Movement:** The principle requires that the movements used should be those, which can be performed most naturally by the body. The application of the principle includes the use of other organs like limbs, fingers etc., so that the workload is spread over those parts of the body best fitted to the work. This principle also concerned with the correct use of muscles and posture when lifting the weight.
4. **Rhythmical Movement:** This principle states that the **rhythm** should be present in movements. Rhythm may be described as the regular repetition of a movement pattern. When rhythm is established, hesitations are eliminated and movements are carried out at higher speeds with less fatigue.
5. **Habitual Movements:** This principle states that the movement pattern should be arranged so that it becomes habitual. Human beings possess a natural ability to form habits. When a set of movements performed habitually, less fatigue is caused and the movements are carried out almost in a relaxed mood.
6. **Continuous Movements:** Always smooth and continuous movements are preferable, as they cause less fatigue and inconvenience to the worker than movements involving sharp changes in direction. This is because, before hand changes its direction it must slow down and stop and subsequently accelerate again to its normal pace. Smooth and continuous movements employ natural momentum and do not involve muscular strain.

In considering the characteristics of easy movements, the field of visions an important factor, which is all too frequently ignored. Where inspection work is involved it must take place within the field of vision of the worker. Once, the improved method is decided with all the changes and improvements, the chart are constructed and now it is ready to submit it to the management with report.

Submit the proposed method to the management

Once the improved method has been developed with the help of specialists in the department and other technical personnel, a report of the proposed method has to be presented to the top management. The report must consist of the following headings in its summary.

(a) Recommendations
(b) Reasons for recommendations, and
(c) Results expected from the recommendations. The detailed report must consist of the following titles:

1. Summary,
2. Summary of recommendations,
3. Introduction,
4. Acknowledgements,
5. Description of the existing situation and its drawbacks,
6. The work-study approach to the present situation,
7. Extraction and evaluation of relevant factors,
8. Recommendations,
9. Implication for management.

3.21. INSTALL AND MAINTAIN

To install the new method, first thing is to get co-operation of every person concerned with the job and then educate them about the benefits of the improved method and train them to accustom to new movements (better to have as many as demonstrations desired). Once it is evident that everybody is following the new method, it is put into practice.

NOTE: Therbligs are symbols used in method study, especially in micro motion study.

Some of the symbols used are given below for reference.

S. No.	Therblig	Symbol	Letter Code
1.	Search		Sh
2.	Found		Fd
3.	Assemble		A
4.	Transport empty		TE
5.	Transport loaded or Hold		TL
6.	Unload		UL
7.	Thinking		T
8.	Sitting Idle		St
9.	Dissemble		DA

Fig. 3.20. Therbligs

WORK MEASUREMENT (TIME STUDY)

3.22. INTRODUCTION

In order to keep up the delivery promises, the plan and schedules prepared for human work must be perfect. The usual practice is to prepare plans by previous experience. But sometimes, planning by previous experience may put the manager in difficulty. In case the manager has an idea about the amount of work involved and time required to complete the job, his plans are workable and he will be in a better position to meet the delivery promises. Work measurement or time study is a technique or a tool by which a manager can set times required to carry out the required work and set time targets by taking into account all the allowances required by the worker while doing work. By definition **work measurement is the application of techniques designed to establish the time or a qualified worker to carry out a specified job at a defined level of performance.** In fact, work measurement is a prerequisite to method study. It is because, without knowing the time required to do the work, there is no meaning in saying a particular method is a right method of doing work.

3.23. OBJECTIVES OF WORK MEASUREMENT

The objectives of fixing the target times for works by the application of work measurement are:

It assists in:

1. Comparing the methods desired by method studies of doing a particular work and selects the best method.
2. To allocate the labours to the jobs in proportion to the work involved having a proper balance of the labour on the job.
3. In the preparation of realistic incentive scheme.
4. In the organization of labour by comparing the actual time taken and the targeted time for doing the work.
5. In the preparation of labour budget and control the same.
6. In preparing the estimates for present and future work.

3.24. WORK MEASUREMENT TECHNIQUES

The work under question may repetitive type or non-repetitive type. In repetitive operations, the element of operation will repeat many times during the study. In non-repetitive works, work cycle is hardly repeated; the examples of such work are maintenance work and construction work. Depending on the type of work, i.e. repetitive or non-repetitive proper method of work measurement is selected. Basically, there are eight methods of work measurement. They are:

1. Stop watch time study,
2. Synthesis,
3. Predetermined Motion Time Systems (PMTS),
4. Analytical estimating,
5. Comparative estimating,
6. Estimating,
7. Activity sampling, and
8. Rated activity sampling.

Before going to deal with the actual methods of work measurement, let us try to understand some of the terms we come across very frequently during the study.

3.25. RATE OF WORKING

If you observe a worker doing a work, you notice that sometimes he works faster and sometimes he works very slowly or if you observe a group of workers, doing some work, you see that some of them working faster and some of them very slowly. This may be due to various reasons. But our interest here is **the actual time taken to do a job depends on the rate of working maintained by the individual concerned.** To facilitate the calculation, work measurement values, unless otherwise stated, are always related to what is termed as **standard performance.** Standard performance mans optimum rate of output that can be achieved by a **qualified worker** on an average for the shift or working day, due allowances being made for the necessary time required for rest. A qualified worker is one who is physically and mentally suited to the job given to him and having necessary qualification, skill and knowledge to carry out the work efficiently.

3.26. THE UNIT OF WORK

In order to represent human work content of various jobs of different types on a common time scale the unit of work is used. In this unit of work provision is made both for the effort required to do work and the allowances required related to the concept of **standard rate of working.** When expressed in units of work the work content of any job should be related to its most suitable characteristic for planning, control, costing, payment and other purposes and in this form it may be compared with other jobs on a quantitative basis. Let us consider for example, three persons working on three different jobs. Mr. A is sitting in an air-conditioned office and involved in decision-making work. Mr. B is involved in some clerical work and sitting in a room with moderate comfort. Mr. C, who is working in hot sun, whose work needs physical exercise. If we consider one unit of work of all the above three persons, they appear as shown in the figure.

A unit of work consists partly of effort and partly of rest, the proportion of rest varying with the nature of the job. Units of work for light, medium and heavy jobs having relaxation allowances of 10 percent, 20 percent and 30 percent respectively. Regarding the dimension of unit of work at standard performance is one minute, which is known as **standard minute** or simply **SM**. Therefore, on SM = 1/60th of an hour. In addition other dimensions are also used such as 80 and 133 units of work per hour at standard performance. Here, SM is unit of quantity and not of time. That means it measures the quantity of human work in a job. SM may be converted into time if the rate of performance is known.

3.27. STEPS IN WORK MEASUREMENT (TIME STUDY) OR PROCEDURE FOR CONDUCTING WORK MEASUREMENT

1. Break the job into recognizable pieces, known as **elements**, whose size should be convenient to measure the time by the method selected.
2. Measure the time by stopwatch. To get the accurate results, the time is measured convenient number of times and the average is worked out. This time is known as **observed time.**

   Observed time $= t_1 + t_2 + t_3 + \ldots\ldots\ldots\ldots\ldots + t_{10}/10 = t_0$

3. The time required to carry out these elements at the standard rate of performance is measured by some means and this time is known as **basic time for the element.**

Basic time or Normal time = (Observed time × Observed rating) / Standard rating.

Standard rating is taken as 100 unless it is given as something else.

Mr. A (Officer sitting in A.C. Room)

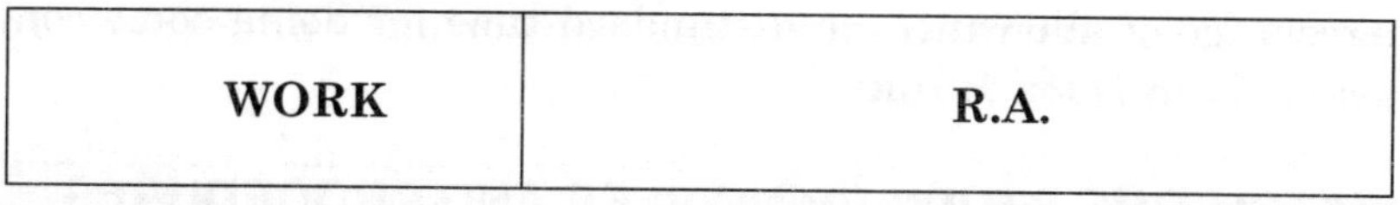

Note: R.A = Relaxation

Mr. B (Clerk sitting in room with moderate comfort). Allowance.

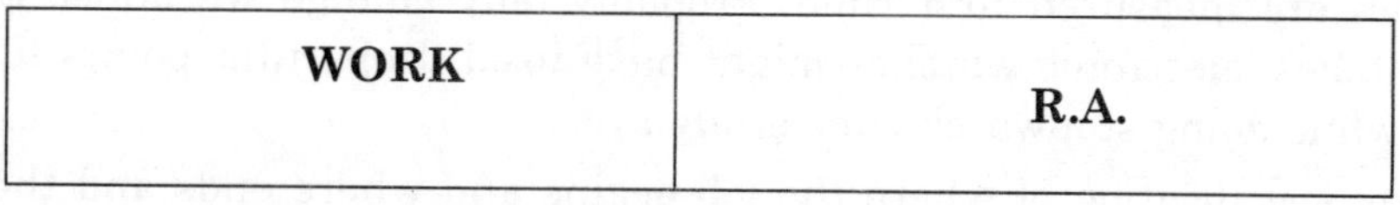

Mr. C (Worker working in hot sun)

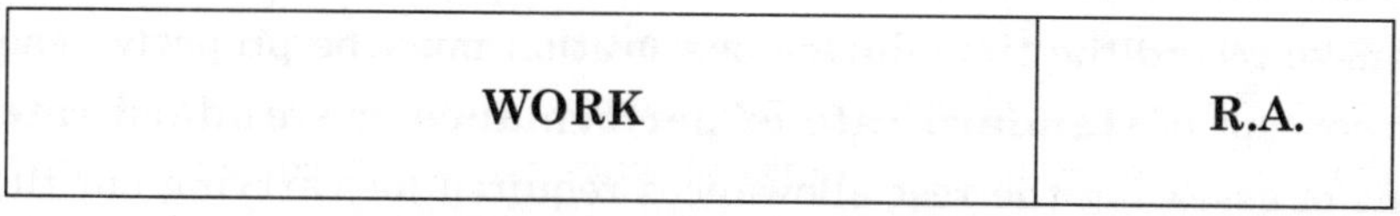

One unit of work

Fig. 3.21. One Unit of Work

Basic time or Normal time = (Observed time × Observed rating) / Standard rating.

Standard rating is taken as 100 unless it is given as something else.

4. Percentage of basic time is added to the basic time individually or for the work as a whole, as the case may be to allow for recovery from the effort induced by doing the work. This is generally known as relaxation allowance. When added we get what is known as **standard time.** This is the quantity of human work in the job expressed in terms of **standard minutes.**

Many a time the work measurement team may find it is not appropriate to use the same method of time measurement to all the elements and also they may notice that there may be some common elements, whose work content may be same. In such cases, they may build-up time from various technique available. In practice the following steps are followed:

1. The job is broken down into its measurable and recognizable elements.
2. For elements involving human work, the records for basic time are consulted for getting basic time for the element.
3. For those elements for which there is no basic time already available, the time is measured by appropriate technique, for example stopwatch time study.
4. In case it is seen that the element, whose time is measured, reoccurs in some other job, the element's time is added to the records of basic time for future reference.

5. The rest allowances are taken from the table and the required parentage of time is added to the time calculated in step (3) above, to arrive at the time for doing the work at standard rate of performance.
6. In addition, any relaxation allowance is deserved; they may be added as a percentage to this time.

Required percentage of allowances and standard time for doing some common elements of a work are available in **Data Banks.**

3.28. STOPWATCH TIME STUDY PRINCIPLES AND PROCEDURES

Measuring time by using stopwatch is good old method and is adapted to measure time for elements, which are measured first time. Probably only change we notice that instead of mechanical watches, electronic watches might have used. Important points to be taken into consideration while doing stopwatch time study are:

(i) Accurate specification of where the job begins and where ends and the method used to carry out the element,

(ii) A system to record the time during observation must be properly designed.

(iii) A clear concept of **standard rate of performance** or **standard rate of working.**

(iv) A means of assessing the rest allowances required for carrying out the elements.

3.28.1. Time Scales and Stopwatches

In the stopwatches used in time study, one hour is divided into 100 equal parts. Also a minute and a second are also divided into 100 equal parts. Each part is known as **centiminute (CM) and centisecond (CS)** respectively. The hour is known as **Centihour (CH).** The stopwatch dial is divided into 100 parts to enable the observer to note down the time in centiminutes. These watches are known as **Decimal minute watches or Decimal hour stopwatches.** In decimal hour stopwatches, the sweep hand makes 100 revolutions per hour or one in every 36 seconds of conventional watches. One hundredths of an hour can be described as a **decimal hour unit** and abbreviated as **CH**. The figure shows the decimal hour watch.

3.28.2. Standard Rate of Working

The time observed and noted is known as **observed time.** The time study men must assess the rate at which the worker is working. He must have enough experience to assess the rate of working. Generally, he compares the work of the worker with a man walking at a speed 6 miles per hour. A man can walk six miles per hour without much strain and effort. Suppose, he rates the speed of a man walking at 6 miles per hour as 100 and compares the speed of the worker and rates 80, it means that the worker's speed is below the standard performance. In case he rates it as 120, then the rate of performance of the worker is above the normal performance. Generally rating scale of 0 – 100 is used. The observer must note the time as well as rate at which worker is performing the element/job simultaneously. There are different rate of scales available, such as 0 to 100, 0 to 80 and 0 to 133 and 0.00 to 1.00. But 0 to 100 scales are commonly used.

Fig. 3.22. Showing Decimal Hour Stopwatch

3.28.3. To Break the Task into Elements

The work measurement man may notice that the rate of working of a worker will be varying for the same element in each cycle. Hence, it will be very difficult for him to find the time required to perform the element. Generally, while dividing any job into elements, it is customary to see that the element is of short time and may be in the range of 10 to 50 centiminutes (6 to 30 seconds on conventional time). The following principles are observed to divide the job into elements:

1. Element should be clearly distinguishable and it should be of the size that it takes not more than 10 to 50 centiminutes.
2. Separate elements, which are identical from those, which are variable in the work they comprise.
3. Separate heavy work (element) from light work (element).
4. When convenient, use audible points in the work, such as the snap of a switch or the sound of an article dropping into a container, as element break point.

When we have some elements taking more than half a minute, or longer than 50 centiminutes, and no break point are available, then break point are arbitrarily made every half minute and the rating recorded. The rating for the whole element will be the weighted average of the rating for the portions of the element. Such elements are known as **long-cycle repetitive elements.** In some cases, we may come across certain elements, whose total time may be less than 10 centiminutes. In such cases, time of a number of cycles of exactly similar elements occurring in succession is taken and an overall rating is made. The observed time for one of the cycles or elements can then be obtained by dividing this overall time by the number of elements observed. Or the element is observed in isolation, without including it in main study and the time is recorded. Such elements are known as **short-cycle repetitive elements.**

3.28.4. Rating and Basic Times

Once the observer does the rating of the element, the observed time can be converted into **basic time.** Basic time is one which would have been by had the work been done at the standard rate of performance, i.e. at 100 rate, without any relaxation allowance being taken.

$$\text{Basic time} = \frac{[(\text{Observed time}) \times (\text{Observed rating})]}{\text{Standard rating}}$$

(Here standard rating is taken as 100).

For example, if the observed time is 10 centiminutes, and the observed rating is 80, then the basic time is given by:

(10 × 80)/100 = 8 centiminutes.

If the observed time is 10 centiminutes, and the observed rating is 120, then the basic time is = (10 × 120)/100 = 12 CM.

In the first case the worker has taken 10 CM for an element, which needs only 8 CM i.e. the rate of performance is slow. In the second case the worker has taken 10 CM for an element, which needs 12 CM that is the rate of performance is fast. It is appropriate to fix up most desirable motion pattern and train worker in that pattern and observe the time and rate of performance. For satisfactory rating the following condition must be satisfied.

(i) There must be ample supply of work to be available.

(ii) Rating should not be influenced by restrictions imposed by the nature of the work,

(iii) While rating, one must see that the required quality specifications are met with.

However, there are certain factors, which affect the rating, some of them may be out of control of the worker and some of them may be controlled.

3.28.5. Factors Affecting Rating

The time taken to do a job depends on various factors, such as conditions of the machine environment conditions, attitude of the worker, quality of the material supplied etc. Depending on the conditions stated above the performance rate will differ. In addition to the above, effectiveness of a man's work is affected by certain controllable factors and certain uncontrollable factors. Some of them are:

1. Variations in quality or specification of the material used,
2. Changes in operating efficiency of tools and/or equipment,
3. Minor changes in methods, and
4. Variation in mental attention necessary for the job.

All these will influence the rate of working. These are outside the control of the worker. Factors like alteration in the quality within the specification given, worker's skill and attitude of worker's mind affect the rate of doing work. These are under the control of the worker. The speed at which the worker works will depend on the effort demanded by the job and the care required on the part of the worker while doing the work.

3.29. TIME STUDY PROCEDURE

All the workers, whose work is affected by the time study, is informed regarding the purpose of time study and the advantages of time study well in advance to get their co-operation during the study. Permission from the management also sought. The time study man must go round the shop and have acquaintance with the workers. Better the management personnel accompany the time study man. After having introduced himself to all concerned workers, he has to plan regarding the breakdown of job into elements, element breakdown points and establishing synthetic data both for cycle and element times.

3.29.1. Tools of Time Study

(a) **Stopwatch:** There are two types of stopwatches used for time study in general. In one of the type the winding knob returns both hands to zero when pressed and immediately pressure is released, the watch restarts. It can be made to stop completely by means of a slide alongside the winder, which halts the hands at the position they were in, at the moment of bringing the slide into action. This type of watch is known as **fly back stopwatch.** It must be checked now and then for its accuracy. This type of watch is always clipped to the time study board and after the use watch is allowed to run down to releases the pressure of the spring. Another type of watch is **continuous type stopwatch.** In this watch, the time is recorded continuously. If we press the knob, the watch handle stops at the point where it is. The second pressing takes the handle to zero. The recording on this watch is known as a **cumulative time record.**

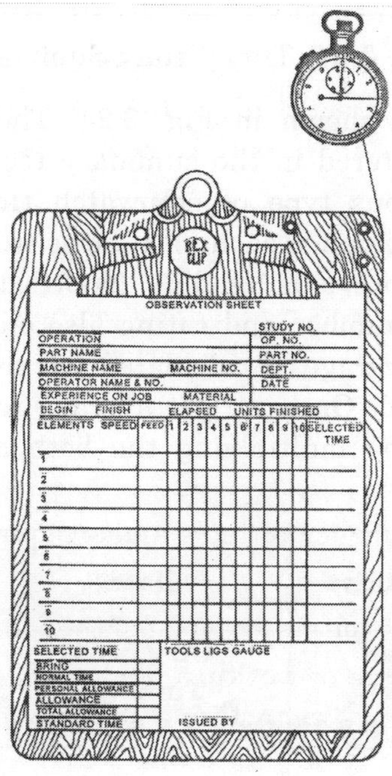

Fig. 3.23. Stop Watch and Observation Sheet on a Clip Board

(b) **Time Study Board:** The study board is used to hold recording sheets and a clip to hold the watch. The board is designed well to size and shape, so that it is convenient to hold in the hand while taking reading. A specimen record sheet is shown in the figure.

STUDY SUMMARY RECORD				
Study reference:				
Time study:	Work:	Page No.		
Production study:	Department:	Date:		
Location:	Taken at:	Labour classification:		
Time clerk:	Operation description:..			
Started time:	Finished time:	Elapsed time:	Total recorded time:	Error:
Materials:	Machine:	Quality:	Quantity:	

S. No.	Element Description	Number of Occasions	Basic Time	Relaxation factors A B C D E F G H	Total

Fig. 3.24. Time Study Summary Sheet

Time study record sheet is shown in Fig. 3.24. The basic time and average rating calculated from this sheet is entered in the summary record sheet shown in figure. Using fly back stopwatch or continuous type of stopwatch time may be recorded. If we use cumulative type recording, the time for each element is worked out by taking the difference between current reading and previous reading (subtract the previous reading from the current reading). The element number and rating also entered. For each element, number of readings is taken and the average is calculated for getting **observed time.** Similarly, average rating is also calculated. Once we get average rating and average observed time, the **basic time** is calculated by multiplying the both and dividing the product by the standard rating (=100).

Observation Record (Time Study)			Date	Study Reference		Page
S. No.	Element Description	Observed Time (x) 1 2 3 4 5 6 7 8 9 10	Observed Time (y) 1 2 3 4 5 6 7 8 9 10	Observed Rating	Average Observed Time	Average Time

Fig. 3.25. Observation Record for Time Study

Once the study is over the stopwatch is left running until it is compared with the clock by which it was started. The procedure for calculating the basic time from the recorded time and recorded rating is known as **extension.**

$$\frac{\{(\text{Observed time}) \times (\text{Observed rating})\}}{\text{Standard rating } (= 100)} = \text{Basic Time.}$$

When the time for an element is observed, each time rating is also recorded. If we calculate basic time for each observation, we may find the basic time will vary for each reading. In such case, we can take the average of the basic times. Best way is to take the average of observed time and observed rating and calculate the basic time. There are many methods for finding the average. One such method is finding graphic average.

3.30. RELAXATION AND CONTINGENCY ALLOWANCES (RA)

After calculating the basic time, relaxation allowances and contingency allowances are to be added to basic time to get **standard time.** Relaxation allowances (RA) are added to the basic time to meet the personal needs and to recover from fatigue caused during the work. The relaxation allowances depend on the nature of work, work environment, gender and age of the worker. There are charts available showing the allowances required (which have been calculated taking all factors such as nature of work, age and sex of worker and environmental factors). Relaxation allowance is expressed as a percentage of basic time. These allowances are classified as:

Relaxation Allowances:

Table 3.6. Showing the List of Relaxation Allowances

Letter Code	Allowance for	Letter Code	Allowance for
A	Energy output	E	Personal needs
B	Posture	F	Thermal conditions
C	Motions	G	Atmospheric conditions
D	Visual fatigue	H	Other influence of environment

3.31. CALCULATION OF STANDARD TIME

Once the basic time for an element is calculated, then allowances to be added are decided depending on the nature of work and workmen and tables of relaxation allowance are referred and recommended percentage of allowances are added to find the percentage of allowances required. Then that much percentage of basic time is added to the basic time to find the **standard time** or **the work content of the element** or **the job.** Some jobs need certain contingency allowance (also expressed as percentage of basic time). These allowances are added to take care of number of minor activities, which may be so spasmodic or infrequent that work measurement cannot be done economically. To get the standard time contingency allowances is also added to the basic time. **The total sum of basic time, relaxation allowances and contingency allowance will give the standard time or the work content of the element or the job.**

Problem: 3.2

In one of the operations, the following elemental times were observed with corresponding ratings. Give 10 percent relaxation allowance and 5 percent contingency allowance. Calculate the standard time for the operation and find out the weekly production, assuming 8 hour per day and 6 days a week. The required data is given below.

Element Number	Element Description	Average Observed Time in Minutes	Average Rating
1	Pick up gasket and element.	0.25	120
2	Pick up gasket and apply adhesive to it and keep it on the conveyor.	0.15	90
3	Pick up element and apply adhesive to it and keep it on the table.	0.15	90
4	Drying.	1.00	----
5	Pick up gasket and element, fix them together and place in bin.	0.10	110

Solution:

Element Number	Average Observed Time in Minutes	Average Rating	(Observed Time x Observed Rating) Standard Rating
1	0.25	120	(0.25 × 120) / 100 = 0.300
2	0.15	90	(0.15 × 90) / 100 = 0.135
3	0.15	90	(0.15 × 90) / 100 = 0.135
4	1.00	----	= 1.000
5	0.10	110	(0.10 × 110) / 100 = 0.110
6	**Total Time**	-------	**1.680**

Relaxation allowance = 10% of basic time = 1.680 × 0.1 = 0.168

Contingency allowance = 5% of basic time = 1.680 × 0.05 = 0.084

Total allowance = 0.168 + 0.084 = 0. 252 minutes.

Therefore **work content or standard time = 1.680 + 0.252 = 1.932 minutes.**

Total number of hours in a week = 6 days × 8 hours = **48 hours.**

This is equal to 48 × 100 = 4800 centiminutes.

Output for 48 hours = 4800/1.932 = **2484.47** Approximately = **2485 units.**

Problem: 3.3

A summary of a time study taken by you on the assembly of three terminal blocks with two screws each to a chassis gives the following result:

S. No.	Description of the Element	Normal Time in Minutes	Frequency
1.	Pick up 4 kg. chassis and place on table and position	0.10	1
2.	Pick up and align one terminal on chassis	0.20	3
3.	Pick up two screws and fix terminal by hand	0.40	3
4.	Pick up tool and position on screws	0.10	1
5.	Tighten screws	0.10	6
6.	Reposition tool on next screw	0.05	5
7.	Aside tool	0.05	1
8.	Aside chassis (4 kg.)	0.10	1

The company works on 8-hours shift, which includes two tea breaks of 15 minutes each and half hour lunch time. Working conditions in the factory are good. Establish the standard time for this operation giving appropriate allowances as applicable. Show the breakdown of the allowances given by you.

Solution:

S. No.	Normal Time	Freq-uency	Total Normal Time	Allowances			Total %	Allow-ances	Standard Time
				Posture	Motion	Energy			
1.	0.1	1	0.1	0.05	0.05	0.05	0.15	0.015	0.115
2.	0.2	3	0.6	0.04	0.04	0.04	0.12	0.072	0.672
3.	0.4	3	1.2	0.03	0.03	0.04	0.10	0.120	1.320
4.	0.1	1	0.1	0.03	0.03	0.04	0.10	0.010	0.110
5.	0.1	6	0.6	0.04	0.04	0.04	0.12	0.072	0.672
6.	0.05	5	0.25	0.03	0.03	0.04	0.10	0.025	0.275
7.	0.05	1	0.05	0.03	0.03	0.04	0.10	0.005	0.055
8.	0.10	1	0.10	0.04	0.04	0.04	0.12	0.012	0.112
9.				TOTAL					**3.331**

Add 5% Contingency allowance = 0.05 × 3.331 = 0.16655

Total time = Standard time = 3.331 + 0.16655

= 3.49755 minutes. Say approximately 3.5 minutes.

Total time available = 8 hours – 30 minutes

= 7 hours 30 minutes. This is equal to 700 + 50 centiminutes.

Hence productivity = 750 minutes/3.5 minutes = 241.28 i.e. approximately 241 units.

3.32. SYNTHESIS FROM ELEMENTAL DATA

In production work or work of any nature, we may find some operations will be commonly appearing with other operations necessary for the work. Say for example, a worker picking up a bolt from a box and another worker picking up a machine component of same size and weight from a tray. Both operations involve picking up and the workers may use same type of hand motions. Though the works are different, the hand motions required for both will be same. It is similar to spelling of many words, wherein same letters will appear in spelling in different order but the letters remain same. In such cases, one have time data for repetitive or non-repetitive operations, it can be used for building up of time of an operation, which consists the element for which the **synthesized** time data is available. In large companies large accumulated data may be available and time for many common operations may be picked up from such accumulated data. Once the time for commonly used operations are available, other operations are subjected to time study and the total time required for the entire operation may be build up. Some organizations, may do time study on some common operations/elements and supply the basic times for the element or operations for which the necessary allowances are added depending on the situation to get the standard times. Building up of times for elements or operations in this manner is known as **synthesis from elemental data.** While measuring time for small elements if we isolate the element and measure the data it is known as **selective timing** and if we club the small element with some large element and measure the time and the time for small element is worked out by taking the difference, then it is known as **differential timing.** But the best way for getting the time for every small element is to use **predetermined motion time system (PMTS).**

3.33. PREDETERMINED MOTION TIME SYSTEM (PMTS)

In addition to synthetic data arrived at by time study of job elements, there are several system of standards based on the elementary human motions on which all human work is based. In the year 1934 a well-known system being called **work-factor** was developed. The objective of this system was to avoid human judgment in conventional stopwatch time study. The basic time values and the means of modifying the values for different classes of motion were developed through thousands of observations involving special measuring devices. In 1941, the **Methods Engineering Council** at **Pittsburgh** made some refinements in the system hitherto made public and a parallel work was done by the **Methods – Time Measurement Association (MTM).** Work factor recognizes certain basic motions, which are modified by elements of difficulty, all of which tend to make movements slower. Factors, which make motions, are weight or resistance, directional control, the need for care, change of direction and stopping a motion by manual control. Each such factor is called a **"work factor"** and modifies the basic time value. In MTM the basic motions are analyzed in greater detail and the predetermined times, therefore, need no modifications. Many companies are using this system under common label **PMTS** or **PREDETERMINED MOTION TIME SYSTEMS.** The theory behind the system is that manual work in industrial conditions can be regarded as consisting of different combinations of a relatively small number of basic motions. Since it has been demonstrated that within partial limits the time required for skilled worker to perform any one of these basic motions is constant, then by synthesis it is possible to construct patterns of basic motions for such work and to build-up time values for them.

The MTM data were obtained from studies of operations working normal industrial conditions. Accurate observations of the motions and their times were made by means of a special type of **synchronous cine-camera.** The data were based on a large sample of different type of operators, of various ages and both sexes, working in different localities. In order to bring the times for all motions to a common level, it was necessary to rate operations while the film recording is being made. This was done on each occasion by at least three trained observers who rated each job as it was being filmed. By analyzing the leveled times, isolating suitable **basic motions** and determining the importance and effect of the variables, a shortcut comprehensive table of data was constructed. There are 23 basic motions used in MTM. In conventional time study, normally the basic times will have value from 0.10 to 0.50 minutes. But in PMTS the basic times fall between 0.001 to 0.04 minutes. The data are thus of the order of milliminutes and are expressed in **time measurement units or TMUs.** One TMU is one hundred thousandth part of an hour. This way of measuring time has become very successful.

In order to improve methods research work being carried out. This work has led to what is now the **family of MTM techniques,** each with particular characteristics and suitable for different work measurement situations. These are labeled as **MTM-1, MTM-2** and **MTM-3**.

3.34. ANALYTICAL ESTIMATING

Analytical estimating is used for measuring non-repetitive work, when it has not been possible to compile sufficient data to enable basic times to be synthesized for all the elements involved. The same principle of breaking the job down into elements is observed as in other work measurement techniques, except that those elements for which times are to be estimated are of longer duration than the elements for timing and rating. The technique serves all the basic purposes of other work measurement techniques, though it is slightly less precise owing to the greater reliance on judgment. It is being satisfactorily used in engineering maintenance as well as in engineering construction; and its use is likely to be extended to many aspects of process work and other fields. When need arises, synthetic data used.

3.35. COMPARATIVE ESTIMATING

The development of analytical estimating enables work measurement to be applied to fields that had hitherto been considered inappropriate for the techniques. This technique requires specialist work-study personnel in the form of estimators to be attached permanently to the unit. An estimator may be attached with 10 to 20 workers for observation. Many a time it is very difficult to see that one estimator is permanently attached to the work-study always. To overcome this difficulty **comparative estimating** is in proactive. The term **universal maintenance standards** or **UMS** has been used for the idea in the United States. British Standards defines comparative estimating as **"A work measuring technique in which the time for a job is evaluated by comparing the work in it with the work in a series of similar jobs or bench marks, the work content of which has been measured".** The arrangement of jobs into broad bands of time is referred to as **slotting,** which reveals the basis of the technique. Each band will show the time in minutes and average work value. For each band there will be a representative selection of job whose work content falls within the range of whose work content has been measured by an appropriate technique (time study or MTM). These will be sample jobs or benchmarks of their band.

When we want to prescribe time for a new job, it is compared with the benchmark jobs and a judgment is made as to which band of jobs it most nearly compares with. It is then judged to be of this band and the appropriate work value from the band is taken as being the work value applicable. Many a times we come across people who are professionally good in some work, and ask what time it takes to complete a particular work (which is similar with the work of the man whom we consult). He by his experience compares the work referred to a similar type of work and spell out the time.

3.36. ACTIVITY SAMPLING

In certain types of work it may not be practicable to use the work measurement techniques discussed above, either to establish work contents directly or for the purpose of building up a fund of synthetic data. The type of work of this category is: large number of people working in an office, or number of workers operating different machines in a production shop. Quite often, management wants to know what is taking place in such situations in terms of the proportion of time being devoted to each type of activity. In such cases, it is better to go for a technique similar to that of **statistical quality control.** In statistical quality control, by observing the result of a small sample, it is decided whether to accept the lot or reject the lot.

In **Activity Sampling** also the work-study man go round the office/workshop and note down what exactly happens at a particular workstation when he visits. He note down whether the worker/machine is **working/idle**. He has to plan his work. First he must decide what should be the sample size. His work may take one day or number of days. Say for example, he conducts study for one day of 8 hours. He found that during 8 hours, he has collected 100 samples (working or not working).

(a) In case he observes that the worker is idle (Not working) for a period of 2 hours, the non-working time as a percentage of total time is (2/8) × 100 = 25%.

(b) Random observations made = 100. In case non-working time observations recorded as 25, then the percentage of idle time is (25/100) = 25%.

That is proportion of non-working time estimated, as a percentage of total time is 25 percent.

Accuracy of Results: It is true that results obtained by activity sampling method differ from that of continuous study. If the sample selected by observer were more, than the result would have been very nearer to that of the time given by time study. The number of random samples selected by the observer depends on the accuracy desired. **In practice, it has been found that ninety-five percent guarantees of the specified limits of accuracy (commonly known as "ninety five percent confidence limits") are acceptable for most purposes.** This means, in effect that the accuracy of the figure obtained can be guaranteed to obtain within ± L nineteen times out of twenty; L represents the limits of permitted variation stated as a percentage of total time. The number of observations (N) necessary to achieve such result is obtained by using the formula:

$$\mathbf{N = [4p\,(100 - p)]/L^2 \text{ OR } L = 2\sqrt{\{p(100 - p)\}/N}}$$

Where p is the occurrence of the specified activity expressed as a percentage of N.

As the technique requires only spot observations, it is possible to use it to study groups by visiting the individuals in sequence, recording in each case what activity of delay is occurring at the instant of observation. Activity sampling is a cheaper method of obtaining information about groups than continuous observation, since small number of observers can cover relatively large groups. The advantage of using activity sampling is that the required observations can be spread over a longer periods than would be economical when continuous studies are carried out. To find the required number of observations, let us consider about 75 per cent of the total time of a group of men or machines are devoted to various activity (p = 75), then if a satisfactory degree of accuracy would be ± 3 per cent of the total time (L = 3) with 95 per cent confidence, the required number of observations is given by:

N = (4pq)/L², Where q = (1 – p) or (100 – p), i.e. [4 × 75 (100 – 75)/3² = 833. Say approximately 850 observations.

Note: For solving problems in activity sampling, knowledge of statistics is essential. Given below are some of the formulae used from statistics while solving the problems.

In sampling process, if there are 'n' independent trials, with constant probability of success 'p', then expected number of successes = np; and the standard deviation or standard error of the number of success is

$\sqrt{\mathbf{npq}}$. where q = (1 – p). Hence mean standard deviation = $\sqrt{\mathbf{npq/n^2}} = \sqrt{\{\mathbf{p(1-p)}\}/\mathbf{n}}$.

Where p = probability of success, q = probability of failure and n = sample size.

The theory of sampling is concerned with:

(i) Estimating the properties or parameters of the population,

(ii) Assigning the limits with which the parameters of the population are expected to lie with a specified degree of confidence.

In normal distribution curve the area covered by normal curve covered by ± 1 sigma = 68.27%, Plus or minus 2 sigma = 96.45% and plus or minus 3 sigma = 99.73%. The concept of normal curve is related to assigning the limits with which the parameters of the population are expected to lie with specified degree of confidence, i.e. how much area should be covered by the chance phenomenon? Therefore, it is essential to decide the level of confidence. Generally the management as their policy matter takes this decision. Once the confidence level is decided the number of observations can be computed. For 68 per cent of confidence level, the probability is 68 per cent that the observation will present facts and 32 per cent they will not. Hence, the number of observations should be for a certain confidence level with certain degree of accuracy. Most commonly and accepted confidence of level is 95 per cent plus or minus 2 sigma limits and plus or minus 5 per cent accuracy.

Plus or minus 5 per cent accuracy can be expressed as standard error (represented by S) i.e. S = plus or minus 0.05. If 'p' is known or can be estimated with the help of past data or trial study, the number of random observations 'n' can be computed.

Example 3.4

The management is interested to know the percentage of idle time of an automatic machines section. Work sampling study was conducted assuming level of confidence 95 per cent and the accuracy of plus or minus 5 per cent. Calculate the number of observations required to obtain the desired results. In order to estimate the value of 'p', a trial study was conducted consisting of 1000 random observations. 250 observations showed that the machine was idle.

Solution:

Obviously the percentage of the idle time would be 25 per cent, i.e. p = 0.25, hence, the number of observations

$$N = [4p \times (1 - p)]/0.005 \times p^2 = [4 \times 0.25 \times 0.75]/[0.0025 \times 0.00625]$$

$$= \text{Approximately 4800 observations.}$$

(**Note:** The number of observations can also be computed with the help of alignment charts or the tables and nomograms which are prepared for 95 per cent confidence level and plus or minus 5 per cent confidence level).

If it is desired 99 per cent confidence level with plus or minus 2 per cent accuracy, the N can be obtained by changing the formula accordingly. 99 per cent confidence level is approximately 3 sigma limits, hence the formula will be:

$$S \times p = 3 \times \sqrt{[p \times (1-p)]}$$

$$= (0.02 \times p)^2$$

$$= \{9 \times p \times (1-p)\}/n$$

$$\text{OR } n = \{9 \times p(1-p)\})/\{0.004 \times p^2\}$$

Therefore, with the help of this formula, the number of observations desired can be calculated for a given confidence level and accuracy.

Suppose we want to know whether the results are within the desired accuracy or not, it can be done by calculating **S** in the formula instead of 'n' as had previously done.

3.37. RATED ACTIVITY SAMPLING

As an extension of the normal uses of activity sampling, attempts have been made to modify this technique so that it may be used to determine the work content, and standard times for jobs. After recording the appropriate activities, observers have made rating assessments by watching workers for short periods of time; the assumption has then been made that such ratings are applicable to the corresponding activities recorded; the difficulties of such a procedure will be apparent. The main problem, however, is that because activity sampling recorded in general terms only what actually happens, even if workers were rated the broad context of existing methods of working must be accepted. The technique, to which the name **rated activity sampling** is given, has been used successfully to establish standard times for jobs where groups of workers are employed on a wide range of activities.

QUESTIONS

1. What is work-study? Why one should study his work? What benefits does studying the work derive? Give examples.
2. What is scientific management? Who is the originator of scientific management? What are his contributions to work-study?
3. Explain the methods of improving productivity in contrast to work-study.
4. Define the following and write a brief note on them; (a) Work-study, (b) Method Study and (c) Work Measurement or Time Study.

5. Briefly explain the method of Introducing Method Study in an organization.
6. Explain the various symbols used in recording the facts in method study and explain teri significance.
7. Write a brief note on diagrams and models and charts used in recording the facts in method study.
8. Explain the points to be remembered while writing charts and diagrams in method study.
9. Give a specimen of Flow Process Chart.
10. Write a Brief note on: (a) Two hand process chart, (b) Multiple activity chart, (c) String diagram, (d) Flow diagram, (e) Cyclograph.
11. Briefly explain the process of critical examination.
12. What factors you consider while developing a new method from the facts you got from method study.
13. Briefly explain the principle of motion economy.
14. Write a brief note on thribligs.
15. What is work measurement? Why should we measure the work? Briefly explain the objectives of work measurement.
16. List out various methods of work measurement and explain any two of them in detail giving their suitability, advantages and limitations.
17. Write a brief note on: (a) Rate of working, (b) Standard rate of working, (c) Observed time, (d) Standard time (e) Unit of work (f) Relaxation and contingency allowances.
18. Explain in detail the method of measuring time by using stopwatch, giving a neat sketch of stopwatch and various tools used.
19. Briefly explain work measurement by Predetermined Motion Time System method.
20. Write note on: (a) Analytical estimating, (b) Comparative estimating and (c) Activity sampling.

MULTIPLE CHOICE QUESTIONS

1. The person who evolved the principle of breaking the job into detailed elements to determine the time is :

(a) Elton Mayo (b) Gilberth
(c) F.W. Taylor (d) H.L. Gantt

2. The person who did work on shoveling and designed optimal size of the shovel is:

(a) F.W.Taylor (b) H.L. Gantt
(c) Lillian Gilberth (d) Elton Mayo

3. The relationship between inputs used and outputs produced is known as;

(a) Production (b) Product
(c) Manufacturing (d) Productivity

4. A management service uses method study and work measurement to study human work is known as:
   (a) Productivity study (b) Measurement of production
   (c) Work-study (d) Time study
5. A technique used to establish time for a qualified worker to do work at standard rate is known as:
   (a) Method study (b) Work-study
   (c) Production study (d) Work measurement
6. One of the objectives of method study is:
   (a) To find the time to do the work
   (b) To give training to the worker
   (c) To use automatic machines only in production
   (d) To improve the working procedure
7. The first step in method study is:
   (a) Critical examination (b) Select the job for study
   (c) Record the facts (d) To save the material
8. The symbol used in recording the facts in method study represents:
   (a) Doing the work (b) Movement
   (c) Inspection (d) Storage
9. The symbol → used for Inspection in recording the facts in method study is:
   (a) O (b) →
   (c) □ (d) D
10. Out line process charts uses these symbols only to overall study:
    (a) O, D (b) →, □
    (c) D, → (d) O, □
11. In two hand process chart the symbol △ is used to represent;
    (a) Hold (b) Store
    (c) Do not move (d) Arrest movement
12. For recording high speed, short cycle operations the technique used is:
    (a) Sting diagram (b) Flow chart
    (c) Cyclograph (d) Multiple activity charts
13. When we want to record the activities of a group of people the chart used is:
    (a) Activity chart (b) Travel chart
    (c) Multiple activity charts (d) Man machine chart
14. When activities of man and machine are recorded on the same chart it is known as:
    (a) Man machine charts (b) Multiple operator charts
    (c) Memo motion chart (d) Control charts

15. SIMO chart represents:
(a) Single inside motion chart (b) Simultaneous motion chart
(c) Simultaneous machine chart

16. The actual time taken by the worker to do a job depends on:
(a) Rate of working maintained by him
(b) Type of facilities provided to him
(c) The quality of raw material
(d) Worker's qualification

17. In a stopwatch if an hour is divided into 100 parts it is known as:
(a) Percent hour (b) Centihour
(c) 100 part hour (c) None

18. [(Observed time × Observed Rating)] /(Standard rating) is known as:
(a) Standard time (b) Rated time
(c) Basic time (d) Observed time

19. Basic time + Allowances is known as:
(a) Standard time (b) Allowed time
(c) Time taken (d) Rated time

20. PMTS means:
(a) Predetermined Time (b) Predetermined motion time system
(c) Perfect measured time schedule (d) None

ANSWERS

1. (c) **2.** (a) **3.** (d) **4.** (c) **5.** (d) **6.** (d) **7.** (b) **8.** (b)
9. (c) **10.** (d) **11.** (a) **12.** (c) **13.** (c) **14.** (a) **15.** (b) **16.** (a)
17. (b) **18.** (c) **19.** (a) **20.** (b).

❍❍❍

STATISTICAL QUALITY CONTROL (SQC)

3.38. INTRODUCTION

Quality control is as old as industry itself. It started with the time the man started manufacture of articles/products because he is interested to see that the customer purchases his products or articles. The interest on quality control technique increased as the number of manufacturing units is increased and due to the competition in the market. Every manufacturer is concerned with the quality of his product at the same time he is interested in supplying the needs of the market and optimal utilization of the resources available. The manufacturer is interested in customer satisfaction through the supply of desired quality and quantity of the products at the right time and at the right price. Stiff competition in national and international market and consumer awareness of the quality of the product made it a mandatory to the manufacturer to mention the level of quality of his product or service. To run the business at the desired economic level and to satisfy the customer, the management has to integrate quality development, quality maintenance and quality improvement of the product, which is possible through a sound quality control system.

3.39. MEANING OF QUALITY

Quality is a relative term and it is generally used with reference to the end use of the product. Any product when it meets the desired specifications, we say it is of good quality. The quality is thus defined as the fitness for use/purpose at the most economic level. The quality depends on the perception of a person in a given situation. The situation may be user oriented, cost oriented or supplier oriented. Since the customer manufactures the product for the use, the requirement (specifications) of the customer dictates the quality of the product. Quality has to be planned, achieved, controlled and achieved continuously. The word **quality** has quite good number of meanings. Some of them are:

(a) **Fitness for purpose:** The component/product is said to be of good quality; if it works or functions properly give the service needed by the customer, when needed. Hence quality can be defined as **fitness for purpose/use.**

(b) **Conformance to the requirement or specifications:** Quality is the ability of material or component or product to perform satisfactorily in an application for which the user intends it. Quality of the product thus means **conformance to requirements.** Consumer needs have to be assessed and translated into specifications, and these specifications will be the yardsticks to assess the quality.

(c) Other terms, which are used in reference to the quality and to assess the quality, are: **grade, degree of performance, degree of excellence and measure of fulfillment of promises.**

3.40. QUALITY CONTROL

Quality control is the process through which we measure the actual quality performance and compare it with the standards and take corrective action. It is systematic control of various factors such as material, tools, labour used during production that affects the quality of the product. It is effective system for integrating the quality development, quality maintenance and quality improvement efforts of the various groups in an organization, so as to enable production and service at the most economical level which allow full customer satisfaction.

3.41. AIMS AND OBJECTIVES OF QUALITY CONTROL

1. To make the company's product more acceptable by the customers and thereby increasing the sales of the company.
2. To reduce the cost of production by proper control of outgoing product by reducing the defects.
3. To achieve interchangeability.
4. To develop quality consciousness in organization.

3.42. QUALITY CHARACTERISTICS

Physical or Chemical property of a product or dimension, temperature or pressure or taste or smell or any other requirement used to define the nature of the product or service (which contributes the quality aspect of the product) may be termed as quality characteristic. They may be classified as:

(a) **Technical:** Length, frequency, diameter, viscosity, etc.,

(b) **Psychological:** Sensory qualities such as taste, odor and beauty,

(c) **Time based items:** Such as reliability, maintainability, life, etc.,

(d) **Contractual terms:** Such as guarantee, safety and

(e) **Ethical terms:** Such as honesty, integrity, etc.

3.43. QUALITY CONTROL AND INSPECTION

Quality control should not be confused with inspection. Inspection means checking of material, product or component of a product at various stages, with reference to certain **predetermined factors** and detecting and sorting out of faulty or defective items. In inspection activity, the emphasis is placed on the quality of the past production or products already produced. Here inspector is concerned with, whether the product conforms to the quality characteristics or not? On the other hand, **quality control** is a broad term; it involves inspection at particular stage but mere inspection does not mean quality control. As opposed to the inspection, in the quality control more emphasis is placed on the future production. The most effective way of controlling quality is to use statistical means to control the incoming material, process, so that if anything found incorrect, immediate steps are taken to rectify the mistake and continue the production. This will help to a greater extent that only good products will leave the manufacturing unit. The lesson learnt from the inspection of the sample is used as a basis to ascertain whether the quality of the product is as per specification or not. **In short, in inspection quality of past production is ascertained and in quality control, quality of future production is regulated.** Also, inspection is merely an act of checking and sorting out the defective items whereas quality control is a broad term which includes number of activities in order to provide quality products/service to the customer. The following table gives the differences between quality control and inspection:

Table 3.7. Showing Difference between Inspection and Quality Control

S. No.	Parameter	Inspection	Quality Control
1.	Scope	Inspection is a part of quality control.	Quality control is a broad term, involves inspection at particular stages, but mere inspection does not mean quality control.
2.	Definition	Inspection is an act of checking materials, components, or products at various sages in manufacturing and sorting out defective items from good items.	Quality control is an effective system for integrating quality development, quality maintenance and quality improvement efforts of various groups in an organization to enable the production to be carried out at most economical level to achieve satisfaction of customers.

Contd...

S. No.	Parameter	Inspection	Quality Control
3.	Devices used	Inspection uses precision measuring instruments such as Vernier Calipers, Micrometer, etc., and devices such as Tool Maker's Microscope and Flaw detectors.	Quality control uses devices such as Statistics, Control charts, Acceptance sampling, Process capability study, quality audit and Field complaints.
4.	Acceptability	Inspection is concerned with past production to judge conformance with specification and sorting out defective items form good items.	Quality control is concerned with the quality of future production. For example, a sample is taken from the production run and tested for quality. In case the sample shows that the quality is deteriorating, the process is stopped to make corrections and after correction, the process is restarted, assuring only good quality of products from production run.
5.	Concern	Inspection is mainly the concern of the inspector.	Everybody working in the organization is responsible for quality of products produced.

3.44. QUALITY POLICY

Quality policy refers to the basic principles, which are used to guide the action of the company, in order to meet the quality objectives. However, economy may be the additional factor while determining the quality policy. Quite logically, the costs of production will increase the level of accuracy and quality of product is raised. Thus, functional use of the product and cost should be considered simultaneously while formulating the quality requirement or policy. While formulating quality policy the effect of policy on manufacturing process, effect on sales, customer profile, cost of inspection and optimal utilization of available resources should be considered.

3.45. STATISTICAL QUALITY CONTROL (SQC)

A quality control system, which performs inspection, testing and analysis, to ensure that the quality of the product produced is as per the laid down quality standards (or specifications) is known as **Statistical Quality Control,** when statistical methods are used for control of quality. SQC, controls, improves and maintains quality or solves the problem related with quality. Statistics is the collection, organization, analysis, interpretation and presentation of the data. It is based on the law of large numbers and mathematical theory of probability it is just one of the many tools necessary to solve the quality related problems. It takes into account the existence of variation. It is in this sense that the adjective **statistical** is used in the expression **Statistical Quality Control.** Building an information system to satisfy the concept of **'prevention'** and **'control'** and improvement of product quality requires the use of statistical methods.

Statistical quality control is systematic as compared to guesswork of haphazard process inspection and the mathematical or statistical approach neutralizes personal bias and uncovers poor judgment. SQC consists of the following activities:

1. Systematic collection and graphic recording of accurate data.
2. Analysis of the data.

3. Practical engineering or management action, if the information obtained indicates significant deviation from the specified limits.

3.46. CAUSES OF VARIATION IN QUALITY

The departure from specified or standard quality is due to **'chance'** factor or due to **'assignable'** causes. So long as only the chance factors are in operation, the manufacturing process is deemed to be under control. It means that all the departures form the standard or specification does not indicate lack of control, but only those departures, which are due to assignable causes, show that the production process is not under control. Quality would be deemed to be under control even when goods produced are not of an exactly identical nature, up to the standard or specification so long as the deficiency is due to causes natural and inherent in the process of manufacture and, therefore, termed as **chance factors.** These causes being natural or inherent are neither preventable nor assignable, nor it is not necessary to prevent them; for they are within limits, known as **tolerance limits.** These variations may be due to the variation in skill of the worker, wear and tear of the tool and variation in the quality of material. To accommodate all these variations, the designers will provide upper limit and lower limit to various characteristics of the product, so that as far as the characteristic does out cross these limits, we say the product is within the limit and the error is due to chance and not of an assignable cause. For example, take a dimension of the product is given limits as 10.00 ± 0.001. When the product is getting processed, the dimension may lie between $10.00 + 0.001$ and $10.00 - 0.001$. As far as the dimensions are within these two limits, we say the product is satisfying the specification. Once the dimension crosses these limits, then we have to find out the cause of the variation as it is out of limit. This cause may be wear in tool or misalignment of machine or any other reason. This mistake is to be rectified and process is to be restored.

3.47. THE PURPOSE OF SQC

When SQC techniques are not in use; the defects in quality were detected by inspection after the finished goods were available. Obviously, there was very little that could be done to improve the quality. SQC techniques, which permit constant inspection during the process of manufacture and enable the SQC man to know almost immediately as soon as the process of manufacture goes out of control. This is a sort of **'built in manufacture'** technique. The management can then takes remedial measure, restore control and redeem the quality of the product. SQC technique involves the application of the theory of probability and theory of sampling, the study of mean and variations. By the application of above methods and theories, it is possible to isolate the chance factors from those of the assignable causes and take appropriate measures. Thus SQC is a collection of specialized techniques used to improve the technical efficiency of production.

3.48. DEVELOPMENT OF SQC

The movement for quality control dates back to the period of Second World War (1934–45), when the needs of modern warfare required turning out highly standardized machine parts and other goods according to strict specifications. Before the growth of SQC, the practice was of post manufacture inspections, which led to waste of large amounts of scarce resources and man-hours. Further, a cent percent manual inspection besides being costly is also no guarantee against defective manufacture of some pieces passing undetected.

3.49. ADVANTAGES OF SQC

The Chief Advantages of SQC are:

1. It saves precious and scarce resources in terms of men and material and enables the goods of a **standard and uniform quality** being supplied from the manufacturing unit.
2. This inspection is much more **economical** as compared to 100 percent manual inspection.
3. From the technical point of view the greatest advantage is, since the control is exercised through carefully selected sample, **it is possible to apply the technique to such cases, where an inspection is of destructive nature.** Also it can be applied to such cases where **margin of error** can be specified in advance.
4. The SQC technique enables to find out the extent to which a change in production techniques would result in an improvement in quality and whether the cost would be justified.
5. SQC techniques enable to distinguish the good worker from the bad worker on the basis of the quality of the products produced by them.

3.50. THEORY AND TECHNIQUES OF SQC

In the techniques of quality control the first thing is the determination of a standard quality or laying down the specification. This is done with reference to the production techniques and other considerations such as cost of production, selling price and skill of the worker, specification of raw materials and the function of the product. One must be careful while laying down the specifications, which has its effect on the cost of product. If we fix up very close limits, the cost of meeting that specification will be very high, because of the technology and skill to be used to get the desired quality. If the specifications are very coarse, the product may not function properly, though the cost of production is low. Hence, the specifications must be specified appropriately. The figure below illustrates the cost and quality.

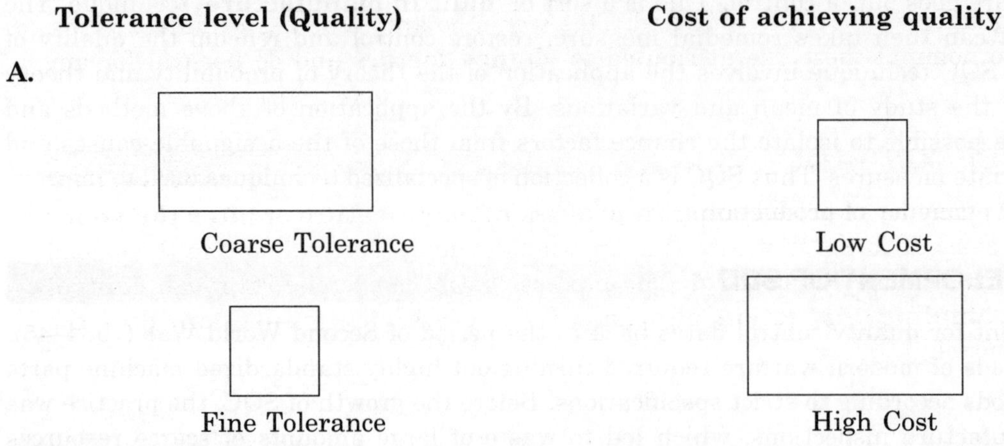

Fig. 3.26. Cost and Quality.

Consider an example of a bolt of 20 mm diameter and 50 mm length. When this bolt is to be used in the assembly of an aero engine, because of the operating conditions of the engine, finer tolerances are to be provided, and hence the cost of the bolt will be considerably high. In case the same sized bolt is to be used the assembly of a tractor engine, the bolt need not be given fine tolerances, as the operating conditions of the engine is totally different. In this case the cost of the bolt is much less than the above.

How to know that the quality of outturn has varied beyond limit is a vital question. It involves the consideration of the theoretical distribution under a normal curve. It is known on a **priory** basis that 99.73 percent of the items would lie between the mean x and 3σ on either side of the mean as shown in the Fig. 3.27.

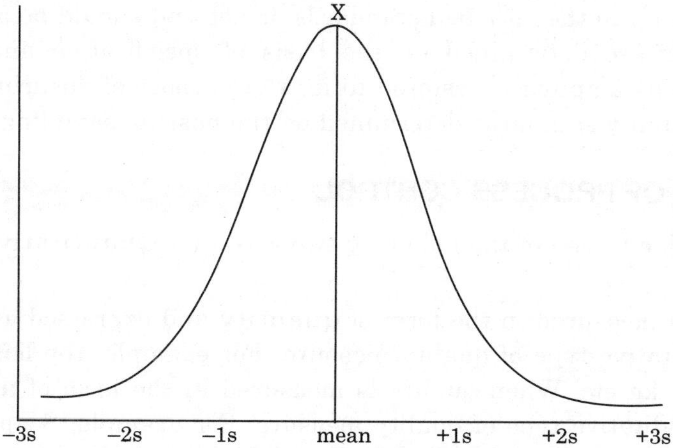

Fig. 3.27. Normal Distribution.

Thus **x** ± **3σ** gives limits, which are referred to as **empirical control limits.** A constant watch would be kept on the process by taking out the samples of the product from the production line occasionally and finding out their standard deviations. If the **3σ** limits on either side of **x** were beyond the limit of variations predetermined by the manufacturing or quality control departments it would indicate that the process has strayed out of control. If a really satisfactory SQC system were in vogue, the fault would be detected at once. Causes of variation in quality would be investigated. This would be known as **assignable causes.** If variations are nominal these are attributed to **chance factors** and do not call for any action.

3.51. TYPES OF CONTROL

Control of quality may be exercised either **in process of manufacture** or **after the goods have been processed.** In the first case it is known as **process control,** and in the second it is known as **product or lot control.** The process control is exercised through **control charts,** while **sampling inspection** also known as **acceptance inspection,** does the product or lot control.

3.51.1. Process Control

Process control is a method of exercising control to determine whether the process of manufacture is within control or not. It is a constant system of control exercised **during the process of manufacture** to maintain and preserve standards of quality by detecting assignable causes. In this method standard of goods is inherent in the system of manufacture and in the plant that is used for manufacturing. Here continuous vigil is maintained on the process of manufacture by drawing and examining samples from the production line to ensure that the process of manufacture has not gone out of control.

3.51.2. Acceptance Inspection

In acceptance inspection a decision has to be taken to determine whether the goods **already manufactured** are up to the specified standards or not and should be accepted or rejected. Here the standards are determined on the basis of specification and requirements. In acceptance inspection sampling is restored to for the purpose of ensuring the acceptance of lots of a specified quality standards determined on the basis of sampling plan.

3.52. METHODS OF PROCESS CONTROL

Quality is measurable in one of the following two ways: **(i) Quantitatively** and **(ii) Qualitatively.**

When quality is measured in the form of **quantity** and expressed as a variable, then it is known as quantitative type of quality measure. For example, the length of an article in mm, or strength in kg etc. When quality is measured in the form of **attribute,** then it is referred to as a qualitative type of quality measure. For example, Soap cakes containing a larger than the standard proportion of soda etc.

Sometimes we come across a situation where both qualitative and quantitative measures can be employed to express the quality of the product. When we are dealing with the length of an object, when expressed that it is 10 mm shorter or greater than the required, it is quantitative measure. When we say it is larger or shorter and reject, then it is qualitative measure of quality.

3.52.1. Control Charts and their Applications

Control charts are based on statistical sampling theory, according to which an adequate sized sample drawn, at random, from a lot represents the lot. All processes, whether semi-automatic or automatic are susceptible to variations, which in turn result in changes the dimensions of the products. These variations occur due to either chance causes or assignable causes. Variation diameter of spindle, being manufactured on lathe may be either due to tool wear or non-homogeneity of bar stock or changes in machine setting, etc. The purpose of control chart is to detect these changes in dimensions and indicates if the component parts being manufactured are within the specified tolerance or not.

3.52.2. Definition and Concept of Control Charts

Control charts are (day-to-day) graphical representations of the collected information. The information pertains to the measured or otherwise judged quality characteristics of the item or the samples. A control chart detects variations in the processing and warns if there is any departure from the specified tolerance limits. A control chart primarily is a diagnostic technique. It is dynamic in nature, i.e., it is kept current and up to date as per the changes processing conditions. It depicts whether there is any change in the characteristics of items since the start of the production run. Successively revised and plotted control chart immediately tells and undesired variations and it helps a lot in exploring the cause and eliminating manufacturing troubles.

Let us take an example of producing a shaft of diameter of 20 mm. After manufacturing the required number of shafts say, 1000 numbers, and their dimensions are measured and plotted on a graph. The graph appears like that shown in Fig. 3.27. Certain measured diameter values lie quite close to the desired dimension, i.e. 20.00 mm. This diameter is known as **mean diameter** or **mean value**, whereas other diameter values are quite far from the mean value. Because of the fact that variations are inherent in all processes and therefore in product dimensions, it becomes necessary to accept all those pieces which fall under a set of specified tolerance limits or control limits; otherwise, if we stick to the mean dimensions of 20.00 mm only then there will be more rejected shafts. As soon as the control limits are incorporated, which are shown as **upper limit** and **lower limit,** the graph becomes a control chart. These limits can be 1σ, 2σ or 3σ depending upon whether the confidence level is 68.27 percent, 95.45 percent or 99.73 percent. Normally 3σ limits are taken for plotting control charts, and (3σ + 3σ), i.e. 6σ, is the spread and is known as **basic spread.** Besides 3σ control limits certain control charts also show **warning limits spread** at 4σ spread. Warning limits inform the manufacturer that the items in the sample are approaching the danger level so that he can take an action before the process goes out of control.

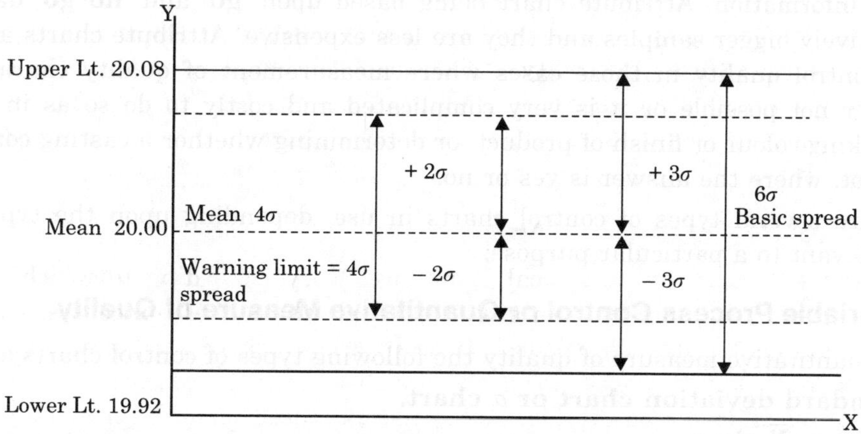

Fig. 3.28. Control Chart

3.52.3. Advantages of Control Charts

The advantages of control charts are:

(a) A control chart indicates whether the process is in control or out of control.

(b) It determines process variability and detects unusual variations taking place in the process.

(c) It ensures product quality level.

(d) It warns in time, and if the process is rectified at that time, scrap or percentage of rejections can be reduced.

(e) It provides information about the selection of process and setting of tolerance limits.

(f) Control charts build-up the reputation of the organization through customer's satisfaction.

3.53. TYPES OF CONTROL CHARTS

All the control charts are based on **attributes** and **variables.** In other words, quality can be controlled either through actual measurement of dimensions, weights, strength etc., or through attributes as **yes** or **no** criteria. A good example for this is use of limit gauges used in mass production to see whether the manufactured article is within limits or not. The gauge will not reveal the actual dimension, but one can judge, whether the dimension under examination is under control or not. The properties of variable chart and attribute charts are:

1. Variable chart involve the measurement of the job dimensions and an item is accepted or rejected if its dimensions are within or beyond the fixed tolerance limit. Variable charts are more detailed and contain more information compared to attribute chart. Variable charts are relatively expensive because of greater cost of collecting measured data.
2. Attribute charts only differentiate between a defective item and a non-defective item without going into the measurement of its dimensions. These charts contain less information. Attribute chart being based upon **'go'** and **'no go'** data requires relatively bigger samples and they are less expensive. Attribute charts are only way to control quality in those cases where measurement of quality characteristics is either not possible or it is very complicated and costly to do so as in the case of checking colour or finish of product, or determining whether a casting contain cracks or not, where the answer is yes or no.

There are several types of control charts in use, depending upon the type of quality measure relevant to a particular purpose.

3.53.1. Variable Process Control or Quantitative Measure of Quality

In case of quantitative measure of quality the following types of control charts are used:

1. **Standard deviation chart or σ chart.**
2. **Mean or $\overline{X}$ chart.**
3. **Range or R charts.**

Attribute process control or qualitative measure of quality: When qualities are expressed as attributes the following types of control charts are used.

1. **Fraction defective charts or p-defective charts,**
2. **Number defective chart or np-chart,**
3. **Number defective per unit chart or C chart.**

3.53.2. Standard Deviation Chart or σ Chart

When standards of manufacture and **allowances** or **tolerance limits** are not specified, a σ chart is prepared to determine whether the process is under control or not. The method consists of finding out a mean quantity and the standard deviation by taking a large number of items. This is necessary to determine the standards as none have been specified in advance. The standard error of σ would give us the control limit, depending upon the degree of accuracy required. Having determined the control limits we will be applying quality control to samples, which are taken from the production run with regular frequency.

Problem. 3.5:

It is required to determine whether an automatic device for cutting candies is in order or not and remain so or not throughout the process of manufacture or not. For this, a sample of 4 candies is taken soon after the cutting device is fixed to cut the candies. The average of the sample is found to be 20 mm with a standard deviation of 0.01 mm. Find the control limits and draw the graph.

Solution:

Suppose it is decided that every time, a sample of 4 is taken to test the process. The standard error of mean would be $\bar{X} = \sigma / \sqrt{n} = 0.01 / \sqrt{4} = 0.005\,\text{mm}$.

The $\overline{3\sigma}$ distance on either side of the mean 20 mm would determine the limits, i.e. 20 ± 3 × 0.005 = 19.985 and 20.015, within which the size of the candies can vary to enable the manufacturing department to claim, that the process is under control.

For this purpose subsequent samples of size 4 would be taken at regular intervals, and plotted on chart known as control chart which is a graphical method of representing the size characters of a sequence of samples and showing the upper control limit (UCL) and the lower control limit (LCL) within which the item sizes can vary in order to regard the process under control.

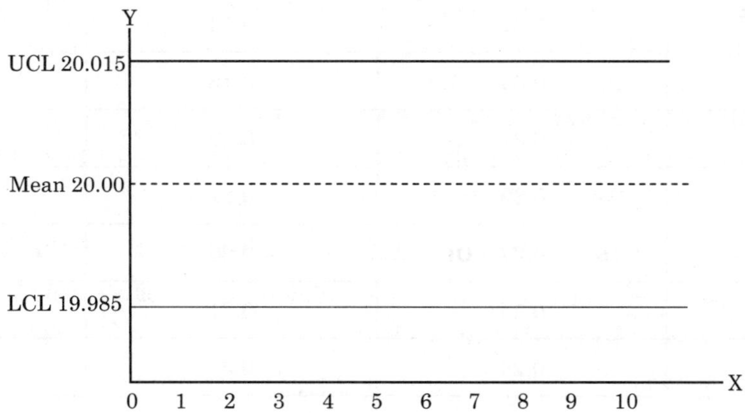

Fig. 3.29. Control Chart

Procedure: Find the mean $\overline{\mathbf{X}}$, find the standard deviation, σ, find the standards error of mean, find 3σ and then workout the limits and then draw the charts and mark the samples.

3.53.3. Mean or $\overline{X}$ Chart

This shows changes in process average and is affected change process variability. This chart is used for measuring control tendency. It shows erratic or cyclic shifts in the process, it also detracts steady process changes, like tool wear. It is most commonly used chart in quality control. When used with $\overline{\mathbf{R}}$ chart, it tells when to leave the process alone and when to chase and go for the causes leading variations, it secures information in establishing or modifying process, specification or inspection procedures. It can be used along with $\overline{\mathbf{R}}$ chart to control the incoming materials.

$\overline{\mathbf{R}}$ chart: It controls general variability of the process and is affected by changes in process variability. It also measure spread. It is, generally used along with $\overline{\mathbf{X}}$ chart. The main disadvantages of these charts are that they require the use of tables of **factors.** These tables are very much useful in the construction of control charts.

Table 3.8. Showing Factors for Estimating 3σ Control Limits for $\overline{\mathbf{X}}$ and $\overline{\mathbf{R}}$ Charts

Number of Observations	Factor for $\overline{X}$ Chart	Factor for $\overline{R}$ Chart	
		LCL D_3	UCL D_4
2	1.88	0	3.27
3	1.20	0	2.57
4	0.73	0	2.28
5	0.58	0	2.11
6	0.48	0	2.00
7	0.42	0.08	1.92
8	0.37	0.14	1.82
9	0.34	0.18	1.78
10	0.31	0.22	1.74
11	0.29	0.22	1.74
12	0.27	0.28	1.69
13	0.25	0.31	1.67
14	0.24	0.33	1.67
15	0.22	–	0.35
16	0.21	–	0.36
17	0.20	–	0.38

Number of Observations	Factor for $\overline{X}$ Chart	Factor for $\overline{R}$ Chart	
		LCL D_3	UCL D_4
18	0.19	–	0.39
19	0.19	–	0.40
20	0.18	–	0

$\overline{R}$ = Average Ranges of samples and $\overline{X}$ = Average of sample
Lower Control Limit for $\overline{X}$ chart = $\overline{X} - A_2\,\overline{R}$ and Upper Control Limit for $\overline{X}$ chart = $\overline{X} + A_2\,\overline{R}$
Lower Control Limit for $\overline{R}$ chart = $D_2\,\overline{R}$ and Upper Control Limit for $\overline{R}$ chart = $D_4\,\overline{R}$

3.53.4. Plotting of $\overline{X}$ and $\overline{R}$ Charts

A good number of sample of items coming-out of the machine are collected at random at different intervals of items and their quality characteristics (diameter or length or any other) are measured. For each sample the mean value and range is found out. For example, if you have five diameters, then mean is given by sum of the diameters divided by the number of items. And the range is given by the difference between maximum diameter and the minimum diameter. Then the average and ranges are tabulated. The procedure to draw the chart is illustrated by means of an example.

Problem. 3.6:

Draw $\overline{X}$ chart and $\overline{R}$ chart for the given data.

Sample size = 5	X	R
1	7.00	2
2	7.50	2
3	8.00	2
4	10.00	2
5	9.50	3
6	11.00	3
7	11.50	4
8	4.00	2
9	3.50	3
10	4.00	2
TOTAL	76.00	26

$\overline{\overline{X}} = \sum \overline{X}/n$, = 76/10 = 7.6 and $\overline{R} = \sum \overline{R}/n$ = 26/10 = 2.6,

Where n = 5

For $\overline{X}$ chart: LCL $= \overline{X} - A_2\,\overline{R} = 7.6 - 0.58 \times 2.6 = 6.092$

UCL $= \overline{X} + A_2\,\overline{R} = 7.6 + 0.58 \times 2.6 = 8.658$

For $\overline{R}$ chart: LCL $= D_2\,\overline{R} = 0 \times 2.6 = 0$ and

UCL $= D_4\,\overline{R} = 2.11 \times 2.6 = 5.486$ approximately.

3.53.5. Fraction Defective Chart or p-Defective Chart

Quality control is also exercised through the construction of fraction defective chart or p-chart, the object being control the proportion of defective according to specified attributes. If attribute standard is not specified, it is inferred by finding the average of fraction defectives. It can be a fraction defective chart or percent defective chart (percent defective chart or 100 p-chart). Each item is classified as good (non-defective) or bad (defective) item. This chart is used to control the general quality of the component parts and it checks if the fluctuations in product quality (level) are due to chance causes alone. It can be used even if sample size is variable (i.e. different for all samples), but calculating control limits for each samples rather cumbersome. p-chart is plotted by calculating, first, the fraction defectives and then the control limits. The process is said to be in control if fraction defective values fall within the control limits. In case the process is out of control an investigation to hunt for the cause becomes necessary.

Problem. 3.7:

A quality controller examines a sample of 1000 items each and finds the number of defectives as follows, calculate control limits of p-chart.

Sample Number	Number of Defectives	Sample Number	Number of Defectives
1	215	11	285
2	227	12	287
3	220	13	312
4	180	14	195
5	320	15	180
6	240	16	190
7	218	17	215
8	195	18	210
9	280	19	215
10	310	20	240

Solution:

On the p-defective chart, the control line is given by the average of fraction defectives, i.e. 0.2367 and the UCL and LCL is calculated by using the formula:

Limits are: = Sp ± 3√(pq/n, where p = Average of fraction defectives and q = average of fraction not defectives. q = 1 – p and n = number of items in each sample.

S. No.	Number of Defectives	Number of Fraction Defectives	S. No.	Number of Defectives	Number of Fraction Defectives
1	215	0.215	11	285	0.285
2	227	0.227	12	287	0.287
3	220	0.220	13	312	0.312
4	180	0.180	14	195	0.195
5	320	0.320	15	180	0.180
6	240	0.240	16	190	0.190
7	218	0.218	17	215	0.215
8	195	0.195	18	210	0.210
9	280	0.280	19	215	0.215
10	310	0.310	20	240	0.240
TOTAL				**4374**	**4.374**
AVERAGE				**236.7**	**0.2367**

Now, $3\sqrt{pq/n} = 3 \times \sqrt{[0.2367\ (1 - 0.2367)]/1000} = 0.0402$.

Therefore, UCL = 0.2367 + 0.0402 = 0.2769 and LCL = 0.2367 – 0.0402 = 0. 1965 and the central line on the graph = 0.2367. The fraction defective for each sample is calculated as shown in table and plotted on the graph. The points outside the limits would indicate that the process of manufacture is out of control.

3.53.6. Number Defective or np-Defective Chart

Sometimes it is simpler to prepare a number defective chart. This chart dispenses with the necessity of calculating the proportion or fraction of defectives in each sample. Consider the above example, where the sample size is 1000; hence it is easy to calculate the fraction defectives. Instead, if the sample size is other than 1000 (or 10 and multiples of 10), say any number like 879, the calculation of fraction would have been a tremendous task by itself. In such cases, number defective chart is easier for construction.

The limits are found from the formulae: $n\bar{p} \pm 3\sqrt{n\bar{p}\,(1 - p)}$

Problem. 3.8:

In a manufacturing process, the number of defectives found in the inspection of 15 lots of 400 items each is given below. Determine the trial control limits for **np** chart and state whether the process is in control or not.

Lot Number	Number of Defectives	Lot Number	Number of Defectives
1	2	9	18
2	5	10	8
3	0	11	6
4	14	12	0

contd.....)

Lot Number	Number of Defectives	Lot Number	Number of Defectives
5	3	13	3
6	0	14	0
7	1	15	6
8	0	–	–
TOTAL			66

Solution

$\sum np$ = Total number of defectives = 66

$\sum n$ = Total number inspected = 400 × 15 = 6000

Hence, $\bar{p} = \sum np / \sum n = 66/6000 = 0.011$

$n = 400$, hence $n\bar{p} = 400 \times 0.011 = 4.4$

therefore, $UCL = n\bar{p} + 3\sqrt{n\bar{p}}\, q = 4.4 + 3\sqrt{4.4 \times 0.989} = 10.65$

and LCL = 4.4 – 6.25 = a negative value, hence the lower limit is zero, i.e. the X-axis is the line. If you plot the curve, you see that lot numbers 4 and 9 are out of control. Hence, the process is not in statistical control.

3.53.7. Number Defective Per Unit Chart or C-Chart

Sometimes, it is more convenient to make a per unit number defective chart. In p-chart, we have seen that the number of items in each sample was uniform. If, however, the sample consists of no uniform number of items, the limits on the control chart cannot be laid out, as **n** would vary. In such a case, a fraction or a number defective chart cannot be used and the number defective per unit chart has to be constructed.

It is the control chart in which number of defects in a piece or a sample is plotted. It controls the number of defects observed per unit or per sample. Here sample size is uniform. The chart is used where average number of defects is much less than the number of defects, which would occur otherwise if everything possible goes wrong. Whereas, p-chart considers the number of defective pieces in given sample, and C-chart takes into account the number of defects in each defective piece or in a given sample. A defective piece may contain more than one defect. For example, cast part may have blowholes and surface cracks at the same time. The C-chart is preferred for large and complex parts, such as parts being few and limited however restrict the field of use for C-chart as compared to p-chart. The chart is plotted in the same manner as p-chart except that the control limits are based on poisson distribution, which describes more approximately the distribution of defects.

Example 3.9:

The following figures show the number of defective items discovered in 10 samples taken on 10 consecutive days in a month.

Month: January

Date	1	2	3	4	5	6	7	8	9	10
Number of defectives per unit of sample	1	2	4	16	4	3	5	20	16	4

Construct a control chart for the number of defective per unit from the above data.

Solution:

The total number of defectives = 75, Average number of defectives = 75 /10 = 7.5 = $\overline{\mathbf{C}}$

Control Limits are given by $\overline{\mathbf{C}} \pm 3\sqrt{\overline{\mathbf{C}}}$, hence $\sqrt{\overline{\mathbf{C}}} = \sqrt{7.5} = 2.7$

UCL = 7.5 + 3 × 2.7 = 15.6

and LCL = 7.5 – 8.1 = a negative number. Hence X-axis is the line for lower control limit.

When the chart is drawn it shows sample number 4,8 and 9th are out of control.

Where to use charts?

(a) Final assemblies use attribute charts (i.e. $\overline{p}$ and $n\overline{p}$ charts).

(b) Manufactured components such as shafts, spindles, balls, pins, holes and slots use variable charts (i.e. σ, $\overline{\mathbf{X}}$ and $\overline{\mathbf{R}}$ charts).

(c) Bullets and shells use attribute charts.

(d) Soldered joints use attribute charts.

(e) Castings and cloth lengths use attribute ad C-charts.

(f) Defects in components made of glass use attribute and C-charts.

(g) For studying tool wear use variable chart.

(h) Punch press works, forming, spot welding works use attribute chart.

(i) Incoming materials use attribute charts and variable charts.

(j) Large and complex products like power plant enginees and turbines use C-chart.

3.53.8. Care to be taken While Using Control Charts

So far we have discussed about the control charts. It is understood that when the points fall outside the control limits, we should say that point fall outside the control limits, we would say that the process is out of control. It does not follow from this that if the points are within control limits the process is fully under control and shows no abnormality whatsoever, so far as the process of manufacture is concerned. It is quite possible that the process may lead for trouble and assignable causes may be in existence. A careful SQC man would immediately take note of the pattern of such points. All the points falling in almost a line indicating a downward or upward trend that is an index of progressive deterioration in process conditions. Another pattern of points, which is regarded as unusual, is when points fall on one side of the central line near the UCL or LCL. When points are uniformly scattered within limits will indicate the usual pattern. Any departure from this will all for attention of the SQC person.

3.54 ACCEPTANCE INSPECTION

Acceptance inspection consists in judging the quality of the goods, which have already been manufactured. The goods, thus, subjected to test are known as a **lot** and the action of judging is known as **inspection,** after which inspected goods are **accepted** or **rejected.** Acceptance inspection is done **only after the goods have been produced and not during the process of manufacture as in the case of process control.**

Acceptance inspection is done on the basis of samples and it is that area of quality control, which determines whether a particular lot should be accepted or rejected, on the basis of a specified quality standards. In connection with the application of acceptance inspection techniques certain expressions are used, the implication of which may be understood at the outset.

3.54.1. Inspection

Any item or component or product, which is manufactured, is required to perform certain functions. The act of checking whether a component actually does so or not is called **inspection.** In other words, inspection means checking the acceptability of the manufactured product. The action of inspection serves two purposes. First, it separates defective components from non-defective ones and thus ensures the adequate quality of the product. Secondly, inspection locates defects in raw materials and flaws in processes which otherwise cause problems at the final stage. For example, detecting the parts, not having proper tolerances during processing itself will minimize the troubles arising at the time of assembly. To check some products, sampling inspection is only the way. For example, the agricultural products cannot be tested until they are harvested.

3.54.2. Sampling

Sampling is an act of drawing samples from a batch on random basis. Sampling depends upon statistical probability and therefore, samples must be collected from all sides and from different depths of box or heap containing the lot or batch (of components or parts) so that every part has an equal chance of being selected. The samples should be collected at regular intervals from the entire production run. The purpose is to obtain a sample truly representative of the lot. The **sample size** normally increases with the lot size and depends upon the degree of quality to be assured. The sample size can be found from re-formulated statistical tables. The following relation also serves as a good guide for calculating sample size. **If N is the batch or lot size, then the sample size equals to $\sqrt{2N}$.**

3.54.3. Producer's Risk

When items are inspected, there is the risk of sometimes rejecting satisfactory items, i.e. those items that are satisfactory according to the standards of the **producer**. This is known as **producer's risk** or **Acceptance Quality Level (AQL)** as adopted by him at the level of fraction defective (indicated by **p** in process control fraction defective chart). Such a situation is described as **producer's risk,** represented by $\mathbf{P_p}$.

3.54.4. Consumer's Risk

Compared to the above, when opposite is the situation, i.e. that there is a risk of sometimes accepting unsatisfactory items, such as those items which are not satisfactory according to **lot tolerance fraction defective level**, showing the maximum, allowable fraction defective, then, it is known as **consumer risk** and is indicated by $\mathbf{P_c}$. Often the allowable **fraction defective** is indicated as **percent defectives**, in which case lot tolerance percent defective (P_c or LTPD) or **Rejectable Quality Level (RQL)** is the standard on the basis of which the items are accepted.

Acceptable Quality Level (AQL)

It indicates a small proportion of bad components in a lot such that the lots having less than this proportion of bad components have a high probability of getting accepted.

Lot Tolerance Percent Defective (LTPD) or Limiting Quality (LQ)

It indicates a small proportion of bad components somewhat larger than acceptable quality level in a lot such that the lots having more than this proportion of defective components have a small probability of getting accepted.

3.55. SAMPLING INSPECTION

Sampling inspection is a technique to determine whether a lot or population should be rejected or accepted on the basis of the number of defective parts found in a random sample drawn from the lot. If the number of defective parts exceeds a predefined level, the lot is rejected. As compared to 100 percent inspection the sampling inspection claims the following advantages:

(i) It involves less amount of inspection to achieve a predefined degree of certainty about the quality.

(ii) It takes less time and is less expensive.

(iii) Fatigue and boredom incurred by the inspection is much less hence their operating efficiency much high.

(iv) It is more accurate because in 100 percent inspection, errors get introduced because of the fatigue and boredom incurred by the inspectors due to large inspection work of repetitive nature.

(v) Since fewer pieces are inspected, no damage is done to the remaining pieces of the lot, as they are not handled.

(vi) In certain cases, where the components are to be inspected by destructive testing or where a powder is to be chemically analyzed, 100 percent inspection can never be employed.

(vii) Rejection of complete batch on the basis of sample decidedly pressurizes for improvement in quality.

3.55.1. Classification of Sampling Inspection

Sampling inspection and sampling plans may be classified as follows:

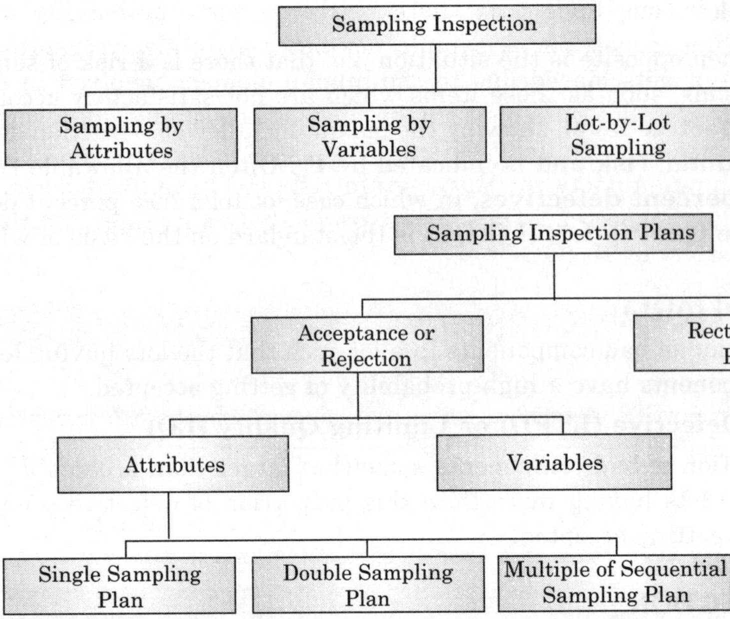

Fig. 3.30. Sampling Techniques.

3.55.2. Acceptance Sampling Inspection by Attributes

Attributes (yes or no) inspection is used to differentiate between a defective and a non-defective part, the part is rejected or accepted without using quantitative measure. For example, if out of a sample taken from a lot a predefined number of bullets fire, the lot is accepted otherwise rejected. Attribute inspection is very important and also very common. The parts can be inspected at an isolated calm place away from the production floor. Finally, **attribute inspection** is used where components are obviously defective and non-defective. Secondly, where it is very difficult and costly to measure each quality characteristic of a product (for example, paints, refrigerator etc.). Thirdly, attribute inspection finds application where the manufacturer does not see any need to measure the exact job dimensions and he feels that **'go'** and **'no go'** type of inspection can serve his purpose. Large part of sampling inspection is done by attributes.

Suppose, a manufactured lot contains **'N'** components, and the purchaser would like that the lot should contain non-defective components but the manufacturer know that the under normal conditions the defective parts are not likely to be eliminated completely, then, both the manufacturer and purchaser have to strike a balance and come to an agreement that if the lot contains more than, say **'X'** number of defective components, the lot will be rejected. One way of finding the number of defective parts is 100 percent inspection, which is costly, and this cost again in one way or the other is recovered from the purchaser. Considering the above both parties bring sampling inspection into picture.

By going into the details, one finds that there is always some probability or doubt associated with the sampling inspection. A sample not necessarily always represent the true condition of the lot as it gets biased due to the human element involved in drawing the sample from the lot. It is quite possible that by chance the sample may contain all good components, but otherwise the lot may be excellent. So, it involves a risk of both to the purchaser as well as the manufacturer. But, certain risk will have to be borne by two parties if they go for sampling inspection. These risks are plotted on a graph and the result is **Operating Characteristic Curve (OCC).**

3.56. STEPS INVOLVED IN INSPECTION BY ATTRIBUTES

1. Select a Sampling Plan

First we have to fix the proportion defective which will decide whether to accept a lot or to reject it. A purchaser always thinks about the cost of making the wrong decision, i.e. the loss he will have to bear in case he accepts a bad lot on the basis of a good sample. By changing the parameters of an OC curve he can easily choose the most appropriate curve for him, the one that involves minimum purchaser's risk, as shown in the curve shown. On the X-axis of the OC curve the percent defectives are represented. Percent defective means the defective components that can be tolerated in a sample. Different curves are drawn for different samples. On Y-axis shown the probability of accepting the sample. We can see on the graph, that as the percent defectives is less the probability of accepting the lot is more and vice versa. Hence, both the parties must be careful enough while selecting the sample size and the percent defectives.

If a batch contains **N** pieces and a sample containing **'n'** of them is taken out, the batch will be accepted if the number of defective pieces (d) does not exceed the acceptance number (a). Both **a** and **n** are the parameters of OC curve. If the batch size is large as compared to lot size, which is commonly the situation in industrial applications, the operating characteristic curve is independent of the batch size. However, 'n' and 'a' influence the shape of an OC curves. As 'n' and 'a' both increase, the OC curve shifts inside towards **K** as in the Fig. 2.30. The dotted inner curve is for a grater value of 'n' as compared to that of the outer OC curve.

2. Determine the Operating Characteristic Curve for the Chosen Sampling Plan

As described above, a single sampling plan involves two parameters, 'n' = the sample size and '*a*' = the acceptance number; and a batch is rejected or accepted depending upon the criteria whether the number of defective components **'d'** in a sample of **'n'** components is more than the acceptance number **'a'** are not.

The shape of the OCC depends upon the value of 'a' and 'n' and accordingly it defines the risk involved or the probabilities of a good lot being rejected and a bad lot being accepted. A balance has to strike regarding the value of 'n'. Large sample size raises the cost of selecting, handling and inspection. A small size does not truly represent the lot; the OC curve shifts away from the ideal curve ABOZ and chance of error increases.

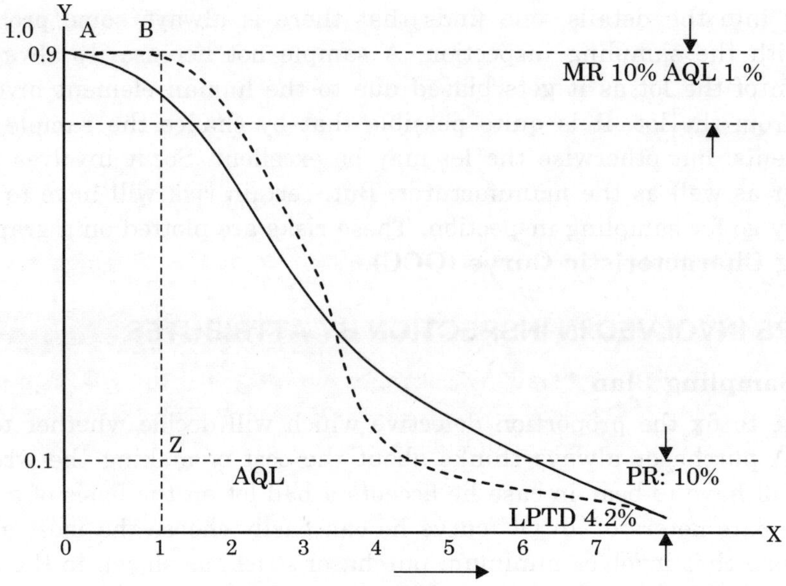

Fig. 3.31. OC Curve

Manufacturer's risk = MR 10%, AQL = 1.0

MR = Manufacturer's risk,

Pa = Probability of batch being accepted,

p = Percent defectives,

AQL = Acceptance Quality Level,

LTPD = Lot Tolerance Percent Defective, and

PR = Purchaser's risk.

The concept of ideal OC curve having rectangular operating characteristics (ABOZ) is that the lots having not more than 1 percent defective components will definitely be accepted and others with more than 1 percent defectives will certainly be rejected.

3.57. SAMPLING BY VARIABLES

When measuring the quality characteristic of a product carries out inspection, for example, by measuring the length or diameter or weight etc., it is called inspection by variables. Variables involve the averages of measurements where as attributes deal with percentage of parts rejected. Inspection using variable is mostly done on the shop floor and is important for the control of operations. Inspection using variables is more detailed, contains more information, but involves higher inspection and other costs per unit, as compared to attribute inspection. The manufacturer has to decide at some stage, which inspection to use, of course, depending upon the requirements of his product.

3.58. SAMPLING PLANS

Sampling plans using attributes or variables are:

3.58.1. Single Sampling Plan

In this plan a lot is accepted or rejected on the basis of a **single sample** drawn from the lot. The procedure is:

(i) Draw a single sample of size 'n', i.e. take out 'n' components which may be calculated or taken from statistical tables.

(ii) Inspect the sample and find the number of defective components.

(iii) If defective pieces exceed the acceptance number **'c'**, the lot is rejected. In case the defective pieces are less than **'c'**, the lot is accepted by replacing the defective components by non-defective components.

(iv) In case the lot is rejected, inspect each and every component (100 percent inspection) of the lot and replace the defective parts and salvage or correct the defective parts by reprocessing them.

The characteristics of single sampling plan are:

(i) A single sampling plan is easy to design, explain and administer.

(ii) It is the only practical type of sampling plan under conveyorized production conditions when only one sample can be selected.

(iii) It involves lower cost of training and supervising employees, transporting and sorting samples.

(iv) It estimates lot quality very accurately.

(v) It is more economical than double sampling plan when lots have their percent defectives close to each AQL.

(vi) It involves a bigger sample size than the double sampling plan.

(vii) It involves record keeping less than that of double and multiple sampling plans.

(viii) A single sampling plan provides maximum information concerning the lot quality because each sample can be plotted on the control chart.

3.58.2. Double Sampling Plan

Sometimes it will be very difficult to decide the fate of a lot on the basis of the first sample, a second sample is drawn out of the same lot and the decision whether to accept or reject the lot is taken on the basis of the combined results of the first and second sample. The procedure is as follows:

The following table gives the characteristics of the two samples.

Particulars	Sample Number 1 = n_1	Sample Number 2 = n_2
Sample size	n_1	n_2
Acceptance number as decided by both the parties	C_1	C_2 ($C_2 > C_1$)
Number of defectives found	K_1	K_2

1. Take a sample of size n_1 from the lot and inspect the same. Let K_1 be the number of defective units found in the sample.
2. If K_1 is greater than C_1, reject the sample or do 100 percent inspection and replace defective items.
3. If K_1 is less than C_1 then accept the lot by replacing K_1, the defective items.
4. If C_1 is less than K_1 and less than or equals to C_2 then draw a second sample of size n_2.
5. Now total number of sample size is $n_1 + n_2$. Inspect the same and let the total defective parts is $K_1 + K_2$.
6. If $K_1 + K_2$ is greater than C_2, and then reject the lot. Or do 100 percent inspection and replace all the defective items.
7. If $K_1 + K_2$ is less than C_2, then accept the lot by replacing the defective items.

Characteristics of double sampling plan are as follows:

(i) A double sampling plan is more expensive to administer compared to single sampling plan.

(ii) Double sampling plan is easier to sell to the personnel because psychologically the idea of giving a second chance to a lot before rejecting it exercises popular appeal.

(iii) It involves less inspection than that required for a sequential sampling plan.

(iv) It permits a smaller first sample than it called for by the sample size of the corresponding single sampling plan.

(v) It involves more record keeping than a single sampling plan.

(vi) It does not give as accurate estimation of lot quality as it provided by a single sampling plan.

In sequential sampling plan more samples are drawn and the above procedure (as that of second sampling plan) is extended.

Before concluding this topic, it is better to expose the students to some of the topics in statistical quality control, though not in detail, at least briefly.

3.59. TOTAL QUALITY MANAGEMENT

The quality of the incoming material and during the process and until the product is shipped and delivered to the customer the quality is to be checked and assured **at every step of the company's activities.** Quality management is a company-wide activity and various functional departments contribute to its success. Total quality management activities starts at **market research stage and ends at after sales service**, to give maximum satisfaction to the customer. This means to say that all the functional departments are involved in assuring the quality product to the customer and quality service to the customer, **the total quality management efforts be properly organized to coordinate the various contributing aspect to quality.** Without such co-ordination, there may be a chaotic situation, and although the quality is everybody's concern, it may become nobody's concern. To get good results, it is better that the quality management should be headed and monitored by a separate functional head.

3.60. ZERO DEFECT PROGRAMME

The best example of the motivational aspect of quality management could be given by means of the relatively novel ideas generated by the **zero defect programme** and **quality circles.** The philosophy behind the zero defects is to negate the commonly held views that **"to err is human".** Instead, zero defect philosophy believes in total perfection or **"to do the job right the first time".** It believes that errors are caused by two factors i.e., (a) Lack of knowledge and (b) Lack of attention. While the former factor can be taken care of by imparting more knowledge, the latter is an attitudinal problem.

3.61. QUALITY CIRCLES

Zero defects promoters motivate individually, **quality circle** is a collective effort, where 3 to 15 volunteers from the workers form a group and meet regularly, may be weekly or bi-weekly for about an hour, in order to identify, analyze and search for solutions to work-related problems and the ways of implementing the solutions. The meetings, which are generally supervised (usually by a foreman) address themselves to technical problems and follow to strict problem-solving approach (workers and management are trained in it), so that the meetings do not fritter the time away and become forums to handle grievances. Quality circles should encourage participation by all members and should foster creativity. The idea is to **develop talents** of the workers and to **develop leadership** besides getting a bunch of good ideas to sole problems by tapping the collective intellect and creative genius of the working staff.

QUESTIONS

1. What is the meaning of quality? Explain its characteristics.
2. Why should we control quality? Distinguish between quality control and inspection.
3. What are the causes of variation in quality? Explain the difference between Quality Control and Statistical Quality Control.
4. Explain the purpose, Development and Advantages of Statistical Quality Control.
5. Explain the theory and techniques of Statistical Quality Control.
6. What is Process Control? Briefly explain the methods used for Process Control with respect to Quality Control.
7. Explain the concept of Control Charts and their application in Statistical Quality Control.
8. Briefly explain the types of Quality Control Charts and mention their advantages and limitations.
9. Explain how do you construct Standard Deviation Chart or σ Chart.
10. Explain the method of construction Mean Chart and Range Chart.
11. What are fraction defective chart and how they are constructed?
12. Explain the method of construction number defective chart or np-chart.
13. How a number defective per unit chart is constructed?

14. What is the significance of Inspection? Briefly explain the below mentioned terms: (a) Acceptance Inspection, (b) Sampling, (c) Producer's Risk, (d) consumer's Risk, (e) Acceptance Quality Level (AQL) and (f) Lot Tolerance Percent Defective.
15. Write a note on Sampling Inspection giving various types of sampling inspection and briefly explain Double Sampling Plan.
16. Briefly explain how an Operating Characteristic Curve is constructed and explain its significance.
17. Briefly write note on Total Quality Management.
18. Explain the concept of Zero Defects Program.
19. What is a Quality Circle? Explain in detail its uses and functioning.

QUALITY CONTROL

1. Quality is:
   (a) Well defied term (b) Confusing term
   (c) Relative term (d) None
2. One of the meanings of quality is:
   (a) Fitness for purpose (b) A term used for control
   (c) A term used for testing (d) None
3. A process through which we measure the actual quality performance and compare it with standards is termed as:
   (a) Maintenance of quality (b) Design for quality
   (c) Quality control (d) Quality assurance
4. Length, diameter and viscosity are .... quality characteristics.
   (a) Contractual (b) Time based
   (c) Technical (d) Ethical
5. Checking the materials, products, and components at various stages, with reference to predetermined factors is known as:
   (a) Quality control (b) Statistical quality control
   (c) Comparing (d) Inspection
6. Inspection is a part of:
   (a) Manufacturing (b) Quality control
   (c) Testing (d) Supervision
7. Inspection is concerned with the quality of:
   (a) Present production (b) Past production
   (c) Future production (d) After storing the product
8. Quality control is the concern of:
   (a) Inspector (b) Quality controller
   (c) None (d) Everybody in the organization

9. When variation in quality arises due to tool wear or defective material it can be classified as:
   (a) Chance cause (b) Assignable cause
   (c) Exclusive cause (d) None
10. A control technique exercised during the product is being manufactured is known as:
   (a) Product control (b) Variable control
   (c) Process control (d) Attribute control
11. The inspection done on past production to decide the quality is known as:
   (a) Acceptance inspection (b) Process inspection
   (c) In process inspection (d) Variable inspection
12. The control tool, which indicates whether the process is in control or out of control is known as:
   (a) Quality meter (b) Inspection
   (c) Quality control (d) Control chart
13. The control charts which distinguish between a defective item and a non-defective item with out going to technical aspects is known as;
   (a) Attribute chart (b) Variable chart
   (c) O.C.C. chart (d) Process chart
14. When standards of manufacture and allowable or tolerance limits are not specified to determine whether the process is under control or not the chart used us:
   (a) Mean chart (b) Range chart
   (c) Sigma chart (d) p-chart
15. In range chart the limits LCL and UCL are given by:
   (a) $D_3 \overline{R}$, $D_4 \overline{R}$ (b) D_4, $\overline{R}$ D_3 $\overline{R}$
   (c) $\overline{X} - A_2 \overline{R}$ (d) $\overline{R} + A_2 \overline{R}$
16. The risk of rejecting the items, which are satisfactory according to the producer is known as:
   (a) Product risk (b) Process risk
   (c) Producer's risk (d) Consumer's risk
17. Risk of accepting unsatisfactory items is known as:
   (a) Consumer's risk (b) Producer's risk
   (c) Inspector's risk (d) Product risk
18. O.C.C. means:
   (a) Operating Circumstance Curve
   (b) Operating Characteristic Curve
   (c) Operating Control Curve
   (d) Operating Control Chart

19. The philosophy of worker's direct involvement in solving problems that affect their work, output and work place is known as:

(a) Quality philosophy (b) Zero defects program

(c) Total quality management (d) Quality circles

20. Zero defects program promotes motivation ....

(a) Individually (b) Group

(c) Inspectors (d) Managers

ANSWERS

1. (c)	**2.** (a)	**3.** (c)	**4.** (c)	**5.** (d)	**6.** (b)	**7.** (b)	**8.** (d)
9. (b)	**10.** (c)	**11.** (a)	**12.** (d)	**13.** (a)	**14.** (c)	**15.** (a)	**16.** (c)
17. (a)	**18.** (b)	**19.** (d)	**20.** (a).				

❍❍❍

Unit 4 Material Management and Inventory Control

4.1. INTRODUCTION

One of the basic functions of management is to employ capital efficiently so as to yield maximum results. This can be done in anyone of the two ways or by both ways.

1. By maximizing the margin of profit, or
2. By maximizing the productivity, i.e. maximizing the production with a given amount of capital. That is the management has to utilize the capital optimally.

However, this is all to often forgotten, much time and ingenuity is devoted to make only labour to work harder. In the process, the capital turnover and hence the productivity of capital is often totally neglected. Several new techniques have been developed and employed by modern managers to remedy this deficiency. Among these, **materials management** had become one of the most attractive techniques.

Materials management is a body of knowledge, which helps the manager to improve the productivity of capital by reducing material costs, preventing large amounts of capital benign locked up for long periods and improving the capital — turnover ratio. The techniques of materials management were evolved and developed during and after Second World War and have helped the more industrially developed countries to make spectacular progress in improving productivity.

Materials management is a comparatively new concept in our country. In the early sixties, managers in India directed their attention towards the materials management. Until early sixties, they were concentrating on items such as Purchasing, Transporting and Store keeping. Since, last four decades, that an increasing understanding of the importance of materials management is slowly finding its way among management circles in India. Since last ten years, materials management has been recognized as a major functional area of management. In western advanced countries this field of management has been recognized as most powerful area in increasing capital productivity and increasing the profit margin.

Materials management covers all aspects of material costs, materials supply and utilization. It covers the whole range of functions involved in converting raw materials and ancillary supplies into finished products. It is concerned with the planning and programming of materials and equipment, market research for purchases, pre-design value analysis, procurement of all materials including capital goods, raw materials, components and assemblies, finished goods, packaging and packing, stores control and inventory control, transportation of materials, materials handling, value analysis, disposal of scrap and surplus, salvage and operations research for materials. Many managers, many a time refer materials management to inventory control or materials handling or material control. But materials management covers a wider area regarding materials. Though materials management is a widely accepted term, some organizations use **'supply management'** and specially, defense organizations use word **'logistic management'**, which is concerned with the functions of materials management.

While the field of materials management covers all aspects of material costs, supply and utilization, opinion is divided as to what functions should be included under the unified direction of the materials manager. The question here is what should be the scope of materials management? And what functions should be included under the duties of materials manager? It is up to an organization to allocate the functions to the materials manager. Some companies can allocate even production control also under materials manager, because of entire production is involved with utilization of materials and materials cost play a major role in the cost of production.

The importance of materials management arises from the fact that materials account for 60 to 65 percent of the sales value of the product, that is to say from every rupee of the sales revenue, 60 to 65 paise are spent on materials. Hence, small changes in material cost can result in large sums of money saved or lost. Materials management should, therefore, be considered as a function of prime importance for our industrial economy. Materials cost form the bulk of the total cost of a manufactured product. A survey in India revealed that in major industries the materials cost on an average works out to 64 paise per rupee, the balance of 36 paise being accounted for the wages and salaries, overheads and profits. In material intensive production industries, the share of materials cost may be still higher. If we take material carrying charges, procurement charges into consideration, the percentage may be still higher. Materials management provides tools and techniques, most of which are very simple, to reduce material costs substantially. As a large chunk of the revenue, i.e. 64 percent is exposed to these techniques, correspondingly large savings result when they are applied, than when attempts are made to save on other items of expenditure like wages and salaries, which are about 16 percent or overheads which may be around 20 percent. As the resultant savings are of a recurring nature, the advantages gained are enormous and lasting. In addition to this savings, efficient materials management also brings a substantial reduction in foreign exchange or reduced value of imports. Industrial managers have been slow in appreciating the importance of materials management, as they have been preoccupied with other matters such as finding new markets, labour problems and so on. Materials management brings about increased profits without any trouble from labour or any other source. It results in increased productivity of capital by preventing large amounts of capital being locked up for long periods in inventories.

4.2. OBJECTIVES OF MATERIALS MANAGEMENT

Materials management function is a staff function and it has to support the objectives of the undertaking as a whole they are:

(i) Survival and growth.

(ii) Maximum satisfaction to customers.

(iii) Good working conditions to employees.

(iv) Technological lead over competitor.

In addition the objectives of materials management are:

(i) Maintaining continuity of productive operations by ensuring a uniform flow of material.

(ii) Reducing materials cost by using systematic inventory control techniques.

(iii) Releasing working capital for productive purposes, by efficient control of inventories.

(iv) Increasing the competitiveness of end products by ensuring right quality at right price in both national and international markets.

(v) Saving foreign exchange through economic use of foreign purchases and import substitutes.

(vi) Establishing good buyer and seller relations.

(vii) Ensuring low departmental costs and high efficiency.

(viii) Setting high ethical values.

By careful financial analysis, it can be shown that a 5 percent reduction in materials cost will result in an increased profits equivalent to a 36 percent increase in sales. Reduction of materials cost is more preferable by a manager than achieving increase in sales. To increase sales, lot of efforts are to be made as it deals with external environment and uncertainties, it will be easier to tackle the problem of reducing the materials cost.

4.3. METHODS OF INVENTORY CONTROL

After considering the importance of materials management, now it is worthwhile to consider some of the important methods of controlling inventory. They are discussed below:

4.3.1. ABC Analysis

ABC analysis is a basic technique of materials management and is recognized as the starting point of materials management. The applicability of this technique extends over almost all aspects of materials management, such as purchasing, receiving and inspection of materials. In fact, this technique can be applied to any aspects of a business or individual problems to control the costs. The origin of ABC analysis is **Pareto's 80–20 rule.** The rule says that **80 percent of country's economy is controlled by 20 percent of people.** If we apply this rule to verify its correctness, the results say that it is correct. Let us consider some examples.

(i) List out all the expenses we do over a period of time and arrange them in the order from highest to the lowest. Find the total of expenses. Work out the cumulative total of the expenses listed above. Workout the percentage of each cumulative total with respect to the total amount. We see that only 20 percent of the items consume 80 percent of total expenses.

(ii) We have 24 hours in a day. List out the times you have spent on each activity and arrange them in descending order and find the cumulative times. Work out the percentage with 24 hours. We find that 20 percent of the items covers 80 percent of the time.

(iii) Take the example of any office and conduct ABC analysis on the salary bill of the office. We find that 80 percent of the bill refers to 20 percent of the staff and rest 80 percent to others. Like this we can apply the principles of ABC analysis to an aspect of business or life.

ABC analysis, VED analysis, FSN analysis and periodic revision classification comes under **selective inventory control.** The principle of management by exception is a better term under which can classify ABC analysis. Items of inventory are classified into ABC or other class for **selective management control**. Controls applied **selectively** to contribute to a better management, in most cases avoiding wastages of precious management time and importantly avoiding the confusion resulting from excessive controls. The degree and characteristics of controls to be exercised by the management should depend upon:

(i) The necessity of control,

(ii) The relative necessity of the material to be placed under control, and

(iii) The particular characteristics of the material.

Materials may be divided into three categories or three classes for selective management control. More grades than this may not give fruitful results. These three grades in which materials are classified is known as **A-class materials, B-class materials and C-class materials.** In fact, any item under classification may be classified like this. In reality A, B, C stands for three different classes of items. But many a time this classification is known as **Always Best Control.** ABC analysis is based on the relative importance of the materials. Therefore, there are various bases for ABC classification. They are **material consumption cost, material's criticality, availability status of materials, material's physical characteristics such as size and weight, frequency of material's usage etc.** Depending on the situation and importance of above said characteristics, classification is made. Conventionally, however, the **basis for ABC analysis** is **"annual consumption value"** of the material. Here one should understand clearly, that annual consumption value does not refer to the unit price of the material and it refers to the annual consumption value of the material. For example, consider the firm is using a component whose unit cost is ₹ 1000/-. It uses 3 units of the component in year. Hence, the annual consumption value is ₹ 1000 × 3 = ₹ 3000/-. Now consider another item for example a bolt whose unit price is ₹ 1/- used by the firm. The firm is using 10,000 bolts in a year. Hence, the annual consumption value of bolts is ₹ 10,000/-. Here the bolt is considered to be item of higher annual consumption value than the other item referred above. It has been found in many industries that a small number of items account for a large proportion of annual turnover (money) of the inventory. These items should attract the materials manager's attention immediately. Such items are known as **A-class items.** It is also observed in industries that very large number of items of inventory accounts for a small portion of the annual turnover or annual consumption value of the materials. These are classified as **C-class materials.** *There are many items contributing very little to the ultimate problem of managing the working capital investment.* Naturally, materials manager should turn his attention to those items only after he has **taken care of annual high consumption value items, i.e. A-class materials.** Class B-items belong to the **in-between** category; neither their total consumption value high nor the total number of items is high. The above-discussed phenomenon occurs in almost all industries and therefore the conventional ABC classification can be applied in most of the industries.

4.3.1.1. Procedure for ABC analysis

1. List out all the materials used in the company (all types of materials are to be considered, whether they are used for manufacturing product or they may be indirect materials).
2. Workout their annual consumption value, which is given by the product of number of units used in a year and the unit price of the material.
3. Arrange all the items in the descending order of their annual consumption value.
4. Add all the annual consumption values and get the total annual inventory cost.
5. Write the cumulative consumption values and find the percentage of this cumulated consumption value with that of annual consumption value.
6. Note down the percentage thus got in step 5 against respective item.

Write dividing lines at 70% and 90% points.

7. All the items, which fall under 70 per cent are 'A' Class items and those fall between 70 and 90 per cent are 'B' class items and others, which are between 90 and 100 per cent are 'C' class items. This is shown in figure 4.1 below.

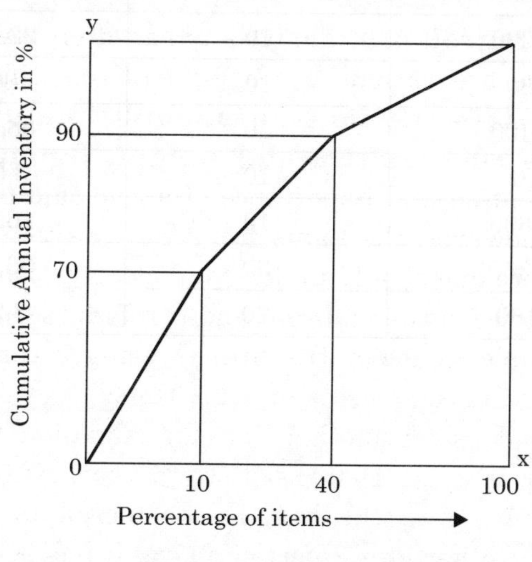

Fig. 4.1. ABC Analysis

Example 4.1.

Management of a company has the following information about its inventory stock. Find the percentage of items management should place in each class according to ABC classification method.

Item Number	Annual usage (number of pieces)	Unit Price in ₹
1	600	20
2	5600	30
3	60	20
4	2200	10
5	80	10
6	4400	20
7	300	10
8	1600	10
9	1200	30
10	160	20

Solution:

First step is to calculate annual consumption value and rank them. Afterwards they are arranged in descending order and cumulative percentages are calculated. The following two tables show the same. We can see that only two items will be A class items and next 6 are B class items and rest are C class items.

Item Number (1)	Annual Usage (2)	Unit price in ₹ (3)	Annual usage value 2 × 3 = (4)	Ranking (5)
1	600	20	12,000	6
2	5600	30	1,68,000	1
3	60	20	1,200	9
4	2200	10	22,000	4
5	80	10	800	10
6	4400	20	88,000	2
7	300	10	3,000	8
8	1600	10	16,000	5
9	1200	30	36,000	3
10	160	20	3,200	7

Item Number	Annual Usage in Percentage of units	Cumulative usage value in ₹	Cumulative percentage of usage value	Category
2	10	1,68,000	47.97	
6	20	2,56,000	73.10	A
9	30	2,92,000	83.38	
4	40	3,14,000	89.66	
8	50	3,30,000	94.23	B
1	60	3,42,000	97.66	
10	70	3,45,200	98.57	
7	80	3,48,200	99.43	
3	90	3,49,400	99.77	
5	100	3,50,200	100.00	C

4.3.2. Periodic Revision of Classification

ABC Classification depends not only on the cost of the unit, but also on the number of units consumed over the year. Because, in this classification, we are dealing with the annual consumption value. Therefore, if the value of items were to increase or if the amount of annual consumption of the item were would increase. Hence, the classification of an item may change from one class to other. This is to say that ABC classification is not done once for all and to be used the same all time, the classification need to be monitored periodically and any changes need to be incorporated accordingly. A proper ABC analysis will lead to better control over materials and consequent reduction in costs associated with inventories.

4.3.3. VED Analysis

In addition to the intrinsic or market value of materials, which is invested in the materials, there is sometimes a **nuisance** value to the materials. In ABC analysis, we have seen that annual consumption value; quantity of material consumed and the unit cost play a vital role. This means that **ABC analysis deal with the annual consumption value of the item due to their presence and not any other aspect such as the criticality of the material or the nuisance value of the material.** The nuisance value is the cost associated with materials due to their absence. Some of the materials are important by their absence and not merely by their presence. In case they are not available, whole production system may come to standstill and involve high cost of loss of production. Here the cost of the item is not the question, but the availability is the matter. The investment in these materials may be small but for non-availability of the item the cost or losses that the company going to involve will be very high. These are **critical items,** which are required in adequate quantity.

With the above discussion, we can understand that materials may be classified depending on their **criticality**, i.e. on **functional basis.** The degree of criticality can be stated as whether the material is **Vital** to the process of production or **Essential** to the process of production or **Desirable** to the process of production. This type of classification is known as **VED analysis. V** stands for **Vital, E** stands for **Essential,** and **D** stands for

Desirable items. In addition to the conventional ABC analysis, VED analysis also plays an important role in materials management. VED ranking may be done on the basis of the shortage costs of materials, which can be either quantified or qualitatively expressed.

4.3.4. Combination of ABC and VED Analysis

ABC and VED analysis, used for classification, one depending on the annual consumption (or consumption) value and the other on the criticality of the item both are important in the process of inventory control. In case we combine both and classify the materials depending both on the consumption value and the criticality, it will give us a fruitful result. This can be made in nine ways, which is shown in the matrix given below:

	V	E	D
A	AV	AE	AD
B	BV	BE	BD
C	CV	CE	CD

ABC – VED Classification Matrix

	V	E	D
A	90%	80%	70%
B	95%	85%	75%
C	99%	90%	80%

ABC – VED Matrix showing the service level

This type of classification helps the management to decide the material policy and what service levels are expected to see that no difficulty is faced. An item belongs to both V class and A class, is costlier (more annual consumption value), at the same time of higher criticality, the management should see that it should be available anytime the need arises and the stock levels to be controlled properly to see that inventory carrying costs are kept under control. The services to be maintained are shown in the matrix for various combinations.

4.3.5. Fast Moving, Slow Moving and Non-Moving Analysis (FSN Analysis)

This analysis relates to the demand for the materials and stock-moving pattern. Fast moving materials are to be stoked nearer to the storekeeper and slow moving items are stocked at a considerable distance and the non-moving materials are stocked in a place without causing incontinence to day-to-day movement of men and materials. Similarly, fast moving materials must be kept in a place easily reached by the storekeeper. Non-moving materials are kept in a remote place, as they are not required for use. This analysis (FSN analysis) will help for optimal utilization of space available and materials handling time of the storekeeper.

In addition to the above analysis, we can also use some of the characteristics of material for classification. For example, **perishable** or **obsolescence** materials. These characteristics are particularly helpful for chemicals and drugs, which have low shelf life. Here classification is made on the basis of shelf life as **Long shelf life, Medium shelf life** and **Short shelf life.** This classification is known as **PQR Classification.** Sometimes the bulk versus weight of the materials is of importance in terms of providing space for the materials in the stores and therefore another classification i.e. **XYZ Classification** is used. Here the classification is **Bulky, Medium Bulky and Lighter materials.**

While storing items, heavy and weighty materials are kept at floor level, so that they can be handled easily. Medium weight materials are kept in shelves depending on their weight, lighter weight materials at the top rack and the heavy materials in the bottom rack etc. This type of arrangement, will save good amount of storekeeper's time and reduces handling costs, also avoids accidents and causalities at the time of handling the materials.

4.4. QUANTITATIVE METHODS FOR INVENTORY CONTROL

In this section, we shall see types of inventories, necessity of maintaining inventory, costs associated with inventory and certain inventory models used to maintain inventory costs at minimum. In addition, let us discuss briefly some important topics of inventory control. (For more details, readers are advised to refer to a book on **OPERATIONS RESEARCH**).

4.4.1. Types of Inventory

Inventory consists of usable but idle resources, such as men, machines and materials and money. When resources involved are material, the **inventory** is also called **stock of materials.** When we talk of men, we call it as **Human resource.** When we deal with living being, other than men, we call it as **live stock** inventory and when it is money, we deal with management of **funds.** In this chapter, we are much concerned with the materials only. An inventory problem is said to exist if either the resources are subjected to control or if there is at least one such cost that decreases as inventory increase. The objective is to minimize total (actual or expected) cost. However, in situation where inventory affects demand the objective may also be to maximize the profit. Inventory may be classified as:

(i) **Raw Material Inventory:** Materials used in manufacturing a product are generally known as **Raw Materials.** For example, Sugar cane is the raw material for manufacturing sugar. Iron ore and coal are the raw materials used for manufacturing iron and so on. These raw materials are bought and stocked in stores room. When demand arises, they are drawn from stores and processed or the use value is added during the process and finally finished product comes out of production system.

(ii) **Semi-Finished Goods:** When the material being processed, it may have to wait between two processes because of non availability of machine, such materials which are waiting for further processing are known as **semi-finished goods, or semi-finished material or work-in-process inventory.**

(iii) **Components:** The parts used in assembly of product, are known as components. These components are purchased from a supplier and used for assembling the product. These are also known as bought out components or bought out materials.

(iv) **Spare Parts Inventory:** When manufacturing or servicing facility breakdown, it is to be repaired. In such case, the defective or worn-out parts of the machine are to be replaced by new one. These new parts of the machine are known as **Spares or Spare parts inventory.**

(v) **Obsolete Inventory:** When any facility becomes unserviceable and it is to be replaced by a new one, after replacing, the old machine/facility is to be disposed. Such machines, which have become useless, are termed as obsolete inventory.

(vi) **Waste, Scrap and Rejects:** This type of inventory occurs in manufacturing firms or in service organizations. While processing materials, chips are produced and it is of no use for the organization and it is to be disposed. Similarly, defective components, which cannot be reprocessed (rejects) and materials, which cannot be used in any way in the organization (waste), all these are to be disposed. They may not be having any use value for the organization, but they may be reprocessed by some other organizations to produce a useful product.

4.4.2. Necessity for Maintaining Inventory

Though inventory of materials is an idle resource (as they are not used immediately and stocked for future use), almost every business must maintain it for efficient and smooth running of its operations. If an enterprise has no inventory of material at all, on receiving a manufacturing order, it will have to place order for purchase of raw material, wait for arrival and receive the material and then start production. The customer will have to wait for a long time for the delivery of goods and may get frustrated and turn to anther manufacturer.

Maintaining of inventory becomes necessary for the following reasons:

(i) It helps in smooth and efficient running of the production system and the enterprise. It decouples the production from the customers and vendors and simplifies the otherwise complex organization for manufacture and reduce co-ordination effort.

(ii) It provides service to the customers at a short notice. Timely deliveries may increase the goodwill for the company.

(iii) In the absence of inventory, the enterprise may have to pay very high prices because of piecemeal purchasing. Maintaining inventory may earn price discounts on bulk purchase. It also takes advantage of favourable market.

(iv) It reduces the product cost, since there is an added advantage of batch production and mass production runs.

(v) It acts as a buffer stock when raw materials are received late.

(vi) Process and movement inventories (also known as pipeline inventories) are quite necessary in big enterprises where significant amounts of time are required to transship items from one location to another.

(vii) Bulk purchases reduce the number of orders and hence less clerical work.

(viii) As many of customers and vendors are away from the organization, it is better to have stock of inventory to continue production during the lead period.

(ix) It helps in maintaining economy by absorbing some of the fluctuations when the demand for an item fluctuates or is seasonal.

However, too often inventories are wrongly used as a substitute answer for management problems. For example, if there are large finished goods inventories, inaccurate sales forecasting by marketing department, may never be apparent. Similarly, a production foreman who has large in-process inventors may be able to hide his poor planning, since there is always something to manufacture. Furthermore, inventory means unproductive and **tied up capital** of the enterprise. The capital could be usefully utilized in other venture as well. With large inventories there is always likelihood of obsolescence too. Also maintenance of inventory costs additional money to be spent on personnel, equipment, insurance, etc. Thus excess inventories are not desirable. This necessitates controlling the inventories in the most useful way.

4.4.3. Causes of Poor Inventory Control

There are certain instances; which leads to poor inventory control. They are:

(i) Over buying without regard to the forecast or proper estimate of demand to take advantage of favorable market.

(ii) Excess production or production of goods much before the customer requires them.

(iii) Over stocking may also result from the desire to provide better service to the customers. Bulk production to cut down production costs also will result in large inventories.

(iv) Cancellation of orders and minimum quantity stipulations by the suppliers may also give rise to large inventories.

4.4.4. Costs Associated with Inventories

The three important costs considered in controlling inventory costs are:

4.4.4.1. Inventory carrying costs or stock holding costs (C_1)

Inventory carrying costs arise on account of maintaining the stocks and the interest paid to the capital tied up with the stock of material in the stores. These costs vary directly with the size of the inventory as well as the time the item is held in stock. Various components of stock holding costs are:

(a) Cost of money or capital tied up in inventories: This is, by far, the most important component. Money borrowed from the bank may cost of about 18 to 20 percent. But usually the problem is viewed in a slightly different way, i.e. how much the organization would have earned, had the capital been invested in an alternative project such as developing a new product, etc. It is generally taken somewhat around 15 to 20 percent of the value of the inventories (Average value of the inventory is considered – this will be explained later).

(b) Cost of storage space: This consists of rent for the space occupied by the inventory. Besides space expense, this will also include heating and lighting and other atmospheric control expenses. Typical value will be from 1 to 3 percent of the inventory value.

(c) Depreciation and deterioration charges: These are especially important for fashion items or items undergoing chemical changes during storage. Fragile items such as crockery, which is liable to damage, breakage, etc. This may range from 0.2 to1.0 percent of the inventory cost.

(d) Pilferage cost: It depends on the nature of the item. Valuable items may be more tempting, while there is hardly any possibility of heavy castings or forgings being stolen. This may be around 1.0 percent of the inventory value.

(e) Obsolescence cost: It depends upon the nature of the item in stock. Electronic and computer components are likely to be fast outdated. Changes in design also lead to obsolescence. It may be possible to quantify the percentage loss due to obsolescence and it may be taken at 5.0 percent of the stock value.

(f) **Handling cost:** This include all the costs associated with movement of stock, such as cost of labour, overhead cranes, gantries and other machinery used of the purpose.

(g) **Record keeping and administrative costs:** Various records are to be maintained by the storekeeper to have a proper account of the inventories on hand and inventories issued, all the cost involved in keeping these records will be included in carrying cost. This may amount to 0.05 to 1.0 percent.

(a) **Taxes and insurance:** Taxes paid on inventories and insurance coverage for the inventory in stock is taken into account. This may amount to 1 to 2 percent of the inventory cost.

As it is very difficult to calculate the inventory carrying cost day-to-day, the average inventory concept is used in calculating the inventory carrying costs. This is to say that in a cycle if the initial inventory is **'q'** and at the end of the cycle is **'zero'** the average inventory is **(0 + q)/2 = q/2.** The inventory carrying cost is calculated for the average inventory.

4.4.4.2. Procurement cost of set-up cost (C_3)

This includes the fixed and variable costs associated with placing of an order. In case of purchase models, it is known as **Ordering Cost.** In case of manufacturing model, it is known as **Set-up cost.** To place an order certain paper work is to be done. The cost of this paper work is taken as cost of ordering. In case of manufacturing, before starting production, the machine is to be set-up (or prepare the machine for production or set the tools etc.). Only on setting of the machine, the material is loaded and the production is started. The ordering cost is distributed over the items purchased in that order. Similarly, the set-up cost is distributed over the items purchased in that order. Similarly, the set-up cost is distributed equally over the products manufactured in that set-up. This cost is also known as **replenishment cost.**

4.4.4.3. Shortage cost or stock-out costs (C_2)

These costs are associated with either a delay in meeting demand or the inability to meet it at all. Therefore, shortage costs are usually interpreted in two ways. In case the unfilled demand can be filled at a later stages **(backlog case),** these costs are proportional to quantity that is short as well as the delay time. The represent loss of goodwill and cost of idle equipment. In case of unfilled demand is lost **(no back log case),** these costs become proportional to only the quantity that is short. These results in cancelled orders lost sales, foregone profit and even the business itself.

4.5. INVENTORY CONTROL PROBLEMS

Two basic factors, which we have to answer when dealing with inventory problems, are (i) When to order (produce or purchase)? (ii) How much to order or purchase?

4.5.1. When to Order?

This is related to the lead-time of an item. Lead-time may be defined as the time interval between the placement of an order and the receipt of the material. It may be replenishment order on an outside firm or within the workshop (work order, is the order placed for manufacturing the component within in the firm). There should be enough stock for each item so that customer's order (or demand from assembly line) can be met from this stock until replenishment. This stock level, known as **reorder level,** has, therefore, to be determined for each item. It is determined by compromising the cost of maintaining these stocks and the disservice to the customer if his order is not fulfilled in time.

4.5.2. How Much to Order?

Each order is associated with the ordering cost. To keep it low, the number of orders should be as few as possible, i.e. the order size should be large. But larger the size of the order, higher will be the inventory carrying cost. These two are contradictory to each other. Hence, a balance is achieved by selecting the right quantity for each order. This quantity is known as **'Economic Order Quantity (EOQ)'**, when dealing with purchase models and **'Economic Batch Quantity (EBQ)'**, when dealing with manufacturing models. Next section deals with some important inventory model. Here the demand is taken as deterministic. When you go for advanced courses, you deal with different inventory models, which depend on the nature of demand. Here we are concerned with only deterministic demand and the model is known as **'inventory model for deterministic demand'.** When the demand is probabilistic in nature, the models are known as **'probabilistic models'.** Before going to discuss models, let us try to understand two important inventory control terms

(i) Fixed Quantity System, and

(ii) Fixed Order System.

They are generally known as **'p-system'** and **'q-system'.** These two are inventory control models.

(i) p-System or Fixed Period System: Here orders for materials are placed every time at a fixed period, say on every first of the month or once in every 15 days and so on. But the quantity for which order is placed will differ from order to order depending on the demand or the rate of consumption. That is the period of order is fixed but the quantity varies.

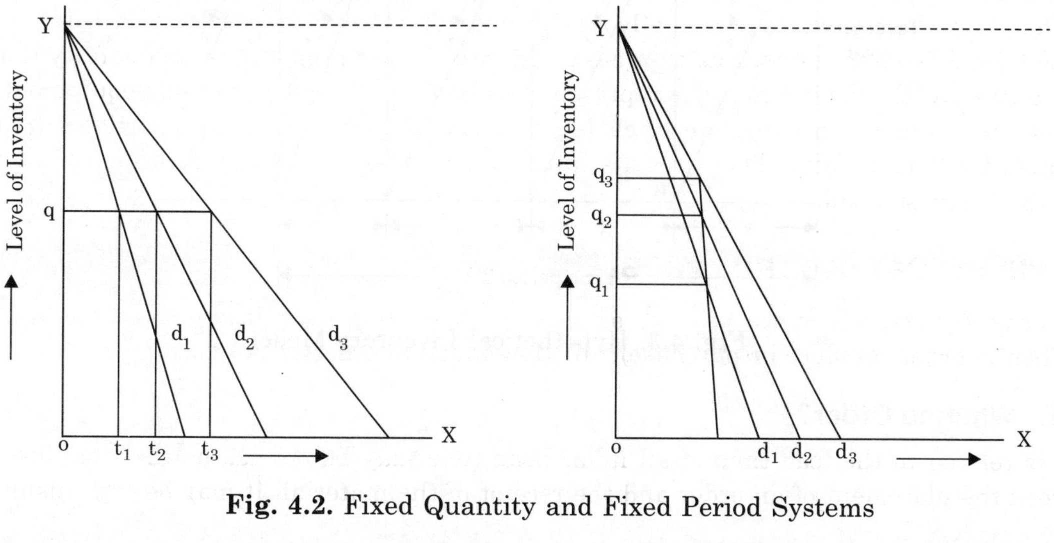

Fig. 4.2. Fixed Quantity and Fixed Period Systems

(ii) q-System or Fixed Quantity System: In this system, the order quantity remains same with all orders placed for a material but the period of placing order for the material will differ. This period once again depends on the demand or the rate of consumption. This is also known as **Two-Bin System.** Both are shown in the Fig.4.2.

4.6. DETERMINISTIC INVENTORY CONTROL MODEL (EOQ OR EBQ MODEL)

Symbols used in the model:

C_1 = Inventory carrying cost of the average inventory cost in rupees.

C_2 = Stock out cost or shortage cost in rupees.

C_3 = Ordering cost in rupees or set-up cost in rupees.

i = Rate of inventory carrying charges, as a percentage of average inventory cost. (for purchase model).

p = Unit cost of the materials or component in rupees per unit.

t = Time period.

r = Rate of demand or rate of consumption in units per time period.

λ = Demand per year in units per year.

q_0 = Optimal order quantity or optimal batch quantity.

t_0 = Optimal time for placing order.

τ = Lead-time.

Deterministic demand or Infinite production rate, where ordering cost is C_3 and inventory carrying cost is C_1 and immediate replenishment, i.e. lead time is zero and shortage cost C_2 is also zero.

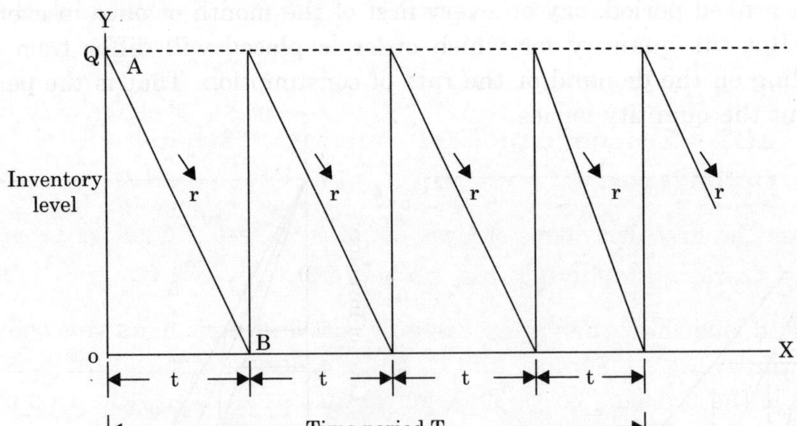

Fig. 4.3. Hypothetical Inventory Model

If the production run is made at the intervals t, a quantity q = rt must be produced for the manufacturing model (in case we are dealing with purchase model q = rt is to be purchased). If the inventory is maintained for a period 't' then the total inventory for the period 't' = q × t = qt. Hence, the average inventory = qt/2 or it may be worked out as below:

Area of the triangle AOB = ½ × Base × Altitude = ½ × t × q = qt/2.

Inventory carrying cost = C_1 × qt/2

Ordering cost = C_3

Total cost = Inventory carrying cost + Ordering cost = (qt/2) × C_1 + C_3.

Total inventory cost per unit of time = $C_q = \{ (qt/2)\, C_1 + C_3\}/ t = (q/2)\, C_1 + C_3/t$

We know that q = rt or t = q /r , substituting this in the above equation of C_q , we get

$C_q = (qC_1)/2 + C_3\, r/q$ ....(1) . **This is known as Cost Equation.**

This should be minimized. Equating the first derivative of C_q to zero can do this.

The first derivative = $dC_q/d_q = C_1/2 - C_3\, r/q^2$. Equating this to zero, and simplifying we get, $q = \sqrt{2C_3r/C_1}$. This is known as **Square root formula** or **Harries formula** or **Economic Order Quantity formula (EOQ) or Economic Batch Quantity Formula (EBQ).**

$q_0 = \sqrt{2C_3r/C_1}$ substituting this in **q = rt** and simplifying we get,

$t_0 = \sqrt{2C_3/C_1r}$ = Time for placing order.

Optimal cost of inventory $C_0 = \sqrt{2C_1/C_3r}$. In case we are dealing with purchase model, then the annual demand = λ units per year, Inventory carrying charges = i , and the unit cost of the item = ₹ p per unit and the ordering cost = C_3. Then the model for q_0, t_0, and C_0 will be as follows:

EOQ = $\sqrt{2C_3\, \lambda/ip}$

EOT = Economic time for ordering = $\sqrt{2C_3/ip\lambda}$

Optimal cost $C_0 = \sqrt{2C_3\lambda ip}$

Note: When the first derivative of C_q is equated to zero, we get ½ $C_1 - C_3r/q^2 = 0$ i.e. ½ $C_1 = C_3\, r/q^2$. Simplifying this, we get $(q/2)\, C_1 = (r/q)\, C_3$.

The left hand side shows inventory carrying cost and right hand side shows the ordering cost (as q/2 is the average inventory and C_1 is the ordering cost and r/q gives the number of orders and C_3 is the ordering cost). This shows that at EOQ (q_0) the **inventory carrying cost = ordering cost.** This can be shown by means of a graph.

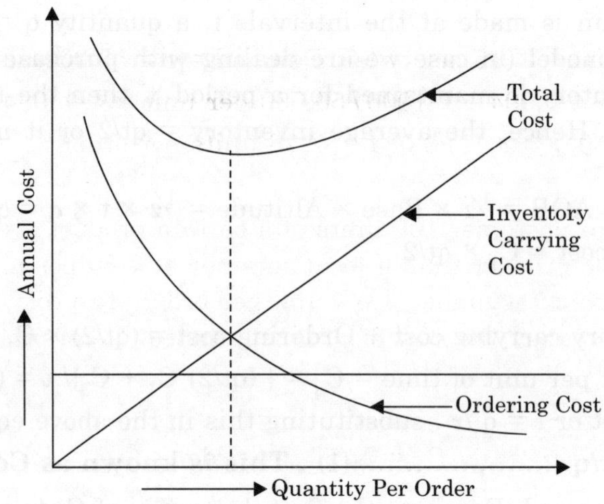

Fig. 4.4. Economic Order Quantity

Problem 4.2.

In a production shop the assembly line has a demand of 200 components per month, the storage cost per component is ₹ 1/- per month. The set up cost per run is ₹ 25/-. The production is instantaneous. Find the Economic Batch Quantity and the optimal for replenishment of inventory.

Solution:

Given data is C_1 = ₹ 1/- per item per month.

Demand for item is 200 units per month = r

Set-up cost = C_3 = ₹ 25/- per run.

(Students must remember that all the data should be on one time scale either day or week or month or year)

$q_0 = \sqrt{2C_3\, r/C_1} = \sqrt{(2 \times 25 \times 200)/1} = 100$ units.

$t_0 = \sqrt{(2C_3)/rC_1} = \sqrt{2 \times 25/1 \times 200} = ½$ month or 15 days.

This can be worked out as follows:

$t_0 = q_0/r = 100/200 = ½$ month.

Here the cost of inventory = Carrying cost + Set-up cost = 1 × 100 + 25 = ₹ 125 per run.

Problem 4.3.

A precision engineering company consumes 50,000 units of a component per year. The ordering, receiving and handling costs are ₹ 3/- per order, while the trucking costs are ₹ 12/- per order. Further details are as follows:

(i) Interest cost is ₹ 0.06 per unit per year,

(ii) Deterioration and obsolescence cost is ₹ 0.004 per unit per year,

(iii) Storage cost is ₹ 1000/- per year for 50,000 units. Calculate the economic order quantity.

Solution:

Data: C_3 = ₹ 3 + ₹ 12 = ₹ 15 per order. Demand = r = 50,000 units per year.

C_1 = ₹ 0.06 + ₹ 0.004 + ₹ 1000 / 50,000 per unit = ₹ 0. 084 per unit. Therefore,

EOQ = √(2 × 50,000 × 15)/0.084 = 4226 units per order.

Problem 4.4.

You have to supply your customer 100 units of a certain product every Monday and only on Monday. You obtain the product from a local supplier at ₹ 60 per unit. The cost of ordering and transportation from the supplier are ₹ 150 per order. The cost of carrying inventory is estimated at 15% per year of the cost of product carried. Determine Economic lot size and optimal cost.

Solution:

Data: r = 100 units per week, C_3 = ₹ 150 per order.

C_1 = 15% if ₹ 60/- per year = {15/100 × 60 × 1/52} per week. = 9/52 per week.

q_0 = √2 × C_3 × r/C_1 = √(2 × 150 × 100 × 25)/9 = **416 units per order.**

C_0 = ₹ (60 × r + √2 C_1 C_3 r) = ₹ (60 × 100 + √2 × (9/25) × 150 × 100 = ₹ **6072/-.**

Problem 4.5.

A shopkeeper has a uniform demand of an item at the rate of 50 units per month. He buys from supplier at a cost of ₹ 6/- per item and the cost of ordering is ₹ 10/- each time. If the stock-holding costs are 20% per year of stock value, how frequently should he replenish his stocks? What is economic order quantity and what is the optimal cost including the cost of material.

Solution:

Data: λ = 50 × 12 = 600 units per year,

i = 0.20. C_3 = ₹ 10 per order and p = ₹ 6 per item.

q_0 = √(2 × C_3 × λ)/i × p = √(2 × 10 × 600) / 0.20 × 6 = 100 items.

t_0 = q_0 / λ = 100 / 600 = 1/6 of an year = 2 months.

C_0 = √2 × C_3 × λ × ip = √2 × 10 × 600 × 0.20 × 6 = ₹ 120

Total cost = Inventory cost + Material cost = 120 + 6 × 600 = ₹ **3720/-**

(It can be done other way also. There are 6 orders, hence ordering cost

= ₹ 10 × 6 = ₹ 60)

Every time the inventory = 100 units.

Average inventory = 100/2 = 50 units.

Hence carrying cost = 50 × 0.20 × 6 = ₹ 60.

Therefore, total cost = Carrying cost + Ordering cost = ₹ 60 + ₹ 60 = ₹ 120/-

Material cost = ₹ 600 × 6 = ₹ 3600.

The total cost = ₹ 3600 + 120 = ₹ **3720/-**

Problem 4.6.

A company uses annually 24,000 units of a component, which costs ₹ 1.25 per unit. Placing each order costs ₹ 22.50 and the carrying cost is 5.4 percent of the average inventory. Find the economic size and the total inventory cost including the cost of material.

Solution:

Data: $\lambda = 24{,}000$ units. $C_3 = ₹\ 22.50$ per order,

$p = ₹\ 1.25$ per unit, and

$i = 5.40/100 = 0.054.$

$q_0 = \sqrt{(2 \times C_3 \times \lambda)/ip} = \sqrt{(2 \times 22.50 \times 24000)/(0.054 \times 1.25} = 4000$ units.

Optimal time of replenishment = q_0/λ = 4000/24,000 = 1/6 of an year = 2 months.

Optimal inventory cost = $C_0 = \sqrt{2 \times C_3 \times ip \times \lambda}$

$= \sqrt{2 \times 22.50 \times 0.054 \times 1.25 \times 24000}$ = ₹ 270/-

σ Material cost = ₹ 1.25 × 24,000 = ₹ 30,000.

Total cost = ₹ 30,000 + ₹ 270 = ₹ 30,270/-

(As EOQ = 4000 units, there will be 24000/4000 = 6 orders.

Ordering cost = ₹ 22.50 × 6 = ₹ 135.

Inventory carrying cost = 0.054 × 1.25 × (4000/2) = ₹ 135.

Therefore, Material cost + Inventory cost = ₹ 30,000 + 135 + 135 = ₹ 30270/-)

QUESTIONS

1. What do you mean by managing the materials? What advantages are derived from managing the materials? What are the objectives of Materials Management?
2. What is Inventory? What are the various methods of Controlling Inventory? List all the methods and explain them briefly.
3. By means of a neat sketch explain ABC Control of Inventory and explain its relevance Pareto Rule.
4. Explain the Procedure of ABC Control.
5. What is VED analysis and FSN analysis? Explain them briefly and compare them with ABC analysis.
6. Explain the various types of Inventory maintained in industries.
7. Explain the necessity of Maintaining Inventory in stores and explain the reasons of poor inventory control.
8. Explain the various costs associated with inventory maintenance.
9. Explain what do you mean by EOQ and EBQ. Derive a formula for Economic Order quantity with usual symbols. Give a neat sketch of hypothetical inventory model.
10. Explain Fixed Period System (p-System) and fixed Quantity System (q-System) of inventory control. And explain their suitability.

❍❍❍

PURCHASE FUNCTION

4.7. INTRODUCTION

In any organization or industry purchases means buying of equipment, materials, parts, tools and stores etc. Required for the smooth running of business in which the organization is involved. As one of the first acts of manufacturing business is to purchase materials, hence purchasing is a primary function. Competitive sales cannot be made unless the materials used for manufacturing or for resale, are purchased at ultimate cost which is commensurate with that available to competitors.

The importance of purchasing function varies with the nature and size of industry. In small factories, this function is performed by Works Manager or sometimes by the manager of the company depending on the size of the business or sometimes by the entrepreneur himself. In large and multi product industries, where large quantities of materials are consumed, the buying function is given to a separate functional department, known as **purchase department** under a highly competent executive designated as **Purchase Manager or Chief Buyer.**

The cost of direct materials and indirect materials form a part of the prime cost of the product. Careful buying helps in reducing the cost of materials and thereby increasing the margin of profits.

4.8. OBJECTIVES OF PURCHASING DEPARTMENT

The main objectives of purchasing department are:

(i) To purchase the required material of right specification desired by the manufacturing department i.e. **to purchase right quality. (What to purchase?)**

(ii) The purchase department must see that the required material is available for manufacturing department when it is required (when the demand arises), i.e. **Purchase at right time. (When to Purchase?)**

(iii) The department must try to purchase the materials from reliable source or vendor, so that incoming materials inspection cost, rejecting the supply and associated costs, rejects from the manufacturing line and cost of rejects can be minimized, i.e. **Purchase from Right Source or Reliable Supplier (Where to purchase?).**

(iv) It must purchase right quantity so that production can be carried out smoothly and to keep inventory costs at minimum. It has to take both **economic order quantity** and **Service level** into consideration while working for the quantity to purchase. **(How much to purchase?).**

(v) The purchase department has to negotiate with the vendors and purchase the materials at economic price. In case discounts on bulk purchases are available and it is advantageous to the organization it must use such opportunities.

(At what price the materials are to be purchased?)

To achieve these above objectives, certain functions are to be performed by the purchasing department. They are discussed below:

4.9. DUTIES OF PURCHASE MANAGER (PURCHASING OFFICER)

The most important and essential duties of a purchasing officer are:

(i) To maintain the standard of quality of product by selecting right quality of materials during purchases. The quality of product manufactured depends on the raw materials used. Also low quality material used for production increases the processing time and increase in production rejects. This will unnecessarily increases the production cost and the organization cannot stand in the competitive market. Also, low quality of product will not encourage the customer to purchase the product.

(ii) To organize and direct the purchasing department for efficient working. Proper planning of activities of the department and co-ordination among the employees of the department will help in promoting the efficiency of the department.

(iii) To represent his organization with other organizations during purchasing contracts.

(iv) He should maintain the reputation of the concern for integrity and fair dealings with others while negotiating.

(v) He must be able to supply the desired material for manufacturing at right time without causing inconvenience for production.

(vi) When the materials are received from the vendors and while issuing the materials to the production shops on indent, he must check properly whether receiving/issuing the correct material (right specification and right quantity) or not.

(vii) He must act as an executive of the firm or as a partner while preparing the purchase budgets.

(viii) To spend money on purchases very carefully and wisely.

(ix) To suggest, the materials which can economically be produced in the concern instead of purchasing and vice versa.

(x) Must have a continuous eye on latest research materials on materials and take advantage of least cost materials, which do not sacrifice the functional and quality aspect of the product.

(xi) He must take active part in value analysis/value engineering stages to help the analyzer to think of alternate materials or reduce the specifications of the material, so that the value of the product is increased.

4.10. FUNCTIONS OF PURCHASING DEPARTMENT

(i) To purchase the materials on a properly authorized material requisition. Without purchase requisition no materials are to be purchased. The authorized person or manager must sign the purchase requisition.

(ii) It must search for right vendor/supplier and negotiate with them and place orders for the requisitioned material.

(iii) To purchase right quality and right quantity of goods at economic price (right price) at right time.

(iv) To see that all the materials are received from the supplier end within time.

(v) On the receipt of material, it has to check, whether received consignment are according to the order not. It has to conduct quality inspection before taking delivery of materials.

(vi) To advise the management regarding possible economics to be maintained by manufacturing an item instead of purchasing or vice versa.

(vii) To study market conditions and enter into a rate contract with the large suppliers to ensure availability of materials all the time.

(viii) To study various sources of supply and decide upon the most convenient as well as alternate supplies.

(ix) To maintain the list of available and reliable suppliers and maintain contact with them whenever necessary.

(x) To keep the list of articles needed in the organization up to date with their normal quantities and placing orders.

(xi) To prepare specifications, to obtain quotations and compare these quotations and place the orders with most favorable supplier.

(xii) To see that the bills of the suppliers are made in time and promptly and good public relations are maintained.

(xiii) To purchase all the items which have low annual consumption value directly without going for quotations.

(xiv) It must work in the interest of the organization.

(xv) It must work to develop and maintain the increased purchase standards.

(xvi) It must conduct ABC, VED, and FSN analysis periodically to assist purchasing and storing the materials.

4.11. METHODS OF PURCHASING

The following are the various methods used for purchasing:

1. Purchase strictly by requirement.
2. Purchasing for a specified period.
3. Market Purchasing.
4. Contract Purchasing.
5. Central Purchasing Organization.
6. Purchase through Directorate General of Supplies and Disposals (DGSD).

1. **Purchase Strictly by Requirement:** This is also known as **hand to mouth** purchasing. When the job is taken for production, then the required quantity of material is estimated and purchased. This is generally suitable for job production workshops and for the firms, which have sufficient working capital. But the purchases are to be made locally. Otherwise, the firm cannot meet the delivery dates. Suppose the material

required is of special type i.e. having special specifications, it cannot be purchased by this method. The advantages of this method are market fluctuations will not affect the cost of production as the costing is based on the market price. Inventory carrying charges are at minimum. The limitations are as the quantity involved is small; one cannot go for bargaining the price. If the availability of material is difficult, sudden demands cannot be met with.

2. **Purchase for a Specified Period:** The materials, generally known as **general purpose materials, or standard materials**, which are regularly used, are purchased in quantities that will be sufficient for a particular future period, say for 3 months or 6 months. These materials are required by many jobs, examples of such materials are bolts, nuts, screws and welding rods etc. The advantages are, as the materials are available on demand, production of an order will not suffer. The market fluctuations will affect to certain extent. The disadvantages are it needs certain storage space and some amount of working capital is locked up in the form of inventory.
3. **Market Purchasing:** The requirement for materials depending on the production plan is worked out and the present market conditions are analyzed and then purchases are made keeping the benefits of the firm in mind. This method takes the advantages of bulk purchasing and bargaining and reduces the procurement cost of the materials. The advantages are, the reduced transportation and procurement cost of the materials. The disadvantage is if the market is highly fluctuating one, there is a chance of loss. In case bulk purchases are made, inventory-carrying costs are more.
4. **Contract Purchasing:** Contracts are given to suppliers for large amounts of future requirements, for a certain period, say 2 to 3 years, subject to revise and cancellation with an approximate period of notice. While calling quotations the approximate quantity and time etc. are specified. Many concerns that use large quantities of basic materials such as pig iron, coal, coke etc. have found it very desirable to contract for the entire supply of such materials for a considerable period of time. While placing the order, specifications about quality and quantity and delivery time and cost of materials are clearly specified. This is sometimes known as **Blanket Purchasing.** The advantages are, as the materials are received in time the problem of storage cost and inventory cost can be avoided. It gives a measure of safety to suppliers as well as the purchasers can be sure of meeting the delivery dates of their customers, as there is no shortage of materials. Market fluctuations will not affect the cost of the material. The disadvantage is in case if the supplier cannot keep up his delivery promise, due to problem in transportation system, there arises a problem of shortage of materials.
5. **Central Purchase Organization:** In large concerns or in certain big government concerns may have section-wise stores at different places and each section may have a separate stores. In such cases there arises a problem as to whether each store should make its own purchases or whether purchases should be made by the central stores or central purchase department, which will supply the needs of each section. If the local sectional stores is allowed to make its own purchases, there would be no delay and the shops can get materials very soon after they have sent their requisition. But local purchases may sometimes lead to malpractice. The purchase officer may have some kind

of understanding with the local dealers and this may result in purchase at very high rates. Now-a-days Centralized purchasing has become a common practice. Centralized purchasing is a method of procurement of all types of materials, supplies, equipment etc. through a single department under the direct control and superintendence of one responsible person. In a single-plant organization the central buying section makes all types of purchases. In the multi-plant organizations with numerous locations, the central buying section of the head office makes all purchases. In such organizations, sometimes regional or branch purchasing agents are employed to make purchases in local markets, but they are doing so always under the jurisdiction, co-ordination and control of the centralized purchasing department. The centralized purchase department purchases materials, which are used by more than one plant. However, the regional or branch purchase agents are allowed to buy the materials from the local market if they are available and involve freight advantage. They are also authorized to make emergency buying.

Advantages of Centralized Purchasing: The centralized purchasing avails the following advantages:

(i) The cost of purchase function will be relatively less and it will be managed efficiently.

(ii) The superintendents of manufacturing departments, departmental heads and office managers are relieved from the responsibility of purchasing their own requirements. They can concentrate in their assigned areas of activities in better way.

(iii) It is possible to tap the advantages of the specialized skill of the buying staff.

(iv) Bulk buying strengthens the bargaining position of the buyer. Moreover, the advantage of the quantity discount can be tapped. Direct contact with the suppliers will be possible which will eliminate the link of intermediaries.

(v) It enables to develop and maintain good relations with the suppliers.

(vi) It will enable the purchase of standardized items through standardized procedure.

(vii) It will reduce the inventory carrying costs. The minimum level of inventories is not maintained at different centers but at centralized center, which reduces investments, in inventories along with the other incidental storing costs.

(viii) The inter-section requirements of the materials can be easily adjusted.

Disadvantages of Centralized Purchasing: The centralized purchasing suffers from the following limitations:

(i) The specific requirements of the individual items may not be attended successfully. At times, it may result into absence of matching of mind between the needy section and the buying section resulting into wrong buying.

(ii) The centralized standard procedure may result into delays in receiving the materials.

(iii) It is likely that the centralized buying staff may not be expert in buying various types of items.

(iv) In case of multi-plant units located at distant places and receiving their requirements from centralized storing, it may not be possible to tap the local resources. However, this situation can be handled effectively by authorizing the regional purchase agents to make local purchases if they involve cost advantage.

(v) Possibilities are there that it affects the employee morale.

6. **Purchase Through Directorate General of Supplies and Disposals (DGSD):** To avoid unpleasant situation in the various government departments for purchasing materials and equipment, there is a Central Purchasing Organization, which provides the supplies at very cheap rates. This relieves a lot of botheration to the individual departments. This department enters into contract with various firms for supply of certain martial to government departments during the year at agreed rates. These firms have to certify that they are not supplying to others the same materials at rates lesser than that mentioned in the rate contract. This is called **'Rate Contract'**.

   The various government departments as and when required place orders on the firm for the supply of material at the rate contract prices. For the Central Government Departments, Directorate General of Supplies and Disposals with various branches in the country and the Central Purchase Departments for State Government Departments are the organizations.

4.12. VARIOUS PURCHASING SYSTEMS

The following are the various purchase systems that are used in medium and large-scale industrial units:

1. **Local Purchase System:** In purchasing small items or in case of emergency, the material is purchased locally by cash payment or without obtaining quotations. The rates may be confirmed orally or by phone or by some other means and order is placed on the spot. This system contains no clerical work and time, quality and availability are the prime considerations than price. This system is adopted mostly in hand-to-mouth purchasing.
2. **Single Tender System:** When the quality is of extreme importance only a reliable firm will be asked to supply and rates are fixed by mutual acceptance. In this case, when the sales are to decline, the supplier will be very happy to receive orders for the material, he can supply and the firm will also try to increase the turnover by placing orders on the customer at a slightly higher rates.
3. **Closed Tender System:** When material is required, firms, which are registered, will be invited to tender their rates and the most economic offer will be given order for the supplies. In this system, the tenders are invited only from some limited firms, as the purchase order does not exceed a limit (this limit depends on the size of the firm and type of material). Hence, this system is also called as **'Limited Tender System'.** The last date to tender the rates is given; the terms and conditions of supply and payments are mentioned in the tender notice. If the rates are almost same, the orders are to be

placed on a known reliable firm. It will improve co-operation and understanding. Always economic value of the items and not the rates should be given prime consideration. Here after receiving the tenders in sealed covers, they are opened in the presence of representatives of the firms given tenders.

4. **Open Tender System:** This system is also known as **'Unlimited Tender System'**, since the quantities to be purchased involves large amounts. A tender notice in trade journals or newspapers is published, so that wide publicity can be given. All the interested firms will apply for the tender forms. These tender forms contain date of receiving and opening the tenders, the approximate quantity required, period and place of delivery, specifications and other terms and conditions etc. for supply. The tender forms are sold at certain price and only those, who purchase this, can tender. This makes the supply on open competition and because of its high amounts; only established firms will be able to participate. A deposit will be received at the time of tendering to ensure that the supplier does not back out after his rates are approved. Also at the time of payment, a certain security deposit will be withheld till the warranty period is over.

4.12.1. The Format of the Tender

Most usually used format of the tender is given below. The format may vary depending on the purpose. The purpose may be:

(a) Purchase of Material,
(b) Purchase of Machinery,
(c) To undertake certain work like — Construction of a structure, Laying of roads, Repair works etc.,

The contents of tender is:

(a) Name of the Office/Department issuing the tender,
(b) Web address,
(c) Tender number,
(d) Date of issue of tender,
(e) Name of the work,
(f) Approximate value of the work/material/Machinery, etc.
(g) Approximate quantity required,
(h) Earnest money deposit,
(i) Cost of tender,
(j) Conditions,
(k) Opening date of the tender, and
(l) Signature/Designation of the issuing authority.

The following is the format of the tender.

XYZ MUNICIPALITY
www. XYZ MUNICIPALITY.GOV.IN
Tender Notice No. 131/XYZ/MUN/ of 01/01/2011.
CONSTRUCTION OF PEDA HOUSES.

The undersigned invites sealed tenders for the works mentioned below up to 15.30 hours of 30.01.2011.

S. No.	Tender I.D.	PH	Description of the work	Approx. Value in ₹	EMD in ₹
1.	1403	N	XYZ Municipality – Poor village construction of houses for poor people. Cost of tender form inclusive of ST in ₹ 3,435/-	26,05,303/-	57,310/-
2.	1404	N	Laying out roads of type – A in Poor village and construct two water tank of W – type as per drawing. Cost of tender form inclusive of ST in ₹ 5,725	52,75,624/-	1,05,520/-

1. The venue of tender opening: Tender Hall, Room No. 111, Municipal Vikas Bhavan, Commissioner's Office, pattabhipuram, XYZ city, ABC district.

   Tender documents duly filled in all respect shall be dropped in the tender box kept for the purpose in the tender hall furnished above or may be sent by post to Municipal Engineer (Works), XYZ Municipality, Pattabhipuram, XYZ city,. XXX XXX. Municipality is not responsible for any delay in transit (or) loss of ender form sent / received by post.

   Date and time of opening tender: 01.02. 2011 at 16.00 hours.

   Last date for issue of tender schedules in person: 29.01.2011 up to 17.45 hours.

   Note: If the last date of receipt and opening is declared holiday for Municipality, Tender will be received and opened at the same time on the next working day.

2. The prospective tenderers are advised to visit website **www. Municipal tenders.gov. in** three days before he tender opening to note any changes/ corrigenda for tenders. **A0605 Municipal Commissioner, XYZ city.**

For further under conditions / details (available in the tender documents) and for downloading the tender documents, please visit our website at **http://municipal *tenders.gov.in***
SMS TO 81212822 22 for any Tender complaint / Suggestion.

4.13. PURCHASE PROCEDURE (OR STEPS OF PURCHASING)

There are various steps in purchasing system. The procedure may slightly vary from firm to firm depending on the size of the firm and need of purchase. But below mentioned steps are mostly used in many firms. It should be noted that various types of forms and records are used to effectuate the purchase procedure. Forms and records are the tools, which simplify the purchase activity and assist in implementing the procedure and policies. The popular forms which are used in the purchase procedure are: Purchase Requisition, Purchase order, purchase Contract form, Follow-up form, Receiving Slip, Inspection Report form and Rejection note etc.

Steps in Purchasing are:

1. Recognition of the need.
2. Selection of the supplier.
3. Placing the order.
4. Comparative statement.
5. Follow-up of the order.
6. Receiving the materials.
7. Payment of the invoice.
8. Maintenance of the records.
9. Maintenance of vendor relations.

1. **Recognition of the Need:** The initial awareness of the need comes from the user department, which is communicated in the **form of requisition**, which is sent to the purchase department directly or routed through the stores department. Thus through the purchase requisition, the need item is officially brought to the notice of the purchase department. Purchase requisition fully describes the quantity and quality of the needed item and it proves the basic data for the action to be taken by the purchase department. The specimen of the typical purchase requisition can be given in this section.

   It should be specified by way of policy that who could make out the purchase requisition and who can authorize the expenditure by countersigning the requisition form. A list of authorized signatories should be made available in the purchase department along with the specification of any limitation on the authority; for example, the supervisor may be authorized to countersign the requisition for the requirement of tools and spares up to ₹ 500/- and above this limit, it must be countersigned by the works manager. The needy department for new items prepares the purchase requisition or the items not available from the stores department or the stores department for the new items and the items, which have reached re-ordering point, may prepare it. In a job-order industry where each piece of product is made according to the specifications of the customer, the **'bill of materials'** serves as a requisitioning document. A bill of materials is a list of all items, which are required to complete one specific order. It is also used for the purchase of standard parts and small, expendable tools. Generally the low value sundries and items of common use are purchased for stock, while the costly and special items are purchased according to the production programmes. The purchase requisition prepared in duplicate, the original copy is sent to the purchase department while the duplicate one is kept by the originating department for the recording purpose. The purchase of the supplies and consumable stores is handled in the same way through the purchase requisition. However, the purchase of plant and machinery and such capital expenditure items are treated in a different manner. Generally, the authorized signatories of such purchases are the persons of corporate level, generally, the director or a committee of directors. Sometimes the purchase of capital nature items has to be approved by the Board of Directors in advance. The reference of the Board approval is mentioned on the requisition and a copy of the requisition is sent to the secretary for the purpose of overall planning and budgeting.

2. **Selection of the Supplier:** After the need of the items has been recognized and described, the attempts should be made to select the best source of the supply. This is the negative process in the sense that the big list of the potential suppliers is reduced to selected few. For the repetitive orders, the buying records of the previous suppliers should be referred and the supplier should be selected on the basis of the satisfactory performance in the past. In case of blanket orders, any backlog of the order may be covered through fresh requirements. In a research conducted by Hugh Bucknet on **'How British Industry Buys'**, it was revealed that, "Approximately half the persons involved in purchasing would not change from their best supplier; to by an identical product from a new supplier for a price reduction of less than 5%. Approximately one fifth would not change for less than 10% reduction in price".

ABC MANUFACTURING COMPANY
No.2, ABC Street, MUMBAI 48
PURCHASE REQUISITION
Number:.................... Department:.................... Date:...................

To,
The Purchase Department (Through Stores Department),
Please obtain the below mentioned material/Tools/Spares. These are required to Job order Number..................... Whose delivery date is .... This department requires the material on ....

S. No.	Suggested Supplier	Specification	Quality	Quantity	Price in ₹	Remarks

Required By: Authorized By:

Fig. 4.5. Purchase Requisition.

In absence of any existing supplier, the procedure for the selection of the supplier would be slightly different. Generally, it is the usual practice of the buyer to maintain as up-to-date list of potential suppliers. The information about the supplier is available from the directories, advertisement in trade journals or direct mailing by the supplier. Out of the given sources, a short list of the appropriate suppliers should be selected. They may be asked for their quotations of price, delivery and other terms and conditions. The comparative statement of the quotations should be prepared. The keen study of the comparative statement will reveal the best supplier out of the available ones. It should be noted that the low bidder is not always the best supplier. When everything except the price is equal, the low bidder would be selected. However, there **'everything'** is not always equal in practice. While selecting the supplier, along with the price the other relevant considerations like his ability to supply the required volume or quantity, maintenance of the quality standards ability to deliver as per schedules, financial standing etc. are also given due importance.

The price of the item is determined by the different methods. The most popular methods are as under:

(i) **Catalogue Price:** For the standard items, generally, the supplier prepares the catalogue and price lists, which are applicable to all types of buyers.

(ii) **Negotiated Price:** Negotiation implies the haggling between the supplier and the buyer. Negotiations are a technique and a good buyer can use it for the benefit of the organization. In other words the supplier and the buyer sit together and bargain the price and other conditions.

(iii) **Tender Price:** The tenders are invited from the different suppliers who are bidding their prices. The bids are opened at specified time and the lowest bidder is selected.

3. **Placing the Order:** After the selection of the supplier, the order is placed with him. The standard purchase order forms are used for placing the order. The format of the order form varies from company to company. One such format is given in below:

The purchase order specifics the name of the supplier, date, specification of the item; any special instructions for packing, quantity required the price and other relevant terms. The authorized persons sign it. Purchase order is an official announcement of the intention of the buyer addressed to the supplier to receive the specified material.

Generally, all purchases are made through purchase order. When emergency purchases are made through telephone or telegraph, the purchases are confirmed by sending a regular purchase orders, following the telephone or telegram. Such purchase order should be marked as "confirmation" so that any misunderstanding on the part of the supplier treating it as a fresh order can be avoided. It is not proper to specify the preparation of the number of copies of the purchase order. The number of copies is closely related with the complexities of the purchase organization. However, the copies of the purchase order are genially required as under.

The original copy is sent to the supplier. Sometimes, an additional copy is also sent to the supplier who is supposed to return the same signifying his acceptance of the order. Such procedure ensures that the supplier has received the order and that he accepts the buyer's terms and conditions. Copy may also be sent to the receiving department, the accounting department, the initiating department, the stores department, inspection department and the follow-up department. The purchase department for record retains one copy. It should be noted that the outstanding orders should be separated from the completed orders. They should be filed properly. Generally, the outstanding orders should be filed alphabetically, while the completed orders should be filed numerically. It is highly essential to develop a system for tackling the small orders as quickly and as cheaply as possible. One important technique is the ABC analysis. It is also popularly known as **"the 80–20 relationship"**. According to this rule, 80% of any organization's purchase expenditure tends to go on about 20% of the items it purchases. These are popularly known as **"A-Class items"**. Generally, more than 75% of the orders placed tend to account for less than 20% of the total expenditure. Such items are denoted as **'C–Class items"**. Since, the firm spends most of its money on a relatively small number of bought items, it will get better result by concentrating on those few items. The buying practice for the low-value, small-order items can be devised as under:

XYZ COMPANY, CHENNAI **Phone:**

From:	To,
The Purchase Manager,	The Supply Manager,
M/S XYZ Company,	M/S ABC Company,
CHENNAI.	**MUMBAI.**

Ref.No: P.O.No: / Mfg/ 2011 / Dt:

Your Ref: ABC / Qtn / XYZ / 2011 / Dt:

Sir,
Kindly supply the material listed below as per the specification mentioned. This purchase order has reference to your quotation mentioned under reference above. The material must reach this office on or before .... Please mark the package as **ABC – XYZ – P.O. No........**

S. No.	Name of the Material	Specification	Special Instructions	Quantity Rate in ₹	Amount in ₹

Requisition Dept. I/C:........... Checked By:........... Purchase Manager:..............

Fig. 4.6. Supply Order Form

(i) To buy from the intermediaries like wholesalers or retailers, rather than from the manufacturers.

(ii) To place a standing order with the supplier. Standing order is an arrangement under which the supplier continues to supply the article at regular intervals until he is told to stop.

(iii) To place a blanket order with the supplier. The blanket order is a period contract made with the supplier to supply the items at agreed terms against the requisition made by the buyer.

(iv) The arrangement of cash limit purchases. Under this system, the staff is authorized to make the direct purchases up to certain limits, e.g. special order pads marked

"Not valid for orders over ₹ 50/-" can authorize the subordinate staff to order directly for meeting the routine requirements.

(v) The junior executive or the order clerk can be delegated the authority to handle all types of purchases of this nature.

Generally, it is the usual practice to all the purchases should be made through the purchase department. However, sometimes the authority is delegated to certain key staff for the emergency purchases; e.g. the maintenance foreman should be empowered to make emergency purchase to meet any unforeseen breakdown in the machines. However, the usual practice is to limit the authorized persons, occasions and amount of emergency purchases and the purchase department at later stages should confirm it.

4. **Comparative Statement:** Once the quotations are received, the concerned officer in purchase department will open them before the purchase committee and get the countersigned by the purchase manager. The purchase manager ask the officer to submit along with comparative statement to enable him to recommend the supplier to the supplier and place orders.

   The comparative statement is a document showing the supply conditions of various suppliers who have sent the quotations in response to the request for quotations for the purchase of material. The below shown is the format of comparative statement.

NAME AND ADDRESS OF THE COMPANY.

Purchase of materials for the company (Name of the materials)

Purchase requisition No: .... Date: .... From:

COMPARATIVE STATEMENT

S. No.	Materials with Specification	Particulars	Supplier No. 1 with Address	Supplier No. 2 with Address	Purchase Manager's Remarks
1.	Material 1 specifications	(a) Cost in ₹ Taxes: Transport cost: Delivery spot: Packing and forwarding cost: Insurance; Payment conditions			
2.	Material 2 Specifications	(a) Cost in ₹ Taxes: Transport cost: Delivery spot: Packing and forwarding cost: Insurance; Payment conditions			

Contd....

S. No.	Materials with Specification	Particulars	Supplier No. 1 with Address	Supplier No. 2 with Address	Purchase Manager's Remarks
3.	Material 3 Specifications	(a) Cost in ₹ Taxes: Transport cost: Delivery spot: Packing and forwarding cost: Insurance; Payment conditions			
4.	Material 4 Specifications	(a) Cost in ₹ Taxes: Transport cost: Delivery spot: Packing and forwarding cost: Insurance; Payment conditions			
5.	Remarks				

(**Note:** Number of columns depends on the number of suppliers who have sent quotations).

5. **Follow-up of the Order:** Getting the materials at the right time and right place are the important ingredients of effective purchasing. Simply, the placing of the order with the supplier does not ensure that the material will be made available where and when they are wanted. So, follow-up or expediting the purchase order is considered as an essential step in the purchase procedure. It should be noted that it is not necessary to chase all types of purchase orders. It would be sufficient if the follow-up function were confined to the key components and materials, which directly affect the smoothness of the production flow. It is not worthwhile to follow-up the purchase of standardized items, which can be procured at eleventh hour and from an alternate source. Similarly, the items of low-value having no direct bearing on the production process can be precluded from the costly follow-up procedure. As a principle, follow-up procedure should be employed where the costs and risks resulting from the delayed deliveries of materials are greater than the cost of follow-up procedure. The follow-up procedure tries to see that the supplier confirms the purchase order and the deliveries are promised. It is also necessary to review the outstanding orders at regular intervals and communicate with the supplier in case of need. Generally, a routine urge is made to the supplier by ending a printed post card or a circular letter asking him to confirm that the delivery is on the way or will be made as per the agreement. In absence of any reply or unsatisfactory reply, the supplier may be contacted through personal letter, phone, telegram or even a personal visit.

The follow-up function varies from company to company. It is handled through recording relevant particulars on the copy of the purchase order or maintaining a desk dairy for the follow-up or handling of outstanding orders with the help of progress-card or by establishing a separate position of expediter in the purchase organization. The timings of the follow-up also depend on the circumstances of each case. It may be the due date of the order, a week earlier to that or at each sate of the implementation of the purchase order till execution.

6. **Receiving the Materials:** The receiving department receives the materials supplied by the vendor. The quantity and quality (specifications) are verified and tallied with the purchase order. The receipt of the material is recorded on the specially designed receiving slip or forms, which also specify the name of the vendor and the purchase order number. It also records any discrepancy, damaged condition of the consignment or inferiority of the materials. The purchase department is informed immediately about the receipt of the materials. Usually a copy of the receiving slip is sent to the purchase department. If the materials require any quality control or inspection, the inspection report should be sent to the purchasing department along with the purchase slip. Receiving function is usually of a routine nature and sometime it is kept independent of purchase department. However, it is desirable to treat the receiving department as a subordinate function of purchase department due to following reasons:
   (i) Before the settlement of the invoice, the purchase department has to verify that the consignment agrees with the purchase order in all respects. This can be verified only with the help of the receiving department.
   (ii) When the shipment is received in damaged condition, the purchase department must have first hand prompt information about this, so that it can imitate immediate legal action against the vendor or the carrier. It can also take necessary action for taping the substitute source of the supply for the urgently needed materials.
   (iii) In case of the short-shipment from the suppliers, the rush orders can be managed so that the work stoppages caused by the lack of materials can be eliminated.
7. **Payment of the Invoice:** When goods are received in satisfactory condition, the invoice is checked before it is approved for the payment. Generally, the invoice is checked to see that the goods were duly authorized to purchase, they were properly ordered, they are priced as per the agreed terms, the quantity and quality confirms to the order, the calculations are arithmetically correct etc. It is a matter of controversy, whether the invoice should be checked by the purchase department or by the accounting department? The popular arguments in favour of purchase department are:
   (i) It is the purchaser who can accurately verify that the consignment is billed properly.
   (ii) As the purchaser is familiar with the routine details and terms and conditions of the order, he can correct and adjust any discrepancy in the execution of the order before invoice is paid.
   (iii) It allows the purchaser to watch the price of the material closely increasing his consciousness for the future purchases.

The arguments in favour of the invoice checking by the accounting department are as under:

(i) Invoicing is an accounting procedure which can be handled efficiently by the accounting department. This is not a sound argument because invoice checking is not merely a routine clerical checking but it also involves certain constructive checking like quality of materials, terms of the purchases etc.

(ii) The prompt processing of invoice by accounting department will enable to tap any possibility of cash discount. However, the efficient purchase department through the prompt clearance of the invoices can as well manage this.

(iii) It facilitates the internal checks. The accounting department verifies the accuracy of purchase department. However, where the systems is internal auditing is in operation, such type of internal checking would not serve any purpose because such verification is bound to be undertaken by the accounting department at some later time.

After the proper verification of the invoice, it is approved for the payment. It is the duty of the accounting department to make the payment in time. In case of the damaged consignment or short supply or supply of inferior goods, the adjustments should be made with the supplier before the payments are made for the invoice. The usual adjustments are – to return the goods to the supplier at his cost, to scrap them on the site, to accept the damaged goods at reduced price with the consent of the supplier, to correct the goods at the cost of the supplier. The payment of the invoice should be made only after the settlement is made with the supplier.

8. **Maintenance of the Records:** Maintenance of records is an important part and parcel of the efficient purchase function. In the industrial firms most of the purchases are repeat orders and hence, the past records serve as a good guide for the future action. They are very useful for deciding the timings of the purchases and in selecting the best source of supply. The maintenance of records is advantageous as under:

(i) It acts as a guide for future action. The person may change, however, the system prevails.

(ii) It provides the authentic records about the inventory, which is essentially needed for the inventory control.

(iii) The maintenance of records is also desirable from the viewpoint of legal proceedings, which may take place in future. The purchase order and its acceptance are legal documents and hence should be preserved till they possess any legal significance.

Purchase requisitions are also important documents so they should be preserved because they constitute the authority on the basis of which the purchase department initiated the buying action.

9. **Maintenance of Vendor Relations:** The quantum and frequency of the transactions with some key suppliers provide a platform for the purchase department to establish and maintain good relations with them. Good relations develop mutual trust and confidence in the course of time, which is beneficial to both the parties. The efficiency of the purchase department can be measured by the amount of the goodwill it has with its suppliers.

4.14. BILL OF MATERIALS

This is the list containing all materials and other parts required in manufacturing a product. It also gives the specification of the materials with their required quantities. When a manufacturing order is issued by Production Planning Department, it also prepares the **"Bill of Materials"**, with two columns.

(i) In stock, and

(ii) Out of stock.

It is then passed on to the Stores Department for checking which of the materials are available in store. The storekeeper makes entries in the **"in stock"** column of the available materials and then sends it to the Purchase Department. The Purchase Department will now make purchases for the materials in the **"out of stock"** column. The bill of materials has got an advantage that purchase department gets an advance information of the various requirements of shops. Secondly, the purchase can be directly made on the Bill of Materials, which saves lot of clerical work and time. Thirdly, only correct requirements are purchased, based on manufacturing order.

4.15. THE ORGANIZATION OF THE PURCHASING DEPARTMENT

Though purchasing is an important function, its independent existence should be justified on the basis of the type and volume of the purchase activities and the economic benefits available from its independent existence. The purchase function is generally organized on the basis of the size of the organization and the volume of the purchase activities. In the small organization, the purchase function is organized in any of the following forms.

(a) Purchasing as a division of manufacturing, and

(b) Purchasing as subsidiary to sales.

In the medium sized organizations, generally purchasing and store keeping functions are combined to form on separate department, generically reporting to the production department. In the large organizations, purchasing is treated as a major function and is departmentalized separately. Even under such organizations the functional division of the purchase department varies substantially. The place of the purchase department in the overall company organizational structure is largely dictated by the degree of centralization of the purchasing function and the divisions of the executive position and authorities to which the head of the purchase department is responsible. The typical organizational structure of the purchase function of a large organization would be as under in the Fig. 4.7.

Generally, the purchase department is organized on the line basis and the purchase manager heads it. In practice the head of the purchase department is designated differently like, purchase manager, purchase officer, purchase agent, director of purchasing, materials director etc. The split up of the purchase department is made in the light of the following activities. The further split up or combination is decided on the basis of the need, cost and convince of the organization.

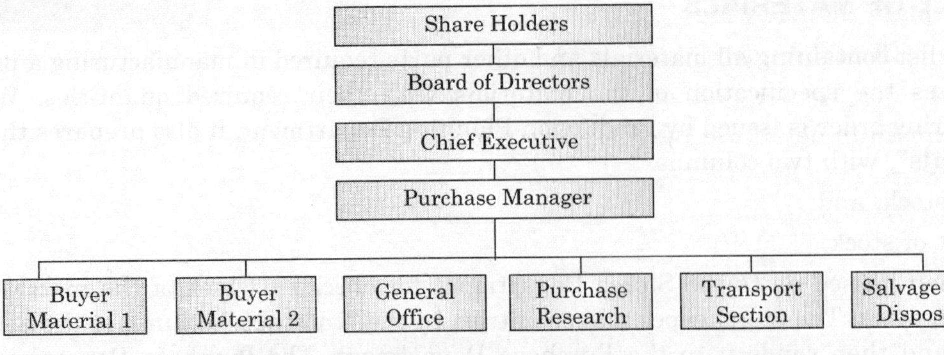

Fig. 4.7. Organization Chart for Purchase

(i) Buying Section: This is the core function of the purchase department and requires specialized skill in buying. It is sub-division according to specialized lines.

(ii) Follow-up Section: The follow-up of the purchase order is important function. This can be separate section in large organizations.

(iii) Invoice Section: the invoice clerk in the large companies checks the invoices. In the small company they are checked by the buyer or purchasing agent. Sometimes, it is also grouped with accounting department.

(iv) General Clerical Section: This section performs the routine clerical work involved in purchase activities like inward and outward of posts, typing, records and filing.

(v) Purchase Research Section: This section is generally organized in large companies. It mainly looks after the development of sources of supply, development of substitute materials, technological developments and its cost impact on manufacturing activities, etc.

(vi) Traffic Section (or Transport Section): In large organizations, the problem of incoming materials and outgoing shipments require special attention, which is usually handled by the traffic section or transport section.

(vii) Disposal and Salvage Section: In the large organizations, the responsibility of the disposal of the salvage is attached to the purchasing department. This section handles the entire salvage work, starting from collecting the salvage and scrap, their reconditioning and subsequent disposal.

QUESTIONS

1. What are the objectives of a good purchasing department?
2. What are the duties of a Purchase manager?
3. Explain the functions of Purchase Department.
4. List out various methods of Purchasing and explain any three of them in detail.
5. Explain Centralized Purchasing and De-centralized Purchasing giving their suitability and advantages and limitations.
6. Mention various Purchasing Systems and explain any two of them in detail.

7. Explain the following:
   (a) Closed Tender System, and
   (b) Pen Tender System.
8. Explain in detail the Purchase Procedure.
9. Write a note on:
   (a) Follow-up-the order
   (b) Payment of the invoice
   (c) Maintenance of vendor relations.
10. Give a neat sketch of: (a) Purchase Requisition, (b) Supply order form.
11. Explain what is Bill of Materials.
12. Sketch the Organization Chart for purchase Department.

OOO

STORES MANAGEMENT AND STORES RECORDS

4.16. INTRODUCTION

The **"Store Keeping"** or **"Stores Function"** is the most vital function of the **Materials Management**. The primary objective of the stores function is to provide the most efficient stores keeping services at minimum costs. The main facets of the store keeping services are **receiving, recording, storing and preserving, issuing, replenishing and controlling the materials.** Store keeping is a service function. It provides a valuable service to the production functions in the manufacturing organization. The stores function is headed by the storekeeper, who is reporting to the materials manager or to the purchase manager or to the works manager according to the type of the organization and the flow of the authorities and responsibilities. The storekeeper is the organizational head of the stores department and he acts as a custodian of all the items in the storeroom.

In the storeroom, the inventories like raw materials, work in process materials, components, and finished goods, bought out components or spares, consumable stores are stored (Finished goods storeroom is generally known as stock room). It should be noted that storing is a service function and costs heavily to the organization. Moreover, the inventories, which are, stored in the storeroom, represent the idle investment of the capital resources. So, sometimes it is argued that the one can do away without the storing function? The answer is negative. In fact store keeping has become an indispensable activity in all the organizations. (But in modern inventory management, we have Just In Time technique, which slashed down the store keeping heavily).

In small factories or concerns, the storeroom and stock room (the room where finished goods are stored or stocked) may be one and under the control of one office but in a big organization both are separate and are separately controlled. The organization of the stores department is as follows: (See Figure 4.8).

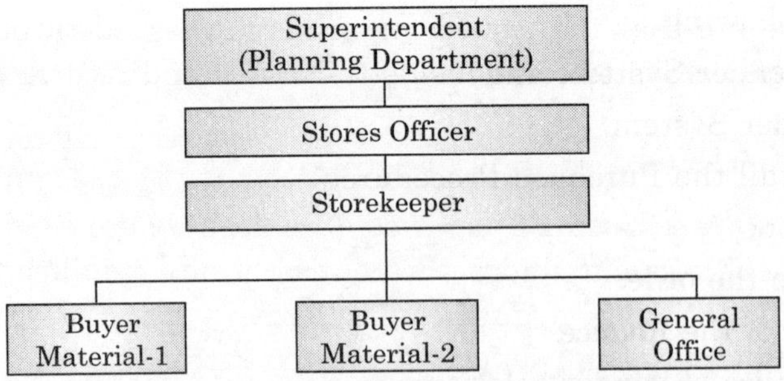

Fig. 4.8. Organization for Stores

The storekeeper is very important figure in this organization and he is as much responsible for the articles in his charge as a cashier is for the cash.

4.17. PURPOSE OF STORE KEEPING

1. To see that the stock of no item at any time falls below the prescribed minimum (re-order level) or goes in excess of fixed maximum quantity.
2. To examine carefully all goods and materials on receipt.
3. To arrange for a systematic and efficient storing of materials.
4. To maintain accurate and prompt distribution of all items to departments as and when required under Issue Requisition Notes.
5. To maintain efficient quantity records of movement of stock and to account for all goods those have come under their charge.
6. To prevent any theft, wastage or deterioration of stock.

4.18. DUTIES OF STOREKEEPER

The important functional duties of storekeeper are as follows:

1 He has to plan the stores. The available space of the stores is to be used optimally and he has to use all the three dimensions properly to store the material. He has to adopt FSN analysis while allocating space for materials.
2. To maintain the records of stores and enter the cost of the stores properly so as to help the costing.
3. Whenever requisitions are received from shops, they are checked and if found correct, materials are issued and entries are made in the required register immediately.
4. He has to check the balance of materials from time to time and see that desired quantities are available for use.
5. Whenever the existing stock of any item is likely to be exhausted, he should send its information to Stores Officer, who in turn will inform to purchase section for its purchase.
6. He has to prevent leakage, theft, wastage and deterioration.
7. He has to see that material is issued only against written requisition.

8. He should not allow any unauthorized persons to enter and handle the stock of materials. Also see that the issued materials are issued through issue window and do not allow the person to come inside the stores and receive the materials.

4.19. STORES LOCATION

(a) Centralized Stores: In small factories, it is desirable to centralize the materials so that they may be brought under the control of one storekeeper and the storeroom should as far as possible near the place, where materials is to be used. If there are several manufacturing departments, the storeroom will be most conveniently situated, where it is near to all the departments. This will reduce the handling and a lot of manual work is eliminated. This type of location is known as **centralized location.**

(b) Decentralized Stores: In large factories, where there are several departments, each using a different type of materials, it becomes beneficial to separate the stores. For example, near the welding department, store the materials required for welding; near the foundry department, store, foundry materials are stored and near assembly shop have the stores of components used for storing and so on. Some stores that are common to several or other departments should be kept in central stores. This type of arrangement is known as **decentralized stores.**

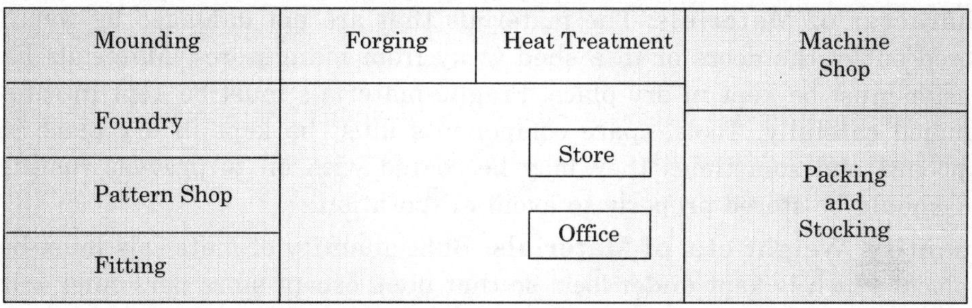

Fig. 4.9. Centralized Stores

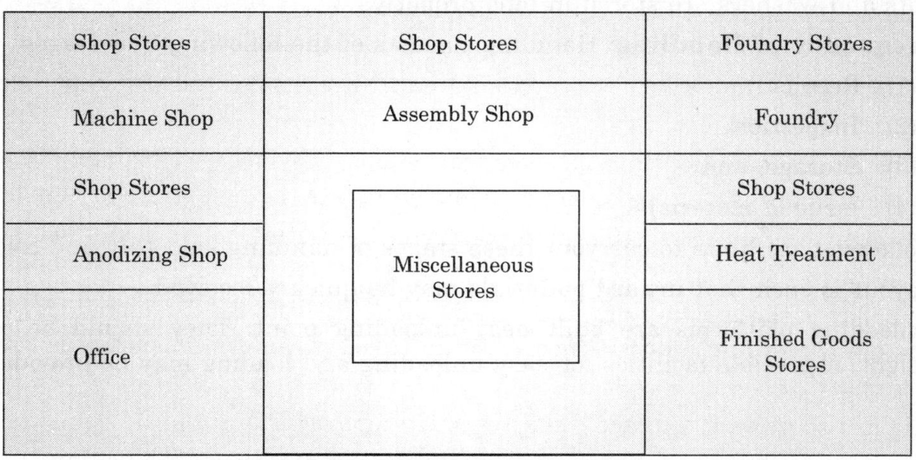

Fig. 4.10. Decentralized Stores

4.20. SYSTEMS OF LOCATION OF MATERIALS

In small factories, where there is one small store, the storekeeper may remember the location of material but in a large factory where he handles several thousand of items, memory would become unreliable. Hence to facilitate the work of storekeeper, it is, therefore, necessary to set up a system of numbering or coding the locations. Under this system, all locations in a storeroom are numbered and these numbers are entered in the index register against the items which are located.

Suppose code number for an item is 10 –12E – 42 means, the location is in storeroom10, aisle 12, rack E and bin 42. By this system, man approaches the correct place and correct material and issuing becomes quick and easy.

Layout of Stores: The layout of stores depends on the following factors:

1. **Flow of Materials:** The principle of this factor is to minimize the movement of materials, so as to minimize the materials handling cost. We can have FSN (Fast moving, Slow moving and non-moving materials) analysis to fix the position of materials in the stores. Fast moving materials are kept nearer to storekeeper such that they are easily assessable, which minimizes the issuing time. Slow moving materials are kept at a distance from issue window, so that they will not cause inconvenience to the movement of store personnel. Non-moving materials are kept outside and away from stores, so that they will not waste storage space available.
2. **Character of Materials:** The materials that are not damaged by weather can be stored out of the doors or in a shed away from main stores. Materials like cement, plaster must be kept in dry place. Fragile materials must be kept in safe place and handled carefully. Tools, spare components must be kept in dry place in a locked cupboard and sometimes they may be coated with oil to prevent rusting. Fuel oil etc. should be stored properly to avoid evaporation.
3. **Quantity, Weight etc. of Materials:** Bulk quantity of materials must be stored in a place, which is kept under lock, so that none except store personnel will enter the room. Light materials are placed at a height whereas heavy materials are stored at ground level. Small components are stored in racks of a cupboard. Items like bolts, nuts and washers are stored in bins properly.
4. **Frequency of Handling:** Handling consists of the following four stages:
   (1) Receipt,
   (2) Inspection,
   (3) Storage, and
   (4) Issue of materials.

The following are hints to carryout these stages of handling smoothly and correctly:

1. Layout is such that inward materials may be quickly received.
2. Unloading platforms are built near unloading point. They should be of suitable height, if possible facilities for easy unloading and loading may be provided.

3. All around the stores there is through siding. If trucks are used for transporting the material, sufficient parking space is provided.
4. For moving heavy materials, equipment, proper handling equipment must be available.
5. It is to be seen that each section of the store has sufficient allotting space. The material is to be arranged in such a way that inward and outward movement of supplies can be carried out smoothly.

4.21. METHOD OF STORING

It depends upon the type of products to be stored. The products can be classified in the following categories:

(a) Raw Materials, (b) Components, (c) General supplies, (d) Tools, (e) Fuels and oils (f) Spare parts and (g) Finished goods. In the central stores or in departmental stores, separate place is allotted the materials of different categories as mentioned. This will enable the storekeeper to reach the materials early at the time of issue or at the time of storing the arrivals.

4.22. BIN CARD

This is a card, which is attached to each bin, rack, shelf or other container for storing items. In fact, a bin is a container or a rack used for keeping materials. A record of all materials entering or leaving the bin and balance of material in hand is kept in this card. It represents a stores ledger. The storekeeper will enter the entries in the card and only the quantities will be recorded. These should agree with the quantities of material as shown in the relevant account in the stores ledger. This will enable the storekeeper to ascertain the quantity of any material in stock and remind him to requisition of fresh stock, when the minimum stock has been reached. In some factories duplicate bin cards are being used. In such cases one card is attached to the bin and the storekeeper on his table for ready reference keeps the duplicate card. Bin cards are checked time-to-time by the inspectors and they put their initials on these cards and take down the discrepancies. The specimen of bin card is given below:

Now-a-days in industries where, imported spare parts are used, which sometime may take longer period to get the material, in such cases to avoid delay in production, an ordering level or safety level is also introduced between the maximum quantity and minimum quantity. At this ordering level orders are placed for the purchase of material and if by chance material is not received and minimum quantity is reached in the stores then some alternative arrangements are urgently made.

4.23. INDENT ON STORES

It is also known as **material issue requisition.** An important rule, which should be strictly followed, is not to allow any material to pass from the store department into the work except upon the authority of written requisition. These indents on stores are demands upon the storekeeper signed by the authorized persons to issue to bearer, to be charged to a particular job or department signified therein. The specimen of indent form is given below:

BIN CARD							
Bin Number......		Minimum Quantity		Maximum Quantity		Ordering Quantity	
Date	Quantity Received	Quantity Issued	BALANCE	Date	Quantity Received	Quantity Issued	BALANCE
Checked By:				Checked By:			

Fig. 4.11. Bin Card

Such indents on stores are made out in triplicate from bound books, and are supplied to each department. They contain the date, the necessity particulars of the stores requisitioned, such as quantity and description, order or the job number to which the material is to be charged department number, signature of the party making it, space for the initials of the issuing storekeeper, and the signature of the person receiving the material. As it is in triplicate, the original copy is sent to the cost department for costing, and the duplicate to the storekeeper and triplicate in the bound book by the indenter by way of a permanent record.

4.24. MATERIAL REQUISITION NOTE

Materials issued for departmental use but sometimes not required and returned to the storekeeper must be properly recorded, so that they may be duly entered in the store records and their values may be credited to the accounts of the department concerned by the cost department.

For this purpose, **Material returned Notes** are written out in triplicate. Two copies being sent to the storekeeper along with the returned material, one of these is returned to the foreman with the storekeeper's acknowledgement. The copy retained by storekeeper is entered by him on the bin cards and then passed on to the stores accountant to be priced and entered by him in the relative stores card. The cost department, the accountant of the department concerned being given credit in respect thereof, will then deal it with. The specimen of the material return note is given above.

MATERIAL REQUISITION NOTE

Book No:..... Indent No:........ Shop/Department:................. Date:................

To,

Storekeeper,

Please issue the under mentioned materials/Components/Spares for the Job No.

S. No.	Material With Specification	Quantity		Stores Register Keeper	Initials of Store-keeper	Rate in ₹	Cost in ₹	Remarks
		Demanded	Supplied					

Total Number of Items:................ Received By:.............. Indenter:.....................

Fig. 4.12. Material Requisition Note

MATERIAL RETURN NOTE

S. No.:.......... From Work Order No. .... Date:...............

Please receive under mentioned materials and acknowledge.

Description of Materials	Reasoning For Returning	Quantity / ₹	Rate in ₹	Value	Stores Ledger Folio	Bin Card Number

Received By:.................... Signature of Foreman:........................

Fig. 4.13. Material Return Note

4.25. ACCOUNTS OF STORES

Mostly stores accounts are referred to the details pertaining to the material, which is not for re-sale. A better stores procedure is a safeguard against waste of material and theft etc. In order to maintain an efficient record of stores, the following books and records will be required and these are maintained separately for different types of materials. Some of the important records are discussed below:

(a) **Inward and Outward Registers:** When the supplier through rail dispatches the material; he will send its receipt issued by the railway authority, generally called **"RR"** (RR means Railway Receipt). On the production of that receipt on railway, the customer can receive material. {In case the materials are dispatched by road transport through a lorry the document is known as **"LR"** (Lorry Receipt). It serves the same purpose of RR}. A separate register is maintained by storekeeper, in which daily entries of RR received are made and is known as **Inward Register.**

In the same way, when some material goes out of the stores to other place, its entries of RR or LR are made by storekeeper in **Outward Register** and that RR or LR is sent to the customer. By production of which, he can take delivery of materials from the concerned.

(b) **Stock Register:** These are:

(i) **Dead Stock or Non-Consumable Register:** This is maintained by storekeeper, in which entries of non-consumable articles such as machines, equipment and furniture etc. are made. The register shows complete details of article together with accessories. The different items are entered in different pages. All the transactions about a particular item are entered in one page. Other details entered in the register are, date of purchase, name of the supplier, purchase order number and date, number of pieces ordered, number of pieces received, rate, cost of item etc. Any maintenance, repairs or replacement of stores of the item is entered in respective page. The location of the item in the production shop is also shown in the register. In one word, the register gives complete history of machine from the date of purchase to date.

(ii) **Consumable Register:** In this, storekeeper maintains record of consumable stores received, such as wood, iron, bolts, nuts, fuels and oils etc. A page in the register is reserved for one material and all the transaction of the material is entered as and when it happens. The date of purchase, specification, rate, quantity, cost and the name of the supplier are entered in the concerned page of the item in the book. When one looks into the book, can easily know what is the existing stock.

(iii) **Daily Receipt Register:** This may be in a register or loose leaf form. Whenever any material comes in the store, it is entered date wise in the daily receipt register. Material is then inspected and if found suitable is entered in stock register. It analogs with a journal used in accounts and the stock register is similar to ledger used in accounts. Sometimes the stores register is also known as stores ledger. If the material is found defective, it will be rejected and either the material or its report will be sent to the supplier.

The incidental changes that are incurred will also be noted in daily receipt register.

(iv) Issue Register: This may be in the register or loose leaf form. All stores issued are entered date wise in it by storekeeper. From the receipt and issue register store ledger is prepared by accounts section.

(v) Surplus Stock Register: Sometimes, purchases of certain materials are made that the material will not come in use for a long time, say 2 to 3 years. Such materials are then declared surplus and are recorded in a separate register called surplus stock register. Thus unnecessary material is removed from that of the stock register, to facilitate easy handling.

(vi) Suspense Register: The defective items or items receive in excess should not be placed in the bins but should be placed in **suspense cell.** Storekeeper maintains a separate register for all such issues placed in suspense and is known as suspense register.

(vii) Condemned Article Register: Unserviceable material after use or absolute material which is recommended to be condemned by authorized persons, is entered in this register and will be shown as stock until disposed off some way. The balance of condemned article will be taken out from store ledger and will be shown condemned.

(viii) Loan Register: Sometimes non-consumable material is issued from store on loan for temporary period by the production of slip of authority on **use and return basis.** Before issuing material is entered in this register and signature of the bearer is taken in the register and slip of authority is kept safe and when material is returned, it is entered in the register and also on the slip and returned to the department, which has sent the slip.

(ix) Empty Containers and Packages Register: The record of empty containers and packages is kept in this register by storekeeper. They should be disposed off at convenient intervals by auction or otherwise to the best of advantage.

The above are the various records, which must be kept by any storekeeper for easy and smooth handling of stores.

4.26. ADVANTAGES OF GOOD STORE KEEPING AND STORE RECORDING

When stores are kept accurately and records are kept up to date, the organization will enjoy certain advantages. They are:

1. Ready record of all materials and stores purchases may be obtained.
2. As the materials are arranged in a systematic way in racks and in bins handling of stores becomes very easy.
3. Unnecessary confusion and delay in issue of material is avoided.
4. It helps to operate shops and production efficiently.
5. Overstocking is avoided and delay due to lack of materials are prevented.
6. Wastages of time and labour, leakage, thefts and pilferages of stores are reduced to their minimum.

7. Classification of receipts and issues are made easy.
8. Each item issued can be traced to its respective department, so as to ensure correct costing.
9. Safety of all the materials lying in stores is guaranteed.

4.27. VALUATION OF MATERIALS ISSUED FROM THE STORES

To find out the cost of materials issued from stores, to a particular job so as to charge the amount to the respective job in accounting several methods are used. The choice of the method should be based on the nature of material and the type of business. Following are some important methods, which are commonly used.

1. First in First Out Method.
2. Last in First Out (LIFO) Method.
3. Average Price Method.
4. Replacement Price Method.
5. Fixed Price Method.
6. Actual Price Method.
7. Inflated Price Method.

1. **First In First Out Method:** This method is also known as **"original cost method"**. In this system goods received are entered in the stores records at actual cost plus other charges such as freight, taxes and insurance etc. In this system; the materials first received are issued first. Materials from second lot are issued only when first lot is exhausted. The prices are charged at the cost at which that lot was purchased. As soon as the oldest lot is exhausted, the issue is priced at cost price of the next oldest lot in the sequence. The following transactions occurred during the first week of May 2001:

May 1, 2001 — 200 units purchased at ₹ 5/- per unit.
May 3, 2001 — 500 units purchased at ₹ 6/- per unit.
May 5, 2001 — 500 units issued to Job No. 506.

The cost of material issued to Job No. 506 is as follows: 200 units at ₹ 5/- + 300 units at ₹ 6/- = ₹ 1,600. The value of closing stock of 400 units will be ₹ 6 × 400 units = ₹ 4, 800. The ledger transactions appear like below:

FIRST IN FIRST OUT (FIFO) METHOD
STORES LEDGER SHEET

Date	RECEIPTS			ISSUES			BALANCE		
	Quantity	Price in ₹	Amount in ₹	Quantity	Price in ₹	Amount in ₹	Quantity	Price in ₹	Amount in ₹
April									
1	200	5	1000				200	5	1000
3	500	6	3000				700	(5, 6)	4000
5				500	200 × 5 300 × 6	1000 1800	200	6	1200

Fig. 4.14. Stores Ledger for FIFO

It should be noted that the actual physical handling of the materials in the bins and the shelves in the sequence of purchases is imaginary under the FIFO method. This method of pricing issued material can be followed irrespective of the physical arrangements of the materials. However, the sequential arrangement is desirable in case of materials, which are subject to deterioration, obsolescence and decay or style changes. FIFO method can be used effectively where the prices tend to be stable, frequency of purchases and issues are less and costlier materials are used. This is also useful where the production is rapid. The **advantages** of this method are:

(a) The method of calculation is simple and does not require lengthy calculation.

(b) The materials are priced at their actual cost.

(c) In case of falling prices, this method inflates the issue price.

The **limitations** of this method are:

(a) The cost comparison between two similar jobs, using the same material is distorted, if issues are made from different lots having different unit prices.

(b) The treatment of excess materials returned from the production shops pose a specific problem. The same will be the case of the materials returned to the vendor.

(c) It presupposes the specific type of stores arrangements; e.g. front and back door, horizontal arrangement instead of vertical stacking etc.

(d) The price charged for the issues have no relation with the current market price, and so it becomes difficult to quote the most competitive prices.

But in many businesses, as the promoter of business do not wants to run the business to get losses, he will be cautious enough to market prices into considerations while sending quotations. As we know, theory differs from practice.

2. **Last In First Out (LIFO) Method:** LIFO method reverses the procedure as followed under FIFO. The cost of the last lot of materials received is used to price the issues until that consignment is exhausted, then the next lot of pricing is used and so on through the successive lots. This method is based on the premise that the materials which are issued to the jobs should carry the cost of the most recently purchased materials, and that is why it is also known as the **replacement cost** method. It should be noted that like FIFO method, the actual physical handling of the materials in the bins and shelves in the sequence of purchase is imaginary. It is considered only for pricing the issues made from the stores. The following transactions show the method of FIFO.

   May 1, 2002: 500 units purchased at ₹ 5/- per unit.

   May 3, 2002: 300 units purchased at ₹ 6/- per unit.

   May 6, 2002: 400 units issued to Job number 206.

LAST IN FIRST OUT (LIFO) STORES LEDGER										
Date	RECEIPTS			ISSUES			BALANCE			Remarks
	Quantity	Price in ₹	Cost in ₹	Quantity	Price in ₹	Cost in ₹	Quantity	Price in ₹	Cost in ₹	
May										
1	500	5	2500	–	–	–	500	5	2500	
3	300	6	1800	–	–	–	800	(5,6)	4300	
6	–	–	–	300	6	1800				
				100	5	500	400	(5,6)	2300	
8				300	5	1500	100	5	500	

Fig. 4.15. Stores Ledger for LIFO

Advantages:

(a) The issue price is in consistency with the prevailing market price and thus enables to quote the most competitive prices.

(b) In the rising prices, the jobs are priced at inflated rates, which reflect the business prudence of conservatism.

Disadvantages:

(a) The issue price has no relation with the purchase price of the material issued.

(b) Like FIFO, the cost comparison of two similar jobs using the same type of materials is distorted if issues are made from two different lots having different unit prices.

(c) Like FIFO, the treatment of excess materials returned from the production shops or materials returned to the vendor pose a specific problem.

(d) Under falling prices, the profit figures tend to be inflated due to under pricing of materials, which is not desirable form the viewpoint of financial management.

(e) The physical sequence is followed under the LIFO principle; it is likely that the oldest stock may deteriorate or may become obsolete.

3. **Average Price Method:** Under this method, the issues are charged at a price ascertained from the common pool made up of the varied prices of several lots. It is advantageous to use this method when the prices are subject to constant changes. In the periods of rise or fall of materials prices, an average cost tends to even out the extreme price changes. The upward and downward trends are moderate as contrasted with the step rise or fall under the FIFO and LIFO methods. The average price is calculated in different ways as under:

   1. Simple average of the stock on hand at the price of the issue.
   2. On the basis of the simple average cost of each kind of material on hand at the close of each month and to apply it for all issues made during the following month.
   3. On the basis of simple moving average wherein the earliest price is dropped, the moment the new purchase are made and the cost of such fresh purchase will be included while arriving at the new average.

It should be noted that instead of the simple average wherein only the unit cost is considered for calculating the average cost to be charged, to the issues, weighted average cost could also be used. Under the weighted average cost, along with the unit cost the quantity of the units are also considered.

As an example consider the following transactions: The lots are purchased during the month of April 2001.

(a) 1000 units at ₹ 3/- and (b) 5000 units at ₹ 5/-.

The simple average cost would be ₹ 3 + ₹ 5/- = ₹ 8/- . The average is ₹ 8/ 2 = ₹ 4/-.

The weighted average cost would be as under:

WEIGHTED AVERAGE COST METHOD			
S. No.	**Unit Cost in ₹**	**Weight**	**Weighted Cost in ₹**
1	3	1,000	3,000
2	5	5,000	25,000
	Total	6,000	28,000

Fig. 4.15 (a) Weighted Average Method

Weighted average cost = 28,000/6000 = ₹ 4.67

4. **Replacement Price Method:** This method is also known as **Market Price Method** under which the material issues are priced at the prevailing market price on the date of the issue. This method is based on the principle that the materials issued for any job on a particular day should be charged at the rate at which they could be replaced immediately from the fresh purchases on the same day. In short, material issues are priced at the prevailing market price on the day of consumption. This method is applicable to the raw materials of standardized grades and is traded at the commodity exchanges, such as cotton, cereals, certain metals etc, because the prices of the items are quoted in the newspapers and it is relatively easier to ascertain the current market price. The main advantage of this method is that it considers the current market price, which is more significant for the purpose of pricing policies. It enables the comparison of the operating efficiency with those of the competitive units. The comparison between the purchase price and the issue price (i.e. the market price) reflects on the efficiency or otherwise of the purchase department. The main drawback of this method is that it distorts the data for the accounting purposes, which necessitates the adjustments in the stores ledger. There is bound to be a discrepancy between the purchase price and the issue price. The difference between the market price and the purchase price is adjusted to the *price fluctuation reserve account*, which indicates the efficiency or inefficiency of the purchase department. (This method is also known as **current price method).**

5. **Fixed Price Method:** In this method, the materials are charged at a predetermined, budgeted or estimated price, which reflects a normal or an effected future price. Generally, standard price is fixed after the careful examination of the current market price, trend of the price, market conditions etc., so that a fairly correct average standard price may be predetermined. The standard price is made applicable for a

definite period as a month, a quarter or a year. The material receipts are recorded at the actual price, while the material issues are charged at the predetermined standard price. So, there is bound to be the discrepancies between the standard and the actual price. The difference between the actual price paid and the standard price charged is recorded to a separate **price variance account.** The standard price is revised periodically, if the discrepancies go beyond a particular limit. The main advantage of this method is that the pricing of issues becomes a simplified function. Like FIFO, LIFO and average method, the issue price need not be ascertained after each receipt or issue of materials. However, it is not advised if the materials involve frequent and substantial price fluctuations.

6. **Actual Price Method:** In this method, the material issues are priced at the actual acquisition cost of the respective materials. This method is applicable where the purchases are made for the specific jobs and are kept physically separate in the storeroom. Each material receipt is recorded in separate stores ledger card and the material issues are charged at the actual acquisition cost. This method is relatively awkward, however, it is advised where few costly items are used in he processing and where non-standardized materials are purchased to meet the customer's specifications. It is more suitable to the job work industries.
7. **Inflated Price Method:** This method of pricing is based on the principle of uniform spreading of normal wastages on the residual units; there are certain types of normal wastages, which are incidental to materials usage (for example, the wastage in the form of chip while cutting the material or breaking a bulk etc.). The good units through charging the material issues at inflated price, absorbs the cost of such normal wastage, for example, 100 units at ₹ 15 were purchased. This material is subjected to 10% normal wastage, so the cost of ₹ 1500/- (100 units × ₹ 15) will be spread over 90 units (100 units–a normal wastage of 10 units), which are good units. And the issue of the materials will be charged at an inflated price of ₹ 16.67 (₹ 1500/ 90 units) instead of ₹ 15/-.

To conclude, it should be noted that the material pricing should be done on the basis of the acquisition cost of the materials. The acquisition cost should consider the net invoice price of the supplier and the transportation charges, which are **the visible costs.** Certain invisible costs are also to be considered such as the cost of ordering, receiving, unpacking, inspection, insurance and storing etc.

QUESTIONS

Stores Management and Stores Records

1. Discuss the purpose of store keeping and give its organizational structure.
2. Discuses the duties of a storekeeper.
3. Discuss the following and give their suitability, advantages and disadvantages and layout:

   (a) Centralized store (b) Decentralized store.

4. Briefly describe the systems of storing the materials in stores.
5. Discuss the four methods of storing the materials in stores.
6. Give a neat sketch of bin card and discuss its uses and advantages.
7. Give a neat sketch of:
   (a) Indent on stores
   (b) Material requisition note
   (c) Material return note.
8. Write a notes on the following:
   (a) Inward register
   (b) Consumable stock register
   (c) Non consumable register
   (d) Issue register
   (e) Surplus stock register
   (f) Condemned article register.
9. Discuss the advantages of good store keeping.
10. Discuss the following methods of store evaluation:
    (a) First in first out method
    (b) Last in first out method
    (c) In flated price method.
11. Discuss the following methods of evaluation of stores:
    (a) Fixed price method
    (b) Actual cost method
    (c) Current value method
    (d) Average cost method.

MULTIPLE CHOICE QUESTIONS

Materials Management: (Purchasing and Store Keeping)

1. One of the functions of management is to employ capital efficiently to yield maximum result. Preferred way to achieve this is:
   (a) Produce good products
   (b) Maximize the margin of profit
   (c) Maximize the productivity of the capital
   (d) Use skilled labour.
2. Material management function is a
   (a) Staff function
   (b) Line function
   (c) Line and staff function
   (d) None.
3. The origin of ABC analysis is:
   (a) Taylor's 20–80 rule
   (b) Pareto's 80–20 rule
   (c) Pareto's 20–80 rule
   (d) Taylor's 80–20 rule.
4. ABC analysis depends on:
   (a) Price of material
   (b) Piece rate of material
   (c) Importance of material
   (d) Annual consumption value of the material.

5. ABC control means:
   (a) Any time better control
   (b) Control of A-class, B-class and C-class material
   (c) Avoid bad control
   (d) Always beer cost.
6. The logic of ABC analysis is
   (a) 80% of materials consume 80% of annual material cost
   (b) 20 % of materials consume 20% of annual material cost
   (c) 20% of materials consume 80% of annual material cost
   (d) None of the above.
7. In VED analysis the letter V stands for:
   (a) Value (b)Variety
   (c) Vitality (d) Vital
8. VED analysis depends on:
   (a) Annual consumption value of materials
   (b) Unit price of the martial
   (c) Durability of materials
   (d) Criticality of materials.
9. In FSN analysis the letter S stands for
   (a) Sluggish (b) Slow moving
   (c) Selected material (d) Smooth material.
10. FSN analysis depends on:
    (a) Position of the stock in stores (b) Scarcity of material
    (c) Materials movement pattern (d) Fragility of materials.
11. One of the causes of poor inventory is:
    (a) High cost of the materials (b) Over production before demand arises
    (c) Negligence of Storekeeper (d) Negligence of General Manager.
12. In inventory control, the procurement cost is represented by:
    (a) C_1 (b) C_3
    (c) C_2 (d) C_4.
13. In p-system:
    (a) Order is placed at fixed period
    (b) Order is placed at quantity
    (c) Order is placed at fixed Price
    (d) Order is placed as per fixed instructions.
14. q–system means:
    (a) Fixed quota system (b) Fixed cost system
    (c) Fixed quantity system (d) Fixed quality system.

15. MRP means:

(a) Material Route Planning
(b) Material Redirect Procedure
(c) Material Research Procedure
(d) Materials Requirement Planning.

16. Total cost of inventory is:

(a) Inventory carrying cost
(b) Inventory carrying cost + Ordering cost
(c) Total material cost
(d) Inventory carrying cost + Ordering cost + Material cost

17. Pareto rule says that .... percent of country's economy is controlled by .... percent of people.

(a) 80, 20
(b) 20, 80
(c) 80, 50
(d) 50, 50.

18. The list of all materials with specification required manufacturing a product and issued by Production Management Department is known as:

(a) List of specification
(b) List of materials
(c) Bill of materials
(d) Production requirements.

19. Indent on stores is known as:

(a) Material issue requisition
(b) Bill of materials required
(c) Request card
(d) Material note.

20. Materials taken from stores but not used are returned to stores by a note. This is known as:

(a) Material not used note
(b) Material return note
(c) Scrap marital note
(d) Material back note.

ANSWERS

1. (c)	**2.** (a)	**3.** (b)	**4.** (d)	**5.** (b)	**6.** (c)	**7.** (d)	**8.** (d)
9. (b)	**10.** (c)	**11.** (b)	**12.** (b)	**13.** (a)	**14.** (c)	**15.** (d)	**16.** (d)
17. (a)	**18.** (c)	**19.** (a)	**20.** (b).				

❍❍❍

MARKETING

Marketing: Functions of Marketing – Marketing Mix – Marketing strategies based on Product Life Cycle – Channels of Distribution.

4.28. INTRODUCTION

Every manufacturing organization manufactures its product and service industries offer services for the consumption of human being. The people must know that the desired product is available in the market. For this the manufacturing company has to market its product. Marketing consists of those efforts, which affect the transfer of ownership of goods and care for their physical distribution. **American Marketing Association defines marketing as the performance of business activities that directs the flow of goods and services from producer to consumer or user.** This shows that activities such as advertising, warehousing, transport and marketing research etc. will come under marketing. Whereas Sales Management is defined as **" the planning, direction and control of personal selling activities of a business unit, including recruiting, selecting, training, equipping, assigning, routing, supervising, paying and motivating as these tasks apply to the personal sales force".** These definitions do help in distinguishing between the functions of the Sales Manager, who plans, directs and controls the activities of salesmen, i.e. conducts the personal selling activities of the business, and is superior who has charge of all the marketing activities and is variously designated as Marketing Manager, or Director of Marketing etc. when two such separate executives exist as they do in case of large companies. However, the defect of this definition of "marketing" is that it does not indicate that marketing thinking should commence even before production activities are undertaken. Besides, the marketing activities should not end once the goods have reached the consumer or user as ensuring customer satisfaction may necessitate, for instance, after sales service so important for repeat sales. This definition is production oriented.

4.29. TRADITIONAL MARKETING CONCEPT

To use economic terminology marketing covers those activities, which relate to the creation of time, place and possession utilities. This says that firstly, goods have to be made available at the time when they are needed. Thus creating time utility of them. Secondly, the need for the product may exist at a far off place and the product is to be transported to that place. Thirdly, once the goods are produced or transported to the destination, it may have to lie in a salable position for a period of time (may be in godowns (ware houses) or transshipment stores) until the consumer desires it. In such a case, **the transfer of possession of the goods to the consumer will create possession utility**. Hence, we can say, that Marketing consists in moving goods from the manufacturer, at a time when they are required to the place where they are to be used, and for those who are to use them for various purposes.

4.30. THE MODERN MARKETING CONCEPT

Above it is discussed, as the marketing is a description of the physical activities involved in the process of distribution of goods. However, marketing is more than a mere physical process or a set of activities. It represents a distinct philosophy of business that has come up in the present marketing scenario. It is customer oriented thinking. It says that the process of a business is to create a customer, i.e. the creation of a customer is the function of marketing. It stresses the importance of marketing function of a business. Here, simply it is mentioned that the **creation of a customer**. It refers to the identification of customer needs and organizing the business to convert the needs of a customer into a product idea and produce the goods to meet the customer needs and the manufactured goods is transferred to the market so that customer can get the product when he needs the service of the product. The objective of modern marketing is **customer satisfaction.** All activities of marketing are oriented towards giving maximum satisfaction to the customer. This is known as **buyer's market orientation.**

4.31. MARKETING AND SELLING

As we have seen above, marketing is done to give maximum satisfaction; it is better at this stage to distinguish between the two terms **marketing** and **selling.** Market in its wider sense includes and embraces the function of selling in the sense of distribution or dispersion of goods and service. However, more important than this is the distinction between the marketing as a philosophy and policy of a business firm and selling as an alternative to it.

Marketing refers to the functions and activities involved in producing and distribution of goods and services to the place of the customer or user as and when he needs it. To be simpler, marketing **gives product awareness to the customer; motivate him to purchase the product.** Whereas **selling is the act of transferring the ownership of the product to the consumer by taking the price of the product.** Hence, fundamental concepts are:

1. That the company's policies and operations should be customer oriented, and
2. That the goal of the organization should be profitable sales.

4.32. MARKETING FUNCTIONS

Production activity exists because of consumption and consumption is the sole end and purpose of all production. Hence, the task of marketing system is to adjust the production of goods and services to the needs of the consumers. Having decided upon the marketing strategy, the marketer has to consider the question of the journey that his product has to cover and pass through many operations and hands before it reaches the ultimate consumer. All the various activities and operations done to fulfill the above are usually termed as marketing functions.

Broadly speaking, marketing function comprise two processes: (a) Concentration and (b) Dispersal or dispersion. The process of concentration consists of gathering and putting together into large quantities of raw materials or finished goods at central points or market places to the ultimate consumers. Dispersion means distribution of goods from market places to the ultimate consumers. These processes also involve a number of other marketing functions of auxiliary nature, which facilitate the total marketing of goods. Marketing functions may be grouped as:

A. Merchandising Function: This involves

1. **Buying:**
   - (a) Determining needs;
   - (b) Finding a seller or seeking out source of supply;
   - (c) Negotiating price and other terms;
   - (d) Transfer of title; and
   - (e) Payment, or arranging for credit.
2. Assembling or its converse disbursing.
3. Standardizing or Grading.
4. Storing or warehousing i.e. creation of time utility.
5. Transporting i.e. creation of place utility.
6. Dividing, Packing, Packaging and Processing.

B. Auxiliary or General Business Functions:

7. Financing.
8. Risk taking — Insurance or Future Trading.
9. Recording.
10. Sale Functions.

Selling:
- (a) Creating demand;
- (b) Finding a buyer;
- (c) Advice to buyer as to the use of product;
- (d) Negotiating price and other terms;
- (e) Transfer of titles;
- (f) Collection, or extension of credit.

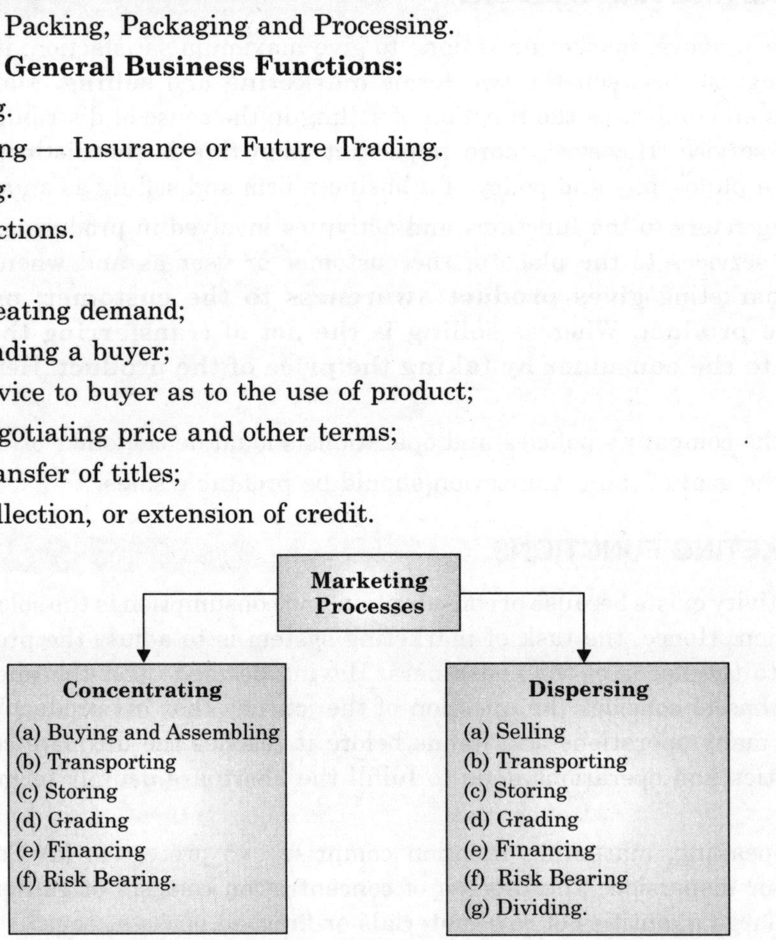

Fig. 4.16. Chart Showing the Functions of Marketing

1. **Buying:** The buying activities of marketing are complementary to selling efforts. Buying includes the determination of one's needs, the seeking out of sources of

supply, the negotiating of prices and other terms, and the transfer of title from the seller to the buyer. Buying is an important function and occupies of the time of both business concerns and ultimate consumers. The ultimate purpose of buying is to bring commodities together where they are wanted for immediate use in production or in personal consumption.

2. **Modes of Purchasing:** Goods may be purchased in any of the four ways. Namely,
   (a) By inspection, (b) By sample,
   (c) By description or (d) By grading.

   (a) Purchasing by Inspection: This means purchasing after the buyer has examined the goods to determine their quality and their adaptability to his needs. This is the oldest type of purchase and is still widely used in retail and wholesale transactions.

   (b) Purchase by Sample: The purchase is made after the buyer examines a sample of goods, it being understood that the entire quality is to be of as good as quality of the sample.

   (c) Purchase by Description or Brand: Purchase is made when the buyer examines a catalogue or obtains description of the goods by some other means, e.g. a brand or trade name. The bulk supplied is required to correspond with the description.

   (d) Purchase by Grade: Purchase is made when the buyer buys a stated quantity of a given grade of a specified product, for example cotton, egg and fruits etc. This method is used largely as a basic of futures trading.

4.33. ASSEMBLING

Assembling is not buying; it is merely putting together of goods to secure larger lots for shipment, for sale, or for manufacture. Assembling plays an important part in the marketing of agricultural goods, which are normally grown in small quantities by large number of producers in territories spread over vast areas. Concentration of raw materials is necessary, because they are to be used in larger quantities by manufacturers, and who require a regular supply of standardized materials. Assembling assures this.

4.34. STANDARDIZING AND GRADING

To grade is to assort goods into lots which are approximately alike in variety, size and quality. To standardize is to give permanence to grades by means of inspection of commodities. When goods, as produced, are not standardized and when the standard to which they conform is unknown, grading or classification is necessary. The object of these efforts is to prepare goods so that a common standardized nomenclature of grade can be utilized in bringing about an understanding between buyer and seller. Grading may be based on size, colour, appearance, chemical contents, strength, shape, specific gravity, amount of, moisture, ripeness, sweetness, or length of fiber etc. A grade carries the idea of uniformity. Therefore, a standard or grade often means that the goods are of certain quality regardless of the producer.

4.35. BRANDING

Besides general gradation, individual producers establish their own standards, commonly known as brands. Branding is the process of identifying the name of the producer with the product. Affixing to the product or its container the trade name or brand represented by words or design usually does this. Branding is very common with consumption goods and with equipment. A brand conveys an idea of permanence, subject to the possibility of change for improvement in quality. As a rule, in selecting a brand name or design consideration should be given to the following points.

1. The name or word should be simple and easy to pronounce so that it can be remembered.
2. The name or design should possess its own distinctive feature to avoid its being confused with some other name or design.
3. It should not lend itself to easy imitation.
4. It should suggestive of good quality.
5. It should not be changed frequently.

4.35.1. Advantages of Grading and Branding

There are number of advantages in grading or branding the product. They are:

1. Purchase and sale are simplified when they are made on the basis of sample, grade, description or symbol.
2. Grading according to definite standards decrease marketing costs and often means higher prices to the producers and lower process to the consumers.
3. Graded products can be marketed more cheaply owing to lessening of risks, and increase in the ease of financing the necessary transactions; a reduction in transportation and storage costs; a decrease in the costs of demand creation; and saving in the time of buyers and sellers in making purchases and sales.
4. Standard goods command wider market than the non-standardized goods.
5. Grading makes possible dealing for future delivery so that hedging transaction can be easily made.
6. Since standardized goods are of known quality and price the owner desiring to borrow money on them may store them in public warehouses and deposit the warehouse receipt at the bank as collaterals for loans. Banks will often lend almost the full market value of such goods.
7. This facility enables owners to carry their goods until they can obtain higher prices for them. Most eggs in cold storage are carried in this way for a number of months.
8. Grading lessons Transport and storage costs. Inferior or unmarketable goods may be discarded so that no transport or storage expenses are incurred on goods not wanted by the consumers.
9. Development of grading widens the market and facilitates dissemination of accurate market knowledge.
10. Grading leads to greater uniformity of production types and tends to eliminate or at least reduce the heterogeneous number of varieties and trade descriptions.
11. Pooling is made possible by restoring to grading and standardization. As selling of lots is uneconomical, goods of one grade can be pooled together to reap the benefits of large scale selling.

12. Grading introduces greater equity or justice. A farmer who sells the commodity, which is not standardized, does not realize the exact price. But by grading all cultivators can get full price for the quality they sell.

4.36. PACKING AND PACKAGING

Packing refers to the wrapping and creating necessary for the transport or storage of goods. Many goods must be packed in order to be preserved or delivered to the buyers. Liquids must be placed in barrels, bottles or cans. Bulky fabrics are compressed into bales. Heavy goods are often crated for handling for protection during transportation. Goods must be place in boxes for delivery to dealers, while the retailers often wrap goods or place them in bags for delivery to ultimate consumers. Fragile goods must often be packed in special containers.

PACKAGING means placing the product in small packages — boxes, cartons, bottles or cans — for sale to the ultimate consumer. It is axiomatic that the job of packaging is to sell; and the major purpose of any package is to influence or controls the location of product storage within the marketing channel right to the ultimate consumer.

The functions of product package are:

(a) Protecting the product.

(b) Adapting to product line speeds.

(c) Promoting the product.

(d) Increasing product density, i.e. increasing the ratio of product volume to package volume.

(e) Facilitating the use of the product.

(f) Having re-use value for the consumer.

The successful package is not the one with an intriguing shape or design, but the one who over-all design, shape, colour and printed message delivered an impact that resulted in a personal relationship between the consume and the package on the shelf. Today the package must come alive at the point of the purchase. The salesman has now stepped inside the package. The manufacturer can create and control the salesman in the package. A poorly designed package tells the consumer that the maker of the product does not care. Like an impatient salesman at five minutes before closing time, he is saying, "take it or leave it". But a well-designed package is a proof that the manufacturer really cares about both the customer and the product and is willing to make an extra effort to please. He is employing a friendly, interested salesman. But what is well designed package? The consumer himself is the measure of a good package. Through his emotional needs, the consumer sets up very demanding standards of good packaging. They are:

(a) Convenience: Does the package hold enough of the product to satisfy his needs without being too bulky or too heavy?

(b) Adaptability: How well does the package fit into his cupboard, refrigerator, drawer, or glove compartment of his car?

(c) Security: Does he feel assured that you have given him quality? Does the package make him feel it?

(d) Status of Prestige: Does he feel that by buying your package he is expressing something about himself?

(e) **Dependability:** Does the package let him feel that he can rely upon you, the manufacturer?

(f) **Aesthetic Satisfaction:** Is he pleased and satisfied by the impact of the design?

Actually these six criteria can be described as combining **utility, security and aesthetic appearance.** A good package expresses profile of a product in a dramatic, easily recognizable way. A bad package, on the other hand, contradicts, under-plays, or undermines a product's profile. Therefore, a tasteful design, high in status value will always give a product prestige and the consumer will like to possess it. But like people, packages also grow old and tired. Yet unlike people, they can be renewed. A tired package communicates the profile of a tired product. Today's consumer demands that his favorite product be full of freshness and youth. This calls for a constant renewal of design. A sale does not end with the purchase of a product. Advertising and promotion continual strive to renew the relationship between consumer and product so as to create an uninterrupted flow of sales. The package must resell itself to the consumer everytime he sees it.

4.37. WAREHOUSING

Warehousing or Storage creates time utility. Many goods are not produced regularly at the point where they are wanted for consumption and they must be stored from the time of production to the time of utilization, if they are to be used in satisfying human wants. Goods produced at a distance from the consumer must be transported to the place of consumers. In order to ensure an even supply, a stock of such goods must be maintained near the consumers as protection against delay and uncertainties of transport and to permit transport in economical units. Many agricultural goods produced seasonally are supplied to consumers more or less evenly throughout the year. Cold storage facility enhances the utility of storage function further, especially in the storage of food products and agricultural products. When there is a fluctuating demand exists for products, storage helps as a buffer for the producer to wait for a fair demand and price.

4.37.1. Storage Facilities

In order that goods can be marketed efficiently, it is important that adequate storing facilities should be available. Sufficient space, proper location, adequate equipment to give protection to goods against heat, cold, moisture, dryness, vermin, fire and thieves should be available. A warehouse should be so located and constructed so that goods can be received and shipped at minimum expenses. It is generally desirable that a warehouse, where large quantities of goods are stored, should be located on railway siding or on the harbor according to need. It should have adequate space for the trucks to load and unload and should be situated near the arterial streets or highways. Facilities for handling goods are important. Types of warehouses are:

(a) Private Warehouses,

(b) Public Warehouse, and

(c) Bonded Warehouses.

Private warehouses belong to the owner of goods, usually a wholesaler, so stores his goods there. The owner of the warehouse maintains this. These warehouses have limited utility and value.

A doc authority, harbingers or any member of the public, may own public warehouse. Such warehouse is operated in accordance with law for the purpose of storing goods belonging to other people for a charge. Public warehouses are useful when the load arrive from upcountry when there are no facilities. It is also helpful when it is not convenient for the importer to receive the consignment. Agent and landlord relationship exist between the public warehouse and owner of the goods. The services rendered by public warehouses are:

(a) They are well constructed and well watched by attendants all the 24 hours of the day, which makes less insurance charges.

(b) They have excellent transport facilities for receiving and shipping goods by both rail and road.

(c) The manufacturer who uses these is relived of the necessity of providing capital for creating his own building or of going to the trouble of leasing building owned by others. He pays only for the space used by him.

(d) Goods stored in public warehouses are more easily financed than goods stored in private warehouses. The receipt issued by the public warehouse will be an excellent collateral security for borrowing money from banks.

(e) A public warehouse is particularly adapted to the needs of the persons who wish to carry regional stocks and who does not have enough goods in various storage centers to justify keeping his own warehouse and maintaining his own employees.

(f) Public warehouse enables smaller sellers to carry regional stocks. This is very important in competitive market.

4.37.2. Bonded Warehouses

A Bonded warehouse is one, which is licensed to accept imported gods for storage before payment of customs duties. By storing his goods in a bonded warehouse the importer gains some control without paying the duty. He can make delivery of small quantities of the goods as he sells them merely by paying duty on those portions, which he desires to remove thereby saving paying the full duty. In case of re-exporting the goods, stored in bonded warehouses, saves double work of payment of duty and its refund on re-export and hence, locking up of big amounts till refund.

4.38. INSURANCE

In business, as in private life, there are risks of every kind. Fortunately, most business risks are completely remote, but that does not lessen the loss they involve when they do occur. All prudent men will always catalogue most carefully every possible risk which the business they own or control may be running and consider how best they can prevent each risk materializing or minimize and provide against its effort. Here risk means uncertainty of losses where the loss is caused by accidental and unexpected circumstances beyond the control of the management. Such risks have to be guarded against and one of the ways to cover them is to take insurance. Every prudent business and resorts to insurance. Insurance is really an element of business; without it no vehicle of transport on sea or land or in the air is allowed to move, noting is built and no wheel turns. Insurance may be described as the provision, which a prudent man makes against unexpected or invisible loss or misfortune. It is commercialized form of spreading risk. The risk of loss is spread over a number of persons, each of whom is prepared to bear a fraction of the loss should be eventuality against which the owner of the property wishes to protect himself actually take place. The person who assumes this risk is called **insurer** and he does so in consideration of the payment of a sum of money called **premium** so that those entering into contract of insurance called the **assured,** who suffered damage are compensated from a common fund to which they and others have contributed. Hence, insurance is described as a co-operative way of spreading risk.

4.39. FINANCING OF TRADE

Methods of financing internal trade in different countries are different. Bulk of the Indian trade is financed by the indigenous system, and a little by the modern or western system of banking. Financing agents or the constituents of Money-marketing India is:

1. The numerous and heterogeneous group of indigenous bankers and brokers, called by different names in different parts of the country, such as Shoroffs, Banias, Mahajanas, Sahukars, Marwaris and Chettis, whose operations are almost entirely confined to the interior of India.
2. The co-operative banks, which advances mainly to member-cultivators.
3. The Indian Joint Stock Banks run on European lines, which advance for a short term on collateral securities.
4. Exchange banks, which mainly finance external trade.
5. The State Bank of India. And
6. The Reserve Bank of India.

4.40. MARKETING RESEARCH

The concept of **"marketing research"** is related to the **consumer oriented** modern concept of marketing. If marketing consists in finding out and satisfying consumer needs through the right products, at the right price, at the right place and at the right time, it calls for systematic effort on the part of the management of the firm. Marketing research is part of such effort. Research involves the definition of problems and the various applications of logical methods to find out solutions to them. Marketing research, therefore, **means the careful and objective study of product design, markets and such transfer activities as physical distribution and warehousing, advertising and sales management.** In a broader and more general way, the definition committee of the American Marketing Association defined market research as **"the gathering, recording and analysis of all facts about problems relating to the transfer and sale of goods and services from producer to consumer".** While taking a marketing decision, a manager will be well advised to take the following steps which constitute the process of marketing research: (a) Recognizing and defining the problem, (b) Developing alternate courses of action, (c) Gathering data or generating information necessary for problem solving and (d) Evaluating alternative courses of action against the data collected with a view to arriving at the courses of action that will give the maximum or best results over a period of time. Kinds of marketing researches are:

(a) Research on products and services: This includes research leading to the development of new products in keeping with needs, conveniences and demand of the consumers, development of proper packaging, product line simplification on the basis of feedback from the market.

(b) Research on markets: This involves investigation into the size and character of market, profitability of different markets, shifts in the nature of markets, economic factors operating on markets, territorial sales opportunities etc.

(c) Research on sales methods and policies: This type of marketing research takes the form of examination of price policies, discount structure, distribution costs, effectiveness of salesman and advertising effort, sales compensation and advertising media selection etc.

4.41. PRICING

Pricing is a marketing function whose importance is acknowledged even more easily than that of the other functions. From the point of view of the consumer, the price of a product as compared with the quality, quantity and the package offered by the firm determines whether he will have anything with the firm or not. The pricing policy of a firm, which is basically the responsibility of the marketing department (even though the other departments are associated with its formulation) is a function basically of cost and demand factors. In practice, it is not as simple as it may appear from these two factors indicated here.

4.42. TRANSPORTATION

The chief function of physical distribution is to take goods from the places of production to the places they are to be consumed. This is referred to as the creation of **"place utility"**. Transportation performs this essential function of marketing. Proper management for the transportation of products to markets is, of course, vital to the process of marketing. What is even more important, improvements in transportation and traffic services have always led to a widening of the markets, increase in the scale of production and specialization in industry. Apart from the economic significance of transportation, the social, political and cultural importance of an efferent system of transport is all too well known to be over-emphasized. Of course, let it be clear that transportation is not merely a marketing activity. To use economic terminology transportation contributes **"place utility"** to goods, helps in effecting **"possession utility"** and aids manufacturing processes in creating **"form utility"**. If production is regarded as the creation of utilities, there can be no objection to regarding transportation as a productive activity. As a matter of fact an article is not fully produced in its broadest economic sense until it is in the hands of the ultimate consumer. From this standpoint also transport is a productive function.

4.43. RISK – TAKING

Marketing, like all other business activities, carries a number of risks. Most of these risks are due primarily to fluctuations in prices. Price changes are responsible for actual loss, or the loss of **potential profit** to the owners and buyers of goods. The unforeseen risks caused by such changes and a number of other factors have to be borne by those performing the functions of marketing. The marketing risks are classified as:

1. **Time risk:** Goods may be purchased (by wholesaler or retailer) for sale at a higher price at some later date. There would be risk of loss during the interval of time between the purchase and sale, for the price may either rise a little or not rise at all, or may even fall down.
2. **Place risk:** If goods are purchased at a place when the prices are low to be sold at another place where they are higher, the expected profit will be realized only if the price at the other place meets the seller's anticipation. Otherwise, there can be a chance of loss. Such risks have been reduced to the minimum these days because of development in the field of communication.
3. **Risk of change in demand:** Under the present set-up of production, goods are produced by round — about methods to meet an anticipated amount of demand. If the demand does not come up to the expectations of the producer at the time when the products are to be marketed, the producer's profit may be curtailed.
4. **Risk of competition:** A producer and a merchant have both to face the risk of losing a part of the market to a rival in the field. If, for example, the competitor introduces new use value to his product, it immediately affects the demand of the firm. Hence, any businessman must be in a position to face the business game and play with suitable strategy to counter the opponent's action.
5. **Other risks:** Besides the types of risks mentioned above the businessman who engaged in marketing have to face a number of unrealities and risks. In the first place his business may be affected by natural risks, such as problems arises from nature, like rain, earthquake, fire, lightning etc. Secondly, he must be ready to face the risks due to accidents, bad debts, strikes, lockouts and government activities and business regulations.

4.44. MARKETING MIX OR FOUR Ps IN MARKETING

The marketing manager's job is to ensure that the **Product is** designed to meet the needs of customers and prospects; is **Priced right** in terms of the customer segments aimed at; is **Promoted** adequate advertising, sales promotion and personal selling to create interest and desire for the product among the customers; and is **Physically** distributed to make it available to the customers and prospects at convenient place through the selection of adequate channels of distribution and the provision of appropriate warehousing and transportation facilitates. The marketing functions and activities can thus be conveniently grouped under the following four heads: They are:

1. **Product,** including consideration of **Packaging** and **Branding.**
2. **Pricing.**
3. **Physical Distribution** including Channels of Distribution, Warehousing and Transportation and
4. **Promotion,** including Advertising, Sales Promotion and Personal Selling.

The above four are referred as in modern marketing thinking as **MARKETING MIX OR 4 Ps OF MARKETING.**

MARKETING MIX Or 4 Ps OF MARKETING.

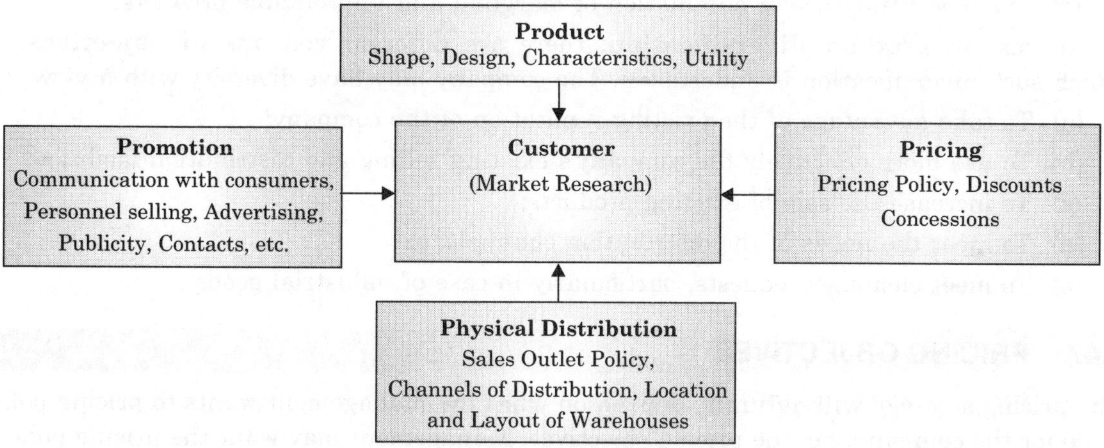

Fig. 4.17. Four Ps of Marketing

4.45. PLANNING IN MARKETING

As the economic and social justification for the company's existence is the satisfaction of customer's wants, the element of the marketing mix i.e. **'four Ps'** in marketing should all be directed towards the customer as shown the figure 4.17. **Planning should be aimed at the customer. It should start with the customer as well as it should finish at the customer in terms of customer satisfaction from the use of the product or service.**

4.46. MARKETING RESEARCH

Systematic marketing, therefore, requires an identification of the needs and preferences of customers as well as research on the effectiveness of the elements of the marketing mix used. This brings to the forefront of the importance of Marketing Research, which alone can ensure that management decisions in the area of marketing are used on facts rather than on hunch or intuition. Marketing research helps the marketing executives to improve their performance and give effective suggestions to the management in matters related to marketing. Market research is **the systematic gathering, recording and analyzing of data about problems relating to the marketing of goods and services.**

4.46.1. Product Planning and Objectives

Product planning can be defined as **"the act of marking out and supervising the search, screening, development and commercialization of new products; the modification of existing lines; and the discontinuance of marginal or unprofitable items".**

Important considerations in product planning are:

(a) Development and introduction of new products;

(b) The modification and improvement of existing line as required by the changing consumer needs and preferences; and

(c) The discontinuance or elimination of marginal and unprofitable products.

In case of **product diversification**, there are different **reasons of objectives** for which such diversification is undertaken. The company may have diversity with a view

(a) To take advantage of the existing reputation of the company;

(b) To use more effectively the company's existing selling and distribution facilities;

(c) To increase the sale of existing products;

(d) To meet the needs of the distribution channels; or

(e) To meet customer requests, particularly in case of industrial goods.

4.47. PRICING OBJECTIVES

The pricing strategy will naturally depend on what the management wants to pricing policy to do for the company, i.e. the pricing objectives. Management may want the pricing policy:

(a) To skim the cream or make huge profits initially as in the case of novelty items with a short life;

(b) To obtain rapid market penetration for the product with a low price;

(c) To discourage potential competitors by pricing low and making it unattractive for them to enter the market;

(d) To achieve the target rate of return on investment or net sales;

(e) To stabilize price over a long period or time;

(f) To meet or follow competition instead of being a price leader; or

(g) To maximize the profits in terms of the demand.

4.48. PHYSICAL DISTRIBUTION OBJECTIVES

To select an appropriate channel of distribution the area of distribution, it is necessary to ascertain the degree of market exposure required. The Physical Distribution Objectives are:

(a) Intensive distribution;

(b) Selective distribution; and

(c) Exclusive distribution.

Some products need widespread distribution, while others need limited distribution. Ideal distribution is one that does not exceed the actual distribution.

Intensive Distribution objective seeks to secure maximum product exposure by selling the product through, as many outlets as are willing to stock it. This policy is normally appropriate in the case of low priced mass consumer convenience goods.

The Selective Distribution policy seeks to restrict the distribution outlets to those who can do an effective job with the product. When selective distributions extended to the extreme, it results in **Exclusive Distribution** where, say only one outlet is selected for a given geographical market. The degree of exposure goes on declining as we move from the intensive to the selective and finally to the exclusive type of distribution strategy.

4.49. PROMOTIONAL OBJECTIVES

In the area of promotion, objectives must also be crystallized. Particularly in the areas of advertising and sales promotions objectives are often not defined clearly and specifically. The objectives and purposes expected to be accomplished by advertising and sales promotion must be clearly determined. Here specific means to say that the objective should not be stated in a vague manner. For example, the objective of advertising is to **increase the sales of product X** is very vague. It must be clearly stated as: To communicate the specific qualities of product X, to gain specific degree of penetration. The Information must reach the specific size of the audience. The advertisement must be published in right time.

The specific objectives may vary with the company and the type of product concerned. The objective of sale should not be viewed as the only objective sought to be achieved. Selling the product is undoubtedly the long run function of good advertising and sales promotion. However, its immediate or short run goals must be narrower and more precise, for example, (i) creating consumer and distributor awareness, (ii) creating favourable image of the company and (iii) inducing immediate sales. In one sentence we can say that the purpose of marketing planning is to crystallize the objectives in each of the **"four Ps"** of marketing and direct them towards the customer with a view to producing both customer satisfaction and profitability for the organization.

4.49.1. Organizing the Produce Strategy and Development

Product strategy relates to the decision to be taken regarding the product line, the introduction of new products, planning obsolescence, packaging and branding.

Diversification:

Most important among product strategy is the product **diversification.** This means *"the manufacture of distribution by a single company of more than one commodity".*

Product diversification may help to increase the sale of the existing product or make a more effective use of the company's selling and distribution facilities. When developing a new product, a committee consisting marketing, production, research and finance personnel may take decision to discuss the consequences of introducing the new product and to visualize competitor's strategies before taking a decision and submit their report.

4.50. PACKAGING

Packaging design is another important aspect of product development. From the manufacture's viewpoint, the two important attributes are generally **"protection"** and **"economy".** However, from the consumer's viewpoint, the question of **"convenience"** is of greater significance. He would also like to be offered options in the form of size and would like packages that open easily. Packaging can also perform a useful **"promotional"** function and help to educate the customers.

4.51. BRANDING

Branding is integral part of the product strategy. A brand is *"a name, term, signs, symbol, or design, or a combination of them which is intended to identity the goods or service of one seller or a group of sellers and to differentiate them form those of competitors"*. A brand includes brand name, a trademark, or both. Rightly or wrongly, customers often believe that products of well-known brands are of higher quality than products of unknown brands. Brands also serve to differentiate products. All the above-mentioned strategies are to be integrated and directed towards the market segments selected to create awareness in customer regarding the product or service.

4.52. PRICING STRATEGY

Pricing should be such that best results are achieved in the market segments.

The steps to be taken are:

(a) Estimate the demand for the product.
(b) Anticipate the competitive reaction.
(c) Establish the expected share of the market.
(d) Select the price strategy to be used to reach the market target.
(e) Consider company policies regarding product, channels and promotion.
(f) Select the specific price.

The pricing strategy for the company must be organized in terms for the needs of the targeted customer segments. Customers differ from the viewpoint of aspects such as decorative trims, variety of operating features and the quality of the material required all of which affect the price to be charged. Accordingly, even when offering a single product, it may become advisable to offer it in a variety of sizes, designs and features at different prices.

4.53. PHYSICAL DISTRIBUTION

In connection with the distribution channels, one must identify the best way to reach the targeted customer segments. It is because; the organization of distribution channels depends on customer characteristics like their geographic distribution, number, frequency of purchase and the nature and extent of planning associated with such purchases.

Product characteristics can also have an important bearing on organizing the channels of distribution. Perishable products must be organized to distribute rapidly through relatively short channels to avoid deterioration caused by delays as well as repeated handling. Bulky products like building materials, requires a minimization of the transportation distance and the number of persons handling them. Company's profile such as size, policy also has effect on distribution.

4.54. ORGANIZING PROMOTIONAL ACTIVITIES

While organizing promotional activities, it is necessary to determine the advertising budget as well as select the optimum media mix. Budget allocation is often determined on the basis of available funds or on the footing of competitive allocations or more commonly as a percentage of sales. It is better to allocate funds in terms of the objectives sought to be attained by the promotional effort. It is also necessary to determine the right media such as press, outdoor publicity, advertising literature, etc. and the number of exposures required. Sales promotion is " *those marketing activities, other than personal selling, advertising and publicity, that stimulate consumer purchasing and dealer effectiveness, such as display, show and exhibitions, demonstrations and various non-recurrent selling efforts not in the ordinary routine*".

Finally personal selling is also to be organized. *"Personal Selling is oral presentation in a conversation with one or more prospective purchasers for the purpose of making sales".*

Personal selling has to be organized around the number of customers sought to be reached, the average number of calls required per customer and the average number of calls it is possible for a salesman to make during a particular period. The salesmen must have adequate training in personal selling. Personal selling is one aspect of sales promotion. All activities such as advertising, personal selling and sales promotion put together is known as **Promotional mix.**

4.55. CHANNELS OF DISTRIBUTION

Distribution may be defined as an operation, or a series of operations, which physically bring goods manufactured or produced by any particular manufacturer into the hands of the final consumer or user. The term "distribution" is sometimes loosely used to mean more or less the same as "marketing" by saying that distribution includes all activities which bring a product form the factory into the hands of the final consumer, which includes the other marketing operations. In fact distribution is an integral part of marketing. Distribution function is to distribute or subdivide the total products of a manufacturer on a geographical basis to various specific markets. There may be State Market or a National Market or even a Global Market for the products. While discussing distribution aspect, we have to deal with two aspects, the first of which is the **organizational aspect of distribution.** This deals with how and through what channels we should distribute? The second one is **operational aspect of distribution** or physical distribution. This is concerned with physical movement of goods from one place to other, includes, warehousing, storing and transportation and costs involved. This aspect is sometimes known as **Logistic of Distribution.**

4.55.1. Distribution Channels

Consider the manufacturer, deciding to distribute his products. He can sell directly:

1. To the consumer (under certain circumstances) or
2. To the retailer or
3. To the wholesalers
4. To a sole distributor or
5. To one or two regional sole distributors or sole selling agents.

If the manufacturer sells to a sole distributor or sole selling agent, the latter in his turn has a similar choice of distribution channels. The sole selling agent or distributor may:

1. Approach the consumer directly or
2. Sell to retailers or
3. Deal with a number of wholesalers who in their turn sell to retailers.

The retailer has really no choice and he sells directly to the consumer. (Here, it is better to understand, from the retailer, the product may go to the hands of customer and then to the consumer. Customer is a person who purchases the product for the self-use or to be used by others related to him.).

Thus there are three **main channels of distribution,** namely:

1. From the Manufacturer or Producer to the Wholesaler, then to the Retailer and finally to the Customer/Consumer.
2. From the Manufacturer or Producer to the Retailer and then to the Consumer (thus avoiding Wholesaler).
3. From the Manufacturer directly to the Consumer.

The chart given below explains the different channels. (Figures 4.18 and 4.19)

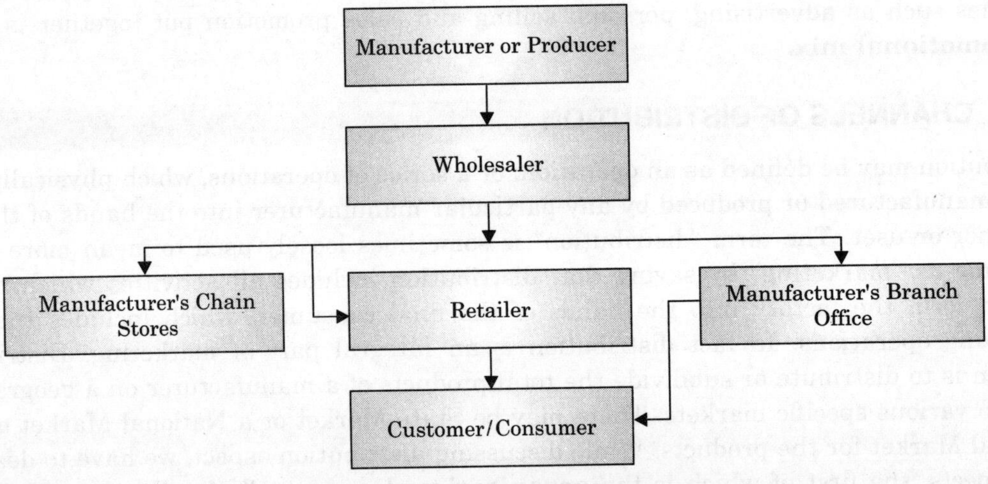

Fig. 4.18. Distribution Channel

The distribution of goods is the last, but the most crucial phase of the process of marketing. A producer or a manufacturer has to take positive steps to bring his products to the notice of potential customers in order to arouse a desire for them and create demand for his products. The term **channel of distribution** is used to refer the various alternative link roads, which connect the producer with the consumer. These channels vary depending on the type of product, consumer and other factors such as environment and available channels. The producer without any intermediary sells sometimes products directly to the user, while others require intermediate step, to being sold through one or more **middlemen** before reaching the consumer. **Middlemen are those merchants who act as intermediaries between the producers and consumers in the distribution of goods among the consumers at large.** The decision to choose a channel or a set of channels for a product is part of the marketing mix — the strategy of the firm in dealing with its market.

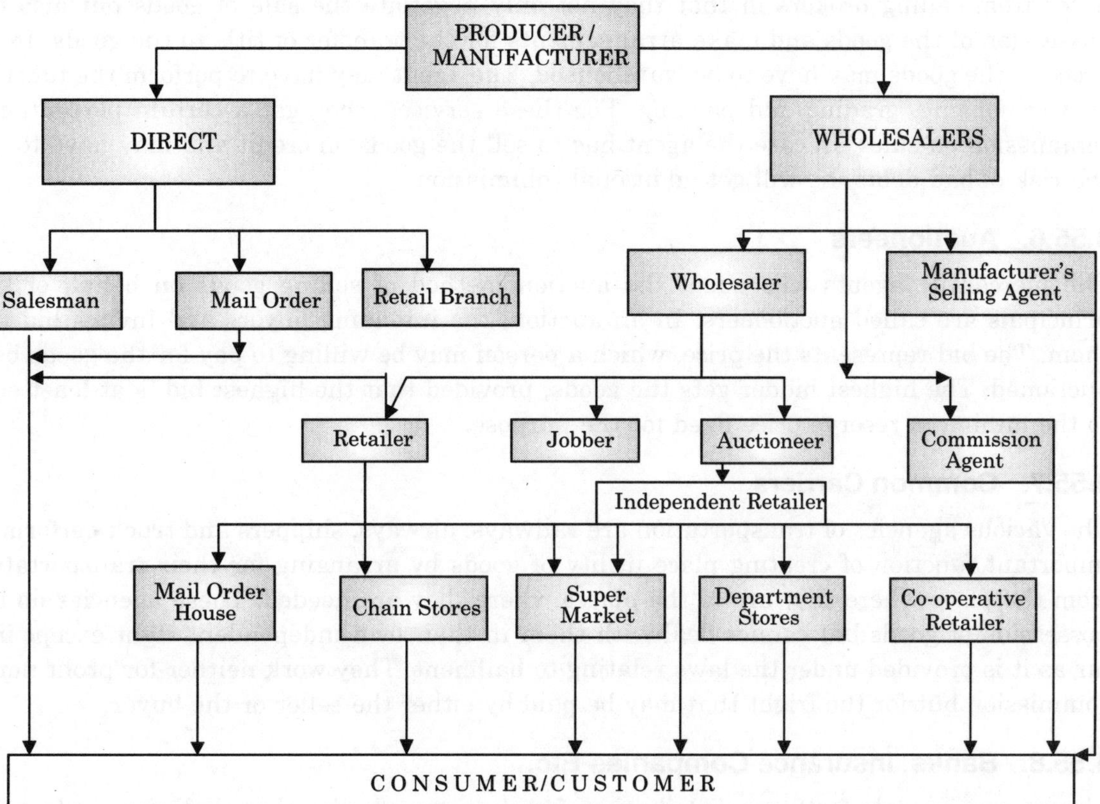

Fig. 4.19. Distribution Channels

4.55.2. Middlemen

Middlemen are the connecting links between the manufacturer on one side and the consumer to the other. A number of agencies exist practically in every country to perform this function. They are called by different names depending on the function offered by them. Mainly there are two groups. (a) Functional middlemen or Mercantile agents, and (b) Merchants.

4.55.3. Functional Middlemen or Mercantile Agents

These are important types of agency houses, which interpose between the producer and the consumers with a view to earning a commission without obtaining the ownership of the goods.

4.55.4. Brokers

Brokers are those mercantile agents who obtain neither the possession nor the ownership of the goods but only serve to bring the buyers and sellers together. They are in fact the intermediaries who negotiate purchase and sale of goods on behalf of other parties.

4.55.5. Commission Agents

The commission agents are also agents who sell goods on behalf of the sellers. But they differ from selling brokers in that they not only negotiate the sale of goods but also take possession of the goods and make arrangements for the transfer of title to the goods. In this process, the goods may have to be warehoused. The agent may have to perform the functions of warehousing, grading and packing. For these services, they get a certain percentage of commission on sales. In case the agent has to sell the goods on credit and may have to bear the risk of bad debts, he will get additional commission.

4.55.6. Auctioneers

The mercantile agents who adopt the auction method of selling goods on behalf of their principals are called auctioneers. In an auction, the intending buyers and invites bid from them. The bid represents the price, which a person may be willing to pay for the goods being auctioned. The highest bidder gets the goods, provided that the highest bid is at least equal to the minimum reserve price fixed for the purpose.

4.55.7. Common Carriers

The various agencies of transportation are railways; airways, shippers and truck perform the important function of creating place utility of goods by arranging for their transportations from the place where they are to the places where they are needed. These agencies do take possession of goods but cannot deal with them in their own independent right except in so far as it is provided under the laws relating to bailment. They work neither for profit nor for commission but for the fright that may be paid by either the seller or the buyer.

4.55.8. Banks, Insurance Companies Etc.

These agencies only facilitate distribution and do not work directly to sell the product. The banks provide the facility of making and receiving payment on account of goods purchased or sold. The insurance companies bare the risk attaching to the goods in warehouses or in transit and thus help in the successful distribution of products.

4.55.9. Merchant Middlemen

The merchant middlemen, who work for profit and acquire the transfer of title to goods in their own right, may be divided into two classes as (a) Wholesalers, and (b) Retailers.

4.55.10. Wholesaler and Distributor

Certain persons consider the wholesaler as a type of unwholesome vulture, feeding the growing rich on the profits of the middlemen. They support this by claiming that if the wholesaler were eliminated the ultimate price of the goods to the consumer would be reduced. It is however elementary economics and common sense that the manufacturers, wholesalers, and retailers should combine with a view to ensure that the public is supplied with goods they want at the most economical price. This argument against middlemen is very similar to the one advanced against advertising, namely, that if advertising were eliminated the savings in advertising costs could be passed on to the consumer in the form of lower selling price. These persons do realizes that mass production can result in a lowering of cost and subsequently the selling price to the consumer. They however shut their eyes to the fact that mass production requires mass distribution for its survival and that advertising and the use of middlemen are necessary to introduce mass distribution. Therefore, let us briefly analyze the utility of the wholesaler.

4.55.10.1. Usefulness of wholesalers

It is sometimes said that intermediaries like the wholesalers result in the increase in the price of the product to the consumer. Whilst there are drawbacks in selecting the wrong type of wholesaler, who may not have appropriate influence or be active enough to push the manufacturer's goods, it must be remembered that the manufacturer who uses a wholesaler is generally assisted by the wholesaler in formulating his policy of manufacture according to the demand. The wholesaler also helps him in securing the market for his goods. He relives the manufacturer from the necessity of having his own sales organization as the wholesaler generally has a ready selling organization of his own. The main functions of these middlemen are selling, providing credit facilities and guiding production in respect of quality and quantity requirements. The manufacturer is also relived from the work of collecting and securing orders. Again the number of accounts the manufacturer has to open is smaller than when dealing directly with retailer or consumers. If all this work has to be done by the manufacturer himself, his cost would be higher as when compared to his relying on wholesalers for performing these activities. In this sense, the use of wholesalers appropriately may even result in a lower price being charged to consumer than would have been charged had the manufacture indulged in all these activities himself. Actually, in terms of costs, the volume of business would determine which method would involve lower cost. Above a certain volume of operations, it would be less costly for the manufacturer to sell directly than through wholesalers. Besides, wholesalers generally enter into forward contracts for supply of goods. They, thus relive the manufacturers of the worry of their goods remaining unsold. Being in close touch with the retailers who are in direct contact with the consumer, the wholesalers can advise the manufacturer as to the changes or alterations to be introduced in their manufacture. They can also exercise a healthy influence on the price in the market by refusing to supply goods to retailers who do not maintain the price fixed by the manufacturer.

Wholesalers are also very useful to the retailers. Retailers cannot invest large sum of money to stock products of various producers. But manufacturers want bulk purchases. He cannot supply in small quantities and he is not prepared to give credit to the retailers. The wholesalers come into picture in between supplier and retailer and invest money to purchase large quantities from the producers and then selling in small quantities to various retailers. In this way wholesaler is useful to the producer to purchase large quantities and sell in small quantities to retailers. This helps retailer to see his investment is small and the goods also remain fresh. As the wholesaler has good experience in this line, he can purchase quality goods from the producers and help the retailers to sell quality goods to the ultimate users. Finally, the wholesaler helps retailer to offer to the consumer a large varieties of lines on a limited stock basis which requires a small capital investment by the retailer. Because of the existence of the wholesaler, consumer is able to get large varieties of goods and different brands in retail shops. Thus, the wholesaler not only assists the manufacturer as well as the retailer but also acts as the link in the chin of distribution between the manufacturer and the consumer for which purpose the wholesaler maintain an efficient and comprehensive organization. The wholesaler has to assess the public demand and see that marketable goods are manufactured thus protecting the, manufacturer from wasteful and indiscriminate production as well as the consumer against goods which are neither satisfactory nor of good value. Stock keeping is an important function of the wholesaler and not that of the manufacturer since the manufacturer must clear his factory of the products as early as possible. On the other hand, the retailer wants to maintain a rapid stock turnover and does not want his capital to be locked up in stock. In this way the wholesaler is useful to manufacturer, retailer and the consumer.

4.55.11. Sole Distributor

A manufacturer often appoints certain wholesaler or large retailers as sole distributors or agent for his goods in particular territories. The manufacturer thus encourages the wholesaler or retailer concerned to push the goods of his manufacture by allowing such a monopoly for the sufficiently lengthened period. Some manufacturers are not keen on granting such local agencies but are prepared to assure the wholesaler or retailer concerned that they will not supply their goods to a competitor of such wholesaler or retailer in that particular locality so long as he maintains a satisfactory level of sales. The sole distributor must however be selected very carefully. The manufacturer must be sure that the sole agent appointed not only has an efficient organization but also has considerable influence in the locality concerned. If this is so, the manufacturer is relieved of considerable expenses in selling and creating goodwill or reputation for his manufacture in the locality. Whilst assigning territory to such a sole agent, the manufacturer should avoid granting too large a territory. The monopoly given must however be for a sufficiently lengthy period. Otherwise the sole distributor will not work hard and provide initial outlay necessary for pushing the goods of the manufacturer because of the risk that his time, effort and outlay may be wasted by cancellation of his agency.

The advantage for the manufacturer is number of account to maintain by him is very small. Besides, large retailers prefer this method as it reduces competition. Very often influential retailers or wholesalers are prepared to act for the manufacturer, who would otherwise have not been interested in acting as only one of a number of distributors. The manufacturer thus enjoys the influence and reputation of such a well-known sole distributing agent. If the agency is worthwhile, the sole distributor is often willing to advertise at his own expense and in any case does mention it in his letterheads and invoices. This amounts to free advertising for the manufacturer. This type of agencies is also useful to the manufacturer wanting to sell his goods in foreign country as this method would considerably decrease the prejudice inherent in the consumer by buying from a foreign country.

The disadvantage of this system is the main one being of sole distributor limits the outlet for sales, thereby possibly limiting the sale volume of the manufacturer in that locality. A single shop in any locality cannot reasonably be expected to attract the whole trade of that locality for a given class of commodity. Besides, the sole distributor may become indifferent and the manufacturer may not be able to terminate the agency until expiry of the period of agency agreed upon. The sole distributor may not have interest in the agency, he may still accept the agency only to prevent his competitors form obtaining and profiting by it. If the sole distributor is unpopular in that area, then the manufacturer will be at a great loss, particularly when the locality is small.

4.55.12. Franchising

Franchising is a system of distribution under a licensing system through which the owner of a product, method or service approaches independent businessmen in selected territories, appoints them as sole franchisee for a particular area and encourages them to make profit for themselves whilst the owner retains control over the technique or style with which the product or service is merchandised. This started as a marketing device used by a few giant companies such as Coca-cola, Pepsi etc. The growing popularity of franchising is due to:

1. The speed at which widespread distribution can be achieved.
2. The offer of immediate access to professional knowledge.
3. The absence of need for previous experience. And
4. The sharing of risk with the franchisee.

4.56. RETAIL OUTLETS

Retail outlets are shops from which the consumer ultimately buys except where the manufacturer sells directly to the consumers. These may be small or giant organizations like the Department Stores and the Chain Stores Organization.

4.56.1. Department Stores

A Department Store is a retail store handling many different lines of merchandise. The main object of such a store is to make it a center of attraction. The department store is like a large shop with a number of smaller shops within its fold. It is akin to a collection of number of smaller shops within its fold. It is akin to a collection of number of tradesman shops under one roof. A visit to such a shop can result in the consumer making a large number of purchases. It is therefore sometimes humorously remarked that **it takes seven tailors to make a man but it does not require seven retailers to break him** — perhaps one department store can do this. The main idea of this type of stores is to have a central shop and attract as many customers as possible to that one location.

4.56.2. Chain Stores or Multiple Shops

Multiple shops or Chain stores constitute a retail-trading organization operating on the system of a chain of branches linked to a central head office. Here a number of shops are opened in different localities and an attempt is made to approach as near the customer as possible. Thus, unlike in the case of departmental stores, an attempt is not made to concentrate the entire business in one center and draw customers to it. The dominating idea is to go as near the customer as possible and thus cater for larger number of customers. Many of the multiple shop organizations had their origin in small retailers opening further shops with their success. Bata stores, DCM stores are the examples.

4.56.3. Super markets

Supermarkets have become very popular. The shop is so arranged that the customer walk from one place to another and picks up the articles, which he wants and finally pays at the checkout counter. Self-service is made easy through adequate stock arrangements and clear price marking. This enables the store to serve more customers with smaller sales personnel. Some of the supermarkets will provide entertainment and refreshment facilities for its customers.

4.56.4. Co-operative Stores

This type of retail outlet is gaining importance today. The co-operative store is generally a shop owned by a society formed of consumers. The members of the society pay small subscription in order to become members. The principle on which business is done in these shops is to supply good quality at a fair price. The surplus remaining after dedicating the cost of goods and other expenses is generally distributed among the members as **"dividend"**. The dominating idea in this type of organization is the pooling of the orders of the members and purchasing at wholesale prices. In this way the profit of the middlemen is sought to be eliminated. These societies usually make their purchases form co-operative wholesale societies formed with the object of avoiding middlemen and wholesalers. Some of these co-operative wholesale societies also work as bankers and financiers for their retail societies.

4.57. FACTORS AFFECTING THE CHOICE OF A PARTICULAR CHANNEL

The question here is **how the manufacturer selects the channel suitable for him?** Various factors have to be taken into consideration before choosing particular channel of distribution. The most important factor is the **type of goods** involved. That is whether the goods are specialty goods or industrial goods (used by limited consumers) or mass consumer goods. In case of industrial goods, retailers are generally excluded and selling is more direct, i.e. through the company's own sales force. In case of a highly technical industrial product there is also the question of technical service, which makes it more desirable to sell direct. In case of perishable products, a speed up through the channels is required. The value – volume relationship should also be considered, as it will have an important bearing on the freight charges as percentage of the value. Generally, the lower the unit value, the longer the channels of distribution. In case of higher unit value or bulky article, physical handling must be minimized.

The next point to be considered is the location of buyers. If all the buyers or users are concentrated in a particular area, a simple distribution system will suffice. Another relevant aspect is the number of buyers for a particular product. Naturally, the distribution system for a mass consumed consumer product like toothpaste or soap has totally different problems when compared with distribution of limited number of people who buy specialized engineering equipment. Next would come the buying habits of the consumers. Do they expect the goods to be delivered at their doorstep (example: newspaper, daily bread, milk etc.,) or do they buy on the mail order system, or do they go to the department stores? What? Another criterion to be considered is the type of retail outlet for the goods. Are the goods sold through general stores, chemists, specialty stores or fashion stores? Again, are the goods convenience goods, shopping goods, or specialty goods?

4.58. PRODUCT LIFE CYCLE CONCEPT

What is the **Product Life Cycle of a Product,** which is being put on the market? Broadly, every product passes through certain different or distinct stages, during the life span of the product. The important stages, from the viewpoint of marketing, they can be grouped into four, namely, **(1) Innovation, (2) Growth, (3) Maturity and (4) Obsolescence.** This is known as ***Product Life Cycle*** as shown in the figure 4.20.

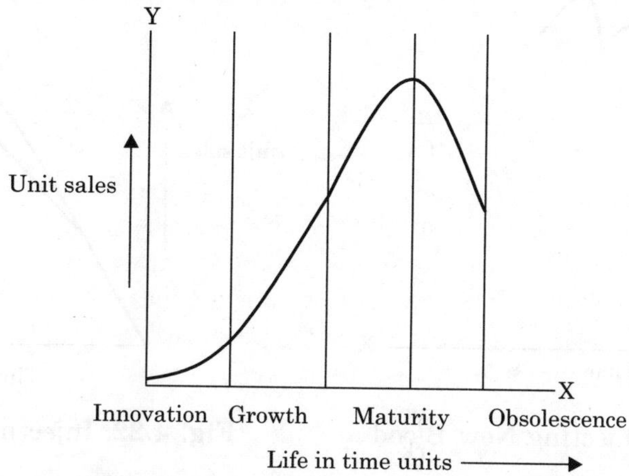

Fig. 4.20. Product Life Cycle

When the product is first is introduced (i.e. at **innovation stage**), the sales will take sometime before they pickup. Once the product gains consumer acceptance, the sales will soar up (which is described as the **Growth stage**). Therefore, as more competitors enter the market, the sales are likely to stop rising and the **maturity stage** or the **saturation point** is reached. Finally, the sales are likely to taper off, which is known as **obsolescence stage.** Time period between "Innovation" and "Obsolescence" however varies between products. When the rate of technological development is very rapid many products will become obsolete even before the plant is constructed to produce them. This is to say that the life of product is small when the rate of technological development is too rapid. In some cases, the life cycle may be many years. Despite such variations in the life span of products, this concept is very useful in deciding the marketing strategy. For example, when a new type of consumer product is introduced in the market, the initial marketing strategy (that is in the innovation stage) would involve heavy advertising, extensive selling and introductory inducements. The sales then pickup in the growth stage. Subsequently as the product gains greater consumer acceptance, competitors are tempted to enter the market. Thus the marketing strategy may shift the emphasizing price appeals and product improvements. Finally, when the sales tend to level off, the organization may merely attempt to recover costs. In the meantime, the research department should have been active enough to come forward with a new product in time.

To ward off the obsolescence stage, the marketing manager should try to

1. Emphasize new uses of the product,
2. Penetrate new markets, and
3. Improve his products.

This may be described as **"injecting the new blood"** technique as shown in figure 4.21. However, this sort of injection of new blood in practice cannot be done permanently. Therefore, particularly in a competitive environment, the company must come out from time to time with a new product so that its sales line will rise steadily. This is termed as **injecting new products** as shown in Fig. 4.22.

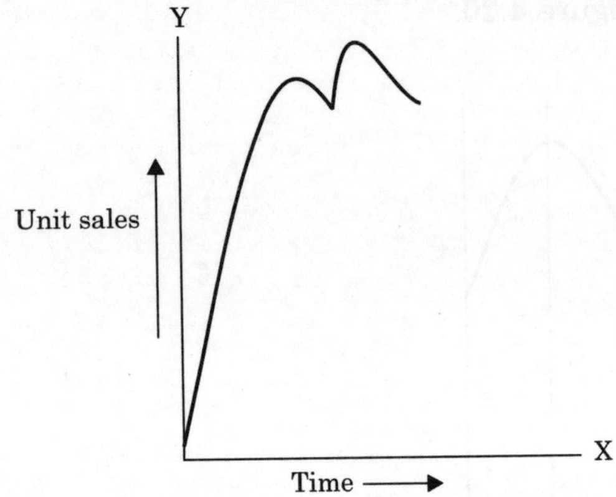

Fig. 4.21. Injecting New Blood

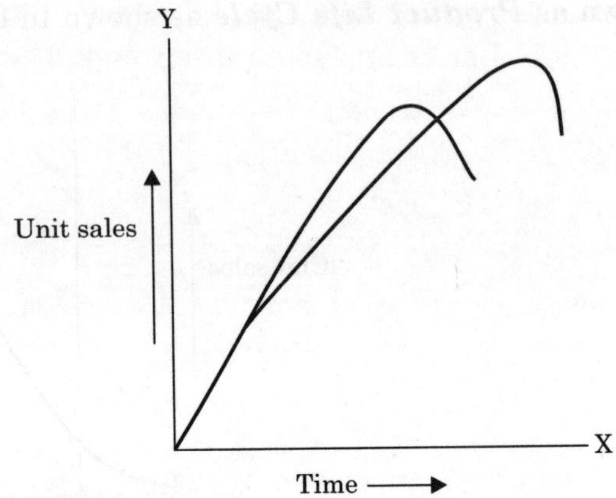

Fig. 4.22. Injecting New Product

QUESTIONS

1. Define Marketing and distinguish between Selling and Marketing.
2. Distinguish between Traditional Marketing and Modern Marketing Concepts.
3. List out the Marketing Functions and discuss any two of them in detail with examples.
4. Discuss the Process of Marketing.
5. What are the various modes of Purchasing?
6. Write short notes on:

   (a) Assembling (b) Branding

   (c) Grading (d) Packing and Packaging.
7. Discuss the advantages of Grading and Branding.
8. Why packing is necessary to a product? What are its uses?
9. Write a note on Warehouse and Warehousing.
10. Write a note on Storage facilities.
11. What is Marketing Research?
12. Write notes on: (a) Risk taking and (b) Pricing.
13. Discuss the four Ps of marketing.
14. Discuss Pricing Objectives.
15. Discuss Physical Distribution Objectives.
16. Discuss Sales Promotional Objectives.

17. What is Channels of Distribution? Give a neat sketch showing the distributional channels.

18. Write Note on:

(a) Brokers (b) Wholesaler

(c) Distributor (d) Merchant middlemen

(e) Banks and Insurance companies.

19. Disuses the usefulness of a wholesaler.

20. Write short notes on:

(a) Sole distributor

(b) Franchising

(c) Retail outlets.

21. Write short notes on:

(a) Supermarkets

(b) Co-operative stores

(c) Chain stores.

22. Clearly explain with a neat sketch the concept of Product Life Cycle.

MULTIPLE CHOICE QUESTIONS

1. The business activities that directs the flow of goods/products and services from producer to the consumer or user is known as:

(a) Selling (b) Transporting

(c) Transfer (d) Marketing.

2. The act of transforming the ownership of the product to the consumer by taking a price to the product is known as:

(a) Selling (b) Marketing

(c) Agreement (d) Give away.

3. Buying, Assembling, Grading are known as:

(a) Selling functions (b) Transfer functions

(c) Merchandising functions (d) Market planning.

4. Putting together the goods to secure larger lots for shipment/for sale/for manufacture is known as:

(a) Piling (b) Roping together

(c) Securing (d) Assembling.

5. The process of identifying the name of the producer by affixing a trade name is termed as:

(a) Grading (b) Branding

(c) Standardizing (d) Fixing the name.

6. The gathering, recording and analysis of all facts about problem relating to the transfer and sale of goods and services from producer to the consumer is termed as:

(a) Marketing (b) Selling

(c) Sales promotion (d) Market research.

7. One of risk the producer has to face in marketing is:

(a) Risk of sales (b) Risk of competition

(c) Financial risk (d) Risk of sales personal.

8. The term used to refer the various alternative link roads, connecting producer and consumer is known as:

(a) Marketing roads (b) Distribution roads

(c) Channels of distribution (d) Routes of marketing.

9. Mercantile agents who obtain neither the possession not the ownership of goods but only serve to bring buyers and sellers together are known as:

(a) Middleman (b) Commission agents

(c) Auctioneers (d) Brokers.

10. The people who works for profit and acquire the transfer of the title to goods in their own right are known as:

(a) Brokers (b) Merchant middlemen

(c) Middlemen (c) Commission agents.

ANSWERS

1. (d) **2.** (a) **3.** (c) **4.** (d) **5.** (b) **6.** (d) **7.** (b) **8.** (c)
9. (d) **10.** (b).

❍❍❍

Unit 5 Human Resources Management (HRM)

5.1. INTRODUCTION

Any organization, aiming at survival and growth, must ***Get the people who can make the organization, Enable them to acquire required capabilities and skills to make the organization successful and motivate them to contribute their resources continuously for running the organization successfully towards the path of growth***. Hence, the manpower or the people with required skills to make an organization are generally referred as ***Human resources.*** In this unit we shall learn about the importance of human resource and ways of developing this resource. Generally, every manager is interested in increasing the material productivity and machine productivity. When we speak of human beings, managers are more concerned with discipline and control. When thinking of increasing the material productivity and machine productivity, we consider them as resources and deal with them, because each of these resources are linked with finance. To increase the productivity of human beings, i.e. ***labour productivity,*** if we think the human beings also as ***resource***, then it will be easy for a manager to tackle the labour productivity problem successfully.

5.2. MEANING AND DEFINITION OF HUMAN RESOURCE MANAGEMENT

Human resource management means employing people, developing their resources, utilizing, maintaining and compensating their services in tune with the job and organizational requirements with a view to contribute to the goal of the organization, individual, society and nation. As planning, organizing, directing and controlling are the functions of management, we can say that the personal management is the field of management which has to do with planning, organizing, directing and controlling the functions of procuring, developing, maintaining and utilizing the labour force so as to fulfil the organizational objectives economically and effectively without sacrificing the objectives of all levels of personnel and national interest. Hence, **Human Resource Management** can be defined as ***"Managing (planning, organizing, directing and controlling) the functions of employing developing and compensating human resources resulting in the creation and development of human relations with a view to contribute proportionately to the organizational, individual and social goals."***

Characteristics of Human Resource Management are:

- Employees both as individuals and as a group, who would like to attain their goal and also with their behaviour, emotions and social aspect.
- Development of human resources, i.e. Knowledge, capability, skills, potentialities and attaining and achieving their goals.
- Covers all levels of employees such as low, middle and higher-level managers. Technical, non-technical professional, clerical and managerial categories of employees.
- It applies to employees in all types of organizations in the world such as industry, trade, service and commerce.
- Human Resource Management is a continuous and never ending process.
- HRM aims at attaining the goals of organization, individual and society in an integrated approach
- HRM is the responsibility of line managers and functions of staff managers in an organization.
- It deals with managing human resources at work and aims at securing unreserved co-operation from all employees in order to satisfy the predetermined goals.

5.3. FUNCTIONS OF HUMAN RESOURCE MANAGEMENT

The functions of HRM may be classified into two categories. They are: (a) Managerial Functions and (b) Operative Functions.

(a) Managerial Functions: Whenever we talk of functions of management, we list out Planning, Organizing, Coordinating, Directing and Controlling. So, also in HRM we have human resource planning, organizing human resources, coordinating human resource, directing human resource and controlling the manpower.

(i) Planning: Manpower Planning and Human resource planning are synonymous. In the past, the phrase manpower planning was widely used, but the new emphasis is on human resource planning which is broader based. Human resource planning is ***"the process by which a management determines how an organization should move from its current manpower position to its desired manpower position.*** Through planning, a management strives to have the right number and the right kind of people at the right places, at the right time to do things, which result in both the organization and the individual receiving the maximum long-range benefit. It is ***forecasting*** future manpower requirements, either in terms of mathematical projections of trends or in terms of judgemental estimates based on the future plans of the organization. It is making an inventory of present manpower resources and assessing the extent to which these resources are employed optimally. Manpower planning consists in projecting future manpower requirements and developing manpower plans for the implementation of the projections. This plan cannot be rigid or static; it is amendable to modification, review and adjustments in accordance with the needs of the organization or changing circumstances. Human resource planning is important because any organization needs more personnel to look after its activities as it grows, to replace persons who have become old, to procure new persons in the place of persons who left the organization and to acquire new skills as desired in the path of expansion and growth.

Manpower planning is done at various levels such as at individual unit level, at industry level, at regional level at state level and at national level. The process of planning consists of (a) Deciding goals or objectives, (b) Estimating future organizational structure and manpower requirements, (c) Auditing human resources, (d) Planning job requirements and job descriptions, and (e) Developing a human resource plan.

(ii) **Organizing:** Every organization has certain objective or objectives. The manager has to strive hard to achieve this or these objectives. This can be done through well-organized manpower. For this he needs a structure of human relations to allocate the work and direct the people. That is why it is said that **organization is a *structure and a process by which a co-operative group of human beings allocates its task among its members, identifies relationships and integrate its activities towards a common objective*.** An organization helps to establish human relationships (organizational) among the employees so as to enable them to contribute their positive efforts to fulfil the organizational goals.

(iii) **Directing:** The function of directing follows immediately after planning and organizing. When a plan is to be executed, the manager has to give proper direction and guide the people towards the achievement of goal. This includes commanding, motivating, leading and activating the people to work as per the laid out plan. Through the act of directing i.e. through motivation and command, manager has to try to tap maximum potentialities of the workmen without harming the individual feelings. Through proper leadership style and directing, manager must make the people to commit to their work in the process of achieving the organizational goals.

(iv) **Controlling:** Once the plans are set and its execution starts, manager has to verify whether all works are being carried out as per plan or not. He and his staff must check the actual and compare with the plan and if they find any deviation, corrective measures are to be taken. The action and operation are adjusted to pre-determined plans and standards through control. Sometimes the deviations may show that something wrong in the original plan. In such cases, the plan is to be revised and accordingly the guidance is given.

Operative functions of human resource management are specific activities of *Personnel Management* and they include employment, development, compensation and relations.

(a) **Employment:** This operative function includes identifying the need, defining the job, specifying the job requirement by careful job analysis, recruiting required personnel, induce the selected personal to the job, give appropriate training to suit the necessity of the organization and internal mobility so as to achieve the goals of the organization.

Job Analysis includes the process of studying, collection of information relating to the operations of the job and responsibilities of the worker in carrying out the job. The personnel department has to collect the information/data regarding the job, men, machine and materials concerned with the job. After collecting necessary information, it has to prepare *job description, job specification and job requirement* on one side and employee specification on the other side, so as to enable the department to select right person for the job on hand.

(i) Recruitment: It is the process of searching for prospective employees and stimulating them to apply for the job in the organization. This includes identifying the sources of prospective applicants, creation of new sources of prospective employees, stimulating the personnel to apply for the posts. Here, the organization has to consider the prospective personnel available in the organization itself and promote them to the higher level, which will create regard in the minds of the employees and it acts as a means of motivation.

(ii) Selection: It is the process of comparing the qualities such as qualification, skill and job knowledge of the applicant and compares them with job specification to appraise the suitability of the candidate for the job. This function includes — designing and developing the blank application forms, inviting application from prospective candidates, scrutinizing the application forms, preparing the list of prospective applicants, designing the appropriate testing and interviewing techniques, arranging interviews, conducting interviews and preparing the list of successful applicants, sending appointment letters.

(iii) Placement*:* Once the selections are made, next thing is to place the selected candidates in respective posts, so that the appointment will match with job requirements. This includes watching the new employees for their performance and counseling the functional managers and foremen regarding the placement and in case of wrong selection, correcting the misplacements and tuning the attitude of new entrants to the objectives of the organization.

(iv) Induction and Orientation: These are the techniques by which a new employee is rehabilitated in the changed surroundings and introduced to the practices, policies, purposes and people etc., of the organization. This includes: Acquaint the employee with the company's philosophy, objectives, policies, career planning and development, opportunities, product, market share, social and community standing, company history and culture, etc. Introduce the employee to the people with whom he has to work such as peers, superiors and subordinates. Molding the employee attitude by orienting him to the new working and social environment.

(b) Human Resource Development: The new employee is like a new tool purchased. Before using it, it should be sharpened and make necessary adjustments made, so as to enable the worker to use it comfortably to perform the desired function. So, also as far as a new employee is concerned, it is the duty of Human Resource Department to improve, mould, change and develop the skills, knowledge, creative ability, aptitude, attitude, values and commitment etc. based on the present and future job and organizational requirements. This function includes:

Performance Appraisal: Here, the performance of the employee on the job is compared with their potential abilities to judge whether the employee is to be rewarded or not or to give further training to the employee. The organization must develop proper policies, procedures and techniques for appraising the performance and help functional managers in this work. Once the appraisal reports are received the department has to consolidate and review the reports and evaluate the effectiveness of various programs.

Training: The new employee may have desired qualification and his performance in the interview may be exceptionally good. But he will not have knowledge of the job he has to perform in the organization. For example, consider a computer programmer. He may know various computer languages, but he lacks the knowledge of application part of the techniques he has learnt at his school. He must be given training by the organization and make him to learn how he has to apply his theoretical and practical knowledge to the job on which he has placed. This includes identification of training needs of the individuals and the company, develops a suitable training programme, help and advises the line managers in conducting the training program, imparting requisite job skills and knowledge to the employees and evaluating the effectiveness of the training programs.

(i) **Management Development:** This is the process of designing and conducting suitable executive development programs so as to develop the managerial and human relations skills of employees. This includes: Designing and conducting the executive development programs, motivating executives, designing special development programs to elevate the employees by promotions and evaluating the effectiveness of the executive development programs.

(ii) **Career Planning and Development:** It is the preparation of career plans of education, training the individual to acquire the job experience and implementing the plans. It includes internal and external mobility. Internal mobility includes vertical and horizontal movement of an employee within an organization. It consists of transfer, promotion and demotion. External mobility includes fresh recruitments and getting the personnel on lean.

(iii) **Organization Development:** It is the procedure for increasing organizational performance through planned interventions. It is an organization wide planned effort to develop the performance of the organization. The aim of this is to change the attitudes, values, organization structure and managerial practices in an effort to improve organizational performance.

(iv) **Compensation:** Here, the objective is to provide equitable and fair remuneration to the employee for the efforts he puts in doing the job. It includes job evaluation, wage and salary administration, incentives, fringe benefits and social security measures.

(v) **Human Relations:** This is the process of interaction among human beings. A human relation is an area of management practice in integrating people into work situation in a way that motivates them to work together to fulfil the objectives of the organization and achieve economic, psychological and social satisfaction.

(vi) **Effectiveness of Human Resource Management:** It is to audit the effectiveness of various HRD (Human Resource Development) programmes designed and implemented by means of organizational health and human resource accounting. Organizational health may be studied by evaluating employee's contribution to achieve the organizational goals and employee job satisfaction. Human resource accounting refers to the measurement of the cost and value of human resource to the organization.

Now let us discuss all the above in detail. Before that we shall see what is the difference between ***Personnel Management* and *Human Resource Management*** by comparing the two.

(a) Personnel Management: As per the Indian Institute of Personnel Management (National Institute of Personnel Management) — Personnel Management or Labour Management or Staff Management means quite simply the task of dealing with human relationships within an organization. Academically the three aspects of Personnel Management are: (i) The *welfare aspect* concerned with working conditions and amenities such as canteens, crèches, housing, personal problems of workers, schools, and recreation; (ii) The *labour or personnel aspect* concerned with recruitment, placement of employees, remuneration, promotion, incentives, productivity, etc., (iii) The *industrial relations aspects* concerned with trade union negotiations, settlement of industrial disputes, joint consultation and collective bargaining. All these aspects are concerned with human element in industry as distinct from the mechanical aspect. As per Lawrence Appley "It is the function of guiding human resources into a dynamic organization that attains its objectives with a high degree of morale and to the satisfaction of those concerned. It is concerned with getting results though people". According to him — all management is *personnel management* as it deals with human beings; its development can be best being discussed in terms of human development, philosophical, psychological, spiritual and physical. From the above, we understand that firstly Personnel Management is concerned with managing people at work. Such people or personnel do not simply refer to *rank and file employees* or *un-unionized labour* but also includes *higher personnel* and *non-unionized labour*. In other words, it covers all levels of personnel, including blue-collared employees and white-collared employees. The shape and form that personnel administrative activity takes, however, may differ greatly from company to company; and to be effective, it must be tailored to fit the individual needs of each organization. Secondly, it is concerned with employees, both as individuals as well as a group, the aim being to get better results with their collaboration and active involvement in the organization's activities i.e. it is a function or process or activity aiding and directing workmen and women in maximizing their personal contributions.

(b) The term ***Human Resource*** at the macro level indicates the sum of all the components of human characteristics possessed by all the people. Here, characteristics refer to skills creative ability, mental and physical stability and other psychological aspects. Human element refers to all the people employed, self-employed, unemployed, employers and owners. Human resource at the organizational level includes all the component resources of all employees like managing director, board of directors, persons who work on honorary basis, experts drawn from various organization and those people (family members) influencing the human resource of the former group. In short it includes the resources of all the people who contribute their services to the attainment of organizational goals and others who constitute their services in order to create hurdles in the attainment of organizational goals. Human resource also includes human values. Thus the term human resource is much more broader compared to the term Personnel either at the component level or at organizational level or even at the macro level. So human resource management at organizational level does mean management of the dynamic components (resources) of all the people at all levels in the organizational hierarchy round the clock and through the year. Though personnel management and human resource management can be differentiated academically, more or less they deal with human aspect of the organization i.e. *the management of men.* In one nutshell, we can say human resource management deals with human being as a resource in production activity rather than an employee. Just as materials manager works with material as a resource required for production, production manager works with machines as resource required for production, so also human resource manager considers human beings (employees) as resource required for production. The difference between human resource and other resources is human resource has mind, brain, thinking and understanding capacity, it can increase its capacity or decrease its capacity as per its will, where as other resources cannot do it by themselves.

Now let us discuss the managerial functions and operating functions in detail.

5.4 HUMAN RESOURCE PLANNING

When man is considered as a *resource,* it is understood, he has some potential characteristics, which can be used to organizational needs in the path of fulfilling the organizational, social and national goals. ***Manpower* or *Human resource* can be considered as *the total knowledge, skills, creative abilities, talents and aptitudes of an organization's work force, as well as the values, attitudes and benefits of an individual involved.*** Among the resources used for production i.e. materials, machines, methods, money and manpower, the most important **M** is manpower resource. When considered as a resource, it is *valuable asset* of the organization. Hence, planning for manpower is as important as planning for other resources.

Manpower Planning or **Human Resource Planning** is synonymous. It is *forecasting* future manpower requirement to cater the needs of the organization. It involves of making an inventory of present manpower resources and assess the extent to which these resources are employed optimally. It consists of projecting future manpower requirements and developing manpower plans for the implementation of the projections. If human resource planning is used properly, it helps in maximum utilization of human resources, reduces excess labour turnover and high absenteeism; improves productivity and excels the organization in achieving the purpose for which it is established. A bad manpower plan may induce dissatisfaction in labour and lead to higher labour turnover, reduces productivity. Human resource planning is essential because of the following reasons.

It provides the required personnel with necessary qualification, skills, knowledge and work experience and aptitude.

To replace the employees who retire, who leave the organization for some reason or the other and to promote/transfer people, proper manpower planning will help the manager.

It helps in estimating the labour turnover and making a forecast and provides adequate supply of labour force in time.

Manpower planning helps the manager to estimate the human resource required for business expansion programs.

Human resource planning helps in planning for training needs due to challenging changes in industrial environment, technology etc.

It helps in identifying areas of surplus or shortage of personnel and making the necessary modifications.

Steps involved in human resource planning are:

- **Deciding goals or objectives**: The ultimate objective of human resource planning is to relate future human resources to future enterprise needs so as to maximize the future return on investment in human resources.
- **Estimating future organizational structure and manpower requirements**: Forecasting of need of different skills required in order to satisfy the growing needs of the organization is a must. Forecasting provides basic premises on which the manpower planning is built and the desired structure is designed. Once this is done, next step is to plan for procurement of human resources to the existing departments and proposed departments.
- **Human resource audit**: Next step is to prepare ***skill inventory***, consisting of data of each employee including his qualification, experience, references, performance and superior's evaluation, which will help the management to chalk out their future needs, keeping in view the present available resources.
- **Planning job requirements and job descriptions**: Once the future need is decided, the next duty is to prepare *job analysis*, which records details of training, skills, qualifications, abilities, experiences and responsibilities etc., which are needed for the job. Job analysis includes the preparation of job descriptions and job specifications.
- **Developing a human resource plan**: This step involves the development and implementation of human resource plan, which aims at finding the labour supply sources and calling for application and selecting the required human resource.

5.5. RECRUITMENT

Adequate staffing is an essential fact for an organization. For this the organization has to find the persons who satisfy the job requirement and must be willing to work. The management must have a list of number of employees of different categories required. This depends upon the scale of production, degree of mechanization and methods of work. The management has to prepare a plan for recruiting the present and future requirement. The prepared plan is thoroughly scrutinized before steps are taken to recruit labour. There are many ways of recruiting the manpower. Recruitment must be conducted in an organized way preferably by *personnel department*. The personnel department will keep in mind the requirements of various departments both as regard to quantity and quality. In small organizations, where there is no personnel department, the concerned departmental managers will recruit the labour force.

5.5.1. Methods of Recruitment

The following are some of the methods used for recruiting the labour force:

1. **Recruitment at the Factory Gates:** In a country, where there are a large number of unemployed people, it is not rare to find job seekers thronging the factory gate. Whenever the need arises, the foreman or the departmental manager scrutinizes in a general way the people who are available at the gate and recruits required number. This method is suitable for recruiting the unskilled workers. One more method used here is to maintain a list of ***badili (alternate)*** workers and whenever a regular worker is absent, then a worker form badili list (Alternate substitute list), who appears near the factory gate every day is selected to do the work. When there is no permanent vacancy, recruitment may be made among the badili workers.
2. **Recommendations of the Existing Employees:** In order to encourage the existing employees, some concerns have made it a policy to recruit further staff only from the relatives of their existing employees. It may be provided that regarding other conditions, equal preference will be given to relatives of the existing employees.
3. **Advertising the Vacancies:** This method is used for recruiting skilled workers, professionals, clerical staff etc. An advertisement is given in leading newspapers, giving job description, so as to enable the potential personnel to apply for the post. The application form for the post advertised may be supplied by the firm or a proforma is given along with the advertisement, so as enable the applicant to copy the same or may ask the employees to send their bio-data. Or they may request the applicant to present directly at a stipulated time at factory recruitment center (Walk-in-interviews).
4. **Employment Exchanges:** In western world, employment exchanges or employment bureaus are quite common. In India also we have government-managed employment exchanges, which will register the names of unemployed, qualified and uneducated youth. The organizations, which have need of human resource, may contact these exchanges and the get the list of candidates suitable for their need and conduct interview to select their need. Now-a-day we have privately organized *Placement offices*, which can cater the need of all categories of human resources of any organization.
5. **Direct Recruitment from Colleges and Universities:** The universities/Colleges affiliated to Universities especially Professional colleges, will have *Placement Offices* or *Placement Centers*, which will have contact with various well established organizations. The personnel department officials of these organizations or factories will visit the placement offices and select the outgoing students of the colleges to fill the posts in their organization. The selection procedure may involve, written test, group discussion, personal interview etc. This method will help to draw the talent available in the universities.

At this stage, it is advisable to discuss about the Labour *turnover*, which will help us to understand one of the reasons of recruitment.

Labour turnover: One of the prominent features of modern factory system is the shifting nature of the labour force. When some workers leave the organization, it is natural that some others will take their place. It is to be remembered here that some labour force is leaving the organization and some other joining the organization. ***Labour turnover refers***

to the changes, which occur in the ranks of workers in a concern over a given period. The rate of turnover, therefore, indicates the extent to which the composition of the labour forces undergone changes. The reasons for labour turnover are:

- **Accessions:** This refers to employment of new workers or the re-employment of former workers or addition to the ranks of the workers.
- **Separations:** This refers to termination of employment or the departure of workers from the organization. The reasons for separations are:
- **Quits:** Workers leaving on their own accord. This may be due to job dissatisfaction or due to acceptance of other jobs or due to ill health or due to some other personal reasons.
- **Discharges:** This refers to dismissal of worker from service by the employer on account of violation of rules, dishonesty, disobedience, laziness', habitual absenteeism etc.
- **Lay-offs:** Suspension of workers owing to lack of adequate work or shortage of materials.

The rate of labour turnover is given by = (Total number of workers leaving per month/Average number of workers on pay roll for a month) × 100

If rate of turnover is high the consequences are:

- **Loss of output:** There will be a loss of output because of various reasons like, filling up of vacancy may take time, or new worker may take some time to accustom to the present job and during that period his slow working speed and loss due to wastage will decrease the output.
- **Loss of training cost:** All the efforts and money spent on training the worker who leaves the organization is a loss. In addition the amount spent on him during selection and the cost of selecting a new worker is a burden on the organization.
- **Overtime costs:** Due to larger turnover, to fulfil the delivery promises of customer will become a problem. In such cases overtime is a strategy, which will put extra cost, which will be added to the cost of the product.
- Because of higher labour turnover the team spirit in the workers and the reputation of the firm will have a great set back.

5.6. EMPLOYEE SELECTION

If an organization wants to survive and grow, it has to select right type of personnel to the jobs in it. A right person for the right job is the proverb. If a person, who is well qualified for the job, handles a job the cost of production will be optimal and the wastages are less. We should see that for any job just right person is to be selected. If we select less qualified person, he cannot cope up with the job. If we select over qualified person for the job, he will get dissatisfied with his work and develop grouse against the management. It is therefore important and necessary that a person who is exactly qualified for it — no more or no less, should do a job. When workers are selected for vocations or jobs in a concern after careful weighing of the requirements of jobs on one hand and assessment and evaluation of the abilities and aptitudes of man on the other hand, it is referred as ***Scientific Vocational***

Selection. Vocational selection requires two things: The first one is ***Knowledge regarding the qualities or traits, which a person should posses in order to do the given job.*** This requires drawing up of **job specifications**. Job specification is a catalogue of various qualities, which a person doing a job should possess. It is based on an analysis of the character of an industrial operation known as **job analysis or occupational analysis.** Secondly, the measurement of qualities possessed by the candidate for the job. The qualities desired by a suitable candidate can be grouped as:

- Educational and Technical qualifications with specialization, if any,
- Intelligence and dexterity,
- Health and physique,
- Responsibility involved and initiative required,
- Ability to command and obey,
- Personality, and
- Ability to work in the conditions in which the job is performed.

Testing the applicant in the above-mentioned qualities vocationally will reveal the fitness of the candidate for the job applied. Vocational selection enables the firm to find a right person for the job on hand.

Job specification: A specification of the job is prepared with the help of people who are getting the things done by the people, i.e. supervisors or foremen and with the co-operation of psychologists or other people who know how the minds of people work. A job analyst will analysis each and every operation of the job and prepares a detailed description of the job and this is known as ***job description.*** This job description includes: (a) What the worker does in a particular job. (b) Duties and responsibilities of the worker, (c) Location of work and equipment used, (d) Working conditions, (e) Training and education needed, (f) Hours of work and (g) Opportunities for promotion.

Job description and job specification will give an idea to the interviewer and understanding of the job on one hand and the qualities to be possessed by the applicant on the other. Basing on these two, selection of right person is done for the right job.

5.7. PROCEDURE FOR RECRUITMENT AND SELECTION

The scientific recruitment procedure will help the personnel department to find a right person for the right job. The procedure of selection depends on the job for which selection is made. An elaborate procedure will be used for jobs, which involve responsibility and decision making, whereas the procedure for selecting a worker in a factory may be simple. Today many organizations are going for scientific vocational selection procedure, for which a separate department is created with psychologists, job specialists and well trained personnel managers.

Step 1 *Requisition:* The first step in the procedure of employing people is *requisition* from the departmental head or foreman concerned regarding the type and number of workers required. While preparing the requisition, the concerned manager must be careful enough to estimate his present and proposed need in the near future. Along with the requisition, he has to give a description of the job, so as to enable the persons in the selection committee to select most suitable person for the job.

Step 2 ***Recruitment*****:** The next step is to identify a proper source, where from they have to select the people. For this depending on the type of job for which they have to select the persons, the recruitment department may contact different sources as follows:

(a) For Casual Workers: The main source for casual workers is *factory gate.* Skilled and semiskilled workers will be waiting for an opportunity at the factory gate. The foreman can go to the factory gate and select the appropriate person the factory needs. Or sometimes, the workers are selected on the recommendations of the permanent employees.

(b) For Skilled Tradesmen: For this category, the recruitment department may approach local employment exchange or local technical training institutes. When they approach employment exchange, the exchange will give a list of candidates registered with them. The company may call these candidates for interview and select their need. When the recruitment department approaches, industrial training institutes, they can conduct various testes to the out going students of the institute to make the selection.

(c) For Clerical Staff: The employment exchanges are the best sources for the candidates for clerical staff, typists etc. Sometimes paper advertisement is also given to tap the talents of the aspirants. Applications received are scrutinized and a list of eligible candidates is prepared for further processing.

(d) For Technical Professionals: Many companies in India go for advertising their requirement and invite applications (may the company supply forms or format prepared by the candidate him or herself). Some of the companies prefer campus selection. These companies visit leading technical institutes or colleges to cater their need. They conduct various tests at the campus and select the promising candidates. Some companies conduct the written tests and other testes at their premises for the applicants to select required personnel.

(e) For Managers: This category also recruited from campus interviews or through advertisement, as above.

(f) Senior Managers: Advertisement is the best source to recruit the senior managers. Job description is given in the advertisement. Candidates applied for the post are called for face-to-face interview and selections are made.

Step 3 ***Application Blanks*****:** When an announcement of vacancies is given in the newspaper, the recruitment department may receive number of applications from the candidates. After careful screening the application forms, a list of eligible candidates is prepared and for them an application form is sent from the company. Or when the company visits the technical institutes for campus recruitment it may get a list of successful candidates who pass the entrance test conducted by the company personnel. The application formant is carefully designed so as to get relevant information from the candidates. The application is so designed to get information regarding the qualification, experience and references. Some questions are involved to test the aptitude of the candidate. After receiving the application form from the candidate, they are carefully examined to prepare the list of prosperous candidates. From this list, few candidates are called for personal interview.

Step 4 ***Trade Tests*****:** This type of tests is generally required when the company wants to recruit tradesmen like welder, carpenter, fitter, etc. Also to recruit people for the posts of stenographer, typist etc. When the company is interested in selecting casual labour, to find for what job the person is suitable, these tests are conducted.

Step 5 ***Psychological Tests*****:** Industrial psychologists have devised certain tests to measure the psychological characteristics of individuals. These tests reveal how an individual behaves while on the job. It consists of giving to the applicant a task, which is representative of the job for which he is being considered. His performance on the job is evaluated relative to that of other candidates. There are different types of tests standardized for jobs at different levels. Examples of such tests are:

(i) **Intelligence tests:** These tests measure the mental capacity of the candidate and enable the examiner to analyze the novel or abstract situations and identify the intellectual and mental suitability of the candidate for the job.

(ii) **Aptitude tests:** These tests are designed to test the inclination of the candidate to learn the skill of the job and his interest on the job for which he is being tested.

(iii) **Dexterity tests:** These tests reveal the individual's capacity to use his fingers and hand while doing the work. It tests individuals grip in holding the tools used for the job. From these tests one can examine the mental balance of the candidate.

(iv) **Achievement test:** These are designed to test the level of knowledge and proficiency in certain skills already achieved by the applicants.

(v) **Personality tests:** These tests will test the emotional balance, maturity and temperamental qualities of a person and also test the physical fitness for the job.

Step 6 ***Interview*****:** Personal interviews are conducted to find out the candidate's mental and social make-up and to know whether the qualities possessed by him make him suitable for the job for which the interview is conducted. For many people interview is a nightmare. They think that interview is conducted to eliminate him from selection by asking unnecessary questions. But in true sense, interview is to be conducted in a friendly atmosphere and the candidate is made to feel at ease. The candidate receives a warm welcome from the committee members so that he can feel free to converse with them. In interview, the questions are asked on the basis of job specifications. Fair chance should be given to the candidate to clarify his doubts, if any, regarding the job and the company. Questions should not be asked in haphazard manner to confuse the candidate. Where written test and other tests are not conducted, job specialists may ask some questions related to the technicality of the job and if necessary may go deep in the subject matter. Matters like hours of work, resting period, working on holidays and overtime should be carefully explained, if necessary, so as to enable the candidate to know all about his work. In many concerns, interview is only the way of examining the candidate for selection. But many a time one cannot judge the ability of the candidate by mere personal interview only. It should be supplemented by some other tests. If interview is only the means, mostly personnel judgement of the committee members will have influence on the selection. Therefore, the disadvantages of interview are,

(a) Some abilities of candidate cannot be judged by members, and

(b) The result of the interview heavily banks on the personal judgement of the committee members.

Step 7 ***Medical Test***: As far as possible, all workers are to be subjected to medical test before selection. It is because, people with poor health may not work to the satisfaction of the management and they may absent frequently from the job, which may have adverse effect on the productivity. Finally, due to ill health he may leave the job, which results in wastage of all the training given to him. When the job demands, good and healthy physic, persons with poor physic may not cope up with job. In case persons employed are having diseases; they may spread it to fellow workers. Hence, it is essential that all applicants, without reference to any cadre, must undergo medical test.

Step 8 ***On-the-Job Test and Selection (OJT)***: Hitherto, many methods of selecting an employee are discussed. Basing on the results of the above tests, applicant may be selected. But before giving him a job on permanent basis, it would be better to try him out for a few weeks in the factory itself. This is because no procedure of selection can find out the whole reality about the personality of the selected candidate. We can judge the candidature by looking carefully the person at work and judge the behaviour with the fellow workers and his effectiveness of his performance of the job. After testing the applicant few weeks on the job, if found suitable, then final selection is made.

5.8. VOCATIONAL GUIDANCE OR COUNSELLING

All the selection procedure mentioned above is to select a right type of person for the right job. From the point of view of employer it is very important to have a suitable person for each job. Also it is equally important from the point of view of employee that he should be placed on a right job for which he is suitable. Hence, the methodology of selecting right person scientifically is known as *scientific selection* or *vocational selection*. **The task of guiding a person as to what sort of job he should have is known as *vocational guidance*.** Vocational guidance and vocational selection are the two sides of a same coin. The purpose of both is to fit a right man on right job. The procedure is as explained below:

(a) The psychologists obtain particulars of the scholastic attainment and proficiency from the teachers and the opinions and wishes of the parents about the candidate under examination.

(b) Analysis of the occupations, which they may adopt, is undertaken with a view to finding out the factors necessary for success at these jobs.

(c) Having the factors of success of the job on hand, the psychologists may give psychological tests to the candidate. These tests, known as *intelligence tests* are so designed to indicate the mental caliber of the candidate and on the basis of the results some jobs are dropped from consideration as being higher or lower than the candidates' general mental level.

(d) Then the candidate is given *Aptitude tests* to find out the special mental and manipulative abilities of the candidate for the jobs for which their suitability is being considered.

(e) Next the candidate is given *Personality tests* to ascertain the temperamental tendencies and their general ability to get along well with co-employees.

(f) To find the health status and fitness of the candidate medical tests are conducted.

(g) Finally candidates own preferences are also ascertained.

Generally, parents or teachers to guide the candidates to go for right type of education. But many parents do not have specialized knowledge about the vocational guidance. Hence, it is better to have vocational guidance from the experts.

5.9. TRAINING

Once the selection of the candidate for a job is over, the next job is to give training to him to make him suitable for the job for which he is selected. Training of the candidate helps him in increasing the aptitude, skills and ability to perform the specific job for which he is selected. It becomes necessary for the organization to train the new employee on the job, so as to enable him to do the job systematically and correctly. The advantages of good training are as mentioned below:

(a) Training improves the skill of the worker. It increases the productivity as the worker does the job in a right way. It improves the quality of work.

(b) Trained workers make the best use of available resources, like materials equipment, which ultimately increases the material productivity and machine productivity.

(c) Good training will not waste supervisory time of manager and he can concentrate on planning and administrative work.

(d) Good training will reveal the mistakes committed at the time of selection. A trainee who has been selected by scientific procedure, will grasp quickly and understand quickly and does not waste material.

(e) Training creates confidence in the minds of the workers. They feel that they are being taken care by the management. This will improve the relationship between workers and management.

If workers are given poor training, it may lead to dissatisfaction in the workers. It has direct affect on productivity in the form of wastage of materials, machine hours and the time. Dissatisfaction of workers may increase labour turnover.

5.9.1. Types of Training

The following are some of the methods by which industrial training is given to the workers:

(a) Induction Training: Induction refers to introduction of new workers to the organization. In this training, the worker is introduced to the organization, so as to enable him to understand his job and know his fellow workers. He is given general idea about the products manufactured by the organization, history of the organization and its rules and regulations and working conditions etc. This training helps the workers to get an idea about the organization and build up confidence in him that he is with the right type of people and right type of organization.

(b) Job Training: This training helps the worker to increase the knowledge about their respective jobs and enable him to increase his efficiency of working. It helps him to understand how to handle tools correctly and operate machine correctly and to know about what precautions he has to take at the time of emergency. This training helps the workers to avoid accidents and to reduce the bottlenecks in the work procedure.

(c) Training for Promotion: In many organizations, executive posts and senior level posts in the operation level are filled up by promotion among the existing workers.

This will create moral obligation in workers and selection costs are reduced on the part of the management. In government organizations, it is a general practice to fill up the higher level posts by promotion only. For many jobs, training is given to the workers, before he takes up new higher-level job on promotion so as to enable him to shoulder the new responsibilities with confidence.

(d) **Refresher Training:** No doubt, the workers are given job training when they have been introduced in the organization. As the time passes, the technology may change and the design of the product may change. Also by nature man may be accustomed to his own way of doing work other than that given during training. This makes the organization to give refresher training — a short-term training course to revive the minds of the workers.

5.9.2. Methods of Training

The following are some of the methods adopted by industries to provide training for their employees:

(a) **On-the-Job Training (OJT):** This type of training was in practice during the World War II, when training was given to large number of workers, by the senior workers. This is particularly suited for labour force and for clerical cadre. Here no school and no teacher will be there. The new worker is trained under the learned senior worker. The efficiency of training depends on the ability of the worker to learn and the ability of the senior worker to teach. The new worker is directly put on the job and senior worker gives training. This is generally known as *Three Position Plan,* which means the worker learns from the man above him and teaches the man below him.

(b) **Vestibule Training:** The literal meaning of *vestibule* is a portico or a forecourt or an entrance hall through which one has to enter before one enters the building. In this type of training, workers are trained well on specific jobs in a special part of the factory. Here an attempt is made to create working conditions very much similar to the actual working conditions. After training here the workers are put to training on the real job under learned workers, so as to acquaint the trained workers to accustom with the actual work. This method was also in practice during World War II. Even today some of the industrial concerns will have vestibule training in practice.

(c) **Apprenticeship Training:** This method of training is suitable for jobs, which are technical in nature, and needs long period to gain proficiency. The trainee is directly put under experts for long periods. They have to work in close associations with experts. They will be under direct supervision of the person under whom they are taking training. The purpose of this type of training is to make worker perfect in the trade. The apprentice is paid remuneration as per apprenticeship act. This is a very costly method. One disadvantage of this method is that there is no guarantee that the worker will continue with the organization after training.

(d) **Internship Training:** Sometimes it is necessary to train the students at Technical Training Institutes to enable them to be useful to the industries. In this connection, both technical training institutes and industries join hands so that students will have even balance of theory and practice. In Internship training, students from technical institutes are sent to factories for practical training, so as to enable them to learn their work in real situation. Only draw back of this method is it takes long time and there may be trouble in maintaining academic schedules. The other way is technical and professional institutes may get the requirement of the industries and accordingly make the desired changes in curriculum, so as to see that outgoing students are useful to the industries. Many institutes, which conduct professional courses in India, adopt this system; say for example, MBA students are sent for summer training to undergo training at factories in the field of their specialization. So, also some IITs and Engineering Colleges also send students for summer training.

(e) **Learner Training:** This type of training is suitable for aspirants who are eligible for semiskilled jobs. These workers will not have any knowledge of basic sciences and technical knowledge regarding the job, which they have to do. In such cases, after selecting, before absorption, they are sent to vocational schools to get basic knowledge of mathematics, especially workshop mathematics and knowledge of working on machines. After the training they are absorbed and placed on production work.

(f) **Supervisory Training:** All the above-mentioned training methods are for training workers. But we must remember one aspect about training, that is, the effectiveness of training mostly depends on the quality of supervisory staff available in the factory/ industry. Hence, it is necessary to give scientific training to the supervisors also. One way of training the executives is to let them learn on the job itself and manage the things. No doubt it is unscientific, but many a time it will reveal the hidden talents of the trainee and make him an efficient leader or executive. The other method is put them in association with senior executives, so that they can see how their executives work and learn from them, so as to get promotion to senior position as and when the vacancies falls. Another method, which is finding place in many industries, is ***Role Playing.*** In this method, in a conference, two trainees given two different roles, say for example one is a *supervisor* and the other is an *employee.* Both of them play their role, which simulates with a problem in the organization. After the role-playing is over, a discussion of their performances takes place. Thus supervisors get training in problem solving. Another outstanding method of training supervisors is ***Training Within Industry (TWI).*** This method was used in USA to train executives during World War II. This TWI course consists of four units of training. Each unit is of ten-hour duration. Totally it is a 40 hours program. They are:

(i) **Job Instruction Training (JIT):** Here the supervisor is trained in preparing instructions and to train him in the method of instructing the trainees.

(ii) **Job Methods Training (JMT):** This training is designed to train the supervisor in the application of and instruction of new methods of work. Here they are given the knowledge of principles of work-study.

(iii) Job Relation Training (JRT): This course is designed to train the supervisor to train him regarding Industrial Relations, which is a must for any executive to maintain a friendly atmosphere between management and workers.

(iv) Program Development Training (PDT): Here the supervisor is given training in method of developing new plans and programs.

In addition to the above, supervisors are also given training through conferences, seminars, lectures and discussions on problems of supervision. They are also trained to handle different situations by what is known as ***Position Rotation Plan,*** where they are placed in different departments/posts, so as to get knowledge of various problems and method of solving the same.

For senior executives, vocational courses or sandwich courses are conducted through ***Executive Training Program***, which are conducted by professional institutions. In India Professional Institutes like Indian Institute of Management and Indian Institute of Technology, National Institute of Industrial Engineering will conduct ***Executive Development Programs***. These programs are of two to three weeks duration.

5.10. PLACEMENT

This is the final stage of selection procedure. Once the selection and training is over, it is the duty of line manager to decide, whether the candidate is to be absorbed or not. Once the line manager approves his selection and appraises his skills shown during training and having a detailed discussion with personnel manager, he gives his nod for the appointment of the candidate. Now the organization will inform to all the candidates regarding their selection either immediately or after sometime through a letter. For successful candidates, an appointment order is sent along with rules and regulations of the organization along with an acceptance letter. In case the candidate agrees with the rules and regulations and job conditions, he can sign on the acceptance form and send it back to the organization informing them his date of joining. Now the candidate joins the organization by giving a joining report to the line manager. The management places the new employee, preferably on probation, before placing him on the right job. Once the probation is over, the management places him on the job for which he is selected. Probation period generally ranges between one to two years. During the probation, if the candidate's performance is not satisfactory, the management may extend the probation period or it may terminate him from the job. Placement is the determination of the job to which an accepted candidate is to be assigned and his assignment to that job.

5.11. PROMOTION, TRANSFERS AND SEPARATION

When an employee elevated to a higher responsible job than the present job, it means to say that he is **promoted**. It refers to an advancement of an employee to a better higher job. The characteristics of promotion are:

- Involves higher responsibility,
- Requires higher degree of skill,
- Commands more prestige and higher status,

- Carries higher pay than the previous one,
- It is a means of filling up of senior posts from the eligible internal candidates, and
- It is a means of motivating the employees.

Promotions increase employee morale and give the employees a hope and faith in the organization. They can put their best effort for the betterment of the organization. If promotions are not there, employees get frustrated and show signs of discontent, which will act against the growth of the organization. When stagnation is there, the employee get frustrated and act against the goals of the organization and almost becomes troublemakers, because they cannot find enough scope to show their talents. When the frustrated employees are promoted to higher posts, it is found that they work for the betterment of the organization with satisfaction and loyal to the organization and they try to put all their efforts to show better results. Hence, organizations encourage employees for promotion, if not for promotion at least for upgradation. Upgradation means fixing higher monitory benefits (advanced scale of pay) in the same post. No doubt in government organizations many of the higher posts are filled up by promotion. But in industrial concerns, which operate on profit motive, always like to have *efficient, knowledge full, experienced and motivated* persons in the senior posts to have effective leadership. Hence, they may encourage external sources for filling up senior level posts rather than promotion, when no suitable candidate is available internally. It is better for any organization to have an optimal blend of external and internal candidates for better performance.

5.11.1. Basis for Promotion (Seniority or Merit)

What should be the criteria for promotion? Whether promotion is to be given on merit or on seniority? The most common policy adopted in government organizations is the sonority or length of service is the measure for promotion. If this policy is adopted in all the organizations, then there will be no problem as far as the labour unions are concerned. Everybody in the organization will be sure of his promotion as and when his chance of seniority comes. Here there is no place for merit, only length of service is considered. In such cases, in case there are really worthy and efficient workers are there; they will get frustrated and may leave the organization. In case Merit is considered as the scale for promotion, then those people who are working in the organization since long time may get frustrated as their juniors are elevated to higher posts. This may cause some problem with unions. Unions always prefer seniority as the basis for promotion. So, it is better if the organization frames a better promotion policy, which takes care of length of service and merit into consideration. A sound promotion policy must include the following elements:

(a) Management must clearly state its intention to filling up vacancies in senior position through promotion from within.

(b) There should be an understanding between management and workers regarding the promotion policy i.e. whether the promotion is based on merit or seniority or a blend of seniority and merit.

(c) By conducting job analysis, a chart is drawn regarding the requirement of the candidate for the post, so that every one will know what their position for promotion is.

(d) Scientific methods of rating workers may be adopted to assess the relative merits of the workers due for promotion.

(e) Recommendations from the immediate supervisors/boss may be considered before deciding the promotion.

Whatever may be the policy, it is very difficult to satisfy unions and employees. Especially, in India, where personal relationship with seniors will work more than all, many a time unwanted persons are promoted to higher level. This is particularly true in government organizations, where political people will play a vital role in promotions and transfers.

5.12. TRANSFERS

If the organization has various departments or units operated in different places, when an employee is moved from one department to another or from one unit to another without any extra commitment, responsibility or higher pay, then it is known as *transfer*. Transfer may be made to punish an employee when he is a headache in the present position. Or transfer may also be done to take advantage of special qualities of the employee in the new unit or new department. Different types of transfers are:

(a) **Production transfer:** When the transfer is made to meet the specific operational needs of the company it is known as production transfer. The employee may have some special skill in a particular aspect. He may be transferred to the other department/unit to train co employees so as to enable them to take up the work independently and confidently. Or if there is heavy workload in one particular department and need some extra people to take up the workload, it is known as production transfer.

(b) **Replacement transfer:** When a senior employee is transferred to replace a junior employee, when the later is laid off as the company cannot provide him job and temporarily set him aside due to some reason or the other, the transfer is known as replacement transfer.

(c) **Versatility transfer:** When an organization wants to train certain employees in various works of the organization, then transfers are made from job to job for a stipulated period. This type of transfers is very common in banks. When some employees go on leave, to cope up with load, these trained workers are very helpful.

(d) **Personnel transfers:** These transfers are made to help the employee. Sometimes when an employee is found not suitable on a job, to save him, he is transferred to other department to utilize him properly. Sometimes, the employees may ask for a transfer due to some family or health problems. In such cases transfer is given to help him and satisfy his need, which create a sense of gratitude in the mind of the employee. Many a time transfers are used to rectify the mistakes made while selection.

(e) **Separation:** Separation is affected when an employee leaves the organization. His separation from parent organization may be due to *promotion, transfer, resignation or death*. Promotion and transfer are dealt above. Resignation of employee is leaving the parent organization due to dissatisfaction or due to in search of better opportunities. As far as possible separation due to resignation should be kept at minimum possible in order to keep labour turnover ratio at a minimum.

5.13. PERFORMANCE APPRAISAL

Performance refers to the degree of accomplishment of the task that makes up an individual's job. Performance appraisal is a method of evaluating the behaviour of employees in the work spot, normally including both the quantitative and qualitative aspects of the job performance. Performance is always measured in terms of results. Important characteristics of performance appraisal are:

- Performance appraisal discloses the job related strengths and weakness of an employee.
- It measures the ability of the employee on the job and gives an idea to establish a plan for improving his performance of the job.
- Appraisal methods are systematic, periodically planned.
- Performance appraisal is different from job evaluation. Performance appraisal evaluates the employee's performance on the job, while job evaluation is used to find the worth of the job to fix up range of pay.
- It is a continuous process and not one time job.
- It is used for administrative purposes to decide promotional/transfer aspect of the employee.

Performance appraisal is needed because it provides information about the performance of the worker to decide about his transfer/promotion etc. It also gives the feedback information about the level of achievement and behaviour of subordinates. This information is helpful in giving suitable training to the worker if needed. The results of performance appraisal help to counsel the employee. Many a time it helps to prevent grievances and in -disciplinary activities.

The purposes of performance appraisal are:

- To create and maintain a satisfactory level of performance.
- To contribute to employee growth and development through training and developmental programs.
- To help superiors to have a proper understanding about the subordinates.
- To guide job changes with the help of continuous ranking.
- To facilitate fair and equitable compensation based on performance.
- To facilitate for testing and validating selection tests, interview techniques through comparing their scores with performance appraisal ranks.
- To set right the work behaviour of the employee basing on the performance appraisal ranks.

Basing on the job analysis the factors to be appraised are decided. Some of the factors appraised are:

(i) Regularity of Attendance,

(ii) Self expression (oral and written),

(iii) Ability to work with others,
(iv) Leadership abilities,
(v) Initiative,
(vi) Technical skill, technical ability, knowledge etc.
(vii) Ability to reason,
(viii) Creative skills,
(ix) Capability of assuming responsibility,
(x) Integrity, and
(xi) Honesty and sincerity.

5.13.1. Who will do Appraisal Work?

The appraiser is a person who has thorough knowledge about the job content, contents to be appraised, standards of contents and who observes the employee while performing a job. He must be in a position to identify the contents of greater importance and lesser importance and evaluate the performance without any pre-conceived ideas. Typical appraisers are: Supervisors, Peers, Subordinates, Employees themselves and Users of service and Specialists. Appraisal schedule may be formal or informal depending on the situation.

Performance Appraisal consists of the following steps:

(i) Establish performance standards based on the job description and job specification incorporating all the factors. Let the standards be as clear and understandable to all the concerned.
(ii) Once the standards are set, they must be made available to all the employees and appraisers.
(iii) The appraisers must follow the instructions given by the management to appraising and appraise the employees through observation, interview and studying the performance records and reports.
(iv) There may be some internal and external factors, which might have influenced the performance of the employee in either way i.e. it, may be positive or negative influence. Appraisers must take these factors into consideration and adjust or scale the performance of the employee accordingly by adopting a scaling factor.
(v) The next step is to compare the performance of the employee with the performance of other workers on the same job or with his previous performance. This will help the appraiser to know what the position of the employee is and what measures to be taken to improve the performance. In case if the performance is improved or better, then what measures to be taken to motivate the employee.
(vi) Compare the performance of the worker with the standards and decide whether there is any deviation from the standard. The deviation may be either positive (improved) or negative (below the standard).
(vii) Inform the employee regarding his performance and deviation. If the deviation is negative, ascertain the reason and discuss the problem with the workers doing the same type of job.

(viii) After coming to a conclusion the appraiser must suggest changes in standards, job analysis, internal and external environment if necessary.

(ix) The last step is to follow up the performance appraisal reports. This includes guiding, counseling, coaching and directing the employee or making arrangements for training and development of the employee in order to ensure improved performance. If the employee is found to be worst, i.e. beyond the scope of any improvement, then suggest removing him from the job.

5.13.2. Appraisal Methods

There are many methods of appraisal. Most important of them are discussed below:

1. **Graphic Rating Scales:** This method is also known as *linear rating scale or simple rating scale.* In this method the appraiser is given a printed form in which a number of objectives, behaviours and traits based qualities and characters to be rated like quality and volume of work, job knowledge, dependability, creative ability, initiative, leadership qualities etc. are printed. These forms contain rating scales. The scale may be continuous i.e. starting from 0 to 10 or may be discontinuous i.e. the appraiser himself may assign a point to each degree of performance. A typical form is given below in Fig. 5.1.

PERFORMANCE APPRAISAL FORM **Name of the Company:** **Department:** **Job:** **Pay Scale:** **Name of the Employee:** **Age:** **Date of Joining:**												
PARTICULARS	SCALE											
	0	1	2	3	4	5	6	7	8	9	10	Remarks
1. Attitude												
2. Job Knowledge												
3. Quality of work												
4. Dependability												
5. Initiative												
6. Cooperativeness												
7. Coordination												
8.												
9.												
10.												

Fig. 5.1. Performance Appraisal Scale

RATING BY DISCONTINUOUS SCALE **Name of the Company:** **Department:** **Job:** **Name of the Worker:** **Pay Scale:** **Age:** **Date of Joining:**		
S. No.	**Particulars**	**Rare (Scale Points) assigned by the Appraiser**
1	Attitude	
2	Job Knowledge	

Cont....

RATING BY DISCONTINUOUS SCALE		
Name of the Company: Name of the Worker: Age:	Department: Pay Scale: Date of Joining:	Job:
S. No.	**Particulars**	**Rare (Scale Points) assigned by the Appraiser**
3	Quality of Work	
4	Dependability	
5	Initiative	
6	Cooperation	
7	Coordination	
8		
9		
10		

Fig. 5.2. Performance Appraising Scale

2. **Ranking Method:** This method is relatively easy and cheap. Hear the appraiser identifies the best worker and worst worker in the group by observing the output of the workers. He scales all other workers in between BEST and WORST. One drawback of method is it raises doubts in the minds of employees and if the appraiser is corruptive then the ranking may be biased. Basing on the observations made, each employee is assigned a rank, which indicates the position of the worker in the group.
3. **Paired Comparison Method:** This is a simple method, where appraiser compares one worker with all other workers in the group, one at a time. This method is more suitable when the number of workers is less. The number of comparisons required is N (N – 1)/2, where N is the number of employees in a group. The drawback of this method is it is time consuming and the workers are simply compared to each other on total performance rather than specific job criteria.
4. **Forced Distribution Method:** It so happens that appraiser may rate the workers either at the higher end of the scale or at the lower end of the scale, i.e. either too high in the scale or too low in the scale. To avoid this, the rater after assigning the points to the performance of each employee has to distribute his rating in pattern to conform to normal frequency distribution. It is similar to the ranking technique. Here, rater has to spread their employee evaluation in a pre described distribution. This method eliminates central tendency and leniency biases. Here, workers are placed in certain ranked categories but not ranked within the categories. Here, the distributions will be made as excellent, average and poor performance.
5. **Checklist Method:** Here appraiser is given a list of statements or words and asked to check statements representing the characteristics and performance of each employee. There are different types of checklists available. They are: (a) Simple checklist, (b) Weighted checklist and (c) Forced checklist.

(a) ***Simple Checklist***: Here the checklist consists of large number of statements concerning the employee behaviour. The appraiser checks the behaviour of the employee as per the statement given in the list and marks *yes or no* or *positive or negative*.

NAME OF THE COMPANY		
Department:..............	**Name of the Employee:..............**	
Designation:..............	**Pay rate:..............**	**Date of Joining:..............**
CHECKLIST	**YES**	**NO**
1. Is the employee regular to his duty? (Attendance)		
2. Is he obedient to the supervisor's instructions?		
3. Is his behavior with co-employees is good?		
4.		
5.		

Fig. 5.3. Simple Checklist

(b) ***Weighted Checklist***: In this method different weights are given to each item in the list depending on their importance in evaluation. The appraiser is expected to look into the question relating to the employee's behaviour, the attached rating scale (or Yes/No type) and tick those traits that closely describe the employee behavior. Often rates are not given to the man who uses the checklist for appraisal, but are computed and tabulated by some others, preferably a responsible person in personnel department. Here, the performance rating is multiplied by the weights of the statement and the coefficients are added up. The cumulative coefficient is the weighted performance score of the employee. Weighted performance score is compared with the overall assessment standards in order to find out the overall performance of the employee. The drawback is it is costlier than the simple checklist and if the appraiser does not know the importance of the items in the checklist, then the evaluation may go wrong.

(c) ***Forced Checklist Method***: In this method a large number of statements in groups are prepared. Each group consists of four descriptive statements, which are known as *tetrad*. These statements are concerned with employee behavior. Two of them will be most descriptive i.e. favorable and two of them are lest descriptive, i.e. unfavorable. Sometimes there may be five statements, one of which will be neutral. The weightages of the statement is kept secret. The appraiser is asked to select one statement that mostly describes employee's behavior out of the two factorable statements and one statement from the two unfavorable statements. The items are usually a mixture of positive and negative statements. This methods aim is to reduce the bias of the appraiser. The statements are designed to discriminate effective from ineffective workers as well as reflect valuable personal qualities.

NAME OF THE COMPANY

Name of the Employee:.............. **Department:..............** **Designation:...............**

Rate of Pay:.............. **Date of Joining:..............**

S. No.	Weighted Checklist Qualities	Weights Assigned	Performance Rating Scale (Scale 1 to 5)				Obtained Performance
			Poor	Average	Above Average	Excellent	8 = 3 × (4/5/6)
1	2	3	4	5	6	7	
1.	Attitude	0.5					
2.	Job Knowledge	1.0					
3.	Dependency	0.5					
4.							
5.							
6.							

Fig. 5.4. Weighted Checklist Method

Model of a Tetrad

Not willing to take up responsibility unless he has full details regarding the job:

Best Least.

- Allows uncertainties of the job to run him down.
- Make snap judgement about the situation.
- Tries to solve the problem in his own way.
- He has not demonstrated his ability.

6. **Critical Incident Method:** All the above methods are discontinuous in nature, i.e. the evaluation is done once or twice in a year. This may reflect overall performance as the appraiser look to the problem for a period of one or two weeks. Hence, it is better to go for *continuous* method of appraising. This method is also known as ***critical incident method***. Here the rater continuously records the critical incidents of the employee performance or behavior relating to all characteristics, both positive and negative in a specially designed notebook. The supervisor rates the performance of his subordinates on the basis of notes taken by him. As the critical incident method does not have necessarily had to be a separate rating system, it can be fruitfully employed as documentation of the reasons why an employee was rated in a certain way. As the appraiser considers the record of performance for evaluating, it is more objective in nature. To be more effective, this method needs that a critical incidence must be clearly

defined so that all raters use the same definition for reference. One drawback of this method is that it consumes valuable time of the executive.

Example of critical incident recording:

CRITICAL INCIDENT RATING			
S. No.	**Subject**	**Target**	**Critical Incident**
1.	Productivity for March 2010	1.2	1.1
2.	Attendance in March 2010	85%	100%
3.			
4.			

Fig. 5.5. Critical Incident Recording

7. **Essay or Free Form Appraisal:** This method consists of writing a short essay describing the performance, behavior of the employee. This is a tedious job and consumes much of the executive time and if number of employees is more, it will be very difficult to write so many essays and use those essays for comparative analysis to rate the workers.
8. **Group Appraisal:** Here the employee is appraised by a group of people, consisting of immediate supervisor, other members who know the work of the employee and the departmental head. The departmental head will act as the chairman of the group and the immediate supervisor act as a coordinator. They can rate the worker by using any of the above methods and compare his performance with the standards set. After evaluation in case they find the employee poor, they suggest the methods for improvement. This method is generally used for promoting an employee.
9. **Behaviourally Anchored Rating Scales (BARS):** This method is a combination of traditional rating method and critical incidents method. BARS are constructed by combining the techniques employed in the critical incident method and weighted checklist rating scale. Much importance is given to the thinking of people who use the scales as evaluators and persons evaluated. Using BARS, job behaviours from critical incidents (effective and ineffective behavior) are described more objectively. This method employs individuals who are familiar with a particular job to identify its major components. They, then rank and validate specific behaviours for each of the components.
10. **Assessment Center:** This method utilizes the services of various experts in evaluating an employee in various aspects by using various techniques. These techniques include those discussed earlier and in addition have role playing, case studies, simulation exercises structured in sight, transactional analysis etc. Evaluation by assessment centers is basically meant for evaluating the potential of candidates to be considered for promotion, training or development. This is a better method of objective evaluation of an employee.

11. **Human Resource Accounting:** This approach basically deals with cost of and contribution of human resource to the organization. Cost of an employee includes cost of manpower planning, recruitment, selection, induction, placement, training and development, wages and benefits etc. Employee contribution is the money value of employee service which can be measured by labour productivity or value added by human resources. Cost of human resources may be taken as standard. Employee performance can be measured in terms of employee contribution to the organization. Employee performance can be taken as positive when contribution is more than the cost and performance can be viewed as negative if cost is more than contribution. Measurements are made in terms of percentage. This is almost similar to cost benefit analysis.
12. **Management By Objectives (MBO):** Refinement of Management By Objectives enabled many organizations to use it as an appraisal tool. In this method the following procedure is used.
    - The subordinate and superior jointly determine goals to be accomplished during the appraisal period and what level of performance is necessary for the subordinate to satisfactorily achieve specific goals.
    - During the appraisal period the superior and subordinate update and alter goals as necessary due to changes in the business environment.
    - The superior and employee determine new goals and performance objectives for the next period based on performance levels.

5.14. JOB EVALUATION AND MERIT RATING

Once employment and placement is over it is the duty of the management to provide an adequate management policy to remedy the mistakes committed during selection process or in promotions or transfers. It may become necessary to an employee to know whether he is fulfilling the expectations of the management. In such situations, it is better if management is provided with an effective and objective tool or system to evaluate and compare the performance of an employee with fellow workers in the group. Industrial psychologists have evolved procedures of ***merit rating*** as an aid to such evaluation and measurement of performance of an employee. *Merit rating can be defined as a systematic evaluation of personality and performance of each employee by his supervisors or some other qualified persons.* Rating techniques are used to comparing individual employee in a work group, in terms of personal qualities or drawbacks and the requirements of their respective jobs. Hence, merit rating or in broad personnel rating is concerned with individual differences among the workers of a workgroup. By objectively comparing and reviewing the industrial performance of the employee it grades or rates an employee. One must understand here that it is *rating of an employee* and not the *rating or evaluation of job as such.* The following are some of the traits, which are evaluated while rating an employee.

(i) Ability to do the work assigned to the employee.

(ii) Knowledge of the job and his performance in engineering and manufacturing operations.

(iii) Work habits and personal characteristics.

(iv) Special qualities.

(v) Supervisory abilities.

5.14.1. Methods of Merit Rating

Various methods of merit rating are there and they are very much same as those discussed while discussing Performance appraisal, such as Ranking method, Graphic rating scales, Forced distribution method, checklist method, Critical incident method etc.

5.14.2. Advantages of Merit Rating

An efficient method of merit rating or performance appraisal may prove advantageous because:

(i) It provides a basis for judging the conduct and performance of every employee of a workgroup by supervisor scientifically.

(ii) As the factors of performance evaluated systematically and scientifically, the merit rating may be used to fix up *fair rates of pay* for the workers basing on their performance.

(iii) As prescribed standards are used to rate the employees, merit rating *brings to light some persons who have special abilities* than others.

(iv) Merit rating may be used as the basis for *transfers*, promotions etc. In fact every thing is done on scientific basis; hence, there will be less industrial disputes.

(v) Merit rating distinguishes between efficient and inefficient workers.

(vi) It reveals the defects of selection procedure.

(vii) As the workers rated scientifically and rewarded are benefited, others will develop a sense of competition (healthy competition, of course) and try to get promotion to higher status. This will definitely has influence on productivity.

(viii) While evaluating, supervisors may get an idea about the difficulties faced by the workers, in general and try to improve the working conditions.

In spite of all the above-mentioned advantages, merit rating cannot be considered as an end in itself. It only compares the performance of an employee against the standards set by the company and ascertains that how far an individual worker is able to cope up with the standards. The chief limitation of merit rating is, its utility depends upon the character of the supervisors who are entrusted with merit rating work.

5.15. JOB EVALUATION

Merit rating helps the management by providing a basis to fix fair wages depending on the performance of the individual employee on the job. In fact Job Evaluation is the outcome of Job analysis. Job analysis provides the information necessary for appraising or evaluating a job or the tasks to be performed in a job, skill required to do the job Knowledge, abilities and aptitude required by an employee to carry out the job responsibility, authority and accountability required by an individual to carry out the job successfully. The various sub-systems of Job evaluation are Job description, Job specification and employee specification. Job description deals with information relating to duties and responsibilities of the job. Job specification gives the information relating to minimum acceptable human qualities like knowledge and skill necessary to perform a job. Employee specification prescribes minimum employee qualifications like physical, educational and behavioral characteristics etc. Job evaluation deals with money and work i.e. it determines the relative worth or money value of a job.

Objectives of Job Evaluation: The objectives of Job Evaluation are:

- To collect the data pertaining to Job description, Job specification and Employee specification.
- To compare the requirements of the job with that of other jobs in the organization.
- To draft the hierarchy and place of various jobs in the organization.
- To determine the ranks and grades of various jobs in the organization.
- To design and assure a fair and equitable wage system depending on the relative worth or value of the job.
- To minimize wage discrimination based on factors like sex, caste and age etc. to minimize the chances of disputes.

5.15.1. Job Evaluation Methods or Techniques

Jobs may be evaluated by using conventional methods or non-conventional methods. Once again conventional methods may be classified as quantitative and qualitative methods. Non-quantitative methods include simple ranking and paired comparison methods, job classifications and grading methods. Quantitative techniques include points rating and factor comparison methods. Non-conventional methods include:

(a) Time-span of discretion theory,

(b) Decision-banding,

(c) Direct consensus method,

(d) Guide-chart profile method,

(e) Problem solving compassable factor,

(f) Guide line method,

(g) Urwick or profile method, and

(h) Profile method.

1. **Ranking Method:** This is simple and easiest method. The evaluator compares one job with the other based on the duties and responsibilities and demands made by the jobs on the job incumbent and the degree of importance of the job to the organization and rank all the jobs from the most important to the least important. The appraiser has to rank the job and not the employee on the job. This is known as ***simple ranking.***

   Generally, the appraiser to reduce his efforts required to rank all the jobs at a time, identifies the key or representative jobs and ranks them first, then identify and rank all other jobs. When he ranks first all the key jobs, then it will become easy for him to rank other jobs. This is known as ***ranking the key jobs.***

   While ranking the jobs it is not advisable or simple to compare a job with all other jobs. To simplify the matter, paired comparison can be adopted. Here the evaluator ranks each job in turn against all other jobs to be appraised, so that a series of paired rankings are produced. This is a comprehensive, logical and reliable compared to the above.

Instead of comparing all the factors of a job (skill, responsibility, effort and working conditions etc.) with that of other job at a time, it is easy to identify most important factor, which influences the performance of each job and compare that factor with the jobs and rank the jobs. The jobs are to be paired after ranking is over. Afterwards the money value of the job is fixed. Once the key jobs are fixed on monitory scale, then ranking of other jobs becomes easy.

The advantages of this method are it is simple and easy, suitable for small organizations. It will be more appropriate to use this method to rank higher-level managerial jobs. It can be used as the first and basic step of job evaluation. The limitations of this method are it does not provide quantities basis for measuring relative worth of one job against the other. The three important elements of job evaluation i.e. job requirement, job specifications and employee specifications are not considered in evaluation.

2. **Job Classifications and Grading Method:** Let us first distinguish between grade and class. As far as this method is concerned the grade refers to group of different jobs of similar difficulty/skill/knowledge requirement for performing the job. Class refers to subdivision of given occupation. For example, senior manager, Manager and Assistant manager are sub classification of manager's post. Generally jobs within a class have fairly similar tasks to be performed, while the jobs within a grade may be different as far as the job is concerned. In this method all the jobs in an organization are clearly graded and classified with clear-cut definitions and descriptions and specifications. The method adopted in grading and classification is:
   - Determine the shape of the organization and draw the organizational structure to understand various levels of jobs existing in the organization.
   - Prepare the Job, Description.
   - Prepare grading of all the jobs depending on the skill, knowledge and effort required to perform the job.
   - Establish the number of job grades and divisions of the organizations.
   - Negotiate with labour unions to get their consent and finalize the grading.
   - Select the key jobs and grade them.
   - Classify the jobs of each grade.
   - Assign money value to each key grade and then to other jobs, relatively.

The advantages of this method are, it takes organization structure into consideration. It is simple and easy to understand. It takes the consent of labour union leaders. The pay grades devised by this method are better and appropriate for comparison with the grades of other companies. The serious limitation is it appears to be sometimes arbitrary. Also it is not that easy to write grade descriptions.

3. **Conventional Quantitative Techniques:** There are two methods employed in quantitative technique. One is points rating method and the other is factor comparison method.

   (a) **Points Rating Method:** Here the job is broken down into components for the sake of comparison. Each component is assigned a numerical value depending on the skill, knowledge, responsibility, working conditions etc. Each factor is divided into degree or levels and point value is assigned to each level. The total of point values assigned to each factor gives the total point values for each job, which can be compared. To avoid defective numbering, the method should be systematically developed and applied methodologically. The process consists of:

- A committee is formulated consisting the expert and representative members from each department to guide in job evaluation.
- Select a sample of jobs and prepare job description, job specification and employee specification.
- Eight to twelve critical factors are selected, which are related to all jobs and these factors are to be most critical in determining the relative degrees of difficulty and responsibility. The factors may be skill, effort, responsibility, job condition etc.
- Determining the weight of each factor according to its relative importance. Assign percentage value to each factor, so that the total percentage of all factors is equal to 100 percent.
- Define each factor specifying the scope.
- Divide each factor into levels and define each level.
- Determine relative value of each level within factors.
- Test the validity of the method by comparing the grading obtained by various other methods for sample of jobs.
- Appraise all the jobs and arrive at a composite numerical value for each job.
- Price the points in order to arrive at a fair wage system.

There are no hard and fast rules for arriving at factors, sub-factors and in assigning the weightage and in deciding the degrees and values. This is only a preliminary step in arriving at an equitable pay structure.

Example of Point Rating System

NAME OF THE COMPANY							
Department:..............		**Job:..............**			**Date: ....**		
S. No.	**Job Factors**	**Weighs**	**Degrees POINTS**				
			1	2	3	4	5
1.	Skill	25					
2.	Knowledge	25					
3.	Training	15					
4.	Experience	15					
5.	Complexity of the job	10					
6.	Cooperation	10					
	Total	100					

Fig. 5.6. Points Rating

After deciding the money value of each job a graph is drawn with points rating on the X-axis and Money value on Y-axis and points are plotted. A correlation line is drawn passing through the middle of the points to fix the trend.

The advantages of this method: We can arrive at same pay scales for the jobs requiring same factors. Jobs are defined and written in applicable terms to jobs. Monetary value is assigned easily and cannot be manipulated. Assignment of points is consistent and accurate. Wage is fair and is according to job content.

The limitations: It is difficult to determine factor levels and assign point values. Technique is not easily understandable and is an expensive method.

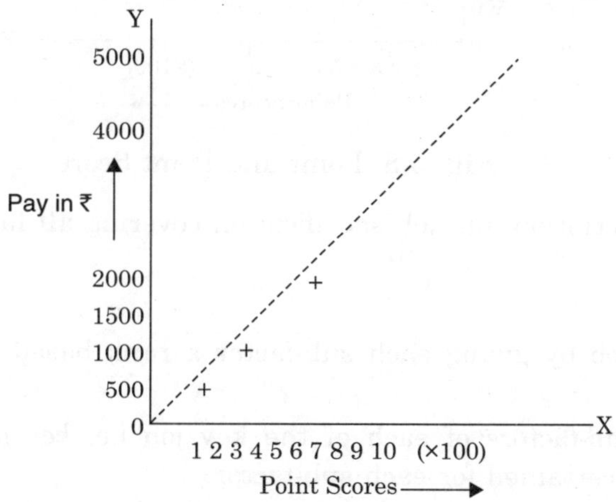

Fig. 5.7. Point Score and Pay

Table 5.1. Showing Relationship between Pay and Job Grades

RELATIONSHIP BETWEEN PAY LEVELS AND JOB GRADES		
GRADES	**PAY SCALES**	
	Minimum (₹)	**Maximum (₹)**
I	1000	1500
II	1500	2000
III	2000	3000
IV	3000	4000
V	4000	6000

(b) The Point Factor or Factor-comparison Method: This method uses the techniques of both *points rating* and *principles of ranking.* Job is broken down into sub-factors or components. First components or sub-divisions are ranked under various factor headings. Next monetary value is assigned to the components or sub-factors. The procedure is:

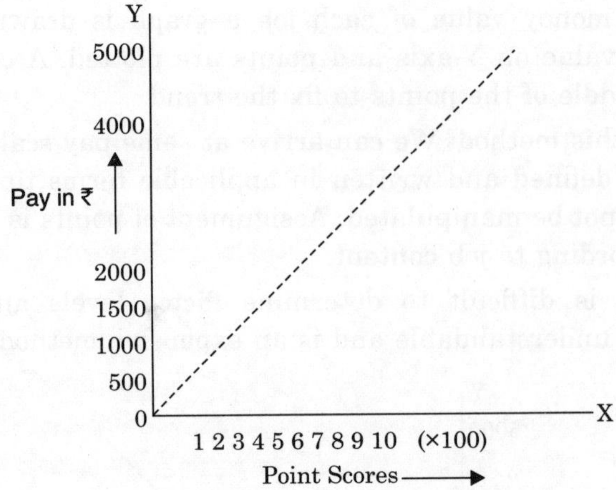

Fig. 5.8. Point and Point Score

- Develop job description and job specification covering all factors like skill, training, knowledge etc.
- Select a key job.
- Rank the key job by giving each sub-factor a rank based on the requirement and specification.
- Evaluate the sub-factors of each of the key job i.e. *key factor evaluation.* Money worth is also ascertained for each sub-factor.
- Integrate the monetary value of sub-factor arrived through factors evaluation with those of ranking of factors.
- Compare all the jobs of the same grade or level, factor by factor with the related key job and establish monetary value to the sub-factors of various jobs based on the monetary value of sub-factors or key jobs.

Example: Two Key Jobs: (a) Fitter (b) Foreman

Factor Ranking of Two Jobs:

Table 5.2. Showing Rank Order and Factor Ranking for Fitter job and Foreman Job.

S. No.	Factors to be Considered	Rank Order	Rank Order	Factor Rating	Factor Rating
		Fitter	Foreman	Fitter	Foreman
1.	Physical requirement	1	5	15	8
2.	Working condition	2	4	05	10
3.	Skill requirement	3	1	10	25
4.	Responsibility	4	3	04	15
5.	Mental requirement	5	2	05	20

The advantages of this method are it is analytical and quantitative. It is the blend of ranking method and factor comparison method. It is easy to operate, reliable and valid. Money value is assigned fairly and objectively.

Limitations of this method are: It is costly, a bit difficult than conventional methods. This method does not consider sub-factors.

5.15.2. Non-Conventional Techniques of Job Evaluation

Let us discuss below some of the non-conventional methods of job evaluation.

(a) Time-Span of Discretion Theory: This method considers *psycho-economic* factors for determining the rates of pay. Professor Elliott Jaques devised this method. He argues that conventional techniques of salary fixing will be based on the bargaining strengths of the parties. He suggested a technique, which will give social, psychological and economic satisfaction to the employee and has a presence of objective and scientific procedure and which would be free from political power and negotiating strengths.

As per his analysis: Let C = Capacity to do certain volume of work,

Actual volume of work turned out by the employee on the job demand = W

Payment made for the work = P

(i) Employee would be in a state of equilibrium when $C = W = P$

(ii) He feels *inequitable treatment* when capacity matches work and payment is below or less i.e. $C = W < P$

(iii) Feels *frustration* when capacity matches with pay and work is below the capacity i.e. $C = P < W$

(iv) He feels stress when pay is greater than work demand and it is greater than his capacity i.e. $P < W < C$

Thus employees *whose capacities are well adjusted to the level of work they do and where work provides them with a subjectively felt equitable level of payment are said to be in a state of* ***psycho-economic equilibrium.*** Professor has devised three systems and they are (i) Time Span discretion, (ii) Equitable work payment scale and (iii) Standard earning progression.

(i) *Time-span discretion*: As per this theory, when level of work (W) is measured in terms of *Time-span* we can introduce a general and universal pay structure. Here work is divided into prescribed and *discretionary* activities. In discretionary activities subordinate exercises his own discretion. Prescribed works are carried out as rules and procedures are fixed by the organization. Here time-span is the longest period of time, which can elapse in a role before a superior can be sure that his subordinate has not been exercising marginally standard discretion continuously in balancing the pace of quality of his work. That is the time-span in hours or days from which the next operator detects an error in sequence of work or by the inspector or supervisor.

(ii) *Equitable work payment scale*: Equitable payment is the common norm, where people in roles on same time-span say that they would considered for a fair pay. When there is an imbalance between C, W and P then the dissatisfaction in employee surfaces.

(iii) ***Standard earning progression:*** This method involves in determining the time-span bracket for each jobholder on assigning the equitable salary bracket. Here considering the pay drawn by the worker, a superior officer evaluates the performance of the worker and adjusts his salary depending on the salary index in the country.

(b) **Decision-Banding Technique:** Paterson devised this method. According to him, conventional methods use subjective measure of work and compare dissimilar jobs. His scheme proposes a single factor — *decision making* for comparing the jobs. His argument is that jobs differ from each other based on the kind of decision to be made in performing the job. The procedure adopted is:

(i) Establish job bands depending upon the decision type and structure.
(ii) Job analysis.
(iii) Job grading and sub grading and ranking of jobs and
(iv) Assessment and assigning money value for each job.

According to Paterson, significant difference among jobs is the quality of decision made and he is of the opinion that every known job can be compared against six basic levels of decision-making. They are:

Policy-making decisions made at the top level: BAND–E

Programming decisions made in the execution of the policy: BAND–D

Interpretive decision made in interpreting the program: BAND–C

Routine decisions made in the execution of the policy: BAND–B

Automatic decision made on the operational aspects of the process such as when, where and how etc. BAND–A

Defined decisions are the decisions permitting very limited discretion: BAND–O

All the bands except Band–O are divided into two groups i.e. Upper level and Lower level.

(c) **Direct Consensus Method:** Associated Industrial Consultants Limited developed this method. This method may be applied to all levels of jobs. In this method the key criteria against which jobs are to be assessed is determined in advance. A committee of assessors will evaluate all jobs by paired comparison and assign money values to jobs.

(d) **Guide Chart Profile Method:** This method is a modification of point method. The accountability of manager's job is a common factor for evaluation. Other important factors considered for evaluation is know-how, Problem-solving skill. These three points are considered as key elements for evaluating a managerial job. Point scales are allocated to know-how and accountability. Each job is rated under each criterion and jobs are plotted on charts to show job structures in quantitative terms. Common scores are calculated and money value is assigned to jobs depending on the score.

(e) **Problem Solving Compensable Factor:** According to Q.W. Charles, jobs can be evaluated on the basis of degree of problem solving skill required to perform the job and he advocates that problem solving skill is a single universal compensable factor and wages should be fixed on the basis of responsibility required by the problem solving activities of the job. He has developed a matrix, which can be used for measurement of amount of responsibility required for problem solving of a job in comparison with those of other jobs.

(f) Guideline Method: This method consists of four elements for grading jobs and they are:

- ***Guideline Scale***: This scale indicates three ranges of pay scale i.e. Minimum, mid-point and maximum and contends that 5 percent differences in the midpoints between pay grades and has flexibility to move a job on the scale.
- ***Scope Data***: This helps in identifying, defining and describing key jobs in order to identify the salaries paid to these jobs in comparable industries.
- ***Market Pricing***: A survey is conducted in industries to find the pay scales fixed for various jobs and compare those jobs with the jobs on hand and fix pay level.
- ***Horizontal Guideline Displays***: Three or more vertical guidelines are used to for ensuring equitable job relationships and are used to develop horizontal guideline displays.

(g) Urwick Orr Profile Method: This is the combination of rating and ranking method devised by Urwick Orr. It is more acceptable in large-scale industries because of its adoptability. The procedure adopted is:

- Select key jobs, which are to be evaluated.
- Rate the jobs basing on six sub-factors viz., responsibility, knowledge, mental demands, social demands, physical demands and work environment. A four-point scale i.e. basic, moderate, high and exceptional may be used to score the sub-factors.
- Rank the key jobs according to total score values of sub-factors.
- Re-rank the jobs on a *whole* job basis.
- Compare and reconcile the ranks based on sub-factor and whole job basis.
- Remove any discrepancies, by reconsidering the weights of sub-factors until a balance is reached.
- Present the evaluated jobs as a profile and point scores.

(h) Profile Method: Here key factors such as general education, technical education, experience, knowledge etc. are considered and given scores depending on the job demand. These scores are totaled and money value is fixed to jobs.

The following table gives the scope and basis of job evaluation methods:

Table 5.3. Showing Job Evaluation Method

BASIS OF COMPARISON	SCOPE OF COMPARISON	
	Job as whole	**Job factors or parts**
1. Job vs. Job	Ranking Method	Factor Comparison Method
2. Job vs. Scale	Job Classification Method	Point Method

Advantages of Job Evaluation: Job evaluation and its accompaniments are means to the establishment of a *rational wage and salary structure*, which will be more satisfying to the workers.

- Disputes and grievances regarding individual rates of wages can be conveniently and satisfactorily settled by reference to the job evaluating machinery.
- The data collected for job evaluation will help management while deciding merit rating, selection and giving training etc.
- The process of determining the wage differentials for different jobs help to set uniform standards to all jobs in a concern.
- Whenever there is a change in responsibility, duties or operations, the wage committee set up may revise the pay for new job conveniently.
- It simplifies the wage administration.

Limitations: In spite of the above-mentioned advantages, management cannot solely relay on the methods as each method has some limitations.

- Many of them lack *scientific precision* because all factors cannot be measured accurately.
- It presumes that job of equal content will be equally attractive to the employee, but it is not correct to make this assumption. This is because the employee has his own way of assessing the jobs while selecting the jobs depending on scope, responsibility, promotional aspects etc.
- If the method does not put emphasis on the wage rate in industry and considers only the unit, it becomes inflexible.
- The evaluation system is an utter failure, if the evaluators are not properly trained in evaluation methods.
- Sometimes it takes long time to evaluate and install wage system it may become costly.

Trade unions always suspect any system and advocate for collective bargaining.

QUESTIONS

1. Why human being is considered as a resource? Explain its significance.
2. Define human resource management and discuss its functions.
3. What is the difference between Human Resource Management and Personal Management?
4. Explain the steps in Human Resource Planning.
5. What is Recruitment? Briefly explain the methods of Recruitment.
6. What is labour turnover? What are the reasons of labour turnover? How to arrest it?
7. What methods are used for Employee Selection? Discuss.
8. Explain in detail the procedure for Recruitment and Selection of workers.
9. Write a note on On-the-Job test.

10. Write a note on Vocational Guidance or Counseling.
11. What is training? Why is it necessary? Discuss the various methods of training employees.
12. Write a short notes on: (a) Placement, (b) Promotion, (c) Transfers, (d) Separation.
13. Discuss the basis for Promotion of an Employee.
14. Discuss the basis for Transfer of an Employee.
15. What is Performance Appraisal? Why is it necessary? What are its advantages?
16. Discuss the various methods used for Performance Appraisal.
17. Explain Graphic rating scales used for Performance Appraisal.
18. Explain Paired Comparison method and Checklist method of Performance Appraisal.
19. Explain briefly what do you understand about Job Evaluation and Merit Rating.
20. What are the advantages of Merit Rating?
21. What are the objectives of Job Evaluation? What methods you use for Job Evaluation? Discuss.

MULTIPLE CHOICE QUESTIONS

1. The manpower or the people with required skills to make an organization are generally known as
   (a) Skilled labour (b) Skilled managers
   (c) Human resource (d) Human power
2. Employing people, developing their skills, maintaining and compensating their services for meeting the objectives of the organization is termed as
   (a) Managing the lobour (b) Human resource management
   (c) Personal management (d) Managing managers
3. The functions of HRM are classified as
   (a) Managerial function and operational function
   (b) Planning and directing function
   (c) Planning and control functions
   (d) Managerial functions and training functions
4. The process by which a management determines how an organization should move from its current manpower position to its desired manpower position is termed as
   (a) Human resource development (b) Manpower development
   (c) Manpower training (d) Human resource planning
5. The process of studying, collection of information relating to the operation of the job and responsibilities of the labour in carrying out the job is known as
   (a) Job analysis (b) Job description
   (c) Job details (d) Job planning

6. The process of searching for a prospective employee and motivate them to apply for the job is known as
   (a) Motivation (b) Searching
   (c) Recruitment (d) Appointment
7. The process of comparing the qualities of applicant and compare them with job specification to appraise the suitability of the applicant for the job is known as
   (a) Selection (b) Recruitment
   (c) Placement (d) Appointment
8. The techniques by which a new employee is rehabilitated in the changed surroundings and introduced to the organization is termed as
   (a) Recruitment and Selection (b) Selection and Training
   (c) Induction and Orientation (d) Selection and Placement
9. The process of comparing the performance of the employee on the job with their potential abilities to judge whether the employee is to be rewarded or not is known as
   (a) Evaluation of performance (b) Job performance
   (c) Employee performance (d) Performance appraisal
10. The process of designing and conducting suitable executive development program to develop managerial and human relation skills is termed as
    (a) Training seniors (b) Management development
    (c) Developing industrial relations (d) Managerial skill improvement
11. To recruit casual workers the main source is:
    (a) Technical institutions (b) Employment exchange
    (c) Rival firms (d) Factory gate
12. To recruit Senior Managers the best source is:
    (a) Factory gate (b) Employment exchange
    (c) Technical colleges (d) Advertisement for requirement
13. The tests which reveal how an individual behave while on the job are known as:
    (a) Trade tests (b) Psychological tests
    (c) Interview (d) Medical test
14. The test which tests the inclination of the candidate to learn the skill of the job and his interest on the job for which he being tested is known as:
    (a) Aptitude test (b) Intelligence tests
    (c) Dexterity test (d) Trade test
15. OJT means:
    (a) One-Job-Training (b) Once-the-Job-Training
    (c) On-The-Job-Test (d) Office-Juniors-Training

16. The task of guiding a person as to what sort of job he should have is known as:

(a) Right placement (b) Training on the job

(c) Guidance (d) Vocational guidance

17. This will help the employee to improve/increase his aptitude, skill, and ability to do the job for which he is selected

(a) Vocational guidance (b) Training

(c) Guidance (d) Strict control

18. A training in which worker is introduced to the organization to enable him to understand his job and to know about fellow workers is known as:

(a) Introduction (b) Job training

(c) Induction training (d) Refresher training

19. In this type of training, students from technical institutes are sent to factories to enable them to learn their work in real situation is known as:

(a) Vestibule training (b) Apprenticeship training

(c) Factory training (d) Internship training

20. JMT means:

(a) Job Methods Training (b) Job Machine Training

(c) Job Material Training (d) None of these

21. When an organization wants to train employees in various works of the organization then transfer is made from job to job this is known as:

(a) Personal transfers (b) Replacement transfer

(c) Versatility transfers (d) Office transfers

22. Method of evaluating quantitative and qualitative behavior of the employee in the work spot is known as:

(a) Performance testing (b) Performance grading

(c) Performance control (d) Performance appraisal

23. A systematic evaluation of personality and performance of each employee by his supervisors or some other qualified persons is known as:

(a) Merit rating (b) Job rating

(c) Performance evaluation (d) Performance rating

ANSWERS

1. (c) **2.** (b) **3.** (a) **4.** (d) **5.** (a) **6.** (c) **7.** (a) **8.** (c)
9. (a) **10.** (b) **11.** (d) **12.** (d) **13.** (b) **14.** (a) **15.** (c) **16.** (d)
17. (b) **18.** (c) **19.** (d) **20.** (a) **21.** (c) **22.** (d) **23.** (a).

❍❍❍

EMPLOYEE REMUNERATION OR WAGE ADMINISTRATION

5.16. INTRODUCTION

When workers are engaged to do work either on day basis, weekly basis or monthly basis, they are to be paid compensation for the work done by them, this compensation paid to them is generally known as *wages*. When paid monthly it is known as *salary*. One of the important factors in human resource management is ***compensation management***. The soundness of compensation management depends upon the amount of wage or salary paid to an employee for a fair days work. The term wage includes any non-pecuniary benefits attached to money payments. This is to say that consider an employee getting a wages of ₹ 20 per day. In addition to his wages he is allowed a concession of ₹ 2/- on food grains his wages will become ₹ 22 per day. When a worker loses his job and compensation paid to him to the effect will not be included in wages. From the point of view of industry, wages constitute that share of the total cost of production, which can be attributed to or allocated to labour. As far as a worker is concerned, wages constitutes the income by which he lives. Man sells his labour to an employer for bread, though bread alone is not the means of living. The standard of living of a worker depends on the money he earns. Workers attitude towards the employer depends on the extent to which he is satisfied with the wages. It does not mean wages is only the important factor of employee satisfaction. There are many factors, which influence the workers satisfaction. But the wage has higher influence on the satisfaction of worker. If wages one gets is not sufficient, it acts as a factor influencing dissatisfaction. So, it is considered as both *satisfier* and *non-satisfier* factor. Satisfiers are used as motivating factors only after dissatisfiers are taken care of. Hence, the management is very much interested in satisfying the workers by giving satisfactory remuneration, before thinking of other ways of motivation. Wages that too fair wages is the single factor in which both labour and unions are interested. Also many disputes in industries cluster around the wages and wage system. Whatever may be the system adopted and wages paid, however fair it may be labour unions always have suspicious eyes on the decisions taken by management regarding wages and wage system.

Wage rates are influenced by many factors and they are:

- ***Demand and Supply***: Depending on the availability of labours, the wage rate may fluctuate. If there is a shortage in supply of labour, then the labours will demand higher wage rate for their work. In case, there is a surplus in the demand, then the management is having a higher hand and can give lower wage rates.
- ***Bargaining Capacity***: Many a time wage rate will demand on the bargaining power of an employee and the unions. If unions are strong enough to influence the management, then the rates fixed will be higher otherwise, if the management is having a higher hand, the wage rates fixed may not be attractive.
- ***Cost of Living***: Though both management and labour unions take advantage of situation as far as the wages are concerned, if they are really progressive in thinking, they take notice of cost of living while fixing the wages. While fixing wages, both

management and unions should consider the existing wage index and fix fair wages so that the labour will have dignified way of living.

- ***Conditions of Product Market***: If the products manufactured by the company have a larger share of market and it has a good demand in the market, then market returns will be sound and the financial positions of the company will also be good and it helps the management to give higher rates of remuneration. In case the company's product does not have market then the position of company will be bad, hence, the wage rates may be not encouraging.
- ***Government's Regulations***: When the bargaining powers of workers is very week and management is exploiting the workers, then the government will interfere in the matter and press the industries to fix fair minimum wages.

5.17. SYSTEM OF WAGE PAYMENT

Mainly one can identify two systems of wage payment that are adopted in industrial concerns. One is labour is paid on the basis of time spent on the job i.e. ***time rate system***. Second one is wage is paid for the quantity of work that the worker performs i.e. ***quantity base system*** or ***payment by results.*** We see that most of the systems adopted in industries are modifications of time rate system or payment by results system or combination of the two. In time rate system, more importance is given to time that the worker spends on the work and time is taken as the basis of remunerating the labour. In payment by results system, the output is taken as the basis of payment rather than the time taken for the job.

5.17.1. Time Wage System or Time Rate System

This method of wage payment is oldest one and simple one. It is also known as ***day work system of wages,*** because in olden days day was considered to be convenient unit for the calculation of wages of the worker. But in modern industrial system, the management hires the worker or buys his time in convenient unit of time such as hour, day of 8 hours, week of 6 or 5 days or a month. It means to say that the worker is paid according to the time he spends on the work. Consider the following example.

Problem 5.1.

Wage is fixed at ₹ 10 per hour and the worker spends 5 hours on the work. What is his wage?

Solution:

Hourly rate = ₹ 10/-

Number of hours spent on the work = 5 hrs

Wage = Time rate × Time spent = 10 × 5 = ₹ 50

Problem 5.2.

A workers wage is fixed at ₹ 50 per day of 8 hours. If he spends 7 days on the work what is his wage?

Solution:

Daily rate = ₹ 50/-

Number of days worked = 7 days

Wage = Time rate × Time = 50 × 7 = ₹ 350/-

In general, if time rate = R and the time spent = T, Wage = T × R

While payment is made, the quality and quantity of output is not considered. But in general, manager or foreman will have a look on the work of the worker. If they find the worker is inefficient, then he will be sacked. If the worker is an efficient one, while merit rating due consideration will be given for wage hike.

The advantages of this system are:

- This system gives a sense of security to the worker because his wages for the time spent is guaranteed. This is necessary for a worker to show his interest in the work. Sometimes due to ill health or worries, his efficiency may fall down temporarily; in such case his wages are not cut.
- If the nature of the work is such that, quality is utmost important, which depends on the skill and devotion of the worker, he can concentrate on the quality of work and not consider time as his time wage is guaranteed.
- As the worker spends his time on the work with devotion, he will not run the machine at over speed or load the machine heavily, which may result breakdown of machines or tool wear out, which will unnecessarily increase the cost of production. This is because he is paid time rate, which is independent of production.
- The system is simple and easily understandable by the worker. It is easy to maintain records. The operating cost of the system is negligible.
- Where the production is not standardized and the production of the worker cannot be measured correctly, time rate system is the best method of payment.
- Where the industry follows mass production system or assembly line production, the workers production rate is controlled by the machine speed or speed of the assembly line. In such cases, time rate system of payment is more suitable.
- This system is most acceptable by the trade unions, because this system does not create any distinctions in the ranks of workers on account of difference in efficiency.

Limitations or disadvantage of the system are:

- As the wages paid on time rate and not on the quality and quantity of production, it does not distinguish between efficient and inefficient or honest and dishonest worker. Naturally, efficient workers also may loose interest in the work.
- Superior and skilled workers get frustrated as they are also paid on par with inefficient workers.
- It is very difficult to workout the cost of production per unit as the payment is not made on the result of the work.
- The system works effectively, when there is good and effective supervision.

This method is more suitable in situations like

- When we have to pay indirect workers, who spend their time on different works, this is the best system of payment.

- Where quality of work is utmost important.
- When the worker is learning the work.
- When the operator has no control on the operation, i.e. Automatic and semiautomatic production system.

5.17.2. Graduated Time Rate System or Modified Time Rate Wage System

In the above system time rate is guaranteed and no consideration is given to the production aspect of the worker. In the modified time rate system different time rates are given to the workers depending on the rate of their production giving due consideration to the quality of the work produced. This will give due consideration to the skill and efficiency of the worker and avoid dissatisfaction in workers who are more committed to work than casual and general workers. Under this plan the rates are adjusted to suit general or particular economic circumstances or to allow for different personal qualities in the workers. The time rate may also be suitably adjusted by the cost of living index or award for the merits of the individual workers.

5.18. PIECE RATE SYSTEM OR PIECE WAGE SYSTEM

In piece rate system worker is paid for the amount of work done by him rather than for the time spent on the job. Here amount of work refers to the specific amount of work measured in terms of number of components, Kg. Of material etc. a specific rate is fixed in terms of money for each unit of work and the remuneration is paid accordingly. The wage paid depends on the production or the amount of work done and not on the time i.e. wage paid is independent of time. As the wage depends on the output, there will be a tendency of worker working very fast to show higher results. But the quality of work is taken into consideration. In case unnecessarily, worker takes longer time than the required, the employer after noticing, may caution the worker to improve his work. The wage paid is calculated as shown below:

Problem 5.3.

Let the wage fixed per piece of output is ₹ 10/-, and the worker produces 25 pieces in a day, then his wage is ₹ 10 × 25 = ₹ 250/-. If R is the piece rate fixed in ₹ and N is the number of pieces produced by the worker, then the wage paid to the worker = ₹ R × N. The advantages of this method are:

- This method of payment distinguishes between efficient worker and inefficient worker. As the payment depends on the result, the workers will be happy. Efficient workers feel that due regard is given to their efficiency.
- It ensures fairness to everybody and there will be no disputes. In this system people with poor performance will be penalized.
- It is very easy to prepare wage bill and it is easily understandable by everybody and the cost of production can easily be calculated.
- As the workers are interested in earning more and the output is measured in terms of number by taking quality of work into consideration, strict supervision is not necessary.

The limitations or drawbacks of this method are:

- As the amount paid depends on the quality output, if the efficiency of worker falls below the expected level due to factors out of his control, his wages are reduced.
- Worker will not have any guarantee about his earnings; he feels a sense of lack of security to his earnings.
- With fluctuating wages, worker cannot fulfil his bare minimum desires.
- To check the quality of work, strict quality control measures are to be imposed, it adds to the cost of the product.
- To attain the desired quality of product, the worker has to put too much of emphasis on attaining the desired quality, in this process, he may not attain the desired quality. It is loss to the worker and to the organization.
- To increase the output, worker may sometimes work with over speeds on the machine and which may cause higher wear and tear and need frequent maintenance.
- If the workers are not able to get the required output due to faulty set up of machines or faulty material, they will get frustrated because it is not their fault. They are penalized due to fault of management. This may lead to dissatisfaction among workers and the relationship between workers and management may get strained.
- To fix up wage rate per piece, all work standards are to be fixed by work-study. Even the management conducts work-study and takes all cares in fixing the wage rate the labour unions will have suspicious eye.

This method is most suitable to industries, where work is of standard nature and is repetitive in nature. It is also suitable when there is urgent need to increase the production, of course without sacrificing the quality. Suitable to industries, where individual output can easily be measured.

5.19. BALANCE AND DEBT SYSTEM

This method is an extension to or adoption of piece-wage system. It considers both time rate and piece rate into consideration. Let us consider, the daily output fixed per day is 20 units (= N) and piece rate is ₹ 5 per unit (R). Also time rate fixed is ₹ 100 per day. If the worker completes 20 pieces he is paid an amount = N × R i.e. ₹ 5 × 20 = ₹ 100. Suppose for some reason or the other the worker is not able to complete 20 pieces and completes only 18 pieces, he is paid time rate i.e. ₹ 100/- per day. Here actually, depending on his production, the worker is eligible for ₹ 90/- (18 × 5 = ₹ 90/- i.e. piece rate). But he is paid ₹ 100/- computed on daily rate basis with a condition that on any day if he produces more than 20 pieces, the wages paid extra (in this example ₹ 10/-) will be recovered from his earnings due to extra output. Here is worker is guaranteed about his wages on time basis but would be paid on piece basis, if these are higher subject to the condition that excess amount paid will be recovered from excess production on successive days.

Let us consider the following example. The time rate is ₹ 100 per day. The piece rate is ₹ 5/- per unit and the standard of output fixed at 20 units per day. The wages will be calculated as follows:

Solution:

Day	Number of Pieces	Wage According to Piece Rate (₹)	Daily Wages (₹)	Excess Paid (₹)	Excess Recovered (₹)	Amount to be Paid in (₹)
1	20	20 x 5	100	---	---	100
2	18	18 x 5 = 90	100	10	--	100
3	21	21 x 5 = 105	100	---	5	100
4	20	20 x 5 = 100	100	---	----	100
5	22	22 x 5 =110	100	----	5	105

We can see from the table that an excess of wages paid i.e. ₹ 10/- on second day is recovered from the extra wages earned due to extra pieces produced on 3rd and 5th days. While recovering, one must remember that the wages paid after deduction should not be less than the wages calculated on hourly or time basis. Here worker is guaranteed his daily wages as per hourly rate an if he does extra work, he will be paid extra amount calculated on the basis of piece rate system. The advantage of this method is that worker will be happy, as he is sure of getting his daily wages. This method is suitable to the industries, where the work on each day will be uneven.

5.20. THE STANDARD HOUR SYSTEM

This system is an extension to piece rate system. This system is also known as ***One Hundred Percent Gain Sharing System.*** The time for a job is fixed through work-study techniques. This time is known as standard time. This time is allowed to do a specified work for which the time is standardized. Say for example, that the time allowed for the work is T = 10 hours. A time rate is also fixed for the work. For example, for the above-mentioned work, let us say ₹ 5/- per hour. i.e. R = ₹ 5/-.

If the worker completes the job in standard time (T) or less than standard time, say in 8 hours, the worker is paid for his standard time at the pre specified rate per hour i.e. the worker is paid for T = 10 hrs at the rate of ₹ 5/- per hour i.e. ₹ 50/-. Here worker is getting ₹ 50/- though he worked on the job for 8 hours only. ₹ 10/- he will get as bonus for the time saved. In case worker takes much time than the standard time say 12 hours instead of 10 hours, he will be paid guaranteed time rate for the time he spends on the job. That is the worker will get ₹ 5/- × 12 hr = ₹ 60/-. If there is no guaranteed time rate, he will be paid only for standard time.

5.21. INCENTIVE PLANS

We have studied the advantages and limitations of time wage system and piece rate system. The piece rate offers no guarantee of a consistently reasonable wage and passes the gains or losses due to variation in productivity of worker to worker himself. Whereas, in time rate system, the time rate is guaranteed to the worker and the loss or gain due to variations in productivity is transferred to the employer. In *Incentive plans* both *time* and *piece* rate systems are blended together to encourage the worker to increase his earnings, at the same time employer also shares the benefit with the worker.

5.22. PROPERTIES OF A GOOD INCENTIVE SCHEME

Any incentive system must be designed to motivate the worker to put his best effort on the work and increase his earnings, at the same time must make the relationship between management and the workers strong enough to have a smooth industrial relationship. It must be possible by a good incentive scheme to put a full stop for laziness in workers, mistrust and indifference between management and workers. While accepting an incentive scheme one must see whether the system has the following characteristics or not.

(i) ***Simplicity***: The scheme should be simple and easily understandable by the workers. The workers need not have any mathematical background to calculate the wages. It must be possible for a worker to make the wage calculations on fingerer tips.

(ii) ***Direct effort-reward relationship***: The reward under a monitory incentive plan must be as nearly related to effort as possible both in amount paid and in the time of payment. **That is *the wage should increase above a minimum limit in the same proportion as increases in output as far as possible. It is because, variable relationship at different levels of output are confusing and therefore, undesirable*.** Once the system is not understandable by the workers, they may feel they are not getting as much as effort they put on the work and get confused regarding the calculation of wages and get dissatisfied. Any incentive system must be such that the reward is paid immediately after the effort is put and not after a long time. If incentive is paid immediately, it will encourage the workers to give better performance.

(iii) ***Justice***: The scheme must be acceptable by both workers and employers. It should be economical to the management and at the same time it must encourage the workers to put their effort honestly to increase their earnings.

(iv) ***Scientific base***: The task involved in doing a job should be set by scientific methods such as method study and work measurement and the work conditions are set as per norms set by state and the system must be such that one should measure the performance very clearly and easily to set up the earnings or remuneration for the worker. Sometimes when it is not possible to have time study, at least referring to past records the performance standards is to be set so that it can be easily understandable by all concerned. One must set the standards in such a way that standards set are attainable by a normal worker. Both employees and employer will accept a well-set standard.

(v) ***Guaranteed time rate***: As time rate system gives a security sense to a worker, it is better to see that the worker earns his daily or hourly rate for the work he has done. Using job evaluation methods manager may set the wages. In general the incentive schemes are set in such a way that the worker can earn 10 to 15 percent more than his earnings when wages are set by piece rate system.

(vi) ***Definiteness***: Once the system is set, it should not be set very often. The changes should be implemented when there is a remarkable change in the process, method, materials, or equipment. While changes are made they should be done on scientific basis and see it should not create any doubt in the minds of workers.

(vii) ***Comprehensive coverage***: Incentives should be fixed on scientific basis for all the jobs eligible for incentive. If any job not considered, the workers doing left jobs may develop grievance against management. Any incentive scheme or wage scheme must be designed in such a way, so that the worker is paid depending on the performance of the worker (output basis) at the same time the earnings should be equal to the earnings by a guaranteed day rate system.

5.23. INCENTIVE PLANS

Now let us discuss some of the important incentive wage payment systems, which are in practice.

5.23.1. Halsey Plan

This incentive plan originated by F.A. Halsey (USA) to encourage the workers to use their skill effectively while guaranteeing them wages according to time basis. The standard time required to do the job is determined scientifically by using the work-study. When that is not possible, standard time for the work is set depending on the previous records or experience. When a worker does the work earlier than the standard time, he is paid a bonus for the time saved. In case worker takes more than the standard time, he is not punished, but paid wages on the basis of time rate system. In case the standard time for the work is fixed on the previous experience or from the previous records, then the total earnings of a worker who finishes his work earlier than that of standard time is equal to ***wages for the time he spent on the work plus 33 ½ percent of money value of the time saved***. In case the standard time set on the basis of work-study, the earnings of the worker will be equal to the ***time wages for the time spent on the job plus 50 % of the money value of the time saved.***

Problem 5.4.

The time wages of a worker is ₹ 2/- per hour. The standard time set for the work is 10 hours. Calculate the wages earned by the worker under following conditions.

(i) Earnings of a worker when he takes 10 hours to do the job.

(ii) Earnings of the worker, when the standard time is set by previous experience and the worker complete his work in 8 hours.

(iii) When the time standard is set by work-study and the worker completes his work in 8 hours.

Solution:

Data: Hourly rate = ₹ 2/- per hour. Standard time = 10 hours.

(i) Time taken by the worker = 10 hours. Hence the wages = 2 × 10 = ₹ 20/-.

(ii) Time taken by the worker = 8 hours. Time set by previous experience.

Hence the wages = Time taken × Hourly rate + 33½ % money value of time saved. As time saved = 2 hours. Wages = 8 × 2 + 33½ % × 2 × 2 = 16 + 33½ % × 4 = 16 + 1.34 = ₹ 17.34.

(iii) When the time is set by work-study the wages of the worker = Time wage for 8 hours + 50% of money value of time saved.

$$= 8 \times 2 + 0.50 \times 2 \times 2 = 16 + 2 = ₹\ 18/-.$$

A slightly modified version of the above method, which was adopted at M/s Weir Engineering Works of Britain, is known as ***Halsey-Weir Plan***. According to this plan, the bonus is 30% of money value of time saved. The wages of a worker according to this system in the above problem is equal to

$$8 \times 2 + 0.30 \times 2 \times 2 = 16 + 0.30 \times 4 = 16 + 1.20 = ₹\ 17.20.$$

Advantages or merits of this system are:

- It assures time rate wages for the worker for the time spent on the work and he has a sense of guaranteed wages and security.
- A bonus is given to efficient workers depending on the time saved by them. This gives encouragement to workers to earn more.
- When a worker finishes the first job early and takes more time for the second job, his earnings are calculated separately i.e. his wages for the first work is time wages for the time spent plus bonus for the time saved. His wages for the second work is time wages for the time taken. The time saved on one job is not adjusted against the extra time taken on the second job. Both are treated separately.
- When time set on scientific basis, the wages of the time spent is shared equally between the worker and the management. When the time set by previous experience, a greater share is given to the management.
- The wage calculation is easy and the worker can calculate his earnings without any difficulty and there is no room for misunderstanding and bickering on this score.
- As the scheme gives more importance for the time saved rather than the increase output, there will be no resistance from the workers side, because the worker gets the time wages for the time spent and the reward for the time saved.

The main disadvantage/criticism of this system is that the time is saved by the worker because of his efficiency and his effort and hence, the larger share of the benefit of the time saved must go to worker but only 50% is given to him rather than more than 50%. Here the argument is if the worker alone is responsible for the time saved the above statement will hold good. But management will argue that it is because of the good facilities, tools, equipment provided by the management may also contribute much for the worker's efficiency. Hence, there is justice in sharing the benefit equally by both the worker and the management. Another drawback of this method is that the worker to earn higher bonus, may work very lastly, without caring for the quality of the job and wastage of material. Hence management argues that there must be a check on the quality of the work done by the worker while due consideration is given to the efficiency of the worker.

This method is suitable where the time for the work is standardized by the application of work-study or where the job is standardized.

5.23.2. Rowan Incentive Plan

James Rowan of M/s David Rowan and Sons, Glasgow, England has introduced this scheme in 1901 and is very popular in England. In this system also the time required by a job is fixed scientifically before hand. The time rate is guaranteed for the worker for the time spent on the work hence the slow workers are not punished. The fast and efficient workers are paid bonus based on the time saved. The method of calculating the bonus is as follows. One important difference between Halsey plan and this plan is here the bonus earned by the worker bears a relationship with both time taken and the standard time.

Wages earned = Time spent on work × Time rate + Time saved × Time rate × (Time taken/Standard time).

Problem 5.5.

If the hourly rate is ₹ 2/- per hour and the standard time is 10 hours and the worker takes 8 hours to complete the work calculate the earnings of the worker. Also calculate the earnings when the worker takes 6 hours to complete the work. Give your comments.

Solution:

Data: Hourly rate = ₹ 2/- per hour. Standard time = 10 hours. Time taken = 8 hours.

Wages earned = 8 × 2 + 2 × 2 (8/10) = 16 + 4 × 0.8 = 16 + 3.20 = ₹ 19.20.

When the worker takes 6 hours the time saved is 4 hours.

Hence the wages earned = 2 × 6 + 4 × (6/10) × 2

= 12 + 0.60 × 2 = 12 + 1.20 = ₹ 13.20.

This shows as the time saved increases, the wages earned reduces. Hence there is a check on the worker to see that he also cares for quality of the work.

Advantages and Disadvantages of the System

As the time taken reduces the 'time saved increases and the bonus which depends on the ratio of time taken and the standard time, goes on reducing. This will definitely have check on the worker's performance. As the bonus decreases it saves much time, then he will be in right time to produce the quality goods. More efficient workers are not benefited from this system. If the worker saves, say whole of his time (an impossible case), his bonus is zero. But this system will have a check on the performance of the worker. The calculation of bonus is somewhat not straightforward to be understandable by uneducated workers. The workers may have suspicious look on the management.

5.23.3. Taylor's Differential Piece Wage Plan

Fredric Winslow Taylor (F.W. Taylor), father of scientific management and founder of Work measurement (Time Study) has devised this plan in the year 1880. He was against to the payment of wages based on the time rate i.e. under his system there is no guarantee of wages earned by the worker depending on the time spent on the work. Taylor is of the opinion that a worker's output and performance can be fixed accurately and correctly by the application of time study. Under Taylor's system, standard of output can be fixed per hour or per day and the piece rate is also fixed. The system works as under:

When the worker exceeds the standard or just attains it he is paid a higher piece rate of wages. When the worker fails to attain the standard, he is paid a lower piece rate system. Let us say for example, that standard fixed per day is 10 units (a day of 8 hours is considered) and the piece rate is Re.1/- per piece when the worker does not attain the standard and ₹ 1.25 when he exceeds the standard. When the worker produces 10 units are greater than

10 units, he will get the wages at a rate of ₹ 1.25 per piece. And if he produces less than 10 units, say 9 units, he will be paid at the rate of ₹ 1/- per unit. This makes the worker to work hard to produce the standard fixed i.e. 10 units. Once he produces 10 units, he is entitled for full piece rate and he will get the full rate even if he produces more than the standard fixed. He and the management as in the case of other incentive schemes do not share the extra earning.

Critical Review of Taylor's Method

This method distinguishes between efficient worker and inefficient workers by fixing a penalty for slow and inefficient worker. The standard of work is fixed scientifically by the application of work-study techniques. Work environment and conditions are standardized, so as to make an above average worker to attain standard. It encourages high standard of performance. The most important thing is that if the system is adopted in any industrial concern for sometime, it will automatically weed out inefficiency in workers. It is argued that the system is too harsh for relatively slow workers. The penalty for attaining less than the standard set, even one unit less than the standard set will be heavy and it creates frustrations in workers. There is no guaranteed wages for the worker and hence no security. Even for efficient workers the system does not provide any extraordinary benefits and simply treat them as cog in the wheel. It gives no concern if the reduction in worker's output is due to illness of the worker or due to bad working conditions. The trade union will not accept such system because it may create difference between workers and lead to industrial unrest. But this method has become a basis for many incentive schemes, which provide bonus on output rather than the time saved.

5.23.4. Merrick Differential or Multiple Piece-Rate Incentive Plan

Merrick Differential Piece rate Incentive plan is an extension to Tailor's Differential Piece Wage Plan. Here Taylor's plan is modified. The difference is that the Taylor's plan prescribes two wage rates i.e. one for the slow workers and the other for efficient workers. Merrick Plan prescribes three-piece rates. They are first one for the beginners, the second one for developing workers and the third one for highly skilled and efficient workers. In this method also like Taylor's plan the standards are set by scientific methods and also provide scientifically set work environment, so as to enable that above average worker will be in a position to attain the standard. The wage standards set by this method are: (a) No guaranteed time wage for the time spent in the factory. (b) Those who are able to produce up to 83% of the standard output becomes eligible for the lowest wage rate. (c) Those workers who have their output reached above 83% of the standard set but not reach the standard are entitled for the second wage rate set which includes a 10% increase in first wage rate, (d) Those who attain or exceeds the standards set, will get the third rate set, which includes further 10% increase in wages (standard set). Let us take for example, the standard set is 100 pieces per day of 8 hours, and the wage rate fixed is ₹ 1.00 per piece.

(a) If the worker produces less than 83 pieces, he will get ₹ 1.00/- per unit. Say if produces 78 pieces, he will get his wages as per the first wage rate, i.e. He will get ₹ 78/- as his wages for the day.

(b) If the worker produces 83 pieces or more than 83 pieces but less than 100 pieces he will get his wage as per the second wage rate, i.e. 10% hike in his wage rate i.e. he will get at ₹ 1.10 per piece. Say he completes 90 pieces; his wages will be ₹ 1.10 × 90 = ₹ 99/-.

(c) If the worker produces 100 or above 100 pieces he will get his wages with an additional increase in piece rate, i.e. his piece rate is ₹ 1.20 per pieces. Say he completes 105 pieces. His wages = 105 × ₹ 1.20 = ₹ 126/-.

Critical View

This method also distinguishes the workers and workers will feel frustrated when they earn less and this aspect may lead to industrial dispute. Trade unions will not accept this method whole-heartedly. But one thing we notice in this method is there is no sudden increase of wages between efficient and inefficient workers. Considerations are given to beginners. This method also if adopted, will weed out inefficient workers.

5.23.5. Emerson's Efficiency Plan

Emerson was also belonging to school of scientific management thought. He devised this incentive plans to encourage the efficient workers and not punish slow and inefficient workers. In this system there is a guaranteed time rate system. So for the workers, whose output is less than the standard set there is no punishment as they get the wages for the time spent on the work. For workers who produce more than the standard set or up to the standard set, will get a bonus. In this system, the standards for measuring efficiency are set scientifically. This may be set basing the time basis or basing the output basis. This is to say that either a standard time per piece is fixed or number of pieces to be produced per hour is fixed scientifically. The actual performance is compared with the standard performance set and the bonus is paid accordingly. The details of the system are:

(a) If the efficiency of a worker is less than 66 2/3% no bonus is paid to the worker.

(b) At an efficiency of 66 2/3%, a bonus of 1% is paid on the wages calculated on time rate basis.

(c) Bonus increases with the increase in the efficiency. At 90% efficiency, the bonus is 10% on the time rate and at 100% efficiency, the bonus will be 20% of the wage and above 100% efficiency, the bonus rate will be 30% of the wage earned on time basis.

Problem 5.6.

If the standard set per day of 8 hours is 100 pieces and the time rate per day is ₹ 30 per day, calculate wages earned by the worker as Emerson plan when he produces:

(a) He produces 55 pieces.

(b) When he produces 70 pieces.

(c) When he produces 100 pieces.

(d) When he produces 110 pieces.

Solution:

(a) When worker produces 55 pieces. His efficiency is less than $66\frac{2}{3}$ %. Hence, he is not entitled for any bonus. He will get time rate wage i.e. ₹ 30/-.

(b) When the worker produces 70 pieces, his efficiency is greater than $66\frac{2}{3}$ % hence his wages is Time rate wage + 10 percent bonus. ₹ 30 + 0.10 × 30 = ₹ 33/-.

(c) When the worker produces 100 pieces, his efficiency is 100 percent. Hence his wages will be Time rate wage + 20 percent of bonus. ₹ 30/- + 0.20 × 30 = ₹ 36/-.

(d) When the worker produces 110 pieces, his efficiency is greater than 100% hence his wages will be Time rate wage + 30 percent of bonus. ₹ 30/- + 0.30 × 30 = ₹ 39/-.

Advantages

It gives encouragement to the workers to increase their efficiency to earn more. It takes care of beginners and gives guarantee for their daily earnings and gives them security. This will definitely encourage the beginners to increase their efficiency. The calculation of efficiency in this method is simple and logical and can be used as fair basis to calculate the incentives for efficient workers. This method may be employed to individual worker of a group of workers as well.

Demerits

People argue that the bonus over and above standard efficiency fixed is very meager. Hence sometimes workers may be tempted to limit their efficiency at 100 percent.

5.23.6. Gantt's Task and Bonus Plan

H.L. Gantt a close associate of F.W. Taylor devised this method. This is basically piece rate system with a guarantee of time rate. The efficiency is calculated as in Emerson's plan. In this plan, if the efficiency of the worker is less than 100 percent, no bonus is paid and only guaranteed time rate is given to him. If the efficiency is 100 percent, then worker will be paid the guaranteed time rate plus a bonus of 20 percent on the wages earned. If the efficiency exceeds 100 percent then the worker is paid piece rate system rather than time basis wage.

Problem 5.7.

The time fixed for the work is 8 hours and the hourly rate fixed is ₹ 10 per hour and the piece rate fixed is ₹110/- Calculate the earnings of the worker when he (a) Takes 10 hours to complete the work, (b) Takes 8 hours to complete the work, (c) Takes 7 hours to complete the work.

Solution:

(a) When worker takes 10 hours. As the method guarantees the time rate his wages will be 10 hrs. × ₹ 10/- = ₹ 100/-.

(b) When worker takes 8 hours, his efficiency is 100%, hence his wages will be ₹ 10 × 8 + 0.20 × 80 = 80 + 16 = ₹ 96/-.

(c) When the worker takes 7 hours, his efficiency is greater than 100 percent, hence he is paid pieced rate for his work i.e. His wages = ₹ 110/-.

Merits

- The method is simple, easily understandable by the workers. Can be easily introduced in the organization and convince the unions.
- It gives security to workers, by guaranteeing the time rate and also for efficient workers it provides bonus. This method encourages workers to increase their efficiency. For really worthy worker, by fixing piece rate system, it does justice to highly skilled labour.
- This method encourages a better supervision to see that obstacles for the worker are removed and a more convenient working atmosphere is provided so that worker

earns more by increasing his efficiency. Foreman is also given incentive depending on the (proportional to) bonus earned by the workers under him.

- Workers are well satisfied under this system as they have security and due considerations are given to their efficiency.
- When the overheads are high, this system helps the employer to spread the overheads on the large number of jobs produced by the workers, to keep unit price of the object under control.
- Gantt has recommended special training to the beginners to improve their efficiency to earn more.

Demerits

The proverb that all accepts no method and no method is rejected by all holds good here. Every group of people has their own interest. If any method is against to their interest, then they find fault of the method or the system. It is quite natural. As fare Gantt's scheme of incentives the argument is as the time rate is guaranteed, the workers may not show interest in increasing the productivity, which is a negative element for the management. This is particularly true, when higher time rate is fixed under the pressure of labour unions.

5.23.7. Bedeaux Point Premium Plan

In this method, the time required to do a job is fixed scientifically before the job is allocated to the workers. Here the time expressed in ***standard B's.*** Each B is equivalent to one minute. Thus, if a job requires one hour to complete it is expressed as 60 B's. One more difference here is that both worker and the foreman share the bonus earned by the worker by saving the time. The idea here is that the worker and the supervision of the foreman is responsible for good and quality work. Hence both the worker and the foreman share the bonus. 75% of the bonus on the time saved goes to worker and 25% of bonus goes to foreman. The standard B's of various jobs completed by the worker in a given time is added and compared with the standard B's set by the management, i.e. the actual time taken is compared with the standard time. If the actual time exceeds the standard time set the worker gets wages on the time basis. Here time wages of the worker is guaranteed. If the standard B's exceeds the actual time taken, the difference is divided by 60 to give standard hours saved and then 75% of the wages of the time saved goes to the worker concerned and 25% to the foreman.

Problem 5.8.

A worker completes four works in a week. The standard time set for job is expressed in standard B's in the table below. If the hourly wages of the worker is ₹ 5.00 and the actual time taken by the worker is as given in the table calculate the earnings by the worker and the incentive for foreman as per Bedeaux premium plan.

Solution:

S. No. of the Job	Standard Time in Hours	Standard Time in B's	Actual Time in B's	Time Saved by Worker
1	8	480	400	80
2	10	600	580	20

Contd....

S. No. of the Job	Standard Time in Hours	Standard Time in B's	Actual Time in B's	Time Saved by Worker
3	6	360	360	–
4	8	480	450	30
Total	32	1920	1790	130

Time saved by the worker = 130 B's. = 130/60 = 1.625.

The worker's hourly wages = ₹ 5.00, then the worker's wages

= Time rate for the time spent on the work + 75% of the wages of the time saved.

= 1790/60 = 29.83 × ₹ 5

= ₹ 149.17 + 0.75 × 130/60 × 5 = ₹ 8.125

The wages = ₹ 28.83 + ₹ 8.125 = ₹ 36.96 = ₹ 37.00

Foreman's incentive = 0.25 × 130/60 × 5 = ₹ 2.70.

Critical Review

Though the plan guarantees the time wages and the bonus for the worker for the time saved, the drawback of the method is the fixation of time and calculation of time. Worker do not know how time is fixed and what a B is. At the same time the foreman shares the time saved by him in the form of bonus. This may displease the worker. But much depends on the attitude of the worker.

5.23.8. Hayne's Plan

This is very much similar to Bedeaux point system. Here the standard time for a job is fixed scientifically. Especially for work of repetitive nature, the time is fixed scientifically. If the job is of non-repetitive type, i.e. the process required to do the job does not re-occur and then the time is fixed by estimation. The time set is expressed in terms of **MANITS.** Manits is the short form of **MAN-MINUTES**. In this plan, the time basis wage is guaranteed. The worker is paid his time wages for the time he spends on the work. The procedure for bonus calculation is as follows:

(a) Find the total mantis spent by the worker on the job. Divide the total mantis by 60 to convert into hours. This will give us the time spent by the worker on the job.

(b) Add the standard mantis of the jobs to get the standard time set for the jobs. Divide it by 60 to get the time in hours.

(c) Calculate the difference between standard time and actual time. This will give us time saved by the worker or the excess time taken by the worker.

(d) If the actual time taken by the worker is more then the worker will get his wages as per time rate for the time spent on the jobs.

(e) If the worker has taken less time than the standards manits, then time saved is calculated and converted into hours by dividing by 60.

(f) The wages earned by the worker = Wages for the time spent on the job as per time rate + Bonus or incentive.

(g) The incentive is calculated as follows:

- If the work is standardized, i.e. the repetitive type work and the time set scientifically, then 5/6 of the wages of the time saved will go to worker and 1/6 will goes to foreman. The foreman's share is credited into a fund, where as the worker is paid incentive in cash.

If the worker is non-standardized, the bonus is divided as under:

(i) 5/10 wages of time saved to the worker,

(ii) 1/10 of the wages of the times saved by the worker to the foreman,

(iii) 4/10 of the wages of the time saved to the management.

Here the bonus payable to the foreman is credited into a fund. If the worker looses time due to the fault of the foreman, then the incentive due to the worker is given from this fund (i.e. the worker has to be paid for the idle time from the fund).

- No manits are credited to the worker for a product that does not pass inspection.

Critical review

The calculation of bonus is cumbersome. Maintenance of fund of the foreman and calculation of incentive is complicated. Worker will get a doubt about the system. The time calculation in manits is also confusion. In general, trade unions will oppose the system. But one advantage is the time rate wage is guaranteed for the worker for the spent on the job.

Problem 5.9.

Calculate the earnings of a worker, foreman and the management under the following conditions:

Job is standardized and the standard manits is 480 manits. Hourly rate is ₹ 10/-. The time taken by the worker is 420 minutes.

Also calculate the bonus when the job is not standardized.

Solution:

When the job is standardized:

Standard time	= 480/60 = 8 hours
Time taken by the worker	= 420/60 = 7 hours
Time saved	= 480 – 420 = 60 manits = 60/60 = 1 hour
Incentive for worker	= 5/6 × 1 × ₹ 10/- = ₹ 50/6 = ₹ 8.35
Wages	= 7 hours × ₹ 10 + ₹ 8.35 = ₹ 78.35
Bonus for the foreman	= 1/6 × 1 × 10 = 10/6
	= ₹ 1.65 which is credited to a fund.

When the work is not standardized:

Earnings of the worker	= time wages for 7 hours + 5 /10 of wage of time saved
	= 7 hrs × 10 + 0.5 × 1 hr × 10 = 70 + 5 = ₹ 75.00
Incentive for foreman	= 1/10 × 1 hr × ₹ 10 = ₹ 1.00
Incentive for management	= 4/10 × 1 hr × ₹ 10/- = ₹ 4.00

5.23.9. Priestman Bonus System

In this system individual efficiency of the worker is not considered. But the overall increase or decrease in efficiency is taken into consideration to decide the incentive to workers. Productivity of the unit/factory/organization is considered for deciding the quantum of incentive and not the individual efficiency of the worker. Say for example the present year's productivity is 12% higher than the previous years productivity or this year's output raises above the standard output set by the management, say that the standard output per worker is 10 units per hour and at the end of the day/week/month/the standard output is slightly higher than the standard put of 10 units, say 11 units (a 10% increase), then the worker's wages is also increased by same proportion. If the output is below the standard set, then the time wage is guaranteed. The standards of work are to be set scientifically.

Critical Review

In this method, individual efficiency is not considered; hence the workers may not show interest in increasing the productivity. But they know, that there is benefit from increased productivity hence they may contribute their efforts to increase the productivity.

Problem 5.10.

In the year 2000 the production of an organization was 2000 units per year. With the same resources, the company has produced 2,200 units in the year 2001. Suppose the wages of a worker is ₹ 50/- per day what will be the wages of that worker in the year 2001.

Solution:

Increase in productivity = Production in 2001 – Production in 2000
(Same resources are used)
= 2,200 – 2000 = 200 units

Increase in productivity = (200/2000) × 100 = 10 percent

Hence the wages of the worker = ₹ 50.00 + 10% of ₹ 50 = ₹ 55.00 per day.

5.23.10. Barth Variable Sharing Plan

In this plan there is no guarantee of time rate. It is very much similar to Halsey and Rowan plan. Here the wages are calculated as per the formula given below:

$$\text{Wages of a worker} = \sqrt{\text{Standard hours} \times \text{Actual hours} \times \text{Rate per hour.}}$$

Here the wages of the worker rises steeply at a decreasing rate. This method is suitable for the learners. It can be used to encourage less skilled workers. This method is not suitable where highly skilled workers are working and the management wants to increase the productivity of skilled workers.

Problem 5.11.

The time set for a job is 8 hours. But the worker will complete the work in 7 hours. The hourly rate of the worker is ₹ 10/- find the wages of the worker as per Bart Variable sharing system. Suppose the worker completes the work in 6 hours what is his wage.

Solution:

$$\text{Wages} = \sqrt{8 \times 7 \times 10} = 7.6 \times 10 = ₹\ 76/-$$

When the worker completes the work in 6 hours the wages = $\sqrt{8 \times 6 \times 10}$

$$= 6.9 \times 10 = ₹\ 69/-$$

5.23.11. Group Incentive Plans

All the incentive plans discussed above are the incentive schemes applicable to individuals. There are some works, which are completed by a group of workers. Say for example construction of a house or laying of a road, where many people are involved in completing the work. In case they complete the work well before the standard time set, then an incentive is to be paid to the group or workers. This type of incentive payment is known as ***Group incentive payment.*** Group incentive plans are designed to motivate the workers to work efficiently in completing a work by a group of workers. One drawback of this method is all the workers of the group receive the incentive on the same basis; even some of the workers do not contribute their effort in completing the work before the time set. Hence sometimes group incentive scheme may have adverse effect on the morale of the workers. But one must be careful enough while designing the group incentive plans. Many a time fixing a piece rate for the entire job for all the workers does it, we can avoid trouble. Then care should be taken to divide the piece rate bonus of the job among the members depending on the skill shown by the worker and the time devoted by an individual. The procedure of calculating earnings of a worker is as follows:

(a) First calculate the wages depending on the time basis system.

(b) Divide the extra group bonus, which is earned by the group among the workers (members of the group), in the ratio of their time wages.

Critical review

This method is suitable where the work is done by a group of workers. As the group shares the incentive, even inefficient workers also get incentive. This may have adverse effect on the morale of the efficient workers. As the piece rate is fixed for the entire job and the difference between total wage of all workers calculated on time basis and the piece rate is treated as bonus and is shared by the members of the group in their ratio of their earned time wages, this may do some justice to efficient workers.

Problem 5.12.

Four workers, A, B, C and D, do a job. Their hourly wages are ₹ 15, 12, 10 and ₹ 8/- respectively. The piece rate fixed to the work is ₹ 600/-. If the time spent by the workers is A and B spends 10 hours on the job and C and D spends 12 hours each on the job, calculate the wages earned by the workers.

Solution:

First let us calculate the earnings of the workers on time basis. The wages of A, B, C and D on time basis are: A and B spend 10 hours on the job. Hence their earnings are:

A = ₹ 15/- × 10 = ₹ 150/-

B = ₹ 12/- × 10 = ₹ 120/-

C and D spends 12 hours on the job hence their wages are:

C = ₹ 10/- × 10 = ₹ 100/-

D = ₹ 8/- × 10 = ₹ 80/-

Total time basis wages of all the members = ₹ 150 + 120 + 100 + 80 = ₹ 450/-

But the piece rate fixed for the job is ₹ 600/-, Hence the extra amount that should be considered as bonus = ₹ 150/-. This amount is shared by the members in the ratio of 150:120:100:80 or 15:12:10:8. Hence the bonus of each worker is as follows:

A will get: (150/450) × 150 = ₹ 50.00
B will get: (120/450) × 150 = ₹ 40.00
C will get: (100/450) × 150 = ₹ 33.35
D will get: (80/450) × 150 = ₹ 26.65

Total wages of A = ₹ 150 + 50 = 200, Wages of B = ₹ 120 + 40 = 160. Wages of C = ₹ 100 + 33.35 = ₹ 133.35 and wages of D = ₹ 80 + 26.65 = ₹ 106.65.

5.23.12. The Scanlon Plan

This is a popular plan devised by Mr. Joseph Scanlon of United Steel Works of U.S.A. This plan aims at sharing the gains from the improved productivity. Scanlon and his associates argue that the formula for bonus and wage payment should be based on the conditions exists on the shop floor. But the plan is well implemented in Lapointe Machine Tool Company. According to this plan, all the employees covered by this plan will get 1% of participating bonus for every 1% increase in productive efficiency. All employees excepting the top management will share the bonus. Thus the lower level managers like, supervisors, foremen, engineers have a recognized part in the plan. The operation of the plan is as follows. The workers who were on piece rate basis are guaranteed time rate wage plus the bonus (incentive earnings). One half of the first 15% of any bonus earned in any month is set aside as reserve fund. The reserve fund thus pooled up is to be used to meet fluctuations in labour costs. Any *unused portion* of this reserve by November of a given year is paid out in December and a new reserve fund is created for future operations.

5.23.13. Profit Sharing

Now a day the word ***Profit Sharing*** has become so popular in industrial scene in democratic countries. Moreover Profit Sharing has become very popular than any other group incentive plans of labour remuneration. As far as economically concerned, the profit is the compensation for the entrepreneur or the owner of the organization for the risk taken by him in organizing the unit. As per the profit sharing plan, profit is no more considered as the exclusive right of the capitalist. The workers are considered as the partners in an enterprise and therefore, a share of the profit made by the concern with their active co-operation is considered to be their rightful due. In this system, workers are paid a share in the profit over and above the wages earned by them. In fact *"Profit sharing is a method of industrial remuneration under which an employer undertakes to pay his employees a share in the* ***net profits*** *of the enterprise, in addition to their* ***regular wages.*** This means any bonus or gratuity paid by the employer at his own discretion will not be included in profit sharing. Profit sharing is neither based on time basis wages or piece rate wages it should be distinguished from the method of wage/ incentive payment discussed earlier. ***In true sense it is a form of added remuneration.*** The share of the profit that is to be given to the workers is decided well before the profits are calculated and distributed. While introducing this plan, the management has to face certain problems or difficulties. They are:

(a) It has to decide *on what basis the profit is to be shared* i.e. whether in the ratio of the wages of the labour? Or whether depending on the results produced by the worker etc.

- ***Individual basis***: Whether the worker individually may be paid that share of the profit, which the unit has earned due to his effort.
- ***Unit basis***: Here the workers working in each particular industrial unit share the profit earned by the unit. Here the efforts of workers and management are considered while deciding the distribution of the profit.
- ***Departmental basis***: Here the profit earned due to the efforts of a particular department is considered and the workers working in the department will share the profit of that department.
- ***Locality basis***: Here the profit of all the industrial units is pooled up and then the workers and the management of all the units share it. But this is very difficult to decide the contribution of each unit because different types of industrial units may be functioning in that area.
- ***Industry basis***: In this method, all the profits earned by the units of a particular industry (for example: Textile, Jute, Paints industries) are pooled up and is shared by the employers (Management) and the labours of the industry. Even if one particular unit make no profit or under loss, the workers of that unit will not be made to suffer. But the drawback is that they are sharing the profit of other units.
- ***Industry cum locality basis***: Here the profits earned by a particular industry in a particular area are considered and they are pooled up and shared by the workers and management of various units of that industry in that area. Though there are various methods of profit sharing, the best method is, the workers and the management of an industrial unit must share the profits of a particular unit in which they are working.

(b) ***Ascertaining the net profit***: The divisible profit is to be decided correctly and well in advance. The profits are generally calculated on commercial basis. Here one has to decide provision is to be made to meet interest on capital, depreciation on reserves. Also decision is to be taken to charge revenue items to profit or not (revenue items like: debenture interest, income-tax and dividend of preference shares etc.).

(c) ***Fixing the share of profit to be given to workers***: The share of the profit that is to be shared by the workers is to be decided well in advance and announced. The best method of sharing is the profit is divided in the ratio of *total capital invested and the total wage bill of the unit*. It is understood that if this rule is followed, the management will get ¾ share of the profit, while the workers will get ¼ share. When there is a loss, very rarely it is shared. Many a time losses are not shared at all.

(d) ***Deciding individual worker's share***: Once the worker's share of the profit is decided, now management has to decide how that should share is to be distributed among individual workers. Various methods are adopted to distribute the money.

They are:

(i) Length of service may be taken as a measure.

(ii) Wages earned by the worker may be taken as basis of distribution.

(iii) Productivity and attendance may be taken as the basis of distribution.

(iv) Number of hours worked may be taken as a measure to distribute the amount.

(v) *Form of distribution*: The money share of the profit that is to be given to the worker may be given to the worker in a suitable form, which must be helpful to him.

- ***Cash***: The amount due to him may be paid in the form of cash. Unions and workers accept this method and this is the most common and easy and simple way of distribution of the share.
- ***Transfer of worker's share to pension or provident fund***: Many a time, employer wishes to credit the share of profit of an employee to his provident fund or pension account. The disadvantage is worker cannot use the money immediately. It will not fulfil his immediate needs. One advantage is that, if money is given immediately, worker spends on luxuries and spends money without thinking of future. The need for money in old age will be much. If he saves the share of profit in his provident fund or pension account, the money along with the interest will be available to him in his old age. If it is in provident fund account, he can take loan when need arises. Many a time all will like immediate cash disbursement.
- ***Cash and Shares***: Here workers share of profit is partly paid in cash and partly by means of bonus shares, which will earn dividend, by this; workers will become shareholders of the company and becomes partners of the company. This makes the workers to commit more to their work and they have feeling that they are working in their own unit. They will have a voice in management affairs and hence they behave more responsible and extend their co-operation for the welfare of the unit. This type of share distribution by shares is also known as ***co-partnership***. And this co-partnership is a viable solution or a means to avoid much of the industrial problems between management and the workers.

Advantages of Profit Sharing

- ***Increased productivity***: Profit sharing creates in workers the awareness and desire to work wholeheartedly for the organization to increase the profit. It is because, as the profit of the organization increases, their share of bonus also increases. They voluntarily try to arrest the cost of production by avoiding wastage of productive resources and try to increase the productivity.
- ***Improved industrial relations***: Profit sharing is a means to avoid much of the industrial problems. By introducing the profit sharing, the misunderstandings between management and the labour class is reduced and both try to co-operate each other to increase the profit, by increasing the productivity.
- ***Increased earnings of worker***: Through profit sharing, worker will get economical stability as it gives additional earnings. As his earnings will be increased when the profit rises, he voluntarily contributes to the material welfare of the company.

- ***Stabilization of labour force***: For sharing the profit, labour must have a minimum experience and stayed with the company for a long time. If the worker leaves the company in the middle, he looses the claim of his share in the profit. Hence this may motivate the workers to continue with the company, thus labour turnover can be drastically reduced, which promotes labour force stabilization.
- ***Improved supervision and administration***: As the workers will get a share in the profit, they co-operate with the management and to try to build up their work morale and do not need strict supervision. Even with mild supervision, they can maintain quality and increase productivity. Because of the co-operation of the workers and their high work morale, standards of administration will be of higher standards.
- ***Realization of social justice***: Profit sharing promotes some measure of social justice by relating the worker's earnings to the financial position of the company. If a portion of profit distributed as a bonus share, their social status is increased and they can identify themselves with the company. In fact, profit sharing is a step towards equitable distribution of income between the two major components of the society i.e. *labours force and the capitalists.*

Disadvantages of Profit Sharing

- ***Concept of profit***: Basically, profit sharing is not well founded because the availability of capital and the efforts of labour force are not only the causes of profit. Profit is a function of effort of management, market conditions and demand for the product, location aspects and host of others, which are beyond the control of employees. Profit sharing does not maintain any relationship between effort and reward, because, in some years, the workers might have contributed sincerely but due to market conditions and competitions, the profits may show declining trend. In such times it may have adverse effect on the morale of the workers.
- ***Profit sharing does not distinguish between efficient and inefficient workers***: As all workers are covered by the scheme, both efficient and inefficient workers will be benefited. In this sense, the efficient workers may get frustrated. When profit sharing is done by industry basis, the less efficient workers working in less prosperous company may get benefit whereas the efficient workers working in a prosperous company may feel that other workers share their effort who are not really worth for a share in the profit.
- ***Time of payment of share***: The reward for the work if paid immediately after work i.e. either weekly or monthly it will have more meaning and usefulness to the working class. But in profit sharing, the reward is given either half yearly or yearly. That is reward comes to the worker after a long time after the utilization of his efforts. The reward he gets will not have desired effect.
- ***Disadvantages during depression period***: During the years, when the sales are showing decline trend, the profit may reach its low or sometimes losses may occur. In such situation, either the share of the profit is very meager or there may not be any share. This may cause dissatisfaction in working class. They may suspect management and do not co-operate in developmental activities. This may not

be the case always. There are persons in working class who can understand the situation and may cooperate with the management in growth activities. But if we have workers who change their mind according to the share of the profit, the profit sharing may itself become a cause for industrial disputes.

- ***Decision regarding the share of the profit to be distributed to workers***: Deciding the actual profit earned and the share that is to be distributed to the workers may pose number of problems. Workers may suspect the management as far as accounts and the calculation of profit is concerned. Sometimes deliberately the management may try to adjust the accounts to show low profits. Even the management is honest; unions may create a problem and make labour class unrest.
- ***Attitude of trade unions***: Trade unions may strongly oppose the profit sharing stating that it is a deliberate capitalistic move to create disunity in the working classes. Workers of industrial units, which are making good profit, may not like to join the trade union and may not react with trade union movements.
- ***Employer's attitude***: Sometimes employers do not fully accept the basic principles underlying profit sharing. Their argument is that the profit is a reward for the risk of the promoters and it must come to them only and it is illegal to share with the employees, who are paid wages according to certain agreement. If profit is to be shared, why not losses at the time of depression period. The argument from the labour side is that they cannot share losses from the wages they are getting.

Conclusion

But one thing we have to remember, for any system to be successful, all the parties involved must sit together and decide about the implementation of an incentive plan. The discussion must be made from all angles of humanitarian considerations. Let us now ask some questions to ourselves to judge whether the profit sharing scheme is really a worthy scheme to both the working class and the management?

(i) Can profit sharing be used to increase the efficiency and the output of the workers?

In fact profit sharing scheme helps the workers to earn more not due to their efficiency or increase of individual output. But the incentive is due to overall increase in the productivity. Both efficient and inefficient workers are treated alike. This may hurt the feelings of efficient and hard working workers. But if the incentive given in the form of shares, then the working class will become the partners of the organization and they may feel more responsible and feel own ness in the company and put all their effort to increase the productivity. They work for their welfare and not for the welfare of the capitalists. This is a right attitude desired from the working class. Though people argue that the incentive comes to the worker after a long time and the inefficient workers are also equally considered the method has got its own advantages and also limitations. For any method to be successful it should be understood well by all the parties involved and cooperate with each other with right attitude for the success of the plan.

(ii) Will profit sharing really promotes industrial peace?

No doubt if profit sharing implemented in its true sense, it definitely promote industrial piece. In fact workers attitude towards management and management's attitude towards workers should properly be oriented and negative view of each class should be eliminated. The profit calculation and workers share in it should be clearly defined well before, so that there will be no scope for manipulation. If profit sharing is not implemented properly, it becomes first cause of industrial disputes. Moreover trade unions view is very important. Once the workers become owners of the company the hold of unions will become diluted. If unions also think in right sense, then really profit sharing will help for the betterment of working class.

(iii) Will profit sharing promote industrial democracy?

Mere profit sharing cannot promote industrial democracy. Unless workers are given co-partnership and take part in decision-making process, we cannot say that there is industrial democracy. Of course there are some industries, which are successful where workers are co-partners and take part in decision-making. Simple profit sharing cannot bring industrial democracy. Until active participation of workers is introduced, the profit sharing will simply remain as an incentive scheme and nothing more.

To conclude, we can say that an incentive scheme must provide

- Guaranteed time rate.
- Incentive depending on the output.
- Profit sharing at the end of the year.

5.24. RECOMMENDATIONS OF BONUS COMMISSION

To decide the quantum of bonus, modus of payment etc. Government of India has appointed a commission in the year December 1961. In its report the commission has recommended the following recommendations:

- A minimum of 4 percent of worker's total annual wages including dearness allowances be paid as bonus in all industrial employments;
- The maximum limit of bonus of an industrial worker is fixed at 20 percent of his annual earnings.
- That a 7 percent return on capital and 4% of reserve funds be provided out of profits before calculating bonus;
- The bonus should constitute 60 percent of the balance of profits after providing the depreciation, taxes and returns on the capital and that the remaining 40 percent of the balance of profits should go to the employers.

5.25. PAYMENT OF BONUS ACT 1965

The Government of India after accepting major recommendations of the commission the bill is passed in the parliament and made an act known as **Payment of Bonus Act 1965.** An ordinance by president was signed on 20th May 1965. The provisions of the Act may be listed as below:

- The provisions of the Act apply to every factory irrespective of the number of employees and to other establishments employing twenty or more persons in India except Jammu and Kashmir.

- An employee who has been in employment for not less than 30 days in the particular year and drawing ₹ 1,600 is eligible for payment of bonus. However, earnings of ₹ 750/- per month or more will be taken as ₹ 750/- only for bonus calculation.
- Every employer is bound to pay to every employee a minimum bonus of 4% of salary or wage earned by the employee in a year or ₹ 40/- (₹ 25/- in case of persons under 15 years) which ever is higher, irrespective of the availability of profits. The minimum amount of bonus that can be paid in any year out of the surplus available for allocation has been fixed at 20% of salary or wage. Salary or wage includes the basic wage rate plus dearness allowance.
- The allocation surplus for any year shall be the gross profit less prior charges including (a) remuneration for working partners and proprietors, (b) Depreciation and Development Rebate admissible under the Income Tax Act. (c) All direct taxes (d) Actual dividends payable on preference share capital and (e) A return of 8.5% on equity capital and 6% on reserves (7.5% on equity capital and 5% on reserves for banks).
- Sixty percent of the allocated surplus as determined in the above manner (67% in case of foreign companies) shall be available for bonus payment in the form of Bonus Fund.
- If allocated surplus is in excess of what is required for paying the maximum, bonus, the excess will be *set on* and added to the surplus for the succeeding lean years. On the contrary, if there is a deficiency in the Bonus Fund, it can be *set off* during the following years of relative prosperity, again, subject to a maximum period of four years.
- The provisions of the Act take effect from the accounting year commencing on any day in 1964.

The act recognizes bonus as a matter of right in the nature of deferred wage. It must be paid within eight months from the close of the accounting year.

The above provisions of the Bonus Act was reviewed and revised by the Bonus Review Committee and amendment bills are passed in the parliament subsequently.

5.26. WAGE POLICY

To have a strong nation and healthy society, a sound and rational wage policy is essential. In case we do not have a sound wage policy, exploitation of workers by the management and discontent among working class and class conflict in the society are the result. Hence it is better to have a good and sound wage policy to be followed by the industries in order to avoid evil effects.

What are Wages?

Wage is the remuneration paid to the worker for the work done by him either on time basis or on result basis. There are three types of wages to be discussed in the wage policy.

They are (a) Minimum wage, (b) Fair wage and (c) Living wage. These are broadly based on the needs of the workers and the capacity of the employers to pay as also on the general economic conditions prevailing in the country.

(a) Minimum Wage: *Minimum wage may be defined as a wage, which makes funds available to the worker for keeping his body and soul together.* The committee on fair wages regarded the minimum wage as an irreducible (minimum) amount considered necessary for the sustenance of the worker and his family and for the preservation of efficiency at work. Minimum wage is generally fixed by an agreement between the worker and the employer. But where is the guarantee that the employer fixes really, the minimum required? He may use all his best to exploit the working class. Hence generally the minimum wage is fixed by legislation. The scene in the organized and large scale industries is different, because, there will be strong trade unions, which fight for the welfare of the worker and management also yields to the demand of the unions in many cases. But unorganized industries, where there are no unions, Government has to interfere to fix the minimum wage for the workers, so that they are not exploited. While fixing the minimum wage, along with the requirement of the worker, other factors like skill needed, strain involved and capacity of the industry to pay are to be considered. It is because; sometimes the industry will not be in a position to pay the bare minimum wage required. In such cases better to closedown the industry.

(b) Fair Wage: Fair wage is another concept used in connection with wage policy. Everybody supports that fair wage is to be paid to the worker. But what is preciously the *Fair wage?* Economists explain fair wage in their own way, some of them are:

- Wages could be regarded as fair if they were the same for jobs of equal disagreeableness of unpleasantness. i.e. differences in wages in a locality could be regarded as fair only if more dangerous or disagreeable jobs fetched higher wages than others.
- There are two degrees of fairness in judgeing a wage rate. In the narrow sense, a wage rate is fair if it is equal to the rate of prevailing in the same trade and in neighbourhood for similar work. In wider sense, it will be fair if it is equal to the predominant rate for similar work throughout the country and in the generality of trades.

These concepts say that the fair wages can be fixed only by comparison with an accepted standard of wages. Such a standard can be determined with reference to those industries where labour is well organized and has been able to bargain well with the employers.

The wages tend to be unfair due to the following reasons:

- When there is excess in the supply of labour in a trade or when the labour in certain locality is not willing to move to other places to take advantage of higher wages, then the situation warns unfair wages. *Thus, the concentration of the labour and the immobility of labour cause the wage to be unfair.*
- When the labour is unorganized and cannot bargain or when the labour class is unaware of the prevailing wages of similar trades in nearby area, the wages tend to be unfair. *Thus when workers are unaware of prevailing wages and are unorganized the wage tend to be unfair.*
- When the employers in an area come to an agreement that they should not compete to get the labours or bid against other to get the labour, then the wage rates will

be unfair. *Thus agreement between the employers not to bid against one another for labour, the wage rate will be unfair.*

When the above-discussed evils are eliminated from the industrial scene, the wage rates tend to be fair.

(c) Living Wage: Living wage is higher than the fair wage, which enables the worker to provide a measure of comfort for himself and his family after meeting the essentials of life. It is wage appropriate for the normal needs of the average employee regarded as human being living in a civilized community. The living wage includes the provisions for the following: (a) Absolute essentials such as food, clothing and shelter, (b) A condition of frugal comfort according to the current human standards, (c) to meet the difficulties of evil days and (d) The special skill of an artisan if he has any. It is also described that the wage, which cannot allow a married life and maintenance of over five persons in a home cannot be regarded as living wage.

In India, several adhoc committees appointed by Sate Government and Industrial Tributes as defined the concept of living wage: *Living wage should enable the male earner to provide for himself and his family not merely the basic essentials of food, clothing and shelter but a measure of frugal comfort including.*

(i) Education for the children, (ii) Protection against ill health, (iii) Requirements of essential social needs and (iv) A measure of insurance against the more important milestone including the old age. But the concept of living wage has become unrealistic if it is altogether divorced from the economic conditions of the country. Moreover the living wage concept varies from country to country depending on the prevailing economic conditions in that country. To conclude, we can say that the fair wage may be fixed between minimum wage and living wage.

(d) Need for Wage Policy in India: Government of India felt that it is necessary to take care of large working class and their welfare by fixing a minimum wage. In 1920 it took first step to think about minimum wage for an industrial worker but could not do anything due to prevailing economic and social conditions in the country. In 1920 I.L.O adopted the draft convention on minimum wage fixing machinery. This has given strength to the working class and in 1931, which started demanding minimum wages. Payment of wages act was passed in the year 1936, which came into force from March 1937. The act was applicable to those workers whose earnings is less than ₹ 400 per month. It also said that wages to be paid within 7 days of the beginning of the month (in industries where the strength of the working class is less than 1000) and within 10 days in other cases and also said that wage interval should not exceed one month. The act also dictates that the management should not deduct any unauthorized deductions from the salary. Authorized deductions are:

- Any fines notified due to misconduct (after giving a chance for worker to show the reasons of such act). The fine to be deducted is 3 Ps. Per rupee for the labour who is above 15 years.
- Deductions due to absence from duty of such amount as he would have earned for such period.

- Actual cost of damages made by the worker i.e. loss of goods or money for which worker is responsible.
- Other deductions, such as recovery of loan or adjustments against prepaid wages, provident fund, insurance and post office savings etc.

During II World War, due to increase in cost of living Government of India appointed an investigation commission in 1944 to collect statistical data regarding the earnings of the worker. The committee revealed that the industrial wages in textile industry at Ahamdabad were standardized. Various industries appointed after world war examined the conditions and submitted a report regarding minimum wage, poverty level, subsistence level and the comfort level. The committee held the view the *basic living wage or the minimum living wage must confirm the* ***subsistence plus level***. Subsistence plus level is described as the level where income is sufficient for meeting: (a) Physiological existence (b) Medical attention (c) Transport expenses (d) Insurance (e) Recreation (f) Clothing compatible with self respect and to provide protection (g) Elementary education for children and (h) Expenses for self improvement.

5.27. MINIMUM WAGE ACT

Government of India has introduced the Minimum Wage Act in the year 1948. The objective of the Act was to introduce minimum wages in the industries, where labours are being exploited. Act is made applicable to both organized and unorganized industries (Woolen, Carpet making, Shawl weaving units, Rice mills, Doll mills, Bidi manufacturing units, Plantations, Oil mills, Stone crushing units, Lac manufacturing units, Mica works, Public motor transport units, Leather units and Agriculture farms). Gradually, the Act was made applicable to other industries also. The Act empowers both State and Central Government to fix minimum rates of wages payable to employees in industries. In case any industry or manufacturing units have not included in the purview of the Act, the concerned State Government may include such industries also in the fold of Minimum Wage Act. As per the Act, minimum wage may be: (a) Minimum Time Rate, (b) Minimum Piece Rate, (c) a guaranteed time rate, and (d) an overtime rate for different occupations, localities or classes of work and for adults, adolescents, children and apprentices.

It may consist of (a) Basic rate of wage and a cost of living allowances, (b) A basic rate of wages, with or without cost of living allowances and the cash value of concession in respect of essential commodities supplied at concession rates, or (c) An all-inclusive rate. The Act empowers State Government to appoint an advisory boards, committees and sub-committees to modify the wages and enquire into grievances. An Advisory Board appointed by the Central Government coordinates the activities of these committees. All these bodies and committees are composed of members/officials of Government, employers and employees. A provision is also made to set up a *competent Authority* to compute the cost of living index numbers for the scheduled industries. (At the time of introducing the Act, the minimum wage has been fixed ranging from ₹ 1.12 per day to ₹ 2/- per day).

Though the objective of Act is to bring the minimum wage into force in sweated industries, yet it has not succeeded in bringing about uniformity in the standards of minimum wage fixation over the different regions of the country. The constitution of India which came into force on 26th January, 1950 has given due place to the question of wage policy and the Article 43 lays it down as the directives for wage policy. In the year 1956, the Government of India formally ratified the I.L.O Convention NO. 26 concerning Minimum Wage Fixing Machinery (Industry) 1928. At the 15th Session in 1957, the Indian Labour Conference accepted and commanded the following norms as a guideline for all wage-fixing authorities.

Norms for Wage Fixing

1. The standard working class family should be regarded as comprising three consumption units, while calculating minimum wages.
2. The minimum food requirements should be calculated on the net intake of calories recommended by Dr. Aykroyd.
3. Clothing requirements should be calculated at the per capita consumption rate of 18 yards. (52 yards for the standard family 4 persons).
4. The rent corresponding to area provided for under the Government Industrial Housing Scheme should be taken into consideration in fixing the minimum, wages.
5. Fuel, lighting and other miscellaneous items of expenditure should constitute 20 percent of the total minimum earnings.

QUESTIONS

1. What factors influence the Wage Rates? Discuss.
2. List out all Wage Payment Systems and discuss any two of them in detail with examples.
3. Discuss:
   (a) Modified Time Rate Wage System.
   (b) Piece Wage System.
4. Discuss: Balance and Debt System and Standard hour System.
5. What is Incentive? Distinguish between Wage and Incentive.
6. Discuss the properties of a good Incentive Scheme.
7. Write a note on:
   (a) Halsey Incentive Plan.
   (b) Rowan Incentive Plan.
8. Write short notes on:
   (a) Taylor's Differential Piece Wage Plan.
   (b) Merrick Differential Piece Rate Incentive Plan.
9. Write notes on:
   (a) Emerson's Efficiency Plan.
   (b) Gantt's Task and Bonus Plan.

10. Write notes on:
    (a) Bedeaux Point Premium Plan.
    (b) Hayne's Incentive Plan.
11. Write notes on:
    (a) Priestman Bonus System.
    (b) Barth Variable Sharing Plan.
12. Write notes on:
    (a) Group Incentive Plan.
    (b) The Scanlon Incentive Plan
13. Briefly discuss Profit sharing system of Incentives. Giving advantages and disadvantages.
14. Briefly discuss the Payment of Bonus Act 1965.
15. What is a Wage? Discuss the Wage Policy.
16. Discuss the provisions of Minimum Wage Act.

MULTIPLE CHOICE QUESTIONS

1. One of the factors influencing the wage rate is:
   (a) Skill of the worker
   (b) Job evaluation
   (c) Demand and supply situation of labour
   (d) Personal qualities of manager.
2. The system in which worker is paid for the amount of work done by him is known as:
   (a) Work rate system   (b) Piece rate system
   (c) Quality system   (d) Capacity system
3. The system in which earnings of a worker is equal to *wage for the time he spent on the job+ 33.5% of the money value of the time saved by him is known as*
   (a) Halsey incentive plan   (b) Rowan incentive plan
   (c) Taylor's incentive plan   (d) Emerson efficiency plan
4. The system in which **wage earned = Time spent on the work × time rate + Time saved × time rate (Time taken/Standard time)** is:
   (a) Taylor's Incentive plan   (b) Halsey Incentive plan
   (c) Rowan Incentive plan   (d) Emerson's efficiency plan
5. Remuneration paid to the worker for the work done by him either on the basis or result basis is known as:
   (a) Reward   (b) Bonus
   (c) Incentive   (d) Wage

6. The wage, which makes funds available to the worker for keeping his body and soul together, is known as:
   (a) Fair wage (b) Real wage
   (c) Minimum wage (d) Living wage
7. A wage, which enables the worker to provide measure of comfort for himself and his family after meeting the essentials of life, is known as:
   (a) Excess wage (b) Living wage
   (c) Real wage (d) Luxury wage

ANSWERS

1. (c) 2. (b) 3. (a) 4. (c) 5. (d) 6. (a) 7. (b).

○○○

Unit 6 Programme Evaluation and Review Technique and Critical Path Method (PERT and CPM)

6.1. INTRODUCTION

Programme Evaluation and Review Technique and Critical Path Method (PERT and CPM) are two techniques that are widely used in planning and scheduling the large projects. A project is a combination of various activities. For example, Construction of a house can be considered as a project. Similarly conducting a public meeting may also be considered as a project. In the above examples, construction of a house includes various activities such as searching for a suitable site, arranging the finance, purchase of materials, digging the foundation, construction of superstructure etc. Conducting a meeting includes, printing of invitation cards, distribution of cards, arrangement of platform, chairs for audience etc. In planning and scheduling the activities of large sized projects, the two network techniques – PERT and CPM are used conveniently to estimate and evaluate the project completion time and control the resources to see that the project is completed within the stipulated time and at minimum possible cost. Many managers, who use the PERT and CPM techniques have claimed that these techniques drastically reduce the project completion time. But it is wrong to think that network analysis is a solution to all bad management problems. In the present chapter, let us discuss how PERT and CPM are used to schedule the projects.

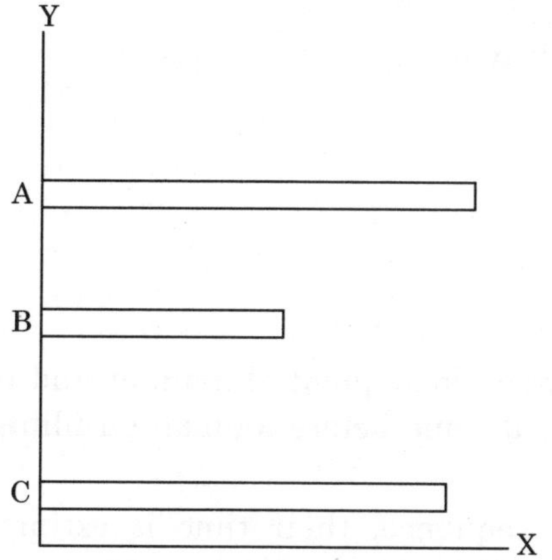

Fig. 6.1. Bar Chart

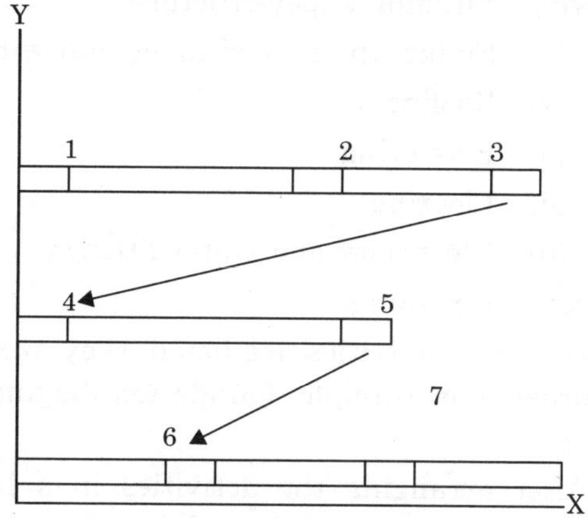

Fig. 6.2. Milestone Chart

Initially, projects were represented by **milestone** chart and **bar chart**. But they had little use in controlling the project activities. ***Bar chart*** simply represents each activity by bars of length equal to the time taken on a common time scale as shown in Figure 6.1. This chart does not show interrelationship between activities. It is very difficult to show the progress of work in these charts. An improvement in bar charts is ***milestone chart.*** In milestone chart, key events of activities are identified and each activity is connected to its preceding and succeeding activities to show the logical relationship between activities. Here each key event is represented by a node (a circle) and arrows instead of bars represent activities, as shown in Fig. 6.2. The extension of milestone chart is PERT and CPM network methods.

6.2. PERT AND CPM

In PERT and CPM the milestones are represented as ***events.*** Event or node is either starting of an activity or ending of an activity. Activity is represented by means of an arrow, which is resource consuming. Activity consumes resources like time, money and, materials. Event will not consume any resource, but it simply represents either starting or ending of an activity. Event cam also be represented by rectangles or triangles. When all activities and events in a project are connected logically and sequentially, they form a ***network,*** which is the basic document in network-based management. The basic steps for writing a network are:

(a) List out all the activities involved in a project. Say for example, in building construction, the activities are:

- (i) Site selection,
- (ii) Arrangement of finance,
- (iii) Preparation of building plan,
- (iv) Approval of plan by municipal authorities,
- (v) Purchase of materials,
- (vi) Digging of foundation,
- (vii) Filling up of foundation,
- (viii) Building superstructure,
- (ix) Fixing up of doorframes and window frames,
- (x) Roofing,
- (xi) Plastering,
- (xii) Flooring,
- (xiii) Electricity and water fittings,
- (xiv) Finishing.

(b) Once the activities are listed, they are arranged in sequential manner and in logical order. For example, foundation digging should come before foundation filling and so on.

(c) After arranging the activities in a logical sequence, their time is estimated and written against each activity. For example: Foundation digging: 10 days, or $1\frac{1}{2}$ weeks.

(d) Some of the activities do not have any logical relationship, in such cases; we can start those activities simultaneously. For example, Foundation digging and purchase of materials do not have any logical relationship. Hence, both of them can be started simultaneously. Suppose foundation digging takes 10 days and purchase of materials takes 7 days, both of them can be finished in 10 days. And the successive activity, say foundation filling, which has logical relationship with both of the above, can be started after 10 days. Otherwise, foundation digging and purchase of materials are done one after the other; filling of foundation should be started after 17 days.

(e) Activities are added to the network, depending upon the logical relationship to complete the project network.

Some of the points are to be remembered while drawing the network is

- There must be only one beginning and one end for the network, as shown in the Fig. 6.3.

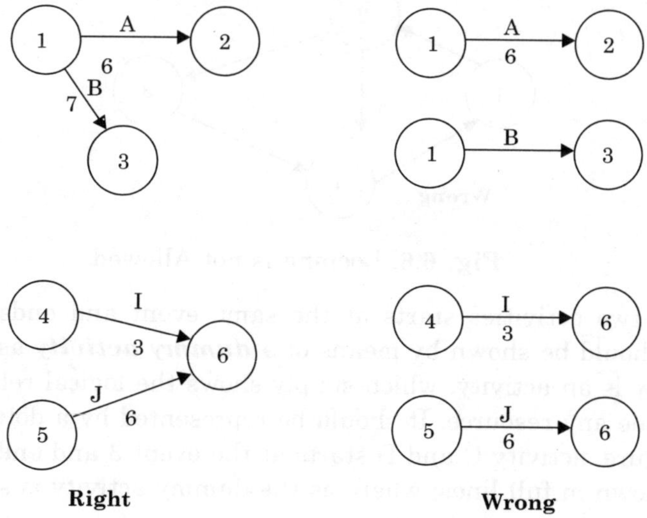

Fig. 6.3. Writing the Network.

(i) Event number should be written inside the circle or node (or triangle/square/ rectangle etc). Activity name should be capital alphabetical letters and would be written above the arrow. The time required for the activity should be written below the arrow as in Fig. 6.4.

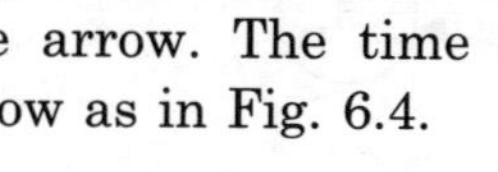

Fig. 6.4. Numbering and Naming the Activities.

(ii) While writing network, see that activities should not cross each other. And arcs or loops as in Fig. 6.5 should not join activities.

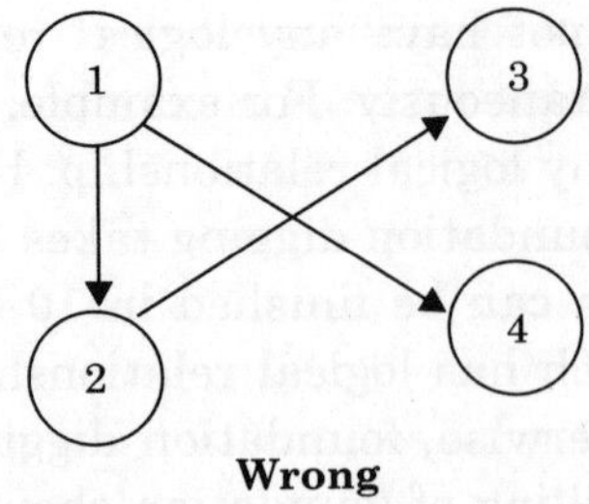

Fig. 6.5. Crossing of Activities not Allowed

(iii) While writing network, looping should be avoided. This is to say that, the network arrows should move in one direction, i.e. starting from the beginning should move towards the end, as in Fig. 6.6.

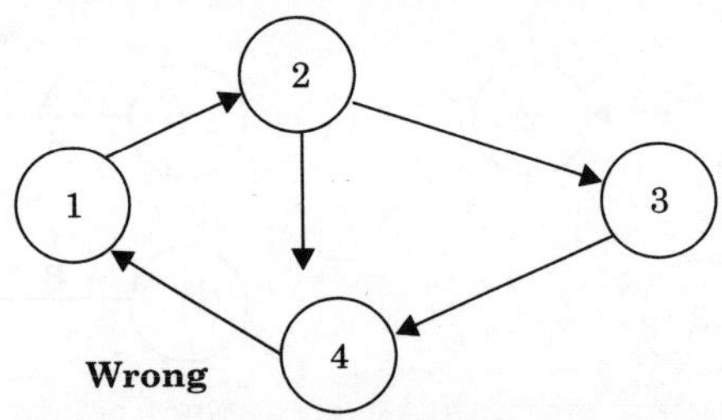

Fig. 6.6. Looping is not Allowed

(iv) When two activities starts at the same event and ends at the same event, they should be shown by means of a ***dummy activity*** as in Fig. 6.7. Dummy activity is an activity, which simply shows the logical relationship and do not consume any resource. It should be represented by a dotted line as shown. In the figure, activity C and D starts at the event 3 and end at event 4. C and D are shown in full lines; where as the dummy activity is shown in dotted line.

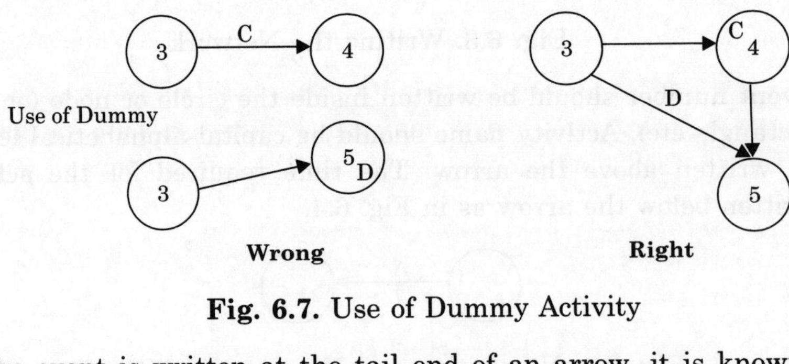

Fig. 6.7. Use of Dummy Activity

(f) When the event is written at the tail end of an arrow, it is known as ***tail event***. If event is written on the head side of the arrow it is known as ***head event.*** A tail event may have any number of arrows (activities) emerging from it. This is to say that an event may be a tail event to any number of activities. Similarly a head event may be a head event for any number of activities. This is to say that many activities may conclude at one event. This is shown in Fig. 6.8.

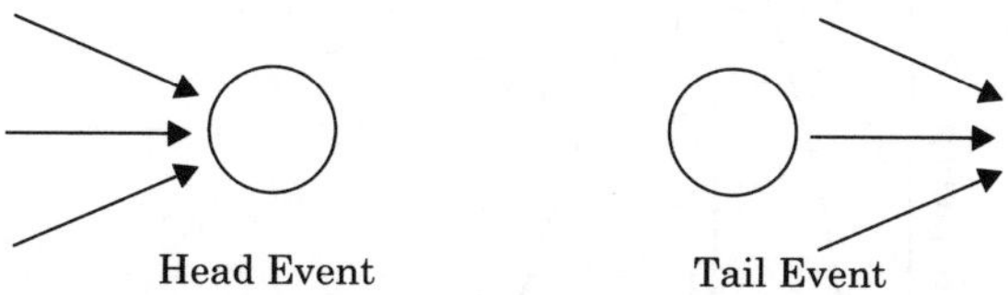

Fig. 6.8. Tail Event and Head Event.

The academic differences between PERT network and CPM network are:

(a) PERT is event oriented and CPM is activity oriented. This is to say that while discussing about PERT network, we say that, Activity 1–2, Activity 2–3 and so on. Or event 2 occurs after event 1 and event 5 occurs after event 3 and so on. While discussing CPM network, we say that Activity A follows activity B and activity C follows activity B and so on. Referring to the network shown in Fig. 9, we can discuss as under.

PERT way: Event 1 is the predecessor to event 2 or event 2 is the successor to event 1. Events 3 and 4 are successors to event 2 or event 2 is the predecessor to events 3 and 4.

CPM way: Activity 1–2 is the predecessor to activities 2–3 and 2–4 or activities 2–3 and 2–4 are successors to activity 1–2.

(b) PERT activities are probabilistic in nature. The time required to complete the PERT activity cannot be specified correctly. Because of uncertainties in carrying out the activity, the time cannot be specified correctly. Say for example, if you ask a contractor, how much time it takes to construct the house, he may answer you that it may take 5 to 6 months. This is because of his expectation of uncertainty in carrying out each one of the activities in the construction of the house. Another example is if somebody asks you how much time you require to reach railway station from your house, you may say that it may take 1 to $1\frac{1}{2}$ hour. This is because; you may think that you may not get a transport facility in time. Or on the way to station, you may come across certain work, which may cause delay in your journey from house to station. Hence, PERT network is used when the activity times are probabilistic.

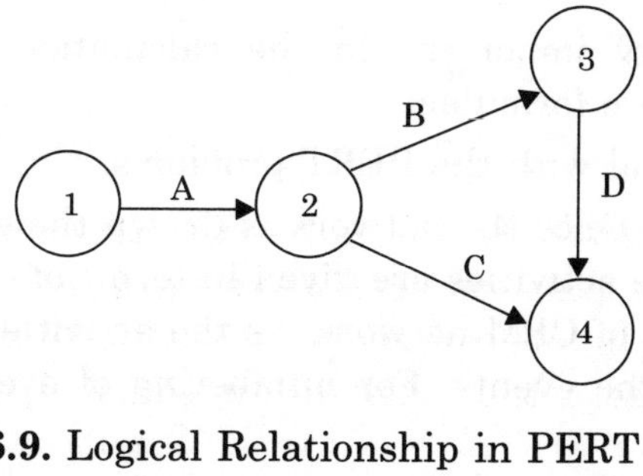

Fig. 6.9. Logical Relationship in PERT and CPM

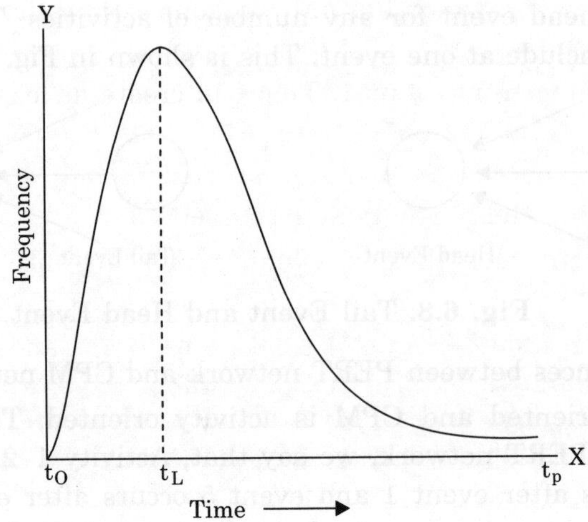

Fig. 6.10. Three Time Estimates.

There are three time estimates in PERT, they are:

(a) Optimistic time: Optimistic time is represented by t_O. Here the estimator thinks that everything goes on well and he will not come across any sort of uncertainties and estimates lowest time as far as possible. He is *optimistic* in his thinking.

(b) Pessimistic time: This is represented by t_P. Here estimator thinks that everything goes wrong and expects all sorts of uncertainties and estimates highest possible time. He is pessimistic in his thinking.

(c) Likely time: This is represented by t_L. This time is in between optimistic and pessimistic time. Here the estimator expects he may come across some sort of uncertainties and many a time the things will go right.

So while estimating the time for a PERT activity, the estimator will give the three time estimates. When these three estimates are plotted on a graph, the probability distribution that we get is closely associated with ***Beta Distribution curve.*** For a Beta distribution curve as shown in Fig. 6.10, the characteristics are:

Standard deviation $= (t_P - t_O)/6 = \sigma$, $t_P - t_O$ **is known as range.**

Variance $= \{(t_P - t_O)/6\}^2 = \sigma^2$

Expected Time or Average Time $= t_E = (t_O + 4t_L + t_P)/6$

These equations are very important in the calculation of PERT times. Hence, the student has to remember these formulae.

Now let us see how to deal with the PERT problems.

(g) Numbering of events: Once the network is drawn the events are to be numbered. In PERT network, as the activities are given in terms of events, we may not experience difficulty. But in case of CPM network, as the activities are specified by their name, we have to number the events. For numbering of events, we use D.R. Fulkerson's rule. As per this rule:

An initial event is an event, which has only outgoing arrows from it and no arrow enters it. Number that event as 1.

Delete all arrows coming from event 1. This will create at least one more initial event. Number these initial events as 2, 3 etc.

Delete all the outgoing arrows from the numbered element and which will create some more initial events. Number these events as discussed above.

Continue this until you reach the last event, which has only incoming arrows and no outgoing arrows.

While numbering, one should not use negative numbers and the initial event should not be assigned 'zero'. When the project is considerably large, at the time of execution of the project, the project manager may come to know that some of the activities have been forgotten and they are to be shown in the current network. In such cases, if we use **skip numbering,** it will be helpful. Skip numbering means, skipping of some numbers and these numbers may be made use to represent the events forgotten. We can skip off numbers like 5, 10, 15 etc. or 10, 20 and 30 or 2, 12, 22 etc. Another way of numbering the network is start with 10 and the second event is 20 and so on. This is a better way of numbering the events.

Let now see how to write network and find the project completion time by soloing some typical problems.

Problem 6.1.

A project consists of 9 activities and the three time estimates are given below. Find the project completion time (T_E).

1. Write the network for the given project and find the project completion time?

Activities		Days		
i	j	T_O	T_L	T_P
10	20	5	12	17
10	30	8	10	13
10	40	9	11	12
20	30	5	8	9
20	50	9	11	13
40	60	14	18	22
30	70	21	25	30
60	70	8	13	17
60	80	14	17	21
70	80	6	9	12

Solution:

In PERT network, it is easy to write network diagram, because the successor and predecessor event relation ships can easily be identified. While calculating the project completion time, we have to calculate t_E i.e. expected completion time for each activity from the given three-time estimates. In case, we calculate project completion time by using t_O or t_L or t_P separately, we will have three completion times. Hence, it is advisable to calculate t_E expected completion time for each activity and then the project completion time. Now let us work out expected project completion time.

Predecessor event	Successor event	Time in days			$T_E = (t_O + 4t_L + t_P)/6$	Range $t_P - t_O$	S.D. (σ) $(t_P - t_O)/6$	Variance σ^2
10	20	5	12	11	11.67 (12)	12	2	4.0
10	30	8	10	13	10.17 (10)	5	0.83	0.69
10	40	9	11	12	10.83 (11)	3	0.5	0.25
20	30	5	8	9	7.67 (8)	4	0.66	0.44
20	50	9	11	13	11.00 (11)	4	0.66	0.44
40	60	14	18	22	18.00 (18)	8	1.33	1.78
30	70	21	25	30	25.18 (25)	9	1.5	2.25
60	70	8	13	17	12.83 (13)	9	1.5	2.25
50	80	14	17	21	17.17 (17)	7	1.16	1.36
70	80	6	9	12	9.00 (9)	6	1.0	1.0

For the purpose of convenience the t_E got by calculation may be rounded off to nearest whole number (the same should be clearly mentioned in the table). The round off time is shown in the brackets. In this book, in the problems, the decimal, will be rounded off to nearest whole number.

To write the network program, start from the beginning i.e. we have 10–20, 10–30 and 10–40. Therefore, from the node 10, three arrows emerge. They are 10–20, 10–30 and 10– 40. Next from the node 20, two arrows emerge and they are 20–30 and 20–50. Like thus the network is constructed. The following convention is used in writing network in this book.

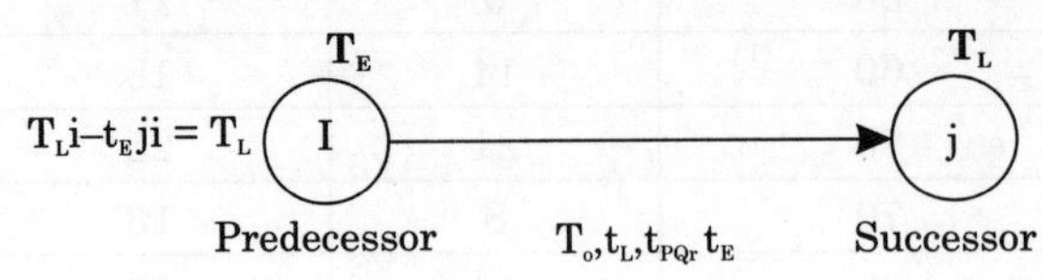

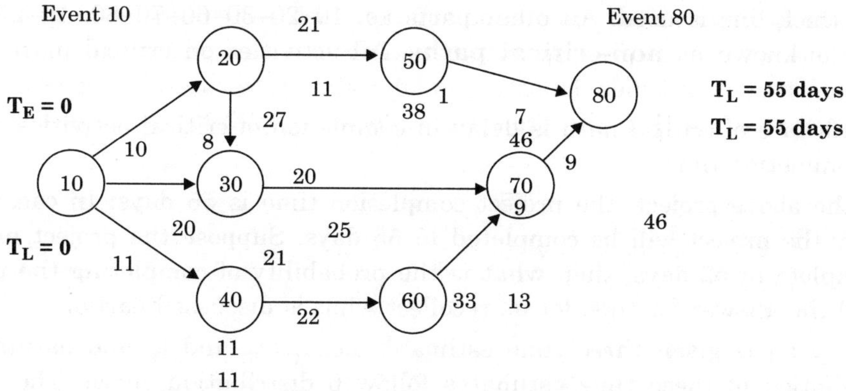

Fig. 6.11. Network for Problem 6.1

Let us start the event 10 at 0th time i.e. expected time $T_E = 0$. Here T_E represents the occurrence time of the event, where as t_E, is the duration taken by the activities. T_E belongs to event, and t_E belongs to activity.

$$T_E^{10} = 0$$

$$T_E^{20} = T_E^{10} + t_E^{10-20} = 0 + 12 = 12 \text{ days}$$

$$T_E^{30} = T_E^{10} + t_E^{10-30} = 0 + 10 = 10 \text{ days}$$

$$T_E^{30} = T_E^{20} + t_E^{20-30} = 12 + 8 = 20 \text{ days}$$

The event 30 will occur only after completion of activities 20–30 and 10–30. There are two routes to event 30. In the **forward pass** i.e. when we start calculation from 1st event and proceed through last event, we have to workout the times for all routes and select the **highest one** and the **reverse** is the case of the **backward pass** i.e. we start from the last event and work back to the first event to find out the occurrence time.

$$T_E^{40} = T_E^{10} + t_E^{10-40} = 0 + 11 = 11 \text{ days}$$

$$T_E^{50} = T_E^{20} + t_E^{20-30} = 12 + 11 = 23 \text{ days}$$

$$T_E^{60} = T_E^{40} + t_E^{40-60} = 11 + 22 = 33 \text{ days}$$

$$T_E^{70} = T_E^{30} + t_E^{30-70} = 20 + 25 = 45 \text{ days}$$

$$T_E^{70} = T_E^{60} + t_E^{60-70} = 33 + 13 = 46 \text{ days}$$

$$T_E^{80} = T_E^{70} + t_E^{70-80} = 46 + 9 = 55 \text{ days}$$

$$T_E^{80} = T_E^{50} + t_E^{50-80} = 23 + 17 = 40 \text{ days}$$

$$T_E^{80} = 55 \text{ days.}$$

Hence, the project completion time is 55 days. The path that gives us 55 days is known as **Critical Path.** Hence, 10-40-60-70-80 is the critical path. Critical Path may be represented by double line (⟹) or thick line (➞) or hatched line (⫻→).

In this book thick line is used. All other parts i.e. 10–20–30–60–70–80, 10–20–50–80 and 10–30–70–80 is known as **non-critical paths**. All activities on critical path are **critical activities.**

The significance of critical path is delay in completion of critical activities will increase the project completion time.

Now in the above project, the project completion time is 55 days. In case every thing goes correctly the project will be completed in 55 days. Suppose the project manager may wants to complete in 52 days, then what is the probability of completing the project in 52 days? To find the answer for this, let us recollect what is discussed earlier.

- Activity i–j is given three time estimates i.e. t_O, t_L and t_P and assumed that the distribution of these time estimates follow β distribution curve. The approximate mean time for each activity given by

$$t_E = (t_O + 4t_L + t_P)/6$$

The meaning of this expected time is that there is a fifty-fifty chance of completing the activities in a time duration t_E as shown in the curve.

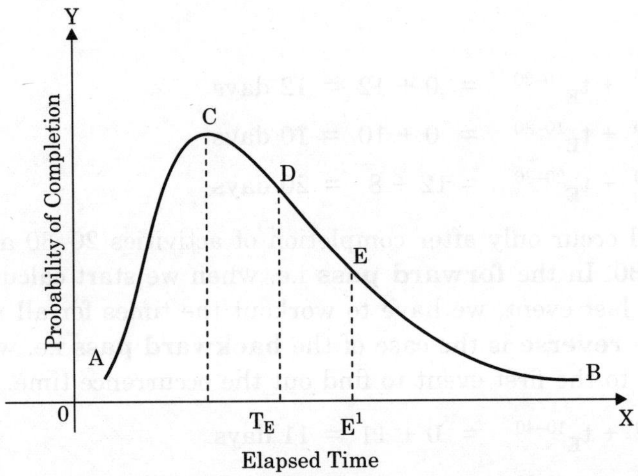

Fig. 6.12

The vertical line at D represents t_E and the chance of completing activities at t_E is ½, suppose we want to find out probabilities of completing the activities at EE[1].

The probability = Area under ACE/Area under ACB

While calculating the probability of completing the project (having number of activities), the following procedure is applied. (Here, we apply central limit theorem).

Step 1: Identify critical path and critical activities.

Step 2: Find variance (σ^2) for critical activities $\sigma_{ij}^2 = [(t_p^{ij} - t_o^{ij})/6]^2$.

Step 3: List out critical activities and their σ^2.

Step 4: Find the sum of variance of critical activities i.e. $\Sigma\sigma^2$.

Step 5: Find the square root of sum of variance i.e. $\sqrt{\Sigma\sigma^2}$.

Step 6: Find the difference between the contractual time (T_L) i.e., time by which the project is to be completed and project completion time T_E, i.e. $T_L - T_E$.

Depending on the value of T_L, this may be + ve or 0 as – ve number. That is

If $T_L = T_E$ then $T_L - T_E = 0$

If $T_L > T_E$ then $T_L - T_E$ = Positive Number

If $T_L < T_E$ then $T_L - T_E$ = Negative Number

Step 7: Find the ratio $(T_L - T_E)/\sqrt{\Sigma\sigma^2} = Z$, this is the length of ordinate at T_L on the curve.

Step 8: Refer to the table 6.1, which gives the height of Z and the probability of completing the project.

If $T_L = T_E$ the probability is $\frac{1}{2}$.

If $T_L > T_E$ then Z is Positive, the probability of completing the project is higher than 0.5.

If $T_L < T_E$ then Z is Negative, the probability of completing the project is lower than 0.5.

Table 6.1. Standard Normal Distribution Function

Z (+)	Probability (P_r) (%)	Z (–)	Probability (P_r) (%)
0	50.0	0	50.0
+ 0.1	53.98	– 0.1	46.02
+ 0.2	57.95	– 0.2	42.07
+ 0.3	61.79	– 0.3	38.21
+ 0.4	65.54	– 0.4	34.46
+ 0.5	69.15	– 0.5	30.85
+ 0.6	72.57	– 0.6	27.43
+ 0.7	75.80	– 0.7	24.20
+ 0.8	78.81	– 0.8	21.19
+ 0.9	81.59	– 0.9	18.41
+ 1.0	84.13	– 1.0	15.87
+ 1.1	86.43	– 1.1	13.57
+ 1.2	88.49	– 1.2	11.51
+ 1.3	90.32	– 1.3	9.68
+ 1.4	91.92	– 1.4	8.08
+ 1.5	93.32	– 1.5	6.68
+ 1.6	94.52	– 1.6	5.48
+ 1.7	95.54	– 1.7	4.46
+ 1.8	96.41	– 1.8	3.59
+ 1.9	97.13	– 1.9	2.87
+ 2.1	98.21	– 2.1	1.79
+ 2.2	96.61	– 2.2	1.39
+ 2.3	98.93	– 2.3	1.07
+ 2.4	99.19	– 2.4	0.82
+ 2.5	99.38	– 2.5	0.62
+ 2.6	99.53	– 2.6	0.47
+ 2.7	99.65	– 2.7	0.35
+ 2.8	99.74	– 2.8	0.26
+ 2.9	99.81	– 2.9	0.19
+ 3.0	99.87	– 3.0	0.13

Now coming to the problem Number 1, given that $T_L = 52$ days.

Critical Activities		$\Sigma\sigma^2$
I	**J**	
10	40	0.50
40	60	1.33
60	70	1.50
70	80	1.00
	$\Sigma\sigma^2$	4.33

$$\sqrt{\Sigma\sigma^2} = \sqrt{4.33} = 2.08$$

$$T_L - T_E = 52 - 55 = -3$$

$$(T_L - T_E)/\sqrt{\Sigma\sigma^2} = -3/2.08 = -1.44 = Z = \text{Normal deviate.}$$

–1.44 falls at probability 8. The probability is very low. Hence, the manager should not accept to complete the project in 52 days.

Say for example given that

$T_L =$ 58 days then $58 - 55 = +3$

$$(T_L - T_E)/\sqrt{\Sigma\sigma^2} = 3/2.08 = 1.44 = Z = \text{Normal deviate.}$$

1.4 falls at 91.9% probability. The probability of completing the project is high. The manager can accept the offer.

Let us continue curve discussion on problem no.1

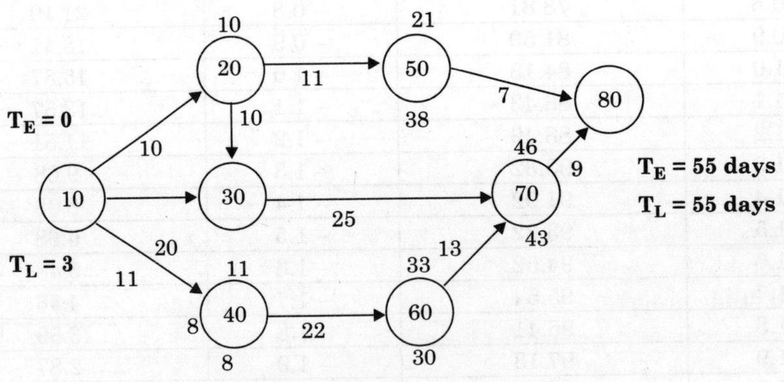

Fig. 6.13

Let us assume that the contractual time = 52 days.

This is written at the end event. Now let us work back to find out when the project should be started if the delivery time is 52 days.

$T_L^{80} = 52$ days

$T_L^{70} = T_L^{80} - t_E^{70-80} = 52 - 9 = 43$ days this we write below the node

$T_L^{50} = T_L^{80} - t_E^{50-80} = 52 - 17 = 35$ days

$T_L^{60} = T_L^{70} - t_E^{60-70} = 43 - 13 = 30$ days

$T_L^{40} = T_L^{60} - t_E^{40-60} = 30 - 22 = 8$ days

$T_L^{20} = T_L^{50} - t_E^{20-50} = 35 - 11 = 24$ days

$T_L^{30} = T_L^{70} - t_E^{30-70} = 43 - 25 = 18$ days

$T_L^{20} = T_L^{30} - t_E^{20-30} = 8 - 8 = 0$ day

T_L^{20} has two values i.e. 24 days and 10 days. Here as we are going back to find out when the project is to be started, take lowest of the two i.e. $T_L^{20} = 10$.

$T_L^{10} = T_L^{20} - t_E^{10-20} = 10 - 12 = -2$ days

$T_L^{10} = T_L^{30} - t_E^{10-30} = 8 - 10 = -2$ days

$T_L^{10} = T_L^{40} - t_E^{10-40} = 8 - 11 = -3$ days

Take $T_L = -3$ days which is lowest. Hence, the project is to be started 3 days before the scheduled starting time.

Now at the critical events calculate $(T_L - T_E)$. For all critical events it is –3 days.

This $(T_L - T_E)$ is known as slack and is represented by Greek letter 'τ'. On the critical path τ remains to be same. In fact slack is the breathing time for the contractor. If $(T_L - T_E)$, slack for all critical events is zero. If $(T_L > T_E)$ it is a positive number and if $(T_L < T_E)$ it will be a negative number for all critical events. For non–critical activities this difference between T_L and T_E i.e. $(T_L - T_E)$ shows the breathing time available to the manager at that activity. For example take the event 50.

For this event $T_L = 35$ days and $T_E = 23$ days i.e. 35–23 = 12 days of time available for this manager. In case of any inconvenience he can start the activity 50–80 any day between 23rd day and 35th day. Now let us work out some more examples.

Problem 6.2

Steps involved in executing an order for a large engine generator set are given below in a jumbled manner. Arrange them in a logical sequence, draw a PERT network and find the expected execution time period.

Activities (not in logical order)	Time in weeks		
	t_O	t_L	t_P
Order and receive engine	1	2	3
Prepare assembly drawings	1	1	1
Receive and study order	1	2	3
Apply and receive import license for generator	3	5	7
Order and receive generator	2	3	5
Study enquiry for engine generator set	1	2	3
Fabricate switch board	2	3	5
Import engine	1	1	1
Assemble engine generator	1	2	3
Submit quotation with drawing and full	1	2	3
Prepare base and completing	2	3	4
Import generator	1	1	1
Order and receive meters, switch gears for switch board	2	3	4
Test assembly	1	1	1

Solution:

As the activities given in the problem are not logical order, first we have to arrange them in a logical manner.

S. No.	Activities	Time in Weeks		
		t_o	t_L	t_p
A	Study enquiry for engine generator set	1	2	3
B	Prepare assembly drawings	1	1	1
C	Submit quotation with drawing and full	1	2	3
D	Receive and study order	1	2	3
E	Apply and receive import license for generator	3	5	7
F	Order and receive engine	1	2	3
G	Order and receive generator	2	3	5
H	Inspect engine	1	1	1
I	Order and receive meters, switch gears for switch board	2	3	4
J	Prepare base	2	3	4
K	Complete assemble engine generator	1	2	3
L	Fabricate switch board	2	3	5
M	Test assembly	1	1	1

Solution:

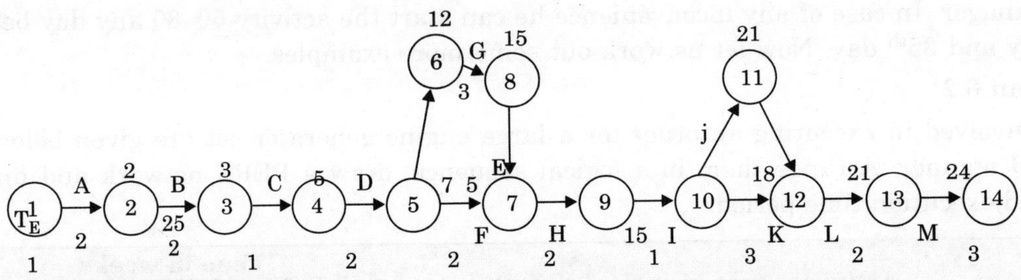

Fig. 6.14

The second step is to write network and number the events

Activities	Predecessor Event	Successor Event	Weeks			$t_E = t_O + 4t_L + t_P/6$	$\sigma = (t_P - t_O)/6$	σ^2
			t_O	t_L	t_P			
A	1	2	1	2	3	2	1/3 = 0.33	0.102
B	2	3	1	1	1	1	0	0
C	3	4	1	2	3	2	0.33	0.102
D	4	5	1	2	3	2	0.33	0.102
E	4	6	3	5	7	5	0.66	0.44
F	4	7	1	2	3	2	0.33	0.102
G	6	9	2	3	5	3	0.5	0.25
H	7	10	1	1	1	1	0	0
I	5	8	2	3	4	3	0.33	0.102

Contd....

Activities	Predecessor Event	Successor Event	Weeks			$t_E = t_O + 4t_L + t_P/6$	$\sigma = (t_P - t_O)/6$	σ^2
			t_O	t_L	t_P			
J	10	11	2	3	4	3	0.33	0.102
K	11	12	1	2	3	2	0.33	0.102
L	8	12	2	3	5	3	0.5	0.25
M	12	13	1	1	1	1	0	0

CRITICAL PATH = 1 – 2 – 3 – 4 – 6 – 8 – 9 – 10 – 11 – 12 – 13

T_E = 25 Weeks

Problem 6.3

A small project is composed of 7 activities whose time estimates are listed below. Activities being identified by their beginning (i) and ending (j) node numbers.

Activities		Time in Weeks		
i	j	t_o	L_1	t_p
1	2	1	1	7
1	3	1	4	7
1	4	2	2	8
2	5	1	1	1
3	5	2	5	14
4	6	2	5	8
5	6	3	6	15

1. Draw the network.
2. Calculate the expected variances fore each.
3. Find the expected project completed time.
4. Calculate the probability that the project will be completed at least 3 weeks than expected.
5. If the project done date is 18 weeks, what is the probability of net meeting the due date?

Solution:

Activities		Weeks			$t_E = t_E + 4t_L + t_P / 6$	t_E	$\sigma = (t_p - t_o)/6$	σ^2
I	j	t_O	t_L	t_P				
1	2	1	1	7	2	6	1	1
1	3	1	4	7	6	6	1	1
1	4	2	2	8	3	6	1	1
2	5	1	1	1	1	0	0	0
3	5	2	5	14	6	12	2	4
4	6	2	5	8	5	6	1	1
5	6	3	6	15	7	12	2	4

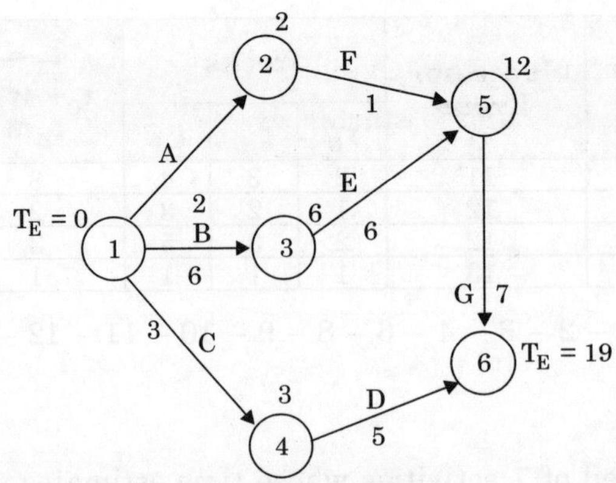

Fig. 6.15

Critical Activities	Variance
1 – 3	1
3 – 5	4
5 – 6	4
$\Sigma\sigma^2$	9

$\sqrt{\Sigma\sigma^2} = \sqrt{9} = 3$

1. Probability of completing the project at least 3 weeks earlier i.e. 16 in weeks

   $T_L = 16$ weeks, $T_E = 19$ weeks.

   $T_L - T_E = -3$ weeks

   $Z = (T_L - T_E)/\sqrt{\Sigma\sigma^2} = -3/3 = -1$

   From table the probability of completing the project = 15.9%

2. If $T_L = 18$ weeks. Probability of completing in 11 weeks is (18–19)/3 = –1/3

   From table probability = 38.2%

   Probability of not meeting due date = 100 – 38.2 = 61.8%

   i.e. 61.8% of the time the manager can not complete the project by due date.

Problem 6.4

There are seven activities in a project and the time estimates are as follows

Activities	Time in Weeks		
	t_O	t_L	t_P
A	2	6	10
B	4	6	12
C	2	3	4
D	2	4	6
E	3	6	9
F	6	10	14
G	1	3	5

The logical of activities are:

1. Activity A and B starts at the beginning of the project.
2. When A is completed C and D starts.
3. E can start when B and D are finished.
4. F can start when B, C and D are completed and is the final activity.
5. G can start when F is finished and s final activity.
   (a) What is the expected time of the duration of the project?
   (b) What is the probability that project will be completed in 22 weeks?

Solution:

First we use to establish predecessor or successor relationship and then find standard deviation σ, variance $σ^2$ and expected time of completing activities, t_E.

Activities	Predecessor Event	Weeks			$t_E = t_O + 4t_L + t_P /6$	$σ = (t_P - t_O)/6$	$σ^2$
		t_O	t_L	t_P			
A	–	2	6	10	6	8/6 = 1.33	1.77
B	–	4	6	12	10	8/6 =1 .33	1.77
C	A	2	3	4	3	2/6 = 0.33	0.11
D	A	2	4	6	4	4/6 = 0.66	0.44
E	B, D	3	6	9	5		1.00
F	B, C, D	6	10	14	10	8/6 = 1.33	1.77
G	F	1	3	5	3	4/6 = 0.66	0.44

Now to write network the logical (predecessor) relationship is considered.

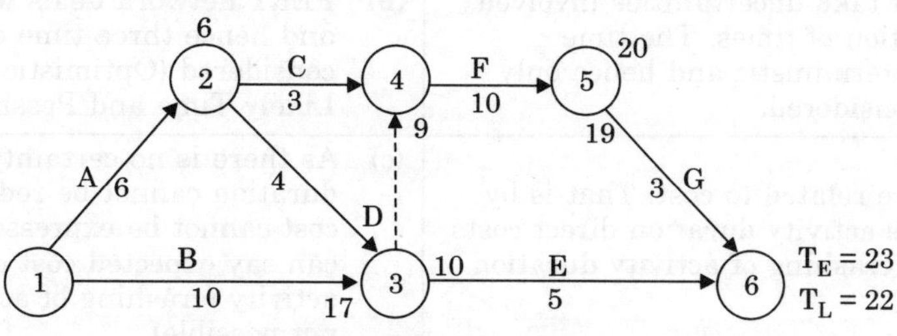

Fig. 6.16

After writing the network, numbering of events and t_E is entered on the network. Next the project completion time is worked out. The project completion time T_E = 23 weeks. This project has two critical paths i.e. A-D-F-G and B-F-G.

(1)

Critical path	Variance (σ^2)
A	1.77
D	0.44
F	1.77
G	0.44
$\Sigma\sigma^2$	4.42

(2)

Critical path	Variance (σ^2)
B	1.77
F	1.77
G	0.44
$\Sigma\sigma^2$	3.98

$\sqrt{\Sigma\sigma^2} = \sqrt{4.42} = 2.10$ $\sqrt{\Sigma\sigma^2} = \sqrt{3.98} = 1.99$

In the problem T_L is given as 22 weeks. Therefore $T_L - T_E = 22 - 23 = -1$

Therefore probability of completing the project in 22 weeks

$-1/2.10 = -0.476$ OR $-1/1.99 = 0.502$

The probability of completing the project is approximately 49%.

6.3. CRITICAL PATH METHOD (CPM) FOR CALCULATING PROJECT COMPLETION TIME

In critical path method, the time duration of activity is deterministic in nature i.e. there will be a single time, rather than three time estimates as in PERT networks. The network is activity oriented. The three ways in which the CPM type of networks differ from PERT networks are

CPM	PERT
(a) Network is constructed on the basis of jobs or activities (activity oriented).	(a) Network is constructed basing on the events. (Event oriented)
(b) CPM does not take uncertainties involved in the estimation of times. The time required is deterministic and hence only one time is considered.	(b) PERT network deals with uncertainties and hence three time estimations are considered (Optimistic Time, Most Likely Time and Pessimistic Time)
(c) CPM times are related to cost. That is by decreasing the activity duration direct costs will increase (crashing of activity duration is possible)	(c) As there is no certainty of time, activity duration cannot be reduced. Hence cost cannot be expressed correctly. We can say expected cost of completion of activity (crashing of activity duration is not possible)

6.3.1. Writing the CPM Network

First, one has to establish the logical relationship between activities. That is predecessor and successor relationship, which activity is to be started after a certain activity. By means of problems let us see how to deal with CPM network and the calculations needed.

Problem 6.5

A company manufacturing plant and equipment for chemical processing is in the process of quoting tender called by public sector undertaking. Help the manager to find the project completion time to participate in the tender.

S. No.	Activities		Days
1	A	–	3
2	B	–	4
3	C	A	5
4	D	A	6
5	E	C	7
6	F	D	8
7	G	B	9
8	H	E, F, G	3

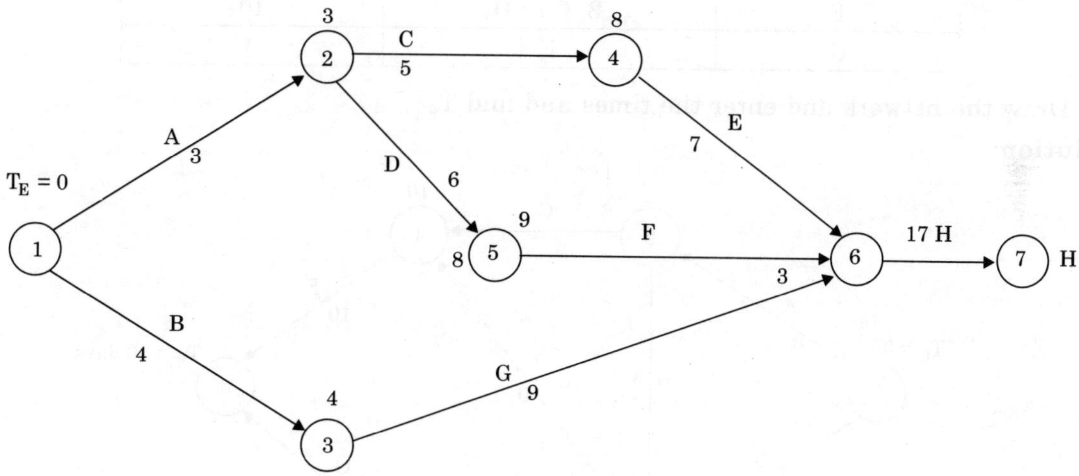

Fig. 6.17

1. Write the network referring to the data.
2. Number the events as discussed earlier.
3. Calculate T_E as done in PERT network $T_E{}^j = (T_E{}^i + T_E{}^{ij})$.
4. Identify the critical path.

Project complete time = 20 weeks and the critical path = A – D – F – H

Problem 6.6

A small project has 7 activities and the time in days for each activity is given below:

Activity	Duration in Days
A	6
B	8
C	3
D	4
E	6
F	10
G	3

Given that activities A and B can start at the beginning of the project. When A is completed C and D can start. E can start only when B and D are finished. F can start when B, C and D are completed and is the final activity. G can start when E is finished and is the final activity. Draw the network and find the project completion time.

Activity	Immediate Predecessor	Time in Days
A	–	6
B	–	8
C	A	3
D	A	4
E	B, D	6
F	B, C or D	10
G	E	3

Draw the network and enter the times and find T_E.

Solution:

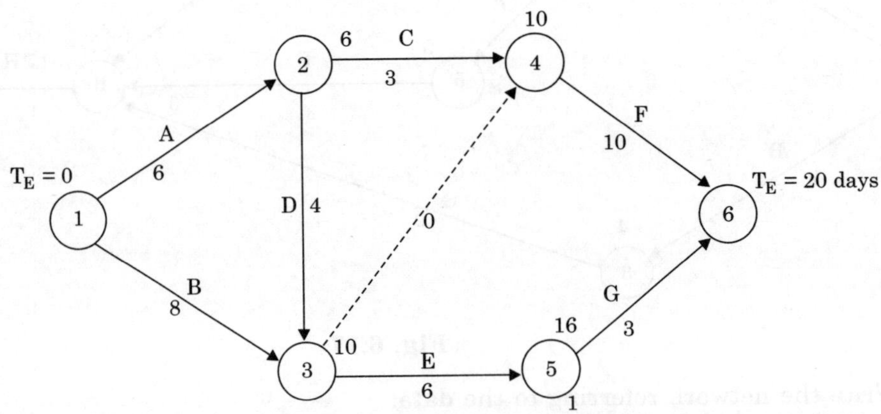

Fig. 6.18

Project completion time = 20 days and critical path is A – D – F

6.3.2. Time Estimation in CPM

Once the network is drawn the next work is to number the events and enter the time duration of each activity and then to calculate the project completion time. As we know, the CPM activities have single time estimates, and no uncertainties are concerned, the system is deterministic in nature. While dealing with CPM networks, we came across the following times.

(a) **Earliest Event Time:** We have defined event as either starting or ending of an activity. Earliest event time means what is the earliest time by which that event occurs. Let us consider a small example to understand this. Consider the Fig. 6.18.

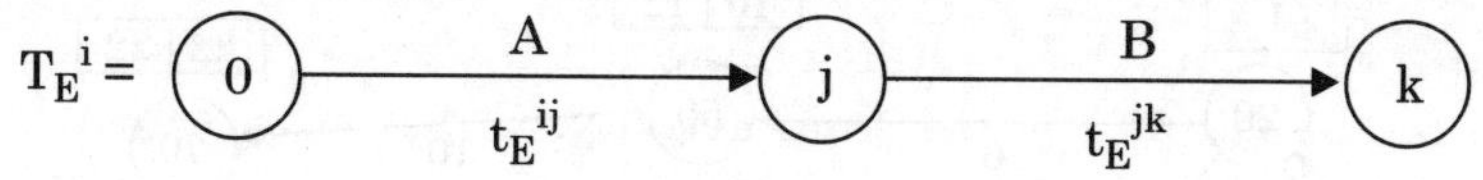

Fig. 6.19

In figure, the network has two activities A and B. Activity A i.e. 'ij' is predecessor to activity B i.e. activity jk. The time taken by activity A is t_E^{ij} and that of B is t_E^{jk}. If the event 'i' occurs at time 0, then event 'j' occurs at the earliest at $0 + t_E^{ij}$ i.e. $t_E^i + t_E^{ij} = t_E^j$ and the earliest time by which event 'k' occurs is $T_E^K = t_E^j + t_E^{jk}$. But when various lines as shown in the Figure 6.19 connect a node, the procedure is as follows.

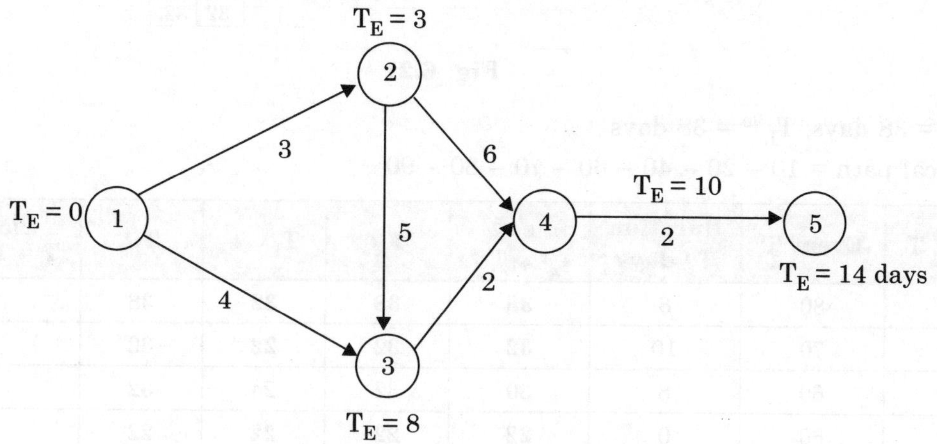

Fig. 6.20

Event 3 is having two routes 1-2-3 and 1-3

$T_E^1 = 0$

$T_E^2 = T_E^1 + t_E^{12} = 0 + 3 = 3$

$T_E^3 = T_E^1 + t_E^{13} = 0 + 4 = 4$ also $T_E^3 = T_E^2 + t_E^{23} = 3 + 5 = 8$

As the rule says that event 3 occurs only after the completion of activities 1-4 and 2-3. Activity 1-3 ends on 4th day and event 2-3 ends on 8th day. Hence event 3 occurs on 8th day. This means the formula for finding T_E is

$$T_E^j = (T_E^i + t_E^{ij})_{max}$$

When the event has more routes, we have to calculate T_E for all routes and taken the maximum of all the routes.

Problem 6.7

Find the slack of each event

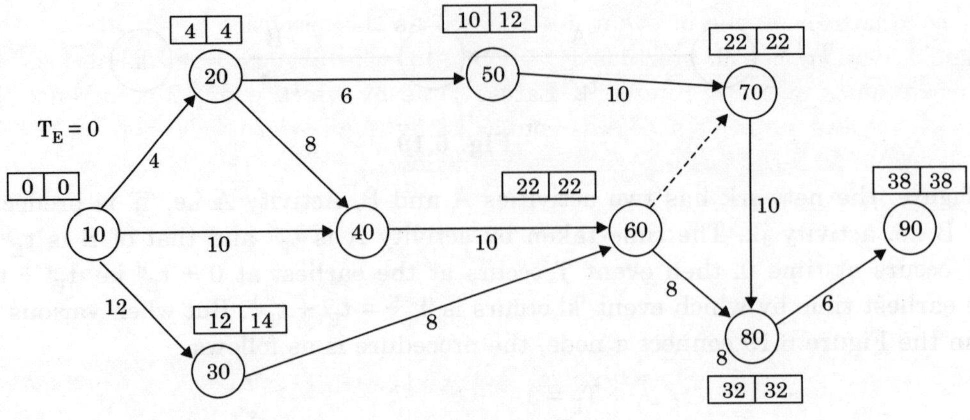

Fig. 6.21

T_E^{90} = 38 days, T_L^{90} = 38 days

Critical path = 10 – 20 – 40 – 60 – 70 – 80 – 90

Event 'i'	Event 'j'	Duration T^{ij} days	$t_E^j = t_E^i + t^{ij}$ ↑	T_E^j	T_L^i ↓	T_L^j	Slack = $T = T_L - T_E$
90	80	6	**38**	38	**32**	38	0
80	70	10	**32**	32	**22**	32	0
80	60	8	30	32	24	32	0
70	60	0	**22**	22	**22**	22	0
70	50	10	20	22	**12**	22	0
60	40	10	**22**	22	**12**	22	0
60	30	8	20	22	**14**	22	0
50	20	6	**10**	10	6	12	+2
40	20	8	**12**	12	**4**	12	0
40	10	10	10	12	2	12	0
30	10	12	12	12	2	14	+2
20	10	4	4	**4**	**0**	4	0

Thick number is Maximum **Thin number is Minimum**

6.3.3. Latest Allowable Occurrence Time

The next one is the Latest Allowable Occurrence time represented by T_L^i. This is illustrated by a simple example.

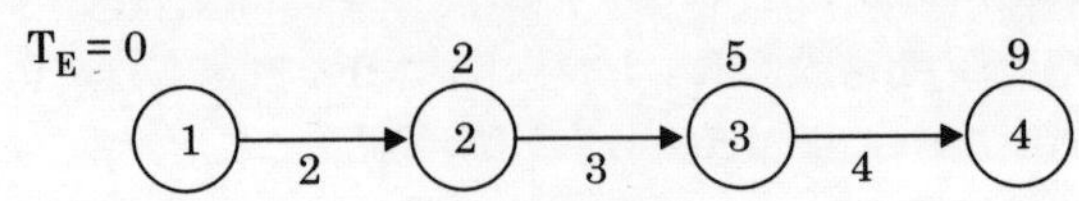

Fig. 6.22

Earliest occurrence time of event 4 = 9 days. As the activities 3 – 4 takes 4 days. The latest time by which activity starts is $T_L^4 - t_E^{34} = 9 - 4 = 5^{th}$ day, which is also the Earliest Occurrence time of event 3. Similarly, Latest Time by which event 2 occurrence in $T_L^3 - t_E^{23} = 5 - 3 = 2$ and so on. If a node is connected by number of paths then we have to find Latest Allowable Occurrence time as discussed below.

Consider the figure given below:

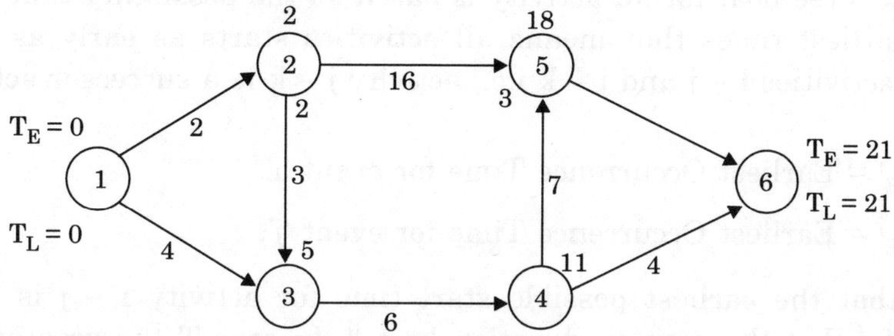

Fig. 6.23

The earliest occurrence time of event 6 is 21 days. As activities 4-6 takes 4 days the earliest occurrence time is

$$T_L^6 - t_E^{46} = 21 - 4 = 17 \text{ days.}$$

But there is another route 6 – 5 – 4. If we Consider this route

$$T_L^5 = T_L^6 - t_E^{56} = 21 - 3 = 18^{th} \text{ day,}$$

$$T_E^4 = T_E^5 - t_E^{54} = 18 - 7 = 11 \text{ days.}$$

As the latest allowable occurrence time for event 4 is 17th day and 11th day. The event 4 will not occur until activities 6 – 4 and 6 –5 are completed. As 11th day is the smallest, the event 4 occurrence on 11th day. Hence, the formula for

$$T_L^i = (T_L^i - t_E^{ij})_{minimum}.$$

6.3.4. Slack Time

Slack time is difference between latest event and the earliest event time i.e. $T_L^i - t_E^i = \tau^i$

Float: Now let us define the times for activities i – j.

(i) **Earliest start time**: This is the earliest occurrence time for the event from which the activity arrow originates and is represented by T_E^i.

(ii) **Earliest finish time**: This is the earliest occurrence time of the event from which the activity arrow originates plus the duration of the activity. $T_E^i + t_E^{ij}$.

(iii) **Latest start time**: This is the latest occurrence time for the node at which the activity arrow terminates minus the duration of activity i.e. $T_L^j - t_E^{ij}$.

(iv) **Latest finish time**: This is the latest occurrence time for the node at which the activity arrow terminates, represented by T_L^j.

(v) Maximum time available for activity is $T_L^j - T_E^i$.

(vi) **Total float**: If the job i – j requires time t^{ij} units, the actual float for jobs i – j is the difference between the maximum time available for the job and the actual time.

$$\text{Total float for } i - j = ({}_{TL}{}^{j} - t_E{}^{i}) - t^{ij}$$
$$= (T_L{}^{j} - t^{ij}) - T_E{}^{i}$$

This is the latest time for the activity minus the earliest start time.

(vii) **Free float**: Free float for an activity is based on the possibility that all events occur at their earliest times that means all activities starts as early as possible. If you have two activities i – j and j – k i.e., activity j – k is a successor activity to activity i – j.

Let $T_E{}^{i}$ = Earliest Occurrence Time for event 'i'.

$T_E{}^{j}$ = Earliest Occurrence Time for event 'j'.

This means that the earliest possible start time for activity i – j is $T_E{}^{i}$ and for the activity j – k is $T_E{}^{j}$. Let the activity duration be $t_E{}^{ij}$. In case $T_E{}^{j}$ is greater than $T_E{}^{i} + t_E{}^{ij}$ activity j – k cannot star until $T_E{}^{j}$. The difference between $T_E{}^{j} - (T_E{}^{i} + t_E{}^{ij})$ is known as Free Float.

Therefore Free Float for activity i – j = $T_E{}^{j} - (T_E{}^{i} + t_E{}^{ij})$. But $(T_E{}^{i} + t_E{}^{ij})$ is earliest finish time for activity i – j. Hence, free float = $T_E{}^{j}$ – Earliest Finish Time of i – j. Free float for activity i – j is the difference between its Earliest Finish Time and Earliest Start time of its successor activity.

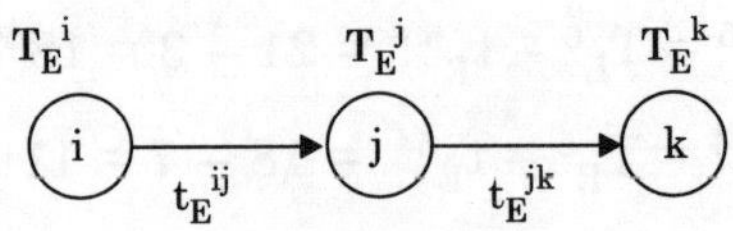

Fig. 6.24

(viii) Another type of float is "Independent Float". Referring to Figure 6.22. Consider the activity i – j. Activity h – i is predecessor to i – j and activity j – k is a successor to activity i – j and $T_L{}^{i}$ is to latest finish time of activity h – i and activity j – k starts at the earliest possible moment i.e. $T_E{}^{j}$. This means activity i – j can take time duration between T_Ei to $T_E{}^{j} - T_L{}^{i}$, without affecting the networks. The difference between the $T_E{}^{j} - T_L{}^{i}$ and $t_E{}^{ij}$ is known as Independent Float.

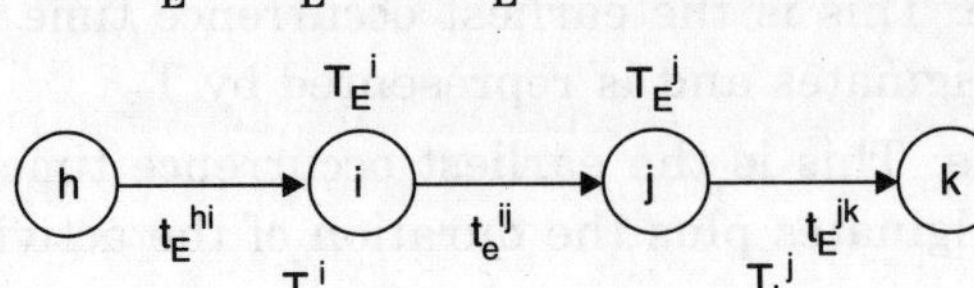

Fig. 6.25

Independent float for $i - j = (T_E^j - T_L^i) - t_E^{ij}$

(ix) Another type of float is Interfering Float. Interference Float is the difference between Total Float and the Free Float. In fact it is head event slack.

Interference float = Total Float – Free Float

$$F_{IT} = F_T - F_F$$

$$F_T = (T_L^j - T_E^j) - t_E^{ij}$$

$$F_F = (T_E^j - T_E^i) - t_E^{ij}$$

$$F_{IT} = (T_L^j - T_E^i - t_E^{ij}) - (T_E^j - T_E^i - t_E^{ij})$$

$$F_{IT} = (T_L^j - T_E^j) = \text{Head event slack.}$$

Summary of float

S. No.	Type of Float		Formulae
1.	Total float (F_T)	Excess of maximum available time over the activity time.	$F_T = (T_L^j - T_E^j) - t_E^{ij}$
2.	Free float (F_F)	Excess of available time over the activity time when all jobs start as early as possible.	$F_F = (T_E^j - T_E^i) - t_E^{ij}$
3.	Independent float F_{ID}	Excess of maximum available time over the activity time.	$F_{ID} = (T_E^j - T_L^i) - t_E^{ij}$
4.	Interfering float (F_{IT})	Difference between total float and free float	$F_{iT} = F_T - F_F$

6.4. PROJECT COST ANALYSIS

So far we have dealt with how to find project completion time in PERT and CPM networks. In CPM network, when the time required by an activity is deterministic in nature, we may come across a situation that we may have to reduce the activity duration. This is not possible in PERT activity; because activity duration is probabilistic in nature and we have three time estimates. Which time (either t_o, t_L or t_P) is to be reduced is a question. Hence, activity time crashing is possible in critical path network only. Before crushing the activity duration, we must understand the costs associated with an activity.

6.4.1. Direct Cost

Direct costs are the costs that can be identified with activity. For example, labour costs, Material Cost etc. When an activity whose duration is to be reduced (crashed), we have to supply extra resources, specially man power. Let us say an activity takes 7 days with 2 men. If 4 men works it can be done in 4 days. The cost of 2 workmen increases. As we go on reducing the activity time, cost goes on increasing as shown in Fig. 6.26.

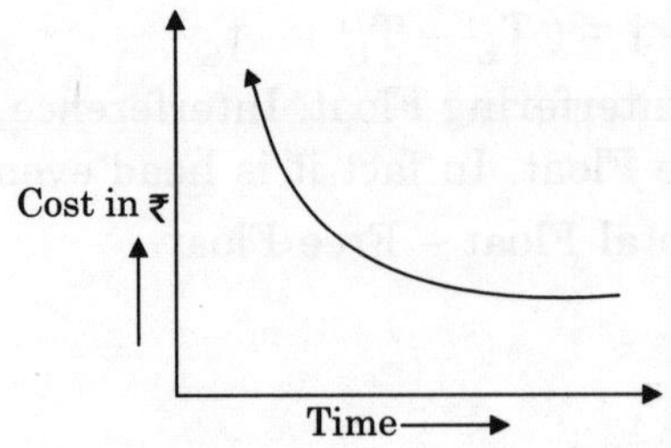

Fig. 6.26. Direct Cost

6.4.2. Indirect Cost

These are the costs, which cannot be identified with the activity. Say the salary of a manager, who is incharge of many projects. Exact amount of his salary that should be charged to a particular project cannot be estimated correctly as it is very difficult to say how much time he has spent on each project. We can express all indirect costs put together in terms of an amount per time period, for example say ₹ 100/- per day. As the indirect costs are expressed as so much of amount per time period, as the duration of project goes on reducing the indirect cost also goes on decreasing as in Fig. 6.27.

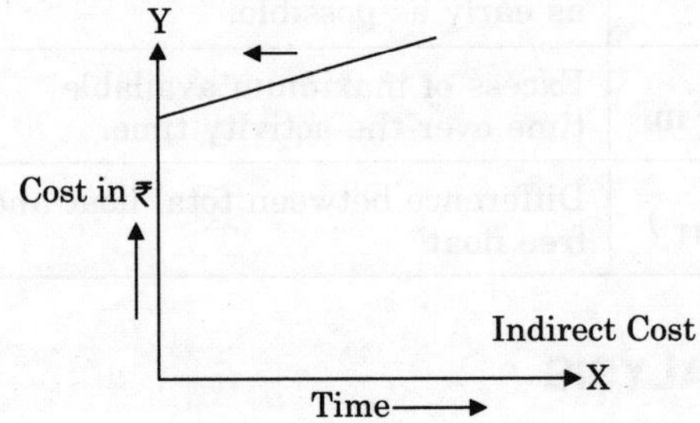

Fig. 6.27. Indirect Cost

6.4.3. Total Cost

The total cost which is the sum of direct cost and indirect cost is shown in the Fig. 6.28. As the project duration goes on reducing the total cost reduces from B to C and if duration is still crashed the total cost increases to A. Hence, our problem here is to find out the optimal duration of the project and optimal cost.

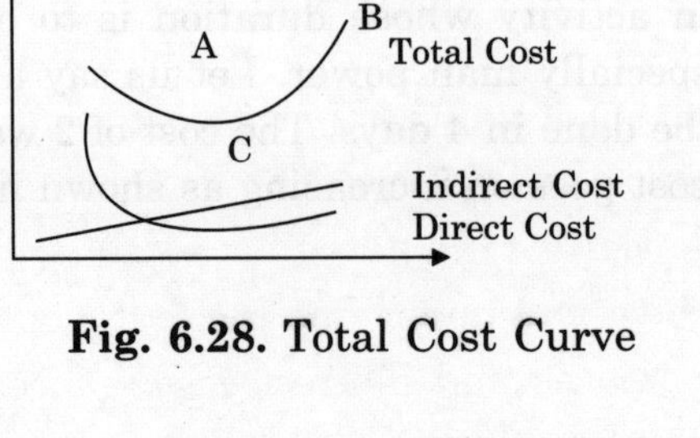

Fig. 6.28. Total Cost Curve

6.4.4. Cost Slope

Consider a small portion of total cost curve and enlarge it. It appears like a straight line as shown in Fig. 6.29.

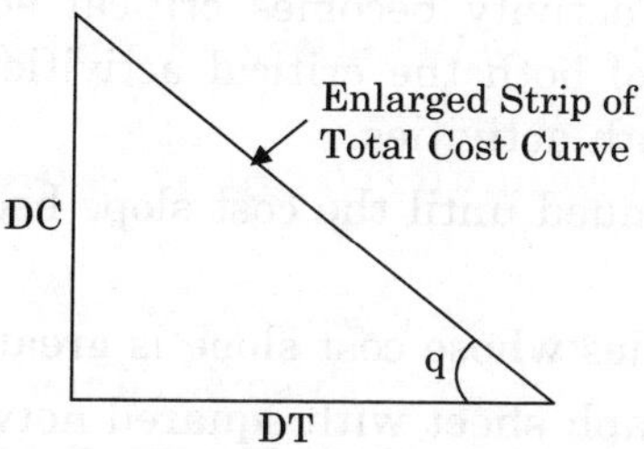

Fig. 6.29. Cost Slope

If θ is the inclination then tan θ = ΔC / Δt. This indicates how much cost increases for crashing a unit of time period.

In this words cost slope is the slope of the direct cost curve, approximated as a straight line. It is given by

$$\textbf{Cost Slope} = \frac{\textbf{Crash cost} - \textbf{Normal cost}}{\textbf{Normal time} - \textbf{Crash time}} = \frac{\Delta c}{\Delta t}$$

Where ΔC = increase in cost, Δt = decrease in time.

Problem 6.8

A project consists of 4 activities. Their logical relationship and time taken is given along with crash time and cost details. If the indirect cost is ₹ 2000/- per week. Find the optimal duration and optimal cost.

Activity	Predecessor	Normal		Crash	
		Time in days	Cost in ₹	Time in days	Cost in ₹
A	–	4	4,000	2	12,000
B	A	5	3,000	2	7,500
C	A	7	3,600	5	6,000
D	B	4	5,000	2	10,000
		TOTAL	15,600		35,500

Solution:

Slopes

1. Find ΔC = Crash cost – Normal cost
2. Find Δt = Normal time – Crash time
3. Find ΔC/Δt = Cost slope.
4. Identify the critical path and under line the cost slops of the critical activities.
5. As the direct cost increases and indirect cost reduces, crash such activities whose cost slops are less than the indirect cost given.

6. Select the lowest cost slope and crash it first, then next highest and so on.
7. Do not crash activities on non-critical path until they become critical activities in the process of crashing.
8. In case any non-critical activity becomes critical activity at the time of crashing consider the cost slopes of both the critical activities, which have same time span and the costs slopes of both activities.
9. Crashing should be continued until the cost slope becomes greater than the indirect cost.
10. Do not crash such activities whose cost slope is greater than the indirect cost.
11. Crashing is done on a graph sheet with squared network drawn to scale.

Activity	Predecessor	Normal		Crash		ΔC	Δt	ΔC /Δt
		Time in days	Cost in ₹	Time in days	Cost in ₹			
A	–	4	4,000	2	12,000	8,000	2	**4,000**
B	A	5	3,000	2	7,500	4,500	3	**1,500**
C	A	7	3,600	5	6,000	2,400	2	1,200
D	B	4	5,000	2	10,000	5,000	2	**2,500**
		TOTAL	15,600		35,500			

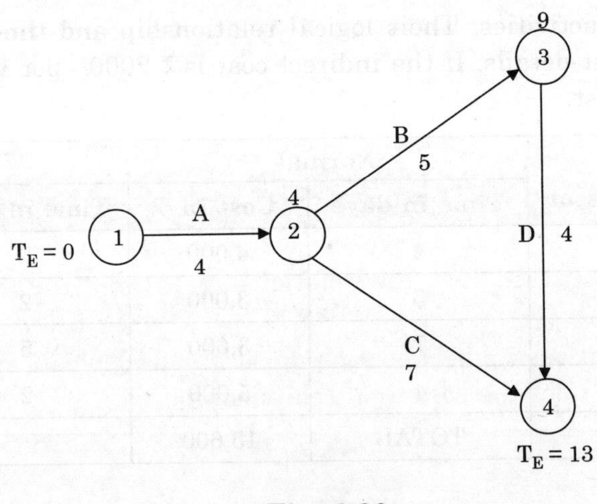

Fig. 6.30

Now activity A, B and D are critical activities. Activity B is only the activity whose cost slope is less than indirect cost. Hence, we can crash only activity B. For crashing we have to write the squared network. While writing squared network critical activities are shown on a horizontal line and non-critical activities are shown as in the figure i.e. above and/or below the critical path as the case may be. That is non-critical path above critical path are shown above vice versa.

Though the activity B can be crashed by 3 days, only 2 days are crashed because after crashing 2 days at 11th day. Activity 2–4(C) also becomes critical activity. At this stage if we want to crash one more day we have to crash activity 2–4 i.e. C also along with 2–3. Now the cost slope of activity B and C are to be considered which will be greater than indirect cost. Hence, no crashing can be done. 11 days is the optimal period and optimal cost is ₹ 39,100/-.

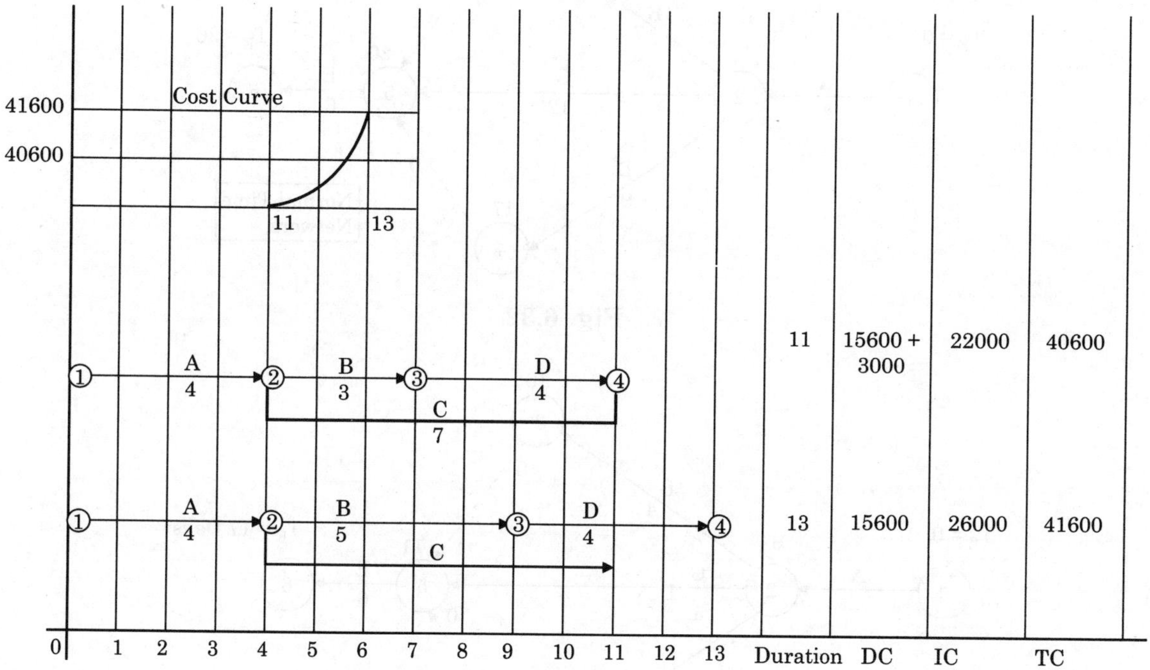

Fig. 6.31

Problem 6.9

(a) A maintenance project has following estimates of times in hours and cost in rupees for jobs. Assuming that jobs can be done either at normal or at fast pace, but not any pace in between. Plot the relationship between project completion time and minimum project cost.

(b) Assuring a relationship between job duration and job cost and with overhead cost of ₹ 25/- per hour, plot the cost time relationship.

Jobs	Predecessor	Normal		Crash	
		Time in hrs.	Cost in ₹	Time in hrs.	Cost in ₹
A	–	8	80	6	100
B	A	7	40	4	94
C	A	12	100	5	184
D	A	9	70	5	102
E	B, C, D	6	50	6	50
		TOTAL	300		530

Solution:

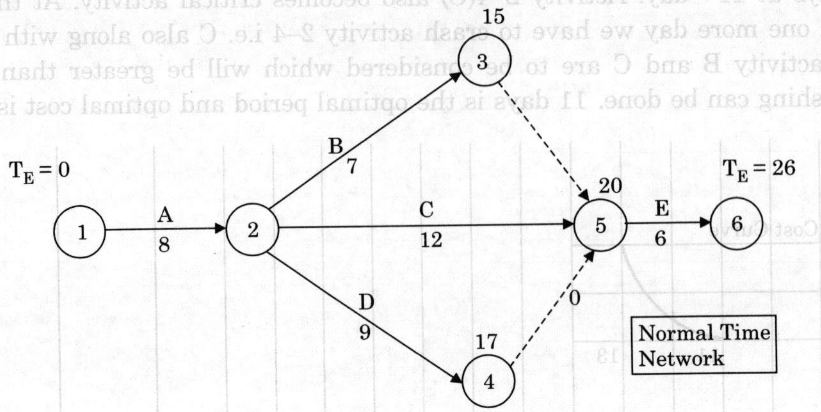

Fig. 6.32

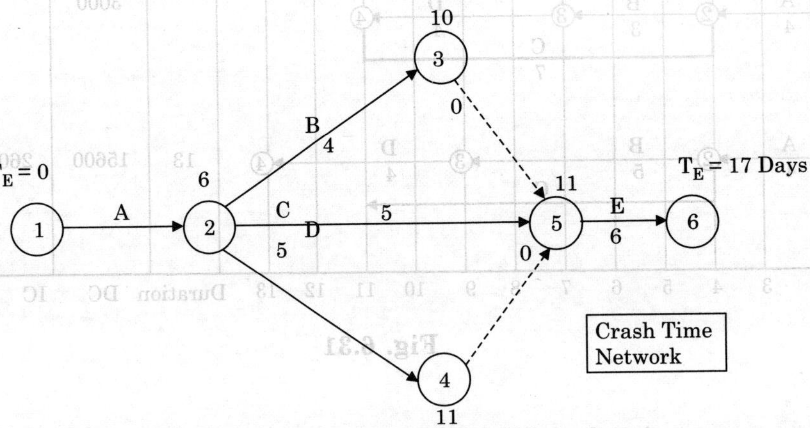

Fig. 6.33

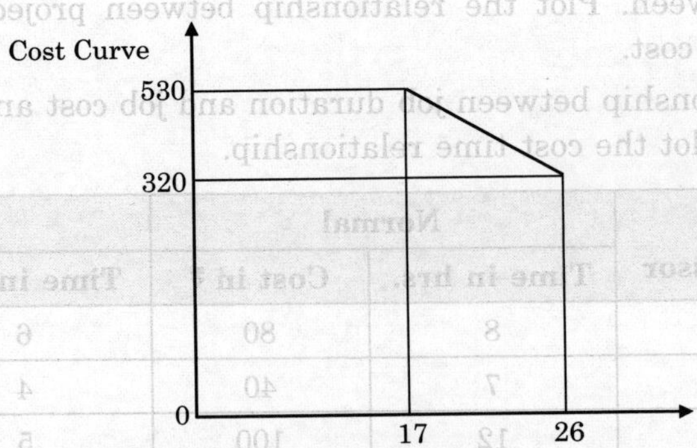

Fig. 6.34

Indirect cost = ₹ 25/- per hour

Jobs	Predecessor	Normal		Crash		ΔC	Δt	$\frac{\Delta C}{\Delta t}$
		Time in hrs.	Cost in ₹	Time in hrs.	Cost in ₹			
A	–	8	80	6	100	2	20	10
B	A	7	40	4	94	3	54	18
C	A	12	100	5	184	7	84	12
D	A	9	70	5	102	4	32	8
E	B, C, D	6	50	6	50	–	–	–
		Total	300		530			

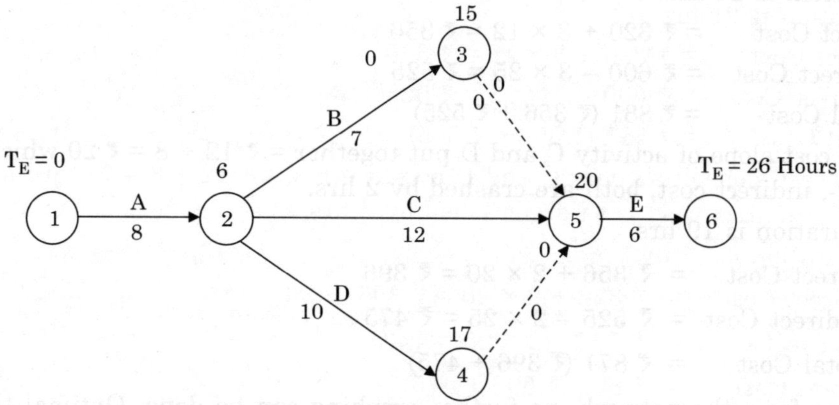

Fig. 6.35

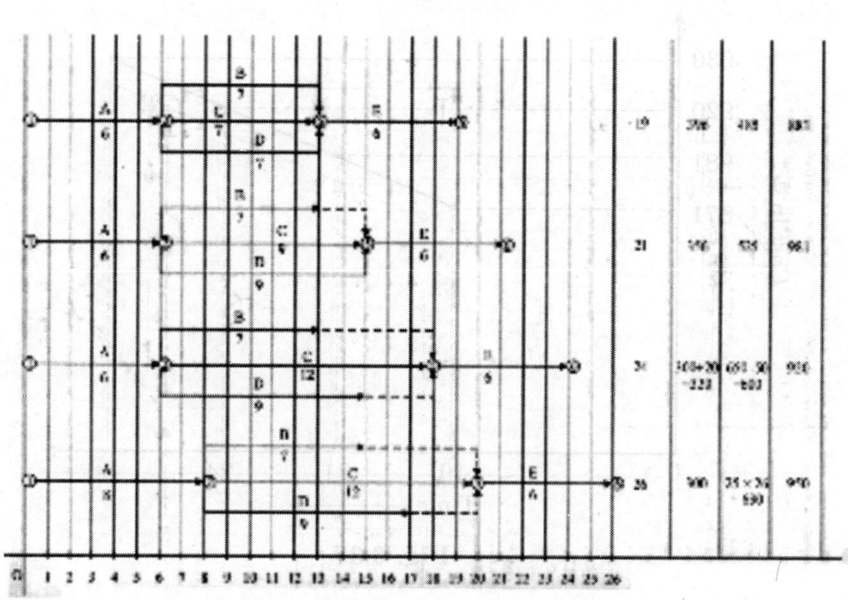

Fig. 6.36. Squared Network for Problem 6.9

(a) Figure 6.36 shows the squared net work.

(b) As critical activity A has got cost slope of ₹ 10/-, which is less than the indirect cost it is crashed by 2 days.

Hence duration is 24 hrs.

Direct Cost = ₹ 300 + 2 × 10 = ₹ 320

Indirect Cost = ₹ 650 – 2 × 25 = ₹ 600

Total Cost = ₹ 920

(c) Next, critical activity C has got a cost slope 12, which is less than 25. This is crashed by 3 days, though it can be crashed 7 days. This is because, if we crash further, activity D become critical activity, hence, its cost slope also to be considered.

Duration is 21 hrs.

Direct Cost = ₹ 320 + 3 × 12 = ₹ 356

Indirect Cost = ₹ 600 – 3 × 25 = ₹ 525

Total Cost = ₹ 881 (₹ 356 + ₹ 525)

(d) Now cost slope of activity C and D put together = ₹ 12 + 8 = ₹ 20 which is less than ₹ 25/-, indirect cost, both are crashed by 2 hrs.

Duration is 19 hrs.

Direct Cost = ₹ 356 + 2 × 20 = ₹ 396

Indirect Cost = ₹ 525 – 2 × 25 = ₹ 475

Total Cost = ₹ 871 (₹ 396 + 475)

As we see from the network, no further crashing can be done. Optimal time = 19 hrs. and optimal cost = ₹ 871/-.

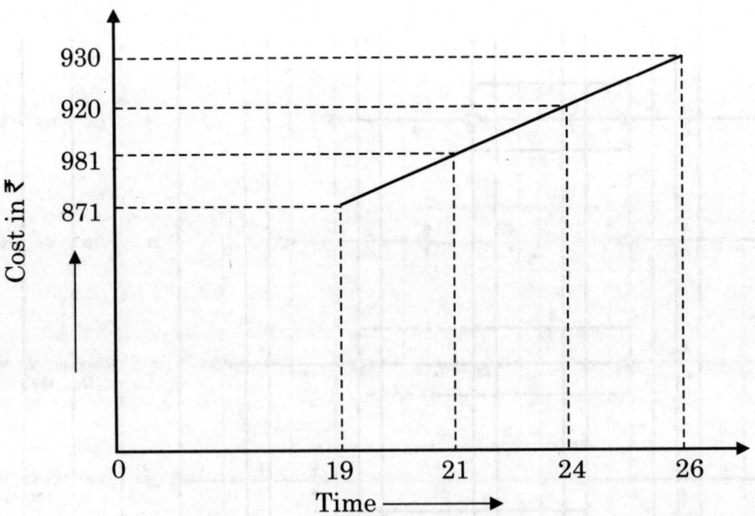

Fig. 6.37

The following details pertains to a job, which is to be scheduled to optimal cost

Jobs	Predecessor	Normal		Crash		ΔC	Δt	$\frac{\Delta C}{\Delta t}$
		Time in hrs.	Cost in ₹	Time in hrs.	Cost in ₹			
A	–	3	1,400	2	2,100	700	1	700
B	C	6	2,150	5	2,750	600	1	**600**
C	–	2	1,600	1	2,400	800	1	**800**
D	A, B	4	1,300	3	1,800	500	1	**500**
E	C	2	1,700	1	2,500	800	1	800
F	D	7	1,650	4	2,850	400	3	**133**
G	E, F	4	2,100	3	2,900	800	1	**800**
H	D	3	1,100	2	1,800	500	1	500
		TOTAL	13,000		18,900			

We can enter Δt in last column.

Assume that indirect cost is ₹ 1100/- per day. Draw least cost schedule. The related network is shown below:

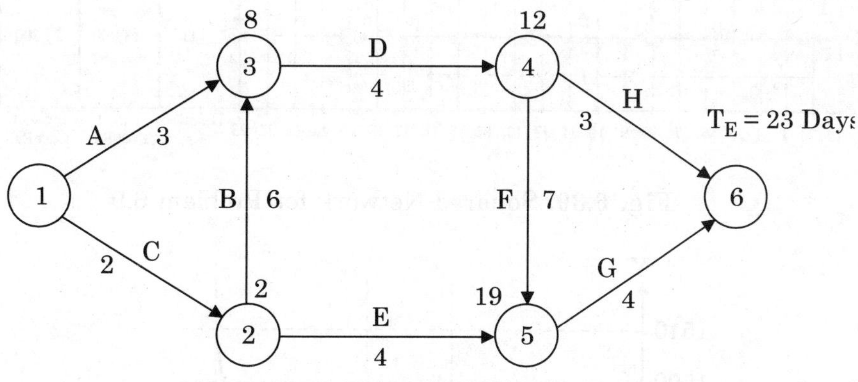

Fig. 6.38

Project completion time is 23 days. Critical path is C-B-D-F-G. Lowest cost slope is ₹ 133 for critical activity F; this can be crashed by 3 days.

Next cost slope is ₹ 500/- for activity D. This can be crashed by 1 day.

Next cost slope is ₹ 600/- for activity B. This can be crashed by 1 day. Next lower cost slope is ₹ 800/- for critical activity C and G. C can be crashed by 1 day and G can be crashed by 1 day.

All critical activities have been crashed and non-critical activities have slack. Hence, they are not to be crashed. Hence, optimal cost is ₹ 33699 and optimal time is 16 days.

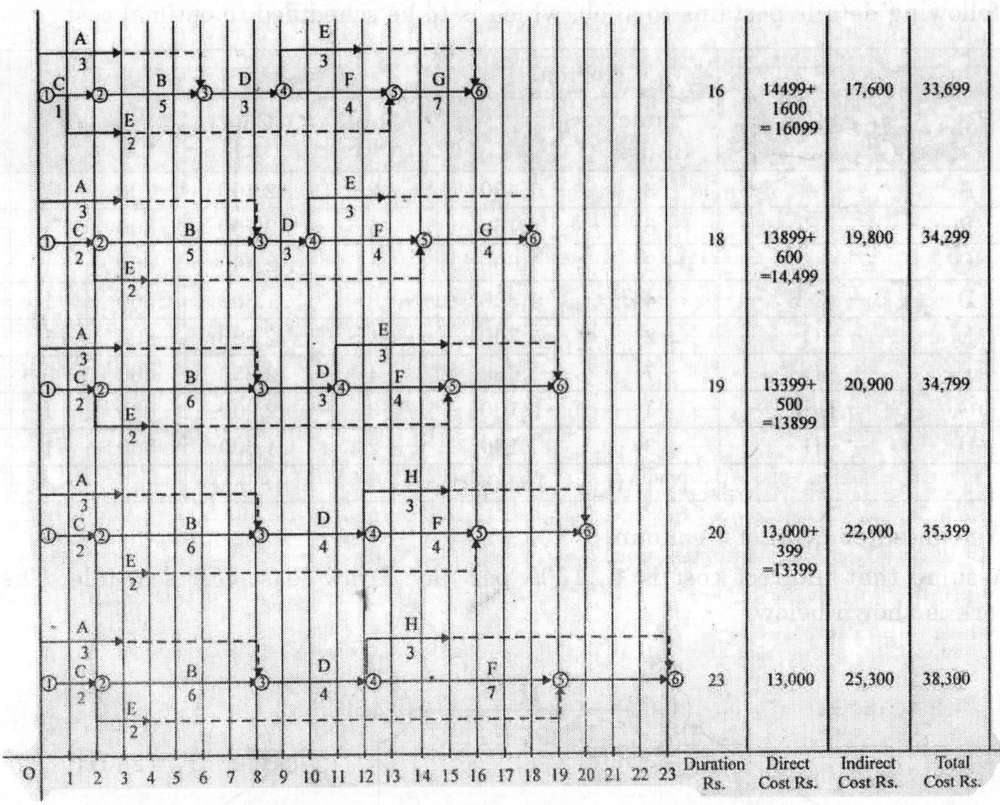

Fig. 6.39. Squared Network for Problem 6.9

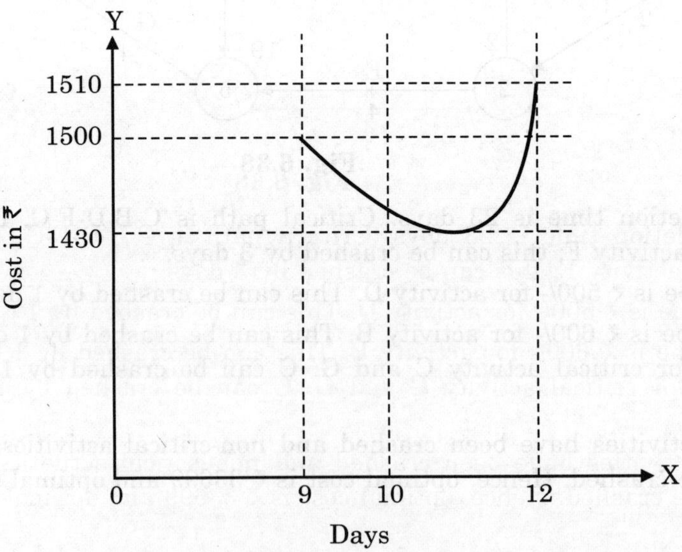

Fig. 6.40. Cost Curve

Problem 6.10

Given below are network data and time cost trade off data for small maintenance work.

Jobs	Predecessor	Normal		Crash	Cost slope ₹ / day ΔC
		Time in hrs.	Cost in ₹	Time in hrs.	
A	–	3	50	2	**50**
B	–	6	140	4	60
C	–	2	50	1	30
D	A	5	100	2	**40**
E	C	2	55	2	–
F	A	7	115	5	30
G	B, D	4	100	2	**70**
		TOTAL	610		

Assume that the indirect cost including the cost of lost production and associated costs to be as given below:

Project duration in days	12	11	10	9	8	7
Indirect cost in ₹	900	820	740	700	660	620

Work out the minimum total cost for various project duration and suggest the duration for minimum total cost.

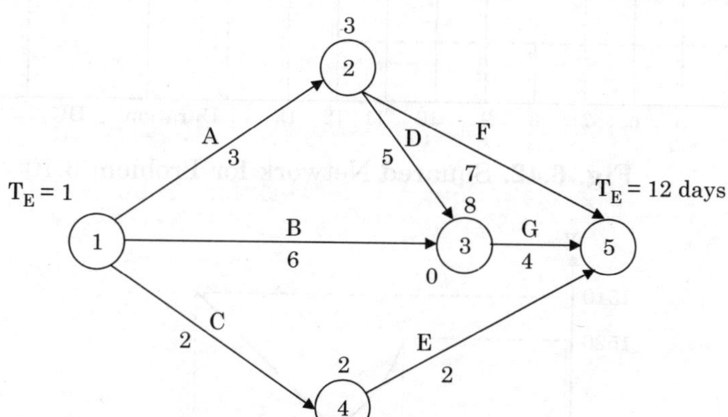

Fig. 6.41

A-D-G = critical path, TE = 12 days.

(a) Activity D has lowest cost slope. It can be crashed by 3 days. It is less than the cost slope for 12 days i.e. ₹ 980/-. By crashing activity D by 3 days, activity F and B have become critical activities.

(b) Next we can crash activity A, whose cost slope is ₹ 50/-, it can be crashed by 1 day, but we have to crash activity B also along with A.

Total cost slope = ₹ 110/- per day.

Here the total cost increases. Hence, optimal duration is 10 days and optimal cost is ₹ 1430/-.

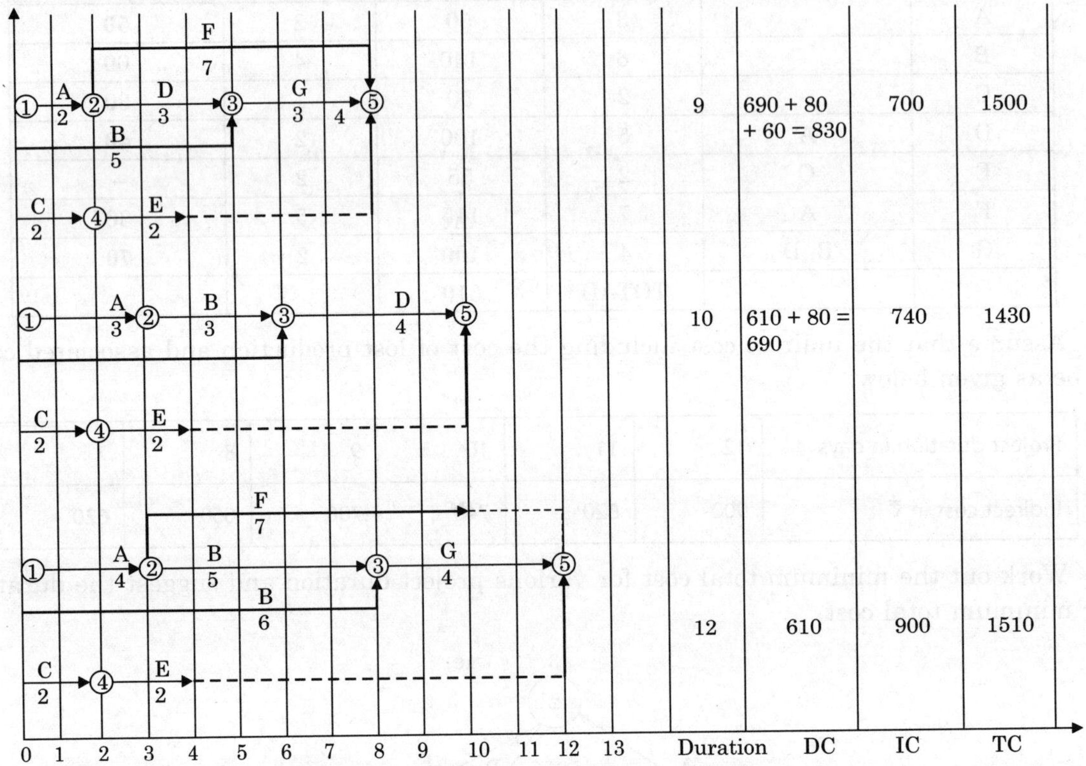

Fig. 6.42. Squared Network for Problem 6.10

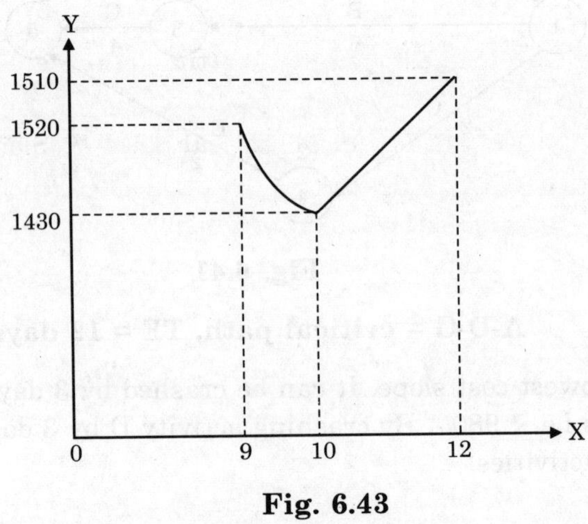

Fig. 6.43

Before concluding this chapter, it is better to introduce the students to further developments or advanced topics in network techniques.

1. **Updating the network:** In large project works, as the project progresses, we may came across situation like
   (a) The time estimates made before may be wrong that a particular activity may take less or more time. And we may also sense that, we have forgotten certain activities. In such cases, we have to **update the project.**
   (b) Leaving the executed activities, remaining activities may have to be modified and the remaining network is redrawn. This is known as updating the network.
2. **Resource leveling and Resource smoothing:** When we have to manage project with available resources, we have two options. First one is resource leveling. Here when the resources availability is less than the maximum resources required for an activity, then delay the job having largest float and divert the resources to critical activities. When two or more jobs compete for same resource, first try to allocate to an activity, which is of short duration and next to the activity which having next highest duration. Here available resource is **a constraint.** The **project duration time may increase** during the process.
3. **Resource smoothing:** Here total project duration is **maintained to the minimum level**. By shifting the activities having floats the demand for resources are smoothened. Here main **constraint** is **project duration time.**

QUESTIONS

1. Explain what do you mean by PERT and CPM. What are it uses? Where they are used? What benefits you derive from using them?
2. Write a note on: (a) Milestone Chart, (b) Event, (c) Activity, (d) Head Event, (e) Tail Event, and (f) Dummy Activity.
3. What are three time estimates? Explain them with examples.
4. How do you number the events? What is skip numbering? Why it is used?
5. Clearly explain the similarities and differences between PERT and CPM.
6. Explain what are: (a) Earliest completion time, (b) Latest allowable occurrence time.
7. Write note on: (a) Critical path, (b) Sub critical path, (c) Slack time and (d) Float.
8. Explain the different types of floats.
9. What is cost slope? How do you find that? What is the use of cost slope?
10. Explain the process of crashing an activity. Can you crash dummy activity? Can critical activity be crashed?

11. Explain what is squared network diagram. When it is used? What is the use of adopting this diagram?
12. Write short notes on: (a) Updating the network, (b) Resource smoothening, (c) Resource leveling.

MULTIPLE CHOICE QUESTIONS

1. Expand PERT:
   (a) Program Evaluation and Reading Technique
   (b) Program Estimation and Reading Technique
   (c) Program Estimation and Review Technique
   (d) Program Evaluation and Review Technique
2. Expand C.P.M.
   (a) Control Path Method (b) Critical Path Method
   (c) Critical Program Method (d) Control Program Method
3. CPM is .... oriented technique.
   (a) Activity (b) Event
   (c) Both a and b (d) None of these
4. PERT is .... oriented.
   (a) Activity (b) Event
   (c) Both a and b (d) None of these
5. Event consume:
   (a) Time only (b) Physical resources only
   (c) Does not consume any resources (d) None of these
6. Activity consume:
   (a) Money only (b) Time only
   (c) Does not consume any resources (d) Consume all resources
7. On the critical path:
   (a) EST = LST (b) EFT = LFT
   (c) EST = LFT (d) EST = LST
   (Where, EST = Earliest start time, EFT = Earliest finish time,
   LST = Latest start time, LFT = Latest finish time)
8. Which of the following is correct:
   (a) EFT = EST + Duration of the activity
   (b) EFT = LST + Duration of the activity
   (c) EFT = EST + LST
   (d) EFT – LST = EST

9. Which of the following is correct:
   (a) LST = LFT + duration of the activity
   (b) LST = LFT – Duration of the activity
   (c) Both a and b
   (d) None of these
10. Total Float is:
   (a) LST – EST (b) LFT – EFT
   (c) LFT × EST (d) LFT × EST
11. CPM is
   (a) Deterministic in nature (b) Probabilistic in nature
   (c) Optimistic in nature (d) Pessimistic in nature
12. PERT is
   (a) Deterministic in nature (b) Optimistic in nature
   (c) Pessimistic in nature (d) Probabilistic in nature.
13. Average time estimate in PERT is given by:
   (a) $(t_O + 4t_L - t_P)/6$ (b) $(t_O + 4t_L + t_P) \times 6$
   (c) $(t_O + t_L + 4t_P)/6$ (d) $(t_O + 4t_L + t_P)/6$
14. Range in PERT is given by:
   (a) $(t_P - t_O)$ (b) $(t_O - t_P)$
   (c) $(t_P + t_O)$ (d) (t_P/t_O)
15. In Project crashing the crashing of .... is considered.
   (a) Event (b) Activity
   (c) Critical activity (d) Critical path
16. As we go on crashing the activities the direct cost goes on ....
   (a) Does not change (b) Increases
   (c) Decreases (d) Both (b) and (c)
17. As we go on crashing the activities, indirect cost goes on ....
   (a) Does not change (b) Increases
   (c) Decreases (d) Fluctuates
18. ....Value of cost slope of critical activity is considered while crashing
   (a) Average cost (b) Lowest cost
   (c) Highest cost (d) Imputed cost
19. While calculating the cost slope, change in cost is expressed as:
   (a) Crash cost – Normal cost (b) Normal cost – Crash cost
   (c) Normal cost + Crash cost (d) Normal cost/Crash cost

20. An initial event is an event which has

(a) Only incoming arrows (b) Both incoming and outgoing arrows

(c) Which is at the end of network (d) Only outgoing arrows

ANSWERS

1. (d)	**2.** (b)	**3.** (a)	**4.** (b)	**5.** (c)	**6.** (d)	**7.** (b)	**8.** (a)
9. (b)	**10.** (c)	**11.** (a)	**12.** (d)	**13.** (d)	**14.** (a)	**15.** (c)	**16.** (b)
17. (c)	**18.** (b)	**19.** (a)	**20.** (d).				

Unit 7 Strategic Management

7.1. INTRODUCTION

Survival and growth of any organization mostly depends on how it plans its long time objectives and medium range objectives and on its plans of day-to-day activities. Any promoter/promoters has to think in which direction they have to grow from the present position. Planning the goals, activities of the organization as a whole for the future is known as **corporate planning.** Once the plans are ready, they have to think of strategies to meet the goals. The strategy in general means the **courses of action**. Say for example, an organization plans for extending the market to neighboring state. This is known as **corporate objective**. For this they have to decide the **courses of action** to meet the objective in stipulated time. These activities are known as **corporate strategies.**

7.2. CORPORATE PLANNING PROCESS

A key activity of all managers is planning and the work under their direction working with each other and with the people who will carry out the plans, they clarify objectives and set goals for each subdivision of the organization; they establish policies and standard methods to guide those who do the work; and they develop programs, strategies and schedules to keep the work moving towards the goal or objectives. Most of these plans they will have to readjust periodically in the light of new information and changes environment and operating conditions. The basic question that bothers a manager is **how detail the plan should be, who should participate in formulating them,** and how much freedom of action should be given to subordinates? The process of planning be best understood if we first examine the basic stages in making a specific decision: diagnosing the problem, finding the good alternative solutions, projecting the result of each alternative, evaluating them in the light of corporate objectives and environmental constraints, (here better to have SWOT analysis) and selecting the optimal course of action to be followed. Looking at the complication involved, we can understand that the corporate planning and decision making is not the act of an isolated individual; and it takes place in the organization we have established. In fact different persons from various departments may contribute in selection of optimal and major corporate plans of the organization clear plans and sound organization set the stage, but a manager must also provide leadership to the people in his organization and to work together to achieve its goals.

7.3. CORPORATE LEVEL STRATEGIES

The corporate level generic strategies pertain to the question which business (es) the company shall be in? There are four alternative strategies, viz, ***stability, expansion, defense*** and a ***combination.***

7.3.1. Stability Strategy

Stability strategy is used to answer the question whether the company should continue in the existing business or not and is doing well in the business with no scope for growth what to do? The stability strategy is a strategy that a firm pursues when:

1. It continues to serve the customers in the same product or service, market and functional sectors as defined it its business definition, or in every similar sector.
2. Its main strategic decisions focus on incremental improvement of functional performance.

The stability strategy is not a *do nothing* strategy. It involves incremental improvements. It is a strategy, which insists on *doing the same thing better*.

Reasons for Stability Strategy

The important factors why companies pursue the stability strategy is:

1. A company is doing fairly well and it is hopeful of the same in future.
2. A family dominated or private company does not like to expand its business if it amounts to diluting the control or if effective supervision is not possible by the family members.
3. The feeling that sticking to the known business is always better and safe.
4. The company may not have the resources and capabilities for expansion.
5. The company may not want to take the risks of growth and expansion.
6. The company which has core competence in the existing business does not want to take the risk of losing sufficient attention to the current business by going for diversion.
7. The management does not have the mind-set of a strategist to analyze the environmental opportunities and seize opportunities.

7.3.2. Growth Strategy

To decide whether the company has to increase the level of activities of the current business or to enter new business the growth strategy is used. Growth strategy redefines the business by adding new products/services or new markets or by substantially increasing the current business. The company peruses the growth strategy when:

1. It enters new business, functions or markets.
2. Effects major increase in its current business.

A company may pursue either or both internal or external growth strategies. Important factors, which encourage companies to adopt growth strategy, are the following:

1. The current business is perceived as having no future.
2. The current business is unstable or volatile in nature.

3. The current business does not fully utilize the available resources and capabilities.
4. There is a feeling of the need for spreading business risks.
5. In some cases, expansion is a retaliatory move. When a company in another business enters the firm's business the firm retaliates by entering the other company's business.
6. Some firms have a tendency to imitate the growth strategies of competitors.
7. In some cases, growth strategy is the result of the urge to grow.
8. In several cases, the motive for growth is the objective to increase market share or gain dominance.

In many cases growth strategy results from the decision to exploit the environmental opportunities.

7.3.3. Retrenchment Strategy

Retrenchment strategy, also known as **defensive strategy**, involves contraction of the scope of level of business or function. In some cases it amounts a redefinition of the business. A firm pursues defensive strategy when:

1. It drops product line (s), market segment (s) or function (s).
2. It focuses on functional improvements or reversing certain deteriorating trends.

Reasons for Retrenchment Strategy

There are number of situations which necessitate a retrenchment strategy.

1. Certain divisions/product lines/market segments/functions which are not profitable.
2. The profits from a business are less than the target rate.
3. The company's new strategy is to focus on its core business.
4. The company is too diversified/scattered to an extent where effective management is not possible.
5. The company has serious financial problems so that the funds obtained by divestiture can be used for strengthening other businesses.
6. Certain current businesses do not confirm to the company's philosophy/ethics.
7. The company is confronted with deteriorating performance indicators.

Defensive strategies include divestiture, liquidation, becoming a captive and turn-around.

7.3.4. Divestiture

A divestiture strategy is persuaded when a company sells or divests itself a business or part of a business. It may be because of loss, less than target rate of return, urgency to mobilize funds, managerial problems or redefinition of the business of the company.

7.3.5. Liquidation

Liquidation occurs when an entire company is sold or dissolved. The reasons for divestiture mentioned above could also be reasons for liquidation. When there are no buyers for a company, which wants to be sold, its assets may be sold and company may be wound up.

7.3.6. Becoming a Captive

A firm becomes a captive of another firm when it subjects itself to the decision of the other firm in return for a guarantee that a certain amount of the captive's product will be purchased by the other firm.

7.3.7. Turnaround Strategy

A turnaround strategy involves management measures designed to reverse certain negative trends and to bring the firm back to normal health and profitability.

7.3.8. Combination Strategy

A company pursues combination strategy when it adopts more than one grand strategy (i.e. growth, stability and retrenchment) simultaneously or sequentially. The reasons for pursuing combination strategy are the existence of a combination of reasons for any two or more of the other three generic strategies. Under the combination strategy, the company adopts anyone of the following:

1. Stability and growth strategies.
2. Stability and retrenchment strategies.
3. Growth and retrenchment strategies.
4. Growth, retrenchment and stability strategies.

A combination strategy results from environmental changes and redefinition of the business.

7.4. CORPORATE PLANNING

Obviously before doing something, it is better to be clear as to what is to be done and how it should be done. Despite the obvious importance of planning, in practice it is often neglected and managers allow things to happen by themselves, instead of making things to happen. Sometimes excuses are made on the ground that the time required for planning is not available and immediate action is necessary. In fact, many managers are more concerned with putting out fires or solving problems as they arise, rather than wanting to look forward and plan to avoid such problems or fires in the future. The planning function has assumed a great importance in all types of organizations irrespective of business in which it is involved. The organization may be a public sector or a private sector, may be profit earning organization or a non-profit organization. The present day management, where entire business is considered as a system and while planning all factors relating to organization is considered, suggests that before planning an interaction with environment on a continuous basis is essential, as much of the organizational plan depends on what is happening in the external environment. Good planning always helps in keeping this interaction between organization and external environment on a continuous basis and mostly the success or failure of the organization depends on the results of this interaction. For example you can recollect the success of Nirma detergent powder and the success of Lijjat Papad. We can have many more examples of similar nature.

In planning process we decide the future courses of action of an organization. This is done at various levels of organization. The levels of planning are Corporate level, Division level, Departmental level and Sectional level. This means to say that the plan is to be progressive, i.e. it should be done stage by stage at various levels. When planning is done level-by-level (or phase by phase), chances of missing the data required for successful plan will be less. Planning for overall origination is known as corporate planning. The word corporate indicates that the plan is for the whole organization to fulfill the company (corporation) objectives. In planning all level of managers will participate, but more emphasis will be on the top-level managers and board members. The middle level managers and lower level managers will supply the data needed for making optimal decision.

***Definition of Corporate Planning:* "It is the process of formulation of objectives as well as developing and evaluating alternate courses of action to teach these objectives, based on identified external opportunities and threats and internal or corporate strengths and weaknesses".**

It is also defined as the **"establishment of objectives and the formulation, evaluation and selection of policies strategies, tactics and action required to achieve these objectives."**

From the above definitions we can establish the features of corporate planning as:

(i) Corporate planning is concerned with company's objectives, plans and strategies and is the responsibility of top management, though the lower level managers help in supplying the necessary data/information.

(ii) It is concerned with long-range objectives and plans of the enterprise and ways of achieving the same optimally.

(iii) It is a systematic approach in developing and implementing plans at strategic and operational levels. In fact corporate planning is an important tool in improving the functioning of the organization. The advantages of corporate planning are:

Advantages

(a) It helps the organization in increasing its ability to face the changes in the external environment and internal environment and uncertainty in business environment.

(b) It encourages the innovative way of thinking and creativity in the organization.

(c) Corporate planning provides ways and means to improve employee and managerial motivation and job satisfaction among employees.

(d) It helps in improving the co-ordination among various departments of the origination.

(e) The most important advantages is that it improves the quality of managerial decisions and strategic decision-making.

Limitations

In spite of some advantages given above, corporate planning has some limitations, they are:

(a) It is time consuming and expensive process, as it consumes executive time. All the top-level managers are involved in decision-making and they cannot do their regular duties. Along with them their subordinates have to be present in the meeting to supply the necessary information for making decisions. Moreover many sittings may require dealing with critical problems, when the external environment poses problems.

(b) Reduces organizational flexibility.

(c) Corporate planning alone cannot show the way to success.

(d) It cannot be suddenly started and cannot expect overnight success.

(e) The outcome may be very nearer to an accurate solution as it involves the element of judgement by managers.

7.4.1. Classification of Plans

Depending on the personnel involved in planning process, the plans may be classified as **Strategic Plans and Operational Plans.** When top and middle level managers are involved in planning process, the plans are known as **Strategic Plans.** These plans are designed to meet the long time goals of an organization and they are very broad. When the lower level managers are involved in making plans the plans are termed as **Operational Plans** and they are designed to meet the day-to-day needs of the organization. In between the above two plans one more classification may be made depending on the time span, i.e. medium level plan or **tactical plans** in which middle level managers will actively participate and are designed to achieve the goals of strategic plans successfully and implement the operation plans successfully. In corporate objective we have a **broad goal** or **mission statement** based on the organization's planning premises, which gives the purpose of organization, its values, its distinctive competencies and its place in the world. We can identify the organization by its mission statement and it is the driving force behind all its activities and plans.

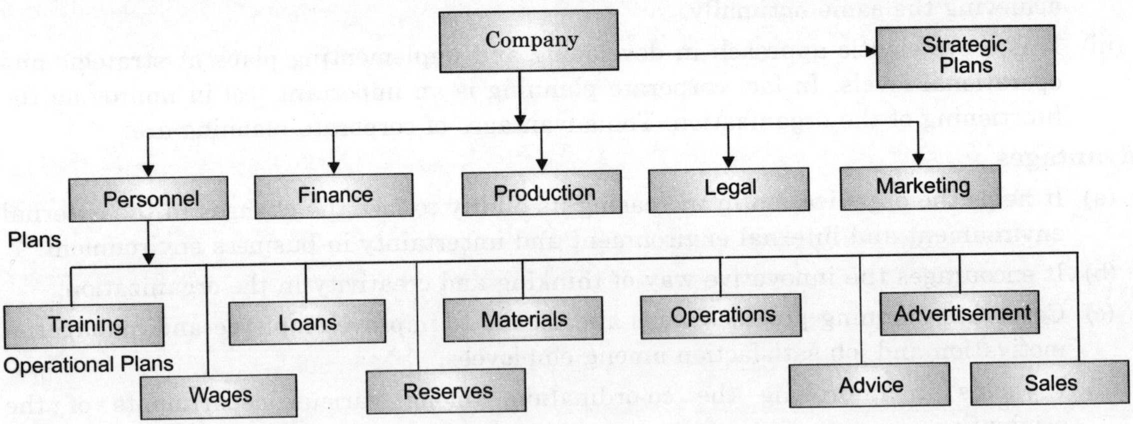

Fig. 7.1. Types of Plans

7.4.1.1. Strategic Plans

Strategic plans are long time plans, which may spread for number of years or decades. They affect a wide range of organizational activities. Top-level managers with the help of middle managers prepare these. They are broad in nature and deceptively simple. These plans are independent and mostly depends on the philosophy of the organization.

7.4.1.2. Operational Plans

Operational plans are short-term plans which may be for a year or less than that. These plans are narrow and limited in scope and deals with coordination of resources to fulfil the delivery promises. Functional managers as per the corporate objectives prepare these plans and with the help of lower level managers they execute the plan. These plans are complex and focus much on functional aspects. They reflect the strategic plans and goals.

The above may be tabulated as follows:

Table 7.1. Types of Plans

S. No.	Feature	Strategic Planning	Operational Planning
1.	Time Span	Long range plans	Short term plans
2.	Scope	Organizational level	Functional level
3.	Concern	Top-level managers	Middle and lower level managers
4.	Complexity	Broad and Simple	Narrow and complex
5.	Dependency	Independent	Depends on strategic plans

7.5. STEPS IN PLANNING OR PLANNING PROCESS

Now let us briefly view the steps generally involved in the planning activity. The following are the major steps in the planning process namely:

1. Crystallizing the opportunity or problem (Goal formulation).
2. Securing and analyzing necessary information. (Environmental analysis).
3. Establishing planning premises and constraints. (Identification of opportunities and threats).
4. Ascertaining alternative courses of action or plans.
5. Selecting the optimum plan. (Decision-making).
6. Determining the derivative plans.
7. Fixing the timing for introduction of plans. (Implementation).
8. Arranging future evaluation of effectiveness of the plan.

The above are briefly discussed below:

7.5.1. Crystallizing the Opportunity or Problems

Naturally the first step in logical planning would be to find out the problem to be provided for or the opportunity to be seized. It is necessary to ascertain clearly what requires improvement for which the plan is visualized. The following questions are asked to get a suitable answer, which may help in planning.

(a) What do we want?

(b) Why is the plan to be formed?

(c) What are we now doing to get what we want?

(d) Is an entirely new plan required or will it be sufficient to modify the existing plan?

(e) If the plan is effective, what will be the benefit to the organization?

This type of crystallization or awareness is necessary to be able to formulate practical and realistic objectives. Understanding the problem will help us in goal formulation, which is very important. The formulated goal alone tells us what we have to achieve. Goal formulation involves reviewing and understanding the organizational mission and then establishing goals that translate the mission in corporate terms. The goal chosen will take up a large amount of organization's available resources and govern so many of its activities. The top-level manager's or the Board of Director's attitude may have crystallizing effect on selection or formulation of goals.

7.5.2. Securing and Analyzing Necessary Information

Adequate information is required to decide on courses of action possible. The information has to be gathered on the type of activity to be planned. It is necessary to determine the nature of information required and where such information will be available. The information so gathered must then be analyzed to establish relationships and tabulate them for adequate interpretation. Knowing the goals of organization and existing strategy provides a framework for defining the aspects of environment that influences the organizational ability to achieve the goal. So, manager must concentrate his attention to scan the environment and get information required and analyze them to frame strategies to achieve the targets set by plan. The purpose of environmental analysis is to identify the factors in external environment, such as, economic, socio-economic, socio-cultural, technological, political and legal factors, competitors, suppliers, customers, government agencies and others can directly or indirectly influence the organization's needs and activities. We can see quite a good number of examples like the manufacturers offering various gifts/offers to promote their sales during certain period to reach the break-even. The manager must be careful enough to list out crucial and non-crucial factors to analyze them to get a better outcome. The relevant information can be gathered from survey, from trade journals and industrial publications and company's forecasts. Today's manager has quite a good number of quantitative techniques on his hand to analyze the collected data to form an optimal plan. Environmental analysis is the process by which the manager monitors the environmental factors to determine opportunities and threats to their firms. Analysis also involves studying the minutes of each factor to find its nature, function and relationship. Strategic manager essentially searches for opportunities and threats, their sources and their impact on the business. Here the manager has to examine the relationship between the company's strategy and the environment. Then the manager compares the strategy with the future environment. If the manager identifies the gap between the two, then he has to revise the business mission and objectives. Systematic environmental analysis and diagnosis is necessary due to the following reasons:

(a) Environmental factors are prime factors that influence the change of strategy.

(b) Environmental analysis and diagnosis provide the time to the strategist to forecast opportunities and to plan to respond aptly to these opportunities.

(c) Environmental analysis and diagnosis help strategic manager to develop an early warning system to prevent threats to develop strategies which can convert a threat into an opportunity.

(d) They help to determine what factor in the environment presents threats to the organization's present strategy and objectives accomplishment.

(e) They help to determine what factors in the environment present opportunities for optimal utilization of resources and achieving of objective effectively.

(f) They also help in identifying the inherent risks involved in utilizing the opportunities as normally, risks are involved in any opportunities.

(g) Systematic analysis and diagnosis enable the managers, to predict the future and to have enough time for other activities. This minimizes the time pressure on the managers of the unanticipated events.

(h) They help the managers to achieve the organizational objectives effectively than other organizations.

The above factors show the importance of environmental factor analysis while preparing plans.

7.5.3. Establishing Planning Premises and Constraints

An analysis of the data so collected will result in the formation of certain assumptions on the basis of which the plan will be ultimately formulated. For example, assumptions regarding the future will be made. Forecasting involves assumptions regarding the future political and economic environments, the possible trends in the market, the probable competitive behaviors and so on. Some of these premises are **uncontrollable** by the organization such as population growth, whereas others are **controllable** such as advertising policy to be adopted by the company itself. **Constraints** such as Governmental control will also exist. Planning will be in the backdrop of such premises and constraints, which must be watched to detect changes and their effect on the plans.

7.5.4. Ascertaining Alternative Courses of Action or Plans

In the light of above analysis the possible alternative courses of action will be ascertained and examined. Generally, in all situations, there is more than one possible course of action ingenuity and imaginations as well as experience are required to be able to ascertain a number of possible alternative courses of action available in a given situation. The manager has to evaluate each alternate course of action in the light of organizational goals, philosophy, and mission and select the best one to achieve the desired goal optimally. There are four criteria for evaluating strategic alternatives. They are:

1. The strategy and its component arts should have consistent goals, objectives and policies.
2. It should focus resources and efforts on the critical issues, identified in the policy formation process and separate them from less important ones.
3. It should deal with sub problems by taking into consideration the organization's available resources and skills.
4. The strategy should be capable of producing the intended results.

In evaluating alternatives, it is also important to focus on a particular product or service and on those competitors who are direct rivals in offering it. A strategy that does not create or exploit the organization's particular advantage over its rivals should be rejected.

7.5.5. Selection of Optimal Plan

Each of the alternative courses of action will then have to be evaluated either by judgement alone or with the help of quantitative techniques and staff assistance to evolve and select the plan or courses of action, which is the optimum or the best considering all the factors in the interest of the company. In choosing among the available possibilities, successful managers select the alternatives that are best suited to the organization's capabilities. New capabilities can be acquired only through investment in human resources and/or equipment and cannot be built up quickly. Therefore, it is seldom advisable to embark on a strategic plan requiring resources or skills that are weak or nonexistent. Instead, recognized strengths should be fully exploited.

7.5.6. Determining the Derivative Plans

From the basis of the strategies selected above, other plans will have to be developed to support the basic plan. These plans are known as **derivative plans.** For example, manpower planning may lead to planning for procuring and selection, training and placement etc. It also helps in planning the production schedules depending on the manpower available.

7.5.7. Fixing the Timing of Introduction of Plan Selected

The question of timing and who will do what, will then be enunciated, an appropriate time schedule will have to be prepared and detailed instructions written for communication of the plan. Much care should be taken to see that the plan is introduced at right time and in right way, which will help the manager to achieve the goals as desired. It is because even the most sophisticated plan or strategy and creative strategy will not benefit the organization unless it is carried out effectively. Effective communication system is desirable to convert strategic plan into the appropriate operational plan.

7.5.8. Arranging Future Evaluation of Effectiveness of the Plan

The ultimate objective of the plan was to achieve certain objectives, results or goals. Have these been achieved? If not, where was the slip up? Such an evaluation, at the earliest possible opportunity, is necessary to ensure adequate controlling to see that the planned objectives are achieved. As the implementation proceeds, manager must check their progress at periodic or at critical stages. Company controllers often play an important role in designing systems of strategic control. These controllers have to check:

(a) Is the strategy being implemented as planned?

(b) Is the strategy achieving the intended results? And what is the deviation of actual from the plan and reasons for deviation?

(c) What course of action is to be taken to reduce the deviations?

The above process is also at times described as the **decision-making process** as planning and decision-making are so closely interrelated.

7.6 TYPES OF PLANS

There are different ways in which plans are classified. The criteria of classification may be **Time span** such as **Short-term plan**, which extends to a time period of one year, **Medium time span** plans whose time span will be from one year to five years and finally **Long range plans** whose time period extends beyond five years. Plans can also be classified depending on the functions like **Production planning, Manpower planning and Marketing planning etc.**

As far as the subject matter concerned here, the plans may be classified as:

1. Objectives or Goals,
2. Strategies and tactics,
3. Standards,
4. Budgets,
5. Policies,
6. Procedures,
7. Programmes,
8. Rules,
9. Methods.

7.6.1. Objectives or Goals

The end results to achieved, or towards which an activity is to be directed are described as **objectives** or **Goals.** Objectives have to be crystallized for the enterprise as a whole, which would constitute the basic plans of the organization (Corporate objectives or Corporate plans). Besides, objectives or goals for each department also have to be enunciated or planned. Thus objectives give direction to the activities and result from planning. Their crystallization requires creative thinking and foresight and constitutes a part of the planning activity.

7.6.2. Strategies and Tactics

While discussing strategy, we have seen that it is distinct from a plan in its deliberate focus on the aspects of winning an advantageous position over an opponent. While plans generally specify direct goals and the ordinary means of achieving them, strategies are aimed at counteracting the actions of the opponent and in that sense strategies are considered to be *special type of plans.* Tactics on the other hand are immediate decisions based on the executive's judgements and experience while facing an actual situation. Terry distinguishes the terms **strategic planning** as being normally used *with reference to fundamental issue, broad perspectives, and long-periods* from **tactical planning** which *deals with determining the most efficient use of the resources that have been allotted for achieving given and specific objectives.* This clarifies that the differences are in time element, that level of the objectives involved and the part of the total enterprise activities covered.

7.6.3. Standards

Standards are well set results (targets), expected to be achieved by implementing plans. When plans are executed, the actual achievement is compared with the standards and the performance is evaluated. Standards are therefore very useful in evaluating deviations from the plans.

7.6.4. Budgets

Budget is described as both a planning and a controlling device. It presents data of reasonable expectancies in a given period. It may be expressed in units of products, machine hours or in financial terms or in any other suitable units depending on the purpose for which the budget is prepared. Budgets are also used as control devices, although making the budget is a planning function. The budget formulation forces the organization to plan ahead and make a numerical, logical compilation to give directions and control limits. Budgets are generally used as controlling devices.

7.6.5. Policies

Policies are general statements aimed at guiding and thinking while making-decisions. They constitute broad boundaries, permitting initiative of the manager to the extent of interpreting the particular policy. Policies need not necessarily be written as they may be implied from the past actions of managers. As example of a policy would be that *promotion must be from within the company or the existing staff.* If such a policy is prescribed, it gives a direction or guidance for future promotions. Both Objectives and Policies guide the mental and physical actions of a manager.

7.6.6. Procedures

A procedure is another kind of plan as it involves a selection and establishment of a logical series of tasks within the framework of predetermined policies and objectives. Procedures are therefore more definite than policies, defining specific activities to be accomplished towards a predetermined goal. Procedures exist throughout the organization. They are generally more in number at lower levels of the hierarchy because of the need for greater control. Say for example an organization may have a policy to allow leave travel concession for its employees once in a year. Whereas the procedures state the guidelines and methods in which the employee should apply for such concession and the various documents to be presented to the management after the completion of such leave.

7.6.7. Programmes

A programme integrates policies; procedures etc. required for effecting a certain course of action. It thus integrates actions, which are diverse but related. It may be looked upon as ***planned actions, integrated into a unity of designed to bring about a stated objectives.***

7.6.8. Rules

Rules are also looked upon as plans as they prescribe the course of action required. Rules are related to procedures as they guide action but there is no time sequence attached to them.

Examples of rules are: (a) *No smoking is allowed in Government Offices and in public places.* (b) *All letters received must be answered on the same day.* The rules allow no deviation.

7.6.9. Methods

The method prescribes specifically and in detail **how a task is to be done constituting the best way of performing the task under question.**

7.7. SWOT ANALYSIS

7.7.1. Introduction

Strategic management involves establishment of proper organizational environment, which matches with organizational factors with the environmental factors. Important duty of strategic management is to analyze organizational factors such as the ***strength and weaknesses of the organization*** and the environmental factors such as ***threats and opportunities in the business environment.***

7.7.2. Swot Analysis

In strategic management analysis or evaluation of companies **STRENGTHS (S),** and **WEAKNESS (W)** and analysis of **OPPORTUNITIES (O)** and **THREATS (T)** of the business environment is an important step while formulating strategies. In addition to this we have **WOTS** (weakness, opportunities, threats and strengths), known as **up analysis, SCOT** (strengths, constraints, opportunities and threats) analysis, **Internal analysis** (Strengths and weakness of the firm), External analysis (environmental threats and opportunities), **ETOP** (environmental threats and opportunities profile), **EFE** (external factor evaluation), **IFE** (internal factor evaluation), and IFE/EFE matrix analysis are also used while formulating strategies. In matrix analysis, key internal and external factors are identified and assigned weightages depending on their influence on the performance of the business and weighted scores are obtained by multiplying the weights with the corresponding ratings.

Analysis of strengths or internal competence like company's image, brand image, business synergies and functional areas such as marketing and finance, personnel and production etc. particularly in comparison to competitors is very important. Similarly, those factors, which tend to decrease the competencies of the firm particularly in comparison with competitors, are known as weaknesses. This may include poor product quality, outdated technology, high production costs, lack of research and development back up, poor distribution infrastructure, poor financial position and weak management etc.

An opportunity of a firm may be a threat for another company and strength of a company may be weakness of another company. For example, let us say that to promote small-scale industries; government is giving protection, so that the small-scale industries enjoy the market. This is strength of these units. In case the government withdraws its protection and gives license for other industries also, then for other industries, this will be an opportunity and strength and for small-scale industries it becomes a threat. The table given below shows the list of strengths and weaknesses of businesses.

Table 7.2. Table Showing Strengths and Weaknesses

S. No.	Strengths	Weaknesses
1.	**Marketing:** Strong brand image. Strong distribution network. Deep Product mix. Efficient and motivated sales force. High quality product. Product offers more utility value. Competitive price.	Poor brand image. Weak distribution network. Narrow product mix. Poor and weak sales force. Poor quality product. Product offers limited or less utility value. High sales price.
2.	**Production:** Economics of scale. State of the art technology. Efficient input sources. Efficient Inventory management. Strong research and development support.	High cost due to small size. Outdated technology. Inefficient input sources. Poor inventory management. Weak research and development support.
	Efficient and good production planning and Control. Efficient industrial engineering support.	Poor and inefficient production planning and control. Poor industrial engineering support.
3.	**Finance:** Comfortable debt-equity ratio. Large internal accruals. High dividends and market capitalization. High credit rating. Good receivables management. Good rate of return.	Lop sided capital structure. Very high interest payments. Poor reserves. Poor credit rating. Poor receivables management. Poor rate of return.
4.	**Human Resource:** Qualified and experienced human resource. Motivated human resource. Good and cordial industrial relation. Efficient human resource management. Good employee morale. Attractive wage and incentive plan.	Redundant human resource. Excess manpower. Poor industrial relation. Poor human resource management. Poor employee morale. Poor wages.
5.	**Management:** Efficient Board of Directors. Good understanding and co-operation between the members of the board and good relation between Board members and top-management team. Efficient managers. Good leadership.	Inefficient Board of Directors. Unhealthy conflict between board members and Conflict between board members and top-management Team. Inefficient managers. Inefficient leadership.

Table 7.3. Table Showing Opportunities and Threats

	Opportunities	Threats
1.	**Regulatory/Political.** Licensing. Reservation. MRTPA implementation. No price control. Liberalization of foreign investments, Technology policy. Capital market reforms. Political stability and stable government.	 De licensing, De reservation. MRTPA relaxation. Control on Selling price. Control on foreign investments and technology policy. Constraints on capital market. Unstable government and politics.
2.	**Economics** Boom in business activities. Steady and fast increase in income. High per capita income.	 Recession in business activities. Economic instability. Low per capita income.
3.	**Social and Demographic** Favorable change in consumer attitude. Healthy increase in population. Change in age composition in population. Growth in consumerism.	 Unfavorable change in consumer attitude. Stagnating/declining population. Unfavorable change in composition of age in population. Decline in consumerism.

7.8. TECHNIQUES FOR ENVIRONMENTAL ANALYSIS

Information gathering and evaluation of gathered information are the two important phases in environmental analysis and organizational analysis i.e. analysis and evaluation of *strengths, weaknesses* (internal environment) and *opportunities, threats* (external environment). Guleck mentions the following steps in environmental analysis, which includes source of information and method of collecting information (first three steps) and using information for visualizing the future scenario (fourth step).

1. **Verbal and Written Information:** Verbal information includes, verbal information obtained by direct talk with people, attending meetings, seminars etc., or through media such as radio and television. Written or documentary information includes both published and unpublished materials.
2. **Searches and Scanning:** This involves research for obtaining the required information.
3. **Spying:** Although it may not be considered ethical, spying to get information about the competitors business and plans is not very uncommon.
4. **Forecasting:** Corporate planners, or other staff personnel or consultants may do forecasting.

7.9. RELATING STRENGTHS, WEAKNESSES AND OPPORTUNITIES, THREATS

Strategy formulation involves relating organizational strengths and weaknesses to environmental threats and opportunities. This is shown in table below:

7.10. SWOT AND STRATEGY

TOWS MATRIX

The **TOWS** matrix devised by Heinz Wethrich is an important and useful strategy formulation and matching tool. It gives four alternative strategies.

Table 7.4. SWOT and Strategies

S. No.	Strengths / Weaknesses	Opportunities / Threats	Strategy
1.	Large internal accruals and High credit rating.	Fast future growth of industry 'X'.	Acquire firms/Establish green field units in industry 'X.'
2.	Gaps in the product mix.	Competitor firm whose Product items can fill the gaps is for sale.	Acquire the competitor's firm.
3.	Obsolete technology.	Increasing competition.	Acquire modern technology or form joint ventures.
4.	Accumulating losses and no Prospects of improvement In one of the businesses.	Increasing competition	Drop the business.
5.	Has technology and Production capability and low Production costs, but no International marketing Capability.	Good demand for the Product in internal and Foreign markets.	Strategic alliance with a foreign firm having marketing muscle.

WT Strategy: The WT strategy, also known as **mini-mini** strategy aims at minimizing the weaknesses and threats. Some of the weaknesses may be overcome or minimized. For example, if any functional area observed to be not functioning properly and happens to be weakness of the company and pose threats, we can replace the manager of that functional area by an efficient and capable manager; it minimizes or overcomes weakness and threats.

Strategic alliance or other types of joint ventures may minimize external threats. Sometimes dropping unprofitable businesses may become very good WT strategy.

WO Strategy: WO or **mini-maxi** strategy focus at minimizing the weaknesses and maximizing the opportunities. Dependency on external resources for the supply of component or material may sometimes be a weakness of the firm. By installing technology and manufacturing will maximize the opportunity.

ST Strategy: The ST or **maxi-mini** strategy attempts to use the organization's strengths to deal with the environmental threats. The company may use all its strengths such as technical, financial, personnel to spoil the game of the competitor.

SO Strategy: SO or **maxi-maxi** strategy, is most desirable and advantageous strategy, aims to make up a firm's strengths to exploit the opportunities.

All the above four strategies are shown in the form of a matrix known as **TOWS MATRIX.**

INTERNAL FACTORS / EXTERNAL FACTORS	INTERNAL FACTORS	
	INTERNAL STRENGTHS (S)	INTERNAL WEAKNESSES (W) ....
INTERNAL OPPORTUNITIES (O) .... ST (Maxi – Mini) EXTERNAL THREATS (T)	So (Maxi – Maxi-Strategy) (Maximize strengths and Opportunities) ST – (Mini – Mini Strategy) Maximize Strengths and minimize threats.	WO (Mini – Maxi Strategy) Minimize weakness and Maximize Strengths) WT (Mini – Mini Strategy) Minimize weakness and Minimize Threats.

Fig. 7.2. Swot Matrix

7.11. ENVIRONMENTAL SCANNING

A business manager has to interact with two types of factors of environments while making a decision. They are **Internal Factors or Internal Environment** and **External Factors or External Environment.** In general when we speak of **Business Environment** it refers to external environment. Now let us deal with both the types of environment to understand the effects of these two types of environment on the work of a business manager. The internal factors or internal environment are generally regarded as **controllable** factors because they are under the control of the organization and its managers. The organization can alter or modify such factors as its personnel, physical facilities, organization and functional means, such as marketing mix, to suit the situation. Compared to internal factors, external factors or external environment, by and large are beyond the control of the company. The external or environmental factors, such as the economic factors, socio-cultural factors, government and legal factors, demographic factors, geo-physical factors etc. are, therefore, generally regarded as **Uncontrollable** factors.

As the external environmental factors are beyond the control of a firm, its success will depend to a very large extent on its adaptability to the environment, i.e., its ability to properly design and adjust the internal or controllable variables to take advantage of the opportunities and to comb the threats in the environment. One of the most critical challenges is to cope up with the environmental dynamics of change, which many a time assumes the nature of turbulence. The challenges an enterprise has to face are the challenges to combat the environmental threats such as intensifications of competitions, declining market, and to exploit the business opportunities. In fact environmental analysis is the first step in Strategic Management or in Corporate Planning process. Environmental Analysis is defined as *the process by which strategists monitor the economic, governmental/legal, market/competitive, supplier/technological, geographic and social settings to determine opportunities and threats to their enterprise.* Environmental diagnosis consists of managerial decisions made by analyzing the significance of the data (opportunities and threats) of the environmental analysis.

7.12. INTERNAL ENVIRONMENT

There are number of internal factors which influence the strategy and other decisions. They are:

7.12.1. Value System

The value system of promoters and those at the helm of affairs has important bearing on the choice of business, the mission and objectives of the organization, business policies and practice. It is a widely acknowledged fact that the extent to which all in the organization shares the value system is an important factor contributing to success. The value system of JRD Tata and the acceptance of it by others who matter were responsible for the voluntary incorporation in the **Article of Association of TISCO its social and moral responsibilities to Employees, shareholders, society and the people.**

7.12.2. Mission and Objectives

The business domain of the company, priorities, direction of development, business philosophy, business policy etc. is guided by the mission and objectives of the enterprise.

7.12.3. Management Structure and Nature

The organizational structure, the composition of the Board of Directors, extent of professionalisation of management etc. are important factors influencing business decisions. We can see those companies who have directors with good technical and professional qualifications who manage the enterprise in a successful way and fulfil the objectives and see that the organization will grow steadily. When the board of directors are selfish and have no moral qualification, they see the end of the organization within no time. The good examples are co-operative banks, which have deceived millions of its customers. (Good examples are some of our Co-operative banks and private financial institutions that have toppled their name boards.)

7.12.4. Internal Power Relationship

Factors like the amount of support the top management enjoys from lower levels and workers, shareholders and Board of Directors have important influence on the decisions and their implementation. The relationship between the members of the Board of Directors is also a critical factor. The differences in the opinion and personal ego and interests are the root causes of failure of any organization.

7.12.5. Human Resource

The characteristics of human resources like skill, quality, morale, commitment, attitudes etc. could contribute to the strength or weakness of an organization. Some organizations find it difficult to carry out manufacturing or modernization because of resistance by employees whereas they are smoothly done in some others. We can recollect here that the employees of LIC of India have agitated, when the organization wanted to install computers in its day-to-day work. But today they are enjoying the benefits of use of computers in data management. The involvement, initiative etc. of people at different levels may vary from organization to organization. The organizational culture and overall environment have bearing on them.

7.12.6. Company Image and Brand Equity

The image of the enterprise matters while raising the resources, especially finance, forming joint ventures or other alliance, soliciting marketing intermediaries, entering purchase or sale contracts, launching new products etc. Brand equity is also relevant in several of these cases. Sometimes a good image may act as a negative factor. For example, when one says NIRMA it gives the image of washing powder. It is because of well-established brand in washing powder. Suppose Nirma organization wants to introduce bathing soap or Nirma cosmetics, the company has to face difficulty to penetrate in the marketing of bathing soap/ cosmetics market. The same happened to Ponds Soap.

7.12.7. Other Factors

There are number of other internal factors which contribute to business success or failure or influence the decision-making. Some of them are

1. ***Physical assets and Facilities***: These are factors like production capacity, technology and efficiency of the productive apparatus; logistics etc. which influence the competitiveness of a firm.
2. ***Research and Development and Technological capabilities***: These will, with other things, determine the ability to innovate and compete in the external environment.
3. ***Marketing resources***: Organization for marketing, quality and commitment of marketing men, brand equity, distribution network etc. has direct bearing on the marketing efficiency. They are important also for brand extension, new product introduction.

7.13. EXTERNAL ENVIRONMENT

External environment may be classified as **Microenvironment and Macroenvironment.**

7.13.1. Microenvironment

Microenvironment consists of performance influencing factors, which are in the company's immediate environment, for example, factors like suppliers, marketing intermediaries, competitors, customers and the public may be considered as microenvironment factors. Against to this macroenvironment consists of the larger societal forces that affect all the actors in the company's microenvironment. Examples of macroenvironment are demographic, economic, natural, technological, political and cultural forces. Microenvironment is also known as **task environment and operating environment.**

Microenvironmental factors are intimately linked with the company's performance than the macroenvironmental factors. The effect of microfactors may vary form company to company in an industry. Some microfactors may have a close relationship with a firm and have higher influence than the other firm. For example, a firm, which depends on a supplier, may have a supplier environment, which is entirely different from that of a firm whose supply source is different. When competing firms in an industry have the same microelements, the relative success of the firm depends on their relative effectiveness in dealing with these elements.

7.13.1.1. Suppliers

Any company needs raw materials for its manufacturing activities. Reliable source of supply is very much essential for smooth running of the company's affairs. If the raw materials are received in time, company can keep up its delivery promises and have good image in the next immediate microenvironmental factor, the customer. Because of importance of reliable supplier, the focus of many companies is on vendor development. Vertical integration may provide a feasible solution regarding this problem. If the suppliers are regular, the company need not maintain large size inventory, which will become burden on the company and unnecessarily increases the production cost. To avoid risk of shortage of inventory, companies should not depend on a single source of supply, as it always affects the performance of the company. At the same time, the company must also have an eye on the changing attitude/ behavior of the supplier. The supply management assumes an important position in a scarcity environment. The best strategy is that the purchasing department might have to **market** itself to **suppliers.**

7.13.1.2. Customers

Customers, in real sense are assets of a company. Customer may be an individual or group of persons or a business organization or government, may belong to the same country or an international customer. It is the primary duty of the company to create and sustain the customer and monitor the customer sensitivity, which is a key to success.

It is not always advisable to depend on a single customer as company will not have bargaining power and in case of differences in terms and conditions, company may have to loose the business. The choice of customer segments should be made by considering a number of factors including the relative profitability, dependability, stability of demand, growth prospects and the extent of competition.

7.13.1.3. Competitors

In strict sense a competitor means another company manufacturing the same product or similar product and selling in the market or offering similar service to the customers. But in broader sense, we have to think of disposable income of the customer. It is particularly true in an economy, where the individual will have limited disposable income and unlimited unsatisfied desires. That is he has various alternative ways to spend disposable money to purchase certain items or to save the same for future spending. Here competitor is considered as those who compete for the discretionary income of the customers. The competitors in this sense may be companies manufacturing same type of goods and selling or other products which satisfies the needs of the customer or financial institutions offering the saving schemes and many more. Say for example, when an individual wants to spend his disposable surplus income to purchase a Television, he can come across an advertisement of a two wheeler, more or less of the same cost with better offers. This makes the customer to change his mind from Television to a Two-wheeler. The competition among such alternatives, which satisfy a particular category of desire, is called **generic competition.** When the consumer decides to purchase a television the next question comes to him is which brand and which make, once this is decided, then comes which type, colour or black and white? If this is answered, then the next question is with remote control or without remote control etc. This is known as **product form competition.** Hence, an implication of these different demands is that a marketer should strive to create **primary** and **selective** demand for his products.

7.13.1.4. Marketing Intermediaries

The links between the producer and the end consumer are known as marketing intermediaries. These include, retailers, wholesalers, middlemen, agencies and physical distribution agencies such as transport organizations and advertising agencies and all those who work for sales promotion of the product of a company. Any company must be careful enough while selecting these intermediaries for their success. A wrong selection may lead the company to close their business.

7.13.1.5. Publics

A public may be defined as any group that has an actual or potential interest in or impact on an organization's ability to achieve its interests. Examples of publics are: Media publics, Citizens action publics and local publics etc. A company maintains its cordial relations with all the publics, especially media public, which gives publicity regarding the product of the company. We see that in some newspapers, information about a financial institution is given regarding the operation of the funds and misuse of funds. This may lead to strong reaction by the public and depositors and the government sometimes. Sometimes the reaction of the public (citizens) may be a threat to the company. It is wrong to think that all publics are threats to business. Some of the actions of the public may cause problems for companies. However, some publics are an opportunity for the business. Some businessmen, for example, regard consumerism as an opportunity for the business. The media public may be used to disseminate useful information. Similarly fruitful cooperation between a company and the local publics may be established for mutual benefit of the company and the local community.

7.13.2. Macroenvironment

A company and the forces in its microenvironment operate in a larger macroenvironment of forces that shape the opportunities and pose threats to the company. The macroforces are, generally, more uncontrollable than the micro forces. Some of the macroenvironmental factors are:

7.13.2.1. Economic Environment

Economic environment of a company consists of Nations economic structure, economic system, and economic policies. Economic determinates of a company deal with nature of economy, the stages of development of the economy, economic resources and level of income, distribution of income and assets. The demand for a certain product depends more on the surplus income a consumer spends to purchase after meeting the basic needs. Hence per capita income is a very powerful factor for deciding the demand for the product. In an economy where investment and income are steadily and rapidly rising, business prospects are generally bright and further investment is encouraged. In a developed economy replacement demand for consumer durable goods plays a vital role than in developing country. It is because, the disposable income in developed economy is considerably high and the consumer wants to replace consumer durables by new design, whereas in developing economy, the consumer cannot go for replacing the goods with him because of meager disposable income. Government's Export and Import Policy will also have effect on the supply and demand of the products. Industrial policy of a nation has direct effect on the performance of the company as government sometimes protects certain industries and sometime it gives subsidy to some industries. In general we can say the scope of private business depends, to a large extent, on the economic system of the nation. The freedom of private enterprise is the greatest in the free market economy.

7.13.2.2. Political and Government Environment

Political and Government environment has close relationship with the economic system and economic policy. It is the government, which makes Industrial policy, permits Industrial Licensing, and gives permissions to start business and formulates laws and regulations for conducting the business. The government is made of elected people's representatives i.e. politicians. Hence, the business, which wants to survive and grow, has to manage with the Government and Politics. Sometimes government may insist laws and regulations to protect consumer interest. Government may also take interest to protect environmental balance and ecological balance, in such cases the business units may have to face some problems. The nation's Standards Organization, for example in India, Indian Standards Organization may have an eye on the standards of the products produced and insist strict measure for quality production.

7.13.2.3. Socio-cultural Environment

While formulating business policies or strategies the socio-cultural fabric, an important macro-environmental factor need to analyzed carefully. The cost of neglecting the socio-cultural factors like, customs, traditions, taboos, tastes and preferences etc. will be very high. The buying and consuming habits of the people, their language beliefs and values, customs and traditions, tastes and preferences, education are all the factors that affect business. When the policy of a business matches with the socio-cultural factors of the people, its performance will be towards success. We can identify Tamil culture in all the business activities in Tamil Nadu. Sometimes the business has to change its brand name to suit the culture in the State/ Nation. The values and beliefs associated with colour vary significantly between different cultures. For example Green is favorite colour for Muslim world, whereas in Malaysia it is associated with illness. Many demographic factors like age and sex composition of population, family size, religion etc., which influence the business. Social environment of the business must encompass its social responsibility and the alertness or vigilance of the consumer and of society at large.

7.13.2.4. Demographic Environment

Demographic environment refers to structure of population. Factors such as size of the population, population growth rate, age composition, life expectancy, family size, spatial dispersal, occupational status, employment pattern, birth rate and death rate and health status of the population affect demand for goods and services. Markets with growing population and income are growth markets. Increasing population is an indication for growing demand for many consumable goods and services. At the same time high growth rate of population may become a vital reason for many economic and social problems. Population poses problem of unemployment, which has influence on socio-economic and socio-cultural problems. It also leads to surplus labour and which has influence on wage structure. The occupational and spatial mobility of population have implications for business and wage rate in industry.

7.13.2.5. Natural Environment

Natural environment consists of geographical and ecological factors, such as natural resources, weather and climate conditions, topographical factors; location aspects in the global context port facilities are very much relevant to growth of business and become factors while formulating business strategies and policies. Ecological factors have assumed a great importance. The depletion of natural resources, environmental pollution and the disturbance of the ecological balance have caused great concern. Unbalanced ecological factors have influence on the agriculture production and which has direct effect on nation's economy, which in turn affects performance of the company.

7.13.2.6. Physical and Technological Environment

Physical factors like geographical and weather conditions play an important role in changing the demand of the product or sometimes demand the redesign of the product. Similarly, technological development may increase the standard of living of people at the same time demand for certain supporting facilities may raise. Say for example introduction of television and refrigerators increased the use of voltage stabilizers. But now due to inbuilt stabilizers affected the demand for stabilizers. Domestic gas connections increased the demand for gas lighters and various other appliances used with gas stove.

7.13.2.7. International Environment

International environment is very much important for the industries dealing with products, which have demand abroad, and the business, which uses the material or components available abroad. The Import and Export policy, control on imports and exports and relaxation of license for importing and exporting by government has its influence on the business. The best example for this is our fuel oil prices, which depend much on oil process abroad.

7.14. STRATEGIC MANAGEMENT

7.14.1. Introduction

STRATEGIC MANAGEMENT: The modern complexity and sophistication of business decision-making requires strategic management. Managing various and multifaceted internal activities is only part of the modern business executive's responsibilities. The firm's immediate external environment poses a second set of challenging factors. This environment includes competitors whenever profits seem possible, suppliers of increasingly scarce resources, government agencies monitoring adherence to an ever-growing number of regulations, and customers whose often-inexplicable preferences must be anticipated. A remote external environment also contributes to the general yet pervasive climate in which a business exists. This environment consists of economic conditions, social change, political priorities and technological developments, each of which must be anticipated, monitored, assessed and incorporated in top-level decision-making. However these influences are often subordinated to the fourth major considerations in executive decision-making—the multiple and often mutually consistent subjective of the stakeholders of the business i.e. owners, top managers, employees, communities customer and country.

To deal effectively with all that affects the ability of a company to grow profitably, executives design strategic management processes they feel will facilitate the optimal positioning of the firm in its competitive environment. Such positioning is possible because these strategic processes allow more accurate anticipation of environmental changes and improved preparedness for reacting to unexpected internal or competitive demands. Broad-scope, large-scale management processes have become dramatically more sophisticated since the end of World War II, principally as a reaction of increases in the sized and number of competing firms; of the expanded intervention of government as a buyer, seller, regulator and competitor in the free enterprise system; and of greater business involvement in international trade. Perhaps the most significant improvement in the management processes came in the year 1970 as ***"long-range planning", "new venture management," " Planning, Programming, budgeting,"*** and ***"business policy"*** were blended with increased emphasis on environmental forecasting and external as well as internal considerations in formulating and implementing plans. This all-encompassing approach is known as ***Strategic management or strategic planning.***

Strategic management is defined as ***the set of decisions and actions resulting in formulation and implementation of strategies (Courses of actions) designed to achieve the objective of an organization.*** It involves attention to no less than nine critical areas:

(a) Determining the mission of the company, including broad statements about its purpose, philosophy and goals.

(b) Developing a company profile that reflects internal conditions and capabilities.

(c) Assessment of company's external environment, in terms of both competitive and general contextual factors.

(d) Analysis of possible options uncovered in the matching of the company profile with the external environment.

(e) Identifying the desired options uncovered when possibilities are considered in light of the company mission.

(f) Strategic choice of a particular set of long-range objectives and grand strategies needed to achieve the desired options.

(g) Development of annual objectives and short-term strategies compatible with long-term objectives and grand strategies.

(h) Implementing strategic choice decisions based on budgeted resource allocations and emphasizing the matching of tasks, people, structures, technologies and reward systems.

(i) Review the evaluation of the success of the strategic process to serve as a basis for control and as an input for future decision-making.

As these nine areas indicate, strategic management involves the planning, directing, organizing and controlling of the strategy-related decisions and actions of the business. By strategy, managers mean their ***large-scale, future-oriented plans for interacting with the competitive environment to optimize achievement of organizational objectives.*** Thus, strategy represents organization's **game plan**. Although it does not precisely detail all future deployments (people, financial and material), it does provide a framework for managerial decisions. A strategy reflects a company's awareness of how to ***compete, against whom, when, where and for what.***

Six important identifiable dimensions of strategic decisions are:

1. Strategic issues require making management decisions.
2. Strategic issues involve the allocation of large amounts of company's resources.
3. Strategic issues are likely to have a significant impact on the long-term prosperity of the firm.
4. Strategic issues are future-oriented.
5. Strategic issues usually have major multifunctional or multi business consequences.
6. Strategic issues necessitates considering factors in the firm's external environment.

7.14.2. Levels of Strategy

The decision-making hierarchy of business firms typically contains three levels. At the top is the corporate level, composed principally of members of the board of directors and the chief executive and administrative officers. They are responsible for the financial performances of the corporation as a whole and for achieving the non-financial goals of the firm (for example, Corporate image and social responsibility). To the large extent, orientations at the corporate level reflect the concern of stockholders and society at large. Particularly in multi business firms, one duty of those at the corporate level is to determine the business in which the company should be involved. Further, corporate officers set objectives and formulate strategies that span the activities of individual businesses in the corporation and the functional area of these businesses. By adopting portfolio approach to strategic management, corporate-level strategic managers attempt to exploit their distinctive competencies within their industries while typically planning over a five-year time horizon.

The second level of the decision-making hierarchy is the business level, composed of principally of business and corporate managers. These managers must translate the general statements of directions and intent generated at the corporate level into concrete, functional objectives and strategies for individual business divisions. In essence, business-level strategic managers must determine the basis on which a company can compete in the selected product-market arena. While so doing, they strive to identify and secure the most profitable and promising market segment. This market segment is the fairly unique piece of the total market that the business can claim and defend because of competitive advantages. Every corporation, even the largest multinational, depends on the strength of market segments for continuing viability.

The third level is functional level, composed principally of managers of product, geographic, and functional areas. It is their responsibility to develop annual objectives and short-term strategies in such areas as production, operations and research & development; finance and accounting; marketing; and human relations. However, their greatest responsibilities are in the implementation or execution of a company's strategic plans. While corporate and business-level managers center their planning concerns on *"doing the right things"*. Thus they directly address such issues as the efficiency and effectiveness of production and marketing systems, the quality and extent of customer service and the success of particular product and service in increasing their market shares.

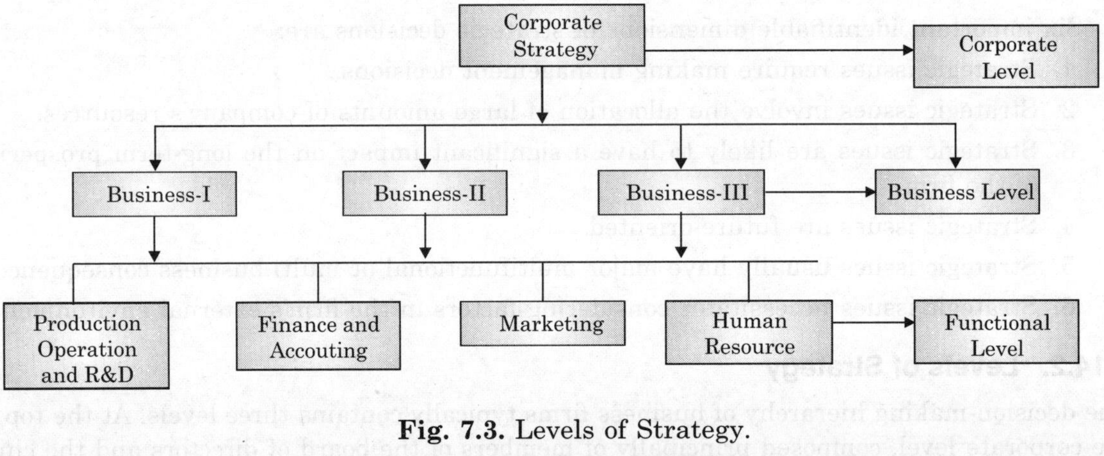

Fig. 7.3. Levels of Strategy.

7.15. CHARACTERISTICS OF STRATEGIC DECISIONS

The characteristics of strategic management decisions vary with the levels strategic activities considered. Corporate-level decisions tend to be value oriented, conceptual, and less concrete than those at the business or functional level of strategy formulation and implementation. Corporate level decisions are also characterized by greater risk, cost and profit potential, as well as by longer time horizons and greater needs for flexibility. These characteristics are logical consequences of the more far-reaching futuristic, innovative and pervasive nature of corporate-level strategic activity (examples are: Choice of Business, Dividend Policy, Source of Long term finance, priorities for growth etc.).

Functional level decisions principally involve action-oriented operational issues. These decisions are made periodically and lead directly to implementation of some part of the overall strategy formulated at the corporate and business levels. Therefore, functional-level decisions are relatively short range and involve low risk and modest costs because they are dependent on available resources. Functional level decisions usually determine actions requiring minimal company wide cooperation. These activities supplement the functional area's present activities and are adaptable to ongoing activities so that minimal cooperation is needed for successful implementation. Because functional-level decisions relatively pertain to operational departments of the organization.

Table 7.5. Table Showing the Characteristics of Strategic Decisions

S. No.	Characteristics	Levels of Strategy	Levels of Strategy	Levels of Strategy
		CORPORATE	BUSINESS	FUNCTIONAL
1	Type	Conceptual	Mixed	Usually quantifiable
2	Measurability	Value judgements	Semi quantifiable	Periodic
3	Frequency	Periodic or Sporadic	Periodic or Sporadic	Periodic
4	Adaptability	Low	Medium	High
5	Relation to present Activities	Innovative	Mixed	Supplementary
6	Risk	Wide range	Moderate	Low
7	Profit potential	Large	Medium	Small
8	Cost	Major	Medium	Modest
9	Time horizon	Long range	Medium range	Short range
10	Flexibility	High	Medium	Low
11	Co-operation Required	Considerable	Moderate	Little

7.16. BENEFITS OF STRATEGIC MANAGEMENT

Strategic management approach emphasizes interaction by managers at all levels of the organizational hierarchy in planning and implementation. As a result, strategic management has certain behavioral consequences that are also characteristics of participative decision-making. Therefore, an accurate assessment of the impact of strategy formulation on organizational performance also requires a set of non-financial evaluation criteria-measures of behavioral based effects. In fact, it can be argued that the manager trained to promote the positive aspects of these behavioral consequences is also well positioned to meet the financial expectation of the firm. Some of the advantages that a firm can gain from strategic management are:

1. Strategy formulation activities should enhance the problem prevention capabilities of the firm. This will make subordinates take rewarding attention to planning considerations and co-ordination.
2. Group based strategic decisions are most likely to reflect the best available alternatives. Because of this, better decisions are made to aid better functioning of the firm.
3. Employee motivation should improve as employees better appreciate the productivity-reward relationship inherent in every strategic plan.
4. Gaps and overlaps in activities between diverse individual and groups should be reduced as participation in strategy formulation leads to a clarification of role differentiations.
5. As required participation helps to eliminate the uncertainty associated with change, which is the root of most of the resistance, thus resistance to change is reduced.

7.17. RISKS OF STRATEGIC MANAGEMENT

Though strategy formulation and implementation helps the firm in certain ways, it also involves three types of unintended negative consequences. They are:

1. First one is, while it is readily recognized that the strategic management process is costly in terms of hours invested by participants, the negative effects of managers spending time away from work is considered less often. Managers must be trained to schedule their duties to provide the necessary time for strategic activates while minimizing any negative impact on operational responsibilities.
2. If the formulation of strategies is not intimately involved in implementation, individual responsibility for input to the decision process and subsequent conclusions can be shirked. Thus strategic managers must be trained to limit their promises to performance that can be delivered by the decision makers and their subordinates.
3. Thirdly, strategic managers must be trained to anticipate, minimize or constructively respond when participating subordinates become disappointed or frustrated over un-attained expectations. Frequently subordinates perceive an implicit guarantee that their involvement in even minor phases of total strategy formulation will result in both acceptance of their preferred plan and an increase in clearly associated rewards. Alternatively, they may erroneously conclude that a strategic manager's solicitation of their input on selected issues will extend to other areas of decision-making. Sensitizing managers to those issues and preparing them with effective means of negating or minimizing such negative consequences will greatly enhance the overall potential of any strategic plan.

7.18. STRATEGY IMPLEMENTATION

Strategy implementation requires disseminating the various components of strategy to different levels; mobilization and allocation of resources needed; structuring authority, responsibility, tasks and flow of information; establishing policies and evaluation and control procedures. Strategy is a blueprint indicating the courses of action to achieve the desired objectives. So effective translation of strategy into effective practice is important one.

Strategy implementation phase has got three components as published by many authors. They are:

1. **Operationalising the strategy:** This includes communicating the strategy to respective levels, setting of annual objectives, developing functional strategies and policies and allocation of desired resources.
2. **Institutionalizing the strategy:** This includes organizational structuring and leadership implementation.
3. **Evaluation and control of the strategy.** Setting up of standards, control procedures and feedback system for evaluation take corrective actions.

As strategy implementation involves a number of executives at different levels, many of them might have not taken part in strategy formulation; hence effective communication of strategy is an important and first step in strategy implementation. Every employee in the organization must be aware of future plans of the organization and what courses of action are to be taken by each and every functional level and what changes are affecting the organization. This is particularly true in growing organizations and to create awareness among employees and create a feeling of belongingness in them. Proper and effective communication of strategy is a prerequisite to successful implementation of the same.

Annual operating objectives designed to contribute to the long-term objectives is a critical step in strategy implementation. Long-term objectives are very broadly stated. While annual objectives very specifically lay down the annual goals for the business and functional areas or sub units of the organization. Annual objectives must be measurable, consistent, reasonable, challenging, clear and communicated throughout the organization.

Functional strategies, which are short-term game plans for the key functional area, are the means to accomplish the annual plans. Functional strategies by clearly specifying the various measures to be taken in different functional areas in different time horizons help in achieving the objectives of grand strategy (long-term strategies).

Making sufficient resources such as finance, manpower, material, technology, supporting facilities etc. are available in time is an essential requirement for effective implementation of the strategy. Without resources, no one can do anything; hence top management's commitments to the strategy will be reflected in the resource allocation.

Effective implementation of strategy requires formulation of policies, i.e. broad, general guide to action, which directs the employees towards the attainment of desired goal of the organization.

To implement a strategy effectively, it is very important to ensure a right organizational structure for the strategy, as **structure follows the strategy** (Alfred Chandler). Many strategies call for change in the organizational structure, which is very common in the industrial world.

Efficient evaluation and control system is very much important for effective implementation of the strategy. Evaluation and control and feedback are essential to check whether the strategy is effectively implemented or not and note down any deviations and take corrective action. Effective implementation needs to motivate the executives, managers and employees by providing rewards and incentives depending on the performance of the persons/departments.

7.19. APPROACH TO STRATEGY IMPLEMENTATION

A clear-cut approach is essential for implementing the strategy. The approach should depend on factors like assessment of change, structure, and culture variables. Five approaches are generally followed in implementing strategy. They are:

(a) Commander approach,

(b) Organizational change approach,

(c) The collaborative approach,

(d) The cultural approach, and

(e) Crescive approach.

(a) Commander Approach: The name indicates that the strategy is formulated at the top and communicated to the lower levels i.e. **top down approach**. The strategy is communicated to subordinates with instructions to execute it and top management oversees it by taking a back seat. This is a very common approach in industries. Here those who implement, the strategy may not be involved in strategy formulation; hence they may not have full commitment. This approach is suitable when the strategy is formulated confidentially or quickly or when the behavioral aspects do not favor other approaches.

(b) Organizational Change Approach: A suitable organization is a prerequisite for effective implementation of the strategy. Hence the management must ensure a right and suitable organizational structure for implementation of the strategy. The organizational change approach, as the name indicates, emphasizes bringing about the required organizational change to implement a strategy. Organizational change approach employs powerful behavioral tools in its operation and is more powerful than Commander Approach and it can implement more difficult strategies.

(c) Collaborative Approach: In implementing strategy, all the managers are involved because this method believe in collective endeavor in strategy development and implementation and expect that all managers contribute their best in achieving the goals. Under this approach brain storming sessions are usually employed for formulation of strategy and implementation of tactics. This is a very effective approach for many businesses. Here goals and strategies are negotiated at top level of the management and provide a forum for share and evaluate information and views contributed by various managers closer to operations and provide a better strategy development process.

(d) Cultural Approach: This is similar to collaborative approach but it uses the democratic element, which provides ways to include lower level managers also in the process. In this approach, the organizational vision and missions are well communicated to the employees so that they become the guideposts to develop strategies. The employees are empowered and encouraged to design their own work activities in pursuit of the mission of the business. Here manager acts as a coach and promotes individual decision-making. In one word we can say that this approach uses **third order control techniques,** i.e. it seeks to influence behavior by shaping the norms, values, symbols and beliefs of which managers and employees base day-to-day decisions. (Note: First order control is direct supervision of the superiors. Second order control is using rules, procedures, and organizational structure to guide behavior). Hence, third order control is more superior and powerful and motivates every person towards the achieving of goal voluntarily.

(e) **Crescive Approach:** Here Crescive means increasing or growing. The Crescive Approach addresses strategy formulation and implementation simultaneously. As against to Commander Approach, this is a **bottom-up approach.** Instead of pushing the strategy downward from the top management or a strategy group, it moves upward from the doers or the worker (operational level) level and then to the lower and middle management level and then to the top management level. Under this approach, instead of the top management taking on itself the entire task of developing the strategy, the subordinates are empowered to develop and implement sound strategies on their own. Goals are stated loosely from top and refined at the bottom level. The top-management team shapes the employee's premises, that is, the employee's notions of what would constitute supportable strategic projects and functions more as a judge evaluating the proposals rather than as a master strategist.

7.20. VALUE CHAIN ANALYSIS

The most important objective of any organization is customer satisfaction. When importance is given to customer value and satisfaction, what does it take to produce and deliver them? The answer to this question needs to discuss the concepts of a **value chain and value delivery-system.**

7.20.1. Value Chain

Michael porter of Harvard proposed the **value chin** as a tool for identifying ways to create more customer value. Every firm is a collection of activities that are performed to design, produce, market, deliver and support its product. The value chain identifies nine strategically relevant activities that create value and cost in a specified business. These nine value-creating activities consist of five primary activities and four support activities.

The primary activities represent the sequence of **bringing materials** into the business, known as inbound logistics, **converting them** into final products by operations, **shipping out** final products known as outbound logistics, **marketing them** through marketing and sales and **servicing them** after sales known as after sales customer care.

The support activities representing **procurement**, **technology development, human resource management** and **firm infrastructure,** are handled in certain specialized departments, supported by some other departments.

Every firm has to examine its costs and performance each value-creating activity and to look for ways to improve it. The firm has to estimate its competitor's costs and performance and take them as benchmarks to compare its own costs and performance and take decisions to improve its value-chain profile by coordinating the activities of all the departments, which is the key to success.

7.21. ALTERNATIVE GENERIC STRATEGIES

Depending on the present position of the business, the top management has to take certain courses of action either to survive or grow. These are known as alternative generic strategies or the courses of action, which are to be taken to develop, expand or diversify the activities of the firm. Below given are some of the **alternative generic strategies.**

(i) Forward integration: Gaining ownership or increased control over distributors or retailers.

(ii) Backward integration: Seeking ownership or increased control of a firm's suppliers.

(iii) Horizontal integration: Seeking ownership or increased control over competitors.

(iv) Market penetration: Seeking increased market share for present products or services present in markets through greater marketing efforts.

(v) Market development: Introducing present products or services into new geographic areas.

(vi) Product development: Seeking increased sales by improving or modifying present products or services.

(vii) Concentric diversification: Adding new, but related, products or services.

(viii) Conglomerate diversification: Adding new, unrelated products or services.

(ix) Horizontal diversification: Adding new, unrelated products or services for present customers.

(x) Joint venture: Two or more sponsoring firms forming a separate organization for cooperative purpose.

(xi) Retrenchment: Regrouping through cost and assets reduction to reverse declining sales and profits.

(xii) Diversiture: Selling a division or part of an organization.

(xiii) Liquidation: Selling of company's assets, in parts, for their tangible worth.

(xiv) Combination: Pursuing two or more strategies simultaneously.

7.21.1. Guidelines for Situations when Particular Strategies are Most Effective

Let us discuss some strategies to see in which situations they are more favorable for an organization.

1. Forwarded Integration

When an organization's recent distributors are especially expensive, or unreliable or incapable of meeting the firm's distribution needs.

When the availability of quality distributors is so limited as to offer a competitive advantage to those firms that integrate forward.

When an organization competes in an industry that is growing and is expected to continue to grow markedly; this is a factor because forward integration reduces an organization's ability to diversify its basic industry activities.

When an organization has both the capital and human resources needed to manage the new business of distributing its own products.

When the advantages of stable production are particularly high; this is a consideration because an organization can increase the predictability of the demand for its output through forward integration.

When present distributors or retailers have high profit margins; this situation suggests that a company could profitably distribute its own products and price them more competitively by integrating forward.

2. Backward Integration

When an organization's present suppliers are especially expensive, or unreliable, or incapable of meeting the firm's needs for parts, components, assemblies or raw materials.

When the numbers of suppliers are few and the numbers of competitors are many.

When an organization competes in an industry that is growing rapidly; this is a factor because integrative-type strategies (forward, backward and horizontal) reduce an organization's ability to diversify in a declining industry.

When an organization has both the capital and human resources needed to manage the new business of supplying its own raw materials.

When the advantage of stable prices is particularly important; this is a factor because an organization can stabilize the cost of its raw materials and the associated price of its products through backward integration.

When present suppliers have high profit margins, which suggests that the business of supplying products or services in the given industry is a worthwhile venture.

When an organization needs to acquire a needed resource quickly.

3. Horizontal Integration

When an organization can gain monopolistic characteristics in a particular area or region without being challenged by the federal government for "tending substantially" to reduce competition.

When an organization competes in a growing industry.

When increased economies of scale provide major competitive advantages.

When an organization has both capital and human talent needed to successfully manage an expanded organization.

When competitors are faltering due to a lack of managerial expertise or a need for particular resources, which your organization possesses; note that horizontal integration would not be appropriate if competitors are doing poorly because overall industry sales are declining.

QUESTIONS

1. Discuss the corporate planning process.
2. What is corporate level strategies? Briefly explain them.
3. Write note on: (a) Stability Strategy, (b) Growth Strategy.
4. Write notes on: (a) Retrenchment Strategies, (b) Divestiture.
5. Write notes on: (a) Turn round Strategy, (b) Combination Strategy.

6. What is corporate planning? Classify them. Briefly explain the advantages of corporate planning.
7. Explain the steps in planning process.
8. What is planning premises and constraints?
9. Explain the types of corporate plans.
10. Write notes on: (a) Standards (b) Rules (c) Methods (d) Budgets and (e) Policies.
11. Briefly explain SWOT analysis and the procedure you adopt in doing this analysis.
12. Assume that you are attending a campus interview. How do you present your strengths, weaknesses to the officer who is interviewing you?
13. What is environmental scanning? What are the factors you consider in selecting the internal environment and external environment of an industrial unit?
14. Discuss microenvironment and macroenvironment.
15. Discuss the role of strategic management.
16. Discuss the different levels of strategy.
17. What are the characteristics of strategic decisions?
18. What are the benefits of strategic management?
19. What are the risks of strategic management?
20. How do you implement a strategy?
21. Write a note on value chain analysis.

MULTIPLE CHOICE QUESTIONS

1. Planning the goals, activities of the organization as a whole for the future is known as:

   (a) Goal setting (b) Goals planning

   (c) Corporate planning (d) Organization planning

2. In general the course of action is known as:

   (a) Action plan (b) Strategy

   (c)) Decision (d) Determination

3. The strategy used to decide whether the company should continue in the present business or not is known as;

   (a) Stability strategy (b) Existence strategy

   (c) Business strategy (d) Life strategy

4. The strategy used to decide whether the company has to increase the level of activity of the current business is known as:

   (a) Stability strategy (b) Divestiture

   (c) Increase strategy (d) Growth strategy

5. The strategy used to decide contraction of the scope of level of business is termed as:

   (a) Stability strategy (b) Retrenchment strategy

   (c) Divestiture (d) Growth strategy

6. Retrenchment strategy is also known as:
   (a) Defensive strategy (b) Offensive strategy
   (c) Divestiture (d) Growth strategy
7. The strategy to decide whether the company sells itself a business or a part of business is known as:
   (a) Divestiture (b) Selling strategy
   (c) Retrenchment strategy (d) Shrink strategy
8. Establishment of objectives and the formulation, evaluation and selection of policies, strategies, tactics and action required to achieve the objectives is known as
   (a) Corporate decisions (b) Corporate objectives
   (c) Corporate planning (d) Corporate policies
9. Strategic plans are:
   (a) Short term plans (b) Mid term plans
   (c) Product plans (d) long term plans
10. Operational plans are in general:
    (a) Long term plans (b) Short term plans
    (c) Decision plans (d) Mid term plans
11. The planning, which is used with reference to fundamental issues broad perspective and long period is termed as:
    (a) Strategic planning (b) Tactical planning
    (c) Departmental planning (d) Operational planning
12. Plan which deals with most efficient use of the resources, that have been allocated for achieving given and specific objectives is termed as:
    (a) Strategic planning (b) Objective planning
    (c) Corporate planning (d) Tactical planning
13. The duty of analyzing organizational factors like strengths and weaknesses and environmental factors like threats and opportunities is function of:
    (a) Production management (b) Personal management
    (c) Strategic management (d) Marketing management
14. In IFE, the letter **'I'** stand for:
    (a) India (b) Internal
    (c) Institutional (d) International
15. In SWOT the letter **'O'** stands for:
    (a) Organization (b) Official
    (c) Objective (d) Opportunity
16. **WT strategy** is also known as:
    (a) Mini-Mini Strategy (b) Maxi-Mini Strategy
    (c) Maxi-Maxi Strategy (d) Mini-Maxi Strategy

17. WO strategy is known as:
(a) Mini-Mini Strategy (b) Maxi-Mini Strategy
(c) Maxi-Maxi Strategy (d) Mini-Maxi Strategy

18. ST strategy is known as:
(a) Mini-Mini Strategy (b) Maxi-Mini Strategy
(c) Maxi-Maxi Strategy (d) Mini-Maxi Strategy

19. SO Strategy is known as:
(a) Mini-Mini Strategy (b) Maxi-Mini Strategy
(c) Maxi-Maxi Strategy (d) Mini-Maxi Strategy

20. The tool for identifying way to create more customer value is termed as:
(a) Value chain (b) Customer chain
(c) Customer promotion (d) Motivate customers

ANSWERS

1. (c) **2.** (b) **3.** (a) **4.** (d) **5.** (b) **6.** (a) **7.** (a) **8.** (c)
9. (d) **10.** (b) **11.** (a) **12.** (d) **13.** (c) **14.** (b) **15.** (d) **16.** (a)
17. (d) **18.** (b) **19.** (c) **20.** (a).

○○○

Unit 8 Contemporary Management Practices

8.1. INTRODUCTION

This chapter consists of heterogeneous topics, which covers wide range of titles that are used in present day management practices. The knowledge of these topics helps the students in their professional work after they get a job in some organization. A brief description about the topics included in the syllabus is made to expose the students to the awareness of the topics.

8.2. MANAGEMENT INFORMATION SYSTEM (MIS)

The present day complicated structure of any business needs proper information for a manager to make decisions. Functional departments supply this information. The data available in each department is collected and required information is prepared and sent to manager's office for further use. **A management information system is used to transform data into useful information as needed to support managerial decision-making with structured decisions (formally called programmed decisions), which are those that are based on predictable patterns of activity.**

The typical Management Information System is based on four major components as listed below:

1. ***Data gathering***: Data relevant and pertinent to the operation of the organization are gathered from both external and internal sources.
2. ***Data entry***: *The above data is fed and stored in data bases as the information processing core of the system,* such as files operated manually or computer files.
3. ***Data transformation***: Collected and stored data is transformed into useful information through the application of computer software programs and judgments made by technical support staff and other system users. (In manual system they are prepared in the form of tables, charts, graphs etc.).
4. ***Information utilization***: The useful information is retrieved as needed by the management and technical personnel and applied to a wide variety of decisions related to the conduct of organizational operations.

Hence, a Management information system is a network of communication channels and information processing centers collecting information from its sources of origin:

(i) Storing, updating, collecting and processing it,

(ii) Supplying the processed information to the various users managing the organization.

8.3. MATERIALS REQUIREMENT PLANNING (MRP)

Generally materials manager will plan for materials using Economic Order Quantity (EOQ) and he will be enough precautious to take care of uncertainties in the delivery of material and make a provision to meet the uncertainties in the form of safety stock. In spite of all the care taken, sometimes he will experience that there is shortage of materials when they are required for assembly of final product. To avoid this situation, he has at his hand a tool known as **Materials Requirement Planning or MRP**, a special technique to plan the requirement for production. Many production managers come across a problem, where raw materials required for production are purchased as per EOQ and still they do not have the availability of materials required for production at the time when demand arises. This is particularly true when the product requires many raw materials or components. Out of many components or materials even, one of them is not available when needed the production cannot be continued. It is because the service levels of each stock of materials are not taken into account.

Let us consider an example that a product requires 10 different components for assembly. The manager has fixed 95% service level for the stock of each component. This means that only 5% of the time there may be a stock out position and 95% of the time the stock available for production. But the manager experiences more stock out position than his expectation. The manager needs 10 components all at one point of time. Each material is stored wit 95% service level. The probability that all the ten materials are available simultaneously is equals to $(0.95)^{10}$ that is approximately equals to 0.60. This shows that all the materials are available only 60% of the time and 40% of the time there will he stock out position. Hence, statistical methods must be understood properly and applied to the situations to avoid difficulty. EOQ and safety stock calculations are made for individual components and not for **bunched** requirement of components. In such cases, instead of adopting statistical safety calculations, better we go for **Materials Requirement Planning.**

Materials Requirement Planning deals with the requirement of raw materials or components, which directly depend upon the requirement of production. It seems, it would be better if we know the production plan or production schedules for the assembly of the finished product and accordingly arrange for all the raw materials that go into the finished products, rater than depending upon the statistics and probabilities and EOQ and safety stock. This is exactly what we do in Materials Requirement Planning (MRP). It is a simple good old system of calculating arithmetically the requirement of the input materials at different points of time based on the actual production plan. In fact production managers used this method earlier. When the factory systems was in infant state, the artisan, who has to produce a product, use to calculate the requirement of material arithmetically depending on the number of products he has to produce and used to purchase that amount of materials and never felt shortage of material during production.

There is no probability involved anywhere, only the derivation of the requirement of input materials base on the requirement or plan for production of the final product. Such a system will work well for materials that have no direct demand of their own, but have only a derived demand. These materials can be called as **dependent demand items.** Finished assembly has the direct demand of its own and therefore, it is an **independent demand item.** In EOQ model the order quantity is calculated by using a formula, which has been worked out by averaging the demand (or the stock of material). The problem of shortage of dependent materials arises because of averaging the consumption of materials. Present day industrial scene shows that industries use hundreds of materials for their products and hence computerized packages are used for calculating the requirement of materials. The success of MRP depends on the pre-requisites of the system. The requisites are:

- The system is suitable for dependent demand materials.
- The demand for dependent materials are derived from the master-schedule for the final finished goods and the requirement should take lead-time into consideration.
- A firm delivery schedule should be available.
- MRP should incorporate flexibility.
- MRP should incorporate self-correcting mechanism depending on the changes in demand.

Better results may be obtained by using MRP and EOQ together.

8.4. JUST-IN-TIME PRODUCTION

Just-in-time production/inventory system is a revolutionary concept becoming very popular in industrial world. Think of a situation that a company produces the required goods **only at the tie when they are needed** and **in the quantity that is needed** (it applies equally to finished goods or components). Now, the company makes an agreement with its vendors or suppliers of raw materials that they should supply the materials and components only at the time of starting the production of the component or part or product and in the quantities needed, by this way the company can eliminate the entire material storing and maintenance responsibility. The raw materials and components are supplied to the point, where they are needed (at point of time). This is known as **just-in-time** or **J.I.T. production system.** Taiichi Ohono, Vice President of Toyota Motor Company, Japan, seeded this system. JIT uses a peculiar material withdrawal and work ordering system, known as **KANBAN** or **MARKER** system.

Another way of adopting the same concept is, consider for example an Industrial Estate having a number of industrial units, manufacturing different types of products using different types of materials. An entrepreneur can take the responsibility of supplying the materials for these industrial units. He can collect the information regarding the requirement of materials from every unit and prepare lists of various materials required by the units and purchase them in bulk and maintain a centralized store. Every unit will indent their requirement daily/weekly/monthly deepening on their production schedules and draw material form this centralized stores. This will help the industrialist in two ways:

(a) They can get rid of all the records, stock registers and the workers in stores.

(b) As the material is available locally, they need not go in search of vendors. Payment for the materials may be made at the agreed period. As there may be many common materials required by many industries, the entrepreneur, managing the stores, could purchase them in bulk quantity and get the advantage of bulk purchase.

8.5. TOTAL QUALITY MANAGEMENT (TQM)

The job of quality management is not just advising a sampling plan for the acceptance or rejection of the incoming material and controlling manufacturing process conditions; it is in fact **a job at every step of the company's activities.**

Quality management is a company-wide activity and various functional departments contribute to its success. The marketing department, especially market research, has information about what quality characteristics the customers desire and to what extent? This is a valuable input for planning quality. Also the information regarding the quality of the manufactured product needs to be presented to the customers. The marketing department also does this. Product design department write the specifications of the product, raw materials used, bought out components. The purchase department makes contact with the suppliers of raw materials, components and selects the appropriate vendors, develops vendors, keeps track of the vendors. Product design and Purchasing have much to contribute to the quality of the final product. Production Engineer selects the process, methods and requirement for the manufacture of the product and can provide valuable information regarding the anticipated difficulties in implementing a certain product quality specification. The contribution of manufacturing line to quality is obvious. They are responsible for actual production and therefore the final product quality depends much upon their skills, motivation to work, and their interpretation of the specifications. Since the finished product may take as much as one year before it reaches the final consumer, the product quality depends upon the design of the packaging and the method of storage in the warehouse. The quality of product also depends on how the product is shipped. The purpose of good product quality is to create a good image of the company and this image should be maintained. Therefore, the company has to attend to the complaints from the customer and provide periodic service to the customers, after sales.

Quality control laboratory/department, which inspects a batch of raw material, coming inside the company or semi-finished components or finished products and approves or rejects them has much to contribute to quality desired. Many a time, the quality control job is misunderstood because of the activity mentioned above. The product quality has inputs form various angles and a total quality control programme should consider all the different aspects contributing to quality. It is stated by many **"quality is everybody's job in a business".** When we take a look at the organizations whose products are of top quality, we always notice that in such organizations all the company employees at all levels and in all functions are motivated to contribute to the total quality establishment effort.

Since each functional department has a contribution to make towards quality, it is imperative that the **total quality management effort be properly organized to coordinate the various contributing aspect to quality.** Without such coordination, there may be a chaotic situation, and although the quality is everybody's concern, it may become nobody's concern. Therefore, quality management should be a separate function headed by a person quite high in the organizational hierarchy so as to facilitate the coordination of the various contributing functions to quality. And, not only should the quality management belong to the top management, but the entire top management should be committed to quality. **In one sentence we can say, to deliver the quality product/ service to the end user or community, every person working in the organization, irrespective of cadre is responsible for the quality of product/service delivered, hence, everybody must work with commitment to fulfil the quality mission.**

8.6. SIX SIGMA AND CAPABILITY MATURITY MODEL (CMM)

It is the objective of a business organization to keep his customer happy by giving him desired quality of service or product to him at the time of need. For this the business organization must evaluate the customers and their desires and deliver them what they need. The companies can manufacture very fine quality of product by using highly skilled labour and sophisticated machines. Each machine has a capacity to produce a certain quality level, which is known as Capacity Capability. More will be the capacity capability; more will be the production cost. But the customer has got his own method of judging the value of the goods. If the product is too costly, he will go to the next quality level. Hence, the firm, which is manufacturing the goods, must provide appropriate quality level to the customer, not more or not less. Depending on the end use of the product manufacturer will give dimensional tolerances for a product to accommodate the variations in three elements of production — material, machine and man. These tolerances must be carefully given so that the desired quality is delivered to the consumer at optimal cost.

In statistics we have a concept given by normal distribution that on a priori basis 99.73% of items would lie between the mean (x) dimension and 3σ on either side of the mean. X ± 3σ gives the limits that are referred to as empirical control limits also the process capability for the process selected.

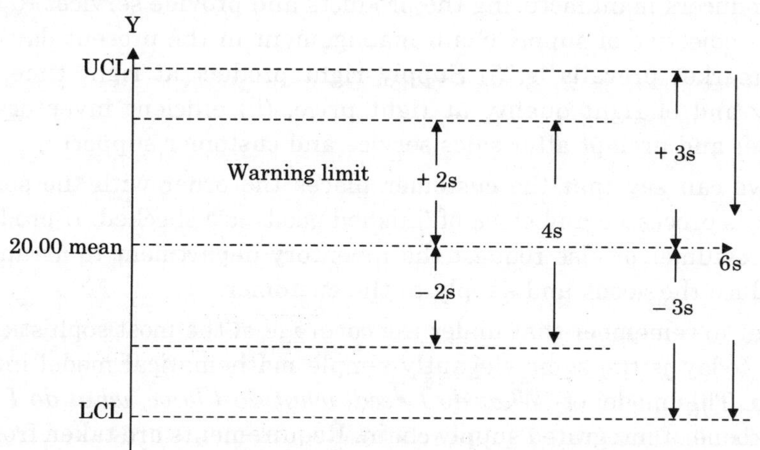

LCL = Lower Control Limit, UCL = Upper Control Limit
4σ = Warning Limit , 6σ = Basic Spread.

Fig. 8.1. 6σ Distributions.

Let us take an example of producing a shaft of diameter of 20.00 mm. After manufacturing the required number of shafts say, 1000 numbers, and their dimensions are measured and plotted on a graph. The graph appears as in figure 8.2. Certain measured diameters values lie quite close to the desired dimension, i.e. 20.00 mm. This diameter is known as **mean diameter,** or **mean value.** The other shafts measured will have a fair distribution having some of the dimensions on one side of the mean and some on another side of the mean. Due to involvement of three elements of production, material, man and machine, the variation in dimension is invariable. Hence to accommodate these variations, **upper control limit** and **lower control limits** are given on either side of the nominal diameter. That is as far as the component manufactured is in between these limits, it is considered that the product is of good quality and once the dimensions cross these limits, it is said that the process is out of control. These limits are to be carefully fixed; depending on the process capability, as the upper control limit and lower control limit indicates the capability of the process to produce. On either side of the mean, the area of the distribution curve is divided as 1σ, 2σ and 3σ on R.H.S and -1σ, -2σ and -3σ on L.H.S. Total spread of the distribution curve is 6σ. This spread is known as **basic spread.** So, under 6σ curve 99.73% of products will be within the specified limits. At 2σ level, that the spread is 4σ 95.45% of the products will be within the specified limits. This 2σ level is known as **warning limit.** The operator can stop the machine at warning limit and rectify the mistake and restart production to see that 100% of the products manufactured will be within the specified limits.

8.7. SUPPLY CHAIN MANAGEMENT

Present day consumer is ruling the product world as he can get his need from any source on earth depending on his need. His behavior led the suppliers to think of globalization of the market and think of the quality of their product to meet the demands of international consumer needs. Producers can satisfy the consumer to the extent he desires only through proper **supply chain management, i.e.** Integrated Logistics system. Supply Chain system consists of the producers manufacturing the products and provide services to the satisfaction of customers. The objective of supply chain management in the present day scenario where globalization of market prevails is: (i) Supply right product at right time, at right place in right quantity and of right quality at right price, (ii) efficient inventory management, (iii) Provide proper and prompt after sales service and customer support.

In one line we can say that the customer places the order with the sales department from where order is processed and stock of finished goods are checked. If product is available it is sent to the costumer or else request the inventory department to arrange for required materials to produce the goods and supply to the customer.

It is important to remember that under the coverage of the most sophisticated enterprise planning system today is the same elegantly simple mathematical model introduced in the first MRP system. This model of "*What do I need, what do I have, what do I need to get and when*" is the backbone of integrated supply chain. Requirements are taken from the customer or internally developed forecasts. These requirements are compared to what is on hand. Finally, a calculation of what is needed is completed including an offset of the estimated lead-time to determine when that item is required form the supplier. **This process of what is needed, what is available, what is required and when is accomplished by**

each link of the supply chain. New technology allows these calculations to be completed very quickly and instantly communicated electronically all along the supply chain. Care must be taken that technology does not totally replace an effective demand management process. Without intelligent demand management, the risk of excess inventory is still very real. In addition, another barrier to full automation of requirements, communication is not a technological constraint but rather the confidence that the calculated requirements are accurate. The accuracy is not dependent on the mathematical computations of the computer. The accuracy dependent on the quality of the data input into the system. This is an issue that cannot be addressed simply by the purchase of a new computer program. This phenomenon has been plaguing software implementations since the invention of the computer.

8.8. ENTERPRISE RESOURCE PLANNING (ERP)

In the manufacturing industry, MRP (Material Requirement Planning) became the fundamental concept of Production Management and Control in the middle of 1970s. At this stage BOM (Bill of Materials), which is purchase order management that utilizes parts list management and parts development was in the main stream. And this concept of MRP unfolded from order inventory management of material to plan and personnel planning and distribution planning which in turn became MRP – II (Manufacturing Resource Planning). This incorporated financial accounting human resource management function and management accounting functions. It came to globally cover all areas of enterprises mainstay business and eventually come to be called **Enterprise Resource Planning – ERP.**

Originally, ERP packages are targeted at the manufacturing industry and consisted mainly functions for planning and managing core businesses such as sales Management, Production Management, Accounting and Financial affairs, etc. However, in recent years, adoption to only to the manufacturing industry, but also to diverse types of industry has become possible and the expansion of implementation and use has been progressing on a global level.

ERP software has been designed to model and automate many of the basic processes of a company, from finance to the shop floor with the goal of integrating information across the company and eliminating complex, expensive links between computer system that were never meant to talk to each other. Figure 8.3. Shows information integration through ERP system.

8.9. BUSINESS PROCESS RE-ENGINEERING

In a competitive Global Market, any organization wants to sustain its new level of operation and grow to highest level to face the competition from its fellow competitors it has to take shelter under the new technique coined by Michael Hammer and James Champy, management consultants i.e. **Business Process Re-engineering (BPR)** and utilize its strength for its betterment. **Business Process Re-engineering (BPR) can be defined as the fundamental rethinking and radical redesign of business processes to achieve dramatic improvement in critical, contemporary measures of performance such as cost, quality and speed of products/services delivered/provided by an organization.**

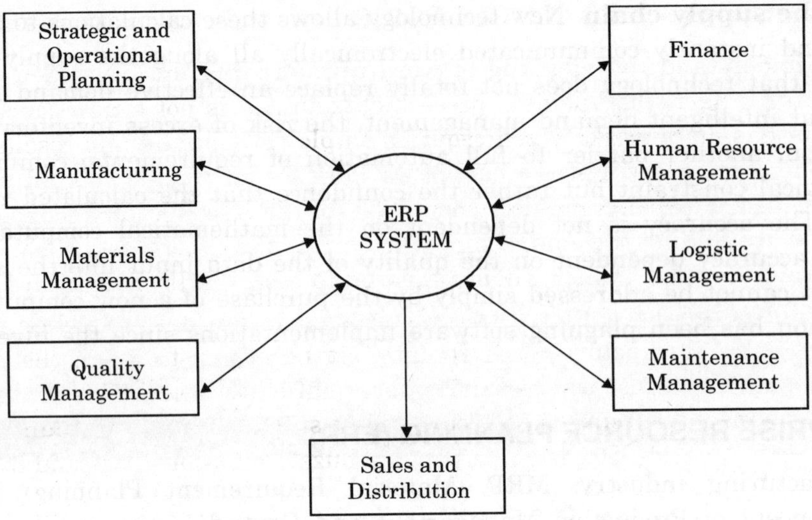

Fig. 8.2. Information Integration through ERP System

8.9.1. Steps in Business Process Re-engineering

Step 1: Development of process vision and determination of process objectives

Today business has become customer focused. Hence a Businessman's ultimate goal is to satisfy the customers by adding more value to his product. Hence in this step, he collects all relevant facts, which provide values and add them to this product to satisfy the customer. Reengineering includes redefinition and simplification of the process of adding value to the product.

Step 2: Definition of processes to be reengineered

Here identify the process to be reengineered and the personnel involved, collect necessary information by asking questions, which will help in the process of reengineering the process.

Step 3: Measurement of existing process

The present process parameters are measured and compared with similar processes and for the process to be reengineered, the performance measurement is done to know the existing level of performance of operation and try to improve performance measure of the operation.

Step 4: Identification of information technology applications

The main objective of reengineering is to have a dramatic improvement in the performance of selected measures of a process. Further it should result in achieving process transformation through appropriate use of Information Technology. For example in Banks, introduction of Teller System, ATM etc.

Step 5: Design of prototype and implementation

Data collected in the above steps enables one to design a prototype and its implementation. Railway Reservation system (from anywhere at anytime) is the best example.

8.10. BUSINESS PROCESS OUTSOURCING

Let us try to understand the meaning of word **outsourcing** and related words **offshore, near shore etc.** In fact, the business process outsourcing is not a new concept. Whenever an organization has more work, which requires employ of more human resource, which is a costly affair, the company will give a part of its work for an outside subcontractor, and gets the things done at a cheaper cost. After the advent of the Information Technology (IT) many American firms are finding the contractors who can do their work at a cheaper cost, as the labor cost at America is far higher when compared to other parts of backward countries.

Outsourcing is the delegation of tasks or jobs from internal production to an external entity (such as a subcontractor). Most recently, it has come to mean the elimination of native staff to staff overseas, where salaries are markedly lower. This is despite the fact that the majority of outsourcing that occurs today still occurs within country boundaries, especially in North America. It became a popular buzzword in business and management in 1990s.

- Where functions previously performed by an organization are supplied under contract from a third party.
- Buying goods or services instead of producing or providing them in-house.
- While outsourcing is not exactly a new innovation, the shifts that have occurred recently in this space are worth noting. As the need for e-learning moves higher up in the IT and corporate training agendas; organizations want to take on the IT management burden of implementing a learning management system (LMS).
- The concept of taking internal company functions and paying outside firms to handle them. Outsourcing is done to save money, improve quality, or free company resources for other activities. Outsourcing was first done in the data – processing industry and has spread to areas, including tele-messaging and calls centers. Outsourcing is the wave of the future.
- A long term, results-oriented relationship with an external resource provider for activities traditionally performed within the company. Outsourcing usually applies to a complete business process. It implies a degree of managerial control and risk on the part of the provider.
- The transfer of components or large segments of an organization's internal IT infrastructure, staff, processes or applications to an external resource such as an Application Service Provider (ASP).

8.10.1. Offshoring

No company accepted definition of **"offshoring"** exists, and the term has been used to include various international trade and foreign investment activities. Services that United States based organizations purchase from abroad are considered imports. They may also be linked to United States firm's investment overseas. For example, United States firms may invest in overseas affiliates as a replacement for, or as an alternative to, domestic production. In recent years, services offshoring have been facilitated by factors, such as the internet, infrastructure growth in developing countries and decreasing data transmission cots. Organization's decisions to offshore services are influenced by potential benefits such as the availability of cheaper skilled labour and access of foreign markets, and by risks, such as geopolitical issues and infrastructure instability in countries that supply the services. "Offshoring of services generally refers to an organization's purchase from other countries of service that it previously produced or purchased domestically, such as software programming or telephone call centers."

8.10.2. Near Shoring

Near shore outsourcing, a form of off shoring is the term used to refer to the practice of getting work done or service performed by people in neighboring countries rather than in your own country.

8.10.3. Insourcing

The act of bringing together a function that was performed outside the organization outsource to being performed inside the organization.

The opposite of outsourcing, that is, a service performed in-house. It is a reaction to outsourcing that conjures up visions of employees aggressively defending their core competencies against cost-cutting senior managers and third party providers.

8.10.4. In-house Outsourcing

We can still notice certain peculiar types of happenings in business. There is an organization, which is famous for manufacturing Carton making machines. The owner of the unit is a Textile Engineering Graduate. Initially, he started his Carton Making unit as a Small Scale Unit, with few employees with him. For discussion let us say he had 10 facilities (machine tools) to manufacture components of the carton-making machine. He has purchased these machine tools and engaged skilled labour to do his work. After certain time, he had an idea of getting his mechanists to be educated, through evening schools and colleges. His idea is it is very easy to convince the educated labour at times of organizational problems. It really worked out nicely. After a decade, he decided to get rid of day-to-day managerial work and called his workmen and told them that the machine tools on which they are working will be given to them for free of cost, with a condition that each worker has to supply the needs of his assembly line (without sacrificing the quality), after which they can take any job works of their desire to earn extra money. They have to draw materials required from stores, make the components, supply it to assembly line and take their labour bill once in a month. By this arrangement, our entrepreneur got rid of his time wasted in supervision of labour and other activities and enabled to concentrate towards doing new things. Labors are also happy that they are the owners of the machine and after fulfilling the needs of the assembly's line they can earn more. This type of arrangement may be coined as **In-house Outsourcing.**

8.11. PERFORMANCE MANAGEMENT

It is customary for any company to know the efficiency at which their units are working. If we want to measure the efficiency of a machine or a labour, it is easy to measure because the ratio of output to input will give it. Similarly, if we want to measure the efficiency of a production organization, by knowing the output and by summing up the inputs of all sorts and if we take the ratio, we can get the efficiency with which the organization has worked.

The input includes all the resources and potential capabilities of the plant, men, materials and machines, as well as organizational abilities; the output is simply the results realized within a certain period of time, generally planning period. But it is not obvious that 'input' and 'output' are rather difficult to define in accurate terms in this case, especially if we are to measure them quantitatively in so many units. Hence, only way in which we can assess the efficiency of the production plant is by comparing the actual performance with targets specified in the specified programme, provided this program is planned in good faith and provided the plant is capable of coping with it.

QUESTIONS

1. Briefly discuss what is management information system.
2. Explain what is material requirement planning.
3. What is just-in-time production?
4. Discuss the features of total quality management.
5. Discuss six sigma and capability maturity model.
6. Discuss supply chain management.
7. Discuss enterprise resource planning.
8. What is re engineering? Discuss business process re engineering.
9. What is business process outsourcing? Discuss.
10. Write short notes on: (a) Offshoring, (b) Near Shoring, (c) Insourcing and (d) In-house outsourcing.

MULTIPLE CHOICE QUESTIONS

1. In **MIS** letter **M** stands for:
   (a) Material (b) Manpower
   (c) Management (d) Manager
2. In **MRP** the letter **M** stands for:
   (a) Material (b) Manpower
   (c) Management (d) Manager
3. **MRP** means:
   (a) Manpower Requirement Planning
   (b) Materials Requirement Planning
   (c) Money Requirement Planning
   (d) Methods Requirement Planning
4. Just-in-Time system uses a Material withdrawal and work ordering system generally known as:
   (a) Withdrawal and Ordering system
   (b) Material and Work order system
   (c) KANMARK system
   (d) Kanban or Marker system

5. **In TQM, the letter Q stands for:**
   (a) Quality (b) Quantity
   (c) Quota (d) None of these
6. **CMM means:**
   (a) Central Management Model (b) Capacity Maturity Model
   (c) Capacity Management Model (d) Capacity Measurement Methods
7. **BPR means:**
   (a) Business Planning Research (b) Business Process Regulations
   (c) Business Premises Regulations (d) Business Process Re engineering
8. **Delegating of tasks from internal production to an External entity is known as:**
   (a) Business Process Contracting (b) Business Process Delegation
   (c) Business Process Outsourcing (d) Business Process Re engineering

ANSWERS

1. (c) **2.** (a) **3.** (b) **4.** (d) **5.** (a) **6.** (b) **7.** (d) **8.** (c).

❍❍❍

University Question Papers

Code: R5320203 **R 5**

III B. Tech. II Semester (R05) Supplementary Examinations, April/May 2011

MANAGEMENT SCIENCE

(Electrical and Electronics Engineering, Electronics and Communication Engineering, Electronics and Computer Engineering)

Time: 3 Hours. *Max. Marks: 80*

Answer any FIVE questions.
All questions carry equal Marks.

---

1. Explain the concept of management and organization and analyze their relationship.
2. What is departmentation? How is it essential for the management of businesses enterprise?
3. Explain "Product Layout", "Process Layout and Combined Layout." State the factors, which influence the selection of one or the other.
4. Write short notes on the following:
   (a) Purchase requisition
   (b) Notice for inviting tenders
   (c) Comparative statements
   (d) Purchase order.
5. Why do organization promote their employees? What should be the criteria for promotion?
6. Define the terms EST, EFT, LST, LFT and calculate with an example.
7. Can strategic management fail? Can it be prevented?
8. What are some of guidelines that can be followed for the purpose of improving MIS?

Code: R7420501 **1**

IV B. Tech. II Semester (R07) Regular Examinations, April 2011

MANAGEMENT SCIENCE

(Common to Computer Science and Engineering. Information Technology and Computer Science and Systems Engineering)

Time: 3 Hours. *Max. Marks: 80*

Answer any FIVE questions.

All questions carry equal Marks.

---

1. (a) Critically evaluate the different leadership stages and an organization.
(b) What are the theories of motivation?

2. (a) What is the need for departmentalism and decentralization?
(b) What factors do you keep in mind for decentralization and what are its merits and limitations?

3. (a) What factors you keep in mind while developing a suitable plant layout?
(b) Distinguish between plant layout and process layout.

4. (a) What are the objects of material control?
(b) Explain the difference between E.O.Q and ABC analysis.

5. Discuss in detail about the methods do you follow for the performance appraisal of an employee.

6. (a) Critically differentiate PERT and CPM.
(b) Project cost analysis.

7. Explain the elements of corporate planning process.

8. (a) What are the basic concepts of Just-in-Time?
(b) Explain enterprise resource planning.

Code: R7420501 **2**

IV B. Tech. II Semester (R07) Regular Examinations, April 2011

MANAGEMENT SCIENCE

(Common to Computer Science and Engineering. Information Technology and Computer Science and Systems Engineering)

Time: 3 Hours. *Max. Marks: 80*

Answer any FIVE questions.

All questions carry equal Marks.

---

1. (a) How do you explain the basic functions of management?

(b) What are the social responsibilities of management? Are they relevant in today's business environment?

2. Explain the significance and advantages of

(a) Functional organization.

(b) Committee organization.

3. (a) What is the significance of plant layout?

(b) Which method do you suggest for optimum result and what are the reasons for it?

4. (a) Briefly explain the functions of marketing.

(b) Distinguish between E.O.Q. and ABC analysis.

5. (a) How do you explain the significance of personal management and industrial relations?

(b) How do you handle the grievances?

6. (a) Distinguish between PERT and CPM.

(b) Project cost analysis.

7. Explain the following:

(a) SWOT analysis.

(b) Environmental scanning.

8. How do you explain the importance of Business Process Outsourcing (BPO) in the corporate sector?

Code: R7420501

3

IV B. Tech. II Semester (R07) Regular Examinations, April 2011

MANAGEMENT SCIENCE

(Common to Computer Science and Engineering. Information Technology and Computer Science and Systems Engineering)

Time: 3 Hours. *Max. Marks: 80*

Answer any FIVE questions.

All questions carry equal Marks.

1. (a) Distinguish between "Administrations, Organization and Management."
   (b) What are the basic principles of management according to Henry Fayol?
2. (a) Differentiate between departmentation and decentralistics.
   (b) Line and staff organization.
3. What are the principles you follow while conducting method study and work measure-ment? What is its important?
4. What is the general purchase procedure you follow in a business enterprise?
5. (a) What is a channel of distribution? What are the channels?
   (b) What factors do you consider while selecting the suitable channel of distribution?
6. (a) How do you emphasis the "Job Evaluation and Merit Rating?"
   (b) Briefly explain the significance of personnel management.
7. (a) What is meant by project cost analysis and project crashing?
   (b) Explain briefly strategy formulation and implementation.
8. Explain:
   (a) Environmental scanning.
   (b) Supply chain management.

Code: R7420501 **4**

IV B. Tech. II Semester (R07) Regular Examinations, April 2011

MANAGEMENT SCIENCE

(Common to Computer Science and Engineering. Information Technology and Computer Science and Systems Engineering)

Time: 3 Hours. *Max. Marks: 80*

Answer any FIVE questions.

All questions carry equal Marks.

---

1. Compare and contrast the Fayol's principles of management and Taylor's scientific management theory.
2. Explain the basic leadership styles. Which of these recommended most? Why?
3. What are the principles and methods of measurement of statistical quality control?
4. (a) What are the functions of stores management?
   (b) What factors you consider while selecting a suitable channels of distribution?
5. Explain about:
   (a) Marketing mix.
   (b) Product cycle and business decisions.
6. (a) Differentiate between PERT and CPM.
   (b) Project cost analysis.
7. Explain the following:
   (a) Performance appraisal.
   (b) Corporate planning process.
8. How do you explain the concept of
   (a) Just-in-Time (JIT).
   (b) SWOT analysis.

1

Code: R7320203

III B. Tech. II Semester (R07) Regular and Supplementary Examinations, April/May 2011

MANAGEMENT SCIENCE

(Electrical and Electronics Engineering, Electronics and Communication Engineering, Electronics and Computer Engineering)

Time: 3 Hours. *Max. Marks: 80*

Answer any FIVE questions.

All questions carry equal Marks.

1. Briefly explain different functions of management.
2. (a) Distinguish between formal and informal organizations.
   (b) Distinguish between line and staff organization.
3. What is process layout? Explain its merits and demerits.
4. What is ABC analysis? Explain the procedure to control inventories based on their value and quantity.
5. Describe the objectives of personal management. Describe the functional and organizational role of personnel manager in achieving the organizational goals.
6. The following details relate to a small project with the help of which compute the probability of completion of project within scheduled time. The expected time of each activities as follows:

S. No.	1	2	3	4	5	6	7	8	9
Activity	1 – 2	1 – 3	2 – 4	3 – 4	4 – 5	5 – 6	3 – 5	5 – 7	6 – 7
Activity Time	6	8	7	12	3	5	7	11	10

7. (a) What is the need for corporate planning?
   (b) Explain the main elements of corporate process.
8. What is portfolio management? Discuss various key aspects in investment decision.

Code: R7320203 **2**

III B. Tech. II Semester (R07) Regular and Supplementary Examinations, April/May 2011

MANAGEMENT SCIENCE

(Electrical and Electronics Engineering, Electronics and Communication Engineering, Electronics and Computer Engineering)

Time: 3 Hours. *Max. Marks: 80*

Answer any FIVE questions.
All questions carry equal Marks.

1. Explain concepts of management and organization and analyze their relationship.
2. What is the need of decentralization? Explain factors determining degree of decentralization.
3. Compare and contrast product and process layouts with suitable examples.
4. (a) What are the objectives of purchasing?
   (b) Explain the various methods of purchasing.
5. Why do organizations promote their employees? What should be the criteria for promotion?
6. Given the following data, compute the expected project duration by drawing a network and indicia critical path. Find total slack of each event.

Activity	T_o	T_m	T_p
1 – 2	2	5	14
1 – 6	2	5	8
2 – 3	5	11	29
2 – 4	1	4	7
3 – 5	5	11	17
4 – 5	2	5	14
6 – 7	3	9	27
5 – 8	2	2	8
7 – 8	7	13	13

7. What do you mean by mission and objectives of the organization? Explain with examples.
8. Explain the philosophy behind total quality management, customer satisfaction and continuous improvement. What are the objectives of TQM?

Code: R7320203 **3**

III B. Tech II Semester (R07) Regular and Supplementary Examinations, April/May 2011

MANAGEMENT SCIENCE

(Electrical and Electronics Engineering, Electronics and Communication Engineering, Electronics and Computer Engineering)

Time: 3 Hours. *Max. Marks: 80*

Answer any FIVE questions.
All questions carry equal Marks.

---

1. Explain the concept of Management, Administration and Organization.
2. Explain the principles of organization.
3. Explain various plant layout based on methods of production.
4. (a) What are the objectives and advantages of inventory control?
   (b) Briefly explain ABC analysis and EOQ.
5. Explain the functions of HR manager in knowledge-based organization such as software developing company.
6. The various time estimates of activities involved in a project are given in table. Determine:
   (a) Determine the expected completion time of the project.
   (b) Determine the variance and standard deviation of the project.
   (c) Determine the probability factor of completing the project within 23 days.

Activity	T_o	T_m	T_p
1 – 2	2	6	10
1 – 3	4	8	12
2 – 4	2	3	4
2 – 3	2	4	6
3 – 4	0	0	0
3 – 5	3	6	9
4 – 6	6	10	14
5 – 6	1	3	5

7. What is environmental scanning and what are the factors affecting external environment?
8. What do you understand by total quality management? How does this concept differ from quality control techniques?

Code: R7320203 **4**

III B. Tech. II Semester (R07) Regular and Supplementary Examinations, April/May 2011

MANAGEMENT SCIENCE

(Electrical and Electronics Engineering, Electronics and Communication Engineering, Electronics and Computer Engineering)

Time: 3 Hours. *Max. Marks: 80*

Answer any FIVE questions.

All questions carry equal Marks.

---

1. State and explain Taylor's scientific management.

2. Discuss the features of line and staff organizations and illustrate their suitability.

3. What are the factors influencing the fixed layout? List out its advantages and dis -advantages.

4. (a) What are the objectives of purchasing?

(b) Explain about the purchasing process.

5. Describe the functions of human resource manager in an industrial setting.

6. Discuss the salient features of network analysis.

7. State the significance of corporate planning. What is the need for planning?

8. What are the major ingredients of total quality management? Are some ingredients more important than the others? Explain.

Code: R7320203 **R 07**

III B. Tech. II Semester (R07) Supplementary Examinations, April/May 2011

MANAGEMENT SCIENCE

(Electrical and Electronics Engineering, Electronics and Communication Engineering, Electronics and Computer Engineering)

Time: 3 Hours. *Max. Marks: 80*

Answer any FIVE questions.

All questions carry equal Marks.

1. Define management and explain it is different from administration.
2. What is the need of decentralization? Explain factors determining the degree of decen-tralization.
3. (a) What are the factors influencing plant layout?
   (b) What are the objectives of plant layout?
4. What is supply chain management? Bring out its significance in materials management.
5. (a) What is the role of human resource manager in development and growth of an organization?
   (b) Explain how "Human Resource Planning" process can be formulated.
6. A project has nine activities. The expected time of each activity is as follows:

S. No.	1	2	3	4	5	6	7	8	9
Activity	1 – 2	1 – 3	2 – 4	3 – 4	4 – 6	5 – 6	3 – 5	5 – 7	6 – 7
Expected Time	6	8	7	12	3	5	7	11	10

   (a) Draw the project network.
   (b) Identify the critical path.
   (c) Find project duration.
   (d) Find slack time at each event.
7. (a) Explain the concept of nature and scope of corporate planning.
   (b) What are the advantages and limitations of corporate planning?
8. Briefly explain the following concepts:
   (a) Business Process Outsourcing (BPO).
   (b) Total Quality Management (TQM).

Code: R7320203 **1**

III B. Tech. II Semester (R07) Regular Examinations, May 2011

MANAGEMENT SCIENCE

(Electrical and Electronics Engineering, Electronics and Communication Engineering, Electronics and Computer Engineering)

Time: 3 Hours. *Max. Marks: 80*

Answer any FIVE questions.

All questions carry equal Marks.

---

1. What are the basic functions of management? Explain them briefly.

2. (a) How do you explain the need and importance of organization?

(b) Briefly explain the principles of organization.

3. Can you explain the line organization and its advantages and disadvantages?

4. (a) What do you understand by good plant layout?

(b) What are the principles of plant layout?

5. (a) What is an importance of materials management?

(b) Briefly explain the functions of materials management.

6. What are the elements in marketing mix? How it is useful in formulating the marketing policies?

7. (a) Distinguish between personnel management and human resource management.

(b) Briefly explain the functions of HR manager.

8. (a) Critically analyze SWOT.

(b) How it is helpful in strengthening the organization?

2

Code: R7320203

III B. Tech. II Semester (R07) Regular Examinations, May 2011

MANAGEMENT SCIENCE

(Electrical and Electronics Engineering, Electronics and Communication Engineering, Electronics and Computer Engineering)

Time: 3 Hours. *Max. Marks: 80*

Answer any FIVE questions.

All questions carry equal Marks.

1. Critically evaluate the Douglas Mc Gregor's theory X and theory Y. What are the assumptions and importance?
2. What do you understand by the functional organization? What are the advantages and disadvantages?
3. How do you explain a plant layout? Explain the types of plant layouts.
4. What do you understand by statistical quality control? What are its advantages, objects and techniques?
5. (a) What is meant by inventory control? What is the purpose?
   (b) Explain the objects and advantages of inventory control.
6. (a) What do you understand by network analysis?
   (b) Briefly explain the uses and limitations.
7. How do you differentiate the PERT and CPM? How they are useful in administration?
8. What is meant by project cost analysis and project crashing? Explain clearly.

Code: R7320203

3

III B.Tech. II Semester (R07) Regular Examinations, May 2011

MANAGEMENT SCIENCE

(Electrical and Electronics Engineering, Electronics and Communication Engineering, Electronics and Computer Engineering)

Time: 3 Hours.

Max. Marks: 80

Answer any FIVE questions.

All questions carry equal Marks.

---

1. What is the contribution made by F.W. Taylor towards the management science? How is it relevant in today's industrial environment?
2. Explain the following:
   (a) Line and staff organization.
   (b) A formal and informal organizations.
3. What is meant by work-study? How is it useful? What are the objectives and methods of work-study?
4. (a) What is meant by selective inventory control?
   (b) Briefly explain the classification of selecting controls.
5. Why is there an increased emphasis on HRM during these days?
6. (a) Compare and contrast job evaluation and merit rating.
   (b) What methods do you follow for performance appraisal?
7. Explain PERT and its importance in network analysis. What are the requirements for application of PERT technique?
8. What do you understand by Just-in-Time system? What are the objectives, features and the key elements?

Code: R7320203 **4**

III B. Tech. II Semester (R07) Regular Examinations, May 2011

MANAGEMENT SCIENCE

(Electrical and Electronics Engineering, Electronics and Communication Engineering, Electronics and Computer Engineering)

Time: 3 Hours. *Max. Marks: 80*

Answer any FIVE questions.

All questions carry equal Marks.

1. Explain the principles of management by Henry Fayol.
2. How do you explain significance of committee organization? How is it distinguished from product organization?
3. (a) What is meant by method study? What are the aims of method study?
   (b) Explain the steps involved in method study.
4. (a) What is meant by ABC analysis?
   (b) Can you explain the methodology of ABC analysis, advantages and limitations?
5. (a) State the functions of channels of distribution.
   (b) What factors affect the selection of particular distribution channel?
6. "PERT provides the framework with which a project can be described, scheduled and then controlled", explain.
7. Explain the basic elements of corporate planning process.
8. (a) What is the importance of environmental scanning?
   (b) Explain the significance of business process outsourcing.

Code: R5320203 **R5**

III B. Tech. II Semester (R05) Supplementary Examinations, December 2010

MANAGEMENT SCIENCE

(Common to Electrical and Electronics Engineering, Electronics and Communication Engineering, Electronics and Control, Electronics and Computer Engineering and Instrumentation and Control Engineering)

Time: 3 Hours. *Max. Marks: 80*

Answer any FIVE questions.

All questions carry equal Marks.

---

1. Define management. State the important characteristics of management.
2. Define organization. Explain the importance of organization in industry.
3. A Hardware storekeeper purchases nails from a manufacturer who produces them in different sizes of lots as given below in the table and also number of rejected pieces. Compute the control limits for each lot and plot the p-chart.

Lot No.	Lot Size (Number of Pieces Inspected)	Number of Pieces Rejected
1	6,000	183
2	6,000	131
3	10,000	184
4	1,780	23
5	3,089	171
6	5,779	65
7	3,000	46
8	2,722	85
Total	38,370	888

4. "Marketing should aim at meeting the given consumer need rather than selling a given product" – comment.
5. What is human resource management? How is it different from personnel management?
6. The following table lists the jobs of a network along with time estimates.

Jobs	Duration in Days		
	Optimistic	Most Likely	Pessimistic
1–4	3	9	27
1–3	3	6	15
1–2	6	12	30
4–5	1	4	7
3–5	3	9	27
3–6	2	5	8

contd.....)

Jobs	Duration in Days		
	Optimistic	Most Likely	Pessimistic
5–6	6	12	30
2–6	4	19	28

(a) Draw the project network.

(b) What is the approximate probability that the jobs on critical path will be completed by the due date of 35 days?

(c) What is your estimate of the probability that the entire project will be completed by the due date? Explain.

(d) What due date has 90% of chance of being met?

7. What are the different types environments that a firm faces? For a firm you are acquainted with, chart the relevant environments.

8. What is supply chain management? Explain the advantages in supply chain management.

Code: R5420501 **1**

IV B. Tech. II Semester (R05) Regular and Supplementary Examinations, April/May 2010

MANAGEMENT SCIENCE

(Common to Computer Science and Engineering. Information Technology and Computer Science and Systems Engineering)

Time: 3 Hours. *Max. Marks: 80*

Answer any FIVE questions.

All questions carry equal Marks.

---

1. What are the principles of management according to Fayol? Are they relevant today?
2. What are different leadership styles? Which of these you recommend most? Why?
3. (a) How do you differentiate line and line staff organizations?
   (b) Differentiate between functional organizational and committee organization.
4. (a) Explain the importance of plant layout.
   (b) What are the various methods of plant layout?
5. What are the basic objects of inventory control? Explain its significance in an industrial enterprise.
6. (a) Briefly explain the basic functions of marketing.
   (b) Write short notes on "Product Life Cycle".
7. Critically analyze the function of human resource manager of an enterprise.
8. (a) Explain the functioning of PERT and CPM.
   (b) Discuss SWOT analysis.

2

Code: R5420501

IV B. Tech. II Semester (R05) Regular and Supplementary Examinations, April/May 2010

MANAGEMENT SCIENCE

(Common to Computer Science and Engineering. Information Technology and Computer Science and Systems Engineering)

Time: 3 Hours. *Max. Marks: 80*

Answer any FIVE questions.

All questions carry equal Marks.

---

1. What are the social responsibilities of management? Are these relevant in present situation?
2. (a) Explain the basic concepts of organization.
   (b) Explain about matrix organization and virtual organization.
3. What are the guidelines you follow while conduction work-study and what is its importance?
4. (a) Explain EOQ and ABC analysis.
   (b) Discuss the importance and functioning of stores management.
5. (a) Critically explain the marketing mix.
   (b) Discuss the channels of distribution and their importance.
6. (a) What steps you take for manpower planning?
   (b) What are the general procedure for recruitment and selection of employee in an enterprise?
7. (a) What is the importance of network analysis?
   (b) What is the significance of PERT?
8. (a) What functions do you consider while establishing the materials requirement planning?
   (b) What is the significance of business process outsourcing?

Code: R5420501 **3**

IV B. Tech. II Semester (R05) Regular and Supplementary Examinations, April/May 2010

MANAGEMENT SCIENCE

(Common to Computer Science & Engineering. Information Technology and Computer Science and Systems Engineering)

Time: 3 Hours. *Max. Marks: 80*

Answer any FIVE questions.

All questions carry equal Marks.

---

1. Explain the importance and the principles of Taylor's scientific management theory.
2. Critically evaluate the line and line and staff organization structure.
3. What are the principles you follow while conducting method-study and work measurement?
4. What is the general purchase procedure you follow in a business enterprise?
5. What is a channel of distribution? What factors you consider while selecting the channel of distribution?
6. (a) What is the significance of personnel management and industrial relations?
   (b) Explain the job evaluation and merit rating.
7. (a) Explain the project cost analysis and project crashing.
   (b) What are steps involved in strategy formulation and implementation.
8. (a) What are the basic concepts of MIS?
   (b) Explain in detail materials requirement planning.

4

Code: R5420501

IV B. Tech. II Semester (R05) Regular and Supplementary Examinations, April/May 2010

MANAGEMENT SCIENCE

(Common to Computer Science and Engineering. Information Technology and Computer Science and Systems Engineering)

Time: 3 Hours. *Max. Marks: 80*

Answer any FIVE questions.
All questions carry equal Marks.

1. Distinguish between administration, organization and management. What are the basic principles of management according to Fayol?
2. (a) Differentiate between departmentation and decentralization.
   (b) Explain line and staff organization.
3. (a) What is the best writable plant layout method? Why do you suggest it?
   (b) Explain statistical quality control, its importance and methods.
4. (a) Critically explain EOQ and ABC analysis.
   (b) What are the stores records that are maintained?
5. What are the basic functions of HR manager?
6. (a) Explain the significance of PERT and CPM.
   (b) Explain project cost analysis.
7. What factors you consider while corporate planning process?
8. (a) Explain environmental scanning – need and importance.
   (b) Supply chain management – significance.

Code: R5320203 **R 5**

III B. Tech II Semester (R05) Supplementary Examinations, May 2010

MANAGEMENT SCIENCE

(Common to Electrical and Electronics Engineering, Electronics and Communication Engineering, Electronics and Control, Electronics and Computer Engineering and Instrumentation and Control Engineering)

Time: 3 Hours. *Max. Marks: 80*

Answer any FIVE questions.

All questions carry equal Marks.

1. State and explain the Taylor's scientific management.
2. Name and describe the principles of organization.
3. Name the various recording techniques used in method study. Give the various symbols used in recording with their meaning.
4. Define purchasing. State the objectives of purchasing.
5. What is the purpose of internal mobility? When are demotions necessitated in organization?
6. The jobs of a project with respective estimates are given in table.

Jobs	T_o	T_m	T_p
1 – 2	3	6	15
1 – 6	2	5	14
2 – 3	6	12	30
2 – 4	2	5	8
3 – 5	5	11	7
4 – 5	3	6	15
6 – 7	3	9	27
5 – 8	1	4	7
7 – 8	4	19	28

(a) Draw the network and calculate the following.

(i) Variance of each job.

(ii) Length of the project.

(iii) Variance of the project.

(b) What is the probability that the jobs on the critical path will be completed by the due date of 42 days.

7. What are the criteria used to determine the corporate strengths and weaknesses? Use these criteria for a company you are familiar with to identify its strengths and weaknesses. Suggest corrective actions.
8. Write short notes on the following:

(a) Bench Marking, (b) Balanced Score Card, (c) End User Computing

R 5

Code: R5320203

III B. Tech. II Semester (R05) Supplementary Examinations, January/February 2010

MANAGEMENT SCIENCE

(Common to Electrical and Electronics Engineering, Electronics and Communication Engineering, Electronics and Control, Electronics and Computer Engineering and Instrumentation and Control Engineering)

Time: 3 Hours. *Max. Marks: 80*

Answer any FIVE questions.
All questions carry equal Marks.

---

1. Define management. State the important characteristics of management.
2. How is informal organization relevant to managers? In what ways, can managers make most effective use of informal organization?
3. Differentiate between process layout and product layout.
4. Name the various types of records maintained in stores and explain them in brief.
5. Why do organizations promote their employees? What should be the criteria for promotions?
6. Explain the uses of variance and expected time in relation to critical path in a PERT network.
7. Does a company have to act selflessly to be considered socially responsible? Discuss.
8. Explain the philosophy behind total quality management, customer satisfaction and continuous improvement. What are the objectives of TQM?

Code: R5320203 **1**

III B. Tech. II Semester (R05) Regular and Supplementary Examinations, April 2009

MANAGEMENT SCIENCE

(Common to Electrical and Electronics Engineering, Electronic and Communication Engineering, Electronics and Control Engineering, Electronic and Computer Engineering, and Instrumentation and Control Engineering)

Time: 3 Hours. *Max. Marks: 80*

Answer any FIVE questions.

All questions carry equal Marks.

1. Define management. State the importance and characteristics of management.
2. Describe various bases for departmentation and suggest a scheme of departmentation for a large marketing company, with a field network all over he country.
3. Differentiate between "Job Order Production" and "Batch Production" systems.
4. Describe briefly the various functions of stores.
5. Discuss HRM and how is it different from personnel management?
6. What do you mean by crashing a network? State step by step procedure for crashing.
7. Distinguish between strategic and operational planning.
8. What are the major ingredients of total quality management? Are some ingredients more important than the others? Explain.

Code: R5320203 **2**

III B. Tech. II Semester (R05) Regular and Supplementary Examinations, April 2009

MANAGEMENT SCIENCE

(Common to Electrical and Electronics Engineering, Electronic and Communication Engineering, Electronics and Control Engineering, Electronic and Computer Engineering, and Instrumentation and Control Engineering)

Time: 3 Hours. *Max. Marks: 80*

Answer any FIVE questions.

All questions carry equal Marks.

---

1. State and explain Taylor's scientific management.
2. What is committee organization? Explain advantages and disadvantages of committee organization.
3. The following are the results of daily inspection of vacuum tube. Compute the value of fraction defective for each day inspection and plot the p-chart.

Year / Date	Lot Size (n)	No. of Defectives
3rd March 2007	1024	30
5th March 2007	2056	48
6th March 2007	16835	86
7th March 2007	16069	108
12th March 2007	7369	59
13th March 2007	8738	29
14th March 2007	1220	10
17th March 2007	16242	112
18th March 2007	15145	76
24th March 2007	5845	88
25th March 2007	13582	154
Total	104125	720

4. "Consumer is the King" comment on the statement in the light of marketing concept.
5. Discuss HRM and how is it different from personal management?
6. The various time estimates of activities involved in a project are given in table; Determine:

(a) The expected completion time of the project.

(b) The variance and standard deviation of the project.

(c) Probability factor of completing the project within 23 days.

Activities	T_o	T_m	T_p
1 – 2	2	6	10
1 – 3	4	8	12
2 – 4	2	3	4
2 – 3	2	4	6
3 – 4	0	0	0
3 – 5	3	6	9
4 – 6	6	10	14
5 –6	1	3	5

7. What are the different types of environments that a firm faces? For a firm you are acquainted with, chart the relevant environments.
8. Explain the seven principles of michael hammer relating to re-engineering.

Code: R5320203 **3**

III B. Tech. II Semester (R05) Regular and Supplementary Examinations, April 2009

MANAGEMENT SCIENCE

(Common to Electrical and Electronics Engineering, Electronic and Communication Engineering, Electronics and Control Engineering, Electronic and Computer Engineering, and Instrumentation and Control Engineering)

Time: 3 Hours. *Max. Marks: 80*

Answer any FIVE questions.
All questions carry equal Marks.

1. Describe the theory of scientific management, and explain how it was criticized?
2. Discuss the features of functional organization structure. What are the benefits and limitations? Discuss the situation under which it is more suitable?
3. The following table gives the number of rivets missing at aircraft final inspection. Prepare appropriate control chart.

S. No.	Air Plane Number	Number of Missing Rivets	S. No.	Air Plane Number	Number of Missing Rivets
1	A	8	15	O	15
2	B	16	16	P	9
3	C	14	17	Q	9
4	D	19	18	R	14
5	E	11	19	S	11
6	F	15	20	T	9
7	G	8	21	U	10
8	H	11	22	V	22
9	I	21	23	W	7
10	J	12	24	X	28
11	K	23	25	Y	9
12	L	16	Total	--	351
13	M	9			
14	N	25			

4. Describe the various functions of marketing.
5. How should one go about identifying training needs in an organization?
6. What is the importance of cost analysis? Account for different types of cost citing examples.
7. List out strategic issues for a software industry in marketing, financial, R&D, and HRM departments.
8. Explain the philosophy behind total quality management, customer satisfaction and continuous improvement. What are the objectives of TQM?

Code: R5320203 **4**

III B. Tech. II Semester (R05) Regular and Supplementary Examinations, April 2009

MANAGEMENT SCIENCE

(Common to Electrical and Electronics Engineering, Electronic and Communication Engineering, Electronics and Control Engineering, Electronic and Computer Engineering, and Instrumentation and Control Engineering)

Time: 3 Hours. *Max. Marks: 80*

Answer any FIVE questions.

All questions carry equal Marks.

1. What are the leadership qualities that you would look for in a manager? Distinguish between innate and acquirable qualities with examples.
2. Describe briefly the various steps involved in organizing procedure.
3. Explain in brief the basic procedure of work measurement.
4. Define consumer behavior. What is its importance in marketing?
5. What environmental change will be the most difficult for HR group to manage?
6. What do you mean by crashing a network? State step by step procedure of crashing.
7. How has information system affected strategic decision-making? What are the issues that have surfaced in the light of rapid change in information technology?
8. What are the different methods of TQM? Explain any two of them briefly.

Code: R5420501

IV B. Tech. II Semester (R05) Advanced Supplementary Examinations, July 2009

MANAGEMENT SCIENCE

(Common to Computer Science and Engineering. Information Technology and Computer Science and Systems Engineering)

Time: 3 Hours. *Max. Marks: 80*

Answer any FIVE questions.
All questions carry equal Marks.

---

1. Define management. Explain important characteristics of management.
2. Define organizations. Explain the importance of organization in an industry.
3. What is plant layout? Explain the advantages of good plant layout.
4. (a) Define work-study and state the objectives.
   (b) What benefits do you derive from work-study?
5. What do you understand by economic order quantity? Derive the formula for determining the economic order quantity.
6. (a) What are the various functions of marketing?
   (b) What factors influence consumer behavior?
7. Discuss in detail the objectives and functions of Human Resource Management (HRM).
8. Briefly explain the concept of selection. What are the different techniques of selection followed by a personnel manager while employing the personnel in an organization?

Code: R5420501 **1**

IV B. Tech. II Semester (R05) Regular Examinations, April/May 2009

MANAGEMENT SCIENCE

(Common to Computer Science and Engineering. Information Technology and Computer Science and Systems Engineering)

Time: 3 Hours. *Max. Marks: 80*

Answer any FIVE questions.

All questions carry equal Marks.

1. State and explain Taylor's scientific management theory.
2. (a) What are the objectives of plant layout?
   (b) Explain the factors influencing plant layout.
3. What are the principles of sound organization structure? Explain.
4. Define consumer behavior. What is its importance in marketing?
5. Explain the functions of HR manager in a knowledge-based organization such as software company.
6. Given the following data, compute the expected project duration by drawing a network and indicate critical path. Find total slack of each event.

Activities	T_o	T_m	T_p [T_p]
1 – 2	2	5	14
1 – 6	2	5	8
2- 3	5	11	29
2 – 4	1	4	7
3 – 5	5	11	17
4 – 5	2	5	14
6 – 7	3	9	27
5 – 8	2	2	8
7 – 8	7	13	13

7. What do you mean by mission and objectives of the organization? Explain with examples.
   (i) What do you understand by total quality management? How does this concept differ from quality control techniques?

Code: R5420501

2

IV B. Tech. II Semester (R05) Regular Examinations, April / May 2009

MANAGEMENT SCIENCE

(Common to Computer Science and Engineering. Information Technology and Computer Science and Systems Engineering)

Time: 3 Hours. *Max. Marks: 80*

Answer any FIVE questions.

All questions carry equal Marks.

1. Explain the concept of management and organization and analyze their relationship.
2. State the essential elements of good organization.
3. (a) What are the objectives of plant layout?
   (b) Explain the factors influencing plant layout.
4. (a) What are the various functions of marketing?
   (b) What factors affect consumer behavior?
5. Explain the functions of HR manager in knowledge-based organization such as software developing company.
6. The following are the activities associated with the event management of new year party. Identify critical path and suggest optimum duration of the project also work out optimum cost considering a daily overheads for ₹ 500/-.

Activities	Time in Days		Cost in ₹	
	Normal	Crash	Normal	Crash
1 – 2	12	8	2000	2800
1 –3	8	6	1000	1600
2 –4	6	4	800	1000
3 – 5	16	12	1800	2400
4 – 5	14	8	1400	1600

7. Explain SWOT analysis. Analyze how SWOT analysis can be used to evolve appropriate corporate strategy?
8. Explain the philosophy behind total quality management, customer satisfaction, and continuous improvement. What are the objectives of total quality management?

Code: R5420501 **3**

IV B.Tech II Semester (R05) Regular Examinations, April/May 2009

MANAGEMENT SCIENCE

(Common to Computer Science and Engineering. Information Technology and Computer Science and Systems Engineering)

Time: 3 Hours. *Max. Marks: 80*

Answer any FIVE questions

All questions carry equal Marks.

---

1. (a) Explain the importance of management.

(b) What are the challenges you have to face as manager? Discuss.

2. State the essential elements of good organization.

3. Define plant layout. Explain the objectives of the good plant layout.

4. (a) What are the various functions of marketing?

(b) What factor influence consumer behavior?

5. Discuss the functions of human resource manager in an industrial setting.

6. Draw the PERT network for the following activities and determine the probability of completing the project in 48 days.

Jobs	Duration in Days		
	Optimistic	Most Likely	Pessimistic
1 – 2	8	8	1
1 – 3	1	3	5
2 – 4	4	6	7
3 – 4	3	7	9
4 – 5	10	20	30
4 – 6	14	18	23
4 – 7	3	6	10
5 – 7	5	9	12
6 – 8	1	4	6
7 – 8	2	5	9

7. Explain SWOT analysis. Analyze how SWOT analysis can be used to evolve appropriate corporate strategy.

8. Write short notes on:

(a) Capability Maturity Model (CMM)

(b) Just-in-Time (JIT)

(c) Balanced Scored Card.

Code: R5420501 **4**

IV B. Tech. II Semester (R05) Regular Examinations, April/May 2009

MANAGEMENT SCIENCE

(Common to Computer Science and Engineering. Information Technology and Computer Science and Systems Engineering)

Time: 3 Hours. *Max. Marks: 80*

Answer any FIVE questions.

All questions carry equal Marks.

1. Define management. Explain its nature and features.
2. State the essential elements of good organization.
3. Define plant layout. Explain the objectives of good plant layout.
4. Define marketing. How is it different from selling? Explain how marketing starts an ends with customer.
5. Discuss the function of human resource manager in an industrial setting.
6. The following table gives required information of a project.

Activity	Normal		Crash	
	Days	Cost in ₹	Days	Cost in ₹
1 – 2	3	50	2	1000
1 – 3	2	750	1	1500
1 – 4	6	1400	4	2600
2 – 4	5	1000	3	1800
2 – 5	7	1150	6	1450
3 –4	2	800	2	800
4 – 5	4	1000	2	2400

The indirect cost is ₹ 60/- per day. Determine optimum cost and time for the project.

7. What is environmental scanning and what are the factors affecting external environment?
8. Write short notes on:
   (a) Capacity maturity Model (CMM)
   (b) Just-in-Time (JIT)
   (c) Balanced Scored Card.

Code: R5320203 **1**

III B. Tech. II Semester (R05) Regular and Supplementary Examinations, April/May 2008

MANAGEMENT SCIENCE

(Common to Electrical and Electronics engineering, Electronic and Communication Engineering, Electronics and Control Engineering, Electronic and Computer Engineering, and Instrumentation and Control Engineering)

Time: 3 Hours. *Max. Marks: 80*

Answer any FIVE questions.

All questions carry equal Marks.

1. Name and describe the various levels of management with their functions.
2. What is departmentation? How is it essential for the management of a business enterprise?
3. Define work measurement. What are its objectives?
4. What do you mean by marketing? How is it different from selling?
5. Explain some of the problems in interview as a method of selection.
6. The following table lists the job of a network along with the time estimates.

Jobs	Duration in Days		
	Optimistic	Most Likely	Pessimistic
1 – 4	3	9	27
1 – 3	3	6	15
1 – 2	6	12	30
4 – 5	1	4	7
3 – 5	3	9	27
3 – 6	2	5	8
5 – 6	6	12	30
2 – 6	4	19	29

(a) Draw the project network.

(b) What is the approximate probability that jobs on the critical path will be completed by the due date of 35 days?

(c) What is your estimate of the probability that the entire project will be completed by the due date? Explain.

(d) What due date has 90% of chance of being met?

7. What are the criteria used to determine the corporate strengths and weaknesses? Use these criteria for a company you are familiar with to identify its strengths and weaknesses. Suggest corrective actions.
8. What is Material Requirement Planning (MRP)? Illustrate.

2

Code: R5320203

III B. Tech. II Semester (R05) Regular and Supplementary Examinations, April/May 2008

MANAGEMENT SCIENCE

(Common to Electrical and Electronics engineering, Electronic and Communication Engineering, Electronics and Control Engineering, Electronic and Computer Engineering, and Instrumentation and Control Engineering)

Time: 3 Hours. *Max. Marks: 80*

Answer any FIVE questions.

All questions carry equal Marks.

1. Explain theory X and theory Y as theories of motivation.
2. Name and describe the principles of organization.
3. A hardware shopkeeper purchases nails from a manufacturer who produces them in different sizes of lots as given below in the table and also the number of rejected pieces. Compute the control limits for lot and plot p-chart.

Lot No.	Lot Size (Number of Pieces Inspected)	Number of Pieces Rejected
1	6,000	183
2	6,000	131
3	10,000	184
4	1,780	23
5	3,089	171
6	5,779	65
7	3,000	46
8	2,722	85
Total	38,370	888

4. What do you mean by marketing? How is it different from selling?
5. What are the best methods of recruitment for position below supervisory level?
6. The following table gives the information relating to a project. By using the given data calculate the optimum duration of the project. Where indirect cost is estimated as ₹ 200/- per day.

Activity	Normal		Crash	
	Time in Days	Cost in ₹	Time in Days	Cost in ₹
1 – 2	4	1000	3	2000
1 – 3	2	1500	1	3500
2 – 4	2	500	1	900
2 – 5	5	1000	3	4000
3 – 4	3	1000	1	2000
4 – 5	2	800	1	1000

(Note: Further question are not available)

Code: R5320203 **3**

III B. Tech. II Semester (R05) Regular and Supplementary Examinations, April/May 2008

MANAGEMENT SCIENCE

(Common to Electrical and Electronics Engineering, Electronic and Communication Engineering, Electronics and Control Engineering, Electronic and Computer Engineering, and Instrumentation and Control Engineering)

Time: 3 Hours. *Max. Marks: 80*

Answer any FIVE questions.

All questions carry equal Marks.

---

1. Discuss the leadership styles with examples, which Indian managers follow. Can you suggest a best style for them? How?
2. What are the various types of organization structures? Explain them with their merits and demerits.
3. Name and describe the various tools and techniques used in layout planning.
4. "Marketing should aim at meeting a given consumer need rather than selling a given product". Comment.
5. Briefly explain the concept of selection. What are the techniques of selection followed by personal manager, while employing the personnel in an organization?
6. What do you mean by crashing a network? State step by step procedure for crashing.
7. Strategic alliances are temporary. Do you agree? Justify.
8. What are the different methods of TQM? Explain any two methods briefly.

Code: R5320203 **4**

III B. Tech. II Semester (R05) Regular and Supplementary Examinations, April/May 2008

MANAGEMENT SCIENCE

(Common to Electrical and Electronics Engineering, Electronic and Communication Engineering, Electronics and Control Engineering, Electronic and Computer Engineering, and Instrumentation and Control Engineering)

Time: 3 Hours. *Max. Marks: 80*

Answer any FIVE questions.

All questions carry equal Marks.

---

1. What are the basic leadership styles and their corresponding effective and ineffective styles?
2. Describe briefly the various steps involved in organizing procedure.
3. Define inspection. What are the kinds of inspection?
4. What do you mean by marketing? How is it different from selling?
5. Highlight the significance of job description in selection.
6. What is the importance of cost analysis? Account for different types of cost citing examples.
7. What is the relationship between corporate governance and social responsibility?
8. What are some of the guidelines that can be followed for the purpose of improving MIS?

Code: RR 320301 **1**

III B. Tech. II Semester (R05) Supplementary Examinations, Aug./Sep. 2008

MANAGEMENT SCIENCE

(Common to Mechanical Engineering, Computer Science and Engineering, Chemical Engineering, Information Technology, Metallurgy and Material Technology, Electronics and Computer Engineering and Production Engineering)

Time: 3 Hours. *Max. Marks: 80*

Answer any FIVE questions.

All questions carry equal Marks.

1. Explain the nature and features of management.

2. (a) Explain and illustrate authority and responsibility. How do you relate and differentiate them?

(b) Explain how do you resolve the conflicts between line and staff managers.

3. A printed circuit assembly shop owner decided to use control charts to monitor the number of defectives in all the boards assembled everyday. The data from the last 12 inspections, in one shift given in the following table. Which chart do you employ? Plot the appropriate chart with control limits and interpret the results.

Pc Number	1	2	3	4	5	6	7	8	9	10	11	12
Number of Defectives	4	3	6	9	6	7	12	9	14	8	2	1

4. (a) Explain the functions of materials manager.

(b) How are the activities need co-ordination with other functional areas?

5. Discuss in detail the objectives and functions of human resource management.

6. Explain how job evaluation can be carried out in an industrial set up.

7. What is environmental scanning? Why is it carried out?

8. For the particulars of project shown in the able below draw a PERT network, determine the critical path and the probability of completion of the project within 72 days.

Activity	**Time in Days**		
	Optimistic Time (T_o)	**Most Likely Time (T_m)**	**Pessimistic Time (T_p)**
10 – 20	6	10	14
10 – 30	2	4	6
20 – 50	12	16	24
30 – 40	16	24	34
40 – 50	0	0	0
50 – 80	10	14	18
40 – 60	12	18	24
40 – 70	6	12	16
60 – 90	2	4	6
80 – 90	6	12	16
70 – 100	16	30	50
90 – 100	4	8	12

2

Code: RR 320301

III B. Tech. II Semester (R05) Supplementary Examinations, Aug./Sep. 2008

MANAGEMENT SCIENCE

(Common to Mechanical Engineering, Computer Science and Engineering, Chemical Engineering, Information Technology, Metallurgy and Material Technology, Electronics and Computer Engineering and Production Engineering)

Time: 3 Hours. *Max. Marks: 80*

Answer any FIVE questions.
All questions carry equal Marks.

---

1. (a) Explain the importance of management.
   (b) What are the challenges you have to face as a manager? Discuss.
2. Explain any four types of organization structures with their suitability.
3. (a) What are the objectives of plant layout?
   (b) Explain the factors influencing plant layout.
4. (a) Explain the concept of economic order quantity.
   (b) Explain the variables that go into the determination of EOQ.
   (c) Show how the formula is derived.
5. Discuss in detail the objectives and functions of human resource management.
6. What do you understand by job evaluation? Explain in detail different methods of job evaluation.
7. (a) What do you understand by environmental scanning?
   (b) What is its importance?
8. Consider the project consisting of nine jobs following precedence relations and average time estimates.

Job	Predecessor	Time in Days
A	-	30
B	-	20
C	A, B	20
D	A, B	20
E	B	10
F	D, E	10
G	C, F	40
H	D, E	20
I	G, H	30

Draw the project network; identify the critical path and total duration for the project.

Code No: RR 310 206 **1**

III B. Tech. I Semester Supplementary Examination, November 2008.

MANAGEMENT SCIENCE

(Common to Electrical and Electronics Engineering, Electronics and Communication/ Engineering, Electronics and Instrumentation Engineering, Bio-Medical Engineering, Electronics and Control Engineering, Mechatronics, Computer Science and Systems Engineering, Instrumentation and Control Engineering)

Time: 3 Hours. *Max. Marks: 80*

Answer any FIVE Questions.

All Questions carry equal marks.

---

1. (a) Can you consider management either as an art or science? Justify your answer.

(b) What are the features of management? Explain.

2. (a) What is a flat organization?

(b) How is it different from matrix organization?

(c) What is its relevance in the present context?

3. (a) What is method study?

(b) Explain the steps involved in carrying it out.

4. (a) Explain the features of good stores layout.

(b) Explain the formats of different documents use in a store.

5. "The success of an organization to a greater extent depends on how the HRD acts" – substantiate.

6. Explain the different methods of On-the-Job training and Off-the-Job training.

7. What are the external factors to be considered while assessing opportunities and threats?

8. Draw the network for the following project; it is further given that project completion time is 42 days. Find the project duration. Also identify critical path.

Activity	Description	Duration in Days
1 –2	Idea generation	7
1 – 3	Market survey	10
2 – 4	Prototype making	7
3 – 5	Advertisement campaign	9
4 – 5	Distribute samples	5
4 – 6	Commencement of production	5
5 – 7	Fixing up sales outlet	7
6 –7	Manufacture	14

Code No: RR 310 206 **2**

III B. Tech. I Semester Supplementary Examination, November 2008.

MANAGEMENT SCIENCE

(Common to Electrical and Electronics Engineering, Electronics and Communication Engineering, Electronics and Instrumentation Engineering, Bio-Medical Engineering, Electronics and Control Engineering, Mechatronics, Computer Science and Systems Engineering, Instrumentation and Control Engineering)

Time: 3 Hours. *Max. Marks: 80*

Answer any FIVE Questions.

All Questions carry equal marks.

1. Explain the nature and features of management.
2. (a) What is flat organization?
   (b) How is it distinct from matrix organization?
   (c) What is its relevance in the present context?
3. (a) What are the objectives of plant layout?
   (b) Explain the factors influencing plant layout.
4. (a) Define market segmentation.
   (b) Explain clearly the basis of market segmentation.
5. What is human resource management? Is it different from Personnel Management and Industrial Relations (PMIR)?
6. (a) What is induction? What is the purpose of induction?
   (b) What is the difference between training and development? Explain.
7. (a) What do you understand by environmental scanning?
   (b) What is its importance?
8. A small project consists of the following activities with the given time estimates.

Project Event Successor Event	Estimated Duration in Months		
	Optimistic Time (t_o)	Most Likely Time (t_m)	Pessimistic Time (t_p)
1 – 2	2	2	14
1 – 3	2	8	14
1 – 4	4	4	16
2 – 5	2	2	2
3 – 5	4	10	28
4 – 6	4	10	16
5 – 6	6	12	30

   (a) Draw the network.
   (b) Calculate average expected time for each activity.
   (c) Calculate the earliest expected time and latest allowable time for each event, and
   (d) Determine the critical path considering project completion time of 36 months.

Code No: RR 310 206 **3**

III B. Tech. I Semester Supplementary Examination, November 2008.

MANAGEMENT SCIENCE

(Common to Electrical and Electronics Engineering, Electronics and Communication Engineering, Electronics and Instrumentation Engineering, Bio-Medical Engineering, Electronics and Control Engineering, Mechatronics, Computer Science and Systems Engineering, Instrumentation and Control Engineering)

Time: 3 Hours. *Max. Marks: 80*

Answer any FIVE Questions.

All Questions carry equal marks.

---

1. Critically evaluate Taylor's theory of scientific management.
2. Compare and contrast formal and informal organization. Why each one is significant?
3. (a) What is method study?
   (b) Explain the steps involved in carrying it out.
4. (a) What do you understand by marketing mix?
   (b) Explain briefly the basic elements of marketing mix.
5. How does globalization make the job of personnel manager more challenging? Substantiate.
6. What is the purpose and importance of merit rating? How do you carry it out?
7. What are the factors of external and internal environmental to be considered for formulating the strategy? Explain.
8. The following is the list of events found in the process of organizing a student's convention. Identify the logical sequence and fix the duration as per the estimate. Draw a PERT network, with assumed data.
   (a) Set connection date.
   (b) Set convention location.
   (c) Set convention chairman.
   (d) Select convention facilities.
   (e) Develop convention program.
   (f) Select convention speakers.
   (g) Set convention cost.
   (h) Notify the members of convention program.
   (i) Print program.
   (j) Notify convention facility of desired set-up of each meeting room.
   (k) Select banquet menu.
   (l) Determine recipient of outstanding member aware.
   (m) Prepare citation for outstanding member award.
   (n) Determine honorarium for speakers.
   (o) Arrange for registration.
   (p) Make boarding and lodging arrangements.
   (q) Arrange transport from airport.
   (r) Await convention.

Code No: RR 310 206 **4**

III B. Tech. I Semester Supplementary Examination, November 2008.

MANAGEMENT SCIENCE

(Common to Electrical and Electronics Engineering, Electronics and Communication Engineering, Electronics and Instrumentation Engineering, Bio-Medical Engineering, Electronics and Control Engineering, Mechatronics, Computer Science and Systems Engineering, Instrumentation and Control Engineering)

Time: 3 Hours. *Max. Marks: 80*

Answer any FIVE Questions.

All Questions carry equal marks.

1. Explain the nature and feature of management.
2. Compare and contrast formal and informal organization. Why each one is significant?
3. (a) What are the objectives of plant layout?
   (b) Explain the factors influencing plant Layout.
4. (a) What are the various functions of marketing?
   (b) What factors influence consumer behavior?
5. Discuss in detail the objectives and functions of human resource management?
6. What is the purpose of training? Explain how training can be imparted?
7. What is SWOT analysis? What is its significance?
8. The following table gives the data relating to a project.

Activity	Normal		Crash	
	Time in Weeks	Direct Cost in ₹	Time in Weeks	Direct Cost in ₹
1 – 2	8	7,000	3	10,000
1 – 3	4	6,000	2	8,000
2 – 3	0	0	0	0
2 – 5	6	9,000	1	11,500
3 – 4	7	2,500	5	3,000
4 – 6	12	10,000	8	16,000
5 – 6	15	12,000	10	16,000
5 – 7	7	12,000	6	14,000
6 – 8	5	10,000	5	10,000
7 – 8	14	6,000	7	7,400
7 – 9	8	6,000	5	12,000
8 – 9	6	6,000	4	7,800

Indirect cost per week is ₹ 1000/-. By using iterative procedure, draw network diagram and determine by trading off between time and cost parameters.

(a) The optimum project completion time

(b) Critical path(s) and

(c) Minimum total cost of project completion.)

Code: RR 320301 **1**

III B. Tech II Semester Supplementary Examinations, Aug./Sep. 2008

MANAGEMENT SCIENCE

(Common to Mechanical Engineering, Computer Science and Engineering, Chemical Engineering, Information Technology, Metallurgy and Material Technology, Electronics and Computer Engineering and Production Engineering)

Time: 3 Hours. *Max. Marks: 80*

Answer any FIVE questions.

All questions carry equal Marks.

1. What are the managerial functions in any service providing organizations like Bharat Sanchar Nigam Limited (BSNL), Life Insurance Corporation of India etc.
2. (a) Explain and evaluate line and staff organizations.
   (b) Where do find it useful?
3. (a) What are the objectives of plant layout?
   (b) Explain the factors influencing plant layout.
4. (a) Define EOQ. What are the factors that determine EOQ?
   (b) A firm requires 1000 units of a particular component. It pays ₹.50/- per component to the vendor. The ordering cost is ₹ 250/- per order. The inventory carrying cost is 20% of the inventory per annum.
   Calculate:
   (i) EOQ, (ii) Number of orders per year, (iii) Total annual cost.
5. What are the key functions of human resource manager?
6. Explain in detail the different methods of job evaluation.
7. What are the external factors to be considered while assessing opportunities and threats?
8. The following are the activities identified in scheduling the time required to install an improved local area network (LAN). Draw the PERT network and identify the critical path.

Activity Identity	Description	Average Duration t_e	Logical Sequence
a	Establish project parameters	2	–
b	Assess present LAN	5	a
c	Present analysis	1	b
d	Refine objectives	3	a
e	Purchase upgradation equipments	6	c,d
f	Test hardware	1	e
g	Test software	2	f
h	Conduct training	4	e
i	Evaluate upgradation	2	g, h

Code: RR 320301 **2**

III B.Tech II Semester Supplementary Examinations, Aug./Sep. 2008

MANAGEMENT SCIENCE

(Common to Mechanical Engineering, Computer Science and Engineering, Chemical Engineering, Information Technology, Metallurgy and Material Technology, Electronics and Computer Engineering and Production Engineering)

Time: 3 Hours. *Max. Marks: 80*

Answer any FIVE questions.

All questions carry equal Marks.

---

1. (a) Why is management considered as a profession and what factors make it a profession?
   (b) If you are appointed as a manager in a medium sized manufacturing company, what activities do you have to perform? Explain.
2. Explain the concept of Line, Staff and Functional organization. Also illustrate.
3. (a) What are the objectives of plant layout?
   (b) Explain the factors influencing plant layout.
4. (a) Explain the concept of economic order quantity.
   (b) Explain the variable that go into the determination of EOQ.
   (c) Show how the formula is derived.
5. (a) What is the role of human resource manager in development and growth of an organization?
   (b) Explain how "human resource planning" process can be formulated.
6. (a) What is induction? What is the purpose of induction?
   (b) What is the difference between training and development? Explain.
7. How do you carry out SWOT analysis for a manufacturing unit? Explain.
8. The following table gives required information of a project.

Activity	Normal Time and Cost		Crash Time and Cost	
	Days	₹	Days	₹
1 – 2	3	500	2	1000
1 – 3	2	750	1	1500
1 – 4	6	1400	4	2600
2 – 4	5	1000	3	1800
2 – 5	7	1150	6	1450
3 – 4	2	800	2	800
4 – 5	4	1000	2	2400

The Indirect cost is ₹ 600/- per day. Determine the optimum cost and time for the project.

Code: RR 320301 **3**

III B. Tech II Semester Supplementary Examinations, Aug./Sep. 2008

MANAGEMENT SCIENCE

(Common to Mechanical Engineering, Computer Science and Engineering, Chemical Engineering, Information Technology, Metallurgy and Material Technology, Electronics and Computer Engineering and Production Engineering)

Time: 3 Hours. *Max. Marks: 80*

Answer any FIVE questions.

All questions carry equal Marks.

1. What is Maslow's hierarchy of human needs? Explain.
2. Compare and contrast formal and informal organization. Why each one is significant?
3. (a) What are the objectives of plant layout?
   (b) Explain the factors influencing plant layout.
4. (a) What are the costs associated with effective inventory control?
   (b) How do you deal with them in modern management?
5. Discuss in detail the objectives and functions of human resource management.
6. Explain different methods of On–the–job training and Off–the–Job training.
7. (a) Explain the concept, nature and scope of corporate planning.
   (b) What are the advantages and limitations of corporate planning?
8. You are given the following data:

Activity	Logical Sequence	Time in Days		
		Optimistic Time (t_o)	Most Likely Time (t_m)	Pessimistic Time (t_p)
A	–	4	8	10
B	–	8	12	18
C	A	6	10	12
D	C	6	8	12
E	B	10	14	18

Draw the network diagram after determining:

(a) Expected task time and their variance.

(b) Earliest and latest expected time to reach each node.

(c) Critical path and

(d) Probability of completing the project in 48 days.

Code: RR 320301

4

III B.Tech II Semester Supplementary Examinations, Aug./Sep. 2008

MANAGEMENT SCIENCE

(Common to Mechanical Engineering, Computer Science and Engineering, Chemical Engineering, Information Technology, Metallurgy and Material Technology, Electronics and Computer Engineering and Production Engineering)

Time: 3 Hours. *Max. Marks: 80*

Answer any FIVE questions.
All questions carry equal Marks.

1. (a) What are the principles of managements outlined by Fayol?
   (b) Explain whether they hold good in today's context.
2. (a) What do you understand by decentralization?
   (b) How do you determine the need for decentralization? Explain.
3. Give the basic procedure involved in work-study.
4. (a) Define EOQ. What are the factors that determine EOQ?
   (b) A firm requires 1000 units of a particular component. It pays ₹ 50/- per component to the vendor. The ordering cost is ₹ 250/- per order. The inventory carrying cost is 20% of the inventory per annum.
   Calculate:
   (i)EOQ, (ii) Number of orders per year, and (iii) Total cost.
5. Discuss in detail the objectives and functions of human resource management.
6. What is grievance and what are the general causes for grievance among workers in an organization? Explain how you can redress them?
7. What is strategic business unit and what is its role and relevance in corporate planning? Illustrate.
8. From the activity details given below, determine the optimal project duration and optimal project cost. Indirect cost is ₹ 75/- per day.

Activity	Normal		Crash	
	Time in Days	Cost in ₹	Time in Days	Cost in ₹
1 – 2	8	100	6	200
1 – 3	4	150	2	350
2 – 4	2	50	1	90
2 –5	10	100	1	400
3 – 4	5	100	1	100
4 – 5	3	80	1	100

Code: RR 320301 **1**

III B.Tech Supplementary Examinations, Aug./Sep. 2008

MANAGEMENT SCIENCE

(Common to Mechanical Engineering, Computer Science and Engineering, Chemical Engineering, Information Technology, Metallurgy and Material Technology, Electronics and Computer Engineering and Production Engineering)

Time: 3 Hours. *Max. Marks: 80*

Answer any FIVE questions.
All questions carry equal Marks.

---

1. (a) Bring out contrast between theory X and theory Y.
(b) Do you find people of these traits around you? Illustrate.

2. What is matrix organization and its uniqueness?

3. (a) What do you understand by product layout?
(b) Analyze the advantages and disadvantages of product layout.
(c) For what type works they can be followed?

4. Discuss the role of purchase manager in formulation and implementation of business decisions.

5. "Human Resource Management in an organization the most challenging function". Do you agree? Justify your answer.

6. What is the purpose of training? Explain how training can be imparted.

7. How do you differentiate mission from vision and what is their importance to organization?

8. A small project consists of the following activities with the given time estimates.

Project Event – Successor Event	Estimated Duration in Months		
	Optimistic time t_o	Most likely time t_m	Pessimistic time t_p
1 – 2	2	2	14
1 – 3	2	8	14
1 – 4	4	4	16
2 – 5	2	2	2
3 – 5	4	10	28
4 – 6	4	10	16
5 – 6	6	12	30

(a) Draw the network.
(b) Calculate the average expected time for the activity.
(c) Calculate the earliest expected time and latest allowable time for each event.
(d) Determine the critical path considering project completion time of 36 months.

Code: RR 320301 **4**

III B.Tech Supplementary Examinations, Aug./Sep. 2008

MANAGEMENT SCIENCE

(Common to Mechanical Engineering, Computer Science and Engineering, Chemical Engineering, Information Technology, Metallurgy and Material Technology, Electronics and Computer Engineering and Production Engineering)

Time: 3 Hours. *Max. Marks: 80*

Answer any FIVE questions.
All questions carry equal Marks.

---

1. (a) What is the need for designing an organization?

(b) Is here any link between "management" and "organization"? Explain.

2. (a) What is organization chart?

(b) What is importance in preparing organization chart?

(c) Give any three different examples.

3. (a) What do you understand by plant layout?

(b) What is its importance?

4. (a) What are the factors that determine the choice of channels of distribution?

(b) Why do manufacturers favor intermediaries?

5. Discuss in detail the objectives and functions of human resource management.

6. Explain the following concepts with appropriate examples:

(a) Job description

(b) Job specification

(c) Job enrichment

(d) Job requirement

7. Identify the factors that are to be diagnosed in external and internal environment of a business organization.

8. Define the terms Slack, Float, EST, EFT, LFT, LST. Explain with an example of your choice.

Code: RR 320301 **1**

III B.Tech Supplementary Examinations, Aug./Sep. 2007

MANAGEMENT SCIENCE

(Common to Mechanical Engineering, Computer Science and Engineering, Chemical Engineering, Information Technology, Metallurgy and Material Technology, Electronics and Computer Engineering and Production Engineering)

Time: 3 Hours. *Max. Marks: 80*

Answer any FIVE questions.

All questions carry equal Marks.

---

1. (a) Why is management considered as a profession and what factors make it a profession?

(b) If you are appointed as a manager in a medium sized manufacturing company, what activities do you perform? Explain.

2. What is matrix organization and what is its uniqueness.

3. (a) What are the objectives of plant layout?

(b) Explain the factors influencing plant layout.

4. (a) Explain the concept of economic order quantity.

(b) Explain the variables that go into the determination of EOQ.

(c) Show how formula is derived.

5. What is human resource management? Is it different from personnel management and industrial relations? (PIMR)?

6. What are the stages in manpower planning? Discuss.

7. (a) What is the need for corporate planning?

(b) Explain the main elements in corporate planning process.

8. The following details relate to a small project with the help of which compute the probability of completion of project within scheduled time. The expected time of each activity is as follows:

Sl. No.	1	2	3	4	5	6	7	8	9
Activity	1 – 2	1 – 3	2 – 4	3 – 4	4 –5	5 – 6	3 – 5	7 – 7	6 – 7
Expected Time in Weeks	6	8	7	12	3	5	7	11	10

Code: RR 320301 **2**

III B. Tech. Supplementary Examinations, Aug./Sep. 2007

MANAGEMENT SCIENCE

(Common to Mechanical Engineering, Computer Science and Engineering, Chemical Engineering, Information Technology, Metallurgy and Material Technology, Electronics and Computer Engineering and Production Engineering)

Time: 3 Hours. *Max. Marks: 80*

Answer any FIVE questions.
All questions carry equal Marks.

1. (a) What are the managerial functions?
   (b) How are they integrated?
2. (a) Why does social responsibility become an important facet of management in the present times?
   (b) How is it discharged?
3. (a) What are the objectives of plant layout?
   (b) Explain the factors influencing the plant layout.
4. (a) Explain the concept of economic order quantity.
   (b) Explain the variables that go into the determination of EOQ.
   (c) Show how the formula is derived.
5. What are the key functions of human resource manager?
6. Explain how manpower planning helps to evolve different HR strategies.
7. Identify the factors that are to be diagnosed in external and internal environment of a business organization.
8. (a) Draw gantt chart for the following program and prepare a milestone chart for the gantt chart.
   (b) Explain the limitations of gantt chart.

Finalize specification	1 week
Prepare engineering drawing	2 weeks
Order materials and equipment	1 week
Receive materials and equipment	3 weeks
Fabricate and assemble	3 weeks
Test and inspect	1 week
Pack and dispatch to customer	1 week

Code: RR 320301 **3**

III B. Tech. Supplementary Examinations, Aug./Sep. 2007

MANAGEMENT SCIENCE

(Common to Mechanical Engineering, Computer Science and Engineering, Chemical Engineering, Information Technology, Metallurgy and Material Technology, Electronics and Computer Engineering and Production Engineering)

Time: 3 Hours. *Max. Marks: 80*

Answer any FIVE questions.

All questions carry equal Marks.

1. Explain the contribution of Frederic W. Taylor in the area of scientific management and its utility to modern managers.
2. (a) What are the advantages and disadvantages of functional organization?
   (b) Draw a block diagram reflecting its philosophy.
3. Check whether the number of observations is adequate of an accuracy or + or – 5% and confidence level of 95% limit if the number of observations of the workers working is 2500 and the number of observations of workers idle is 500.
4. (a) What do you understand by marketing mix?
   (b) Explain briefly the basic elements in marketing mix.(8 + 8)
5. Discuss in detail the objectives and functions of human resource management.
6. Explain the following concepts with appropriate examples.
   (a) Job Description.
   (b) Job Specification
   (c) Job Enrichment
   (d) Job Requirement
7. What are the factors of external and internal environment to be considered for formulating the strategy? Explain.
8. The following are the activities identified in scheduling the time-required to install an improved local area network (LAN). Draw PERT network and identify the critical path.

Activity identity	Description	Average Duration t_e in Days	Logical Sequence
a	Establish Project parameters	2	–
b	Assess present LAN	5	a
c	Present analysis	1	b
d	Refine objectives	3	a
e	Purchase upgradation equipment	6	c, d
f	Test Hardware	1	f
g	Test Software	2	f
h	Conduct Training	4	e
i	Evaluate upgradation	2	g, h

4

Code: RR 320301

III B. Tech. Supplementary Examinations, Aug./Sep. 2007

MANAGEMENT SCIENCE

(Common to Mechanical Engineering, Computer Science and Engineering, Chemical Engineering, Information Technology, Metallurgy and Material Technology, Electronics and Computer Engineering and Production Engineering)

Time: 3 Hours. *Max. Marks: 80*

Answer any FIVE questions.
All questions carry equal Marks.

1. (a) Bring out contrast between theory X and theory Y.

(b) Do you find people of these traits around you? Illustrate.

2. What is matrix organization and what is its uniqueness?

3. (a) What are the objectives of plant layout?

(b) Explain the factors influencing plant layout.

4. (a) What is the need of market research?

(b) Explain how market research can be carried out for formatting marketing strategy?

5. What are the key functions of human resource manager?

6. Explain how manpower planning helps to evolve different HR strategies.

7. How do you differentiae mission from vision and what is their importance to organization?

8. (a) Draw gantt chart for the following program and prepare a milestone chart for the gantt chart.

(b) Explain the limitations of gantt chart.

Finalize Specification	1 week
Prepare Engineering Drawing	2 weeks
Order Materials and Equipment	1 week
Receive Materials and Equipment	3 weeks
Fabricate and Assemble	3 weeks
Test and Inspect	1 week
Pack and Dispatch to Customer	1 week

Index

M

N

O

P

T

U

V

W